Visual Basic® By EXAMPLE

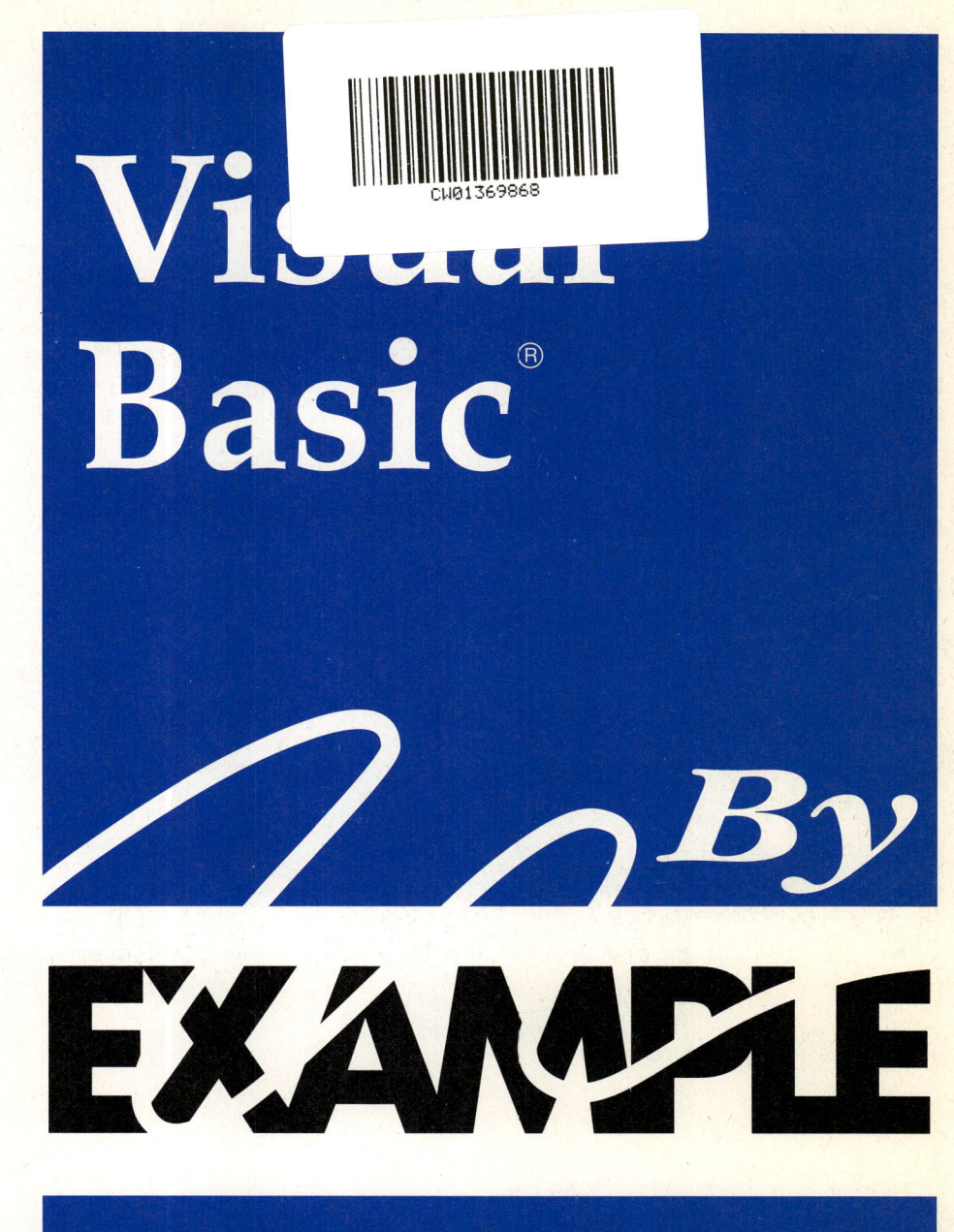

que

D.F. Scott

Visual Basic By Example

© 1992 by Que

All rights reserved. Printed in the United States of America. No part of this book may be used or reproduced, in any form or by any means, or stored in a database or retrieval system, without prior written permission of the publisher except in the case of brief quotations embodied in critical articles and reviews. Making copies of any part of this book for any purpose other than your own personal use is a violation of United States copyright laws. For information, address Que, 11711 N. College Ave., Carmel, IN 46032.

Library of Congress Catalog Card Number: 92-80084

ISBN: 0-88022-904-7

This book is sold *as is*, without warranty of any kind, either express or implied, respecting the contents of this book, including but not limited to implied warranties for the book's quality, performance, merchantability, or fitness for any particular purpose. Neither Que Corporation nor its dealers or distributors shall be liable to the purchaser or any other person or entity with respect to any liability, loss, or damage caused or alleged to be caused directly or indirectly by this book.

95 94 93 92   8 7 6 5 4 3 2 1

Interpretation of the printing code: the rightmost double-digit number is the year of the book's printing; the rightmost single-digit number, the number of the book's printing. For example, a printing code of 92-1 shows that the first printing of the book occurred in 1992.

Publisher
Richard K. Swadley

Publishing Manager
Joseph Wikert

Managing Editor
Neweleen A. Trebnik

Acquisitions Editor
Gregory Croy

Development Editor
Jennifer Flynn

Technical Editor
Gordon Arbuthnot

Production Editor
Tad Ringo

Copy Editor
Lori Cates

Editorial Assistant
Rosemarie Graham

Formatter
San Dee Phillips

Cover Designer
Jean Bisesi

Book Designer
Michele Laseau

Production Manager
Corinne Walls

Page Layout Coordinator
Matthew Morrill

Proofreading/Indexing Coordinator
Joelynn Gifford

Production Analyst
Mary Beth Wakefield

Graphic Image Specialist
Dennis Sheehan

Production
Beth Baker
Paula Carroll
Michelle Cleary
Keith Davenport
Dennis Clay Hager
Carrie Keesling
Phil Kitchel
Laurie Lee
Jay Lesandrini
Anne Owen
Cindy L. Phipps
Caroline Roop
Kelli Widdifield
Lisa Wilson
Phil Worthington

Indexers
Jeanne Clark
Tina Trettin

Composed in Palatino and MCPdigital by Prentice Hall Computer Publishing.
Screen reproductions in this book were created by means of the program Collage Plus from Inner Media, Inc., Hollis, NH.

Dedication

To Kellie, who has given me the courage.

About the Author

D. F. Scott is an independent technical author, artist, musician, and poet living in Oklahoma City. He was Technical Editor of *The Computer Street Journal,* Contributing Editor of *ANALOG Computing* and *ST-Log* magazines, and a contributor to *Computer Monthly*. His insights and observations on alternative computing have appeared in *Computer Shopper* since 1985, where he also served as moderator of the Computer Shopper Information Exchange.

Acknowledgments

My thanks to Al Meadows, who has given me many of the ideas for programs that appear in this book. His enthusiasm for Visual Basic has kept my curiosity high and my mind alert to new possibilities. My thanks also to Christopher Hood, Steve Yeager, and the rest of my "support group" at Info 1 Computers in Oklahoma City for standing by me and, in general, just standing by.

Trademark Acknowledgments

Que Corporation has made every attempt to supply trademark information about company names, products, and services mentioned in the book. Trademarks indicated below were derived from various sources. Que Corporation cannot attest to the accuracy of this information.

Finder is a trademark, and Apple, Apple II, and Disk II are registered trademarks of Apple Computer, Inc.

HyperCard is a registered trademark of Apple Computer, Inc., licensed to Claris Corporation.

Flight Simulator is a registered trademark of Bruce Artwick.

Commodore and Commodore 64 are registered trademarks of Commodore Electronics, Limited.

CorelDRAW! is a trademark of Corel Systems.

DEC is a registered trademark of Digital Equipment Corporation.

PL/1-80 and GEM are trademarks of Digital Research Inc.

GEnie is a trademark of General Electric Company.

CompuServe Incorporated is a registered trademark of H&R Block, Inc.

LaserJet is a registered trademark of Hewlett-Packard Company.

Intel386 is a registered trademark of Intel Corporation.

IBM, IBM 8514/A, and Selectric are registered trademarks of International Business Machines Corporation.

Visual Basic, MS-DOS, GW-BASIC, and Microsoft QuickBASIC are registered trademarks of Microsoft Corporation.

Super Mario Bros. is a registered trademark of Nintendo of America, Inc.

Windows, QBasic, and Word for Windows are trademarks of Microsoft Corporation.

Norton Utilities is a registered trademark of Symantec Corp.

Oracle is a registered trademark of Oracle Corporation.

Radio Shack TRS-80, TRSDOS, and Tandy are registered trademarks of Radio Shack.

Overview

Introduction 1

Part I The Visual Basic Environment 11
   1 What a Program Is 13
   2 The Project 27
   3 Grammar and Linguistics 45
   4 The Development Process 63

Part II Values and Variables 81
   5 Definition and Declaration 83
   6 Formulas 95
   7 Logic 107
   8 Strings 119
   9 Arrays 133
  10 Time and Date 143
  11 Number Systems 153
  12 Value Management 161

Part III Instructions and Groups 173
  13 Primary Program Operation 175
  14 Phraseology 181
  15 Conditional Clauses 189
  16 Loop Clauses 207
  17 Arbitrary Instruction Clusters 221

Part IV Modularization 237
  18 The Module Heirarchy 239
  19 Parameter Passing 253

Part V Graphical Interaction 261
  20 The Form 263
  21 The Window 269
  22 Managing List Boxes 285
  23 Options and Scroll Bars 305
  24 Dialog Boxes 319

- 25 Control Manipulation and Organization 327
- 26 Control Appearance 339
- 27 The Menu Bar 345
- 28 Dragging 353
- 29 The Timer 375
- 30 The Keyboard 381
- 31 The Mouse as Device 395

Part VI Arithmetic Functions 405

- 32 Function Classification 407
- 33 Conversion 413
- 34 Practical Math 423
- 35 String Functions 429
- 36 Composite Variable Types 449
- 37 The Random-Number Generator 457

Part VII Text 463

- 38 Conventional Output 465
- 39 Textual Properties 479
- 40 The Printer 487

Part VIII Bitmapped Graphics 493

- 41 Picture Boxes 495
- 42 Plotting 501

Part IX Error Trapping and Debugging ... 523

- 43 Image Scaling and Integrity 525
- 44 Registering Errors 533

Part X Physical Data 545

- 45 Sequential Access 547
- 46 Random Access 565
- 47 Data File Attributes 579
- 48 Formal Records 591
- 49 Sorting 617

Part XI The Operating System 645

 50 Devices and Directories 647
 51 Windows Instructions 671
   In Closing 685

 A ASCII/ANSI Code Chart 687
 B Answers to Review Questions 695
 C Complete Source Code Listings
   of Major Applications 715

   Glossary 743
   Index 755

Contents

Introduction 1
    Overview 3
    Who Should Use This Book 5
    How to Use This Book 5
    Points of Order 7

Part I The Visual Basic Environment

1 What a Program Is 13
    A Programmer's Credo 13
    Fundamental Terminology 15
    A More Literal Interpretation 17
    The Process of Interaction 20
    Flying Blind is Truly Flying 21
    Concern for the Environment 23
    Summary 25
    Review Questions 26

2 The Project 27
    The Visual Basic Project 27
    Graphic Objects 32
    Property Assessment 38
        The `.Caption` Property 39
    Saving Your Work 41
    Summary 42
    Review Questions 43
    Review Exercise 43

3 Grammar and Linguistics 45
    Modern Syntax 45
    A Matter of Expression 48
    Intrinsic Functions 49
    Groups, Subgroups, Subsubgroups, and So On ... 50
    Subsubsubdivisions, and So On 55
    Visual Basic Symbology 57
    Summary 61
    Review Questions 62

Contents

4 The Development Process 63
　　Instructions on Instructions 63
　　Entering Programs into the Interpreter 65
　　Making the Expressor 68
　　Does Function Follow Form? 73
　　Summary 78
　　Review Questions 79

Part II Values and Variables

5 Definition and Declaration 83
　　Variables and the Universe As We Know It 83
　　I Declare! 85
　　We Hold This Truth To Be Confusing 87
　　Degrees of Precision 90
　　Live and Let Live 92
　　Summary 93
　　Review Questions 94
　　Review Exercises 94

6 Formulas 95
　　The Function of Formulas 95
　　The Order of Evaluation 97
　　In Praise of Parentheses 98
　　Summary 104
　　Review Questions 105
　　Review Exercise 105

7 Logic 107
　　Boolean Logic and Pinball 107
　　Higher-Level Comparisons 110
　　Making Logic Do Something 113
　　Truth and/or Fiction 113
　　Summary 117
　　Review Questions 117

8	**Strings**	**119**
	Value Versus Content	119
	Of ANSI, ASCII, and Other Such Acronyms	121
	Summary	129
	Review Questions	130
	Review Exercise	131
9	**Arrays**	**133**
	The Purpose of Arrays	133
	You're Traveling into Another Dimension	134
	Controlling Arrays	138
	Establishing Bounds	140
	Summary	141
	Review Questions	142
	Review Exercises	142
10	**Time and Date**	**143**
	It's About Time	143
	Times and Dates as Text	149
	Summary	152
	Review Questions	152
11	**Number Systems**	**153**
	Touching Base	153
	Making Spaces for Places	156
	Summary	158
	Review Questions	159
12	**Value Management**	**161**
	Structured Programming, Such As It Is	162
	A Variable's Scope of Existence	163
	Constants	168
	Counting from 0 or 1	170
	Summary	170
	Review Exercise	171

Contents ◆

Part III Instructions and Groups

13   Primary Program Operation 175
   The End 175
   Summary 178
   Review Questions 179

14   Phraseology 181
   Programming Versus the Real World 181
   Subjective Reasoning Versus Objective Reasoning 183
   One Final Remark 186
   Summary 187
   Review Exercise 188

15   Conditional Clauses 189
   The Construction of a Clause 189
   If-Then as a Two-Sided Argument 194
   Natural Selection 197
   In Search of the Pneuma 200
   Summary 203
   Review Questions 204
   Review Exercise 205

16   Loop Clauses 207
   To Loop or Not To Loop 207
   Everybody's Doing It 217
   Summary 219
   Review Questions 220
   Review Exercises 220

17   Arbitrary Instruction Clusters 221
   A Branch of Archaeology 221
   Keeping Context with the Times 228
   Wherefore the Subroutine? 229
   Sequential Branching 232
   Summary 234
   Review Questions 234
   Review Exercise 235

Part IV Modularization

18 The Module Hierarchy 239
- The Origin of Modules 239
- Where Does It All Begin; Where Does It End? 244
- The Form of Forms 247
- Summary 249
- Review Questions 250
- Review Exercise 251

19 Parameter Passing 253
- I Pass 253
- The Natural Order of Things 256
- Summary 259
- Review Questions 259

Part V Graphical Interaction

20 The Form 263
- Where Your Forms Are 263
- Inter-State Transport 265
  - *Form*.`FormName` Property 265
- Summary 268
- Review Questions 268

21 The Window 269
- What is This Thing Called, Love? 269
- Would Someone Open a Window? 270
- The Fine Art of Property Setting 272
  - *Form*.`ControlBox` Property 272
  - *Form*.`MaxButton` Property 273
  - *Form*.`MinButton` Property 273
  - *Control*.`BorderStyle` or *Form*.`BorderStyle` Property 275
- State Determination 280
  - *Form*.`WindowState` Property 281
- Summary 282
- Review Questions 283

XV

Contents ◆

22 Managing List Boxes 285
Gaining Control 285
List Boxes and Combo Boxes 286
   `Combo.Style` Property 286
   `Object.List` Property 290
   `Object.ListCount` Property 290
   `Object.ListIndex` Property 290
   `List.Sorted` or `Combo.Sorted` Property 291
   `Combo_DropDown` Property 296
Taking on a Load 296
   `Drive.Drive` Property 296
   `Dir.Path` Property 297
   `File.FileName` Property 297
   `File.Pattern` Property 297
Natural Selection 298
It's Time for a Change 302
   `Object_Change` Event 302
   `Dir_PathChange` Event 302
   `File_PatternChange` Event 302
Summary 302
Review Questions 303
Review Exercises 304

23 Options and Scroll Bars 305
Grouping Controls Within a Form 305
   `Object.Value` Property 308
Grouping Controls Within the Source Code 310
Scroll Bars 311
   `Scroll.Max` and `Scroll.Min` Properties 312
   `Scroll.SmallChange` and `Scroll.LargeChange` Properties 312
   `Text.ScrollBars` Property 316
Summary 317
Review Questions 318

24 Dialog Boxes 319
Reaching into the Message Box 319
The Input Box 323
Summary 325
Review Questions 325

xvi

Visual Basic By EXAMPLE

25 Control Manipulation and Organization 327
    A Control by Any Other Name 327
        Control.`CtlName` Property 328
        Control.`Index` Property 328
        Control.`Tag` Property 328
    Looking at Things Subjectively 329
    Pulling Tabs 331
        Control.`TabIndex` Property 332
        Control.`TabStop` Property 332
    Monitoring Activity 334
        *Control*_`GotFocus` and *Control*_`LostFocus` Events 335
        *Object*_`Click` and *Object*_`DblClick` Events 337
    Summary 337
    Review Questions 338

26 Control Appearance 339
    Front and Center 339
        Form.`Left` or *Control*.`Left` Property 339
        Form.`Top` or *Control*.`Top` Property 340
        Form.`Width` or *Control*.`Width` Property 340
        Form.`Height` or *Control*.`Height` Property 340
        Object.`Caption` Property 341
        Object.`Text` Property 341
        Control.`BackColor` and *Control*.`ForeColor` Properties 341
    Summary 343
    Review Questions 344

27 The Menu Bar 345
    Le Menu 345
        Control.`Enabled` Property 350
        Control.`Visible` Property 350
        Menu.`Checked` Property 351
    Summary 351
    Review Questions 351

28 Dragging 353
    Dragging Everything Out into the Open 353
        *Control*_`DragDrop` Event 354
        *Control*_`DragOver` Event 355

Contents

	`Control.DragMode` Property	355
	`Control.DragIcon` Property	360
	An Idea for a Lock and Key	364
	Deletion at the OK Corral	368
	Summary	373
	Review Questions	373
	Review Exercises	373
29	**The Timer**	**375**
	Where Did I Leave My Watch?	375
	`Timer_Timer` Event	376
	`Timer.Interval` Property	377
	Summary	379
	Review Questions	379
30	**The Keyboard**	**381**
	The Thing with All the Letter Buttons on It	381
	`Control_KeyDown` and `Control_KeyUp` Events	383
	`Control_KeyPress` Event	386
	Substituting Buttons for Keys	388
	Assigning Keystrokes to Buttons	391
	`Command.Default` and `Command.Cancel` Properties	391
	Summary	392
	Review Questions	392
31	**The Mouse as Device**	**395**
	The Key to Your Mouse	395
	`Control_MouseDown` and `Control_MouseUp` Events	396
	`Object_MouseMove` Event	397
	Whither the Pointer?	401
	`Control.MousePointer` Property	402
	`Control.Pointer` Property	402
	Summary	403
	Review Questions	403

xviii

Part VI Arithmetic Functions

32 Function Classification 407
    The Function of the Matter 407
    I Redeclare! 410
    Summary 412
    Review Questions 412

33 Conversion 413
    "Integize" 413
    String Conversions 415
    Summary 421
    Review Questions 421

34 Practical Math 423
    Algebraic Functions 423
    Summary 426
    Review Questions 427

35 String Functions 429
    String of Pearls 429
    String of Strings 438
    In the Midst of Strings 440
    Summary 446
    Review Questions 447

36 Composite Variable Types 449
    The Composition of Variables 449
    Summary 456
    Review Questions 456

37 The Random-Number Generator 457
    Whether 'tis by Chance or by Circumstance... 457
    Summary 461
    Review Questions 462

Contents ◆

Part VII Text

38 Conventional Output **465**
    In Search of Finer `.Print` 465
    Gobbledygook Made Logical 472
    Summary 477
    Review Questions 478

39 Textual Properties **479**
    Font Characteristics 479
        `Object.FontName` or `Printer.FontName` Property 480
        `Object.FontSize` or `Printer.FontSize` Property 480
        `Label.Alignment` Property 480
        True-False Font Properties 480
    The Curse of the Missing Cursor 481
        `Combo.SelStart` or `Text.SelStart` Property 482
        `Combo.SelLength` or `Text.SelLength` Property 482
        `Object.SelText` or `Text.SelText` Property 483
    Making It All Fit 483
        `Object.CurrentX` or `Printer.CurrentX` and
        `Object.CurrentY` or `Printer.CurrentY` Properties 484
    Summary 484
    Review Questions 485

40 The Printer **487**
    Hard Copy 487
        `Printer.Page` Property 487
    Font Selection 489
        `[Screen].Fonts` or `[Printer].Fonts` Property 489
        `[Screen].FontCount` or `[Printer].FontCount` Property 490
    Sound 490
    Summary 491
    Review Questions 492
    Review Exercise 492

xx

Part VIII Bitmapped Graphics

41 Picture Boxes **495**
    Picture.Picture Revisited 495
    Picture.Picture Property 495
  Summary 499
  Review Questions 499

42 Plotting **501**
  You Have to Draw the Line Someplace 501
  Windows Within Windows 503
  The Color Scheme 504
  The Plot So Far 510
  The Plot Thickens 513
    Form.DrawStyle, *Picture*.DrawStyle, or
      Printer.DrawStyle Property 513
    Form.DrawWidth, *Picture*.DrawWidth, or
      Printer.DrawWidth Property 514
    Form.FillColor, *Picture*.FillColor, or
      Printer.FillColor Property 514
    Form.FillStyle, *Picture*.FillStyle, or
      Printer.FillStyle Property 514
  Summary 520
  Review Questions 521
  Review Exercises 521

Part IX Error Trapping and Debugging

43 Image Scaling and Integrity **525**
  Integrity Properties 525
    Label.AutoSize or *Picture*.AutoSize Property 525
    Form.AutoRedraw or *Picture*.AutoRedraw Property 526
    *Form_*Paint or *Picture_*Paint Event 526
  Rescaling 526
    [Object].ScaleMode or *[Printer]*.ScaleMode Property 527
    .ScaleLeft, .ScaleTop, .ScaleWidth, and
      .ScaleHeight Properties 528
  Summary 531
  Review Questions 532

Contents

44 Registering Errors **533**
    To Err Is Not Only Human 533
    Baiting the Trap 535
    "We Sing the Song of the Sewer…" 540
    Summary 543
    Review Questions 544
    Review Exercises 544

Part X Physical Data

45 Sequential Access **547**
    The Hydrodynamics of Data Files 547
    Sequential Data as Pages 562
    Summary 563
    Review Questions 563
    Review Exercises 564

46 Random Access **565**
    Yippie I/O 565
    Is This On the Record? 573
    Summary 576
    Review Questions 576

47 Data File Attributes **579**
    Now Then, Let's See… Where Exactly Are We? 579
    Data Process Control 583
    Unformatted Data Input 586
    Summary 588
    Review Questions 588

48 Formal Records **591**
    Making NameForm Work 591
    Placing the End in the Middle 599
    Summary 615
    Review Questions 615

49 Sorting 617
Programming as Locomotion 618
Dive! Dive! Dive! 625
    The BubbleSort Algorithm 625
    The Shell/Metzner Sort Algorithm 627
    The QuickSort Algorithm 630
Algorithmic Logic Versus Archie Bunker 638
BubbleSorting and the Real World 641
Summary 643
Review Questions 644

Part XI The Operating System

50 Devices and Directories 647
Dust off Your Hard-Sector Disk Drives 647
    File.Normal Property 650
    File.Hidden Property 651
    File.ReadOnly Property 651
    File.System Property 651
    File.Archive Property 651
Murder or Mere Deletion? You Decide! 665
Summary 668
Review Questions 669

51 Windows Instructions 671
Environmental Control 671
Which Events Take Precedence? 677
System Clipboard Management 679
Summary 683
Review Questions 684

In Closing 685

Contents

A	ASCII/ANSI Code Chart	687
B	Answers to Review Questions	695
C	Complete Source Code Listings of Major Applications	715
	Glossary	743
	Index	755

Introduction

Welcome to the art of programming. The majority of your time working on a microcomputer thus far may have been spent writing documents, composing spreadsheets, and making at least an attempt to balance the corporate account. Up to now, you have interacted with programs in the role of *user*. As such, you have acted out a role, literally, in a script. Each program has given you choices of actions, and for the most part you've composed the data you've entered. Yet your personal interaction with the program has been scripted, planned, and plotted well in advance by programmers who may as well be playwrights. This interaction is, in essence, a dialog between you and the computer, which uses data as its medium of communication.

Microsoft Windows is an elaborate stage for the production and presentation of programs. Windows' visual resources—the various buttons, gadgets, and pointers—are the props for this stage. Naturally, the program itself is the play. The purpose of the program—whether to balance the corporate account or give the user a few moments of stress relief—is the *theme*. A person practicing to become a playwright studies the themes developed by great playwrights—such as Shakespeare, Tennessee Williams, Ferlinghetti, and the Marx Brothers—to determine how an intriguing and meaningful dialog can best be constructed among the characters.

Introduction ◆ Visual Basic

The objective of this book is to teach you to write computer programs in much the same way amateur playwrights learn their craft. In the same way that no great theatrical play (be it tragedy or comedy) can be written without a strong underlying theme, no computer program, whether in Visual Basic or assembly language, can be conceived without a strong underlying purpose or objective. This book cannot give you an objective for your program any more than a book on 20th Century playwrights can supply you with a theme for a play. Yet this is the very thing other books on the subject of programming try to do—tell you what to write, rather than how to write it.

Visual Basic By Example shows you various techniques for writing working programs, allowing you as an amateur Visual Basic programmer to develop your own style. Programming, rather than just a method for translating everyday procedures into logical code, is also a means of expression. To be a user of applications, you assume the role of an actor on a stage. As a programmer, however, you set the stage, conceive the dialog, and in a somewhat detached fashion, direct the actor in how to perform the role of user.

To better understand the role of programmer, imagine the elements of a program—the various modules, procedures, routines, and clauses—as if they were the supporting characters of a play. In other words, the part of the program that figures the totals, the part that draws the lines on the graph, the part that recalls the name of your client, and the part that checks to see if the user pressed a button are all supporting characters, different in purpose although equal in treatment.

The user, however, has the lead role in this production. The dialog between the lead and the rest of the cast comprises the body of the play. If the characters don't interact with each other, their individual identities aren't apparent to the audience, and the message in the play doesn't come through. Likewise, without a high degree of coordination and data exchange between the elements of a program and the user, the program doesn't flow, and its objective may not be completed with ease. Like the confused, disgruntled patron of a theater, the user may choose to walk out in mid-scene.

So you can see that your role as programmer in this drama is both as playwright and stage director. No programming environment to date more closely resembles, analogously speaking, a stage than Visual Basic. There are platforms, props, gadgets, and in a sense, choreography. The stage for each program is arranged and assembled on-screen using the mouse as your stage hand. The production itself, however, is still a script, meticulously executed and thoroughly rehearsed.

Visual Basic By Example explicitly and exhaustively demonstrates the development of programs and program modules from the perspective of the programmer, showing you what decisions are made—both necessary and arbitrary—that lead to a well-planned, thoughtfully prepared, perfectly executed production.

Overview

The first order of business is to comprehend the mechanics and characteristics of the stage where you will produce your programs. In Part I, "The Visual Basic Environment," I take you on an explicitly guided tour of the workspace where you will construct your programs. Once you're settled in and comfortable in your new workspace, you begin to concentrate on your main objective: learning just what a program actually is and how a Visual Basic program differs from a conventional BASIC program or even a C program.

Throughout the book—as its title implies—I show you programs and program modules in various stages of construction, and give you some practice constructing your own modules for real-world purposes. Instead of just showing you a working program or two and saying, "Make yours like mine," Chapter 4, "The Development Process," takes you step-by-step through the construction of a small Visual Basic program, concentrating on what goes through the mind of the programmer and what type of goals programmers set for themselves. Any program, no matter what the language, does not manifest itself in complete, flawless source code like some of the other books might have you believe. Most good programs are the result of bursts of inspiration, separated by several hours of error-trapping and debugging.

When you're comfortable with the setting and the process of programming, you start to examine the verbal and graphic elements of Visual Basic piece by piece. As graphically comprehensive as Visual Basic is, a novice programmer might be led to believe there is

Introduction ▶ Visual Basic

little or no arithmetic left in the programming process. Such is not the case; arithmetic logic and procedural algebra still comprise the crux of all programming. Visual Basic is considerably more adept at interpreting mathematical functions than, for instance, HyperCard or ToolBook. Still, math is not a very glamorous subject. Math can be the most esoteric and paradoxical part of the programming process; so in Part II, "Values and Variables," I carefully introduce you to arithmetic logic and procedural algebra using tangible, real-world terms and analogies.

If you're a veteran of older versions of BASIC, you probably have noticed already how the simple process of printing a line of text has grown from a statement of fact into a complex event of methodology. In Part III, "Instructions and Groups," you examine in detail the reformed syntax of the Visual Basic language. In Part IV, "Modularization," I demonstrate how the overall job of a Visual Basic program is divided and delegated to the various modules and constituent procedures.

The Visual Basic language contains dozens of reserved terms for handling graphic elements and user interaction processes. Each of them is covered in Part V, "Graphical Interaction." Part VI turns to the subject of "Arithmetic Functions." I then cover the more conventional methods of graphic output in Part VII, "Text," and Part VIII, "Bitmapped Graphics."

The Visual Basic interpreter offers a trial-and-error environment for testing programs. It is quite natural for programs to exhibit errors in the early stages of their development; in fact, one of the major factors in the development of a perfectly formed and executed program is the prior existence of errors. In Part IX, "Error Trapping and Debugging," I introduce you to the fine art of correcting yourself—which is probably what you spend half your time doing as a programmer, even after you become an expert.

Comparisons are continually drawn between Visual Basic and graphical database management systems such as PerForm or Oracle. Despite all the enhancements, the Visual Basic methodology for handling data in the form of records—such as records of your clients, or of items of inventory—is still rooted in the old BASIC dialects. I cover the subject in detail—although it's old ground to a BASIC veteran—in Part X, "Physical Data."

Afterwards, you look at how Visual Basic programs communicate with other Visual Basic programs, with Windows, and with DOS itself. In Part XI, "The Operating System," you see how Visual Basic handles functions that are normally dispatched to DOS.

Who Should Use This Book

I assume that you have already used Windows enough that you understand the principles of icons, buttons, and drop-down menus. I also assume that you have already fully installed Visual Basic into your computer, and that it is operating normally. I assume, however, that you have no prior knowledge or experience with BASIC unless stated otherwise.

How to Use This Book

One of the tools I frequently use to show you how the Visual Basic language works is *pseudocode*. In essence, a paragraph of pseudocode states what the program instructions would say if they could state their functions to you out loud, in English. The pseudocode is typeset in *italics,* and a light bulb symbol appears next to the pseudocode.

Actual Visual Basic code is typeset in `monospace`. Placeholders—terms used to represent what you actually type within the code—are typeset in `italic monospace`. Here are two samples, the first of which is written in pure Visual Basic, and the second of which is a pseudocode sample that explains the function of the code fragment preceding it:

```
For C = 1 to 5
     Form1.Print C
Next C
```

Start counting from 1 to 5.
  Print the number you just counted.
Go back to where you started counting, and repeat yourself until you count to 5.

Introduction ▶ Visual Basic

Granted, the preceding segment of pseudocode is a bit verbose, but its purpose is not only to show you what the Visual Basic source code is trying to state for the interpreter, but also at what point in the code it is stated.

Next to many working program modules and fragments is a symbol representing the relative degree of effort and experience required to comprehend the example. Level 1 is the easiest, whereas Level 3 indicates the most difficult examples. A module's size alone is no measure of the extent to which it can be confusing. I hope these symbols help you confirm that, when a particular module is difficult, it was meant to be. The following is a list of the symbols I use for this purpose:

Level 1

Level 2

Level 3

Every once in a while, you encounter a line of Visual Basic source code that is so long that the typesetters didn't have room to fit it all on one line. In such cases, we've used a little rightward-sweeping arrow before a line that is the continuation of the previous one, as in the following example:

```
Declare Function GetSystemDirectory Lib "Kernel" (ByVal
    ↪ lpBuffer As String, ByVal nSize As Integer) As Integer
```

Note also the "Level 3" symbol used next to this example, just to let you know that it's alright to be confused at first by this line of example source code. Believe it or not, if you follow this book through from beginning to end, by the time you get to the chapter that mentions this very line, you'll be able to understand it just as if it were English—or, at least, English shorthand.

In an effort to make every square inch of this book useful to you, we've placed information and diagrams out in the margins. If an

Visual Basic *By* EXAMPLE

Margin notes emphasize important new terms and concepts.

important new term is being introduced that is a crucial part of the Visual Basic conceptual vocabulary, or of the vernacular of computing in general, a definition for that term appears in a *margin note*. Also, where space permits, small *flowcharts* appear to the side of some program examples. These flowcharts have been drawn using modern formatting, to help you visualize the flow and throughput of individual procedures.

At the end of most chapters, you are presented with a short series of review questions and, where applicable, exercises that should challenge your comprehension of the information in that chapter. The difficulty-level symbols are used here, too, giving you fair warning as to the difficulty of the questions. You can find the answers—printed right-side up because we trust you—in Appendix B at the end of the book.

Points of Order

There are a few items concerning English-language syntax worth noting before we proceed. You've probably already observed that we write *Visual Basic*—only initial uppercase letters—with respect to the specific product and *BASIC*—in all uppercase—with respect to the language genre as a whole. This is because BASIC is an acronym that stands for Beginner's All-purpose Symbolic Instruction Code. Microsoft chooses to lowercase *Basic* when it refers to the language; in deference to John Kemeny and Thomas Kurtz who conceived the language as well as its name, however, I choose to leave the acronym as it stands. From time to time, however, *Visual Basic* is abbreviated as *VB*.

The screen shots I show from time to time depict Microsoft Windows running on a standard VGA monochrome monitor at 640 x 480 resolution. Due to slight variations in Windows video display drivers, especially in varying resolutions, your screen may appear slightly different from mine when you perform the same operations.

In the old days of programming, back when things were simpler to describe (for instance, about 1989), you could print a few pages of source code—pure text and numbers back then—type it all in, and you would have a working program. Times have changed,

Introduction ◆ Visual Basic

and now you do not entirely *type in* a Visual Basic program. The positioning and characteristics of graphic objects are activities done with the mouse; you now practically *draw* control windows. When you type one of the programs in this book, it would be unfair for me to simply show you a photograph and say, "Draw your control form like mine." Instead, whenever I give you a complete source code listing, I give you a table showing the name of each graphic object employed in the program, along with the *properties* or characteristics—such as position, size, color, and index number—that have been changed from their default settings. You can then assemble your control form manually using the table as a guide.

All the source code modules, program listings, and property tables in this book are yours to type, manipulate, experiment with, destroy, rebuild, and enhance for whatever purposes you desire. Although D. F. Scott is the original author of these modules, I feel the best way to see how a mechanism—physical or logical—works is to take it apart and put it back together. You shouldn't have to ask permission to experiment with something as basic as BASIC.

A programmer writes programs with the aid of Visual Basic, although Visual Basic is itself a program. This could cause some confusion if I use the phrase *the Visual Basic program* without being specific as to whether I'm referring to the program written in the VB language or to Visual Basic the program. Therefore, I refer to the programs you write using the VB language as *Visual Basic applications*. When I say, *the Visual Basic program*, I am referring to the software you bought in the white and blue box.

With respect to the actions a user makes when operating a program in a graphical environment, I chose to standardize the usage of individual verbs for specific actions. Thus, a menu item is *selected*, an item from a list box is *chosen*, data in a form or window is *indicated*, and a button is *clicked*. Further, a setting, property, or file name typed manually into a text box is a *designation*, and a setting or attribute chosen from a list box is an *assignment*. This choice of terms is consistent throughout the book to reduce confusion.

The standard mouse button used for indicating objects on the screen is the left button; however, Microsoft Windows allows its left-handed users, through the Control Panel, to reconfigure the mouse so that the right button acts as the left. Because the right button can be the left button if you want—and that can create a lot of confusion in print—I use the term *index button* to refer to the mouse button that is used to indicate objects.

I refer to the *cursor* to indicate the blinking vertical line or block that denotes on-screen where text is to appear when it is typed from the keyboard. By contrast, the *pointer* is the arrow that is moved by the mouse.

Finally, I refrain from using the term *user interface,* at the request of an ever-expanding group of engineers and programmers who feel the term *interface* should be limited to mechanical, not visual, devices. Instead, I refer to Microsoft Windows as a *graphical environment,* as stated on the box it comes in. I use no poetic synonyms for forms, windows, controls, graphic objects, or devices.

Now that the stage is set, it is time for us to raise the curtain on Act I.

Part I

The Visual Basic Environment

What a Program Is

In this chapter you are introduced to the concept of the program, with respect to both Visual Basic and the art of computing as a whole. This chapter explains what you as a programmer must know about the behavior of programs in a computer, so that future users of your programs won't have to worry about that themselves. I cover the elementary concepts of programming with a high-level language. If you're already familiar with what such a language is and what it does, feel free to proceed to Chapter 2.

A Programmer's Credo

The objective of all programming is to model or simulate some rationally describable process—be it in the real world or imaginary—as a logical and arithmetic procedure. This process can be completely mathematical like accounting, geometrical like floor planning, or recreational like starship piloting. If you understand the principle behind the process, you already know what your computer program should contain. What you need to do is reconstruct and reorganize this process as a mathematical model. In other words, you have to find a way to describe absolutely every part of the process mathematically.

Chapter 1 ◆ What a Program Is

To explain: Everything about a computer is logical and is comprised of numbers and mathematical methods. It is therefore relatively easy to conceive an accounting program, because the process of accounting is comprised of numbers and numerical methods. Consider, however, a program that renders floor plans and landscaping plans. There geometry plays a role, and some processes that at first may not be viewed as numerical—such as drawing where the trees or shrubbery are to be planted—are simulated with program instructions.

Now consider a program that renders routine medical diagnoses for doctors. The part of the program that maintains a list of symptoms, causes, and medications would be the easiest part to create—you might call this portion the *database manager*. A database is a collection of organized records (such as a doctor's list of patients). A database manager is the part of a program that maintains the database information.

> A *database* is a collection of organized records. A *database manager* is the program that maintains database information.

It's certainly far more difficult for the programmer to simulate the decision-making process than to maintain the lists of symptoms and medications. If you're not already a doctor, you as programmer would need to talk with medical doctors extensively and study the concepts and procedures of diagnosis. You would have to read all the introductory material as if you were a medical student (and, unofficially, you would be one). It is important for a doctor to rely to some degree on gut feelings and intuition when making a clinical diagnosis. Keeping this in mind, you would need to simulate the diagnostic process for the sake of a machine that has no intuition, or for that matter, guts. This is not an impossible task. You can let the program simulate just the "memory" functions and let the doctor provide the intuition.

Leaving the doctor's office behind for now, consider writing a chess program. You probably know from experience that a computer *appears* (note the emphasis) to play chess very well, and grand masters like Gerry Kasparov can appreciate how well these programs play the game (although Kasparov still beats them constantly). What you may not know is that no chess program conceives its own strategy for winning the game. The program reevaluates the board move after move, and the evaluation results are generally discarded after each move is made. When you play chess against a computer,

Visual Basic *By* EXAMPLE

you're playing human strategy versus a bunch of math. Your job as programmer of a chess game is to conceive the bunch of math. Programming a chess game does not require a mastery of chess; however, it does require a mastery of math. You should probably be a reasonably good chess player, but you wouldn't be programming your own strategies into the game because chess programs don't *think*. Instead, you'll define methods for, for instance, the proper position of the Knight 10 moves ahead with respect to all other squares that could be in check by that time.

When conceiving a program that performs work that would otherwise be performed by a human being, it is important that you thoroughly comprehend the fundamentals of the work process and the principles, laws, and mathematics governing that process. It is not necessary for you to master the process itself. In other words, you don't need to be an accountant to write an accounting program or an M.D. to write a clinical diagnosis program. Simply review the fundamentals of the process and *look up the details when you need to*. You should, however, comprehend the jobs of the professionals who will be using your program to a degree that they won't be insulted or aggravated by that program.

When a program is applicable to your business task, we call that program an *application.* Visual Basic is a tool for the development of applications. When using it, keep in mind that your objective is *automation*—taking the logical and arithmetic part of a real-world job such as record-keeping or data analysis and delegating a measure of responsibility for it to the computer. If the applications you write merely invent more work for their users, automation doesn't take place and people will not be compelled to use the applications. An application should take a load off somebody's shoulders, or at least distribute the weight more evenly in the way a word processor organizes documents or a database management system handles records.

Fundamental Terminology

A *program* is the symbolic form of a task.

To comprehend Visual Basic requires more than a modicum of effort; you are trusted to have mastered the mental concept of a *program*. To start you toward this level of mastery, here is a new,

15

broader, but fitting definition for the term *program* in this context: A program is the symbolic form of a task or work process. It is any computing process that is described logically using a fundamental code that is interpretable by both the person reading it and the computer processing it.

Notice that in the preceding definition I did not use the term *language*. Computer programs are generally written using languages. Although there are a few exceptions, the Visual Basic language is certainly not one of them. Nonetheless, we do call the written text of a program its *source code*.

> *Source code* is the written text of a program in its native language.

The source code of a program consists of instructions that are executed in sequence. This sequence is not necessarily top-to-bottom or beginning-to-end, but there is a sequence nonetheless. Because the instructions of a Visual Basic program appear to have sentence structure, and because the sequence of those instructions in a program communicates the purpose of that program to its human reader in a manner more attributable to human language than machine language, we say Visual Basic is a *high-level* programming language. Machine or assembly languages, by contrast, are called *low-level* languages because they more closely resemble the logic of the computer than the reasoning of the mind.

> An *instruction* is any complete directive made within a program.

Although you use something called a *language* to program a computer, the act of programming is not like a conversation or giving orders to an employee or crew member. Unlike communication with a knowledgeable human being, you cannot expect an unprogrammed computer to *intuit* the meaning behind a complex instruction, or have any processing capability ahead of time that's related to the task you're instructing it to perform. If a computer came to you "out of the box" with the capability to do whatever you asked it to do, there would be no need for packaged software.

A machine, scientifically defined, is any device that performs work. A computer is a machine to the extent that it has electronic components that simulate the actions of mechanical ones. A mechanical device such as a watch or a locomotive engine has mechanics that you can assimilate just by looking at it. A computer's mechanics are all electronic. Because you can't see electrons or electric currents, the computer's mechanics must be explained symbolically, both to you as well as the computer. What's different about the computer as a machine is that by changing the arrangement of its symbols, you change its mechanics. This rearrangement is called *programming*.

When one programs a computer using the most rudimentary symbols recognized by its central processing unit (CPU), we say that the program is written in *machine language*, and that the symbolism constitutes a *low-level* program. As a low-level programmer, you could be feeding your computer instructions such as `24`, `62`, `47`.... Imagine how difficult it would be for you as a rational, intelligent human being to have to interpret the meanings behind these digits day after day.

> A *low-level* programming language "talks" directly to the computer in machine code.

This is the reason there is a BASIC programming language. Rational, intelligent people have no time to mess with assembling code that sounds like the emanations from a football quarterback. We have the right to program computers using something more closely resembling human language. BASIC and its descendant Visual Basic both use words as symbols rather than numbers or mnemonics to represent electronic operations logically. This is one reason we call BASIC a *high-level* language.

> A *high-level* programming language resembles written words and must be translated into machine code.

A More Literal Interpretation

An *interpreter* is a program that continually breaks down a program's high-level linguistic symbols into low-level arithmetic symbols. A computer won't execute code until it has been broken down—or *catabolized*—to its lowest level; language of any form is far beyond the capacity of a central processing unit to interpret for itself. Visual Basic is an interpreter that continually breaks down source code into instructions the CPU can recognize, because BASIC instructions must be reinterpreted into machine language before they can be executed.

> An *interpreter* translates high-level linguistic code into low-level numeric code.

If you've programmed a computer using the GW-BASIC or QBasic interpreters supplied with your copy of DOS, you're familiar with the conventional concept of the interpreter. Normally you supply the BASIC interpreter with a list of instructions using a built-in editor, and the interpreter processes each instruction while the program is being executed.

Chapter 1 ◆ What a Program Is

Visual Basic interprets the program as it is written.

With other interpreted languages, the program is translated into machine language one line at a time as the program runs.

On the surface, the Visual Basic interpreter appears to be no different from a standard interpreter, except for the fact that it performs the interpretation process *while the program is being entered into the editor.*

Figure 1.1 illustrates the differences between these processes.

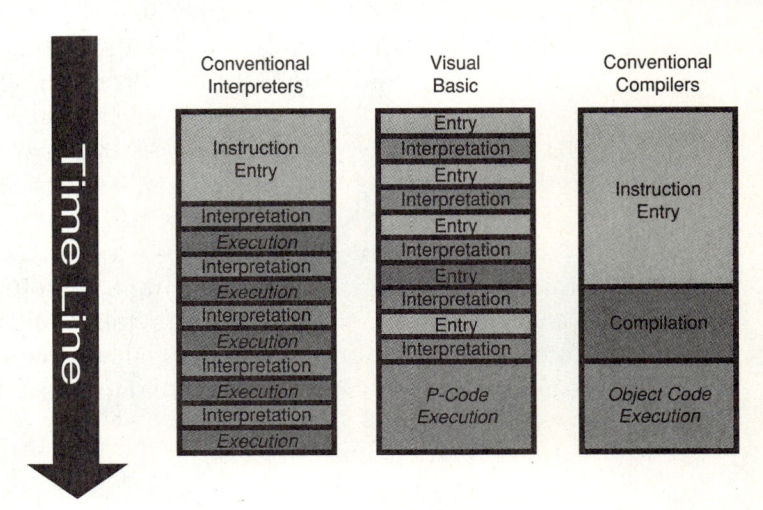

Figure 1.1. Three forms of program generation compared.

Object code (machine code) is comprised of CPU instructions that are not symbolized in any way for human interpretation.

Visual Basic does not actually interpret the program fully while it is being written. The code that Visual Basic generates internally (which you never see) is called *intermediate code* or *p-code.* This code rests in memory, awaiting the execution call from the user or programmer. The p-code is then reinterpreted—or shall I say interpreted the rest of the way—until it becomes *object code* for the CPU. This code is then executed, but is not retained in memory. Instead, the interpreter goes about its business of reinterpreting more p-code.

Visual Basic source code executes quickly in comparison to a standard interpreter because half the interpretation process is already done by the time the programmer gives the order to Run. Still, another program is required at all times in order for the intermediate

18

p-code to be executed, whether that program is the main Visual Basic interpreter or a special, smaller interpreter program without the editor, which is shipped with every copy of Visual Basic and is freely distributable with permission of Microsoft. At the time of this writing, this run-time interpreter was called VBRUN100.DLL.

In contrast to an interpreter, a *compiler* is a program that takes high-level instructions and translates them all at once into a machine-language executable code file. A C compiler produces object code that is executable (able to be run) without the aid of the C compiler, comprising a stand-alone program. When you run a compiled program, there is no interpretation process; the compiler has already completely broken the source code into object code. Most programs or applications you'll ever buy or use are compiled this way.

A *compiler* produces a stand-alone executable program file.

Although compilers give you the benefit of generating pure object code without having to supply an interpreter of some form with your programs, the act of programming with a compiler generally gives you no room for trial and error. If there's an error in your program, execution generally stops, and that's that. Modern compilers such as those currently sold by Microsoft and Borland have eliminated this problem by including with their editors separate p-code interpreters (also called *p-code compilers,* perhaps out of confusion) that work in much the same way Visual Basic works. This way programmers can test their source code to make sure the program works properly before compiling it into pure object code. The standard Visual Basic package does not include an object code compiler.

The VB (Visual Basic) control program or editor can be used to produce a file with the extension .EXE, although this is *not* an executable file by the DOS definition. The "compiled" program file produced by Visual Basic is in fact the preinterpreted high-level p-code that the editor program would normally generate while the VB application is being entered into the editor. All Visual Basic programs, even if they have an .EXE extension, *must* be run with the VB interpreter—either the main interpreter or the VBRUN100.DLL interpreter.

Chapter 1 ◆ What a Program Is

The Process of Interaction

Information is any symbol or message that is meaningful to people. *Data* are the carriers of information within a computer.

Earlier I stated that computing is an *interactive* process. Generally this term implies the exchange of information between parties. We often misstate that information can be shared between a person and a computer. It's important that you draw a vital distinction between the terms *information* and *data.* The formal definition of *information* is any symbol or message that conveys meaning to a person or to people. A computer cannot be *informed* of anything; it's not intelligent, and it cannot be taught. Information is imparted from one party to another through a medium. In the field of computing, data is this medium, or what Marshall McLuhan might call the carrier of the message. A computer stores and retrieves only *data,* which may or may not impart meaning to you or anyone else. Data cannot impart meaning to the computer because the computer is not a thing that reasons.

The exchange that takes place between a person and a computer may be informative, and it may even be conversational. Note, however, that this conversation does not really take place between the computer and the user; it is between the *programmer* and the user. The conversation is merely indirect, the symbols used in the conversation are limited, the topic is chosen in advance, and the responses as delivered by the program are, in effect, prerecorded. In the way syllables and phonemes convey meaning when utilized in a conversation between people, instructions and data convey meaning to the person using an application.

Let's be more specific about this by comparing real-world person-to-person interaction with person-to-computer interaction. Assume you are a small-business owner. You deliver your company's transaction data to a professional accountant (or C.P.A.) and give the accountant instructions on what to do. You are performing the same role as the user of an accounting program—that of data supplier and process initiator. You wouldn't tell the C.P.A. exactly what to do. You would assume his training allows him to determine just what he should be doing, based on the particular data you have given him. You expect the C.P.A. to know the process already.

Switch sides now and assume you're the C.P.A. Your training is based on years of learning and reviewing accounting principles.

Visual Basic *By* EXAMPLE

Along with that, you've gained much business experience. You know the process of recording this small business' account information after you've been given this mountain of data to sift through, because your experience acts as a guide on what to do. The more experienced you are with figuring numbers as an accountant, the more skilled you become.

Still, as a C.P.A. you're *not* performing the role of a computer accounting program. The computer is not an instrument that acquires skill over time or with constant use. The computer's "understanding" of what to do with all this data is constructed beforehand as its program, long before the data is created. The difference between giving a person instructions and giving a computer instructions is that a person has numerous faculties available for *deducing* the proper process. By contrast, you instruct the Visual Basic interpreter using only mathematics, logic, formulas, and comparisons—no specifics, and no examples. You cannot construct an accounting program by taking existing business financial data, feeding that data into the program, and having the computer generate formulas from it. Unlike the way people reason, the computer cannot deduce the process that leads to particular results based on the values of those results.

You can, however, take existing business information as an example for yourself and reasonably deduce the formulas that a C.P.A. would use to analyze and record this data. You would, however, remove any part of those formulas that makes them specific to a particular business at a particular time. You replace these specifics with vague references to unknown or arbitrary values, called *variables*. In other words, you remove everything absolute from the example process, leaving in its place only the algebra, which is entirely figurative.

Flying Blind is Truly Flying

A good analogy for this process—although thankfully not one drawn from the real world—is if you were to use an audio tape to instruct a kindergarten student to pilot a space shuttle. Assume this student is your child; and although she's bright, and has seen things go up into the sky and come down from it—birds, planes, and kites—she hasn't quite differentiated between them yet. Her current idea of a joystick is something you use to make Mario kick the turtle on the video game.

Your first job as narrator for the Better Daycare Through Astrophysics School for Young Pilots is to define the world for this person. What is space, where is it, and why is it so difficult to breathe there? You'll probably need to explain *g-force*, but you'll probably also need to explain that *g* falls between *f* and *h*. Take note that all the referential information a skilled pilot is naturally aware of has absolutely no bearing upon your child's world for the moment. You not only have to define what all this information is, but you have to define the *world* for your child as well.

Should you introduce into the tape the concept of rocket physics? What makes the thing go in the first place? Arguably, a person might not need to know about the combustion engine to drive a car, but an astronaut's survival might depend on this kind of knowledge. It might be possible to tell your young listener something about the universe, the layout of the instrument panel, and the location of certain important valves connected to the flight suit, without necessarily holding true to the absolute facts; and yet, just perhaps, you might impart enough information to your young pilot that she might be able to perform the right procedures at the right time. You don't have to lie to the child, but in the interest of her own safety you may not want to confuse her by attempting to impart all the facts to her. Perhaps most importantly of all, because this is an audio tape programmed in advance of flight time, you as narrator cannot assume your pilot has succeeded or failed in her mission. She therefore cannot draw any conclusions from experience.

Programming in Visual Basic is not always such an impossible or frustrating task as that invented above. Think of the VB interpreter as a program that by itself "flies blind." *You* are its vision. You tell the VB application how to calculate accounting data and generate ledgers without giving it any data except during the testing stage. In terms of piloting, you're flying by instruments only. Yet to be able to fly by instruments makes one a better pilot. To comprehend the work process well enough that you can model it within a computer program not only helps automate your office, but also augments your own understanding of how things work.

Visual Basic *By*

EXAMPLE

Concern for the Environment

The control program *of a computer provides the resources that a program needs to run.*

Almost all computers run more than one program at a time. This is not necessarily multitasking. It is merely the result of the division of responsibilities in a computer. In the history of computing, when the job of computer control was first removed from the human operator and handed over to software, there were as many as two real programs in operation in a computer system at any one time. The *control program* (the operating system of the computer) provided input/output, memory, and storage services to the *user program.* In your computer system running Visual Basic today, there can be six levels of program operation at any one time, with the program at a lower level providing services to the program above it.

Figure 1.2 depicts the structure of all programs in a computer system at all times while Visual Basic is running. The arrows in this figure depict the provision of services from one level of program to the one above it. The resulting strata of environments forms a sort of computing "atmosphere," in which the richest elements shared between tiers in the structure rise to the top.

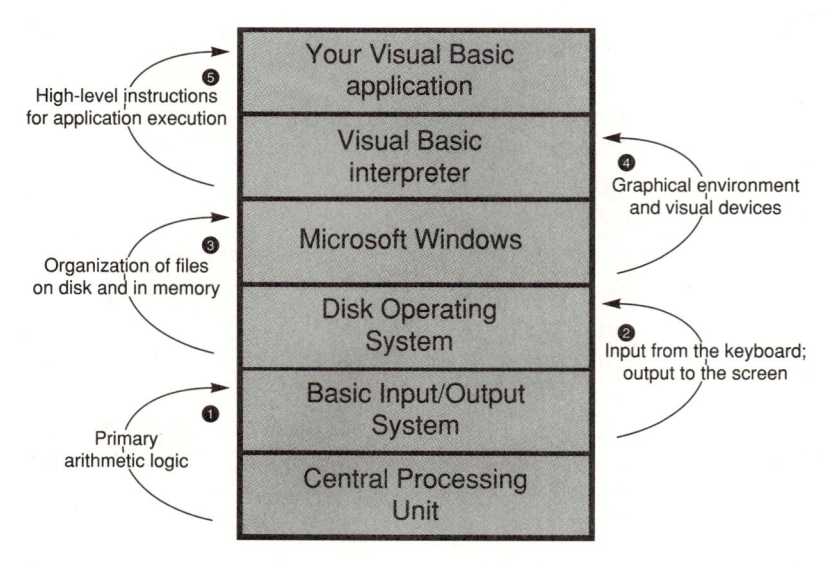

Figure 1.2. The Visual Basic "computing atmosphere."

23

Chapter 1 ◆ What a Program Is

> A *pixel* is the smallest point that can be plotted on your screen at any given resolution.

At the bottom of this structure is the CPU, the core element of any computer system. The primary arithmetic logic of the computer is literally etched into this unit like a drawing. The CPU provides services to the Basic Input/Output System (BIOS), which is officially the lowest-level program in a microcomputer. This is the part that tells your computer that it is a computer, and its job is to *poll* (make a request of) the keyboard and other devices for user input, and to display characters or pixels on the screen as output.

The job of collecting all those characters, pixels, and bytes registered from the BIOS as actual files is delegated to the *disk operating system*. In our particular system, this is some form (or clone) of MS-DOS or PC DOS. Microsoft Windows Version 3.0 borrows many of these file-handling services from DOS, therefore acting as a "visual overlay" on top of DOS that makes DOS easier to use. Version 3.1 of Windows will take over some of the file-handling responsibilities from DOS. Eventually, it is reported, Windows will assume all of the file-handling responsibility currently granted to DOS.

> An *environment* acts as the graphical mediator between the user and the program.

Microsoft calls its Windows product a *graphical environment*, which means that it provides facilities and resources for other programs to operate, cooperate, and share data. Windows provides the environment for Windows applications such as Excel, CorelDRAW!, and Visual Basic.

The facilities and resources Windows provides Visual Basic are significant. Most obviously, the appearance and function of graphic objects such as buttons, menus, and scroll bars is defined for Visual Basic by Windows. Furthermore, the visual display drivers, special considerations for different fonts and type styles, and the drivers for individual printers are all regular provisions of the Windows environment. Visual Basic as a program needs to concentrate only on its main objective as an interpreter of a programmer's instructions.

At the top of the heap, the Visual Basic application is granted use of the resources given to the VB interpreter by Windows. This makes it possible for a programmer to specify the presence, location, and purpose of a button, a drop-down list box, or one of the other Windows graphical controls without having to program the mechanics of that control from scratch. This is the part of Visual Basic that makes it marketable. As a Visual Basic programmer, you will spend less time drawing controls and more time conceiving instructions and organizing information as data. The remainder of this book is organized proportionally with respect to what you as a Visual Basic programmer will do with your time and effort.

Summary

The purpose of programming can either be the automation of a real-world process or the simulation of a new process. A Visual Basic program is a mathematical model of a task that people could most likely perform using pencil and paper in the "old world." If the program is no easier to operate than pencil and paper, or if the program does not otherwise add some measure of functionality to the process, the objective of the program hasn't truly been fulfilled.

To achieve automation of a work process within a program does *not* require the programmer to master this process in the real world; in other words, the author of a legal assistance database manager need not be a lawyer. If the programmer can model just the fundamental principles of a real-world process, that alone will help professionals in their daily business.

The written form of a program is called *source code*. The individual directives within this source code are called *instructions*. A low-level program instruction makes sense to the computer almost instantly, although a high-level program instruction, as in Visual Basic, must first be translated into intermediate instructions or p-code before it can be executed. This is why Visual Basic is called an *interpreted language*. Unlike a conventional interpreter, however, VB source code is completely interpreted prior to the program's execution. In other words, the program is compiled to memory.

All programs exchange data with their users, although a good program exchanges more information with its user using less data. In information theory, data is seen as the carrier of information, like a sound wave over a phone line is seen as the carrier of the message. A mathematical process cannot be described to the interpreter by example or inference—only through algebra. The form of a Visual Basic program certainly doesn't resemble conventional algebra, although its processes are said to be algebraic. The interpreter makes no assumptions as to how any real-world process works. That process must be described using the vocabulary of Visual Basic in advance of the program's execution before that program can be said to work.

An operating environment provides services, functions, and facilities to its programs. Microsoft Windows provides access to its graphic control resources to Visual Basic. Visual Basic recognizes the primary Windows graphic controls and allows the programmer to place these controls into a form at will. Visual Basic receives language-form instructions from the programmer concerning how to operate these graphic controls and interprets these instructions on behalf of Windows.

Review Questions

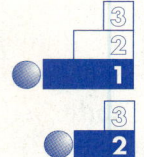

1. Why is BASIC considered a high-level language?
2. What is a "sentence" within a program's source code called?
3. What is the primary low-level language of any computer called?
4. Which program in your computer provides services to Microsoft Windows?
5. If you were to instruct the Visual Basic interpreter that, for the time being and in the proper context, the letter *a* were to represent the number *6*, to what extent can that instruction be considered *informative*?

The Project

In this chapter you are introduced to the methodology by which Visual Basic programs are organized *visually*. A VB application contains many on-screen elements called *controls,* around which the linguistic components of the program are constructed. Each control has its own procedure, which is a part of the overall program. I discuss the more linguistic elements in Chapter 3; for now, we concentrate on the structural and graphical composition of the Visual Basic project.

The Visual Basic Project

Armed with the knowledge of interpreters and environments gained from Chapter 1, let's dive into the Visual Basic environment. Figure 2.1 shows the Visual Basic workspace as it generally appears at startup.

If you're looking for a READY prompt like the one you used to rely on if you programmed in BASIC during the 70s and early 80s, you won't find it here—more to the point, you won't find it anywhere in this decade. Instead, the majority of the tools you need to program are laid out before you as if they were on a drafting table. At the center of this table is Form1, which currently represents the site of the main input/output panel for your future program.

Chapter 2 ◆ The Project

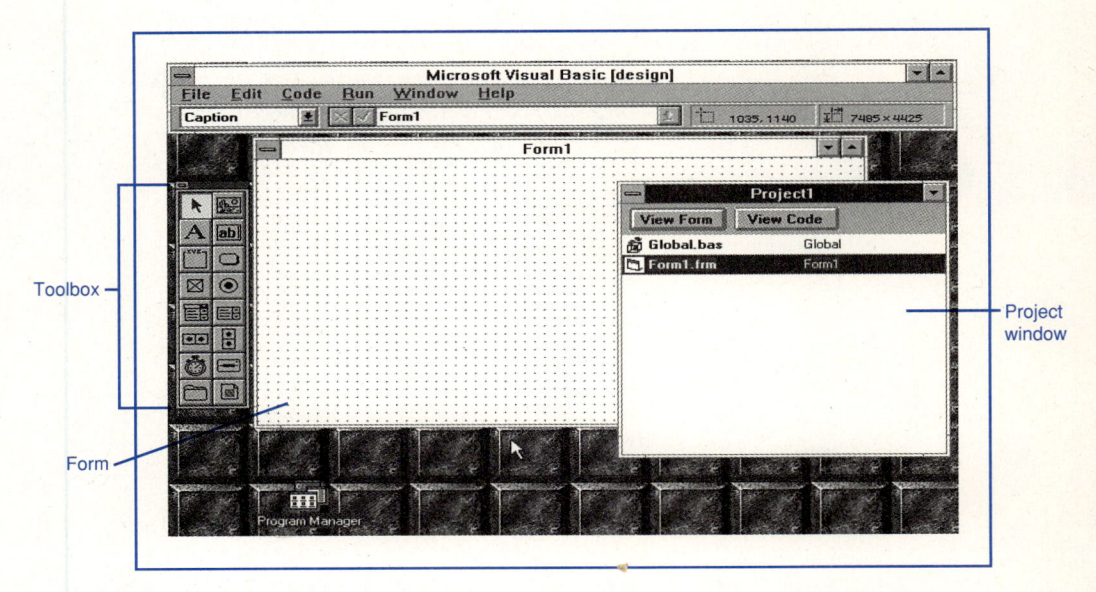

Figure 2.1. The Visual Basic environment in its clean, natural state.

Generally, each Windows application is given its own self-contained window, and all the tools needed to operate that application are placed within that window. Visual Basic violates this law of organization entirely because it has no primary window of its own. Actually, this is for a good reason: The applications you develop should follow the rules of Microsoft Windows, which state that each program is apportioned one primary window. To make this feasible, Visual Basic has to step outside the main window of the application you're developing, because you really shouldn't have two main windows active at the same time.

While a Visual Basic program is under construction, it is called a *project*. This is because the source code of a VB program is distributed among more than one physical file stored on disk; a VB project consists of at least three files: namely, the *global module* that sets the stage for the project's execution; one *form module* that contains the graphic elements of the VB application along with the instructions; and a *general module* that may be empty or contain more instructions.

Along the right side of the Visual Basic screen at startup is the Project window, which contains a list of all files that are a part of the

> A *project* consists of all the files that collectively comprise a Visual Basic program.

Visual Basic *By*
EXAMPLE

project currently being edited. This list comprises a file itself, the name of which appears as the title bar of the project window. When saved to disk, this title becomes the project file name. The example in Figure 2.1 shows the default file name for the project, which is `Project1`.

While programming in Visual Basic, there are basically two things you'll do (besides staring at the screen and waiting for solutions to come to mind): typing instructions for the program and drawing the control forms on the screen. While you're doing the latter, believe it or not, the VB interpreter is helping you with the former by preparing in advance the framework for procedural modules for each graphic object you add to the form.

On startup, Visual Basic displays by default a blank project. At the center of the screen is `Form1`, which is the primary window for your VB application. Each form in a VB project, including this one, has a physical file all to itself. Stored in this file is all the information concerning the appearance, contents, and characteristics of the form, along with the VB instructions for operating each graphic object that is a part of the form.

As you take a guided tour of the visual part of the VB environment, you're invited to follow along on your computer as I show you how to invoke certain facilities and windows. I assume you've already started Visual Basic and that your screen looks somewhat like Figure 2.1. A blank form resides in the center of your screen. Visual Basic reserves a space for the entry of program instructions regarding this form alone. The area where code is entered is called the *Procedure window*.

To examine the instructions pertaining to this form, double-click anywhere within the form window. The procedure window appears, as depicted in Figure 2.2.

A *procedure*—as I discuss in detail in the next chapter—is the core program component of Visual Basic. Each time you add a graphic object to a form, the VB interpreter makes ready a new set of procedure frames. These frames may later contain instructions defining what the graphic object will make the program do whenever anything important happens with respect to that object—for instance, the user clicking it, or the arrow pointer entering it.

The *form* is the input/output window for Visual Basic applications.

Code for your Visual Basic program is entered into the *Procedure window*.

A Visual Basic *procedure* defines what should happen when an event takes place, such as clicking a button.

29

Chapter 2 ◆ The Project

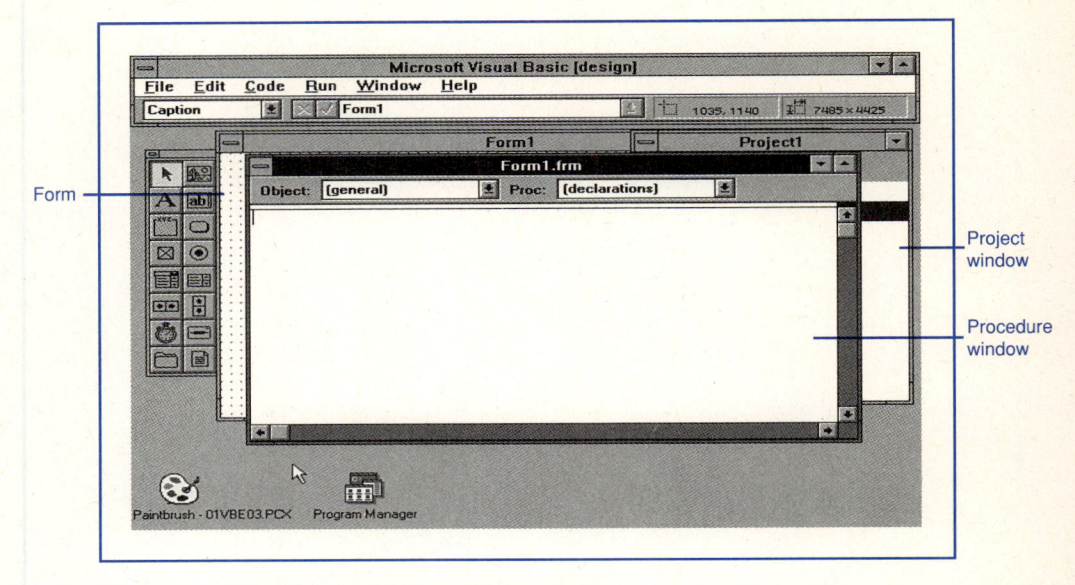

Figure 2.2. The first blank procedure window.

Immediately following the addition of a graphic object to the form, without you ever having to press a key, Visual Basic makes ready for you the *frame* of a formal procedure pertaining to that object. This frame awaits further instructions from you. The opening and closing statements have already been entered into the procedure; the blank line between them denotes where new instructions are to be typed.

You invoked this procedural frame by double-clicking within the area of the blank form; as a result, the procedure Form_Click was called up. In object-oriented syntax, Click is an *event* that acts in this instruction as a verb to the noun Form. The Click event is the default event for this procedure window. Any instructions you type into this procedure frame will be executed whenever the form—or more to the point, the background area within the form window—is clicked once during the program's run time.

> An *event* is some action caused by the user which results in a programmed response.

30

Visual Basic *By*

EXAMPLE

Example

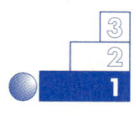

As a test, type the following into the blank line between `Sub Form_Click ()` and `End Sub`:

`Form1.Print "You clicked on the form area."`

You have set up a response to an event; namely, whenever the user of your newly constructed program (yes, you've just written a program) clicks once within the form area during run time, the text within the quotation marks is printed to the form named `Form1`. Written as pseudocode, here's how your first procedure might appear:

Start this procedure whenever this form is clicked.
*Print "You clicked on the form area" to **Form1**.*
End this procedure.

Although you can have several forms on the screen at one time (`Form2`, `Form3`, and so on), you can work on only one Visual Basic project at a time. A project within the VB workspace is in one of three states: design (the startup state), run, and break (or temporary suspension). To see the current project in its running state, follow this procedure.

To run the current VB program:

1. Indicate (click once within the area of) the control window, which is normally along the top of the screen and is currently marked `Microsoft Visual Basic [design]`.

2. From that window's **R**un menu, select **S**tart.

> **NOTE:** If you're a veteran of 1970s BASIC interpreters, the preceding procedure is the modern equivalent of typing RUN at the READY prompt. Alternately, to run a VB program that is currently being edited, you can also press the F5 key.

When a Visual Basic program runs within the interpreter environment, the design palettes and project window disappear, leaving only the control window. The startup form window is redrawn without its spotted grid. The title bar of the VB control window now reads `[run]`.

31

Chapter 2 ◆ The Project

As a test, click once within the area of Form1. Your screen now should look like Figure 2.3. You should notice your message appearing in the upper-left corner of the form. Each successive click should place another message beneath the previous one.

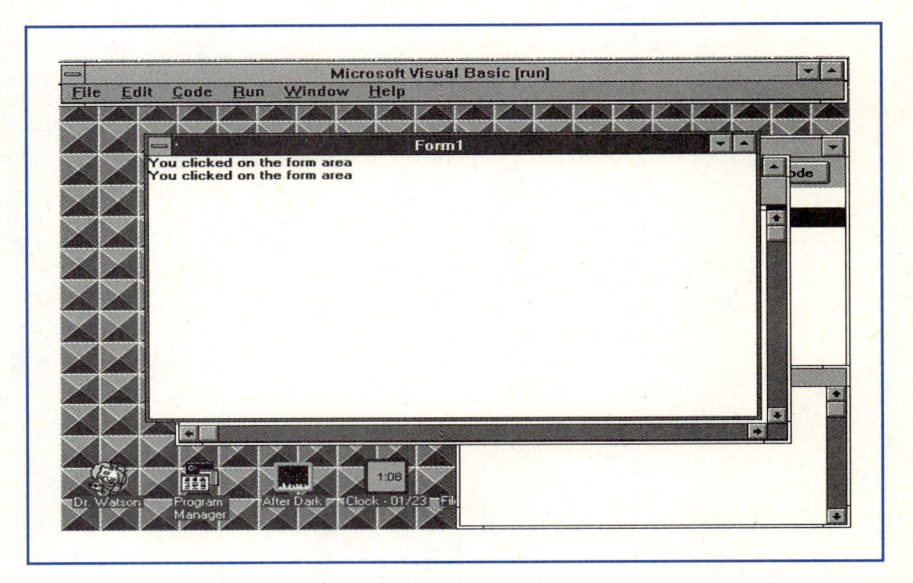

Figure 2.3. The first running program.

To end program execution at any point:

From the **R**un menu of the control window, select **E**nd.

Later, once you've compiled your completed Visual Basic application, you can assign to it an icon and install it into the Windows Program Manager as if it were a standard Windows application.

Graphic Objects

As discussed in Chapter 1, the Visual Basic interpreter receives its instructions on how to handle graphic objects from Microsoft Windows. One such object is the button, which is the grey, bevel-edged device that you generally find within dialog boxes and usually contains `OK`, `Cancel`, or some similar directive. Having received these instructions from Windows, VB can then "hand" you a button from inside its toolbox and let you place that button anywhere on the form.

With the advent of Version 3.0 of Microsoft Windows, buttons were given an animated effect: When clicked, they appear to recede slightly into the framework of the dialog box, as if the box was a wooden panel suspended in space with real metal buttons attached to it. With Visual Basic, whenever programmers need a button for a control panel or dialog box, they can click the button tool in the VB toolbox with the mouse, drag its shape to the input form, and give it a new title by typing that title from the keyboard. Visual Basic thereafter understands that there is a button in this form window, and treats it as a graphic object with all the attributes and animation generally afforded a Windows button.

You do not have to tell Visual Basic how the button recedes into the framework when the user clicks it. In other words, you don't have to tell VB to plot a separate image of the button two pixels to the right and two pixels down to give it the appearance of sinking. Microsoft Windows already knows how to animate a button, and Visual Basic knows how to engage that animation on behalf of the programmer. Several years ago, if you wrote a program even in BASIC, you might have had to write a routine yourself to perform this animation because there wasn't a Windows environment to perform it for you. Moreover, you probably would have had to write a routine which defined a "button" for the sake of your program alone. Every time you wrote a new program, you'd need to port over your old button routines and integrate them into the new contexts.

Part of the beauty of Visual Basic is that programmers have easy access to the most often-used graphic elements of Windows. They can lift those elements from a toolbox with the mouse and place them on the input panel at the points where the user will operate them. This is a far less tedious process for programmers than plotting the identity and coordinates of each element by number, as they might have to do if they were programming in C++.

Figure 2.4 depicts the standard Visual Basic toolbox, where graphic objects are retrieved and added to the form. The toolbox in this figure is set against the background of a form containing examples of the graphic objects that are accessible through the toolbox.

Chapter 2 ◆ The Project

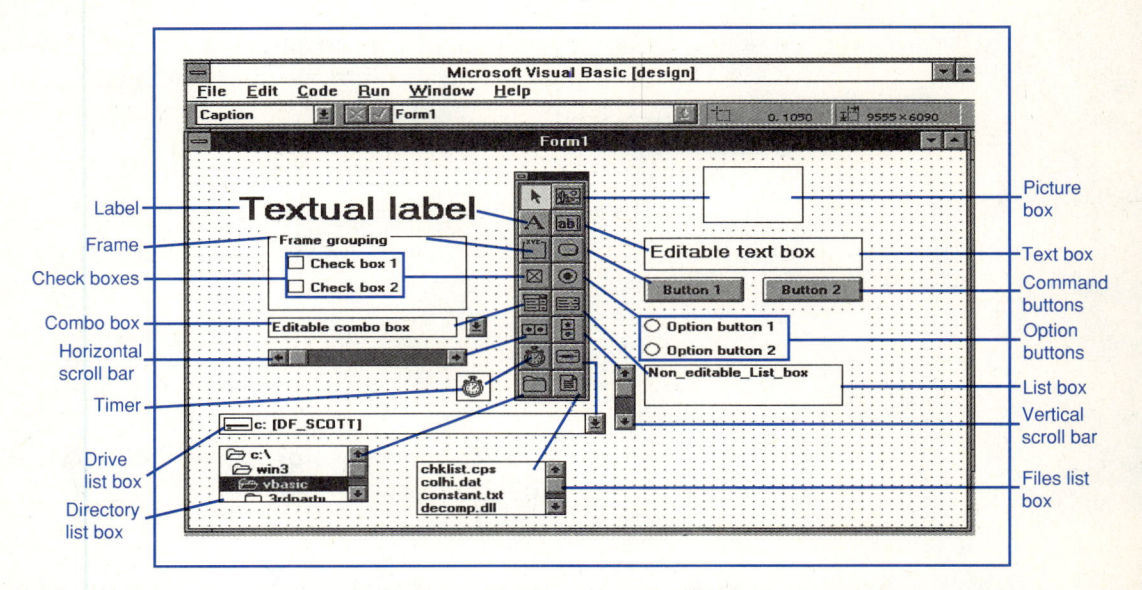

Figure 2.4. The standard Visual Basic toolbox with its component parts.

Each tool within this toolbox is represented by a button. Most of the tools here are symbolic representations of resources you commonly use in Windows; you've probably already spotted the scroll bar tools and list boxes. The primary tool is in the upper-left corner of the box; the left-pointing arrow is the primary indicator of graphic elements already residing on the form. When you wish to point to an existing element of the form, use this tool.

The graphic controls available from the Visual Basic toolbox are as follows:

♦ Picture box—used to display any images, containing pictures or text or both, that are interpretable graphically rather than as text.

♦ Text box—a field for the entry and editing of text.

♦ Label—a field for the display of noneditable text.

♦ Frame—groups related objects together, such as two check boxes.

Visual Basic *By* EXAMPLE

- Command button—will "depress" when clicked. Enables the user to give directives to the VB application, such as `OK`, `Cancel`, or `Options >>`.

- Check box—used to represent the active or "on/off" state of a single item.

- Option button—used in a multiple-choice situation to represent the currently active choice.

- Combo box—gives the user the option of choosing from the list or entering an option of her own within the attached text box.

- List box—used to present a fixed list of choices to the user.

- Horizontal scroll bar—used to represent any numeric selection within a range.

- Vertical scroll bar—used to represent any numeric selection within a range.

- Timer—allows the form to be timed using a real-time clock. Does not display on a form when the program is run.

- Drive list box—displays a list of the user's active storage devices, such as disk drives, RAM disks, and CD-ROM drives.

- Directory list box—displays a list of a device's directories.

- Files list box—displays a list of the user's files within a directory.

Example

With the first test program's initial run ended and the control window reading `[design]`, the next order of business is to add a graphic object to this form—namely, a button that will invoke a small procedure.

To add a button to a form:

1. Click the command button tool in the toolbox. The button you just clicked will stay receded. There is no need to hold down the mouse index button.

35

Chapter 2 ◆ The Project

2. Move the mouse pointer to the form window, and click and hold the index button down on the point that is to be one corner of the button control.

3. With the index button held down, drag the pointer to the opposite corner of the button control area.

4. Release the index button. The button control will appear in the form.

At this point, the VB interpreter has already prepared several frames for procedures relating to this button. The most useful of these procedures, obviously, is the one which is invoked when the button is clicked during run time. To bring up this procedure frame, double-click on the button control in the form.

Visual Basic buttons are said to direct commands to the application; thus they are named `Command1`, `Command2`, and so on, by default. The procedure frame showing now is `Command1_Click`, which will contain the instructions to be executed whenever the button is clicked during run time. The VB interpreter derived the name for this procedure by combining the name given to the button with the name of the event to which this procedure will pertain, joined with the underscore (_) character.

> Visual Basic uses procedure names made up of the object name, an underscore (_), and the event name.

To test this procedure, type the following line into the procedure frame:

```
Form1.Print "You clicked on the Command1 button."
```

Using the steps mentioned earlier, run your program. Notice that you still see `You clicked on the form area.` whenever you click the area of the form that is *not* the button; however, when you click the button, the message reads `You clicked on the Command1 button.` instead. When you are done, end the program by choosing **End** from the **Run** menu.

> An *event* triggers the execution of a procedure.

These tests may not be as exciting as a good game of Asteroids; however, they demonstrate the most important feature distinguishing Visual Basic from its predecessors: The VB language is almost entirely *event-driven*, in that most of its procedures will not be executed until the user gives the computer some sign, signal, or other form of input. This sign can be a waver of the mouse, a press of a key, or perhaps the very act of making the computer wait for five

Visual Basic *By* EXAMPLE

minutes doing nothing. An *event* is a unit of user input utilizing any of the available devices attached to the computer system and employed to trigger the execution of a procedure in response.

Visual Basic already knows how to wait for an event, and also how to discern one event from another. All you have to tell VB as its programmer is what to do to respond to those events. Event-driven procedures will comprise the majority of almost every Visual Basic program you write.

As a test, bring up the procedure window again for Command1_Click by double-clicking the Command1 button. The window for a graphic object's procedure appears. Below its title bar is a control bar containing two drop-down list boxes. Click the down arrow for the list box on the right, which is marked Proc. A list of events attributable to a command button appears, as depicted in Figure 2.5.

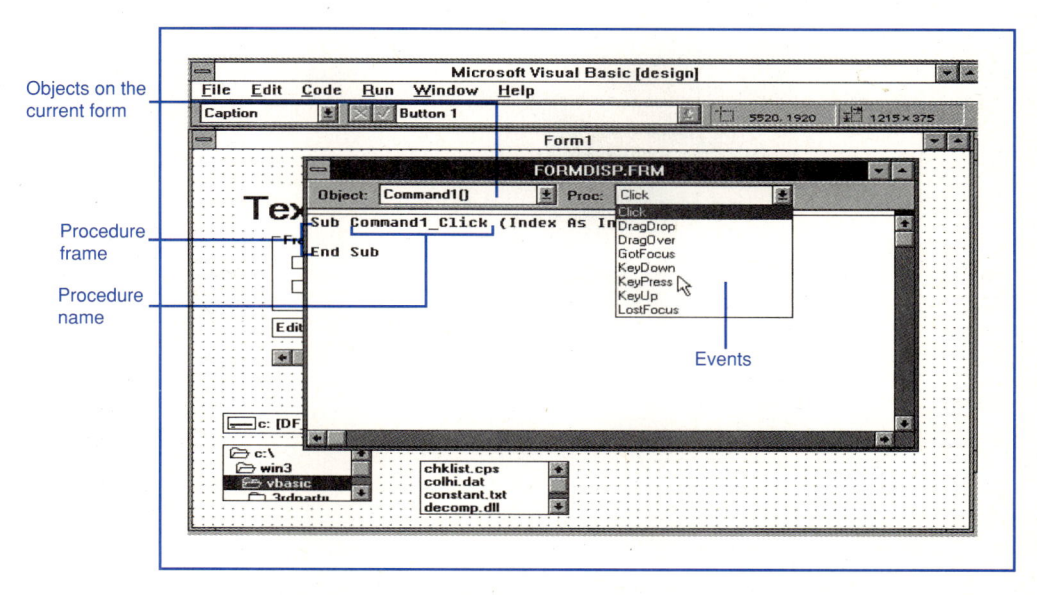

Figure 2.5. Some of the events for a command button.

You can write procedures to be executed on the occurrence of each of these events. Choosing one of these events from the list brings up its event procedure in the code window below. In a sense, you can say the procedures for all the associated events for each object *virtually* exist, although they remain codeless until you give them instructions.

37

The leftmost list box in the procedure window, marked `Object`, displays the names of all the graphic objects belonging to the current form. The form itself is included because Visual Basic considers it a graphic object as well. After choosing a different object from this list, a new set of recognized events is loaded into the `Proc` list. Think of the object list in the procedure window as a display of everything within the form that can have something *done to it,* and the procedure list beside it as a display of everything that *can be done.* The object is the recipient of the action in Visual Basic, just as it is in English grammar. Now you have some idea of the general concept of "object-oriented" syntax.

Property Assessment

A *property* is an attribute of a graphic object which is accessible by name and can be described by a value or term.

As you have witnessed, much of the Visual Basic programming process is accomplished through graphical inference. A button was placed on a form not by typing its coordinates into the source code of the program, but by drawing the button on the form with the mouse. Visual Basic interpreted the act of drawing the button as a directive to the program being constructed. The position, size, and contents of the button were all defined by Visual Basic, for the program, as *properties.*

It is possible to declare these properties using written Visual Basic instructions. I chose not to do so with `Form1`, however, for the simple reason that it was easier at the time not to. The VB environment lets you place a graphic object on the form by pointing to its location and drawing its outline. The position and size of this object instantly become two of its properties. By using the controls located in the VB main design window, as depicted in Figure 2.6, you can access each property of a graphic object by name and assign or change its value, setting, or description.

Visual Basic *By* EXAMPLE

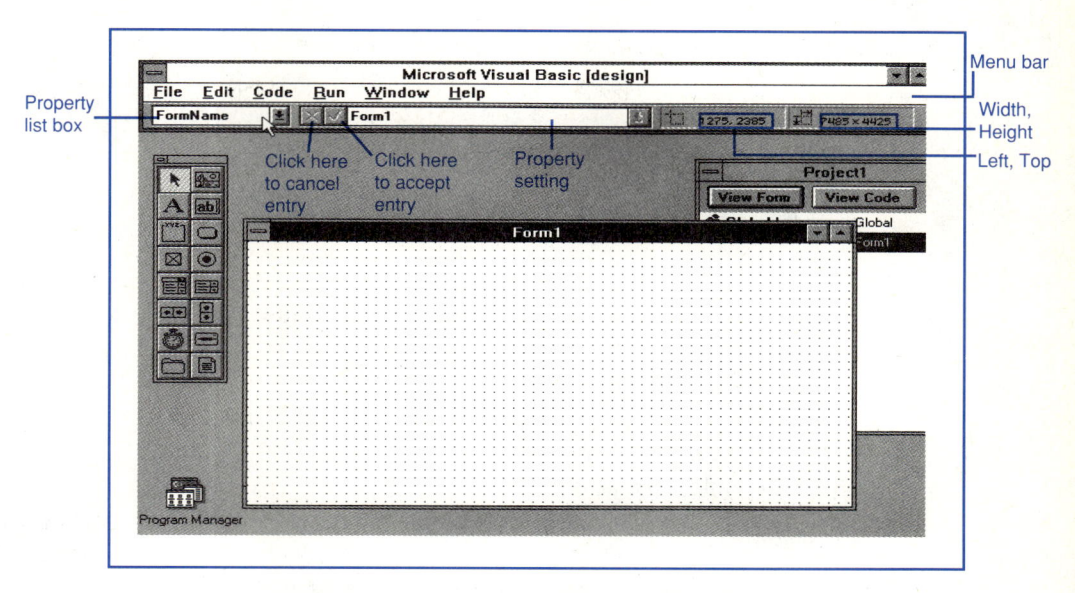

Figure 2.6. The property-setting controls of the VB main window.

The .Caption Property

The .Caption property is used to change the text displayed on an object.

One of the more important properties of a button control is its textual contents, or *caption*. After all, the user of this program probably won't be able to make much sense out of a button simply called Command1. To change the contents of the Command1 button in the current Form1, change its .Caption property to reflect the new contents.

To change the text of a button control:

1. Indicate the button that is to have its text changed by clicking once on that button. Eight *handles* surround the button; these are generally used as controls for resizing the button.

2. In the VB main window, from the list box at the lower-left corner of the properties bar, choose the property .Caption. The text box at the center displays the current contents—for this example, Command1.

39

Chapter 2 ◆ The Project

3. While the pointer is in the center text box, its form becomes an *I-beam*, indicating that it can be used to place the cursor in this box. To replace the existing text, use the pointer to indicate the entire text.

4. Type the replacement text. As you type, the text is echoed into the button control.

5. To complete the entry, either press Enter or click the checkmark button to the left of the text-entry box.

6. To cancel an entry in progress, click the cancel button.

> The `.CtlName` property is used to identify an object by name in the program code.

It's important to note that changing a button control's contents does not change its name throughout the source code. It happens that `Command1` is both the default control name and default caption for the first button in a form. Changing one does not change the other. To change the button's control name from `Command1` to `MainButton`, use the method described previously, but select the property `.CtlName` rather than `.Caption`.

Whenever you change a control's name property, its name in the VB procedures is changed automatically. Notice that the `_Click` procedure for the former `Command1` now reads `Sub MainButton_Click ()`. You can change a control name at any time, and the VB interpreter will make the proper changes to the source code of its associated procedures. By contrast, changing a button's caption does not result in any alteration to procedure code.

> A property's name is made up of the name of the object, a period, and the name of the property.

While I'm on the subject, notice that in the terms I've discussed thus far an event is separated from an object by an underscore character, as in `MainButton_Click`, whereas a property is separated from its object by a period, as in `MainButton.Caption`. This punctuation helps identify the attribute of the object preceding it as an event or a property.

The properties bar can be used, among other purposes, to designate the size of a control by number, to set the color of a control or its background, or to change the font for included text. Throughout this book, you will be continually setting the attributes of properties, setting the stage—at least visually—for each full project you produce. Later in the book, I discuss the more conventional predeclaration of values, variables, and functions for the computational portion of the programs, all of which is done with instructions.

> **NOTE:** Although the job of creating controls and designating their properties can be considered programming in the context of Visual Basic, the act of property-setting is not instructional, and is therefore not reflected in the source code of the program being constructed. When the source code is executed, the VB interpreter expects the properties of the graphic objects referred to in the program to have been set beforehand. If you're a BASIC veteran, this may make reading the source code of the program a bit confusing. Most programmers who have programmed in BASIC for a long time have grown accustomed to modeling all the characteristics of a program with written instructions and reading those characteristics as instructions.

Saving Your Work

Here's the procedure for saving your project to disk for safekeeping:

1. From the **F**ile menu of the control window, select Save Project.... You can alternatively select Save Project As... if you wish to specify a new file name for the project.

2. If the elements of the VB application as they appear in the project window haven't been given formal file names, file selector boxes appear for each element, enabling you to designate the file name of your choice. The state of a form, along with its associated procedure code, is saved in a file with the extension .FRM. You can type a file name for each element or accept the default file name supplied by VB. Click OK.

3. Finally, a file selector box appears asking you to designate a file name for the project itself. Project file names carry the .MAK extension. Either designate a file name or accept the default, then click OK. The project is saved.

Use the preceding method to save the single-button form project to disk, accepting the default file names GLOBAL.BAS and FORM1.FRM for the two project elements and designating TEST1.MAK as the project file name.

One way to save the project as a file independent of the VB control program is to compile it into a separate intermediate p-code file. This way the file can be installed into the Windows Program Manager and run from there by double-clicking its icon or by double-clicking its file name in the Windows File Manager. This p-code file is not a stand-alone program; the VBRUN100.DLL program needs to coexist with the p-code file in the same directory, although it does not need to be installed into Program Manager.

To make a distributable p-code file from a VB project:

1. Save the VB project to disk using the preceding method.

2. From the **F**ile menu, select **M**ake EXE File.... A file selector box appears.

3. Type the eight-letter file name for the p-code file into the text line marked `Filename`. VB automatically attaches the .EXE extension to the file. This file will not overwrite any other file pertaining to the project.

4. Click OK. You now have an intermediate p-code file.

Summary

Visual Basic considers the forms and procedure modules collectively as a project. The programmer does not need to provide the Visual Basic interpreter with extensive instructions for the display and handling of graphic controls. When these controls are placed in the control form, the programmer needs only to tell the Visual Basic interpreter how to respond to the input events attributed to those controls. Each possible event for a graphic object has its own virtual procedure in a VB program. Each object in a VB form, including the form itself, has properties attributed to it, the characteristics of which can be set in advance using the properties bar without specifying any instructions in code.

Review Questions

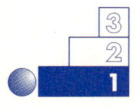

1. In what type of file does Visual Basic store a collective list of forms and their controls, and modules and their procedures?

2. During the run time of your VB application, commands are passed to the application through what graphic control?

3. In a term that joins the object `ClickHere` and the event `DblClick`, what item of punctuation is used between them?

4. In the procedure heading `Sub Form4_Click ()`, what term represents the event?

5. You can tell that your Visual Basic application is not running at the moment by looking where on the screen?

6. When creating a VB application, the interpreter is in what mode?

7. What is the three-letter extension of the name of a file that contains the property settings for a form?

Review Exercise

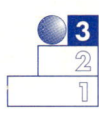

1. Write a procedure that would print the line `Something has happened!` into a form called `Form7` whenever a button called `BobTheButton` is clicked.

Grammar and Linguistics

In this chapter you study the phraseology of the Visual Basic program—in other words, how its terms and keywords are organized and expressed within the source code. You then begin composing more complex examples of programs than those developed (although perhaps "arrived at" would be the better phrase) in the previous chapters. You learn about instructions and how they are constructed. You then learn how instructions are executed, organized, grouped, and modularized.

The topics introduced here are covered in greater detail in later chapters, with each topic given a chapter to itself. This chapter presents the major concepts of program construction so that you can see how these concepts relate to each other. Here, I shine a broad spotlight on all the characters of the Visual Basic stage, instead of shining a narrow penlight on one or two parts.

Modern Syntax

A *variable* represents a unit of data that can be altered.

At the heart of every program you write are logical comparisons between unknown and known numeric values. Whatever overall objective you have in mind for your VB application, the primary business of that application—the stuff that keeps your program busy—is the manipulation of values in memory. As in

Chapter 3 ◆ Grammar and Linguistics

algebra, unknown values are represented within the Visual Basic syntax by variables. A *variable* is an arbitrarily named term that represents a unit of data in memory that can be altered by the program.

A value is assigned to a variable with an equality statement, such as `a = 1` or `items = 27`, on a line by itself. When a Visual Basic instruction can be placed on one line, that instruction is called a *phrase*, partly because the syntax of the instruction resembles that of an English-language phrase or, perhaps, a complete sentence. For example, the syntax of the instruction `If a = 1 Then GoTo More_Help` can be deduced by using some rules of the English language—if not some rules of English slang. The preceding instruction can rightfully be considered a phrase.

Each Visual Basic instruction has a component structure, in much the same way an English sentence can be divided into component phrases. The preceding instructional phrase consists of three statements, all of which rest on one line. Therefore, this phrase is called a *compound instruction.* There is a mathematical expression included in one of the statements: `a = 1`. The words `If`, `Then`, and `GoTo` are some of the primary keywords in all BASIC programming languages. `If-Then` and `GoTo` are considered *statements* because they specify changes in the state of operation of the program. I'll demonstrate just how they work later. For now, let's concentrate on the fact that a statement in programming is a directive made to the interpreter that tells it how things are changing.

The definition of a statement might be confusing at first. (Frankly, it might be confusing later, so be patient.) If someone told you, "If you're through with your insulting remarks, then leave the room!" you would hardly consider that directive a statement. Just because the inference was made that you should leave doesn't mean that you will leave, and it especially does not mean you have already gone.

In the part-metaphysical, part-sociological structure of Visual Basic, what appears to be an order or directive to change the state or value of something is actually interpreted as a statement of fact and a report of the current operating status of the program. In the statement `GoTo Away`, the line marked `Away` is someplace else in the program. Telling the interpreter to *go to* that part in the program,

> A *phrase* is a simple instruction.

> A *statement* is an instruction that specifies a change or deviation in the operating status of the program.

from the interpreter's point of view, is as good as saying it *is* at that point in the program now. You've written what looks like a command, but from the standpoint of the logic of the computer, you've made an unconditional statement.

Suppose, however, that you add a condition to that statement. For instance, assume the VB interpreter comes across the phrase `If count > 1000 Then GoTo Away`. Here `count` is a *variable* or symbol that represents a numeric value, standing in place of that value in the text. For our example, the interpreter first evaluates the variable `count` to determine whether its value is indeed greater than 1000. The two parts of this phrase `If` and `Then` constitute one statement, which we call the `If-Then` statement. It tells the interpreter to make an evaluation—in this case, to see if the value represented by the variable `count` is greater than 1000. The result of this evaluation is logically considered to be "true" or "false." In pseudocode, the statement's general framework might appear as follows:

If what's being said here is true, then execute the statement immediately thereafter.

In this case, if the expression `count > 1000` evaluates true, the interpreter suspends execution and then resumes at the point of the program marked `Away`. The phrase `GoTo Away` is interpreted as a statement only if the expression is true. Otherwise, the interpreter never sees the statement. `If-Then` in this instance appears to be a "command." In earlier versions of BASIC, it was categorized as such. Yet given the understanding that commanding the interpreter to do something is really a metaphorical way of *stating* that it is done already, realistically you can and must consider `If-Then` and `GoTo` as statements.

All computer processes are the result of logical evaluations. Such evaluations are called *binary* because their results can have either one or two states—true or false, or in Visual Basic values, –1 or 0 (negative one is simply how that bit of "true" data is interpreted within a byte by Visual Basic). The purpose of logical evaluation in the real world is to eliminate "grey areas." Nothing, once it is logically evaluated, is "for the most part true." Within the computer, there are no grey areas to begin with. Absolutely everything retained in memory, stored on disk, or undergoing processing within some evaluator chip is describable in its rudimentary form or forms as a *binary state*.

> A *binary state* is the minimum unit of value in a computer, and can be described as either true (–1) or false (0).

Chapter 3 ◆ Grammar and Linguistics

Because there is no in-between state in a logical evaluation, and because logical evaluation is all the computer actually does, the computer cannot understand "change." The concept of one state becoming another state is foreign to the computer; there is simply no logical way to represent it, just as in real-world evaluation there is no way to logically represent grey. The Visual Basic language makes it appear that you are telling the interpreter to change something by giving it instructions that appear to be commands, when in fact you are actually restating the operating conditions for the computer at the present time. The syntax of the language gives you a more tangible and perhaps more realistic method of communication with the computer. In the real world, things change all the time, so it might help you to understand what's happening in the computer if things appear to change. If you were a computer, however, you would believe that nothing ever changed.

A Matter of Expression

The computer can only "think" using on/off binary states, represented by ones and zeroes.

An expression is the assigning of or the comparison between two variables.

In the preceding example, one of the statements within the `If-Then` compound instruction was an expression: `count > 1000`. This expression compared an unknown value to a known value and evaluated the result of that expression. Logically, there can only be two possible results, which may only be expressed as *binary states*.

Whenever an unknown value or variable is compared to a known or unknown value—as in `count > 1000` or `liquidity_ratio = (assets / liabilities)`—we call the statement of that comparison an *expression*. An expression is any of the following:

- ◆ An arithmetic comparison between two values, having a result that is expressed logically as a binary state
- ◆ One or more values or variables arithmetically joined by functions or functional operators
- ◆ An assignment of value to a variable using another value, variable, or another expression

Under the first definition, `count > 1000` is an expression of comparison. If `count` is greater than `1000`, a Boolean value of True (–1) is returned to the interpreter that may trigger the execution of

48

a process. Under the second definition, `a + b * c` and `4 * (n - 3)` are expressions of combination, resulting in a numeral value that can be assigned to a variable. Also under the second definition, `6` is officially an expression—a rather boring one, but an expression nonetheless. Under the third definition, `x = a + b * c` and `liquidity_ratio = (assets / liabilities)` are expressions of assignment, in which the results of the arithmetic combinations are actually stored as variables.

> An *equation* is a statement of equality that assigns a value to a variable.

You could place `liquidity_ratio = (assets / liabilities)` on a line by itself, in which case the expression would be both a statement and an *equation* that assigns the value of `assets` divided by `liabilities` to the variable `liquidity_ratio`. We would then say the preceding expression assigns a value to the variable `liquidity_ratio` using two other variables.

> A *binary operator* is a symbol that represents a mathematical function combining, comparing, or equating two values.

In the preceding equation, the slash (/) is used as an *operator* designating division between the two values it separates. Operators are used within BASIC expressions like the function buttons on a calculator.

When an equality expression is listed on a line by itself, that expression is considered by the interpreter as an assignment of value to a variable. The equal sign in that statement would be considered the *assignment operator*. If you were to state on a line by itself `x = 6` and then later invoke the statement `TextBox.Print x`, the number 6 would appear in the text box. By contrast, when an expression is part of an instruction—as in `If x = 6 Then...`—that expression is treated as a comparison of 6 to x, the result of which is a Boolean value of true (–1) or false (0). The equal sign in a comparison is, naturally, the *comparison operator*. The negative sign (–) preceding the 1 above is called a *unary operator* because it concerns only one value, not two.

Intrinsic Functions

> A *function* returns a value in a single variable.

For arithmetic operations that cannot be described by symbols or operators, Visual Basic maintains a broad vocabulary of intrinsic *functions* that perform arithmetic operations on values or expressions enclosed in parentheses. A function is an arithmetic operation performed on a value, variable, or expression, resulting in an explicit value returned within a single variable.

Chapter 3 ◆ Grammar and Linguistics

A function in Visual Basic has the following syntax:

`Function_name(expression)`

The expression in parentheses is evaluated first, so that the function can operate on one rational value—something more closely resembling `67.5` than `(x + 6)`. There may be more than one expression within the parentheses; in such cases, they will be separated from each other by commas. The specified function is then performed on the value or values between the parentheses.

An *intrinsic function* is a term that is built into the Visual Basic vocabulary (in other words, a *keyword*). Other functions can be programmed by you and added to the functional vocabulary within the scope of a VB project.

> An *intrinsic function* is one that is built into Visual Basic.

Intrinsic functions are actually quite simple. For instance, `Sqr(9)` represents the square root of `9`, so the function is said to *return* a value of `3`. `Int(3.1415927)` returns the value of the expression in parentheses converted to an integer by rounding to the nearest whole number—in this case, `3` again. If the variable `g` has the value `6`, the function `Abs(g - 10)` would return the value `4`, because `g` is `6`, `6 - 10 = -4`, the absolute value of –4 is 4, and thus `Abs(-4) = 4`.

Groups, Subgroups, Subsubgroups, and So On

Over the decades that the BASIC programming language has been developed and redeveloped, those who have been lucky enough to become part of the development process have also managed to break BASIC constructs into an increasing number of parts. There are more parts, or divisions of instruction groups, to a Visual Basic application than perhaps any other BASIC application.

Figure 3.1 depicts the hierarchy of divisions and subdivisions of a Visual Basic application. To explain, I begin with the largest division and work toward the smallest.

> A *module* is a complete set of procedures stored within a single file.

The entire source code of a VB application is considered, of course, the *program*. The first division of a program is the *module*, at least one of which is always attributed to a form window.

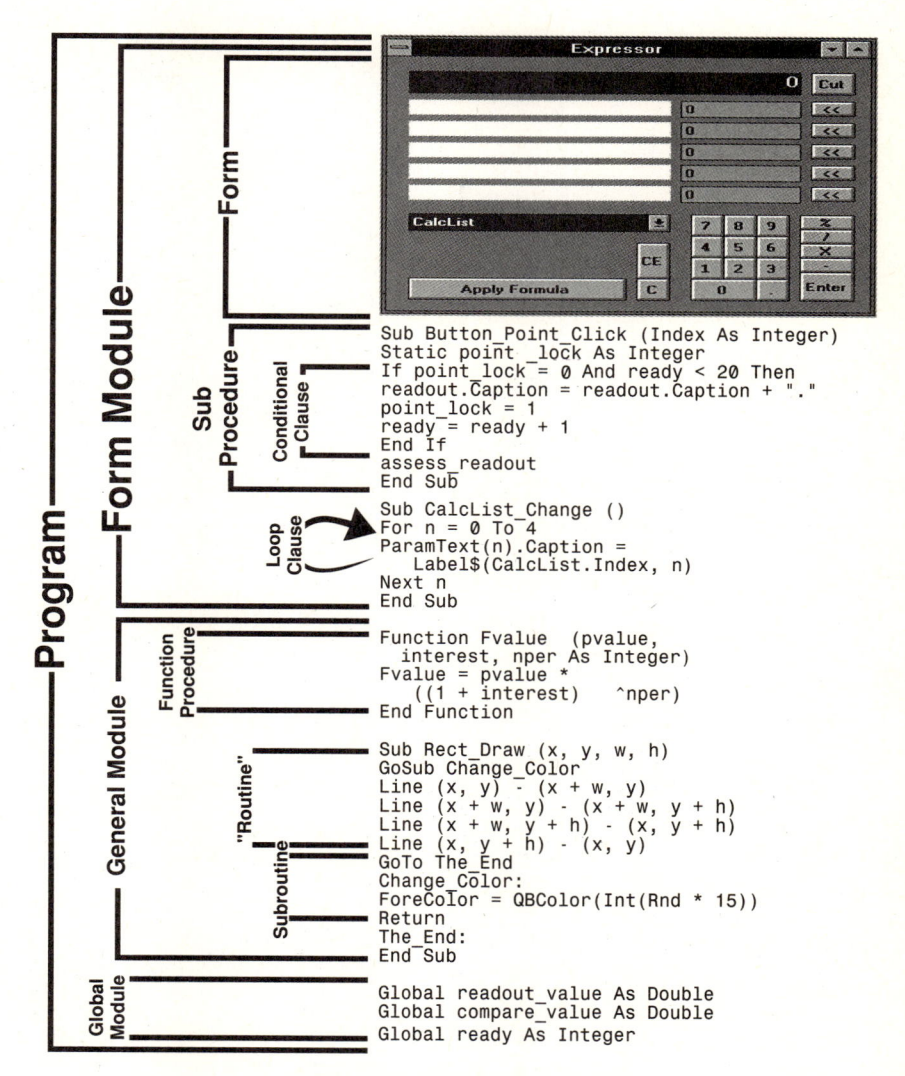

```
Sub Button_Point_Click (Index As Integer)
Static point_lock As Integer
If point_lock = 0 And ready < 20 Then
readout.Caption = readout.Caption + "."
point_lock = 1
ready = ready + 1
End If
assess_readout
End Sub

Sub CalcList_Change ()
For n = 0 To 4
ParamText(n).Caption =
    Label$(CalcList.Index, n)
Next n
End Sub

Function Fvalue  (pvalue,
    interest, nper As Integer)
Fvalue = pvalue *
    ((1 + interest)    ^nper)
End Function

Sub Rect_Draw (x, y, w, h)
GoSub Change_Color
Line (x, y) - (x + w, y)
Line (x + w, y) - (x + w, y + h)
Line (x + w, y + h) - (x, y + h)
Line (x, y + h) - (x, y)
GoTo The_End
Change_Color:
ForeColor = QBColor(Int(Rnd * 15))
Return
The_End:
End Sub

Global readout_value As Double
Global compare_value As Double
Global ready As Integer
```

Figure 3.1. The divisions of a Visual Basic application.

In any VB application, there can be three types of modules:

A *form module* refers to the objects and contents of a particular form window.

The *global module* contains only those declarations of variables and functions that pertain to the program as a whole, thus specifying the context of the entire program.

51

Chapter 3 ◆ Grammar and Linguistics

The *general module* contains the procedures that exist independently of forms or other graphic objects. It can be saved independently or as part of a form module.

A *procedure* is Visual Basic's core program component.

Because a module is by definition a set of procedures, it naturally follows that the program component on the next lower level is the *procedure*. A procedure is the core component of a Visual Basic application, having the purpose of logically describing or modeling at least one task or mathematical function and passing its results to some other component.

The *context* of a procedure defines its relative pertinence to the rest of the program.

When you edit a form or general module using the code editor window, you are looking at only one procedure at a time. The name of that procedure appears within the window's heading, generally beside the term `Sub`. As such, the name also appears in the editor window control bar, in the list box marked `Proc`. We call the `Sub` statement as a whole a *procedure declaration*, because it not only defines the procedure for the rest of the program, but it also helps define the *context* of that procedure—what values and variables are shared with the rest of the program. The context of a procedure is the understanding the interpreter has of which variables and functions pertain only to the procedure, which values and variables are exchanged between this procedure and the one that called it, and which variables and functions pertain to the program as a whole.

A *parameter* is a value or variable passed to a procedure.

The way a `Sub` procedure is structured enables it to accept variables and values as input from the body of the program that called it (in Visual Basic, another procedure) and perform computations using those values. These passed values are called *parameters*.

Any variables created or declared during the procedure are specific to that procedure alone, unless otherwise specified with statements. In other words, each procedure has a variable context all its own, called the *local context*. When the procedure is exited, and some other procedure is being executed, the variables within the local context are deallocated.

Example

As an example, here is a procedure that draws an unfilled rectangle on the screen, given four parameters.

```
Sub Rect_Draw (x As Integer, y As Integer, w As Integer,
    h As Integer)
    Line (x, y) - (x + w, y)
    Line (x + w, y) - (x + w, y + h)
    Line (x + w, y + h) - (x, y + h)
    Line (x, y + h) - (x, y)
End Sub
```

So that you can get a better feel for what the program is doing, here is the preceding procedure translated into pseudocode:

Procedure for drawing a rectangle with its upper-left corner at (x,y), a width of w, and a height of h:
  Draw a line from the upper-left to upper-right corners of the rectangle.
  Extend the line to the lower-right corner.
  Extend the line to the lower-left corner.
  Extend the line back to the origin point.
End of procedure.

The coordinates for the upper-left corner of the rectangle are accepted as x and y. The width and height of the rectangle are accepted as w and h. Here is a procedure with the sole purpose of calling procedure Rect_Draw.

```
Sub Form_Click ()
    Rect_Draw 10, 10, 500, 500
End Sub
```

Notice that the four variables mentioned previously don't exist within the context of procedure Form_Click. Instead, there are four explicit integral values, designated in the same *order* as the variables listed as parameters for Rect_Draw. Whether these values are numerals or variables, by invoking the name of the procedure, these parameters are passed to it. Procedure Rect_Draw then accepts parameters in the order in which they were given and utilizes those parameters within its own context only. This way variable w can refer to *width* in the context of Rect_Draw, and perhaps to *water level* within some other procedure. When Rect_Draw is exited, variables x, y, w, and h no longer exist; but if Form1 is clicked, the rectangle remains.

Chapter 3 ◆ Grammar and Linguistics

A variable's scope *is its pertinence to the rest of the program.*

Within the preceding procedure, the individual variables invoked pertain only to that procedure. The way it is written now, when the procedure is exited, the values of x, y, w, and h are discarded. The names can be used again when the procedure is reentered. This is one example of a set of variables with *local scope;* that is to say, their meaning pertains only to their local procedure. The scope of a variable is the degree to which that variable pertains to the rest of the program; a variable's scope can be broadened to encompass an entire module, or the breadth of the VB application.

Example

A function *passes a value in its own name.*

Another form of procedure is the Function procedure, which is structured like a Sub procedure, except it passes a value *back* to the procedure that called it. Here is an example function that finds the future value of an annuity, given three parameters:

```
Function Fvalue (pvalue, interest, nper As Integer)
    Fvalue = pvalue * ((1 + interest) ^ nper)
End Function
```

Notice how Fvalue is not only the name of the Function procedure, but also a variable to which the computed value is assigned. Here, pvalue is the present value of the annuity or loan, interest is the rate of interest per annum, and nper is the number of payment periods remaining. Here is the procedure that calls this function:

```
Sub Future_Click ()
    FutVal1.Print Fvalue(1000, .1, 3)
    FutVal2.Print "Computation complete."
End Sub
```

Here is the procedure written in pseudocode:

Procedure for clicking the **Future** *button:*
  Execute the procedure **Fvalue** *for a $1000 annuity paid off with a 10 percent interest rate over three years, and print the result within the picture box called* **FutVal1**.

> *Print the message "Computation complete." within picture box called FutVal2.*
> *End of procedure.*

In Visual Basic, a picture box may contain text as well as graphics; so one uses the `.Print` method to print text to a picture box. For a button having the control name `Future`, and for two picture boxes with control names `FutVal1` and `FutVal2`, procedure `Future_Click` will place the future value of a $1000 annuity at 10 percent interest over three years—assuming annual payment periods—into picture box `FutVal1`. The call to `Fvalue` looks and acts like an intrinsic function in the regular Visual Basic vocabulary.

Note that function `Fvalue` will be executed in its entirety *before* the instruction to print the message in picture box `FutVal2` is executed. This is an example of program control being passed between procedures. Further execution of procedure `Future_Click` is suspended when the call to `Fvalue` is made. When `Fvalue` is done, execution of `Future_Click` resumes with the instruction immediately following the call.

Subsubsubdivisions, and So On

Informally speaking, a grouping of instructions from a procedure is called a *routine*. On occasion, I may use as an example a portion of a large procedure, without the headings. If the instructions within that portion perform some whole function or task, I refer to the excerpt as a routine.

In the previous two examples, you saw program control being passed from procedure to procedure. As I've noted before, instructions within modules are not necessarily executed from top to bottom. Within the confines of a procedure, program control can be commanded to branch to another point designated by a *label*. A label is a noninstruction set to a line by itself and followed by a colon (:), designating a branching point.

Formally speaking, a *subroutine* is a series of instructions within a procedure—especially a long one—that can be branched to by calling its label by name. A subroutine allows for automatic branching back to the instruction that follows the one calling the subroutine.

Chapter 3 ◆ Grammar and Linguistics

A clause *contains one or more instructions that are treated as a group.*

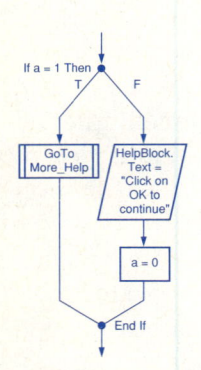

A long instruction broken apart and distributed over several lines is called a *clause*. A clause is a compound instruction containing one or more subordinate instructions distributed in a single group over more than one line.

Here is an example of a small clause:

```
If a = 1 Then
    GoTo More_Help
Else
    HelpBlock.Text = "Click on OK to continue."
    a = 0
End If
```

To be honest, there really is more than one instruction here. All three lines that are inset a few spaces are legitimate instructions by themselves. At the same time, they are part of a greater conditional instruction that tells the VB interpreter, "Either execute *this* group of instructions, or else execute *that* group." These inset phrases are called *nested* instructions. The act of embedding instructions within a clause in this manner is called *nesting*. Still, `If-Then...Else...End If` is treated as a single instruction, and more categorically as a statement.

A loop *is a sequence of instructions that is repeated either a specific number of times or until a condition is true.*

The next most common type of clause after the conditional clause is the loop clause. A *loop* is a sequence of instructions that is executed repetitively either for a specified count or until a condition is evaluated true.

Example

Often, you find you need to execute a set of instructions a certain number of times; or to evaluate functional series, you need to accumulate values using a loop clause. Here's an example loop that uses an array variable and uses its own running count to create an exponential series:

Visual Basic *By*
EXAMPLE

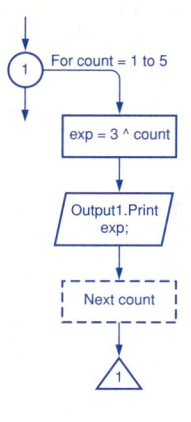

```
For count = 1 to 5
    exp = 3 ^ count
    Output1.Print exp;
Next count
```

Here is the example loop in pseudocode:

Count from 1 to 5, and for each count, do the following:
  Assign the value of 3 raised to the power of the count to the stated variable.
  Print the value of this variable within this output region.
Count the next number and execute all instructions between the beginning and end statement of the loop.

The primary loop clause statement in any BASIC language is the `For-Next` loop. Within it, the variable `count` is created and its value is initially set to 1. The program continues execution in sequence. First, the value of `3 ^ 1` (three to the first power) is evaluated and stored in the variable `exp`. The value of the variable `exp` is then printed to the output region named `Output1`. On reaching the instruction `Next count`, the interpreter increments (adds 1 to) the `count` variable and branches back to the instruction following the `For` statement.

This repetition continues until `count = 5` and `Next count` is reached. At that point, `count` is no longer to be incremented, and execution continues with the instruction following `Next count`. The result is a text region that contains the exponential series 3, 9, 27, 81, and 243.

Visual Basic Symbology

The primary difference between a program written in the original BASIC and one written in a modern dialect such as Visual Basic is that the older program is more conversational, whereas the newer one is more symbological. For instance, a program written in the 1964 edition of BASIC might ask, "HOW WIDE IS THE WOODEN BEAM?" or "WHAT IS THE INTEREST RATE PER ANNUM?" to obtain values for a formula. In a conversational mode, a BASIC program could be executed step-by-step, in a totally predictable manner. From the programmer's point of view, the only unknown element in such a program would

57

Chapter 3 ◆ Grammar and Linguistics

be the answers to the preceding questions. One could argue that it was simpler to program in the era of conversational programs, because the programmer didn't have to consider very deeply what the user intended to do with the program, except perhaps to predict how wide the wooden beam could be.

Figure 3.2 depicts the on-screen appearance of two simple programs from two different eras, but with exactly the same purpose. They calculate the zone of a sphere—or the measure of the area of a strip along the surface of a sphere. The sphere is divided by two parallel planes. Where those planes meet with the surface of the sphere, they form the boundaries of the zone. The area of the zone is calculated by these two programs. The formula is described mathematically as

```
z = 2prh
```

in which p is the symbol for the constant π, r is the radius of the sphere, and h is the distance separating the two planes.

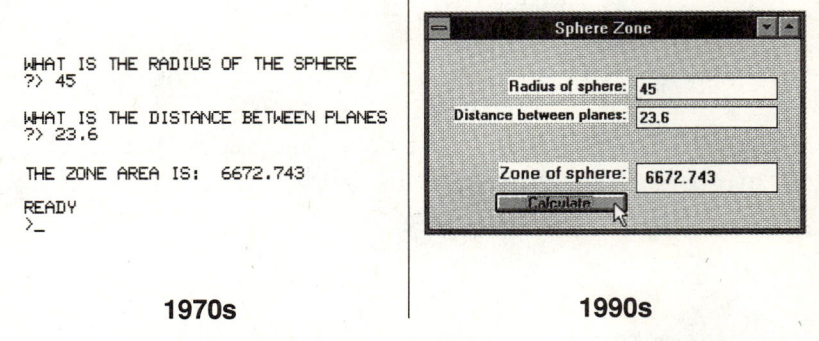

1970s | **1990s**

Figure 3.2. The zone formula, then and now.

Imagine zoning off and measuring the area of the Earth's crust between 20 and 30 degrees north latitude, and you'll get a picture of this formula in your mind.

Visual Basic *By* EXAMPLE

Let's compare the source code of both these programs. The older, conversational program uses the ANSI standard BASIC adopted in the mid 1970s. The newer program is in Visual Basic. So that you can see the simple structure of both programs, I've excluded the error-trapping code that better programmers generally include. First, here is the old BASIC program:

```
10 REM +++ FORMULA FOR ZONE OF A SPHERE +++
20 CLS
30 INPUT "ENTER THE RADIUS OF THE SPHERE";R
40 INPUT "ENTER THE DISTANCE BETWEEN BISECTING PLANES";H
50 Z=(2*3.1415927)*R*H
60 PRINT
70 PRINT "THE ZONE AREA IS ";Z
80 END
```

It's easy to spot in the preceding example which instructions perform the role of conversing with the user: They're marked with the term INPUT. This term is not a part of the Visual Basic vocabulary. Because typed data in VB is entered into predrawn form fields rather than in response to input prompts, the INPUT statement has faded into history as far as Visual Basic is concerned, along with the MAT statement and line numbers.

Looking at modern code, here is the source code and pseudo-code for the only procedure in the VB application:

```
Sub ZoneCalc_Click ()
' Formula for Zone of a Sphere
    r = Val(Radius.Text)
    h = Val(PlaneDist.Text)
    z = (2 * 3.1415927) * r * h
    ZoneSphere.Text = Str$(z)
End Sub
```

Procedure for calculating the area of a sphere zone:
  *Retrieve the value of **r** from a text box **Radius**.*
  *Retrieve the value of **h** from a text box **PlaneDist**.*
  Calculate the sphere zone using the classic formula.
  *Output the results in a text box **ZoneSphere**.*
End of procedure.

Knowing what you know about properties, you should be able to identify `.Text` as a property by looking for the period that separates the property from its graphic object. `Radius`, `PlaneDist`, and `ZoneSphere` are three text boxes in the form. The textual contents of these boxes are addressed by adding `.Text` to their names.

Without going into too much detail (I do that later), let's look at what this program actually does. If you compared the mathematical formula for the area of a sphere zone to either of the two programs, you probably were able to locate the BASIC form of the formula. Notice that it doesn't really appear much different from the algebraic form of the formula—which is partly why we call the theory of high-level programming *procedural algebra*. In both programs, letters were used to represent values; so as in algebra, we call these letters *variables*. In Visual Basic, you can use entire words as variables, as long as these words aren't recognized by VB as instructional terms.

In the first (old BASIC) program, the values for the formula are put into variables that are declared following the `INPUT` statements. In the second (Visual Basic) program, text is extracted from the two input text boxes in the form and translated into values that are used in the formula. The result of the formula is translated back into text and placed in the output text box of the form. Remember that this procedure is not executed until the button named `ZoneCalc` is clicked.

The sphere zone formula itself is the one part of both programs that has kept its syntax over time, partly because procedural algebra is resistant to change. More obviously, there are no line numbers in Visual Basic programs, and lowercase is now prevalent. However, the methodology of user interaction with the BASIC program has changed drastically. As a result of this change, Visual Basic is a very different language from ANSI Standard BASIC, BASICA, GW-BASIC, or even Microsoft QuickBASIC. Note also that the pseudocode element provided applies equally to both examples.

The linguistic portion of Visual Basic is loosely based on the first 1964 Kemeny/Kurtz edition of BASIC—the `If-Then`, `GoTo`/`GoSub`, and `For-Next` statements still abound in VB, although Microsoft has greatly reshaped them to fit their modern roles. With the advent of Visual Basic, Microsoft has introduced object-oriented syntax to the BASIC dialect. Using this syntax, a graphic object, such as a text box or a button, has its own "noun," and processes related to that object (such as printing or resizing) have their own "verbs." An earlier edition of BASIC might express the measurement of whether a mouse button was pressed within an instruction as follows: `IF MOUSE(0)=1 THEN PRINT AT 15,15;"You pressed the mouse button."` In Visual Basic syntax, the value of a pressed mouse button is implied, not expressed directly, as in the following example:

```
Sub Form_Click ()
    Form1.Print "You pressed the mouse button."
End Sub
```

Even if you're a novice programmer, you can tell from the preceding comparison that Visual Basic bears a loose resemblance to its progenitors. If you're a veteran of older BASICs, you probably also noted how the simple process of printing in the event of a mouse-button click has been elevated in stature from a mere clause to a subprogram module.

Summary

A large percentage of all instructions within the source code of a Visual Basic program will consist of comparisons between known and unknown values. The unknown values are represented, as in algebra, by variables. The instruction that compares such values can be classified, among other instructions, as a statement.

The phraseology of a BASIC-language statement is borrowed from English syntax, although more from the syntax of an English command rather than an English statement. A Visual Basic statement may appear to be a command to the computer to change some value or some operating component of the program; but from the point of view of the interpreter, the would-be command states the present value of a variable or the present state of the component, and for this reason we call directive instructions *statements*.

The portion of a statement that actually compares the two values to each other is called an *expression*. An expression is arithmetically reduced by the interpreter to the most fundamental logical value in computing, that being a true/false binary state. A complex statement that assigns a value to a variable is a *formula*. Within formulas, common arithmetic functions may be symbolized by VB function terms, which contain an abbreviation of the function's name followed by a value or expression that the function will operate on.

A Visual Basic project consists of at least one form module, at least one general module (although it may be empty), and absolutely one global module. Within each module are procedures, which are the core components of all VB programs. A procedure describes or models at least one work task, or performs at least one mathematical function.

Within the boundaries of a procedure, a subroutine in Visual Basic is a set of instructions that may be executed repetitively. This repetition is accomplished by branching to that set and then branching back to the instruction following the one that called the subroutine. A more common method of repetitive execution is the loop clause.

Review Questions

1. Write the part of the instruction `If f = 6 Then GoTo Outahere` that is an *expression*.

2. Write the part of the instruction `Total = Int(a + b + c)` that is a *function*.

3. Write the part of the instruction `If quality > 10 then good = 1` that is an expression of assignment.

4. If `x = 5` and `y = 2`, the function `Sqr((x - y) ^ 3)` returns what integral value?

5. The instruction `If coins >= too_many Then Return` ends what type of instruction grouping?

4

The Development Process

This chapter begins by explaining how the source code of Visual Basic applications is presented throughout this book, so that you can follow along, type the examples, and experiment with some working programs. You are then shown how a programmer conceives and develops a Visual Basic application as you take a tour of the development process. You will see a Visual Basic application being written.

Instructions on Instructions

Throughout this book, I highlight individual Visual Basic instructions and demonstrate their best use within the context of the language. Each instruction to be introduced is given a page or so for a summary of its construction and purpose. Toward the beginning of each summary is a line or paragraph devoted to demonstrating example syntax for the instruction. In an example syntax frame, the

Chapter 4 ◆ The Development Process

regular parts of the instruction appear in monospaced (computer output) type. In monospaced italics are placeholders—words that represent the "parts of speech" that appear in a Visual Basic application. Here is an example using the Select Case statement clause:

```
Select Case variable
      Case [Is] comparison1a [To comparison1b]
            instruction block1
      [Case [Is] comparison2a [To comparison2b]]
            [instruction block2]
      .
      .
      .
      [Case Else]
            [instruction blockn]
End Select
```

Here, the words that appear in square brackets represent optional terms that you do not necessarily need to type for the instruction to operate. The italicized words, along with their enclosing brackets, stand in place of real terms and denote the types of terms that would be used in their place. For the preceding example, here is what the italicized words represent:

variable	Any term that can be interpreted as a variable; in other words, not as a keyword. For instance, x or items.
comparison	The value to which a variable is being compared for equality, such as 6 or x.
instruction block	Any number of interpretable instructions.

When more than one term of the same type appears in an example syntax, the terms are differentiated with digits, as in *variable1* and *variable2*. This way, if the same term appears twice within the same syntax, the matching numbers allow you to spot where the terms match as well. Also, when two or more terms within braces are separated with a vertical line—as in {either|or}—only one of the terms within the braces appears in that position. In the example syntax of a clause, a *vertical ellipsis* (three dots, each on its own line, as in the preceding Select Case example) stands in place of any number of interpretable instructions. Finally, punctuation such as brackets ([ ]), braces ({}), or ellipses (...) are not actually typed into the VB instruction or clause.

Entering Programs into the Interpreter

The global module of a Visual Basic project, as I explain in further detail later in the book, is an optional part that contains the variable definitions and functional declarations that have scope and context, respectively, that pertain to the entire program. A general module, by contrast, contains procedures which are not automatically executed when a graphic event takes place, that may be called by such an event procedure.

In just about every other book on programming, it would be easy for the author to present you with a source code example and ask you to type it verbatim, from front to back. In most high-level programming languages such as C or standard BASIC, the source code sequence of any program can be written out all on one spool from beginning to end. C is a modular programming language, and sometimes the order of its modules is arbitrarily defined by the programmer—but at least the order is defined.

In Visual Basic, modules are entities by themselves. As such, the general and object-associated modules have no absolute sequence. When you ask the VB interpreter to list the current project for you—the modern equivalent of the LLIST command in the old Microsoft interpreters—the global module is listed first, followed by the source code and a picture of the default appearance of each form in the project, sorted in alphabetical order by file name. Then each general code module is listed in alphabetical order by file name. Within each code module, the general procedures are listed in alphabetical order by call name. The object procedures are listed in alphabetical order by object name first, event name second.

There are two problems with this listing rationale: First, the code portion of the project is not structured or executed in any sequence relating to the order of the Roman alphabet. Second, at no time are the property settings for the objects in each form—the frame of which is not depicted in the listing, by the way—listed in any

65

form. So the only way a reader could attempt to duplicate someone else's project based on a VB-produced listing alone is by raw estimation or guesswork.

In presenting listings for complete, ready-to-use projects, I am a bit more prudent. Each project listing begins with the source code for the global module, when there is one. This shows the various variable, structure, and function declarations to be used throughout the VB application.

The global module code is followed by the forms' listings. Preceding the source code for each form module is a table showing the property settings for each graphic object in the form, including the form itself, which is listed first. Properties, you remember, are descriptive elements of graphic objects, defining some manner in which the objects appear or behave. Among the properties mentioned are the objects' contents and control names. As for the other properties, the table shows only those properties that have settings changed from their default values.

To enter property settings from the listings:

- If a window for the form mentioned in the "Object type" column is not present, select New Form from the File menu.

- Find and choose each form property listed in the "Property" column from the leftmost drop-down list box in the properties bar of the main Visual Basic window, beneath the menu bar.

- Enter the setting for that property into the center text box in the properties bar. If the setting is textual, type it directly in the box. If the down-arrow button is available (if the arrow is black rather than grey), click it to see the list of current setting choices for that property. If an ellipsis (. . .) appears in place of the down-arrow, click it to see a file selector box from which you can select the file name that acts as the property setting, such as an icon's .ICO file name.

- For each graphic object that is a part of the form, click the VB toolbox button associated with the object type listed. Draw or place the object somewhere within the form for the moment, preferably not overlapping another object. Use the property bar to set the properties for the object, in the same manner as in the preceding step.

For your convenience, the `.CtlName` and `.Caption` or `.Text` properties are listed first, followed by other properties that have been changed from their default values.

The code modules for each form are sorted in order of importance; therefore the main or default form is listed first, and any subsequent forms such as dialog boxes or file selectors follow. Event procedures are arranged in the order of the importance of the event with relation to its object, in the context of the particular program. For instance, the event procedure that responds to typing a key into a text box is probably more important than the one that responds to passing over it with the mouse pointer.

The project listing concludes with the source code for the general code modules (those not related to a specific form), again arranged in order of importance. Procedures within those modules are arranged in order of their relevance, or by their frequency within the source code of the program.

An application is conceived in stages and written in layers, with the heart of the program—the calculation part—written first and the various frills and eccentricities added to it later. You may not yet understand many of the structural details of programming; the rest of this book is devoted to that subject. Still, to understand what you're learning, you need to see a program being built.

A person doesn't learn to paint a portrait with oils by first studying how to hold the paintbrush, then memorizing the chemical composition of the oil paints and the resilience of different brands of canvas, and then by counting the number of brushstrokes to be made per minute. A person learns to paint by watching an artist at work. You do not teach your child how to speak to you by force-feeding him parts of speech—"Look, son, a ball. 'Ball' is a noun. Can you say 'noun?'" He learns by listening to you talk. Programming can be as natural for you as speech—or at least as natural as playing the clarinet, or tennis, or anything else you enjoy.

Programming is a science to the extent that it is studied, analyzed, and theorized on. Programming can be an art inasmuch as it can be practiced, cultivated, and appreciated. You are about to witness a Visual Basic application under construction. If this application were a drawing, it would be a thumbnail sketch. Still, by observing the principles of the programming process being applied, you may be able to obtain a greater understanding of the meaning behind each individual part of the program when you study it in detail.

Making the Expressor

To give you an idea of how the Visual Basic programming process works, here's how I went about programming a special type of scientific formula calculator that I call the *Expressor*. For some time, I've wanted a scientific and financial hand-held calculator from which I could retrieve a formula; type the variables into specific windows that showed me not only each variable I typed, but what it represented with respect to the formula; and see the result of the formula in a separate window. (*Window* was, at one time, what the LED registers on calculators were called, by the way.) Generally when you operate most scientific and financial (sci/fi?) calculators, by the time you've reached the result of your formula, you've lost track of your input parameters because you can't see them anymore.

All "sci/fi" calculators have a storage bank of "memories" that holds values you've typed in at one time or another. My idea for Expressor Mark I was to have five of those "memories" be visible, set apart from the main register, and labeled with terms that relate them to the formula on which you're working. This allows you to calculate the values for the memory parameters independently from the main formula calculation. One input parameter, for instance, may be the sum of several items added together. With the Expressor design, you can calculate the inputs separately and let the Expressor take care of the main formula.

Figure 4.1 is a diagram of the Expressor in its conceptual stage. Programming is a process of trial and error. Many books paint a picture of a logically rosy world where programs can be compiled and executed on the first try. This is simply an unrealistic viewpoint; the better you are at programming, the more errors you will make per program. The reason for this is, the better you are, the bigger and more cumbersome your programs become.

Visual Basic *By* EXAMPLE

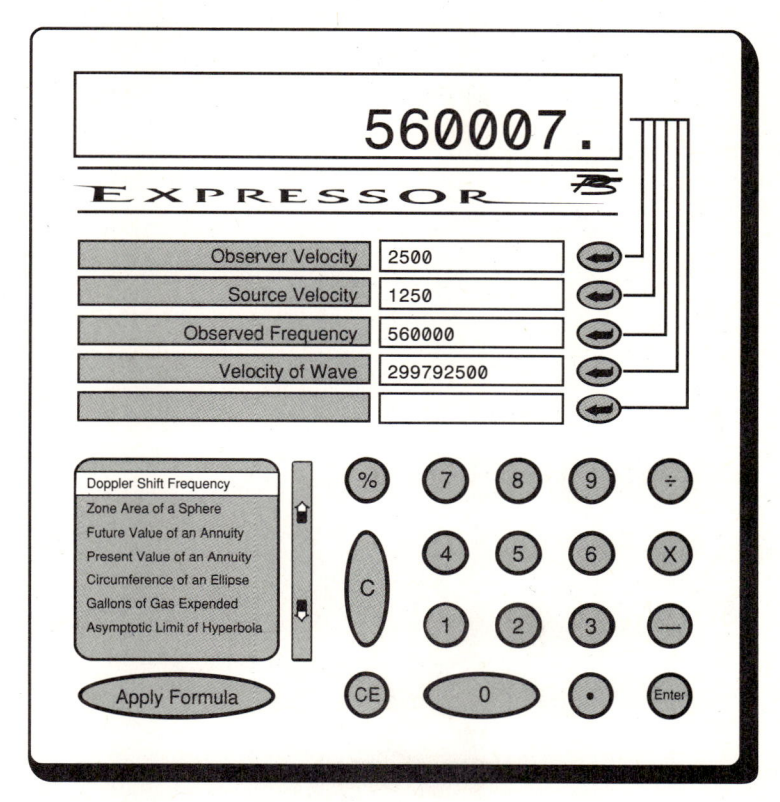

Figure 4.1. A sketch of the Expressor.

Here's how the Expressor works: The calculator portion of the program behaves like a standard RPN four-function calculator. By pressing one of the arrow buttons, the value currently appearing in the readout is copied into the "memory slot" next to the button. Suppose the user wishes to solve a formula for a set of given values. The user selects the name of a formula from a list in the lower-left corner of the device. On doing so, the names of various parameters for this formula appear beside each memory slot. Values can then be copied into the memory slots by making the input parameters appear in the readout, either through calculation or direct entry, and then clicking the arrow button beside the appropriately labeled slot.

When the text for the parameters accurately describes the values that have been inserted into the slots, the user clicks the `Apply`

69

Chapter 4 ◆ The Development Process

`Formula` button. The Expressor then immediately solves the formula for the parameters given and displays the result in the main readout. This method of entry reduces the possibility of error and makes the entry process more fluid and efficient.

The most difficult part of writing a program is in the act of translating those first ideas into logic. Rather than set about right at first imagining the first line of source code, I visualize a potential end product. When I've decided on a partway-feasible goal (and my goals tend to be just that, partway-feasible), the final part of the conception process is creating the beginning of the program.

For the Expressor, I decided my goal would be to write a program the user could operate like a hand-held device. One of the goals of Microsoft Windows is to provide an environment in which programs appear to operate like real-world devices with buttons and gadgets. It is tempting at this point in the Visual Basic programming process to start drawing buttons and gadgets on the screen—to first plot how the user sees the program, and later decide how the computer will see the program. The real-world term for this method of programming is *procrastination.* To construct a program in any language, you do not organize the user control elements (the *shell*) first and try to fill that shell with the yolk of the program later. The first task of a programmer is to determine which elements of the program can be represented numerically as values.

When looking at the Expressor sketch, what do you see beneath the obvious that can be represented numerically as values? If you've ever used a programmable calculator, you know that the specific key you press—whether it be a numeral or function key—is represented numerically. A calculator arithmetically combines the value previously entered into its main window with the one currently being entered, so there are two important values there. The number being typed is different from the one that will be entered into the arithmetic combination, so there is a third important value. The number of digits appearing in the main window is another important value, because you can't enter a number of characters that flows past the leftmost edge of the display.

For the sake of the Expressor, there are five "memory" values held in separate text boxes for use later as parameters for the chosen formula. The formula name appears in a drop-down list box. Which formula is chosen also can be considered a value. The VB interpreter "thinks" in terms of numbers, not gadgets or things. So when you plan a program, you should think in terms of numbers as well.

I know what you may be thinking: A Visual Basic form appears to be a series of pretty objects on the screen which react to events in a programmed way. But at the core of the system, an object has properties that are described numerically; beneath that surface, events are merely the results of continual comparisons of numbers to each other until an expected result is reached. These numbers concern the position of the object, the position of the pointer with relation to the object, the color values within the object, and so on. Objects are not the quanta—or indivisible constituent units—of Visual Basic any more than atoms—as we have learned from the discoveries of subatomic particles and quarks—are the building blocks of matter.

When you've determined what can be represented as values, your next step is to estimate which values will be important throughout the entire program. To explain: Your Visual Basic program will be comprised of numerous procedures, such as those that respond to the user pressing a button, those that apply arithmetic functions to the input values, or the one that stores a displayed number in a "memory slot." Each procedure awaits a certain event that will trigger its execution. When the procedure starts, it needs to be shown those values that are important to its operation. Otherwise, the procedure doesn't know what's going on in the program. Think of each procedure as being asleep until an event wakes it. When the procedure is awake, it suffers from the logical form of insomnia until it has a chance to be briefed concerning the current status of the program.

> The value of a *global variable* is maintained throughout the entire program.

So that my program never forgets its purpose, I declared the most important values the program uses throughout as global variables. The place in the program where I made these declarations is the global module. Figure 4.2 shows where the listing for the global module appears in the Visual Basic project window and shows the global module window itself. I saved the project to disk, so each element of the project has been given its official file name. As is always the case with DOS, I'm limited to an eight-letter filename, so I purposefully removed one *S*.

Chapter 4 ♦ The Development Process

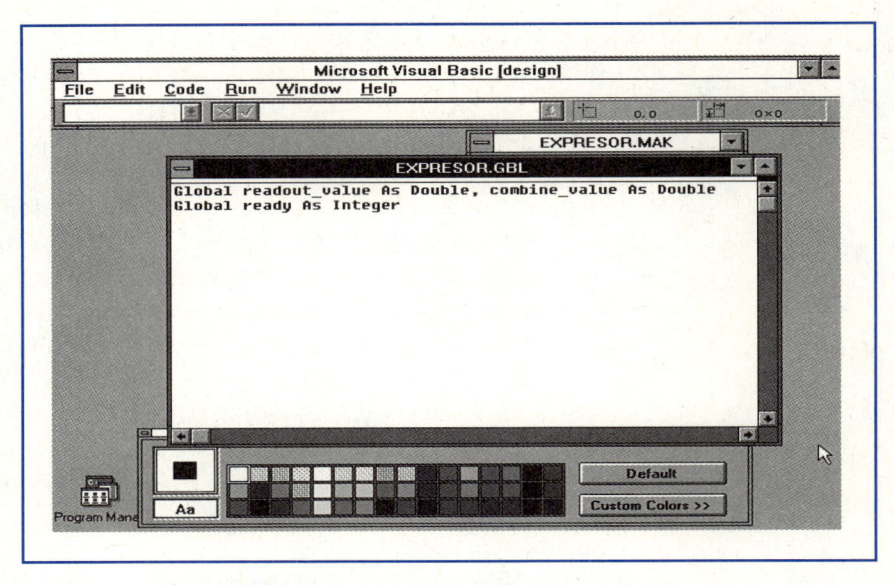

Figure 4.2. The Expressor's main variables in the global module.

The three variables I believe to be pertinent to the program as a whole are the current value in the window, the value with which it is combined, and the number of digits in the "readout" window. I named these variables arbitrarily, as every BASIC programmer has the right to do. I decided to call the window where the main number appears the *readout*, rather than the *window* or the *display*—two words with synonyms that may be confusing for another person to read. I decided to call the values I attributed to the readout `readout_value` and `combine_value`. The underscore character is not part of a Visual Basic convention, but it is instead a replacement for a space, making the variable name easier to read.

In determining which values are global and which, by contrast, are local, one consideration is what values comprise the objective of your program—the sum totals, the statistics concerning the records being kept, and the product of the analysis. Another consideration is which values, unseen by the user, most likely will be shared among several procedures. For the Expressor, the number of digits in the readout is one such value. I named its variable `ready` because it refers both to the readout and to the state of readiness for the readout to receive more digits from the button panel.

The value of a *local variable* is remembered within the procedure that invoked it.

72

Visual Basic *By*
EXAMPLE

The size of the global module shown in Figure 4.2 is an indication of how small this program will be. Throughout the book, I add instructions and procedures to the Expressor program, improving its performance and giving it more capabilities.

Does Function Follow Form?

When writing a program from the beginning, one does not foresee clairvoyantly the modular interrelationship, draw the framework of that interrelationship into the program, and fill that framework with immaculate source code. The technique I choose to use is to select some procedure of the program, make that function work well, and then orient the rest of the procedures around that one. This might not necessarily be the main procedure of the program, although it can be.

When planning your program, start with the most important operational *elements.*

With the Expressor, I chose to make the digit buttons operational first. I could have written the formula-solving routines instead, but to test them out in their running state I would need a number entered into the readout. One rule of programming you generally do not learn from a book (until now) is that the most important *purposeful* elements of a program are not necessarily the most important *operational* elements. Each procedure of a program is like the gear of a mechanism, such as a watch. When you lay out a program using the layered technique, the main gear is wound first. This becomes the engine of the program, in a sense. When the engine is running, it provides the power for the rest of the program, including the gears that perform the true purpose of the program.

The Expressor project is one good example of this principle in action, because the actual formula-solving part of the program was added toward the end of the project. The first stage in the process was to make the digit buttons work. The method I chose in the beginning was to draw the first 11 buttons (digits 0 through 9, and the decimal point), write the procedural source code for one button that would echo its contents into the readout, and copy that code into the procedures for the remaining buttons. I wrote the code for the 7 button, and then copied it into the other procedures, replacing 7 with the appropriate digit. Here's how the procedure looked:

73

Chapter 4 ◆ The Development Process

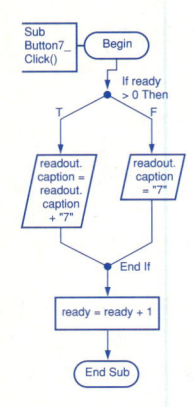

```
Sub Button7_Click ()
If ready > 0 Then
    readout.caption = readout.caption + "7"
Else
    readout.caption = "7"
End If
ready = ready + 1
End Sub
```

Here's the preceding procedure explained as pseudocode:

Procedure for clicking on the 7 button:
If the tally of digits in the readout is one or more,
   Add a "7" to the end of the readout,
Otherwise,
   Make the readout say "7" and nothing else.
End of condition.
Add 1 to the number of digits in the readout tally.
End of procedure.

Notice that this procedure starts to mimic the way a pocket calculator works. When clear, the readout always reads 0, and the first digit typed always replaces that 0—unless you type a decimal point or press the 0 key. In the process of writing a program, you gradually realize what all the exceptions are and add them layer by layer as you go.

The second major principle one learns—and continues to learn—as a programmer is that the simplest code to produce is not necessarily the most efficient. The most efficient BASIC code is generally the most compact. The preceding source code example may look compact, but multiply it by 11 and you may begin to wonder whether one big gear runs better than a handful of smaller ones.

Visual Basic allows for a structure of graphical controls to be established, called a *control array*. Such an array can contain several controls, each of which is accessed using the same control name, and all of which are referenced within the same Sub procedure. Each control in an array, however, is distinguished by its .Index property. To initiate a control array, the first object of the array is placed in the form. After indicating that object and selecting **C**opy from the **E**dit menu, Visual Basic responds by asking you if you want the copies of

---

A *control array* is a group of similar objects (such as command buttons or text boxes) addressed jointly within a single procedure.

this object to form a control array. You respond by clicking the Yes button. At that point, VB sets the original object's .Index property to 0, and each clone thereafter to 1, 2, 3, and so on.

Here's how a programmer thinks: The .Index property of elements of a control array is a number. The purpose of each button in this particular array is to pass a digit—which is a number, after all—to the readout. If that number is always a single digit, you can write a generic procedure for the entire control array. The procedure will pass some distinct value, whatever it is, to the readout whenever one of the buttons in the array is pressed. You don't need several separate-but-equal procedures to define the pressing of buttons when one procedure does the job just as well. The one element of distinction here is the .Index property of each button, so if you make each .Index equal to the number being passed, you can program the procedure to pass the .Index to the readout.

The third thing you learn to do as a programmer is to say, "On second thought..." often. As stated earlier, the 0 and decimal point buttons operate differently on a calculator than the rest of the digit keys, so you can't include these two wayward buttons in the control array. The 1 through 9 buttons are functionally identical, however, so those buttons with positive-valued indices can be included in a control array. Here's the code for the new procedure, rewritten from the 7-button version presented earlier:

```
Sub ButtonPos_Click (Index As Integer)
If ready > 0 Then
    If ready < 20 Then
        readout.caption = readout.caption + Right$(Str$(Index), 1)
        ready = ready + 1
    End If
Else
    readout.caption = Right$(Str$(Index), 1)
    ready = 1
End If
assess_readout
End Sub
```

Notice how this procedure has evolved. Because this procedure belongs to a control array rather than to one control, the Index of that control is automatically passed to the procedure through the

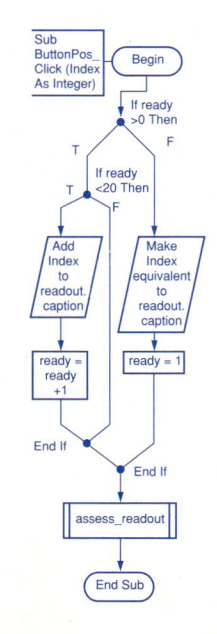

75

Chapter 4 ◆ The Development Process

parentheses within the initial `Sub` statement. `Index` is the parameter passed to the procedure when the user clicks on a positively numbered button. Think of the parentheses within the `Sub` and `Function` statements as a slot through which values—here called *parameters*—are passed.

The function `Right$(Str$(Index), 1)` converts the numeric value of `Index` to textual contents. Visual Basic stores alphanumeric text and real numbers differently; the text may happen to have numbers in it, but VB still cannot evaluate that text. To give numeric text value, it must be converted to a value using the function `Str$()`. The function that, in this instance, encloses that function, `Right$(..., 1)`, removes the leading space character—another bit of alphanumeric text.

Here are the instructions for the new and improved procedure, written as pseudocode:

For all positively numbered buttons, receive the index for the particular button pressed.
If the tally of digits in the readout is one or more,
    Then if this tally is less than 20,
        Add the numeric form of the index to the readout
        and add one to the tally of digits.
    End of this condition.
Otherwise (if there's only one digit in the readout),
    Place the numeric form of the index into the
      readout and make the tally equal 1.
End of the main condition.
Execute the procedure that assesses the readout value.
End of procedure.

Within the "memory bank" portion of the Expressor form, the groups of five value registers, descriptive text boxes, and value-loading buttons were each created as control arrays.

I chose to program the four-function calculator portion of the Expressor using Reverse Polish Notation (also called H.P. or Hewlett Packard notation) primarily because it is easier to implement. If you've ever used a Texas Instruments (T.I.) calculator or one that uses T.I. notation, you know that you enter each element of an arithmetic expression the way it would appear on paper in algebraic notation. Thus *two times three divided by six* is entered in T.I. notation as 2 * 3 / 6, where * is the multiplication operator and / is the division operator.

The downside of T.I. notation is that the previous arithmetic function is implemented whenever the next one is entered. For instance, in 2 * 3 / 6, 2 will actually be multiplied by 3 when the division key is pressed. Subsequently, the division operation takes place when the = key is pressed. To implement this notation in a Visual Basic program, the previous arithmetic function has to be remembered—which means creating another variable and giving each function its own arbitrary index.

For Reverse Polish Notation, the same formula is entered as 2 [Enter] 3 * 6 /. This looks backward on paper—thus the name *Reverse*—but it's easier to implement in a program. Each arithmetic operation takes place at the time its operator is pressed. The Expressor's function buttons can then be programmed to execute the operation the moment the button-pressing event is triggered.

Here's the source code for the procedure that handles the pressing of the multiplication button:

```
Sub Times_Click ()
assess_readout
readout_value = readout_value * combine_value
combine_value = readout_value
readout.caption = Str$(readout_value)
ready = 0
End Sub
```

Here is the same procedure written in pseudocode:

Procedure for clicking the "Times" button:
Execute the procedure that assesses the value of the number in the readout.
Multiply that assessment by the combination value—previous value entered into the readout.
Make the combination value the current value, in the event of future button presses.
Place the textual form of the mathematically combined value into the readout.
Pretend there are no digits in the readout, so that the next digit button pressed will clear it.
End of procedure.

Chapter 4 ◆ The Development Process

Notice the next-to-last statement in the procedure. The way the digit buttons work, a digit replaces the contents of the entire readout if the register of the number of digits, `ready`, is equal to `0`. You know that the solution value in the readout is not likely to be 0. You also know, however, that the next digit button pressed should not add a digit to the solution, but should instead replace it. Therefore, I set the digit-number tally to 0. The real-world term for this form of process-triggering is *lying*.

This is the point in the discussion of the art of programming where I admit to you that I am a "code-as-you-go" programmer. I don't devise the inner schematics of my BASIC programs beforehand. In fact, most of my grand solutions to procedural dilemmas come to me by accident. The setting of `ready` to `0` when there were clearly digits in the readout is one case in point. I could have prepared another variable to act as a register which sets itself to 1 whenever a function button is pressed, and then had my digit button procedures check to see if `register = 1` before proceeding. I would, however, have had to add another comparison to my conditional statements. Furthermore, why make two registers perform similar purposes when one does the job just as well, if not better? When programming, be prepared to abandon at any time whatever process or method you originally *thought* would work in favor of a better way. This really is the way to program.

Summary

Here is an outline of the principles of programming introduced in this chapter, which are utilized throughout the book:

1. When conceiving a program in your mind, start with the end product and work backward toward the beginning.

2. The first task of a programmer is to determine which elements of the program—graphical or logical—can be represented numerically as values.

3. The second task is to determine which values are important to the entire program and which are necessary only within their own local procedures.

4. Make one whole procedure of the program work first, and then write the other procedures to work around it.

5. The most compact code may be the most difficult for a person to read—or, for that matter, write—but it is probably the most efficient code for the interpreter to execute.

6. Prepare to rewrite entire procedures as you discover new methods that work better. You will probably keep less than 30 percent of the original draft of your source code, regardless of how well-written it is.

7. Accept new solutions that come to mind along the way, even if they are devious and the apparent product of a scheming mind.

The Expressor program is far from complete at this point in the development process. In upcoming chapters, however, I pick up on the initial programming process, as well as the revision process. The entire source code for the Expressor appears in Appendix C.

Review Questions

1. In the Expressor program, why were the 0 and period keys not part of the same control array as the keys 1 through 9?

2. Reverse Polish Notation is easier to implement in a computer program for what primary reason?

Part II

Values and Variables

Definition and Declaration

In this chapter you will be introduced to the concept of the variable, which is the logical container for values and text in Visual Basic. You will learn the different categories of variables and experiment with placing values within each type. You will also construct mathematical expressions using variables as components.

Variables and the Universe As We Know It

Every Visual Basic instruction you write manipulates the contents of the computer's memory in one way or another. Even the single-statement instruction Stop—which suspends the program's execution—alters the contents of memory. The Stop statement, however, does not impart to its human reader just what contents are being altered at the time. You as programmer, therefore, are manipulating the computer indirectly. As user you see only the cause of the program's suspension—the "command" Stop—and its seemingly immediate effect. What you don't see are all the values in memory being manipulated, which result in the appearance of stopping the VB application. If you were inside the computer, you

Chapter 5 ◆ Definition and Declaration

A *variable* represents a unit of data.

would discover that by saying Stop, you actually started a myriad of internal processes—for instance, processes that turn over control to the VB environment. These are invisible processes, however, so the VB interpreter doesn't appear to be guilty of insubordination; in other words, it really does respond to the "command" as directed.

A direct statement such as Stop is, in fact, an indirect method of manipulating values in memory. In Visual Basic, the direct method of manipulating values in memory is to represent those values as *variables*. A variable is an arbitrarily named term that represents a unit of data in memory that can be altered by the program.

In the history of the English language, few scientific formulas have ever become cliches. Perhaps the best-known of these formula catchphrases is $E=mc^2$, the formula that explains one of the primary principles of relativity theory. Many people who know this catchphrase have no idea what it means; however, many of these people seem to know that the three letters of this formula represent values of some sort—although they may not be sure just what those values are.

At the time this formula was conceived, c represented what appeared to be a *constant*—that is, an unchanging value. Namely, this value is the speed of light. But recently, physicists have determined that this value is not, in fact, constant at all. We can therefore say with some sense of assurance that the three letters in the famous formula are all variables that represent values that are subject to change. The very fact that fewer people know what values are represented by these variables than know that they are variables underscores the principle of using variables to represent values: Variables are often *unknowns*.

When writing a program, you constantly deal with unknowns—more specifically, with unknown values. For instance, you may write a program that at one point tells the interpreter to solve for the velocity of a jet airplane traveling at so many thousand feet through some level of atmospheric density with the throttle at some percentage level. You do not know the specific attributes of this flight, but you do know the *relationships* between those attributes. In the relativity formula, the particular level of mass (m) is not specified, and the speed of light (c) is no longer specifiable as a constant. Still, the formula denotes what we perceive to be the proportional inter-relationship between mass, light, and energy. Formulas specify relationships; now you know why it's called "relativity" theory.

Visual Basic *By*
EXAMPLE

> A *formula* states the relationship between known and unknown quantities.

A *formula* is an algebraic expression of equality that states the relationships between qualities, quantities, or other such values, whether they be known or unknown. This definition holds true in common conversation as well as with respect to Visual Basic.

I Declare!

> An *expression* can be a comparison between values, a formula, or an assignment of value to a variable.

Visual Basic recognizes variables as unique combinations of alphanumeric characters up to 40 characters long. (It will probably be on extremely rare occasions that you use a 40-character variable.) When the Visual Basic interpreter starts executing a program, no variables exist for that program. In other words, the interpreter maintains several values for the program even at first, although none of them have yet been explicitly claimed by you. To stake your claim on a variable using the informal method, you use that variable for the first time in a mathematical *expression* of equality.

An expression is any of the following:

- An arithmetic comparison between two values, having a result that is expressed logically as a binary state

- One or more values or variables arithmetically joined by functions or functional operators

- An assignment of value to a variable by way of another value, variable, or expression

> In BASIC, a variable is *declared* whenever it is first invoked within the source code.

Whenever a variable is used for the first time within a program, we say that variable is *declared*. A declaration of a variable is the first statement in a program to assign a legitimate value to that variable.

Example

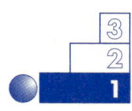

Perhaps the simplest variable declaration is x = 1. The preceding declaration is a mathematical expression that creates the variable x and assigns to it the value 1. From this point on, whenever x appears in the program, the interpreter will evaluate it to be 1 until some instruction explicitly changes the value of x to something else.

85

Chapter 5 ♦ Definition and Declaration

The best way to experiment with variables is to invoke the *Immediate window* from within Visual Basic, as depicted in Figure 5.1. This window contains a command-line interpreter—in other words, a prompted line like the DOS prompt on which you type direct statements as commands. This is the descendant of the READY prompt from the old BASIC interpreters.

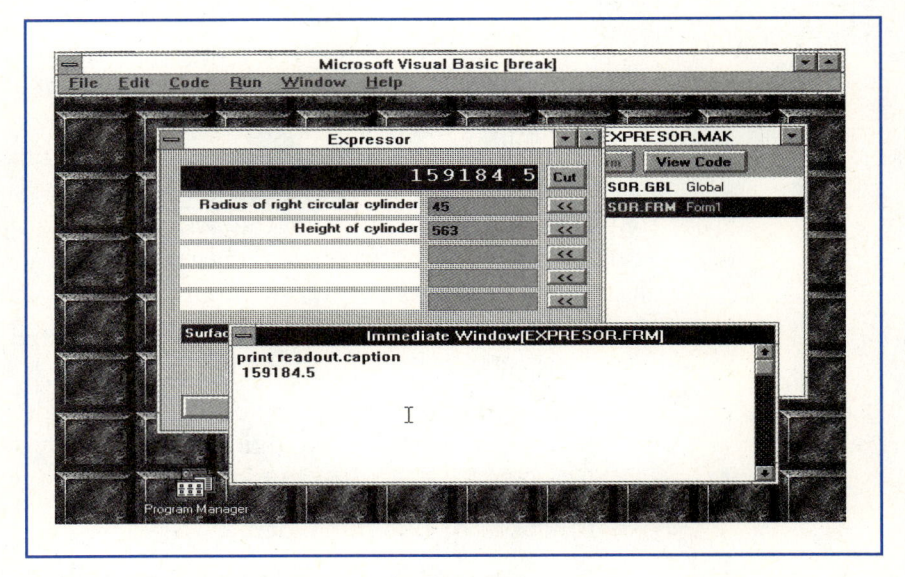

Figure 5.1. The Immediate window in all its glory.

To invoke the Immediate window without loading a program:

1. From the VB **F**ile menu, select **N**ew Project.... Shortly, a blank Form1 is visible.

2. From the **R**un menu, select start. For a moment, Form1 disappears and then reappears without the grid.

3. Select **B**reak from the **R**un menu. The Immediate window appears.

4. Click once anywhere within the area of the Immediate window to begin operating it.

Visual Basic *By*
EXAMPLE

Each instruction you enter here is interpreted immediately, hence the window's name. You may therefore enter x = 1 into this window and start your variable-manipulating career at once.

To test the effectiveness of the Immediate window, enter Print x at the Immediate window prompt. The window should respond with 1 on a line by itself. Likewise at this point, if you enter Print y, the window should respond with 0 because no real value has yet been loaded into a variable y. All variables that have never been officially declared are "virtually" equal to 0; in other words, if a variable is invoked in a formula that has never had a value assigned to it, the variable is evaluated as 0.

The statement x = 1 is an expression of assignment, in that the value 1 is assigned to x. It is also a declaration of the existence of x if and only if the expression is the first instruction within the VB program to use x.

We Hold This Truth To Be Confusing

The fact that a program is made workable by continually assigning and reassigning values to variables is not self-evident—in fact, little in the art of programming is ever self-evident. I could stop here in the text and say, "Now that you've made x equal to 1, you know how to make value assignments," and then skip merrily away to the next topic. Such methods of explanation through assumption lend themselves to such widely-read and underappreciated works as the Federal Budget.

As stated earlier, an expression of equality—an *equation*—specifies the relationships between values as well as their proportions, ratios, and limits. The Visual Basic application is, in the purely logical sense, a mechanism that utilizes equations as instructions for the construction and assembly of a product. This product is not the program, mind you, but the data "manufactured" by that program. The data are always, in their root form, a set of numbers. In its tangible form, the product of a program is a record of names, a graph, a mathematical series, or the destruction of the Xamphoid Empire. Whatever its guise, the product of any program is really a bunch of numbers.

Chapter 5 ◆ Definition and Declaration

In order for the mechanism to work, the instructions to be interpretable, and the final product to be manufactured, at some point the programmer must draw out a parts list. These are the elements that are *seeded* into the formulas and procedures, and that, when they are combined, produce solutions. Lo and behold, these parts are a bunch of numbers. If you're beginning to get the impression that all a computer program does is take one group of numbers and reconstitute it with formulas so that it is another group of numbers, you're beginning to think like a programmer.

Example

Here's an example of this principle in practice. Suppose there is a formula you use in your business to determine whether the price you charge for an item is excessive. You figure your cost for the item is equal to the actual wholesale cost you paid for it as a retailer, plus your costs for shipping, employee maintenance time, and time the item spent consuming your shelf space. This formula is fixed, but your percentage of markup over your costs varies, perhaps by the day.

Here's how your formula might appear:

```
Sub Analyze_Markup (sale_price, shipping, manhours,
    shelf_time, markup_ceiling)
total_cost = shipping + manhours + shelf_time
ratio = (sale_price / total_cost - 1) * 100
If ratio > markup_ceiling Then
    too_high = 1
End If
End Sub
```

Here is the task the VB interpreter is being instructed to perform, rendered as pseudocode:

Procedure for analyzing the fairness of the markup value, taking into account the current sale price, costs for materials shipping, production hours, shelf time, and the current markup ceiling:

*Calculate the total cost of producing the item as equal to the shipping
   cost for raw material, plus the number of production hours, plus
   the time the item will rest on the shelf.
Calculate the percentage ratio of sale price to this total cost.
If this ratio is higher than the maximum allowable markup ceiling, then
     Set the "too high" flag.
End of condition.
End of procedure.*

There are three value assignments in the preceding procedure. You add all the operating costs and expenditures to arrive at the total cost per item. The next procedure is a formula that determines the percentage of price markup. The third procedure, which is executed conditionally, is the simplest of all. It assigns a value directly to a variable, as a flag, in case the markup is too much.

Suppose that before you execute this procedure, in lieu of acquiring inputs from a form, you *seed* the formula with the following statements appearing in the midst of another procedure:

```
.
.
.
shipping = 2.90
manhours = (av_salary / no_boxes) * 8
shelf_time = .25 * no_days
markup_ceiling = 33
.
.
.
```

You can interpret these statements as a sort of parts list for the "assembly manual" that is `Sub Analyze_Markup ()`. These statements, or some such assignment of value to these variables referred to in `Sub Analyze_Markup ()`, are essential to the operation of the program. Otherwise, Visual Basic will not be able to execute the procedure. The variable `total_cost` cannot be allowed to equal `0` because the interpreter will "error out" if it attempts to divide another value by 0.

Chapter 5 ♦ Definition and Declaration

Because some of the preceding ingredients are, in fact, formulas, we could take this seeding process one step further with the following initial statements:

```
av_salary = 6.50
no_boxes = 1300
no_days = 5
```

As stated before, the programming process sometimes works best backward. Direct assignment statements act as the fuel for the arithmetic engine of the program. The programmer can easily change the values within these statements.

Degrees of Precision

A byte is comprised of eight bits.

When the Visual Basic interpreter sees a variable for the first time, it allots a space for that variable in memory. Computers do not "think" in terms of decimal numbers (numbers in the base 10 numeral system). Therefore, the VB interpreter does not place into memory numbers like the kind we are accustomed to using. A unit of memory, as mentioned in the preceding chapter, is a *byte*—the primary memory storage unit for all forms of data in a computer system. A byte is comprised of eight binary digits (bits).

Each eight-bit byte can hold any absolute integral value between 0 and 511 and any signed value between –256 and 255.

As you've seen, variables can have fractional values. Bytes, however, do not have fractional values; so when apportioning space for a variable that may at some time become fractional, the Visual Basic interpreter, by default, apportions extra memory for both fractional and whole-number values to be maintained for each variable.

A floating-point value may or may not be fractional.

In fractional value storage, the interpreter maintains a separate register for each value that could possibly be fractional. This register specifies the placement of the decimal point in the binary, or base 2, form of the number. The whole-number and fractional parts of the number are then translated into base 10 separately. This type of number is referred to as a *floating-point* number. The term *floating-point* refers to the storage format for a value that is possibly fractional, where the position of its decimal point is stored as a separate value.

Table 5.1 shows the five numeric precision types that Visual Basic supports and the number of bytes apportioned for each type. The table also shows the special characters used for addressing these different classes. These characters are placed immediately following the variable name, to denote the variable's precision type throughout the source code.

Table 5.1. **Numeric precision types.**

Variable type	Symbol	Memory Usage	Fractional Value Storage
Integer	%	2 bytes	None
Long Integer	&	4 bytes	None
Single-precision floating-point	!	4 bytes	Includes 2 bytes of fractional value storage
Double-precision floating-point	#	8 bytes	Includes 4 bytes of fraction value storage
Currency	@	8 bytes	Includes 2 bytes of fractional value storage

Keep in mind that a *kilobyte* (K) is equal to 1,024 bytes, and that a *megabyte* (M) is equal to 1.024 kilobytes. With the amount of a computer's installed memory now being measured commonly in megabytes rather than in multiples of 16K, it might seem a bit out of fashion to consider conserving memory for variable usage two bytes at a time. Those who concur that it is out of fashion may very well be the authors of programs that do less with two megabytes than some late-70s applications did with 32K.

The degree to which you conserve memory when writing programs should not be dictated by the deflating dollar value of memory on the open market. Furthermore, if you've ever tried to write a book with a huge word processor, while testing programs with a high-level interpreter, while also running background utilities all in the same environment, you most likely have come to appreciate small, efficient programs.

One way to tighten the object code or threaded p-code of a program is to eliminate the "trailing zeros" from unnecessarily decimalized integers, or whole numbers with two or four bytes of

An *integer* is any whole number that has no fractional value.

decimal values all set to zero. Another might be to determine which variables will always be described as whole numbers—for instance, the number of work-hours expended in the earlier example—and declare those variables as integers rather than as floating-point (possibly fractional) variables.

Example

Here's the last group of assignment expressions, edited, in the interest of conserving space, to specify their new variable type:

```
av_salary@ = 6.50
no_boxes& = 1300
no_days% = 5
```

For those values that you know will never be fractional—for instance, any variable that represents a number of units—you should consider using the % integer symbol to use two bytes for the variable instead of four, or the & long integer symbol for anything you keep in stock that may number in the billions.

Live and Let Live

Optionally, a statement of assignment or an informal declaration can be written as a formal Visual Basic statement using the keyword Let, as introduced here:

`[Let] variable = expression`

The interpreter first evaluates the expression on the right side of the equation. If that expression evaluates to be a rational arithmetic value, that value is assigned to the variable stated. If that expression evaluates to be a legal textual string, that string is assigned to the string variable stated. If the expression can be evaluated rationally, and the statement of the variable is the first instance of that variable within the code of the procedure, the stated variable is considered officially declared, either as a single-precision number or a string, with its scope set to local.

Example

Here are the three values of assignment revised again to appear as formal `Let` statements:

```
Let av_salary@ = 6.50
Let no_boxes& = 1300
Let no_days% = 5
```

Using `Let` gives your instructions more of a sentence-like structure. Beyond that, the term does nothing more of importance for the instruction; for that reason, I tend to avoid using it. In the 1960s versions of BASIC, `Let` was a mandatory term to be used before statements of assignment. Perhaps because there is no word `Let` in algebra, usage of the term was dropped in the mid-70s. In deference to those who prefer the older structures, `Let` is maintained in Visual Basic as an optional keyword. Almost no other part of BASIC looks like it did in 1964; so consider the `Let` statement the syntactic equivalent of your own body's appendix.

In upcoming chapters, you'll learn about textual strings and variable scopes.

Summary

A computer program of any type, written with any language, works by manipulating values in memory. The result of this value manipulation is the production of data. In Visual Basic, values used within a program that are not subject to change are represented using numerals, and are called *constants*. Values that are subject to change are represented using alphanumeric characters, and are called *variables*.

In Visual Basic, a value is automatically assigned to a variable once that variable is invoked within a program, even if that value is zero. When a variable is formally declared, its initial value will be zero. A variable may be informally declared by means of its invocation within a formula. Such a formula will assign a specific value to a variable, whether by means of direct assignment or calculation.

The primary program element used to assign a value to or assess the value of a variable is the *expression*. In an expression, a variable on the left side is compared to a variable or value on the right side. If one value is being compared to another within an expression for equality, the equal sign (=) is used between the two.

Review Questions

1. The result or solution of an expression of comparison is described logically as what?

2. The `Print` instruction to the Immediate window falls under what category of instruction?

3. If one instruction sets the value of y to 12, what type of instruction is required to set it to some other value?

4. How many binary digits (bits) are there in a long integer variable?

5. Estimate why an unsigned byte can hold a value between 0 and 511, but a signed byte can hold a value between –256 and 255. Why not between –512 and 511? Why is the positive maximum value odd?

Review Exercises

1. Write five instructions that set the variables `prime1`, `prime2`, and so on equal to the first five prime numbers.

2. Write expressions of assignment for arbitrarily named variables. Assign the following values to those variables. Use symbols for those variables that direct the interpreter to allocate the least number of bytes feasible for each value.

   A. 17.725

   B. 1 3/8

   C. –16

   D. 0.176470588235294

   E. $56.25

   F. 152,587,890,625

Formulas

In this chapter you experiment with equations and formulas that involve values and arithmetic functions. You learn how values are derived from elsewhere in the program and assigned to a variable with an expression of assignment. You study the order of evaluation of simple arithmetic functions and begin to incorporate more complex, intrinsic Visual Basic functions into formulas.

The Function of Formulas

Although Visual Basic uses procedural algebra to encode its own applications, it really doesn't use algebra to its full extent in evaluating mathematical expressions. Algebraic equations deal primarily with unknown values. As you saw in the previous chapter, no variable in Visual Basic has an unknown value. Even if a variable was never declared and you asked the interpreter to print its value to a form, VB would respond with *0*—a known value.

If you've studied algebra, you know that each algebraic statement is an equation. Likewise, each statement of value assignment in Visual Basic is an equation. An *equation* is a statement of equality that assigns a value—whether it is a numeral or an arithmetically derived value—to a variable.

> An *equation* is a statement that assigns a value to a variable.

Chapter 6 ◆ Formulas

The elementary syntax of a Visual Basic equation is as follows:

`variable = value1 [[operator1] [value2]...]`

When you assign a value to a variable, through direct specification (as in x = 1) or through indirect reference by way of other variables (as in x = y + 1), you use an equation. Here are some valid Visual Basic equations:

```
a = n + 1

lifeboats = crewmen / 15

Energy = mass * light_speed ^ 2

sphere_volume = (4/3) * 3.1415927 * r ^ 3
```

Notice that in the preceding expressions the left side of the equation is always a single variable. Arithmetic functions are placed on the right side of the equation. It would be invalid, therefore, to state n + 1 = x / 6 and expect the interpreter to solve for n. Although Visual Basic uses algebraic notation, it is not so figurative in its evaluation. In other words, the interpreter does not simplify algebraic terms in the way the equation $6y^2 = 3y$ is simplified to $2y = 1$ and then to $y = 1/2$.

> **NOTE:** The solution to a Visual Basic equation is always a known value, and is always assigned to a single variable by itself on the left side of the equation.

An *operator* is a symbol (+, –, *, /) that represents a mathematical function.

In the preceding example VB equations, the variables and numbers were each separated by arithmetic symbols. You probably recognize some of these symbols; however, there are some you may not recognize if you're a newcomer to BASIC. These symbols are called *operators*, and their purpose is to represent simple arithmetic functions. A *binary operator* is a symbol that represents a mathematical function that combines, compares, or equates two values.

Table 6.1 lists operators used in Visual Basic expressions. The third column of this table lists solutions to the expression 2 *operator* 3, where *operator* is replaced with the specific arithmetic operator to the left of each solution.

Table 6.1. Arithmetic functional operators.

Operator	Function	2 operator 3
^	Exponentiation (raising to a power)	8
*	Multiplication	6
/	Division	.66666666
+	Addition	5
–	Subtraction	-1

The Order of Evaluation

In Table 6.1, the operators are listed in the order of their evaluation in a formula. When you type numbers and functions into a pocket calculator, the evaluation generally takes place as each button is pressed, so the order of evaluation—also called the operator *precedence*—is generally front-to-back.

Examples

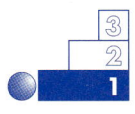

With Visual Basic, the entire expression is stated within an instruction before evaluation takes place. A Visual Basic expression is in many ways a restatement of an algebraic formula or equation. To understand why the order of evaluation in VB is the way it is, examine an equation stated in pure algebraic notation, followed by an equivalent Visual Basic expression:

$$c = y^3 + \frac{5y^2}{4}$$

c = y ^ 3 + 5 * y ^ 2 / 4

In algebra, a variable raised to an exponent—such as y^3—is considered to be one term rather than a function relating y to 3. Thus, if the entire equation is to be solved rationally, "y to the third" is solved first. If the term is to be multiplied by a whole number, that number is the term's coefficient. In algebra, "5y squared" is rarely stated as "5 *times* y squared," although it would be correct to do so. Multiplication of this nature is generally presumed in algebra to exist almost by default, so the function has taken on a virtual priority just below exponentiation.

In the preceding algebraic equation, "5y squared over 4" is considered to be a fraction. Fractional values in Visual Basic are stated as functions of division, as in "5 times y raised to the power of 2 *divided by* 4." Nonetheless, a fractional term in algebra is one term, rather than two terms separated by a division symbol. Therefore, to maintain the algebraic hierarchy, division operations are performed at the same time as multiplication.

Addition and subtraction symbols separate terms in algebraic notation. Because they do, those functions are evaluated last. To understand why, take the first part of the preceding Visual Basic equation: `c = y ^ 3 + 5`.... Logically speaking, the solution for just this part of the equation should be the same if you instead stated it as `c = 5 + y ^ 3`.... If addition were to be performed first rather than exponentiation, then in the first example, `3 + 5` is evaluated first. The solution for the first three VB terms would be the value, algebraically speaking, of y^8 rather than y^3—"y to the eighth power" (the `3 + 5` power) rather than "y to the third."

In the second example, if addition were to be evaluated first, the solution would reflect the value of $(5+y)^3$ rather than $5+y^3$. In other words, y and 5 would be added together and then the result would be cubed, instead of the cube of y being added to 5. There would be a discrepancy of 120 in the final solution.

In Praise of Parentheses

A *delimiter* separates elements of an expression from each other.

If you want to evaluate the value of `5 + y` added and cubed, just as in the algebraic instance in the previous paragraph, place parentheses around the part of the expression you want the interpreter to evaluate before the other parts. You would therefore write `(5 + y) ^ 3`. In such an expression, the parentheses act as *delimiters* for the interpreter. A *delimiter* is a punctuation mark used to distinguish or separate elements of an expression from each other.

Example

Here's an example of a real-world formula in which parentheses are necessary. A formula for depreciation of the monetary value of an asset over a given period follows:

`dep@ = ((init_value@ - prior_dep@) * factor%) / life%`

Figure 6.1 depicts a "parenthetical mountain" for this formula. At the summit of this mountain is the smallest enclosure of terms within parentheses. Evaluation of this formula starts at the summit and works its way toward the foot of the mountain. Notice that I included the type designators (such as `@` and `%`) beside each variable. I didn't have to include them, but the formula now consumes less memory.

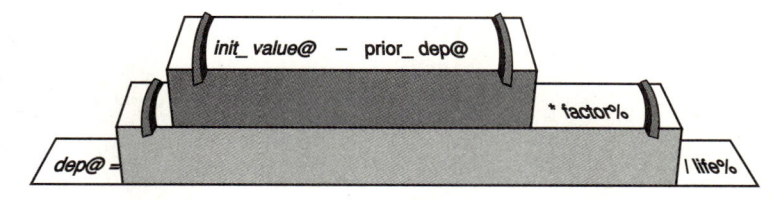

Figure 6.1. A mountain of depreciation.

The first order of business for this formula is to subtract any depreciation of the asset `prior_dep@` from the initial value of that asset `init_value@`. The remainder is multiplied by the factor at which the balance declines `factor%` before it is divided by the life span of the depreciation in equivalent periods `life%`. The solution is rendered to the depreciation variable `dep@`. Variable `dep@` is obviously a currency value, so the result is limited to four decimal places.

Here is an example session—a "conversation"—using the Immediate window. You can test this formula without having to devise an entire project for it.

Chapter 6 ◆ Formulas

```
init_value@=2400
prior_dep@=500
factor%=2
life%=12
dep@=((init_value@-prior_dep@)*factor%)/life%
?dep@
 316.6667
```

Every now and then, you use the VB Immediate window to test formulas. BASIC formulas have been tested and proven this way for years, and there is no reason for that to change now. I've left out the spaces between terms, operators, and delimiters in the preceding code. Visual Basic does not require these spaces, especially within the Immediate window.

CLI (command-line interpreter) is another name for Visual Basic's Immediate window.

The first four lines seed the variables for the formula in the fifth line. The statement `?dep@` is on the sixth line. Here, the `?` is an abbreviation for the `Print` statement. Since the 70s, `?` has stood in place of `Print`, primarily for the reason that in conversations with the *command-line interpreter* (*CLI*) such as the preceding one, `?` is easier to type when you're in a hurry and you're "quizzing" the interpreter. Hereafter, I refer to the Immediate window as the CLI. Take note, however, that `?` does not substitute for the `.Print` method in a procedure window.

In the first six lines of the conversation, the CLI does not type a response. Only after the quizzing statement does the CLI respond with `316.6667`. In the text of such conversations, the CLI adds a leading space to distinguish its responses from your statements.

Example

For the next example, I construct a working Visual Basic project. This project concerns coordinate geometry. Its objective is to allow you to figure the distance between two points with Cartesian (x, y) coordinates—such as (0, 0) or (16, 5)—on a plane. Figure 6.2 shows the form for the two-dimensional Cartesian calculator, along with a graph that shows two points on a Cartesian plane and the distance between them.

Visual Basic *By* EXAMPLE

Again, to add controls and graphic objects to a form, click the symbol button for that object on the toolbar, and move the pointer to the form area. Click and hold down the index button, and drag the pointer from one corner of the control to the opposite corner. Upon releasing the button, the object will appear on the form. You can alter its shape or position by dragging any of the eight indicator nodes that surround it. Properties such as textual contents can be changed using the combo box in VB's main properties bar.

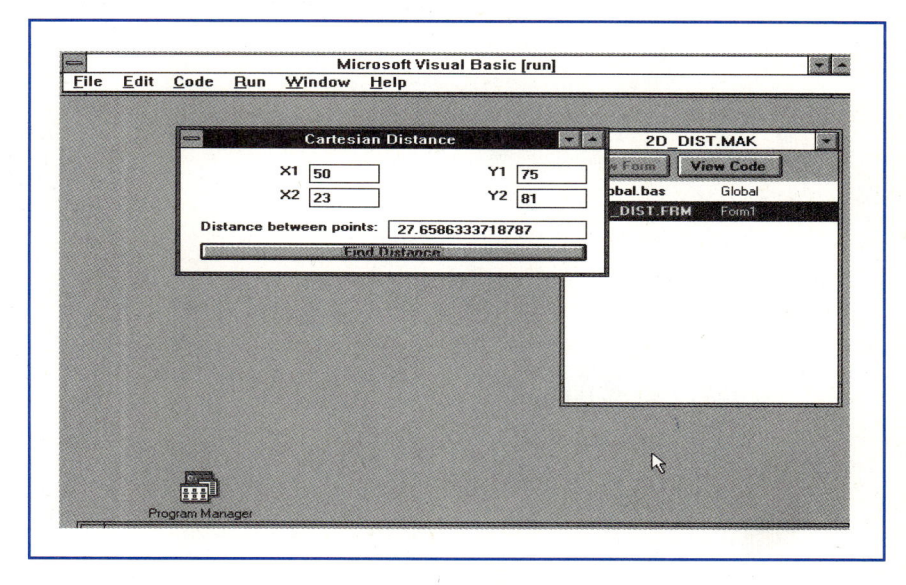

Figure 6.2. The Cartesian calculator.

Using Figure 6.2 and the following table as guides, draw five text boxes, five labels, and one command button on the form. Change the properties of each object as indicated. Here is the extended listing for the two-dimensional calculator:

101

Chapter 6 ◆ Formulas

2D Cartesian Coordinates Calculator

PROJECT NAME
2D_DIST.MAK

CONSTITUENT FILES
2D_DIST.FRM

Object type	Property	Setting
Form	.Width	5265
	.Height	2280
	.Caption	Cartesian Distance
Text box	.CtlName	Box_x1
	.Text	(blank)
	.TabIndex	0
Text box	.CtlName	Box_y1
	.Text	(blank)
	.TabIndex	1
Text box	.CtlName	Box_x2
	.Text	(blank)
	.TabIndex	2
Text box	.CtlName	Box_y2
	.Text	(blank)
	.TabIndex	3
Text box	.CtlName	Distance
	.Text	(blank)
Label	.Caption	X1
	.Alignment	1 - Right Justify
Label	.Caption	Y1
	.Alignment	1 - Right Justify
Label	.Caption	X2
	.Alignment	1 - Right Justify
Label	.Caption	Y2
	.Alignment	1 - Right Justify
Label	.Caption	Distance between points:
	.Alignment	1 - Right Justify
Button	.CtlName	Go
	.Caption	Find Distance

Visual Basic *By*
EXAMPLE

To enter the following procedure, double-click the `Go` command button in the newly drawn form, and type the following:

```
Sub Go_Click ()
x1 = Val(Box_x1.Text)
x2 = Val(Box_x2.Text)
y1 = Val(Box_y1.Text)
y2 = Val(Box_y2.Text)
d# = Sqr((x2 - x1) ^ 2 + (y2 - y1) ^ 2)
Distance.Text = Str$(d#)
End Sub
```

To help you understand what's going on, here is the above procedure written in pseudocode:

*Procedure for clicking on the **Go** button:*
Retrieve the four values from their respective text boxes.
.
.
.
Calculate the zone of the given sphere using the specified coordinates.
*Place the result in the text box called **Distance**.*
End of procedure.

Like the sphere zone calculator from Chapter 4, this program has only one formula to maintain and one procedure to execute. After clicking the `Find Distance` button given the control name `Go`, the alphanumeric contents of the four text boxes are converted to real numbers using the Visual Basic function `Val()`. Four variables are derived from this process, which are referenced in the formula for variable `d#`. The formula solves for `d#`—a double-precision floating-point number. Then the solution is converted back to text using the VB function `Str$()`. The string is then placed in the text box named `Distance`.

When examining a formula with multiple sets of parentheses, you should try to imagine it in three dimensions, as a terraced platform seen from above. Visualize each parenthesis as a stairstep, with the left parenthesis leading up toward you and the right leading down away from you. If you can project a complex formula that way, those parts of the formula that solve first should telescope themselves toward you, perhaps in breathtaking CinemaScope.

103

Chapter 6 ◆ Formulas

Let's put on our 3-D glasses now and stare closely at the preceding Cartesian distance formula. The two expressions (x2 - x1) and (y2 - y1) solve first because they appear to jut out furthest toward you. Geometrically speaking, these two expressions each represent the difference between coordinates along one axis. So the difference between the x-coordinates and the difference between the y-coordinates are solved separately. The solutions to those two expressions are squared, then added to each other in the part of the equation which solves next. *Squaring* a value, geometrically speaking, gives it form or dimension.

Along the final tier, the base platform of the equation, the sum of the two squares is then "rooted" once more back to a linear value, using the square-root function Sqr(). This value is the distance between two points along a Cartesian grid, which is assigned to the double-precision variable d#.

The distance-finding formula can be used for the coordinate systems of any two points appearing on a map. Compare the Visual Basic version of the formula to the algebraic version that appears here:

$$D = \sqrt{(x_2 - x_1)^2 + (y_2 - y_1)^2}$$

Summary

Values are assigned to variables in Visual Basic by way of equations. In equations that arithmetically combine values, simple arithmetic functions are represented by operators and complex functions are evaluated using intrinsic Visual Basic function terms. A Visual Basic equation is an expression of assignment, and therefore it has only one term on the left side of the equation, that being the variable receiving the solution value to the equation. The solution is always a known value.

The simple arithmetic functions in Visual Basic equations have a natural order of evaluation which is based on the way terms are evaluated in algebra. This natural order can be overridden through the use of parentheses as delimiters in an equation. These delimiters reestablish the precedence of terms' evaluation; offsetting an expression in parentheses raises its precedence.

Review Questions

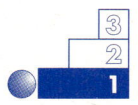

1. Predict the solution values to the following equations:

   A. x = 4 + 6 ^ 2 / 5 * 6

   B. x = (4 + 6) ^ 2 / (5 * 6)

   C. x = (4 + 6 ^ 2) / 5 * 6

2. Convert the following algebraic expressions to Visual Basic equations:

   A. $v = \frac{1}{3} \pi r^2 h$ (where π = 3.1415927)

   B. $P = \dfrac{F}{(1 + i)^n}$

Review Exercise

Using 2D_DIST.MAK as a framework, revise the project so that it displays the distance between coordinates in three-dimensional space. As a guide, here are the formulas for distances in two-dimensional and three-dimensional space:

$$D_2 = \sqrt{(x_2 - x_1)^2 + (y_2 - y_1)^2}$$

$$D_3 = \sqrt{(x_2 - x_1)^2 + (y_2 - y_1)^2 + (z_2 - z_1)^2}$$

Logic

In this chapter you dive directly into the heart of all computer operations, exploring the functions that result in true or false (–1 or 0) values. First, you explore how logic constitutes every part of a computer's operation, both numerically and mechanically. Next, you construct expressions of comparison that have solutions that are true or false values. I then introduce Boolean logical operations, separating "black" from "white" using truth tables.

Boolean Logic and Pinball

<aside>A bit can only be true (1 or ON) or false (0 or OFF).</aside>

The only thing a computer does is compare two binary digits and render the state of that comparison as another binary digit. This is the basis of all logic. As stated in Chapter 2, the logic of a computer is such that it can interpret only states—more to the point, it evaluates the presence or absence of electrical current in its own integrated circuits. A binary state represents the presence or absence of current as the simplest digit within a computer—a bit. The term *bit* is short for *binary digit*, which is the elementary unit of value within a computer, which represents a logical state of true (1 or ON) or false (0 or OFF).

A current, electrically speaking, is a constant change or flux. The computer does not know this, however, because it looks only for

Chapter 7 ◆ Logic

the presence of this flux. This presence is treated as if it were a physical object in the machine.

Imagine the central processor of the computer as a converted upright pachinko machine, with slots for eight marbles positioned along a horizontal chute at the top of the machine. A lever is pulled, which releases the marbles from the chute absolutely all at once. As they drop, they hit various pins, dampers, and levers that flip up on one end as marbles strike them on the opposite end. The moved levers can cause other marbles to change course and fall in some other direction. When struck, some levers open gates through which other marbles can pass. Others open traps that cause marbles to become stuck. At the bottom of the machine is a series of collector slots that catch the marbles that have survived the obstacle course.

Suppose the operator of this machine loads marbles into the top eight slots at random. She may fill some slots and leave others blank as she wishes. In other words, she selects the pattern in which she loads the marbles into the chute. After the marbles are released, she keeps track of which marbles accumulate in the slots at the bottom. Assuming the following things:

> The pachinko machine remains upright at all times
>
> The machine is bolted to something firm
>
> The marbles have identical mass, shape, and weight
>
> The various levers and gates are all set to their starting positions
>
> Gravity remains a constant

it should follow that for each particular random marble-loading pattern, there should be one predictable falling pattern as a result. To restate, as long as you maintain identical conditions for the machine, each loading pattern must result in one and only one falling pattern.

Suppose the lady at the pachinko machine attributes a specific number to each pattern. There is an easy way to do this: Each slot in the loading chute either contains a marble or it doesn't; the same holds true for the accumulator at the bottom. Each slot can therefore be described by a binary digit—1 for presence and 0 for absence. The

A *byte* is comprised of eight bits.

opening chute and closing slots can thus be described by eight-digit binary numbers—in other words, by bytes. In computing, a *byte* is the primary memory storage unit for all forms of data in a computer system, and is comprised of eight binary digits (bits).

Here's how each pattern is enumerated: You're familiar with the decimal system of numbers (also called *base 10*), in which digits from 0 through 9 each have their own place—or slot—in the number. The value of each place is described by increasing powers of 10 (10^0, 10^1, 10^2, 10^3, and so on). Thus there is the *ones* place followed by the *tens* place, *hundreds* place, *thousands* place, and so on.

There are 10 digits in the decimal system, thus the alternate name *base 10*. In the binary number system, or *base 2*, there are two digits (0 and 1). Each place is described by increasing powers of 2 (2^0, 2^1, 2^2, 2^3, and so on). Thus there is the *ones* place, followed by the *twos* place, *fours* place, *eights* place, and so on by powers of two.

Figure 7.1 depicts a potential marble-loading pattern, represented as an eight-digit binary number. The powers of two for each place are listed beside each slot so that you can better comprehend the arithmetic behind the conversion of a binary number to a decimal number.

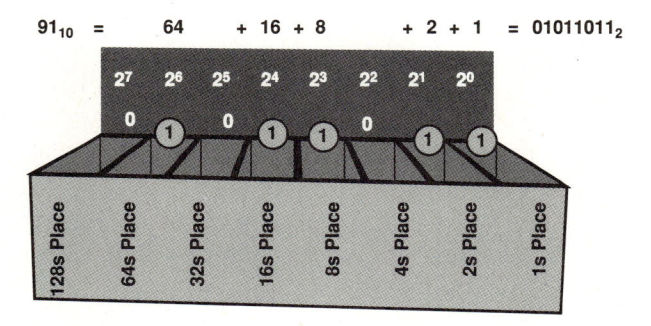

91_{10} = 64 + 16 + 8 + 2 + 1 = 01011011_2

Figure 7.1. A somewhat overbearing view of a byte.

Suppose the marble-loader pays careful attention to the starting position of the devices—the pins, levers, gates, and traps—before loading marbles into the chute. She could give each setting pattern its own number as well. Conceivably, therefore, for each particular pattern of loaded marbles and for each particular pattern of device settings, there is one predictable fallout pattern of marbles in the bottom accumulator. Resetting the devices' loading positions by their pattern numbers would have a direct, perhaps measurable, effect on the outcome of the fallout pattern. The term for this type of device-resetting by pattern number is *programming*.

For all intents and purposes, you have just witnessed what a computer and its programmer actually do, except that the marbles are really electric currents, the various devices are actually logic gates, and both the loading chute and the fallout accumulator can be described as memory. An instruction in machine language is literally a device-setting pattern. The sequence of these patterns is a program. If you consider patterns to be instructions and you give each pattern a number corresponding logically to the construction of that pattern, every logical arrangement of those patterns yields a predictable result. This is how a computer works.

Higher-Level Comparisons

In Visual Basic, the results you have in mind for your program are complex. The tools you use to achieve those results are complex as well. This complexity is necessary in order for you to be able to program with instructions like `If-Then` rather than `00101101`. Still, the most fundamental tools of programming—logical comparisons between two states—are at your disposal in the Visual Basic vernacular.

> Visual Basic assumes true to be equal to –1, and false to be equal to 0.

I begin with arithmetic operators of comparison, which are used in expressions of comparison to derive logical results. Think of these operators as the high-level language version of pins, traps, gates, and levers. As you've learned, Visual Basic recognizes the values –1 and 0 to be true and false, respectively. An expression of comparison always results in a true or false value.

Table 7.1 shows the logical operators of comparison in Visual Basic. Beside each operator is the logical solution to the expression `6 operator 3`.

Visual Basic *By* EXAMPLE

Table 7.1. Comparison operators.

Operator	Function	6 operator 3
=	Is equal to	0 (False)
>	Greater than	-1 (True)
<	Less than	0 (False)
>=	Greater than or equal to	-1 (True)
<=	Less than or equal to	0 (False)

The order of the symbols in both <= and >= can be swapped; so you can state =< and => just as easily and the VB interpreter won't mind.

Example

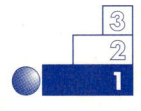

For the first example of comparison operators in action, let's go to the CLI in the Immediate window. Here's an example conversation which evaluates the logic of b=4.

```
b=4
?b=4
-1
```

It might seem odd at first to use the equality operator = in an expression that is not an equation, but you'll soon get used to it. After b was set to 4, I quizzed the CLI whether b=4. The CLI's response was -1, which means that it is true.

Suppose we quiz the CLI whether b<3. Here is its response:

```
?b<3
0
```

Zero is the response for false.

Understand that –1 and 0 are not just the CLI's way of saying *yes* and *no;* these are in fact the evaluated values of the expression and are real numbers. Thus this dialog:

Chapter 7 ◆ Logic

```
?(b=4)-1
-2
```

Now, -2 is not a symbol for *more true than true.* By subtracting 1 from –1—the value of (b=4)—you've made the expression part logical and part arithmetic. The parentheses in this expression are important. Look what would happen if you removed them:

```
?b=4-1
0
```

The CLI evaluated 4-1 first, derived 3, and compared b to 3 rather than to 4. The traps were set in the wrong order.

While I'm on the subject of order of evaluation, can truth be evaluated for the presence of truth? This bit of dialogue proves that it can be done. Remember that b=4.

```
?b=4=-1
-1
```

Yes, there can be two equality operators within a single expression, just as long as you realize it's not an equation. The value of b=4, which you already know to be –1, was compared next to –1 for equality. Naturally, the result was nothing but the truth: -1. Suppose you change the order of evaluation, however, by placing the latter comparison in parentheses, as in:

```
?b=(4=-1)
0
```

The first thing the CLI did this time was compare 4 to -1 for equality. The result, of course, was 0, which was compared to the value of b (4) for equality, and that too was false.

I realize that the preceding comparison of 4 to -1 was, to borrow a phrase, "stupid," and not something you'd ever want to write during the course of a real program. However, it did prove the point about the importance of ordinance in a compound logical comparison. If you ever used the expression b=(c=d) in a program, and c=4 and d=-1, the result of that expression would still be 0, and this time it might not be so stupid. I simplified this expression by using real numbers so that you can understand the role of the operators in the instruction.

Visual Basic *By*

EXAMPLE

Making Logic Do Something

In Visual Basic, you use comparison expressions most frequently within the `If-Then` comparison clause statement. Here, an expression is evaluated for truth. A set of instructions following the term `Then` will be executed if the result of the expression is logically true. Alternatively, another set of instructions that may follow the term `Else` can be executed if the result of the expression is logically false.

Example

You'll study the construction of conditional clauses in greater detail in Chapter 15. For now, let's concentrate on the logical part of the `If-Then` statement. Assuming `b` is still equal to `4`, let's give a conditional instruction to the CLI:

```
if b=4 then ?"Works for me."
Works for me.
```

The bottom line is the CLI's response to the instruction on the top line. First, the interpreter evaluates the expression `b=4` for truth. As you've already learned, the value of that expression at present is `-1`. The interpreter will execute the instruction following the term `then` if the result of the expression is `-1`. This is proven by the following test instruction fed to the CLI:

```
if b=3 then ?"Probably won't see this line again."
```

The prediction is correct because, as you can see, the CLI did not make any visible response to this instruction.

Truth and/or Fiction

A *Boolean operator* compares one binary value to another.

The second category of logical operators in Visual Basic is *Boolean operators*. These are terms used to compare one binary value to another, and to derive a single binary value as a result.

The purpose of Boolean operators is to evaluate expressions comparing two values that are *already* binary in nature. For instance, `-1 AND -1 = -1`, whereas `-1 AND 0 = 0`. Here, AND is the Boolean operator,

113

and will be capitalized where it appears in a paragraph from here on out in the text to distinguish it from the everyday word "and." The result of the expression x AND y will be true if and only if x is true *and* y is true—otherwise the result is logically false.

Example

As an example, here is yet another dialog with the command-line interpreter:

```
x=3
y=5
?x=3 and y=5
-1
```

First, I seeded variables x and y with the nonbinary values 3 and 5, respectively. On the third line is the compound logical comparison. Here, the values of x=3 and y=5 are obtained first. They are both -1, which satisfies the conditions for the AND comparison to equal -1, as printed on the fourth line by the CLI. In the preceding quizzing statement, it is important to leave spaces around the Boolean operator so that the interpreter won't confuse it with just another variable.

Example

Assuming you leave x and y as they are, you can apply the preceding compound logical expression in a conditional execution clause:

```
If x = 3 and y = 5 Then
    Form1.Print "It's true!  It really is!"
Else
    Form1.Print "Oh, well, forget it."
End If
```

The logical expression is evaluated and its result triggers the execution of one or the other set of instructions in the If-Then clause. If-Then really does not evaluate the expression. In truth, all it is looking for is a –1 or a 0. One way or the other, a logical expression simplifies to one of those two possible values. When that's done, `If-Then` takes off.

By introducing the Boolean operator `OR`, you now can have a logical expression that has a true result (–1) if one or the other value is true.

Example

As usual, the best way to test a function is through a dialog with the CLI:

```
x=4
y=10
?x=4 or y=9
-1
```

Obviously the result can be true if one of the compared values is true. As a quick test, let's see if it works if both comparisons are true:

```
?x=4 or y=10
-1
```

The result is still true. The only way you can obtain a false value is if both comparisons are false:

```
?x=3 or y=9
0
```

Example

A related Boolean operator `XOR` (exclusive-or) returns a true value if one or the other comparison evaluates true, but not both. In other words, the compared values can't match. Let's leave `x=4` and `y=10` for a moment and retry a few of the preceding evaluations, using `XOR` instead of `OR`.

```
?x=4 xor y=9
-1
```

115

Chapter 7 ◆ Logic

```
?x=4 xor y=10
0
?x=3 xor y=9
0
```

Notice that when both comparisons evaluated true, the result of the XOR comparison was false. An exclusive-or comparison really does want one or the other to be true.

Example

Combining the ANDs and ORs and taking advantage of what you know about the usefulness of parentheses, let's examine a complex logical comparison, first using the CLI:

```
x=6
y=7
z=9
?(x=6 and y=3) or z=9
-1
?(x=6 or y=3) and z=9
-1
?(x=6 and y=3) or z=10
0
```

The values within parentheses, as always, are evaluated first. The result of that comparison is itself compared using another Boolean operator to the expression outside the parentheses. When you integrate one of these compound comparison expressions into the source code sample you created a few pages back, you have the following:

```
If (x = 6 and y = 3) or z = 9 Then
    Form1.Print "It's true!  It really is!"
Else
    Form1.Print "Oh, well, forget it."
End If
```

If the two compared values of a Boolean expression are not binary, the Boolean operators will compare the bitwise values of each bit of both values in their respective places and render their results in the same place of the solution variable. In other words, the binary value of the third binary place in one variable (representing 23) will be compared to the value in the third binary place in a second variable, with the binary result rendered in the third binary place of the solution to the expression.

Summary

Logic is the basis of all computing operations. In Visual Basic, logical operations are comparisons between two binary states, the result of which is rendered as a binary state. Logical operations can be compounded by means of further operators and the inclusion of parentheses; however, the result of the expression of logical comparison is still a binary state.

Review Questions

Given x = 5, y = 9, and z = -1, assess the binary truth value of the following:

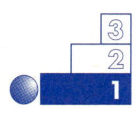

1. (x = 5)
2. (x < y)
3. ((x + z) >= y)
4. (x = 5) and (x < y)
5. ((x < 5) and (z < x)) or (y = 9)
6. (x < 5) and ((z < x) or (y = 9))
7. ((x <= 5) and (y = 3 ^ 3)) xor z

Strings

In this chapter you learn about string variables, which are containers for groupings of alphanumeric characters—letters, words, or entire sentences. You witness how alphanumeric contents of graphic controls are assigned to strings, using what appear to be arithmetic expressions. You then study how patterns of binary numbers form the patterns that comprise alphanumerics.

Next, you see how expressions are used to manipulate the contents of string variables, using the + arithmetic operator as well as intrinsic Visual Basic functions. Finally, you see how properties of graphic objects in Visual Basic forms are treated as string variables.

Value Versus Content

Up to this point, I have discussed the manipulation of data in memory as values—numbers you can use in calculations or substitute for variables in formulas. A value is one way Visual Basic translates data. As you've seen, a byte of data is, at its lowest level, just a sequence of 1s and 0s. *Value* is, in essence, a higher interpretation of data, in the way that *81* is a higher interpretation of *01010001*.

The other common way to interpret data is as text. This form of data in Visual Basic is assigned to string variables. A *string* is a sequence of any number of bytes that are interpreted jointly as text, or alphanumeric characters.

A *string* is a sequence of alphanumeric characters.

Chapter 8 ◆ Strings

A sequence of characters is assigned to a string variable with an expression of assignment, as in the following example:

```
a$ = "Q"
```

Assuming the variable `a$` wasn't declared beforehand, this statement creates it and assigns it the contents Q. A simple expression of assignment for a string variable is stated as an equation, using the following syntax:

```
variable$ = "alphanumerics"
```

The dollar sign ($) is used to distinguish string variables in the way the percentage sign (%) is used to distinguish integer variables.

> **NOTE:** The reason $ was chosen so many years ago for strings is that it looks like an *S* without being one. The currency category for variables was created long after 1964. The $ already had a job, so it couldn't be used to represent money. Thus, Microsoft chose the @ character to distinguish currency variables.

In the preceding expression, the text to be assigned to the string variable is enclosed in quotation marks. These quotation marks do not become part of the string; they are merely used here as delimiters to mark where the string begins and ends. The following are some valid string variable assignments:

```
x$ = "Valid."
alert$ = "RED"
full_name$ = "Hubert H. Humphrey"
sale_price$ = "359.95"
```

Using this syntax, any character can be assigned as part of a string variable, the sole exception being a quotation mark, which is reserved for marking the beginning and end of the string. The contents of `sale_price$` appear to be numeric. Like the three examples preceding it, however, the contents are actually textual. In other words, `sale_price$` is six bytes long, beginning with the character representation for *3*, followed by that for *5*, and so on.

Visual Basic *By*

EXAMPLE

Of ANSI, ASCII, and Other Such Acronyms

When I refer to *character representation*, I mean the pattern of bits in a byte which stand for an alphanumeric character. The decision of which pattern belongs to which character is not exactly arbitrary. If we left this decision to the individual manufacturers, however, we would be left with dozens of incompatible codes. Imagine what would happen if Microsoft's *Q* was Borland's *&*.

Some time ago, the American National Standards Institute (ANSI) devised a coding scheme for the most-used characters in computers and Teletype machines. A subset of that code exists today as the American Standard Code for Information Interchange (ASCII, often pronounced *as'-key*). The ASCII code is the most widely used method for transmission and storage of alphanumeric data in a bitwise form within or between computers.

In the ASCII code, the letter *Q* is represented by the binary form of decimal value 81. Table 8.1 shows the word *QUANTUM* as it appears in its binary form.

Table 8.1. The mechanics of *QUANTUM*.

Alphanumeric Characters	*ANSI*	*Binary*
Q	81	01010001
U	85	01010101
A	65	01000001
N	78	01001110
T	84	01010100
U	85	01010101
M	77	01001101

Notice that no consideration is made for place or value, because you're not dealing with storing a number.

ASCII is a binary code like Morse Code. Both use two symbols interchangeably (*on* and *off*, or *dot* and *dash*) to create patterns that stand for characters. The trouble is, Morse Code was not meant for use

Chapter 8 ◆ Strings

with a computer. Although Morse Code is binary, its sequence of dots and dashes do not follow a binary pattern. If a dot was 0 and a dash was 1, for instance, the code for *E* (one dot alone) would be *0*, and would fall first in line before the rest of the alphabet. Furthermore, Morse Code does not have a set number of symbols per character; ASCII uses a constant number of symbols per character—eight.

A listing of the ANSI character codes used and adapted by Microsoft for use with Windows and Visual Basic is in Appendix A.

Example

As my first example, I start a dialog with the Visual Basic Immediate window CLI.

```
quantum$="Niels Bohr"
?quantum$
Niels Bohr
```

Notice that the syntax of the ? (`Print`) statement doesn't really change when I refer to a string rather than a numeric variable. The expression of assignment (also known as the `Let` statement) is one of the few in which string variables and numeric variables are interchangeable. The CLI's response to the ? on the bottom line is precisely the contents between the quotation marks in the assignment equation.

Example

Strings can also be used in place of values in equations which appear to involve addition, as shown in the following dialog:

```
first_name$="Niels"
last_name$="Bohr"
full_name$=first_name$+" "+last_name$
?full_name$
Niels Bohr
```

Concatenation is the process of joining strings together.

The third line of the preceding dialog constitutes a formula that consists of three elements—two string variables and an explicit string consisting of one space to separate the first name from the last name. The + operator here is used for *concatenation*—joining strings together. This is the only operator symbol allowed in string variable formulas. The minus sign doesn't work here because it wouldn't be reasonable to try to "subtract" the contents `Bohr` from `Niels`.

Example

Certainly the most common practical use of string variables is as containers for people's names and vital information. This test involves the skeleton of a record-entry system. A Visual Basic form acts as the receiver for the individual elements of each person's vital information. A record-keeping system might have to sort each record by the person's last name; when you print these names to envelopes, however, the first name should come before the last name. Such a system that maintains a database, by the formal definition, would need to be capable of resituating elements of data, such as the parts of a person's name, in a list or reference.

Figure 8.1 is a picture of the `NameForm`, which will be the form for our skeletal record-keeping system. For now, examine one particular procedure from this form, which is shown in Figure 8.1.

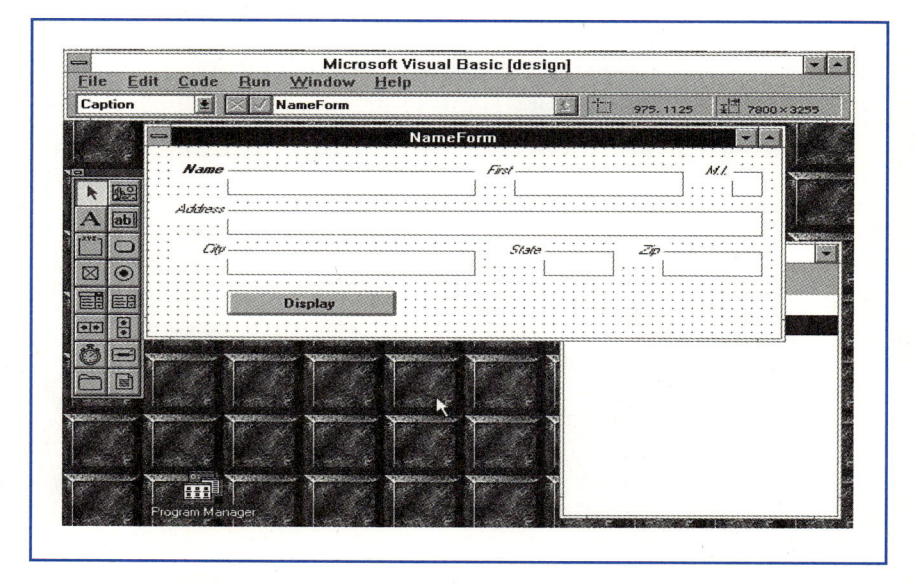

Figure 8.1. The rudimentary `NameForm`.

123

Chapter 8 ◆ Strings

Use Figure 8.1 and the following table to construct the `NameForm` form. Be sure to adjust the properties of objects as needed.

> **NOTE:** The `.Font` property sets the size of the letters that will be typed into the graphic objects.

Name-Only Record-Entry System

PROJECT NAME
NAMEFORM.MAK

CONSTITUENT FILES
NAMEFORM.FRM

Object type	Property	Setting
Form	.Left	960
	.Top	1155
	.Width	7800
	.Height	3255
	.Caption	NameForm
Text Box	.CtlName	LastName
	.Text	(blank)
	.FontSize	9.75
Text Box	.CtlName	FirstName
	.Text	(blank)
	.FontSize	9.75
Text Box	.CtlName	MidInit
	.Text	(blank)
	.FontSize	9.75
Text Box	.CtlName	Address
	.Text	(blank)
	.FontSize	9.75
Text Box	.CtlName	City
	.Text	(blank)
	.FontSize	9.75
Text Box	.CtlName	State
	.Text	(blank)
	.FontSize	9.75
Text Box	.CtlName	Zip

Visual Basic *By* EXAMPLE

		.Text	(blank)
		.FontSize	9.75
	Label	.Caption	Name
		.FontItalic	True
		.FontBold	True
		.Alignment	0 - Right Justify
	Label	.Caption	First
		.FontItalic	True
		.FontBold	False
		.Alignment	0 - Right Justify
	Label	.Caption	M.I.
		.FontItalic	True
		.FontBold	False
		.Alignment	0 - Right Justify
	Label	.Caption	Address
		.FontItalic	True
		.FontBold	False
		.Alignment	0 - Right Justify
	Label	.Caption	City
		.FontItalic	True
		.FontBold	False
		.Alignment	0 - Right Justify
	Label	.Caption	State
		.FontItalic	True
		.FontBold	False
		.Alignment	0 - Right Justify
	Label	.Caption	Zip
		.FontItalic	True
		.FontBold	False
		.Alignment	0 - Right Justify
	Button	.CtlName	Display
		.Caption	Display

125

Chapter 8 ♦ Strings

Double-click the `Display` command button and type the following:

```
Sub Display_Click ()
   FullName$ = FirstName.Text + " " + MidInit.Text + " " +
      LastName.Text
   StreetAddress$ = Address.Text
   Residence$ = City.Text + ", " + State.Text + "  " + Zip.Text
   Next_Line$ = Chr$(13) + Chr$(10)
   Envelope$ = FullName$ + Next_Line$ + StreetAddress$ +
      Next_Line$ + Residence$
   MsgBox Envelope$
End Sub
```

Now here is the preceding procedure rephrased as pseudo-code:

*Procedure for clicking on the **Display** button:*
   The person's full name is the equivalent of his first
      name plus a space, plus his middle initial plus a
      space, plus his last name.
   *Take his street address out of the **Address** box.*
   The location where the person lives is phrased as the
      city, plus a comma and space, plus the state, plus
      two spaces, plus the ZIP code.
   The code for "next line please" is a carriage return
      character plus a line-feed character.
   The name that appears on the envelope is the
      equivalent of the full name, next line please, his
      street address, next line please, plus the locale
      in which he lives.
   Place this data into a message box.
End of procedure.

The property `.Text` is applied to each text box in the form. Therefore, when you refer to the contents of a text box, the name of the box is stated first, followed by `.Text`. Think of this reference as pulling the text that the user typed from the form without placing it in a variable. Although it is considered a reference to an element of text in formulas, object properties such as `FirstName.Text` are not considered string variables; so for many statements, the `.Text` property of an object will not suffice when an explicit string variable is required.

In the first line following the `Sub` statement, a string variable `FullName$` is created that contains the three parts of a person's name—assuming that all people have middle initials. These parts are added using the + concatenation operator. Notice, however, that I've separated the elements with " " spaces. There is exactly one space between the quotation marks, so the words in the string are set apart from each other. Concatenated strings do not space themselves, and for good reason: Suppose you had `part1$ = "Washi"` and `part2$ = "ngton"` in the course of a procedure. If you were to join the two with +, you would not want an automatic space between them. Therefore, when you need a space, Visual Basic has you insert it yourself.

In `Sub Display_Click ()`, the variable `Residence$` is created on the fourth line. Notice that a comma and space together are used to separate the city from the state. As a result, you don't have to make a comma part of every `City` *datum* (unit of data) in order to make the address appear properly in print.

On the fifth line, `Next_Line$` is created purely as a signal string to tell the interpreter to invoke the carriage return (with `Chr$(13)`) and to feed one line down (with `Chr$(10)`). The term `Chr$()` is an intrinsic Visual Basic function which returns the specific ANSI-code character having the number that falls between the parentheses. For example, `Chr$(81)` returns the letter *Q* and `Chr$(51)` returns the digit *3*. `Chr$()` follows the standard intrinsic function syntax *function(expression)*. *Control characters* are handled in memory like regular letters and numbers, though their purpose is—or rather, was—to send some signal to the computer, such as to delete the previous character or end the current line. Control characters comprise part of both the ANSI and ASCII codes, although Microsoft Windows doesn't use all of these characters in either set; thus we say the code is not *true ASCII*. Visual Basic supports the carriage-return (13) and line-feed (10) characters for some textual display areas, although not all.

In `Sub Display_Click ()`, the next-to-last line `MsgBox Envelope$` invokes a message box that displays the contents of `Envelope$`. A *message box* is a small window which contains just a message, often with an accompanying symbol such as a big exclamation point or question mark, and one `OK` button. In the procedure, `Envelope$` was created in the line above the `MsgBox` line by joining all three lines of the person's formal address and separating those lines with `Next_Line$`—the special string which forces the carriage return with the line feed.

> **NOTE:** Carriage returns and line feeds work only within dialog boxes such as message boxes and Visual Basic picture boxes, which are objects capable of displaying both graphics and text. These special characters by default do not work within text boxes; instead, they generate little black blocks which return neither carriage returns nor line feeds. This problem can be eliminated within text boxes by setting their `.MultiLine` property to `True`.

The results of this first effort at concatenation are in Figures 8.2 and 8.3. Figure 8.2 shows the fully filled form, whereas Figure 8.3 shows the contents of this form reorganized as they would appear printed on an envelope. This application is not extremely functional just yet; through the course of this book, however, you will add functionality to it.

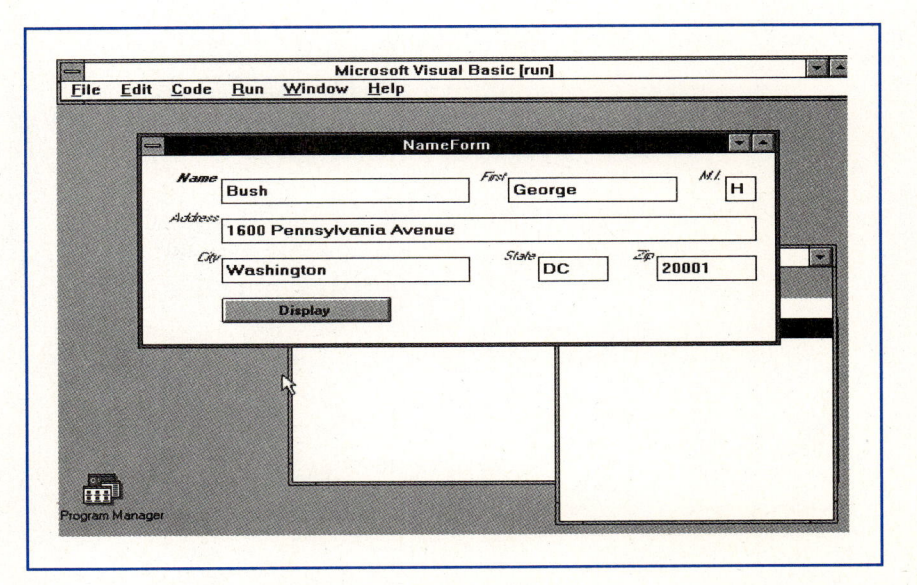

Figure 8.2. `NameForm` **before processing.**

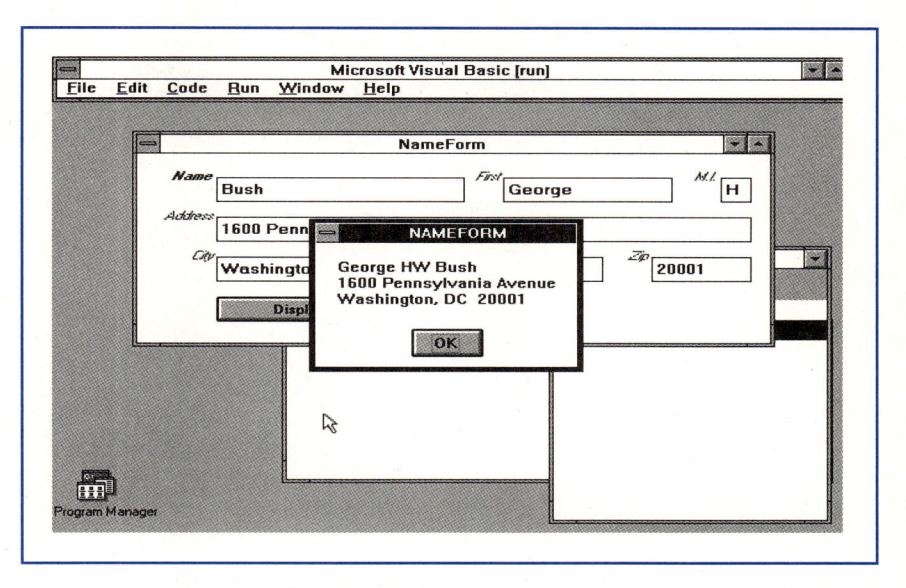

Figure 8.3. `NameForm` after processing.

Summary

A string is a group of alphanumeric characters which are to be considered as text rather than values. Characters in the computer are patterns that have code that is called ANSI or ASCII code. This code consists of logically derived bitwise patterns for the most necessary 256 characters in standard communication between computers. Each character in this code is stored in one byte.

A string variable is an arbitrarily named term used to represent text groupings in an expression. The contents of such a variable are set with an equation, in which the contents to be assigned to the variable are enclosed in quotation marks. String variables are identified within source code by the symbol $, which is not used here to represent currency. Strings can be joined in an expression with the + concatenation operator. Textual properties from user input forms can be assigned to string variables. Names chosen for string variables must not conflict with names chosen for any other string or numeric variables within the same context of the source code.

Chapter 8 ◆ Strings

Review Questions

Figure 8.4 shows the form from the `NameForm` procedure earlier in this chapter, filled with vital information for a fictitious person (in other words, don't attempt to write to this person for assistance). Using the property table and the procedure `Sub Display_Click ()` printed earlier in this chapter as a guide, determine the contents of the items listed below:

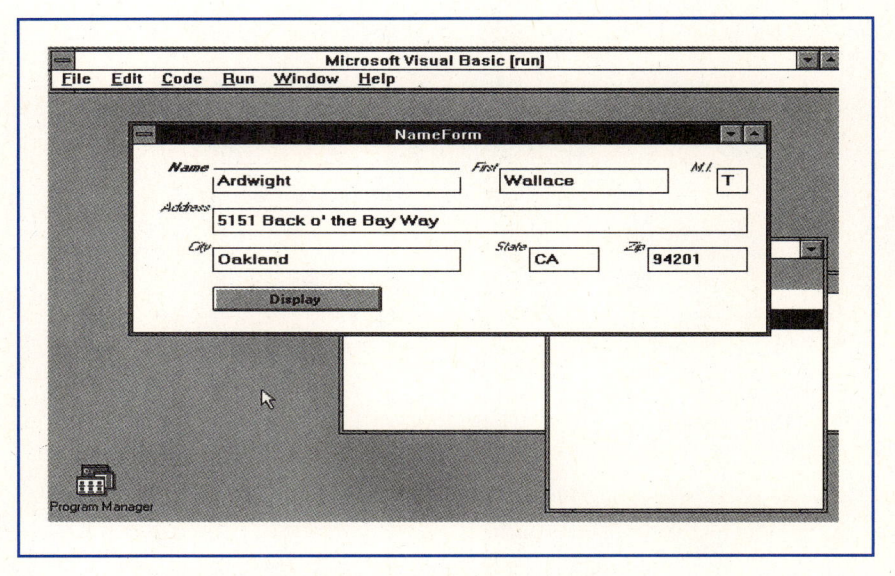

Figure 8.4. `NameForm` filled with fictitious information.

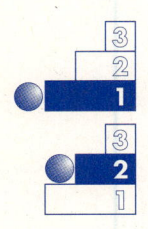

1. `LastName.Text`
2. `Zip.Text`
3. `FirstName.Text + LastName.Text`
4. `StreetAddress$`
5. `Residence$`
6. `Envelope$`
7. `FullName$ + Next_Line$ + Next_Line$ + Residence$`
8. `"Mr. or Ms. " + FullName$`

130

Review Exercise

Using the `NameForm` example program as a guide, modify the line that prints the person's name so that the last name is printed first and is separated from the first name by a comma.

Arrays

In this chapter you see how Visual Basic processes lists of items in the form of arrays. First you experiment with generating simple item-by-item lists. You then progress to processing values that reside in two-dimensional tables.

The Purpose of Arrays

> An *array* is a list of related values that are referred to by a common term.

In almost every Visual Basic application you write, you find yourself composing a formula or procedure that processes a list of values that each have the same purpose or fulfill the same role individually in a formula. For instance, you might have a formula which returns a value for *a1*, and then at some other time for *a2* and *a3*. Or you may be composing a record-keeping routine that tells the interpreter how and where to print the last name, the first name, and the middle initial—and there will certainly be more than one name on this list. The primary tool you use for referring to lists of values that are somehow related is the *array variable*.

As an example, one array variable may contain the names of the 50 United States in alphabetical order. You could then have `us$(1)="Alabama"`, `us$(2)="Alaska"`, `us$(3)="Arizona"`, and so on until `us$(50)="Wyoming"`. Another procedure in the program might be used to figure the state sales tax on an item printed on an invoice for a company that does business in all 50 states. Instead of having 50 forms, you can program one form which contains "holes" for any state's sales tax. The print line might appear as follows:

```
Form7.Print us$(state); " State sales tax:",tax_pcnt(state)
```

In effect, what you're telling the interpreter to do is this:

*Print to **Form7** the name of the state having its number currently kept by the variable **state**, followed immediately by the words "State sales tax:", followed thereafter by a tab, and then that state's sales tax value.*

Suppose you want to put the tax percentage for Maine on this line. Maine, on the alphabetical list, is the 19th state; so at some point in the program the value of the variable state would be set to 19. The value 19 becomes important because it now stands for Maine in any array variable within this program which pertains to the states. It is as if 19 were equal to Maine. Of course, it can't be in the logical sense, although it can in the symbolic sense. The number 19 is now representative of Maine. Representation in this manner is part of the role of an array variable's subscript. A *subscript* is an integral value or variable within an array variable that represents the place or position of a value in the array's list or table.

> A *subscript* is the position within an array that holds a particular value.

You're Traveling into Another Dimension

A standard variable in Visual Basic with one value can be informally declared by its mere invocation in a formula. As you've seen, you can write state=19 and, by writing state for the first time, you've made that variable exist for the sake of the program. An array variable, on the other hand, cannot be invoked in this manner. Obviously, you couldn't have a statement us$(19)="Maine" as the first instance of us$() in a program and expect the interpreter to know that you want 50 of these things.

BASIC has always handled the matter of declaring array variables with the Dim statement. Dim does not refer here to a low level of light, but rather it is short for *dimension.* In the vernacular of BASIC, the word *dimension* has been used rather liberally—and geometrically, for that matter—as a verb. As a result, to *dimension a variable* is to declare an array and thus make a unit into a list the way one makes a point into a line. In geometry, by drawing a line and understanding it as a sequence of points, you give that line dimension; likewise, extending that line into a plane gives it another dimension. Dimensioning is therefore used analogously in Visual Basic to add a sequential level to a variable.

Here is the conventional syntax and definition for the `Dim` statement:

Dim Statement

Simple one-dimensional syntax:

```
Dim variable(integer)
```

Multivariable one-dimensional array syntax:

```
Dim [Shared] variable1(integer)[, variable2(integer)
    ...variable60(integer)][As type]
```

The most complex two-dimensional form with specified subscript ranges and declared types:

```
Dim [Shared] variable1(integer [To integer]
[,integer [To integer]])[As type][, variable2
(integer [To integer][,integer [To integer]])
[As type],...variable60(integer [To integer]
[,integer [To integer]])[As type]]
```

The `Dim` statement declares at least one array *variable* to be a list or table of values or string contents that are each addressable by number. This number is an *integer* (whole number), and is used as an address to represent the place of a datum in the list. A one-dimensional array, or *list*, is generally declared using one integer (or integral expression) between the parentheses. This integer represents the highest address in the list. Optionally, a one-dimensional array can be declared using two integers, which represent the lowest and highest addresses respectively in the list and are separated by the term `To`.

135

Chapter 9 ◆ Arrays

A two-dimensional array, or *table*, is declared using two integers between the parentheses, separated by a comma. These integers represent the references, or *axes*, of the table, as in a table's x- and y-axes. Both integers represent the highest address along their respective axes, unless the term To is used to distinguish the lowest and highest addresses along either or both axes. A three-dimensional array, or three-axis table, is declared in the same fashion using three sets of integers separated by commas.

Unless otherwise specified, a variable bearing no type symbol is dimensioned as single-precision floating-point. A type can be established for each variable in the dimension list either by attaching a type symbol to the variable or by stating the type as an optional term following the word As. You can declare up to 60 variables within a Dim statement.

Example

As the first example, here's how an array for the 50 states would be dimensioned:

```
Dim us$(50)
```

The minimum address in any array dimensioned in this way is (0), so in fact the preceding statement makes room for 51 states (reserving room, perhaps, for Puerto Rico). Still, it might not make sense at times to refer to states 0 through 49, or to Alabama as the 0th state (it's doubtful that Alabama would appreciate that distinction, anyway). The programmer may choose simply to allocate strings for addresses 1 through 50 and leave address 0 blank.

Example

Here's a simple two-dimensional array being dimensioned:

```
Dim chessboard%(8,8)
```

This statement would be useful within a chess program, perhaps to establish what piece rests on the board at any one time. The array variable `chessboard%` is integral and would symbolize the type of piece that rests on a specifically addressed square. A 0 value would represent an open square; likewise, 1 would represent a Pawn, 2 would represent a Rook, and so on. At opening position with the upper-left corner square considered to be (0,0) (assuming that you played white and the x-axis (file) is to be represented first and the y-axis (rank) second), `chessboard%(4,8)` would be the white Queen.

Example

Here's a compound declaration for a set of array variables I have found myself dimensioning often in my programming career—some might say too often:

```
Dim klingons(299), starfleet$(15), sector_map(7,7) As Integer
```

Perhaps the two most well-known games ever to have been originated in BASIC (or so says legend) are both called *Star Trek*, after the original television series. One version is played on an eight-by-eight grid that is sometimes called a *short range sensor map* or a *sector map*. There are several of these maps in the game—generally 64.

In this dimensioning example, I pay closer attention to the type of variable being declared, as well as the number of units. The variable `klingons` may represent the current energy level given the maximum number of enemy ships in the game—300 of them, numbered 0 through 299. When a ship's energy level reaches 0, it's considered conquered. The energy level may have fractional value. So, knowing that the default setting for a dimensioned array variable is single-precision floating-point—just what I want—I add no extra symbols or type declarations to `klingons`.

The string array `starfleet$` can contain the names of 16 (numbered 0 through 15) friendly starships in the game. The two-dimensional integer array `sector_map` is an eight-by-eight grid (again, remember the number system starts with 0) within which the identities of the individual game pieces (friendly ship, enemy ship, star, planet) are represented. This time I used the term `As Integer` to specify that I wanted whole numbers only; there's no need to have a variable that has a default value that is roughly 0.00000000 when 0 does just as well. I could have dimensioned `sector_map%` instead. Using `As Integer`, however, you can refer to `sector_map` without the accompanying symbol and still have it represent an integral value.

Controlling Arrays

Let's consider some future possibilities for the `NameForm` application. Suppose that at some future date you have this program save and load its data as disk files. When reloading a saved file into memory, you want the contents of the old file to be erased. This can be accomplished with the `Erase` statement.

Erase   Statement

Syntax:

`Erase array[, array...]`

The `Erase` statement clears the values and contents of all specified arrays in the statement. Parentheses are not used in the specification. The length of each erased array previously declared with a `Dim` statement is not affected.

Example

Suppose you're writing the routine in the `NameForm` application for loading a new file into memory. Here's how the `Erase` statement for that application would appear:

`Erase LstName$, FrstName$, MdInit$, Adress$, Cty$,Stat$, Zp$`

Now the contents are clear for entry of new data.

Next, suppose you don't want every file you create to be exactly 1000 records long. Visual Basic has provisions for allocating array variables dynamically; in other words, it has ways for the program itself to change the variables' sizes on demand.

Visual Basic *By* EXAMPLE

ReDim Statement

Simple syntax:

```
ReDim variable(integer)
```

Complex syntax:

```
ReDim [Shared] variable1(integer [To integer]
[,integer [To integer]])[As type][, variable2
(integer [To integer][,integer [To integer]])
[As type],...variable60(integer [To integer]
[,integer [To integer]])[As type]]
```

The `ReDim` statement specifies all previously allocated array variables to be cleared of their values or contents and also is used to redeclare arrays for different limits, type, and scope.

> **CAUTION:** Redeclaration of the variables specified by the `ReDim` statement is possible only if the array variables are first allocated *dynamically*, with the statement `Dim variable()` in precisely this syntax, without any expression specified within the parentheses. Dynamic allocation allows the program to declare an array of any length required at the time by the program.

Example

Suppose you implement within the `NameForm` application a routine that allocates as many units for each array variable as there are records within the file being loaded into memory. This way, there aren't a bunch of null and void records residing in memory following the last one loaded. Within the general module, you would first need to declare the arrays in this manner:

```
Dim LstName$(), FrstName$(), MdInit$(), Adress$(),
    Cty$(), Stat$(), Zp$()
```

139

Chapter 9 ◆ Arrays

When the file is loaded into memory, the first value recognized would be a value that sets the length, in records, of the entire file. This value is then assigned to the variable `FileLength`. The loading procedure would then contain the following statement:

```
ReDim LstName$(FileLength), FrstName$(FileLength),
    MdInit$(FileLength), Adress$(FileLength),
    Cty$(FileLength), Stat$(FileLength), Zp$(FileLength)
```

As a result, each array in the program would be exactly as long as the loaded file.

Establishing Bounds

One problem that might come up when you are dimensioning an array variable for a variable amount, or when you are dimensioning an array dynamically, is that a procedure may not know at any one time just where the array starts and ends. Conventionally, when a list array is dimensioned, one integer is specified within the parentheses, representing the upper limits, or *bounds*, of the array. The lower bounds are assumed to be 0, or 1 if the statement `Option Base 1` appears at the top of the general or global module. Using the term `As`, two integers are declared between the parentheses, which specify both the upper and lower bounds of the array. If you allow both bounds to be variables themselves, the possibility of losing track of that array doubles.

So that a procedure might be reminded how big the arrays are, Visual Basic provides you with two functions suited to the purpose: `LBound()` and `UBound()`.

LBound()   **Function**

Syntax:

`variable% = LBound(array[, dimension])`

Visual Basic *By* EXAMPLE

UBound()   Function

Syntax:

variable% = UBound(*array*[, *dimension*])

These two functions return the lower and upper bounds, respectively, of the specified array. If the array is multidimensional, to return the bounds for a dimensional level, the number of that level is specified as the second parameter of the function. The name of each array is stated without parentheses.

Example

Using the existing `NameForm` program, the following function would return the value 1000 in the variable `FileMax`:

FileMax = UBound(LastName$)

Summary

An array is a list or table of values or text. In Visual Basic, arrays are referred to through the use of array variables, which contain integral subscripts enclosed in parentheses. Each subscript in an array variable acts as the address for a value or string contained within the array. Each subscript in an array variable gives that array an added dimension, or an added axis of a table.

When an array is dimensioned using the `Dim` statement, it is given upper bounds, or the address of the highest element in the array. The lower bounds are by default assumed to be 0, unless lower and upper bounds have been specified in the dimension statement using the `To` term. The type of a variable can also be declared using `Dim` paired with the `As` term. The `ReDim` statement can be used to change the specifications of an array that has been allocated dynamically using `Dim` with empty parameters. The `Erase` statement clears the contents of a dimensioned array without changing its dimensions or type. Upper and lower bounds of a dimensioned array can be returned using the `UBound()` and `LBound()` functions, respectively.

Review Questions

1. Using what you know about the structure and dimensioning of array variables, and using the first example as a guide, what would be the contents of the variable `us$(27)`?

2. In the second example, assuming you are playing black, what piece occupies the square that has its value represented by `chessboard%(6,8)`?

3. Assume that the general procedure of your form contains the statement `Dim GridValue(255, 400 To 1200)`. If `GridHigh = LBound(GridValue, 2)`, what is the value of `GridHigh`?

4. Which of the following three valid statements allocates the dynamic array?

    A. `Dim Aspen As Double`

    B. `Dim Aspen() As Double`

    C. `Dim Aspen(30) As Double`

Review Exercises

Write just the procedure for the `NameForm` application that would accept numeric input from a text box and interpret this number to be the upper bounds of all the array variables used in the program, assuming they were dimensioned dynamically. Have the procedure redimension the array to the upper bounds specified when you click on a button. If possible, reconfigure the right scroll bar so that the lowermost point of its thumb represents the upper bounds of the array.

10

Time and Date

In this chapter you get a brief tour of the timekeeping system of Microsoft Windows and see how Visual Basic uses it.

It's About Time

Your computer system maintains a constantly running clock. Microsoft Windows constantly reinterprets the value held in that clock. The result is a time and date that are stored as a very large double-precision number. This number is updated with each passing millisecond. These data are supplied in turn to Visual Basic, where they may be referenced within a program as if they were global variables.

The most important time-related internal variable used by Visual Basic follows:

Now   **Internal Variable**

Syntax:

Now

The variable Now is assumed to be a double-precision floating-point number. Its contents are interpreted symbolically. The numbers to the left of the value's decimal point represent the number of days that have passed since December 30, 1899. The numbers to the right of the decimal point represent the number of milliseconds that have ticked off since midnight on this day. The date and time presented together in this format can be reinterpreted by Visual Basic later as a *signature* for the date and time that has just passed.

The *time signature* maintained in the internal variable Now is a pattern that the interpreter breaks into parts in order to retrieve such things as the day of the week it represents, or the year. This makes Now interpretable as a pattern; it is not a string, however, because that pattern is interpreted arithmetically and not textually. Here are the functions which extract date-related information from this signature variable:

Day ( )   Function

Syntax:

[*variable%* =]Day(*double*)

Weekday ( )   Function

Syntax:

[*variable%* =]Weekday(*double*)

Month() Function

Syntax:

[*variable%* =]Month(*double*)

Year() Function

Syntax:

[*variable%* =]Year(*double*)

Each function in this set accepts a double-precision value as its parameter, with the format of numbers in this value matching that of the signature format used by the internal variable Now. This signature variable represents a date and time. The function Day() returns the day of the month for the specified date. Likewise, Month() returns the month of the year and Year() returns the current year. Weekday() returns the day number of the week, where 1 is Sunday.

In the same vein, here are the functions that extract time-related information from a signature variable:

Hour() Function

Syntax:

[*variable%* =]Hour(*double*)

Chapter 10 ◆ Time and Date

Minute() — Function

Syntax:

`[variable% = ]Minute(double)`

Second() — Function

Syntax:

`[variable% = ]Second(double)`

Each function in this set accepts a double-precision value as its parameter, with the format of numbers in this value matching that of the signature format used by the internal variable `Now`. This signature variable represents a date and a time. The function `Hour()` returns the hour for the specified time in 24-hour format. Likewise, `Minute()` returns the minute for the specified time, and `Second()` returns the second for that time.

Example

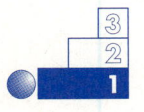

This part of the manuscript was written September 30, 1991. The following dialog took place with the Visual Basic CLI on that day:

```
?day(now)
 30
?month(now)
 9
?year(now)
 1991
?now
 33511.2499652778
```

Notice how difficult it would be to mentally extract *9/30/91* from the number *33511*.

Example

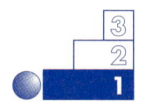

Likewise, here is more of that dialog, wherein the time-related functions were invoked:

```
?hour(now)
 6
?minute(now)
 2
?second(now)
 33
```

This goes to show you how early in the morning some authors tend to work. It's easy to deduce that the time is 6:02:33 a.m.

Given any time and date, a signature value can be reconstructed using the following functions:

DateSerial() — Functions

Syntax:

DateSerial(*year*, *month*, *day*)

TimeSerial() — Functions

Syntax:

TimeSerial(*hour*, *minute*, *second*)

The functions `DateSerial()` and `TimeSerial()` each receive arguments in the same format as given by those functions which return a date and time element from a signature value. `DateSerial()` returns

Chapter 10 ◆ Time and Date

the number of days that have passed since December 30, 1899, or the number to the left of the decimal point in the signature. `TimeSerial()` returns the number of milliseconds that have passed since midnight, or the number to the right of the decimal point in the signature.

Example

When added, the values returned by `DateSerial()` and `TimeSerial()` comprise a double-precision value in the precise format of the signature value maintained in `Now`. Thus the following equation assigns to the variable `once#` a double-precision value representing the time of the previous discussion with the Visual Basic CLI:

```
once# = DateSerial(1991, 9, 30) + TimeSerial(6, 2, 33)
```

Another internal variable that is similar to `Now` although it does not deal with the VB time signature, is the internal variable `Timer`.

Timer   Internal Variable

Syntax:

`Timer`

The `Timer` internal variable is continually set by the interpreter to the number of seconds that have elapsed since midnight, according to the time being kept internally by the computer. This number is expressed as a single-precision floating-point value.

Example

`Timer` can be used in much the same way as `Now`, in timing situations where fractions of a second are not critical. The following example shows how you can determine how many seconds elapsed during the execution of a routine:

```
StartTime = Timer
    .
    .
    .
EndTime = Timer
Elapsed = EndTime - StartTime
e$ = "Total elapsed time: " + Elapsed
TimeDisplay.Text = e$
```

The vertical ellipsis here substitutes for the routine being timed. Notice how both variables `StartTime` and `EndTime` are set to the value of the same internal variable `Timer`. The two variables will have different values, however, because the VB interpreter automatically updates `Timer` to reflect the number of seconds that have elapsed since 12:00 a.m. With `StartTime` subtracted from `EndTime`, the result is a single-precision value denoting the number of seconds elapsed between the execution of the first assignment instruction and the execution of the second one.

> **NOTE:** Later you experiment with the timer control, which is available from the VB toolbox. The `Timer` internal variable, despite its name, has nothing to do with this control.

Times and Dates as Text

The Visual Basic interpreter maintains two internal string variables for printing the current date and time: `Date$` and `Time$`.

Date$ **Internal Variable**

Syntax:

Date$

Chapter 10 ◆ Time and Date

Time$ — Internal Variable

Syntax:

`Time$`

The internal variable `Date$` is always 10 characters long, and is continually maintained automatically so that its contents always reflect the current system date. This date is returned in the format *mm-dd-yyyy*. Likewise, `Time$` always reflects the current system time. This is returned in the format *hh:mm:ss*.

Example

Unlike `Now`, the contents of `Date$` and `Time$` can be changed by directly assigning them new strings that are interpretable as valid dates and times, respectively. As a result, the system date and time are manually reset. Here's how you can reset them from the Immediate window CLI:

```
date$="9/30/91"
time$="6:33:45"
```

Notice that you can use slash marks in the `Date$` assignment in place of dashes; VB accepts either. Also, the current year can be abbreviated to the final two digits.

The reverse of these functions would be to take string data in the proper formats and convert the data to signature value format. This is the purpose of the following functions.

DateValue() — Function

Syntax:

`DateValue(Date$)`

150

Visual Basic *By* EXAMPLE

TimeValue()   Function

Syntax:

TimeValue(*Time$*)

The function DateValue() accepts a validly interpretable date string and converts it to a whole number value. This value follows the time signature format used by the internal variable Now. It represents the number of days that have passed since December 30, 1899. Acceptable date formats are *dd-mm-yyyy*, *dd-mm-yy*, *dd/mm/yyyy*, and *dd/mm/yy*. The function TimeValue() converts a validly interpretable time string to a double-precision fractional value. The format of this value also follows the format used by Now.

Example

Suppose you've loaded data into memory from two files. Their headers have different dates, and you need to know the number of days between the save dates of these files. The headers are in string format, although their date contents follow one of the four formats supported by Visual Basic. The following function procedure can be used to find the number of days between save dates:

```
Function diff_dates (dat1$, dat2$)
dv1 = DateValue(dat1$)
dv2 = DateValue(dat2$)
diff_dates = dv2 - dv1
End Function
```

Here's the preceding procedure written in pseudocode:

Function for solving the difference between two dates:
  Solve for the value of date #1.
  Solve for the value of date #2.
  Subtract the date value of #1 from #2, leaving the
    number of days between the two dates.
End of function.

Chapter 10 ◆ Time and Date

Summary

The Visual Basic interpreter maintains one key internal variable: Now. Now's format is such that the entire system date and time, expressed in intervals from years to milliseconds, can be represented in one double-precision variable. Other Visual Basic functions can be used to extract date and time interval information from this key variable or from any other variable with the same format. The internal variable Timer returns the number of seconds elapsed since the system tolled the stroke of midnight.

Review Questions

The following are sets of input parameters for the functions discussed in this chapter. Determine which functions accept parameters in each format.

1. 1992, 2, 9
2. 15, 12, 49
3. 15:12:49
4. Time$

11

Number Systems

In this chapter you are given further insight into how a computer counts, thus becoming reacquainted with the number systems of mathematics. You then construct an application that utilizes the primary principles of number systems to convert any decimal number to a system of anything from base 2 to base 36.

Touching Base

People normally count using the *decimal*, or base 10, numeral system.

The reason our common system of counting is called *decimal* is because *deci-* is a Greek prefix meaning *ten*. Some people have a tendency to call fractional values *decimal numbers*, perhaps only because such numbers force us to use the *decimal point* to divide the whole-number side of the number from the fractional side.

The number *1495* is a decimal number because we trust it to be written in base 10. At least we assume it is a decimal number, because there is nothing to tell us otherwise. We have a natural tendency to trust numbers for what (we think) they are. Unfortunately, as you become a programmer, you start to lose some of that trust, replacing it with a sort of natural, rational skepticism which, if not controlled carefully, can creep into your entire way of thinking. When you regulate your skepticism, however, you'll be more able to detect how something or some system—mechanical or

Chapter 11 ◆ Number Systems

interpersonal—works and operates, just from observation and logical deduction.

To understand how computers count is to understand the inspiration behind their invention. We could say the concept of modern computing began to take shape in 1854, when British mathematician George Boole wrote a treatise called *Investigation of the Laws of Thought.* In this work, Boole attempted to equate the sciences of mathematics and psychology by theorizing that strictly binary logical processes may be the primary constituents of all reasoning in the human mind. Boole believed—at least at that time—that absolutely all thought could be *catabolized* (broken down) into comparisons of one binary state to another. It is for him that Boolean logic is named.

We generally give Charles Babbage credit for inventing the mechanism of the computer; but the concept was actually brought forth, in large part, by a Hungarian physicist named John von Neumann. In the late 1930's, von Neumann studied Boole's works thoroughly and, employing a natural skepticism for which the world will be forever thankful, bent Boole's logic so that it applied not to mental processes, but to *physical* processes—as in quantum physics and mechanics. Along the way, von Neumann discovered that sequences of electrical currents—as you learned in Chapter 7—can replace mechanical devices such as wheels and levers in a calculation mechanism. The first stored-program computers, for precisely that reason, were called *von Neumann machines.*

Without question, John von Neumann was one of the masters of logical analysis and proofs. One of the things he managed to "prove," using the very types of logic you're starting to deal with now, is that there is no common, everyday world at all—that "ordinary" objects do not exist by our ordinary definition. To some extent, von Neumann proved that we as individuals *create* everything we see just by thinking about it, or by being conscious of it. In other words, the world in which you live is in great measure created within your own mind and soul. Should you ever wish to read von Neumann's proof, it appears in his 1932 book *The Mathematical Foundations of Quantum Mechanics (Die Mathematische Grundlagen der Quantenmechanik).*

If you are (or will be) a good mathematician or programmer, you may at some time, in the midst of a daydream, start disproving the existence of anything and everything. Certainly the only thing that changes by doing so is your perspective. The world continues to exist, no matter how you choose to define *existence*. When you see some principle proven mathematically, yet you still wholeheartedly disagree with it, even if you're the creator of it, you begin to realize that belief—or faith, if you prefer—is actually somewhat stronger than proof. If you realize that, however, you fall right into von Neumann's trap.

This section on places, bases, and powers may cover old ground from your point of view. If it does, I beg your indulgence for just a few pages. One of the things we rely on in the everyday world is the ability to count and to know what a number means when we see it. When we write *1495*, the number is expected to mean *one thousand four hundred and ninety-five*. If this number is written in base 16, however, that isn't what this number means. The *9* is no longer in the tens place, but is instead in the sixteens place.

Computers have a difficult time with decimal, or base 10, numbers. This is because computers are naturally binary and have an easier time dealing with anything that is a factor or multiple of 2 and only 2. Computers have an easier time with base 16, or *hexadecimal*, numbers because *16* factors out to *2 times 2 times 2 times 2*. A computer can easily interpret anything you can describe as a power of 2. The number *10* factors out to *5 times 2* and stops there, because *5* is a prime number. Computers, at their heart, understand only two states—0 and 1—so *5* is as much of a mystery to a computer as a 10-dimensional universe would be to us.

> A *bit* (binary digit) is a single binary state within a computer, which can be described as either on (1) or off (0).

The number *5* is best represented within a computer as a combination of three binary states—three being the number of binary digits, or *bits*, required to represent *5*.

When written in base 2 or binary, *5* appears as *101*. In other words, there's a *1* in the fours place and a *1* in the ones place. What determines the place in any number system is the base of that number system, raised to the number of the place counting from right to left, starting with the zeroth place. Table 11.1 demonstrates this principle in action using the number *1495* (base 10). The \ operator used in Table 11.1 is similar to the regular division (/) operator, but returns an integer without any fractional remainder.

155

Chapter 11 ◆ Number Systems

Table 11.1. Finding one's place in the world.

Conversion of 1495 base 10 to a base 2 number

1495	=	1495	\	1024	=	1
− 1024	=	471	\	512	=	0
	=	471	\	256	=	1
− 256	=	215	\	128	=	1
− 128	=	87	\	64	=	1
− 64	=	23	\	32	=	0
		23	\	16	=	1
− 16	=	7	\	8	=	0
		7	\	4	=	1
− 4	=	3	\	2	=	1
− 2	=	1	\	1	=	1

In any number system, there are as many digits as stated in the base of that system, ranging from 0 to the base minus one. In the decimal system, there are 10 digits ranging from 0 through 9. In octal (base 8), there are eight digits ranging from 0 through 7. In hexadecimal (base 16), however, there are more digits than there are numerals available. Thus the digits for 10 through 15 are represented by the capital letters *A* through *F*. Where no digit (0-9) can represent the value within a place, capital letters are used.

Making Spaces for Places

To put what you know about number systems into action, here is a procedure that takes any base 10 number and converts it to any specified number base from 2 to 36. We picked 36 because it is equal to the number of digits (10) plus the number of letters in the alphabet (26).

Visual Basic By EXAMPLE

```
Function Convert$ (convValue, convBase)
Find_Top:
comp = convBase ^ expn
If comp < convValue Then
    expn = expn + 1
    GoTo Find_Top
End If
For spot = expn To 0 Step -1
    digit% = convValue \ (convBase ^ spot)
    convValue = convValue Mod (convBase ^ spot)
    Convert$ = Convert$ + Right$(Str$(digit%), 1)
Next spot
If Left$(total$, 1) = "0" And Len(Convert$) > 1 Then
    Convert$ = Right$(Convert$, Len(Convert$) - 1)
End If
End Function
```

This is the largest procedure you've worked with thus far, so I explain it in detail. This is a `Function` procedure which accepts two values: the base 10 value being converted (`convValue`) and the base to which it's being converted (`convBase`). The converted number will be expressed as `Convert$`, an alphanumeric string, because it may contain "digits" such as `A` and `F`.

An *implied loop* starts at the point marked `Find_Top`. The purpose of this loop is to determine the number of digit places in the number `convValue` after it is converted to the base specified in `convBase`. The point of this loop is to keep adding power exponentially to the variable `comp` until its value becomes greater than that of the number you're converting (`convValue`). Each time you add power to `comp`, you increment (add 1 to) variable `expn`; so `expn` is counting the number of places in the converted number that will be `Convert$`. When `comp` becomes greater than `convValue`, you know you've gone too far and have counted enough places. You now know there are as many digits in `Convert$` as have been counted by `expn`.

The loop that follows is a conventional `For-Next` loop, wherein you start with the *leftmost* place in `Convert$` and work backward (`Step -1`) to the right toward the ones place. The countdown is kept within the variable `spot`. When `spot = 0`, the loop is complete and the number is nearly converted. We're figuring the value of `Convert$` one

157

digit at a time, starting from the left. For the first iteration of the loop, the leftmost digit is equal to the number of times the value being converted `convValue` goes into the place value being considered (`convBase ^ spot`) evenly. That number of times is the first `digit%` of `Convert$`.

Having converted one digit, I *shave* the amount of the converted digit from `convValue` using *modulo arithmetic*—in other words, I take the *remainder* from the division equation `convValue \ (convBase ^ spot)` and put it back into `convValue`. This remainder is evaluated during the next iteration of the loop. Until then, the converted `digit%` is made into an alphanumeric character using the function `Str$()`, and the leading space Visual Basic attaches to positive values is trimmed from it using the function `Right$()`. Both functions are covered in detail later.

As an example, assume `convValue` is the base 10 number 1495 from the previous table and `convBase` is 2—meaning that you're converting to base 2. The initial `Find_Top` loop will determine that the base 2 form of 1495_{10} is an 11-digit number; so at the end of that loop, `expn = 10`, the power that 2 is raised to at the 11th digit. The `spot` loop counts down from 10 to 0. During the first iteration, `spot = 10`. The value of 2^{10} is 1024, and that goes into 1495 once. This makes 1 the first digit in `Convert$`. The remainder 471, equal to `1495 - 1024`, is derived using the `Mod` modulo arithmetic function, which returns the remainder of a division—in this case, of `1495 \ 1024`. The value 471 becomes the `convValue` for the next iteration of the loop. After the final iteration, `Convert$ = 10111010111`.

> **NOTE:** In Visual Basic, hexadecimal (base 16) values, when written into source code or displayed on the screen, are preceded by the symbol `&H`. Thus `&HFF` is equal to 255.

Summary

The native number system of a computer is binary (base 2). Often certain variables used by the system are expressed as hexadecimal (base 16) because its numbers are shorter, and 16 is a multiple of 2, making conversion between the two bases easy. By comparison, conversion between binary and decimal (base 10) numbers is difficult for the computer. A representation of the digit-by-digit conversion procedure was the example program for this chapter.

Review Questions

Respond to the following questions using the example table and the `Function` procedure presented in this chapter.

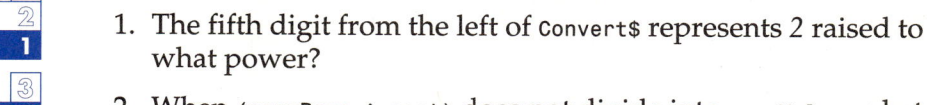

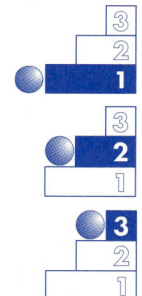

1. The fifth digit from the left of `Convert$` represents 2 raised to what power?

2. When `(convBase ^ spot)` does not divide into `convValue`, what is the value of the `digit%` at the current `spot`?

3. If `convValue` is integral, will there ever be a case in which `Convert$` is a fractional number?

Value Management

In this chapter you see how variables are formally declared in Visual Basic, using explicit statements rather than equations. You learn about the scope of a variable, which is the extent to which the value contained within a variable pertains to the various modules of the program. You see how Visual Basic statements are used to define the scope of variables, and in so doing define the context of the procedures in which they reside.

Next, you see three ways you can set the limits for your program's internal environment:

By applying terms to whole numbers, thus defining them as constants

By creating your own variable types as composites of other types

By setting the base-counting value of the interpreter

Chapter 12 ◆ Value Management

Structured Programming, Such As It Is

BASIC is believed to be the first high-level programming language in which variables can declare themselves. Time after time in this book, I've presented source code examples containing equations such as a = 1 where there was no a before. BASIC has always been smart enough to play catch-up with the programmer; if the programmer says a not only exists but equals 1, it must exist.

The patchwork quilt that has become modern BASIC is comprised of many elements of FORTRAN, PL/I, Pascal, and C. In each of these languages, a variable is formally declared before a value is assigned to it, or before the variable is used in a formula. In other words, the variable is formally introduced to the program with a statement.

> **NOTE:** In BASIC, a declaration of a variable is the first statement in a program to assign a legitimate value to that variable.

For years after its inception, the only real way to declare a variable in BASIC was simply to assign a value to it, as in a = 1. At first, this method of declaration was seen as a true advance in the art of high-level programming. As time passed, and more and more low-level programmers added new structures to BASIC, absolutely every variable of every type could be declared before it was utilized. This was immediately seen as an advance in the art of high-level programming.

You will find after being a programmer for a number of years that there are certain fashion trends to this business. One of these trends concerns the structure of your source code. One frequent argument among programmers is whether to include comment lines. Another debate, although perhaps not as frequent, is whether to declare variables before values are assigned to them.

At the time of this printing, it is currently in fashion to declare variables before a value assignment, even in BASIC and Visual Basic. This, frankly, does not mean you have to do it; I certainly don't. Often when I'm writing a loop clause, I need a quick "utility variable" to keep the count from 1 to 5, so that the program performs some set of instructions five times. I don't care what the count variable is, as long as its name is not currently in use. Sometimes I give it a name from out of the blue, as in the statement `For ralph = 1 To 5`. I'm not about to go out of my way to declare `ralph` in a separate statement (such as `Declare ralph As Integer`) just so `ralph` can count for me.

As you read more about programming, you'll undoubtedly come across the subject of "structured programming." Modularity in source code, conservatism in choosing variable type categories, and explicit variable declaration are three products of discourses and arguments on this topic. "Structured programming" is a redundant statement; all programs are, to some degree, structured. In the interest of preserving "structured programming," some would argue we should all write source code in a specified style. Imagine how such proponents would be received if they applied their arguments to architecture, poetry, or music.

When programming, you should strive for conservative use of memory, efficient use and exchange of values, and an appearance that makes the user want to understand what she's reading. Style is a consideration that comes later, when you start developing a style for yourself. Never allow style to be dictated to you by something that calls itself "the norm." Remember that Hewlett and Packard, Jobs and Wozniak, and Gates and Allen all developed the tools that reshaped this industry partly in defiance of "the norm."

A Variable's Scope of Existence

The scope of a variable defines at what level in the program its value is remembered.

When you create a variable by expressing it within an equation for the first time, the implied declaration for this variable gives the variable a local scope. The *scope* of a variable is the extent to which that variable applies across the various divisions of the source code of the program.

Example

A variable with *local scope* applies only to the procedure in which it is declared, whether it is a specific declaration or an

Chapter 12 ◆ Value Management

inference from an equation. Here's an example from the two-dimensional distance calculator project, 2D_DIST.MAK:

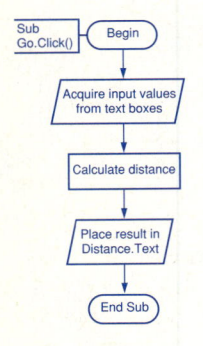

```
Sub Go_Click ()
x1 = Val(Box_x1.Text)
x2 = Val(Box_x2.Text)
y1 = Val(Box_y1.Text)
y2 = Val(Box_y2.Text)
d# = Sqr(Abs((x2 - x1) ^ 2) + Abs((y2 - y1) ^ 2))
Distance.Text = Str$(d#)
End Sub
```

The context *of a body of source code describes its relationship to the rest of the program.*

Here I invoked five variables: `x1`, `x2`, `y1`, `y2`, and `d#`. The purpose of these variables is to reach a result that could be displayed as `Distance.Text`. None of these variables has any purpose beyond the context of this procedure. The *context* of a body of source code is the extent to which the values generated within that body, and the statements made within that body, relate to the rest of the program.

Modular variables are declared in the general module.

Procedures are grouped within a module which may or may not contain a display form. Variables having scope that is declared to be modular pertain to all the procedures within that module. The place for declaring variables with modular scope is in the general module area of the form's source code window, in the procedure window marked (`declarations`). Figure 12.1 shows the general declarations for project NAMEFRM2.MAK, appearing in the proper source code window.

To declare a variable with local scope, use the `Dim` *statement.*

Within this window is a formal declaration for a variable of modular scope but of unit length; in other words, a non-array variable. `Dim Shared RecordNo As Integer` creates the variable `RecordNo` and applies it to all procedures in the module, because the declaration appears in the general module area.

`Dim` Statement

Syntax:

```
Dim [Shared] variable1 [As type][, variable2
  [As type],...variable60 [As type]]
```

This syntax for the `Dim` statement is new to Visual Basic. With this syntax, up to 60 non-array variables can be declared and given type specifications. The scope of the variables declared with this statement is determined by its position in the source code. If `Dim` appears within a `Sub` or `Function` procedure, the variables declared within `Dim` are assumed to have local scope. If `Dim` appears within the general module of a form, in the (declarations) section, the variables declared within `Dim` are assumed to have modular scope and thus apply to all procedures in the module or form. If `Dim` appears within the global module of a project, the variables declared within `Dim` are assumed to have global scope and thus apply to the entire source code.

The term `Shared` is used here as a throwback term to earlier versions of BASIC, to ensure that all variables declared in that statement apply to, or are shared with, all lower orders of division within the source code.

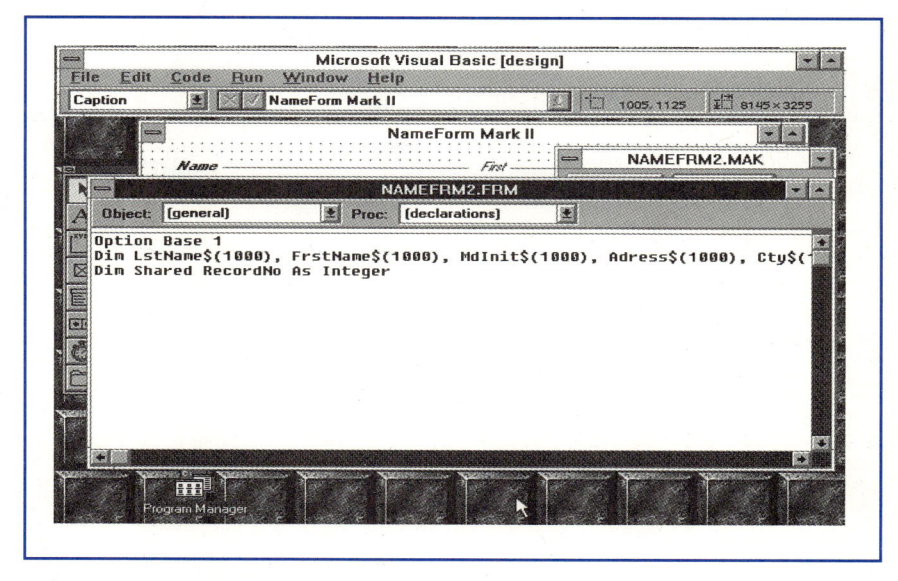

Figure 12.1. Variables with modular scope.

If the project NAMEFRM2.MAK had contained more than one form, I could have easily moved the statements contained currently within the general module of NAMEFRM2.FRM into the global

Chapter 12 ◆ Value Management

module. In fact, I could move the statements to the global module now. Because one module is the extent of the project, however, this would make no difference in the operation of the application.

Table 12.1 lists and defines the three categories of variable scope.

Table 12.1. Scope categories of variables.

Category	Definition
local	Pertaining only to the procedure in which the variable is first invoked or declared, and its value is cleared when the procedure is exited.
static	Pertaining only to the procedure in which the variable is first declared, although its value is maintained after the procedure is exited in case of possible reentry to that same procedure.
modular	Pertaining to all procedures in a module by virtue of having been declared in the general module area of a form module.
global	Pertaining to the entire source code.

To declare a variable with static scope requires a special statement:

Static   **Statement**

Syntax:

```
Static variable1[(integer [To integer]
[,integer [To integer]])][As type][, variable2
[(integer [To integer][,integer [To integer]])]
[As type],...variable60[(integer [To integer]
[,integer [To integer]])][As type]]
```

> To declare a variable with local scope that maintains its value, use the `Static` statement.

The `Static` statement is used in place of `Dim` to declare all of a procedure's unit and array variables having values that are to be maintained by the interpreter after the `End Sub` or `End Function` statement is executed for that procedure. With the exception of the main term itself, `Static`'s syntax is the same as the syntax of the `Dim` statement within a procedure, although it may not include the term `Shared`.

You may remember the following procedure from the Expressor application:

```
Sub Button_Point_Click (Index As Integer)
Static point_lock As Integer
If point_lock = 0 And ready < 20 Then
    readout.caption = readout.caption + "."
    point_lock = 1
    ready = ready + 1
End If
assess_readout
End Sub
```

Here, the variable `point_lock` was declared `Static` because I wanted it to remember whether the user clicked on the decimal point button of the calculator. This way, the decimal point won't appear in the readout twice.

Variables can be declared within the global module through the use of a special statement:

Global Statement

Syntax:

```
Global [variable1(integer [To integer]
[,integer [To integer]])][As type][, variable2
[(integer [To integer][,integer [To integer]])]
[As type],...variable60[(integer [To integer]
[,integer [To integer]])][As type]]
```

167

Chapter 12 ◆ Value Management

To declare a variable with global scope, use the `Global` statement.

The `Global` statement is used in place of `Dim` to declare all unit and array variables within the global module having values that are to apply to the entire source code of the program. With the exception of the main term itself, `Global`'s syntax is the same as the syntax of the `Dim` statement, although it may not include the term `Shared`.

Here again is the global module for the Expressor:

```
Global readout_value As Double, combine_value As Double
Global ready As Integer
```

Now that you understand the syntax of variable declarations, it should be easy for you to determine the purpose of the preceding declarations. The values that pertain to the calculator as a whole are declared within the global module. They may, in some future revision of the application, refer to other forms or separate modules, which is why I declared these variables ahead of time with global scope rather than modular scope.

Constants

Throughout the source code of Visual Basic, arbitrary terms that aren't keywords or instructions can be declared as constants. A *constant* is a term that stands in place of a value in an expression. A constant's value is set only once.

The declarative statement for constants is as follows:

Const   Statement

Syntax:

```
[Global] Const name = expression[, name = expression...]
```

The `Const` statement is used to declare a term to represent a fixed (nonvariable) value for use in expressions. The scope of a constant is determined by the position of its declaration in the source code.

Visual Basic *By* EXAMPLE

A constant declared within a `Sub` or `Function` procedure is said to have local scope. A constant declared within the general module area of a module is said to have modular scope. A constant declared within the global module, using the term `Global`, is said to have global scope.

Example

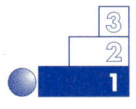

Here is perhaps the most common use for constants within a program:

```
Const TRUE = -1
Const FALSE = 0
```

Now tests of logical expressions can be read more clearly; for instance, `If Form1.Visible = TRUE Then....`

Example

Here is a revised general module area for the Expressor:

```
Dim label$(15, 4), p(4)
Dim readout_value As Single, solution As Single
Const PI = 3.1415927
Const GRAV = 6.6732E-11
```

Here, two universally recognized constants appear: the value of Pi, and the gravitational constant GRAV that is so important to Newtonian laws.

Declaring constants within the global module may prove to be a convenience in cases where it's easier for you to remember a word than a number. For instance, you may prefer to set some control's `.BackColor` background color property to MAGENTA rather than the octal number for magenta. In such a case, you can declare `Const` MAGENTA equal to the octal number once and once only. As a result, you won't find yourself looking up color tables in the middle of late-night programming.

Chapter 12 ◆ Value Management

Counting from 0 or 1

Finally, allow me to introduce one statement that has the sole purpose of changing the default lower bounds address number used by array variables:

Option Base **Statement**

Syntax:

Option Base {0 | 1}

The `Option Base` statement, used within the global module or general module area of an application, establishes whether the starting address of an array variable is to be 0 or 1. This value is specified in the accompanying integer and can be no other value. The default lower bounds value of array variables is 1.

A good place for `Option Base` to appear is at the top of the general module area in the NameForm application:

```
Option Base 1
Dim LstName$(1000), FrstName$(1000), MdInit$(1000),
  Adress$(1000), Cty$(1000), Stat$(1000), Zp$(1000)
Dim Shared RecordNo As Integer
```

This statement may come in handy if you'd like for the first element of your arrays to be element #1 rather than element #0. If you plan to use two-dimensional geometric arrays, however, in which an origin point is element (0,0), you'll want to leave the `Option Base` at 0.

Summary

A variable in Visual Basic can be declared by inference, which means stating it within an expression for the first time within the source code of the program. Variables declared by inference are assumed to have local scope and single-precision floating-point type unless otherwise specified. Formal declaration for local variables on the procedure level, as well as for variables with modular scope, is achieved by using the `Dim` statement's optional syntax. Similarly, variables with global scope can be declared with the `Global` statement. Variables with static scope, which are local to procedures but have values that are constantly maintained, are declared on the procedure level with the `Static` statement.

A constant is an arbitrarily defined term that is assigned a value only once. The constant's value does not change through the course of the program. User-defined types can be declared using the Type clause. A user-defined variable is, in fact, a composite variable that may be comprised of multiple preexistent variables of any currently recognized type with the exception of arrays.

Review Exercise

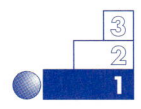

Take the source code for the NameForm application (project name NAMEFORM.MAK) and list on paper each variable invoked, along with the type and scope for that variable.

Part III

Instructions and Groups

13

Primary Program Operation

This chapter is a quick examination of the statements that affect the execution of some defined portion of the application, or the execution of the program as a whole.

The End

The End statement is used to end a clause or procedure.

Thus far, with every complete procedure or multiple-instruction clause I've listed in this book, I've closed the instruction set with some form of the End statement.

End — Statement

Syntax:

`End [{Function ¦ If ¦ Select ¦ Sub ¦ Type}]`

When used on a line by itself, the End statement terminates the program. When used in conjunction with another term, the statement specifies the closing portion of a clause or procedure. There can be only one End statement per clause or procedure.

Chapter 13 ◆ Primary Program Operation

One member of the original BASIC vocabulary which survives in Visual Basic is the `Stop` statement.

Stop Statement

Syntax:

`Stop`

Executing the `Stop` statement suspends program execution, provoking the same response from the interpreter as if the user had selected **R**un/**B**reak from the Visual Basic main menu. The Immediate window CLI becomes available after `Stop` is executed. Program execution may resume at a procedure or line label specified within a statement that the user must issue through the CLI.

Because you can `End` a clause or procedure only once, Visual Basic provides the programmer with a sort of "back door" statement with which execution of a particular instruction set can be terminated:

Exit Statement

Syntax:

`Exit {Do ¦ For ¦ Function ¦ Sub}`

Execution of the `Exit` statement immediately terminates execution of the current procedure or loop clause. In the case of loop clauses, execution of the program resumes with the instruction following the clause closure instruction. In the case of a `Sub` or `Function` procedure, execution resumes with the instruction following the instruction that placed the call to the procedure. If the procedure was not called by another instruction, execution suspends pending the occurrence of a recognized user event.

Visual Basic *By* EXAMPLE

Example

Here is an excerpt from a procedure appearing within the Expressor application introduced in Chapter 4, slightly revised for this chapter to utilize all three of the preceding statements properly:

```
Sub ApplyFormula_Click ()
For in = 0 To 4
p(in) = Val(param(in).text)
Next in
ndx = CalcList.ListIndex + 1
If ndx = -1 Then Exit Sub
On ndx GoTo f1, f2, f3, f4, f5
MsgBox "Trouble processing your request."
Stop
f1:
solution = surf_area_rccyl(p(0), p(1))
GoTo display_result
    .
    .
    .
f5:
solution = dopp_shift(p(0), p(1), p(2), p(3))
display_result:
readout.caption = Str$(solution)
End Sub
```

Here is the preceding procedure written as pseudocode:

Procedure for clicking the **Apply Formula** *button:*
Start counting from 0 to 4.
　Place the value of the input parameter in the memory slot currently being counted, into the stated array variable.
Keep counting.
The number of the formula just chosen is equal to the index of the formula listed in the list box, plus one to account for the fact that the first item is #0.
If no formula appears to be chosen then get out of here.

177

Depending on the index value of the chosen formula, branch to the point in the code corresponding in the list to the index value.
Supposing there was no branch, notify the user that something's wrong.
Then stop the program.
Branchpoint #1:
Go solve the surface area of a cylinder.
Display the result.
.
.
.
Branchpoint #5:
Solve for the Doppler shift equation.
Result-displaying branchpoint:
Place the solution value from the function procedure just executed into the readout.
End of procedure.

If you look closely, you find the instruction `If ndx = -1 Then Exit Sub`. This instruction exits the procedure by itself if there is no formula selected within the drop-down list that the procedure can process. If for some reason the `On ndx GoTo` multiple branch statement fails to work, a message box is displayed to that effect and `Stop` is executed. This works like a break command, and the Immediate window—also called the `Debug` object—is brought up. Execution may resume if the user tells the CLI to `GoTo display_result`.

Summary

In Visual Basic, a conditional clause or procedure is terminated using the `End` statement. This statement acts as the bottom part of an instruction set enclosure, or nest. A loop clause or procedure is exited using the `Exit` statement, without having to execute the statement that closes the clause or procedure. At any time, the programmer can suspend execution of the program with the `Stop` statement.

Review Questions

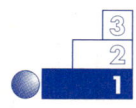

1. What is the difference between the `End Sub` statement and the `Exit Sub` statement?

2. What is the difference between the `End` statement and the `End Sub` statement?

14

Phraseology

This chapter is a review of Visual Basic's many "parts of speech." In the course of this review I expand on many of the principles introduced in Chapter 3, "Grammar and Linguistics." You are then introduced to the principles of object-oriented syntax, which is relatively new to BASIC. Object-oriented syntax may not be entirely new to you, however, because you've been using it since Chapter 2.

Programming Versus the Real World

When you write instructions for another person to follow—for instance, how to construct a filing cabinet—each individual written instruction is generally a complete sentence. Each sentence represents a step in the construction process. For the moment, assume that there is only one way to build a filing cabinet given the tools and materials you've specified that your reader must have ready in order to begin. You have one specific objective or product in mind, for which there is only one design and one method of construction, without variance.

You expect each step in the construction process to follow the previous one in a natural sequence. It's highly unlikely that you'll ever find yourself specifying special cases for what to do if the

Chapter 14 ◆ Phraseology

screws are twice as long as they should be, or if the side panels were sawed to one-half the width of the shelf panels, or how to drive a nail into a shelf panel if the panel happens to be made of aluminum instead of oak. You don't expect to have to write such "conditional" instructions because you assume your reader has acquired precisely the tools and materials you specified and wishes to construct the exact filing cabinet you have in mind. You assume your reader's objective is definite.

When writing instructions for a Visual Basic program, you as a programmer cannot assume that anything related to the user is definite. Suppose you're writing an index card filing program. Your intention is for the user to be able to define the data fields, field labels, and contents for each index card. In effect you're programming a flat-file database manager. Whenever you give the user choices—either in terms of how the user inputs data or how the user manipulates the program—you cannot make assumptions or even predictions as to what that choice will be.

You instead could have written a program that keeps, in a specified format, records concerning some absolute subject, such as baseball cards. It probably would be an easier program for you to write because you wouldn't have to devise a system by which the user could manipulate the record storage format. In making things more definitive and more manageable for yourself as a programmer, you in turn limit the degree of choice the user has, which makes your program less applicable. From a marketing standpoint, you'll have fewer users.

To make your program more applicable to more people, you must write instructions that take possibilities into account. The more generalized you make the purpose of your application, the foggier your view of its intended user becomes. You do not see the world where this user resides, and you aren't sure what this user's job really is. Because of this, as programmer you often have to place yourself in the role of several users, anticipating what each user possibly can do with your application. There is some measure of hypothesis, after all, in programming.

Visual Basic **By**

EXAMPLE

Subjective Reasoning Versus Objective Reasoning

A *statement* is an instruction that specifies a change.

A *function* is an arithmetic operation that returns a single value.

The two primary types of Visual Basic instructions are statements and functions. A *statement* is an instruction that specifies a change or deviation in the operating status of the program.

By contrast, a function is an abbreviated form of an expression or mathematical formula. A function often appears in a formula itself. A *function* is an arithmetic operation performed on a value, variable, or expression, having a result that is returned as a single value.

The two types of instructions are quite distinguishable from each other. In short, a statement performs operations on the computer or the program, whereas a function performs operations on a value or on data. You undoubtedly have noticed that when I formally introduce each instruction term or keyword to you, to the right of the keyword is its "part of speech" or type. To this point, I have introduced many statements, some functions, and the only four internal variables there are in Visual Basic.

An *object* is a data structure that combines the data contents and attributes with the encoded form of its function.

A *handle* is used by a true object-oriented language to manipulate objects.

With the advent of Visual Basic, Microsoft has added object-oriented syntax to the language, particularly with regard to the wide array of graphic objects supported by the interpreter. In the conventional BASIC vernacular, changes are made to some part of the program or to some value by stating the results of those changes as facts. In object-oriented syntax, in contrast, changes are made to some part of the program by specifying the nature of the change.

This is a confusing concept, so here's some more detail. A true data object actually contains the part of the program which states what should be done with the data. More to the point, the structure of a true object defines how that structure is to react or be changed when an action is applied to it. For instance, a true object-oriented sentence (although not in Visual Basic) might be `object1.move`. Part of the program for moving is called when the move action is invoked; however, just how the object is moved is defined by the data object itself. In doing so, the object gives the computer a type of handle with which it can be operated.

Visual Basic is not an object-oriented language in the true sense of the word. It does, however, give the appearance of true object orientation by utilizing its syntax to some degree in VB instructions.

Chapter 14 ◆ Phraseology

Figure 14.1 depicts the interlocking nature of terms in Visual Basic's implementation of object-oriented syntax.

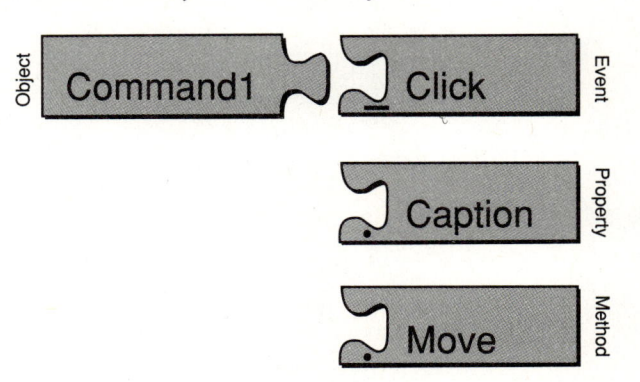

Figure 14.1. Object orientation as a docking maneuver.

A Visual Basic *graphic object* either receives input or displays data.

The only data objects supported by Visual Basic are graphic objects. Many people argue that these are not really objects by the definition subscribed to by the Object Management Group, a coalition of software manufacturers cooperating to define language standards. Microsoft is a member of this group. A *graphic object* in Visual Basic is a data structure that is representable visually, and which behaves to some degree as a device that either receives user input, displays results, or does both.

Each VB graphic object has been given a predefined set of actions called *methods* that are applicable toward that object.

The syntax of a method instruction is as follows:

A *method* is an instruction that directs the interpreter to perform a programmed action on a graphic object.

`object.method [parameters]`

Like an objective-case noun in Latin, the object is stated first, separated from the name for the method—the verb in the Latin sentence—by a period. The BASIC `Print` instruction, which is one of the language's original statements, is reborn in Visual Basic as a method, in such instructions as the following:

`Form1.Print "One more method under way."`

***Properties* are the attributes of graphic objects which can be changed.**

By entering the programs we've listed here into the interpreter, you gain a modicum of experience in manipulating the properties of graphic objects. A *property* is an attribute of a graphic object that has values or contents that can be established or reassigned in the manner of an expression of assignment.

Visual Basic By EXAMPLE

Here's a piece of one of the property tables from a revised version of `NameForm`:

Object Type	Property	Setting
Vertical Scroll Bar	.Top	7800
	.Left	0
	.Width	255
	.Height	2895
	.CtlName	RecordShown
	.LargeChange	10
	.SmallChange	1
	.Max	1000

These properties can alternately be set with source code instructions, as follows:

```
VScroll1.Top = 7800
VScroll1.Left = 0
VScroll1.Width = 255
VScroll1.Height = 2895
VScroll1.CtlName = "RecordShown"
VScroll1.LargeChange = 10
VScroll1.SmallChange = 1
VScroll1.Max = 1000
```

As you can see, the syntax of property assignments is as follows:

`object.property = setting`

> A *setting* is a term which represents the state, appearance, or some aspect of a graphic object.
>
> An *event* is used to trigger the execution of a procedure.

Notice how strings are assigned to object properties by enclosing the string within quotation marks, just as if you were assigning the contents to a string variable. The values or contents assigned here are called *settings*.

As the beneficiary of user input, each graphic object may be the recipient of what object-oriented syntax calls *events*. An *event* is a type of user input applied to a graphic object, which is often used to trigger the execution of a procedure.

Chapter 14 ◆ Phraseology

By now you're familiar with the syntax for attributing an event to a graphic object:

`object_event`

The event is separated from the object by an underscore character, as in `Command1_DblClick`.

One Final Remark

Before you start breaking new ground again, I'd like to introduce you to one statement that is used primarily to add things that are not executed to a program:

Rem   Statement

Syntax:

`{Rem ¦ '} [remark]`

When the interpreter encounters the `Rem` statement on a line, it ignores the remainder of the contents of that line and skips execution to the next line. This allows the programmer to type anything into the source code at random, generally for use as comments. The apostrophe (') can alternatively be used in place of the term `Rem`.

Example

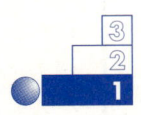

Here's an example of `Rem` in use as the anchor for a bannerhead along the top of the global module of Expressor Mark II:

```
'-----------------------------------------------------
'¦ Expressor Mark II                                 ¦
'¦    by D. F. Scott for Visual Basic By Example     ¦
'-----------------------------------------------------
Global readout_value As Double, combine_value As Double
Global ready As Integer
```

Notice the apostrophes on the far left side of the nonexecutable lines. These characters make room for the programmer to place his signature on his program. What better use for a remark than as a way to promote oneself?

Example

The other major use for remarks is as explanations for people who read your program and would like to know what you're talking about. Here's a revised procedure from the Expressor:

```
Sub Times_Click ()
'Find out what the readout says.
assess_readout
'Multiply the readout by the compared value...
readout_value = readout_value * combine_value
'...and swap values.
combine_value = readout_value
'Display the result.
readout.caption = Str$(readout_value)
'Make the next digit pressed clear the readout.
ready = 0
End Sub
```

Before every instruction in the preceding code is a relatively long comment explaining what's happening. Such comments are not unlike writing pseudocode.

Summary

The two major types of instructions in BASIC and Visual Basic are statements, which operate on elements of the program, and functions, which operate on elements of data. Microsoft has added object-oriented syntax to Visual Basic. In the process, it has classified graphic controls in VB applications as graphic objects. A stated action to be performed on a graphic object is a method. An attribute that an object affects or changes somehow by such an action is a property. An element of user input involving a graphic object is an event. Each of these three "functions" of graphic objects is invoked using its own particular syntax.

187

Chapter 14 ◆ Phraseology

Review Exercise

The following is a procedure from TOUCHBAS.FRM, a more developed form of the number base-converting `Function Convert$()` introduced in Chapter 11. Using what you know about the various types of Visual Basic instructions, write this procedure on paper. Beside each instruction write its type.

```
Sub Convert_Click ()
b10$ = Base10.Text
b10$ = Str$(Int(Val(b10$)))
Base10.Text = b10$
ConvValue = Val(Base10.Text)
Find_Top:
cb = Val(ConvBase.Caption)
comp = cb ^ expn
If comp < ConvValue Then
    expn = expn + 1
    GoTo Find_Top
End If
For spot = expn To 0 Step -1
    digit% = ConvValue \ (cb ^ spot)
    ConvValue = ConvValue Mod (cb ^ spot)
    total$ = total$ + d$(digit%)
Next spot
If Left$(total$, 1) = "0" And Len(total$) > 1 Then
    total$ = Right$(total$, Len(total$) - 1)
End If
Result.Caption = total$
End Sub
```

15

Conditional Clauses

A *condition* is the test of whether an instruction will be executed.

In this chapter you learn about the mechanism that makes the execution of a set of Visual Basic instructions dependent on the results of a test. The test which must be passed for this instruction set to be executed is called a *condition*. When the test is passed, we say the set of instructions is executed *conditionally*. The specific set of instructions which is executed based on the results of the test, or the state of some value in memory, is called a *clause*.

You will construct Visual Basic clauses based on expressions of comparison, which execute sets of instructions based on the results of that comparison. The two major conditional clause statements in Visual Basic are If-Then and Select Case. You use both statements in this chapter.

The Construction of a Clause

A *clause* is a set of instructions which the execution of is in some way dependent upon the value of a variable.

As you become more familiar with Visual Basic, hopefully you'll grow more comfortable with the various ways of referring to sets and sequences of instructions. Visual Basic has many different conventions for referring to instruction sets, some more formal than others and some less formal. A clause is an informal way of referring

Chapter 15 ◆ Conditional Clauses

to an instruction set, although most of the source code of a Visual Basic program can be divided into clauses. A clause is any set of instructions having its execution dependent on the value of a variable in a mathematical expression.

When you read Visual Basic source code instructions from top to bottom in sequence, each clause is bound at its beginning and end by two parts of a clause statement. The following pseudocode shows the general construction of an ordinary clause:

```
Clause statement part1 [expression]
    Instruction1
    Instruction2
    .
    .
    .
    Instructionn
Clause statement part2
```

The dependent instructions between both parts of the clause statement are said to be *nested.* When *nesting* instructions within a clause, many programmers choose to indent them a few spaces or, in Visual Basic, with a tab. This form of typesetting helps clauses stand out and makes them more easily identifiable, although the indention is not necessary in order for the clause to be executed. The instructions in a clause can all be flush against the left margin without affecting the program.

When the clause contains a mathematical expression for evaluation, it appears within the first part of the clause statement. For the most part, expressions are stated outright in the manner you've learned thus far. In a few cases, however, parts of the expression are actually implied within the statement governing the clause, as you'll see later in this chapter.

Example

Here's an ordinary conditional clause the way it might normally appear in a Visual Basic program:

190

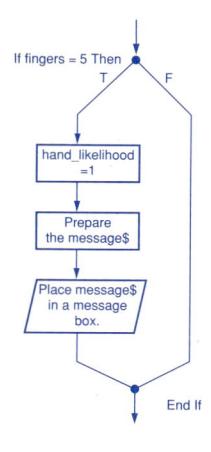

```
If fingers = 5 Then
    hand_likelihood = 1
    message$ = "Five fingers. . . could be an
      ordinary hand."
    MsgBox message$
End If
```

The purpose of this somewhat fictitious code fragment hopefully is self-evident. Suppose you have a program with the purpose of evaluating data pertaining to a sentient being, to determine whether it's human. The preceding fragment is a whole clause because it is bordered at the beginning and end by two parts of an `If-Then` statement. The mathematical expression being tested is `fingers = 5`, where `fingers` is an arbitrarily named variable. The three dependent instructions within the clause will be executed only if this sentient being's data shows that it has five fingers. Within those dependent instructions, a flag variable is declared and a message is displayed to that effect.

The preceding code fragment is an example of the most basic of BASIC conditional clauses: the `If-Then` statement.

If... Then... [ElseIf... Then] [Else...]... End If Statement

Syntax 1:

```
If expression1 Then
    instruction block1
[ElseIf expression2 Then
    instruction block2]
    .
    .
    .
[Else
    instruction blockn]
End If
```

Chapter 15 ♦ Conditional Clauses

The `If-Then` statement tests a mathematical expression to see if it is true. If it is, execution continues with the first dependent instruction below the expression. If the expression is not true, execution skips down to the first instruction outside of the nest. If that instruction is `Else`, the dependent instructions below it will be executed. If that instruction is `ElseIf`, another mathematical expression is evaluated in the same manner as the first. The clause is terminated when `End If` is reached.

There is an alternate syntax for this statement that is used in cases that warrant extreme brevity.

Syntax 2:

`If expression Then instruction1 [Else instruction2]`

The preceding syntax is reserved for single-instruction clauses and can be written all on one line. Notice that the `End If` is excluded from this syntax.

`If-Then` is the fundamental conditional statement of the BASIC programming language. The statement can be described as a mechanism having a trigger that is a mathematical expression. The result of this expression is a Boolean logical value somewhere in memory, which can be interpreted as true or false (–1 or 0). If the expression is true, the first set of instructions in the clause is executed in sequence.

Should there be another set of instructions in the `If-Then` clause following the term `Else` or `ElseIf`, that set will be executed in sequence if the original expression beside the term `If` is false. Written in pseudocode, here is how the general mechanism of a fully developed `If-Then` statement appears:

If this expression evaluates true, then
　Execute this set of instructions;
Otherwise if this other expression evaluates true, then
　Execute this set of instructions instead;
If all else fails to be true, then
　Execute this set of instructions as a last-ditch measure.
End of clause.

Visual Basic *By* EXAMPLE

The mechanism of If-Then is flexible; think of it as an adaptable logical switch. In the conventional structure of If-Then, you can use this switch to have the program *either* perform a process *or* leave things as they are. The mathematical expression being evaluated throws this switch one way or the other. Therefore any process of instructions that can be described as "one way or the other" or "one way or nothing at all" can be modeled by If-Then.

Example

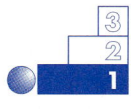

Suppose you have an input form on your screen containing two option buttons marked Active and Inactive, describing the state of some process. You want the users of your program to click Active if they want the process to take place. If-Then can be used to trigger a process if the Active button on the form is set. Here is how the conditional clause might appear:

```
If ActiveButton.Value = -1 Then
    process$ = "Active"
End If
```

Here the value -1 represents the Boolean *true* logical value as defined in Chapter 7, "Logic." If the .Value property of ActiveButton is set to *true* (–1), the contents of string variable process$ are in turn set to read Active. Otherwise, execution of the program skips to the instruction following End If. A word of caution here: If the variable process$ was never formally declared before this clause was executed, and if the state of Active.Button is *false* (0), process$ will not exist as a variable. This may result in an error with any evaluation of that variable later in the program.

The If-Then statement itself is not "cognizant" of the complexity of the mathematical expression being evaluated. In other words, If-Then is not performing the actual evaluation. What the interpreter actually does first is take the included expression and *reduce* it logically to –1 or 0, *true* or *false*. Regardless of how many terms you include in your expression of comparison, If-Then only operates as if you wrote -1 or 0 in place of that expression.

193

Chapter 15 ◆ Conditional Clauses

Example

Suppose a list box on your form is to contain a series of over-the-counter stock issues that have attractively high price-to-earnings ratios and are worth your consideration for investment. Here's how an `If-Then` clause that enters the name of an attractive company to the list might appear:

```
If price(stock) / earnings(stock) > 10 Then
    OTCStock.AddItem ticker_symbol$(stock)
End If
```

In the preceding clause, the subscript variable `stock` was used as an index number for each informal record of stock offerings in the list. Variable `stock` is thus the *key* to each array. For instance, if you're evaluating a stock with index number 143, at some time prior to the execution of this clause the value of `stock` would be set to `143`. The variable is then used as an index for the three array variables in the example. In English, the clause might read: "If the price of stock #143 divided by the earnings of stock #143 is greater than 10, add the ticker symbol of stock #143 to the list of OTC stocks to consider."

`If-Then` as a Two-Sided Argument

If the `If-Then` clause can be likened to a sandwich, when `Else` is included it becomes the Big Mac of clauses, with `If-Then` and `End If` on both sides and `Else` acting as the thin slice of bun in the middle. When `Else` is included in an `If-Then` clause, it acts as a partition between the true part of the instruction set and the false side. `If-Then` is used in such cases to have the interpreter execute *either* one *or* the other set of instructions, depending on the reduced logical value of the expression (−1 or 0). Figure 15.1 demonstrates this point, by breaking an ordinary clause into two *either/or* segments.

Visual Basic *By* EXAMPLE

Example

Suppose there is a number box in the form and you need it to register a value only if it is positive. If the value is negative, you want the box to be left blank, or else made blank. Here is a clause for that purpose:

```
If balance >= 0 Then
    num_box.Text = Str$(balance)
Else
    num_box.Text = ""
End If
```

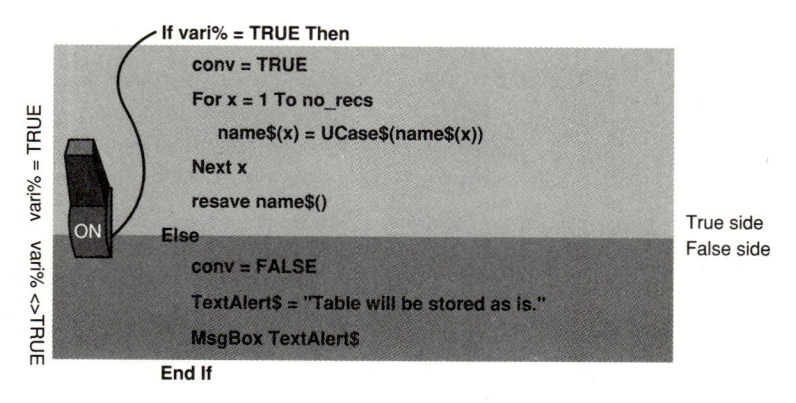

```
If vari% = TRUE Then
    conv = TRUE
    For x = 1 To no_recs
        name$(x) = UCase$(name$(x))
    Next x
    resave name$()
Else
    conv = FALSE
    TextAlert$ = "Table will be stored as is."
    MsgBox TextAlert$
End If
```

vari% = TRUE
vari% <>TRUE
ON

True side
False side

Figure 15.1. Point/Counterpoint.

The clause will set the number box named `num_box` to the textual form of the value of the variable `balance` if the value of `balance` is greater than or equal to 0 (in other words, if `balance` is positive). If the expression contained within `If-Then` evaluates true, the expression preceding `Else` is executed. When `Else` is reached, execution skips to the instruction following `End If`. If the initial expression evaluates false, execution skips to the first term outside of the instruction nest immediately below. In this case, that term is not `End If`, but it is instead `Else`. This tells the interpreter that there is a set of instructions to be executed in the event of falsehood. In this case, the text of `num_box` is set to a null string (made blank). Graphic objects cannot receive numeric values as output assignments—only text or string contents.

Chapter 15 ◆ Conditional Clauses

Example

The mathematical expression being tested within If-Then can be divided into parts by Boolean logical operators. As long as the expression reduces to logical true or false, any operator is allowed within the expression. For instance, imagine that your program is a game which branches to the end if the player has run out of money *or* if time has expired. The clause that triggers that branch might read as follows:

```
If money <= 0 Or time = 0 Then
    GoTo no_win
End If
```

The preceding clause is one example of a *conditional branch*, which jumps the program to the statement beneath the label specified in the GoTo statement only if the condition evaluates true. Here, the condition will evaluate true if the player has beaucoup bucks but no turns left, or if the player has several moves to go but is bankrupt.

> **NOTE:** Although the clause is written like a sentence, the term If is never stated twice—so If money <= 0 Or If time = 0 would be erroneous.

Example

The syntax of a mathematical expression within the first line of the If-Then clause is not restricted to that of an expression of assignment; in other words, the left side of the equation does *not* have to be a single variable. It instead can be an expression, as demonstrated by the following amendment to the no-more-money conditional branch:

```
If money + account <= 0 Or time = 0 Then
    GoTo no_win
End If
```

Suppose a second variable account comes into play in this game, representing an amount the player has stashed away in savings. The player is considered bankrupt if he has no money in his pocket + no money in his account.

> **CAUTION:** In expressions of comparison in Visual Basic, values or contents can be combined on *both* sides of the equation. Keep in mind that this is not true for all versions of BASIC.

Natural Selection

I use the If-Then statement frequently in this book because it comprises a huge portion of all BASIC and Visual Basic programs. There is another conditional clause that is used far less frequently, but which has a form that makes it especially functional in cases of *multiple* evaluated states, and not just one or two. This multiple-evaluative clause is Select Case.

Select Case... Case... End Select   **Statement**

Syntax:
```
Select Case expression
    Case [Is] comparison1a [To comparison1b]
        instruction block1
    [Case [Is] comparison2a [To comparison2b]]
        [instruction block2]
    .
    .
    .
    [Case Else]
        [instruction blockn]
End Select
```

Chapter 15 ◆ Conditional Clauses

The `Select Case` statement compares the value or text contents of an initial expression to that of one or more other expressions for equality. The statement contains several expressions of comparison for equality, although the element being compared is written only once as the initial expression, at the front of the clause. This initial expression can consist of a variable by itself, or even a number by itself; however, it can also contain any number of elements specified or implied, and combined by arithmetic operators.

For each equality comparison, in the event (or `Case`) one of the comparisons between expressions evaluates true, the set of instructions below `Case` is executed. When the next `Case` or `End Select` is reached, execution skips to the instruction immediately following `End Select`.

The purpose of `Select Case` is to give the program a way of assessing options. Written in pseudocode, here's the general mechanism of `Select Case`:

The following clause concerns the logically reduced value of this expression:
 In case the reduction equals this amount,
  Execute this set of instructions;
 On the other hand, in case the reduction equals this amount,
  Execute this set of instructions instead;
 If all else fails, and the reduction equals nothing mentioned thus far,
  Execute this final set of instructions.
End of clause.

The phrase *logically reduced*, with respect to arithmetic, refers to the act of obtaining the solution value to an expression. For instance, if a = 5 and b = 3, the expression 5 - (a - b) logically reduces to 3. Similarly, the expression (a > b) logically reduces to -1 (true). At the present time 5 - (c - b) logically reduces to 8, because you haven't assigned c a value yet, so c is assumed to equal 0, and 5 - (0 - b) equals 5 - (-b) equals 8. As you can see, expressions which contain variables that haven't been formally declared still reduce logically to real-number values.

Visual Basic By EXAMPLE

> **TIP:** The logically reduced value of any validly constructed algebraic-syntax expression appearing at any time within the program is a real-number value.

The most common type of `Select Case` comparison concerns an integer variable having a value that represents one of a handful of possible states. This state could be as simple to comprehend as which button was pressed, the user's selected expert level, or which planet in the solar system is being evaluated for orbital characteristics. Conceivably, you might have several unique sets of instructions for each option—for instance, the formula for sideways orbits applies only to Uranus. The sets of instructions for each option can be included within the `Select Case` clause, with each option specified following the word `Case`.

Example

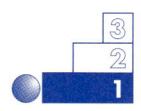

For the first example of `Select Case`, say you're programming a board game with three expert levels (0 = novice, 1 = intermediate, 2 = expert). You need your program to set specific conditions based on which number the user selects. Here's how the code sample might appear:

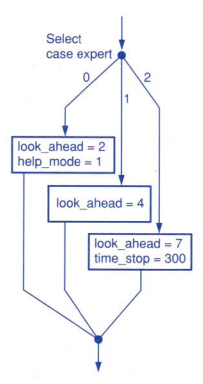

```
Select Case expert
   Case 0
      look_ahead = 2
      help_mode = 1
   Case 1
      look_ahead = 4
   Case 2
      look_ahead = 7
      time_stop = 300
End Select
```

There are three comparisons taking place here: `expert = 0`, `expert = 1`, and `expert = 2`. In each of these cases, however, the equality operator = does not appear. The `Case` term implies that you're comparing the value beside `Case` with the value beside `Select Case` for equality.

199

Example

The same logical mechanism of Select Case can be applied with respect to string variables. Here's an example that creates a currency conversion factor based on the contents of a string variable:

```
Select Case currency$
    Case "pound sterling"
        conv_fact = 1.76
    Case "franc"
        conv_fact = .87
    Case Else
        conv_fact = 1
        currency$ = "dollar"
End Select
```

I could have been more worldly and added more cases; a Select Case clause can handle significantly more than three cases. The preceding clause declares by inference a currency conversion factor conv_fact and assigns to it a value based on the contents of a string variable currency$. Notice the final condition in the clause, headed by Case Else. This final case takes care of the conversion factor in the event that the contents of currency$ aren't anything the program recognizes. You can use Case Else for setting default values or initial conditions for your program in case those conditions cannot be set or determined logically.

In Search of the Pneuma

The key to comprehending a high-level programming language is in recognizing its mechanisms of logic. Often, the more linguistically complex a language such as BASIC becomes, the more difficult it is to discern its logical mechanism from its mesh of phraseology. This is the primary danger in using "fourth-generation" languages, or "graphically objective" languages such as Visual Basic, to perform logically intensive tasks. Perhaps the primary secret to programming *well* in Visual Basic is being able to look beneath the phraseological and graphical *phenomena*, and operating first and foremost with the "old-fashioned" logical mechanism of the language—the soul of any programming language, or what the Greeks call the *pneuma*.

Figure 15.2 depicts the logical mechanism of the `Select Case` clause. Notice how, in the same way `Else` acts as a partition between the true and false sides of the `If-Then` clause, `Case` acts as a partition between multiple potential solutions. It's easy to spot the phraseological difference between `Select Case` and `If-Then`. Recognizing the logical difference between them, however, may make both simpler for you to use. Think of `If-Then` and `Select Case` as two ways of posing questions as on a written test, in which case the two types of clauses are like two categories of questions: `If-Then` is like a true or false question, whereas `Select Case` is multiple choice.

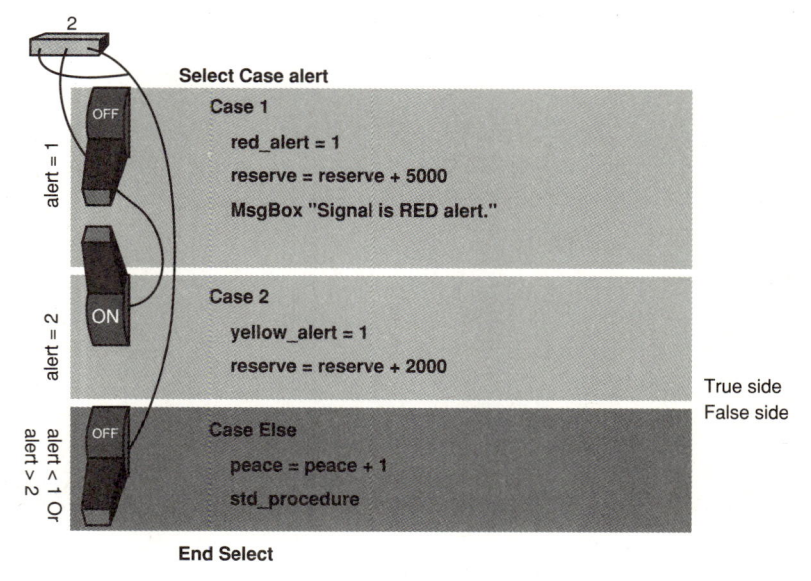

Figure 15.2. The mechanism of `Select Case`.

The way `Select Case` is designed, the interpreter's mission is to compare the reduced value of two expressions for equality. We can fool this mechanism so that it evaluates one expression to see if its value is *greater than or equal to* the reduced value of *several* other expressions. Assume you have a variable `fuel_level#` having a value that may tend to drop over time below three set stages, from *optimal* to *nominal*, then below *marginal*, and then below *critical*. You could establish `Case` ranges for what fuel levels are nominal and what are critical. But for a double-precision variable, you'd have to specify range values to within 308 decimal places. In other words, we couldn't specify `0 To 299` and `300 To 499` as ranges and expect a fuel level of 299.349834923 to fall within one of those ranges. We have to have some way of saying "over and above *this* level" rather than merely specifying ranges and allowing for borderlines to form virtual blind spots.

Example

Here's a way of defeating the "equality only" restriction of the `Select Case` clause:

```
Select Case -1
   Case fuel_level >= 1000
      alert = 0
      status$ = "Optimal"
   Case fuel_level >= 600
      alert = 1
      status$ = "Nominal"
   Case fuel_level >= 200
      alert = 2
      status$ = "Marginal"
   Case fuel_level >= 0
      alert = 3
      status$ = "CRITICAL"
End Select
```

You know `Select Case` compares two expressions for equality, but the depth of the expressions is unlimited. Thus `-1` is an expression; and as you know, −1 stands for logical truth in Visual Basic. Each expression of comparison beside the `Case` term is reduced to a logical value of either −1 or 0. All `Select Case` has to do is keep making comparisons until `-1 = -1`, or in other words, until the reduced value of the expression is equal to logical true. When that happens, the instructions following `Case` are executed until either the next `Case` instruction or `End Select` is reached. I now have multiple ranges with discernible borderlines, and I have also defeated the equality restriction of `Select Case`. If I had used the instruction `Const TRUE = -1` in the global module, the first line of this clause could read `Select Case TRUE` and make even more sense to the human reader.

To be honest, I could have used an `If-Then` clause to achieve much the same results as the `Select Case` clause did previously. In fact, in the interest of full disclosure, here's the substitute clause:

```
If fuel_level >= 1000
   alert = 0
   status$ = "Optimal"
ElseIf fuel_level >= 600
   alert = 1
   status$ = "Nominal"
ElseIf fuel_level >= 200
   alert = 2
   status$ = "Marginal"
ElseIf fuel_level >= 0
   alert = 3
   status$ = "CRITICAL"
End If
```

There's one less line in this clause, and the logical mechanism is much the same. Theoretically, `Select Case` should execute more quickly; however, the difference in speed may be so marginal that it isn't noticeable. Your choice of instructions may be one of style.

Summary

Sets of Visual Basic instructions can be executed conditionally by placing them within clauses. Each conditional clause is contingent on at least one expression evaluating true. Those instructions which are dependent on this expression are called *nested instructions*. In the `If-Then` clause, the crucial expression is one of comparison. Such expressions are said to logically reduce to a value of –1 or 0 (true or false). In the complex form of `If-Then`, the statements preceding `Else` are executed if the expression is true, and the statements following `Else` are executed if the expression is false.

In the `Select Case` clause, the logically reduced values of several expressions are compared with one expression for equality. Several sets of dependent instructions can be nested within `Select Case`, each set being bound by a contingent expression evaluating true. Only one set of instructions is executed within a `Select Case` clause.

Chapter 15 ◆ Conditional Clauses

Review Questions

The following is a fragment of code designed to test your brain. Without using your computer, execute the instructions in your mind. Respond to the following questions by estimating the value or contents of the variable shown at the time the last instruction in the list is executed.

```
x = 15
y = 5
throughput$ = "Go"
logic = -1
If x > 8 Then
    Select Case logic
        Case (x / y) = 3
            logic = 0
            y = 3
        Case (x / y) = 5
            throughput$ = "Stop"
            x = logic
    End Select
ElseIf x > 1 Then
    Select Case y
        Case 5
            throughput$ = "Caution"
        Case 3
            caution$ = "Negative"
    End Select
End If
```

1. `x`

2. `y`

3. `throughput$`

4. `logic`

5. `caution$`

Review Exercise

A variable `velo` represents the velocity of a test rocket-powered automobile. The maximum velocity projected for this vehicle is 305 miles per hour. On the other end of the scale, the minimum safe velocity for the car at maximum power is 120 miles per hour. The Visual Basic automobile simulator will light a yellow alert light when the velocity of the car is within 20 percent of its maximum or minimum speed, and a red light when it is within 10 percent of its maximum or minimum speed. You can say `alert$ = "yellow"` or `alert$ = "red"` to stand for this light. Write a routine that sets `alert$` to its proper contents for any value of `velo`.

16

Loop Clauses

In this chapter you see how Visual Basic interprets instructions that are to be executed a set number of times with the loop clause. A loop is a set of instructions to be repetitively executed in a cycle. This cycle continues from the top of the clause to the bottom of the clause and back to the top again, generally until some condition is met—in other words, until a logical expression evaluates true. If the loop has no condition, execution continues in a cycle indefinitely until the loop is exited manually or the program ends. At the end of this chapter, you'll understand why you would want to repeat yourself so often.

To Loop or Not To Loop

The following is the high-level language definition for the term *loop*. If you read it carefully, it may not be as repetitious as it sounds:

A *loop* is a set of instructions executed repetitively until an expressed mathematical condition is met or until the loop is exited manually.

A *loop* is a set of instructions executed repetitively until a condition is met or until the loop is exited manually.

What Visual Basic instructions are worthy of being executed several times in succession? Suppose you assigned a value to a variable, as in `spare_tires = 15`. Making that assignment five times in succession would result in the value of `spare_tires` being 15—which is what it would have been had you made the assignment only once.

207

Chapter 16 ◆ Loop Clauses

An iteration *is one cycle of execution of the instructions in a loop clause.*

So obviously, in cases of small clusters of instructions, the point of establishing loops must not be for the sake of pure repetition. The secret to the operation of the loop is in repeating the same instructions *without evaluating the same values each time.* The way loops are generally constructed, a separate variable maintains the current count of the number of *iterations* made thus far in the loop.

In the For-Next loop, a variable is maintained by the enclosing statement that is changed with each iteration. Generally, 1 is added to the variable (in other words, the variable is *incremented*) unless some other value is specified. In any event, the count variable changes. It is this change that is reflected in the instructions within the loop. So a For-Next loop, although it is a repetition of the same instructions, is not a repetition of the same interpretations.

For... Next Statement

Syntax:

```
For count = startval To endval [Step addval]
    instruction block1
    [Exit For]
    [instruction block2]
    .
    .
    .
Next [count]
```

The For-Next clause encloses a set of instructions that are to be executed repetitively. At first, the variable *count* is assigned an initial value specified by *startval*. Execution of the clause then proceeds in sequence and can be exited on reaching the statement Exit For.

At Next *count*, a value is added to variable *count*. This is generally 1, unless otherwise specified as *addval* beside the optional term Step. If the augmented value of *count* is less than or equal to *endval* specified at the top of the clause, execution jumps to the instruction immediately following the For line. If *count* is found to be greater than *endval*, the loop is terminated and execution proceeds to the instruction below Next *count*. If no For-Next clause exists within this For-Next clause, specification of *count* following the term Next is optional.

Here's the general construction of a For-Next loop, as expressed in pseudocode:

Start counting between this initial value and this maximum value, keep track of the count, and be prepared to add this amount to the count value.
Execute this block of instructions.
Now add the stated amount to the count. If the result is equal to or less than the maximum value, go back to the beginning of the loop.

As you can see, Next *count* speaks volumes. Figure 16.1 shows the For-Next statement in more visual terms:

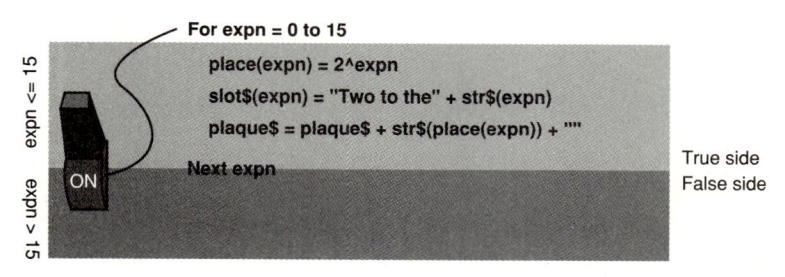

```
For expn = 0 to 15
    place(expn) = 2^expn
    slot$(expn) = "Two to the" + str$(expn)
    plaque$ = plaque$ + str$(place(expn)) + ""
Next expn
```

expn <= 15   True side
expn > 15   False side

Figure 16.1. Who's next?

Example

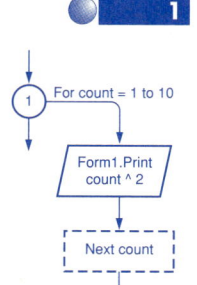

For my first demonstration of a reasonable loop, I show how with each passing iteration the evaluation should change, whereas the instructions remain the same:

```
For count = 1 to 10
    Form1.Print count ^ 2
Next count
```

The result of this loop is a list of the first 10 squared integers. Notice that count was referred to within the loop nest itself. Because count is continually incremented by Next count, each time the expression count ^ 2 is encountered, the result is always different. In almost

209

Chapter 16 ◆ Loop Clauses

every `For-Next` loop you'll write, the variable expressed just after `For` plays a role in the expressions within the nest of the clause.

Example

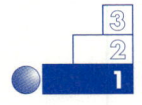

Perhaps the most common use for loop clauses is as a way to address elements of an array in sequence. Here's a loop that writes the contents of one array to a file one datum at a time:

```
For c = 1 to recno
    Print #1, dat$(c)
Next c
```

Here, `recno` is a variable containing the number of records in memory. On the first iteration, the `Print #` statement writes the contents of `dat$(1)` to channel 1, because `c = 1`. (*Channel 1,* by the way, is a logical path to a disk file.) After the first instance of `Next c`, variable `c` is incremented, the loop is reexecuted, and the contents of `dat$(2)` are written to channel 1. This goes on until the contents of `dat$(recno)` are written—the last record in the array. Execution then drops to the instruction below `Next c`.

Example

Suppose you have a variable `resp()` that contains one aspect of a patient's electroencephalographic response level to external stimuli over time. For each second of time, a new reading was taken. These readings of responses over the passing seconds were entered into the `resp()` array. You want to plot these readings to a chart so you can see the rises and falls in response levels. Here's the loop that would plot these levels as vertical lines emerging from the x-axis of the chart for some defined segment of time:

```
For sec = min To max
    Form1.Line (sec, 2500) - (sec, 2500 - resp(sec))
Next sec
```

Visual Basic maintains a coordinate system for graphics, although it is not pixel-oriented. It's based on a relative scale set for each form in advance, in which each unit is affectionately called a

Visual Basic By EXAMPLE

twip. In Windows, the twip coordinate system represents a logical arrangement of points on a graphics screen, whereas the conventional pixel system represents the physical arrangement of points. This particular loop assumes such a coordinate system of twips exists, regardless of the actual size of the form on the screen at the time. The preceding .Line method plots a series of twips between two pairs of screen coordinates, listed within parentheses.

The preceding code fragment starts at the leftmost vertical twip line on the form, starting at line number sec and working line-by-line to the right. The upper-left corner is considered point (0,0), so point (0, 2500) would be at the bottom-left corner of the form. Assuming sec's initial value min is preset to 0, the loop would draw lines starting at (0, 2500), working to (1, 2500), then (2, 2500) and so on until the final value of sec is reached (sec = max).

Each new line is plotted to the right of the previous one and is drawn from the bottom (twip number 2500) up toward twip 2500 - resp(sec). This array variable, by the way, holds the E.E.G. response for each second of testing. Loop variable sec here establishes the relationship between the line being plotted and the response value being tested.

Example

Suppose you want a less precise chart—perhaps a bar chart instead—that shows the patient's reaction over 10-second intervals. The array variable still contains reaction levels over one-second intervals. Here's how the code fragment could be modified:

```
For sec = min To max Step 10
    Form1.Line (sec, 2500) - (sec + 8, 2500 - resp(sec)), , B
Next sec
```

Notice that the .Line method now draws a box (what the capital B stands for at the end of the method). By adding Step to the end of the For instruction, I've changed the additive value from 1—the default—to 10. Now when Next sec is executed, the interpreter adds 10 to sec. In so doing, the origin point of the graph line is moved 10 twips to the right rather than one. The box being plotted is eight twips wide, which accounts for the sec + 8 in the second pair of coordinates.

211

Example

The next example of `For-Next` comes from the Expressor. If you recall, this formula calculator has up to five parameter lines for formulas selected by the user. When the user chooses a formula, a text line appears beside each parameter to describe its purpose in the formula. Here's the procedure that makes those descriptor lines appear:

```
Sub CalcList_Click ()
For n = 0 To 4
    ParamText(n).Caption = label$(CalcList.ListIndex, n)
Next n
Clear_Params
End Sub
```

The event that triggers this routine is clicking the drop-down list of formulas called `CalcList`. The value of the property `CalcList.ListIndex` represents the formula chosen with the index of the formula name as it appears in the list.

The five descriptor lines called `ParamText()` in the Expressor form comprise a *control array*, which is a sequential grouping of graphic objects that have the same purpose. Graphic objects in a control array can be addressed by number, using a subscript in the same manner as with an array variable. The first object in a control array is object `0`, so the loop `For n = 0 to 4` starts there and counts to 4. The string array variable `label$` is two-dimensional; it maintains a set of parameter descriptor strings for each formula and line in the form.

When the loop instruction undergoes its first iteration, `n` is equal to `0`. Therefore, the loop pertains to the first descriptor line. Within the array variable `label$`, `CalcList.ListIndex` points to the chosen formula, and `n` points to the first line (line #0). So the contents of `label$`, for whatever `.ListIndex` number, line 0, are assigned as the setting of property `ParamText(0).Caption`.

The last line in the procedure before `End Sub` is `Clear_Params`, which is a call to yet another looping procedure:

Visual Basic *By* EXAMPLE

```
Sub Clear_Params ()
For pl = 0 To 4
param(pl).text = ""
Next pl
ClearAll_Click
End Sub
```

At this point, you should be able to recognize the loop mechanism at work, even without indentations to demarcate the nest. The control array `param()` consists of the five parameters for the chosen formula. The property `param(pl).text`—not to be confused with `ParamText()`—refers to the textual form of the parameters, because text boxes within a form can contain only what Visual Basic recognizes as text.

> **TIP:** Two quotation marks next to each other—two enclosures that enclose nothing—signify a null string. Setting the textual property of a graphic object to `""` clears that object of its contents.

The preceding procedure clears objects in the `param` control array, numbered 0 through 4, in sequence. The program then proceeds to the procedure, which clears any calculations in progress.

When invoking a count variable for a loop clause, the name you choose for that variable is often not very important—what is important is that you keep whatever name you choose consistent throughout the loop. In the preceding routine, for instance, I could have named the variable `pl` something else—such as `place_where_the_numbers_will_appear`—and the operation of the routine would not have been affected in the least. For small loops, the variable name you choose can be arbitrary. I find myself using `n` or `x` when I'm in one of my pensive moods, and `triumph` or `indomitable` when I'm feeling more literary. My personal programming style can become a bit outrageous when nobody's looking; and because you are, I promise to keep my choice of terms somewhat tame.

213

Chapter 16 ◆ Loop Clauses

Example

A loop clause can be embedded easily within another loop clause, in which case the embedded clause is repeatedly executed itself. Here's an example that creates a textual chessboard:

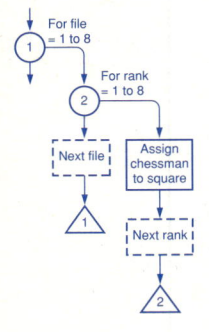

```
For file = 1 to 8
   For rank = 1 to 8
      chessboard$(file, rank) = man$(square_val(file, rank))
   Next rank
Next file
```

Assume `man$()` is an array that contains symbols representing chessmen. Variable `square_val()` maintains the numeric value of the chessman seated on each square in a two-dimensional array, where Pawns are 1s, Rooks are 2s, and so on. The preceding equation assigns the symbol for each chessman to its proper position in the array `chessboard$()`. As a result, the following double-embedded loop displays a symbolic chessboard:

```
For file = 1 to 8
   For rank = 1 to 8
      Form1.Print chessboard$(file, rank); " ";
   Next rank
Next file
```

This is perhaps the oldest way to symbolize chess pieces in computer programs, especially in machines that didn't have graphics or used printers as their main output devices. In both preceding examples, the loop clause for variable `rank` is executed eight times because of its inclusion in the greater loop clause for variable `file`.

Example

Here's an example that tests both the `For-Next` loop and `Select Case` clause structures: Suppose you're keeping records of clients that are sorted in order of their last names. These files are to be stored on disk; however, all the records together would comprise too unmanageable a file. You want to separate the records into four files, with each file designated its own quarter of the alphabet. Before you

214

can perform an alphabetic sort, then, you'll need to assign a file division to each record and then sort each resulting file within its respective division. Here's a routine for establishing this division:

```
For recno = 1 to maxrec
   Select Case LastName$(recno)
      Case "Aaa" To "Fzz"
         division = 1
      Case "Gaa" To "Mzz"
         division = 2
      Case "Naa" To "Szz"
         division = 3
      Case "Taa" To "Zzz"
         division = 4
   End Select
   LNDivided$(rec(division), division) = LastName$(recno)
   FNDivided$(rec(division), division) = FirstName$(recno)
   .
   .
   .
   rec(division) = rec(division) + 1
Next recno
```

Here is the preceding procedure written in pseudocode:

Start counting from the first record to the last record.
　For all possible cases of the current last name:
　　Should the name fall between A and F,
　　　assign the name to division 1.
　　Should the name fall between G and M,
　　　assign the name to division 2.
　　Should the name fall between N and S,
　　　assign the name to division 3.
　　Should the name fall between T and Z,
　　　assign the name to division 4.
　End of possibilities.
　Add the next last name for the previously assigned division to the
　　current list for that division.

Add the next first name for the previously assigned division to the current list for that division.

.
.
.

Increment the current subscript number for this division.
Count the next record.

Visual Basic recognizes alphabetic ranges as valid textual expressions. Thus "A" To "F" would be a range that includes *Aaron, Ezekiel,* and *F. Fenchurch,* however, would not be included since in an alphabetic sort, *Fenchurch* falls after just plain *F.* Because of this, we established ranges with lower-case as and zs in order to include all the pronounceable proper names which may fall within the range. *Sycyznyk* would therefore fall between "Naa" To "Szz" where it would not fall between "N" To "S".

In the preceding For-Next loop clause, the variable maxrec represents the number of the final record to be processed. The loop counts from 1 to this number, with the count kept in the variable recno. There are four files being created within this clause, with each file given its own number addressed by the variable division. Each created "drawn and quartered" file has its own independent count of the amount of records stored within it, which is kept in the array variable rec(). Each time a record is added to a quartered file, the independent count is incremented by 1. In the meantime, the count of records currently being processed by the loop clause is maintained in recno, apart from the independent counts. The statement Next recno increments that variable by 1 and sends execution to the top of the loop to process the next record in the main list.

The way the Select Case clause works, variable LastName$() is an array that contains the surnames of everyone in the list. Variable recno is the key variable here, establishing the sole relation between LastName$() and similar arrays FirstName$(), as well as those that may be addressed in the area represented by the ellipsis. When the contents of LastName$() fall within one of the Case ranges, a file division number is drawn from one of the four *slots.* Execution then skips, naturally, to the instruction following End Select, where the current record contents are assigned to a two-dimensional array in four partitions.

Everybody's Doing It

The other form of loop clause supported by Visual Basic is the Do-Loop clause.

Do [While¦Until]...Loop [While¦Until] Statement

Syntax 1:

```
Do [{While ¦ Until} expression]
    instruction block1
[Exit Do]
    [instruction block2]
    .
    .
    .
Loop
```

Syntax 2:

```
Do
    instruction block1
[Exit Do]
    [instruction block2]
    .
    ..
    .
Loop [{While ¦ Until} expression]
```

The Do-Loop clause repetitively executes the set of instructions enclosed within it. Execution of this set may or may not be dependent on an optional conditional expression. If a condition is expressed, execution of the set can be terminated. If a condition is not expressed, the loop is considered endless and can be exited only with an Exit Do statement.

Under Syntax 1, a conditional expression is made at the beginning of the clause, following Do. If the expression is preceded with While, execution of the instructions within the clause proceeds in sequence as long as the expression evaluates *true*. If the expression is preceded with `Until`, execution proceeds in sequence as long as the expression evaluates *false*—in other words, when the expression is true, the clause is terminated. If the `While` expression is false or the `Until` expression is true, execution skips to the instruction following `Loop`. If this is the first iteration of the loop and execution skips to `Loop`, the instructions within the clause will never have been executed.

Under Syntax 2, a conditional expression is made at the end of the clause, following `Loop`. The rules governing use of `While` and `Until` are the same as for Syntax 1. Under Syntax 2, execution of the instructions within the clause proceeds following the `Do` statement *unconditionally*. The expression will be evaluated when `Loop` is reached; if the loop is to proceed, execution skips to the instruction following `Do`. Otherwise, the loop is terminated and execution proceeds normally.

Example

`Do-Loop` can be used interchangeably with `While-Wend`; in fact, here is that converted implied loop after being given the syntax of `Do-Loop`:

```
Do While cb ^ expn < ConvValue
    expn = expn + 1
Loop
```

Absolutely no logical change has been made to this clause in converting it from `While-Wend` to `Do-Loop`. The only true logical difference in syntax between `While-Wend` and `Do While-Loop` is that the `Do` clause has the option of being exited using the statement `Exit Do`. There is no equivalent *Exit While* statement.

Example

Suppose you have a list in memory of people or organizations who have contributed to your client's political campaign. The names are accompanied by the amount contributed and are arranged in the order in which the contributions were made. You wish to extract from this list the names of contributors of the first $25,000 to your client's campaign for inclusion in a newsletter. Because everyone contributed variable amounts, the only way your application can know when to stop extracting names is by keeping a running tally of contributions as each name is extracted and evaluating that tally each time to see if $25,000 has been exceeded.

Here's the routine that performs the name extraction:

```
Do
    first$(listno) = contrib$(listno)
    famount(listno) = camount(listno)
    tally = tally + camount(listno)
    listno = listno + 1
Loop Until tally >= 25000
```

Here the variable `listno` maintains the current count of which record is being extracted and written to. The array `first$()` will contain the first contributors extracted from array `contrib$()`; likewise, `famount()` will contain the amounts they contributed as extracted from `camount()`. Variable `tally` contains the running amount, which is evaluated at the end of the clause to see if $25,000 has been met or exceeded.

If you're a veteran of other recent editions of BASIC, you may be accustomed to writing `Do` loops that end not with `Loop`, but with `Until` or `While` whenever conditions are expressed. In Visual Basic, the term `Loop` is mandatory when closing a `Do` loop, whether or not a condition is expressed immediately following the `Do` loop.

Summary

A clause that executes instructions repetitively is called a *loop clause*. Each repeated execution of instructions in a loop clause is called an *iteration*. The primary BASIC statement that governs loop clauses is the `For-Next` statement. This statement is dependent on a count variable, which has its value updated each time the `Next` instruction is executed. Generally, 1 is added to the count variable unless a different update value is specified beside the optional `Step` term.

Another loop clause supported by Visual Basic is `Do-Loop`. The `Do-Loop` clause can be far more versatile as a conditional loop clause, allowing conditional expressions to be evaluated either at the beginning or end of the loop, and for either truth or falsehood. The `Do-Loop` clause also allows the loop to be exited manually, if necessary, using `Exit Do`.

Review Questions

Of these types of loop clauses: `For-Next`, `Do While-Loop`, and `Do-Loop Until`, which is best suited for the following routines?

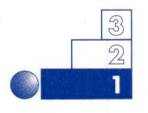

1. Plotting the trajectory of a moving target for each second of movement.

2. Plotting the trajectory of a moving target for each second, until the target travels beyond a specified range.

3. Plotting the trajectory of a moving target for each second, while the target travels within a specified range.

Review Exercises

Write loop clause routines that you feel would be the best-suited to perform the following jobs. You can name your variables according to your personal preference.

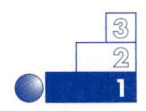

1. Counting the number of people in a list whose last names begin with *S*.

2. Tallying the first 25 people in a list whose last names begin with *S*.

3. Tallying the first 25 people in a list whose last names begin with *S* until there are no more names left in the list.

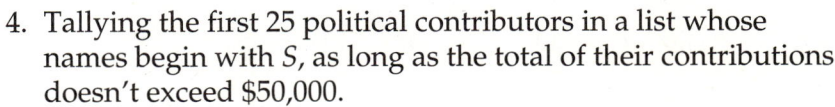

4. Tallying the first 25 political contributors in a list whose names begin with *S*, as long as the total of their contributions doesn't exceed $50,000.

17

Arbitrary Instruction Clusters

In this chapter you learn more about *branching,* or how you can manually and unconditionally make a Visual Basic application's execution jump from one instruction to a distant one. You'll see how the line labeling system works and how it is used to mark the specific landing point of a manual jump. You then examine how a subroutine works and find out how Visual Basic knows to jump back to the instruction just below the one that called the subroutine.

A Branch of Archaeology

When BASIC began, there were two ways to perform a direct branch: with the GOTO "command" and with the GOSUB "command." Back then, each instruction line within the entire program was given its own number in one running sequence, as you saw in Chapter 3, "Grammar and Linguistics." To force a branch, you would "command" BASIC to GOTO a specific line number. Generally, a programmer would number each line in increments of 10; so the first

Chapter 17 ◆ Arbitrary Instruction Clusters

line might be line 10, followed by lines 20, 30, and so on. To add several lines to the middle of a program, the programmer often had to change the numbering sequence of the program entirely. If by some stroke of bad luck the programmer had to add one instruction between lines 17 and 18, he would have to find some way of scooting lines 18, 19, and 20 down one number. Then the programmer would have to edit all the GoTo commands that branched to line 20, making them branch instead to line 21.

Luckily, in Visual Basic you aren't forced to worry about this ongoing, often nightmarish sequence. The modern age has progressed computing to the extent that humans do not have to reteach computers how to count day after day. Line numbers have been replaced, for the most part, by *labels*. A label, with respect to elements of source code, is a noninstruction that appears on a line by itself and is followed by a colon (:). The label designates a branching point.

Branching causes the program to jump to some other specified point.

In Visual Basic, line labels are used as jumping points for branch statements. To *branch* is to direct the interpreter to suspend execution of the normal sequence of instructions and to resume the sequence at some other specified point.

There are some who argue that, along with the passage of time, the GoTo and GoSub statements should also pass into antiquity. Indeed, there are many fully functional modern BASIC programs that contain neither statement anywhere in their source code. In the sample applications Microsoft supplies with Visual Basic, there are no GoTo (except for the error traps) or GoSub statements, nor are there line labels. The main reason for the exclusion of these once-staple elements of BASIC programs is that you can usually make execution of instructions pass seamlessly from procedure to procedure without them. Any point the interpreter might jump to is the start of a formal Sub procedure. Conceivably, every possible use for the GoTo and GoSub can be duplicated by some other clause instruction or procedural declaration.

Yet the statements remain, and this language with which we write programs still contains the word *Basic* in its name, albeit now in lowercase. The role these two statements play in Visual Basic programs today is greatly reduced; they can be used only to branch execution to some other point *within their own procedure* and not outside of it. You may or may not choose to use GoTo and GoSub in your programs, but they still work, and people who have programmed in BASIC for decades still have a tendency to invoke these statements by nature or out of habit. As long as your applications operate efficiently, the matter of your own personal programming style should not be argued.

Enough of causes; here is the GoTo statement explained:

GoTo Statement

Syntax:

GoTo *label*

On being executed, the GoTo statement causes the interpreter to suspend execution and resume with the instruction within the same procedure immediately following the label specified in the statement. The label must appear on a line by itself and must be followed by a colon.

Example

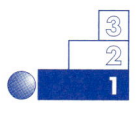

Here's how the manual jump mechanism works. What follows is a fragment from a procedure that has its initial conditions set at the beginning. The branch point for the main body of the procedure follows the setting of those conditions.

```
monkeys = 15
barrels = 3
jump_back:
For mov = 1 to monkeys
    .
    .
    .
Next mov
If monkeys > 0 Then GoTo jump_back
```

Forgive my hypothetical cruelty to animals, but the preceding routine branches back to the instruction immediately following the label `jump_back` as long as there are monkeys left to manipulate (`monkeys > 0`).

Chapter 17 ◆ Arbitrary Instruction Clusters

Example

Here's another valid use of `GoTo`: You have a main procedure that simulates the actions and conditions of a race car on a hot day in Indy. The order in which the procedures are generally executed is maintained within a loop clause. Execution branches to each procedure and returns from it back to the main procedure in the order specified within that loop clause. What if, however, the car were to stop for some reason? You need to exit the main loop and enter a damage control routine that executes corrective procedures based on the current track conditions.

But what routine do you execute? If you use the normal `Exit Do` statement for emergency exit from the main loop, regardless of the condition of the car, execution branches to only one point: the instruction immediately following the `Loop` clause-closing instruction. This would be the same instruction that executes when the car comes to an intentional stop or crosses the finish line under the checkered flag; you would prefer in cases of emergency that the program go someplace else.

Here's a skeletal model of the main procedure, concentrating mainly on the elements of damage control and how the main loop is exited conditionally:

```
Sub Main ()
Up_top:
Do
    full = Fuel_System (gas, temp, velo)
    cool = Cooling_System (water_level, temp, velo)
    intact = Body_Structure (integrity, momentum, velo)
        .
        .
        .
    If velo = 0 Then
        If full < 50 Then GoTo CheckFuel
        If cool > 300 Then GoTo OverHeat
        If intact < 20 Then GoTo DidWeCrash
            .
            .
            .
    End If
Loop Until miles = 500
```

```
GoTo GoodFinish
CheckFuel:
    .
    .
    .
GoTo Status
OverHeat:
    .
    .
    .
GoTo Status
DidWeCrash:
    .
    .
    .
Status:
    If okay >= 10 Then Goto Up_top
Totaled:
    Form1.Cls
    Form1.Print "Damage is beyond repair."
    .
    .
    .
    End
GoodFinish:
    Form1.Cls
    Form1.Print "You finished in ";place$(p);" place."
    .
    .
    .
    End
End Sub
```

Here's the preceding fast-paced circuit written in "encapsulated pseudocode" (EP):

Main procedure:
Top of main loop.
  Copy the main values from the global arrays into some local variables.
  .
  .
  .

Chapter 17 ◆ Arbitrary Instruction Clusters

If there's no speed in this car any more, then
   If we're low on gas, go to the fuel-checking routine.
   If we appear to be overheating, then go to the heat-checking routine.
   If we seem to be falling apart today, then go to the crash-detection routine.
   .
   .
   .
  End of condition.
Keep up the main loop until we've gone 500 miles.
At the end, go to the Good Finish routine.
Here are the branchpoints for all those diagnostic routines introduced earlier.
  .
  .
  .

At the end of each diagnostic routine, go check our overall status.
Overall status checkpoint:
  If we're still alive then go to the top of this procedure and resume execution there.
  Evidently if we're executing this instruction, we're dead, so clear the form.
  State the hopelessness of things.
  .
  .
  .

End of program.
Good Finish branchpoint:
   Clear the form.
   Tell us where we finished overall.
   .
   .
   .

End of program.
End of procedure.

Visual Basic *By*
EXAMPLE

> A *routine* is any arbitrarily bounded sequence of instructions within source code.

The preceding model shows three of the many possible conditional exit points in the main `Do-Loop` clause that would cause execution to branch out of the loop to a specific instruction. This instruction is marked by a label that designates the beginning of the damage assessment routine. I've used the word *routine* frequently already; perhaps it's time I defined it. A *routine* is any arbitrarily bounded sequence of instructions within a body of source code.

There really isn't any formal structure of source code called *routine* that is maintained by the Visual Basic interpreter; but when we humans want to refer to some working set of instructions, we should refer to it as a routine.

In the preceding skeletal model, the `Do-Loop` clause first places calls to `Function` routines (not shown) that return the operating status of certain parts of the car. When these functions are executed, the `If-Then` clause checks to see if for some reason the speed of the car has become 0. If it has, several embedded `If-Then` statements check to see if any variables have fallen below the critical level, indicating a possible need for corrective action. If action is necessary, execution branches to the specified routine. You can (unofficially) refer to a portion of a procedure that is bounded by a line label and a terminating statement as a routine.

The corrective action routines fall below the `Loop` statement that terminates the main loop. To ensure that the interpreter doesn't execute one of these routines by accident when the car reaches the finish line (`miles = 500`), another `GoTo` statement is added that branches to a routine called `GoodFinish:`. Thus you can avoid the program from diagnosing the car at the end of the race.

Each diagnostic routine starts with a line label. Two of the three routines end with—of all things—`GoTo` statements, which take the program to a single routine called `Status:` that decides whether it's safe to continue running the car. The routine called `DidWeCrash:` doesn't need to branch to `Status:` because it falls immediately below the routine anyway. If `Status:` determines 10 or more reasons why it should continue—as indicated by the variable `okay`—execution branches to `Up_top`, which is the start of the main `Do-Loop` clause.

At the end of this procedure are two terminating routines called `Totaled:` and `GoodFinish:`, both of which end with `End` and together represent the extreme worst-case and best-case scenarios as far as the interpreter is concerned.

As you've probably already determined, when you "let in" the GoTo statements, they start to swarm like sparrows in a barnyard. Visual Basic's syntactic structure is based not on the manual tracing of execution paths like old BASIC, but on the natural flow of data between formal procedures. When you add manual branching to a routine, you actually introduce something somewhat foreign to the scheme of things, not unlike damming a river. When you redirect the course of the river, you suddenly become responsible for where the water goes.

> **CAUTION:** If you're new to programming, you may want to be cautious in your use of manual branch statements. If you're a veteran of BASIC, however, you have nothing to fear by using GoTo because Visual Basic only enables you to use it under the confines of local procedures, anyway.

Keeping Context with the Times

Visual Basic is one of the first implementations of BASIC to limit the use of GoTo and GoSub to the local procedure in which they appear. In more common editions of BASIC, *procedures* are defined as routines separate from the "main body" of the program, which generally contains the primary sequence of instruction execution. In Visual Basic, there is no "main body" of the program—just a group of procedures that call one another.

Entry into and exit from each Visual Basic procedure is a closely guarded matter; Visual Basic's procedural syntax is designed to exchange data in the way highways exchange cars at their intersections. The Sub and Function declarations establish clear entries into these procedures, whereas End and Exit Sub ¦ Function define clear exit points. The Visual Basic interpreter can thus easily draw a map for itself, connecting all the procedures that refer to each other and designating the types of data the procedures will exchange when they meet at the intersection.

To arbitrarily force branches between procedures would befuddle this road map somewhat. Such a move would be about as sensible in the context of Visual Basic as placing a teleportation field in the middle of a busy interstate to absorb cars and rematerialize them at a teleportation field in some other state. First of all, if you can teleport, who needs a highway in the first place? Second, and perhaps most important, if you could have the VB application branch between any two arbitrarily defined points in two different procedures, how would the contexts of these procedures be maintained?

In other words, if variable x in one procedure refers to the number of white corpuscles in a cubic centimeter of blood, and in another procedure variable x refers to the number of Brazilians who claim to smoke more than two packs of cigarettes per day, if execution were to branch unconditionally from the middle of one procedure to the middle of the other, how does the Visual Basic interpreter decide, when xs collide, which x is more important? It can't, frankly, nor should it be forced to. You could decide, therefore, to allow x to be used once and only once within a program like in old BASIC, so that these conflicts would not occur. That would, however, place restrictions on the programmer, rather than on the computer where they belong. So GoTo and GoSub are now restricted to making local jumps only.

Wherefore the Subroutine?

A *subroutine* is a set of instructions within a procedure that branch back to the instruction just past the one that called it.

The first formal subdivision of BASIC source code was in the creation of the *subroutine*. A subroutine is a set of instructions within a procedure that is executable repetitively, can be called by name, and the end of which forces a branch back to the instruction just past the one that called it.

The first subroutines had no absolute beginning; a branch to a subroutine was performed by addressing a line number, as in GOSUB 2900. The end of each subroutine was supposed to be more definite, defined with the RETURN "command;" but such commands could be applied in conditional statements such as IF A > 15 THEN RETURN. As a result, subroutines had fuzzy boundaries on both sides—they had no marked point of entry and many possible points of exit.

229

Chapter 17 ◆ Arbitrary Instruction Clusters

GoSub Statement

Syntax:

GoSub `label`

Subroutines in Visual Basic have some differences from their old BASIC counterparts, but not many. On execution of the `GoSub` statement, the interpreter branches to the instruction immediately following the specified label. While execution proceeds in sequence, the interpreter keeps track of the location of the instruction that performed the branch. On executing the `Return` instruction, the interpreter branches back to the instruction immediately following the `GoSub` call.

Example

Suppose your application sends its output directly to your printer. Periodically, you need the program to send the page footer and page eject code to the printer. Here's how you can do this using `GoSub`:

```
Sub PrintTotals ()
Printer.Print "Monthly Totals for Period Ending ";date$
  .
  .
  .
Printer.Print "Totals thus far:    ";total(pageno)
GoSub NextPage
Printer.Print "Advertising Expense Projection"
  .
  .
  .
Printer.Print "Totals thus far:    ";total(pageno)
GoSub NextPage
Printer.Print "Maintenance Expense Projection"
  .
  .
  .
```

```
Exit Sub
NextPage:
   Printer.Print "  Page"; pageno
   pageno = pageno + 1
   Printer.NewPage
Return
End Sub
```

As you can see, more than one `GoSub` call can be placed within the same procedure to the same subroutine. Notice that no parameters are passed; this is true for all `GoSub` statements. In Visual Basic (unlike some other BASIC dialects), no data is exchanged during the branch to a subroutine. Such an exchange isn't really necessary, because the context of a subroutine is identical to the procedure in which it resides; in other words, it shares variables with its procedure. Because all variables belonging to the procedure belong to the subroutine, parameter passing is entirely unnecessary.

Notice that the statement that closes the subroutine is `Return`.

Return Statement

Syntax:

`Return`

When the `Return` statement is processed, a branch is made to the instruction immediately following the most recently executed `GoSub` statement.

Example

Using subroutines, the Indy automotive simulator procedure can be modified so that you can perform multiple diagnoses on the same accident. The branch statements to the diagnostic routines can be rewritten as follows:

Chapter 17 ◆ Arbitrary Instruction Clusters

```
If velo = 0 Then
    If full < 50 Then GoSub CheckFuel
    If cool > 300 Then GoSub OverHeat
    If intact < 20 Then GoSub DidWeCrash
    .
    .
    .
End If
```

Each diagnostic routine branches using a `GoTo` statement to a single point called `Status`, which can be updated as follows:

```
Status:
    If okay >= 10 Then Return
```

Now, if something is wrong when `velo = 0` (the car isn't moving), the branches to each of the diagnostic routines are all `GoSub` statements. The labels of the individual routines have not been altered. The end of each diagnosis routine still branches to `Status:` using `GoTo` statements. At the end of the `Status:` routine, however, is a `Return` marking the end of not only one, but *all* the diagnosis routines. The interpreter knows to branch back to the instruction following the `GoSub` statement that called it, wherever that is. In the case of this procedure, the `Return` branch could be to another conditional `GoSub` branch, which could start this cycle all over again.

Sequential Branching

In the previous example, you saw how a single `Return` can cause a branch back to any of multiple calling points. Visual Basic continues to use a variation of both `GoTo` and `GoSub` for branching from the calling point to any of multiple locations specified in a sequence.

Visual Basic *By* EXAMPLE

On...GoTo
On...GoSub

Statements

Syntax:

On *expression* GoTo *label0*, *label1*[, *label2*,... *label255*]
On *expression* GoSub *label0*, *label1*[, *label2*,... *label255*]

Placing On *expression* before a GoTo or GoSub statement converts that statement into a sequential branch to any of the labels specified in the list following the keyword. Branching is dependent on the value of *expression*. Generally, *expression* consists of one variable by itself. The logically reduced value of *expression*, when rounded to the nearest integer, must equal between 0 and 255, inclusive. This value is equivalent to the place in the list of the *label* that will be the destination of the branch. If the statement placing the branch is GoSub, the branch will be treated as a regular call to a subroutine; on processing Return, execution will proceed to the instruction immediately following On...GoSub.

Example

You may remember seeing On...GoTo used in the Expressor application to branch to any one of the five routines for processing formulas. The branch appeared within Sub ApplyFormula ():

On ndx GoTo f1, f2, f3, f4, f5

Variable ndx in this routine contains the index of a formula selected from a drop-down list box. If a formula was indeed selected, ndx should be equal to an integer from 0 to 4. This makes the list box control a perfect candidate for being evaluated with On...GoTo. In essence, the preceding statement is like making five statements all on one line: If ndx = 0 Then GoTo f1, If ndx = 1 Then Goto f2...and so on.

233

Chapter 17 ◆ Arbitrary Instruction Clusters

Summary

Visual Basic allows for manual branching to other points in a procedure marked by line labels. Such labels are identified by their solitude on an instruction line, and by the colon (:) that follows them. The primary statement for performing a manual branch is `GoTo`. The area of instructions within a procedure that is the recipient of a branch can be called a *routine*, although no such formal structure exists in Visual Basic.

A subroutine is a portion of a procedure that is branched to using the `GoSub` statement. After a subroutine is completed, execution branches back to the statement immediately following the previously executed `GoSub` after processing the `Return` statement. Subroutines are informal structures and often do not have absolute beginning or ending statements. Many subroutines can be closed with a single `Return` statement. The instructions comprising a subroutine need not be adjacent to one another within the context of a procedure.

A conditional sequential branch is possible using `On` *expression* before a `GoTo` or `GoSub` statement. Such a statement branches to any label within a list delimited by commas, having a place in the list that is equal to the rounded value of the *expression* stated beside the `On` term.

Review Questions

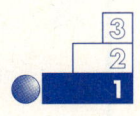

1. Speculate: The interpreter comes across a `Return` instruction within a procedure without having processed a `GoSub` instruction. What happens?

2. What Visual Basic loop clause structure substitutes for the conditional branch used in the following routine?

```
top_loop:
c = c + 1
   .
   .
   .
If c < 4 Then GoTo top_loop
```

3. What Visual Basic loop clause structure substitutes for the conditional branch used in the following routine?

```
top_loop:
If c = 4 Then GoTo out_loop
c = c + 1
 .
 .
 .
GoTo top_loop
out_loop:
 .
 .
 .
```

Review Exercise

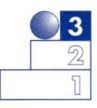

The following is a puzzle that uses `GoTo` and `GoSub` statements. Using your mind and not the computer, follow the branching pattern of this routine as best you can. Here, line numbers are used as labels for each line of the routine. This is the closest thing to a maze I can write in the context of this book and get away with it. The objective is to find the final value of variable c whenever an `End` statement is processed.

```
 1 : GoTo 5
 2 : GoSub 4
 3 : GoTo 25
 4 : Return
 5 : GoSub 10
 6 : a = 4
 7 : GoTo 15
 8 : a = 3
10 : Return
15 : GoSub 8
20 : GoTo 2
25 : On a GoTo 30, 40, 50, 60, 70
30 : b = 4
35 : GoTo 80
40 : Return
```

Chapter 17 ◆ Arbitrary Instruction Clusters

```
 50 : b = 3
 60 : b = 5
 65 : GoTo 80
 70 : b = a
 80 : On b GoSub 100, 110, 120, 130, 140, 150
 90 : Print c
 95 : End
100 : c = 3
105 : Return
110 : c = b
115 : Return
120 : c = 6
125 : Return
130 : Return
140 : c = a
145 : Return
150 : c = c
160 : Return
```

Part IV

Modularization

18

The Module Hierarchy

In this chapter you examine the framework of a Visual Basic application in detail. Because the source code of an application is divided into modules with no obvious sequence of arrangement, it is difficult for a person reading the source code to determine the order of execution for the procedures. Understanding the hierarchical relationship between modules and procedures of an application helps you better determine—or better yet, decipher—the order of execution of those modules.

The Origin of Modules

The first BASIC programs were not divided into modules, procedures, or anything other than *pages*. They consisted of many pages of numbered instructions. A BASIC programmer of the 1970s didn't consider what area or region of the program a variable belonged to, because when a variable was declared—generally informally—the rest of the program had full access to that variable. Compared to the structure of Visual Basic, each old BASIC program consisted of one huge procedure.

Chapter 18 ◆ The Module Hierarchy

In the '70s and early '80s, BASIC programmers wrote subroutines that could be used within several programs and that were integratable into the BASIC source code. This integration was not easy, however. First, the line numbers used by the subroutines could not conflict with any other line numbers used by the program—so programmers often numbered their reusable subroutines starting with an astronomically high number in hopes that the main routine would stay comfortably within the four-digit range.

Secondly, the names of variables invoked within these subroutines could not be duplicates of names used by the main body of the program. Therefore, it was generally not safe to use a simple variable name like X or N for a reusable subroutine; rather, it was often safer to use names like WILBUR and HANK. Imagine writing a reusable subroutine that converted radians to degrees before performing a trigonometry operation. Because your main program—to be written later—would probably use all the variables there are with meaningful names, you had to make sure your variables had meaningless names to avoid future conflicts.

Modular programming languages such as C existed long before BASIC became modular. The original idea behind BASIC was that it would be for beginners. When a programmer became good enough at programming to be concerned about variable conflict reduction, the programmer didn't need BASIC any more. Yet in certain cases, it appeared C programmers were having fewer problems than BASIC programmers; moreover, it is widely agreed that a programmer should spend more time concentrating on the completion of the task at hand and less time on the maintenance of the program itself.

BASIC source code became much easier to manage when line numbers became optional features. The first real modular subdivision made to BASIC source code—the point at which the cell began to split—came with the introduction of *subprograms*. From the point of view of BASIC programmers of the day, a subprogram was an advanced type of subroutine that existed, in a sense, in its own little world. None of the existing variable values and dimensions within the main body of the source code applied to a subprogram, except for those few variables listed within a set of parentheses. Microsoft chose to mark subprograms within BASIC source code with the statement Sub. Although Microsoft doesn't use the term *subprogram* today with respect to Visual Basic, the declarative statement retains the original name Microsoft gave it.

Sub Statement

Syntax:

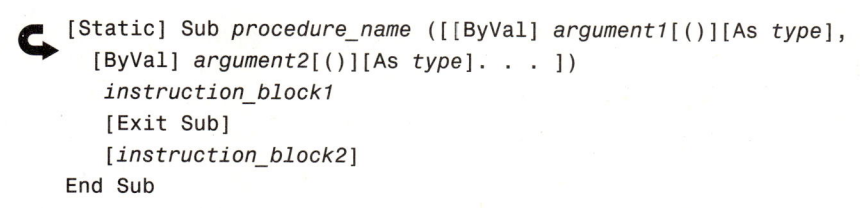

```
[Static] Sub procedure_name ([[ByVal] argument1[()][As type],
  [ByVal] argument2[()][As type]. . . ])
    instruction_block1
    [Exit Sub]
    [instruction_block2]
End Sub
```

`Sub` is the primary procedural declarative statement in the Visual Basic vocabulary. The statement is used to enclose a procedure of a given name *procedure_name*. Execution can branch to this `Sub` statement from any point in the program if you invoke this procedure name within the source code or use the `Call` statement.

A `Sub` procedure is said to receive values from the procedure that called it, as *arguments* or *parameters* (the terms are interchangeable here). When a procedure is called from outside, those values that pertain to that procedure are listed within parentheses, separated by commas. These values are said to be *passed* to the procedure. When a procedure is declared inside, those values are received in the order in which they were passed, and are assigned to variables that have names that may not necessarily be the same as those used for the procedure call. Contents of string variables can be passed in the same manner as values of numeric variables.

If the variable type of an argument is to change, or at least be ensured with specific reference, you can state the term `As` *type* beside that argument. The contents of an entire array can be passed to a procedure as an argument, as long as the variable name of the array is identified with empty parentheses `()`.

Under normal circumstances, any change made to the values of the arguments listed is reflected in the variables used as arguments in the procedure call. This reflection can be overridden for a specific argument by placing the term `ByVal` before that argument; doing so allows the variable used in the procedure call to retain its value even if the value of the variable used to receive the argument has changed within the procedure.

Execution of the instructions within a Sub procedure occurs in sequence. A Sub procedure is terminated whenever an Exit Sub or End Sub is reached during this sequence.

Under normal circumstances, the values of the variables with scopes that are local to the procedure, or that have not been declared as modular or global outside the procedure, are nullified whenever the procedure is exited. Use of the term Static before the Sub term changes the context of the procedure from standard local to static, allowing the interpreter to maintain the values and contents of variables used by the procedure after it is exited.

Microsoft is believed to be the originator of *user-defined functions* within BASIC source code. Originally, the definition of such a function could only be expressed on one line using the statement DEF FN (which stands for *define function*). Later, function definitions were promoted to formal clauses, and are now considered procedures in their own right. In fact, in Visual Basic, any instruction that is not a part of a Sub procedure and is not a global or modular declaration is part of a Function procedure.

Function   Statement

Syntax:

```
[Static] Function procedure_name ([[ByVal] argument1[()]
  [As type], [ByVal] argument2[()][As type]. . . ])
    instruction_block1
    procedure_name = expression1
    [Exit Function]
    [instruction_block2]
    [procedure_name = expression2]
End Function
```

The Function statement acts as the header for the procedures that receive arguments in the same manner as a Sub procedure, but which return a single value or string contents to the procedure that called them in the manner of an equation. The Function statement itself appears to have precisely the same syntax as the Sub statement. One important difference between the syntaxes of the Function and

Sub procedures is that the *procedure_name* of a Function procedure is treated like a variable within the procedure. Toward the termination of the Function procedure, a validly interpretable expression is assigned to that *procedure_name* with an equation. The value of this expression is considered to be the solution or result of the function as declared.

The syntax of arguments expressed within the Function statement is the same as the syntax of arguments within the Sub statement. Under normal circumstances, the values of those variables that have scopes that are local to the procedure, or which have not been declared as modular or global outside the procedure, are nullified whenever the procedure is exited. Use of the term Static before the Function term changes the context of the procedure from standard local to static, allowing the interpreter to maintain the values and contents of variables used by the procedure after it is exited.

A Sub procedure has no specific responsibility to the rest of the program to provide it with any values or results. By contrast, a Function procedure is charged with the responsibility of providing one value or alphanumeric string as the result of the function. Within the Function procedure, between the declaration and the End Function terminator, the name of the function itself—without parentheses—is shown. The name of the function is treated like a variable. The result of the function is assigned to this apparent variable—in fact, the assignment can be made at several different points in the procedure, but it must be made at least once. This way, the function name may represent that variable value *outside* of the function procedure.

For instance, because twist is not a reserved Visual Basic keyword, if one procedure contains the instruction a = twist(c, d), the interpreter checks to see if twist is an array variable or a call to a function procedure. If a function declaration Function twist(x, y) exists someplace in the program, the function procedure twist executes. Like the Sub procedure, variables x and y are treated as inputs. Unlike the Sub procedure, the Function procedure has one output; someplace within the procedure, there *must* be a statement of assignment in the form twist = *formula*. Notice that twist has no parentheses in this assignment. The assignment is made as if twist

243

Chapter 18 ◆ The Module Hierarchy

were a standard variable. This is because, like a variable, the term `twist` represents a value outside of the `Function` procedure.

Where Does It All Begin; Where Does It End?

We writers like to use phrases like "The execution of the program proceeds in sequence." In the case of Visual Basic, however, that sequence is not evident when you consider the all-important matter of which procedure comes first. There is an absolute order to the execution of Visual Basic procedures, as depicted in the hierarchical tower in Figure 18.1.

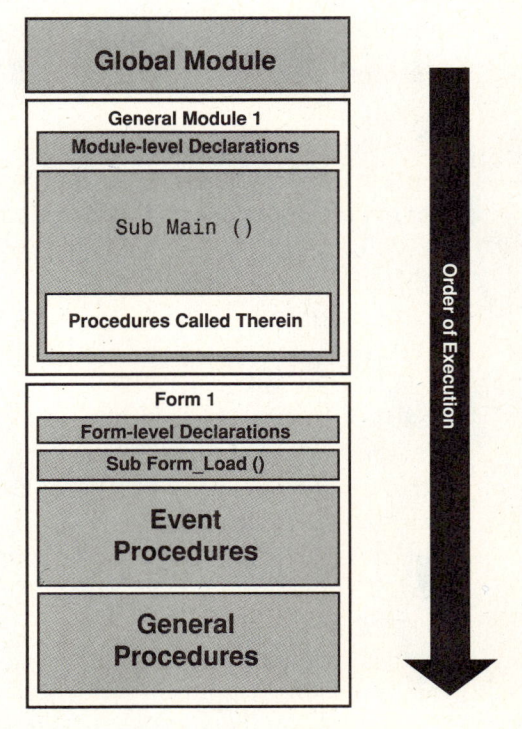

Figure 18.1. The Tower of Procedural Execution.

Visual Basic *By* EXAMPLE

> A *library* is a set of procedures that supplement the Visual Basic procedures.

We start at the top of this tower and, like Ronald Reagan's economic program, trickle down toward the base. The global module, which is shown at the top of Figure 18.1, is always executed first. This module may contain only declarations for global variables or declarations for the forms of procedures that act as extensions to the Visual Basic vocabulary. Visual Basic maintains many keywords, but the vocabulary itself is not limited to those keywords. VB allows *libraries* to be attached to the operating set of recognized instructions for an application. A library is a set of process names that are treated as procedure names by Visual Basic, but that are actually calls to processes within Dynamic Link Libraries outside Visual Basic.

If you plan to extend the Visual Basic vocabulary, you need to state that fact right at the beginning, within the global module of the application.

A general module does not contain forms or graphic objects. Its only purpose is to house procedures that perform arithmetic or analytical tasks or functions. If your application has any procedures that are not responses to graphical events—in other words, they're not executed because the user clicked something with the mouse or typed something on the keyboard—those procedures belong inside a general module. General modules are good places to locate `Function` procedures because none of the event procedures within a form module are `Function` procedures.

A general module is created by selecting **N**ew Module... from the **F**ile menu of Visual Basic's main window. The VB interpreter will give the module its own window, with a default title of `MODULEX.BAS`, with `x` representing the order in which the module was created within the project—having nothing to do with order of execution. At this point, the module has no specific file name; once you enter text into this module and select **F**ile Save **A**s, you give this module a formal file name. General modules, as a standard, although not as a rule, are usually given the extension .BAS. An existing general module may be attached to a project by selecting **F**ile **A**dd Module and choosing the module's file name from the selector box; by default, the selector searches for files ending in .BAS.

When the Visual Basic interpreter executes a program with general modules in it, the file names of those general modules do not effect the execution. In other words, at run time the interpreter views all the procedures of all the general modules belonging to the project

Chapter 18 ◆ The Module Hierarchy

as existing within a sort of conglomerated pool. Therefore, even if there are two or more general modules within a project, no two procedures within the project can share the same name. If you intend to load two preexistent general modules into a project, you should make certain the names of the procedures won't conflict with each other.

Under the default condition of the VB interpreter, no `Sub` or `Function` procedure in any general module executes at all unless a procedure within some form module places a specific call to that procedure. This is because the interpreter usually executes instructions belonging to the *startup* form—the first form module the interpreter executes. By default, this is the first form module entered into the project—the former `Form1`, whatever it may be named now.

The startup *procedure is the first one executed in a VB project.*

Example

An alternative structure is to have a startup procedure within one of your project's general modules, called `Sub Main ()`. Like its counterpart `main()` in the C programming language, `Sub Main ()` is generally used to specify the order of execution of the other major general procedures in the project. Often this order of execution is expressed as a cycle within an unconditional `Do-Loop` clause. Here's an example of a `Sub Main ()` procedure within a general module solely intended in this instance to specify the order of execution of other procedures, in this or other general modules:

```
Sub Main ()
    Do
        LoadRecords()
        GetInput()
        SaveData()
    Loop
End Sub
```

Here we have calls to three arbitrarily named procedures that exist within this or some other general module. They are each called and executed in sequence continuously until program execution is stopped.

A project can contain more than one general module, and there is no limit to how many procedures can exist within a general module. So during run time, from the interpreter's point of view, all general module procedures that are not named `Sub Main ()` exist in one conglomerated pool.

On first entering the `Sub Main ()` procedure into a general module, the interpreter does not automatically recognize it as the startup procedure. To make `Sub Main ()` the startup procedure:

1. While the project is in its design state, from the VB main window's **R**un menu, select **S**et Startup Form. A dialog box will display listing the names of all form modules currently enrolled in the project. Mind you, these names represent the `.FormName` property settings for these forms, not their file names.

2. If one of the general modules in your project contains a procedure named `Sub Main ()`, it, too, will be listed among the other form names. Never mind the fact that `Sub Main ()` is not a form; it's listed anyway. Choose it by double-clicking `Sub Main`.

Once `Sub Main ()` has been made the startup "form" (pardon the faulty nomenclature), when the VB project is executed, no form is loaded into the workspace and displayed unless a specific statement is issued to that effect.

The Form of Forms

Each form module for a project is divided into three sections: the declarations section, the event procedure section, and the general procedure section—listed here in order of their consideration by the VB interpreter. Declarations made within the declarations section of a module use the `Dim` statement and are considered to have modular scope—meaning they pertain to every procedure in the form module.

Following the execution of the declarations section, the interpreter looks next to the event procedures section for the presence of a procedure called `Form_Load ()`. Here, `_Load` is an event; specifically, it is the event of loading the form into the workspace in the first place. If this procedure exists, it is executed next. After `Form_Load ()` is complete, if there are any other event-driven procedures within the form module, Visual Basic suspends execution and waits for an event to occur that activates an event procedure.

If no procedure `Form_Load ()` exists for the first form module in the project, and if any other event procedure exists within that module, VB suspends execution and waits for an event to happen that will execute one of those procedures. If no event procedures exist for this first form in the project, regardless of whether any procedures by any name exist in the general procedures section of the form module, no procedure is executed and the interpreter will be waiting for nothing to happen. This is why you can run a VB application that has no lines of source code in it and still receive a form named `Form1` on the screen while the interpreter waits for an event to occur.

When a general module's procedure addresses a procedure within a form module, the syntax of the address places the `.FormName` property setting of that form first, followed by the procedure name. For an event procedure, this name is the usual `.ControlName` property followed by the event; for a general procedure, the name is arbitrary. All elements of the address are separated from each other by underscore characters. The syntax for such a call is as follows:

`FormName_ControlName_Event`

or

`FormName_GenProcedure`

The procedures that exist within the general procedures section of a form module are executed only when called by name; otherwise, the interpreter never notices them. Likewise, every general module procedure other than the `Sub Main ()` procedure executes only when called by name.

Whenever a form module subsequent to `Form1` is loaded into the workspace using the `Load` statement or the `.Show` method, if a procedure `Form_Load ()` exists for that form, it is immediately executed. If any other event procedures exist for that module, when the window for that module is active on the screen, the VB interpreter awaits an event that triggers the execution of one of those procedures.

The VB interpreter has nothing against you naming one of the procedures within the general *procedures* section of a form module

Sub Main (), unless a Sub Main () procedure exists within one of your general modules. However, a Sub Main () procedure within a form module does not hold the same exclusive distinction as one within a general module; in other words, the interpreter will not view it as a candidate for "startup form," and it will not be executed automatically.

You've just read the general road map for Visual Basic applications. The fact that this road map is defined for you ahead of time by the Visual Basic interpreter may actually make it easier over time for you to design a project with multiple modules and procedures. At first, however, the learning curve for the arrangement of modules and procedures within a VB project can best be described as a steep incline.

Summary

The need for modular divisions within BASIC programs developed from the conflicts programmers faced when adding routines together. These conflicts concerned distinguishing line numbers from each other and making sure variable names weren't duplicated. Visual Basic procedures eliminate both possible areas of conflict by making line numbers optional—although an obsolete option—and having the programmer state specifically which variables are to be shared between procedures.

With the exception of variable and functional declarations sections, all other executable instructions within a Visual Basic project exist within procedures of some sort. The two types of procedure declarations in Visual Basic are Sub and Function. The difference between Sub and Function is that Function returns a specific value within a variable name that doubles as the name of the Function procedure. Both Sub and Function procedures allow for input values between the parentheses of their declaration; however, unlike the Sub procedure, a Function procedure passes a value back to the body of the program from which it was called. The values to be passed between procedures are presented as arguments within the procedure declaration and within the procedure call.

Execution of the procedures in a Visual Basic application proceeds in the following order:

Chapter 18 ♦ The Module Hierarchy

1. Global module
2. `Sub Main ()` of any general module if and only if it is officially declared the startup procedure
3. Any procedures anywhere in the project that are called within `Sub Main ()`
4. The declarations section of `Form1` if that form is loaded into the workspace, or of any form that has been made the startup form in place of `Form1`
5. `Sub Form_Load ()` of the startup form if that form is addressed by `Sub Main ()` or if no `Sub Main ()` exists
6. Any event procedures within the startup form
7. Any procedures called within the general procedures section of the startup form
8. The declarations section of `Form2`, or whatever form was entered into the project following `Form1`
9. `Sub Form_Load ()` of `Form2` if it is loaded into the workspace
10. Event procedures for `Form2`
11. General procedures for `Form2`, and so on

Review Questions

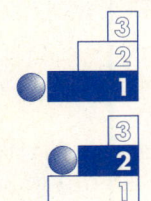

1. What part of a VB project always executes first without exception, whether or not it contains any code?
2. Assuming you've never selected **R**un or **S**et Startup Form, what, by default, is the first procedure executed for an application that contains at least one dialog box?
3. What instruction from `Form1` executes the first procedure of `Form2`?
4. Assume a VB project has no form assigned to it, only a general module. There is no `Sub Main ()` procedure within this module. When you select **R**un or **S**tart, what happens?

250

Review Exercise

The following is a list of procedure names for a Visual Basic project, along with their locations within the modular structure of the project. This list is in random order. Reorganize the list so that it reflects the natural order of execution of these procedures.

Function angle_over (angle, circle)	general module 1
Global module	
Declarations section	Form2 module
Sub Command1_Click ()	Form1 module
Sub blowed_up_good ()	general module 1
Sub main ()	general module 1
Sub Form_Load ()	Form2 module
Declarations section	Form1 module
Sub Form_Load ()	Form1 module

Parameter Passing

In this chapter you get more insight into the logical mechanisms that allow values to be passed and shared between procedures in a Visual Basic application. You'll understand to a greater extent why there are distinctions between different scopes of variables, and why the variables of a VB application are not simply shared among all the procedures and instructions of the program.

I Pass

To this point, when you've placed calls to Sub procedures using instructions within other procedures, all you've needed to do is state the name of the procedure being called in an instruction or phrase by itself, along with any parameters the procedure may take, in a list delimited by commas. Visual Basic provides an optional second method for calling Sub procedures, with an explicit statement:

[Call] Statement

Syntax 1:

```
Call procedure_name ([argument1, argument2. . . ])
```

Chapter 19 ◆ Parameter Passing

Syntax 2:

`procedure_name [argument1, argument2. . .]`

When the `Call` instruction is processed, or when the name of a defined procedure is invoked within source code, a branch is made to the named `Sub` procedure. Any values to be passed to the procedure as arguments are listed beside the `procedure_name` in precisely the order in which they are to be received by the opening statement of the `Sub` procedure.

> **CAUTION:** If the term `Call` is specified, the argument list is enclosed in parentheses. If `Call` is omitted, the argument list is *not* enclosed in parentheses.

Example

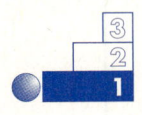

Assume you have a `Sub` procedure called `tri_area` that figures the area of a right triangle, given the lengths of two of its sides. Here are two statements that would result in exactly the same branch to the procedure:

```
tri_area side1, side2
Call tri_area (side1, side2)
```

The procedure that solves for the area of the right triangle might appear as follows:

```
Sub tri_area (base, height)
    area = base * height / 2
End Sub
```

Arguably, this procedure might be expressed better using `Function` rather than `Sub`. As a result, the procedure call can be placed in the midst of a formula rather than placed as a statement by itself. Here's how the `Function` call and the revised procedure might appear:

254

```
Under_incline = tri_area (b, h)
    .
    .
    .
Function tri_area (base, height)
    tri_area = base * height / 2
End Function
```

Another reason the procedure would perform better as a `Function` than as a `Sub` is that in the `Function` syntax, a separate variable `area` need not be declared for modular scope outside of the procedure using `Dim`. This would be necessary with the `Sub` syntax, because the scope of the calculations within a `Sub` procedure are confined to that local procedure. The result of the calculation would have no other way to get out of the confines of the procedure except by having been declared with a scope above local.

To illustrate, in order for `Sub tri_area ()` to pass variable `area` back to the calling body, the instruction `Dim area` would have to be placed in the declarations section of the module containing both the call and `Sub tri_area ()`. However, for `Function tri_area ()`, the programmer is free to place the procedure within a general module completely separate from any procedure that may call it. Upon executing the instruction `a = tri_area (b, h)`, execution proceeds from wherever the call was placed to the general module. Yet there doesn't need to be any `Dim` or `Global` declaration for a variable `tri_area`.

In Chapter 12, "Advanced Value Management," I listed the four variable scopes (no, it's not a new R&B group). To refresh your memory, Table 19.1 shows them again, along with the statements that declare variables for each scope.

Table 19.1. The Four Variable Scopes.

Scope	Statement	Definition
local	Dim	Pertaining only to the procedure in which the variable is first invoked or declared, and having a value that is cleared when the procedure is exited

continues

Table 19.1. continued

Scope	Statement	Definition
static	`Static`	Pertaining only to the procedure in which the variable is first declared, although its value is maintained after the procedure is exited in case of possible reentry
modular	`Dim`	Pertaining to all procedures in a module by virtue of having been declared in the general module area of a form module
global	`Global`	Pertaining to the entire source code

Notice that at the beginning of both of the preceding procedures, the variable names chosen for the procedures are different from the variable names that passed those values to the procedures. This is because the variables themselves are not passed between procedures, just their values. Global variables obviously don't have to be passed as parameters, because every procedure is entitled to know their values or contents. On the other hand, local variables are kept local partly in an attempt to maintain their identity. You can perform the same `Sub` procedure or `Function` on several sets of variables, so the procedure needs to be able to accept its input from several sources. Because the variables in all the sources will be kept separate from each other, it therefore follows that the variables in the procedure that solves for those input variables should be kept separate as well. This is why there are scope distinctions between variables.

The Natural Order of Things

In the right-triangle formula, the parameter-passing order didn't really matter because the two parameters were multiplied together anyway. For most other procedures, however, the order in which the parameters are passed is crucial.

Visual Basic *By*
EXAMPLE

Example

Take for example this procedure call and its formula, which calculates the area of a right-circular cylinder. This procedure call and formula were taken from the Expressor application.

```
f1:
solution = surf_area_rccyl(p(0), p(1))
GoTo display_result

Function surf_area_rccyl (r, h)
surf_area_rccyl = (2 * PI) * r * h
End Function
```

Keep in mind that routine `f1:` and `Function surf_area_rccyl ()` appear in (or as) two different procedures. Notice that the input parameters for the function are stored in an array variable `p()`, whereas on the receiving end their values are assigned simply to unit variables `r` (radius) and `h` (height). Geometrically speaking, these values pertain to two distinctly different aspects of the cylinder, so their order within the parentheses must be maintained. It is the relation between the *order* of parameters in the passing and receiving lists that determines the purpose of those parameters.

Example

From another area of the Expressor is a call to a `Function` procedure that needs more parameters. This is the Doppler shift formula, which determines the frequency of a light or sound wave emanated from a moving source, given the observed shifted frequency of that wave and the velocities of both the source of the wave and its observer:

```
f5:
solution = dopp_shift(p(0), p(1), p(2), p(3))
display_result:
readout.caption = Str$(solution)

Function dopp_shift (vo, vs, fo, c)
dopp_shift = ((c + vo) / (c - vs)) * fo
End Function
```

257

Chapter 19 ◆ Parameter Passing

Again, vo is the velocity of the observer of a wave, vs is the velocity of the source of the wave, fo is the observed frequency of the wave, and c is the velocity of the wave (c is generally representative of the speed of light in physics equations, although the user of the program may wish to substitute the speed of sound here). Again, the values were passed to the function with array variables, but were received by unit variables. You could have used any four valid numeric variables to pass values to Function dopp_shift (), but the result of the equation would have been the same. Here again, it is the *order* of the four variables within the parameter-passing sequences that determines their purpose and relation to each other—not their names. This order can be arbitrarily defined when the procedure is written. Once this order is defined, however, it must be maintained within every call to that procedure.

Here is the standard syntax for calls to a Function procedure:

variable = procedure_name (parameter1, [parameter2...])

The function term formed by *procedure_name()* can also be used within a formula or expression and still be able to call the Function procedure. This is because the called procedure defines for the Visual Basic interpreter how the function term logically reduces to a real value.

Example

When passing parameters between equations, the precision of those parameters must match. Thus a single-precision floating-point variable must pass a value to another single-precision value in the receiving procedure. Suppose, however, for the sake of a receiving Function procedure, we need the formula to work on a rounded integer, although the original variable doing the passing may be fractional. Say variable c is the variable you're rounding. The Function procedure can be written as follows:

```
Function wild_card (x, n, c)
c = Int(c)
.
.
.
End Function
```

Variable c is rounded inside the Function procedure. If the instruction that called it is r = wild_card(u, t, v), not only will c be rounded but v as well. If you want the procedure to leave the passed variable alone, you need to state that right up front at the procedure declaration, using the qualifier term ByVal as follows:

```
Function wild_card (x, n, ByVal c)
```

The term ByVal stands for "only the value of" in this case. Including it means the rounding of c will not in any way affect the value of v in the calling procedure.

Summary

A branch to a Sub procedure is made through the use of a statement that may or may not contain the term Call. A branch to a Function procedure, on the other hand, is made by implication—by stating the procedure name as an element of a mathematical expression or equation.

When passing parameters between procedures, the purpose of those parameters within the procedure is determined not by the name, type, or scope of the parameter, but by the parameter's chosen order within the parameter list. The order of the list in the instruction that calls the procedure and the order of the list in the declaration of the procedure must match for the procedure to operate. When parameters are passed successfully in this fashion, changes made to the variable that received the parameter value are reflected in the variable that passed the parameter value to the procedure. This reflection can be overridden in advance by use of the term ByVal before the variable that has a calling counterpart that is to be left alone.

Review Questions

1. Early in this chapter, you saw two different types of procedures—Sub and Function—perform the same type of arithmetic operation on the same parameters and yield the same results, except in different ways. Why is the instruction that

calls the Sub procedure for this arithmetic operation considered a *statement,* whereas the instruction that calls the Function procedure for the same arithmetic operation is considered a *function*?

2. Syntactically speaking, why does a Call statement enclose its arguments within parentheses, whereas the same statement made without the use of Call omits those parentheses?

Part V

Graphical Interaction

20

The Form

In this chapter you examine the role of the form as a graphic object. In recent chapters, I've discussed forms as source code modules. As you begin Part V, however, I devote more space and time to the graphic, and often more artistic, part of Visual Basic. As you've learned, a project can contain more than one module. At the time the code for that project is being executed, however, not all of these forms may reside in memory. Windows has a tendency to send unused memory items to disk until they become necessary. With Visual Basic, unused forms in a project are already dispensed to disk until they are formally called. You learn more about this process in this chapter.

Where Your Forms Are

Your *workspace* is the area of the screen where forms and tools reside.

As discussed in Chapter 18, "Module Hierarchy," when an application starts running, it executes the declarations within the global module first. If a general module exists within the project and it contains a procedure called `Sub Main()`, that procedure is executed next. Otherwise, the Visual Basic interpreter loads the first form—by default called `Form1` unless otherwise named—into the workspace. The *workspace* is the area of the screen where forms and Visual Basic tools reside—although they may not necessarily appear there—during an application's run time.

263

Chapter 20 ◆ The Form

This is the only instance where the interpreter loads a form into the workspace by itself. To better understand what I mean by *loading into the workspace,* look at Figure 20.1, which depicts the strange hierarchy of states of existence. As I said earlier, sometimes programming is a philosophical exercise; as you are about to witness, it can also be metaphysical.

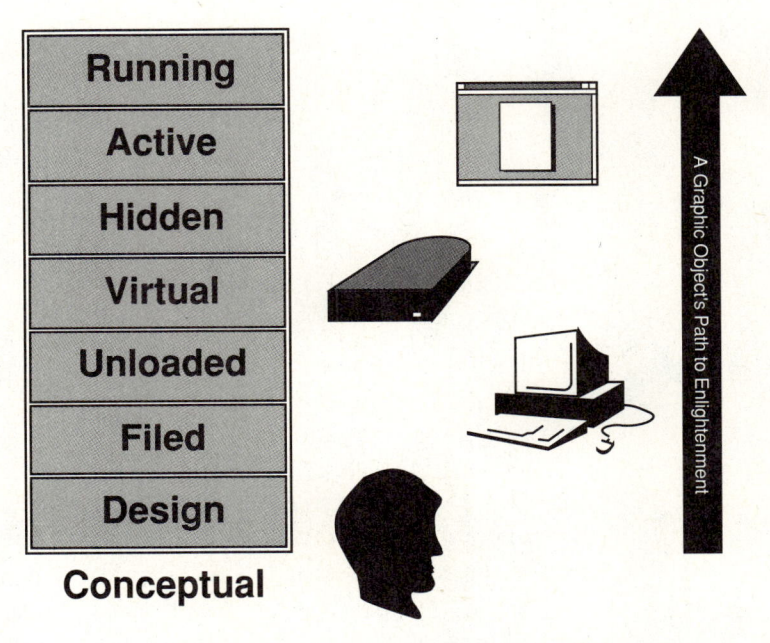

Figure 20.1. The "planes of existence" for a graphic object.

Graphic objects in Visual Basic (forms are VB graphic objects as well as controls) have different levels of existence that are almost like different levels of consciousness, as Figure 20.1 shows. At the base of this multiplane chart is the *design state,* or the level of existence of a graphic object while the VB application is being written by the programmer. When a graphic object becomes part of a form module, it later is stored to disk as part of a file. This is the *filed state* of the graphic object—the next step up the chain of consciousness.

When an application is running—whether it is a Visual Basic project or a compiled .EXE file—the graphic object may be referred to by the source code. Chances are, however, that unless the object belongs to `Form1`, the object has not yet been loaded into memory. It exists in the midst of a running application, but it hasn't yet found its way into the RAM of the computer. In this state, which appears to be somewhere along the proverbial bridge between physical and logical storage, the object is in its *unloaded state*.

When the graphic object or the form containing it is finally loaded, Microsoft Windows might consider it to be in "memory." If it isn't really in use at the time, however, chances are that the object exists in virtual memory—which is really yet another disk file waiting to be translated into RAM. This is the *virtual state* of the graphic object. When Windows deems it necessary, the file containing the virtual memory of the graphic object is at last translated into RAM and *loaded into the workspace*. This doesn't necessarily mean, however, that you can actually see the graphic object yet. The object may be invisible unless specifically told to appear. We call this twilight zone of being the *hidden state*.

It takes an explicitly stated method to make the VB interpreter show this object. At last, we can say the object is in an *active state*. If the graphic object is being manipulated by the user, we can say the object is in a *running state*. From *design state* to *running state*, we can say this graphic object has traversed the Visual Basic equivalent of the Noble Eightfold Path.

Inter-State Transport

When a VB form is in its design state, it can be assigned a name with a property setting. Here is the first listing of a property of a graphic object and how that property is set:

```
Form.Property
```

Form.`FormName` Property

`.FormName` is a textual property that contains the name of the antecedent form as it will appear in the source code. This is not the file name of the form module. `.FormName` must consist of only one

Chapter 20 ◆ The Form

grouping of characters without any spaces. This property may not be set at run time with an equation; it may be set only at design time with the VB properties bar.

Before going on, here is a new term that I use in this book to refer to the graphic object that is the "owner" of the mentioned property: The *antecedent* is the graphic object referred to by a property. It generally appears before the period that separates that property from the graphic object in the property's full name.

> The *antecedent* is the graphic object referred to by a property.

Programming has borrowed this term from English grammar; remember how a pronoun (such as *it*) refers back to its antecedent?

Regardless of what name a form is given at design time, when the project containing that form is running, the form itself can be loaded into memory—whether that is in RAM or in virtual memory (on disk)—using the Load statement.

Load Statement

Syntax:

Load *objectname*

The Load statement addresses a graphic object belonging to the currently running application by name, loads it into memory as well as into the workspace without displaying it, and holds it in suspension until an instruction is executed that forces that object to be shown.

Example

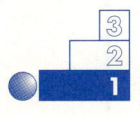

If a form named Panel belongs to your application, here is the instruction that will load it into the workspace:

Load Panel

Note that the form hasn't been displayed yet. To accomplish this feat, use the following method:

.Show — Method

Syntax:

[*formname*.]Show [*style*]

The .Show method displays a loaded form. If the form hasn't been loaded into the workspace yet, it will be loaded automatically. If the *formname* is omitted, the graphic form sharing the current module with the currently executing procedure will be shown. The optional *style* value, when set to 1 (0 is the default), makes the displayed form *modal*—in other words, no other window can accept input from the user until this form is somehow exited.

The two instructions introduced thus far in this chapter have counterpart instructions that are their own undoing. They are as follows:

.Hide — Method

Syntax:

[*formname*.]Hide

The .Hide method takes a form that is currently being shown and removes it from the screen until further notice. It virtually occupies the same coordinates on the screen. Controls on the hidden form may still be referred to within the source code. In other words, operation of the form by the program is not suspended; operation of the form by the user is suspended.

Unload — Statement

Syntax:

Unload *objectname*

Chapter 20 ◆ The Form

The `Unload` statement removes the loaded form or graphic object specified from the workspace, as well as from memory. The object continues to exist as a form within the project and as a stored file on disk if it ever has been stored. This statement is necessary for a compiled Visual Basic application because it will not have the services of the VB interpreter to automatically "shut down" each form once the compiled program is formally exited.

Summary

A form as a graphic object—when its design has been completed and it has been given its `.FormName`—is executed by the Visual Basic interpreter by first loading the form into the workspace using the `Load` statement and then displaying the form with the `.Show` method.

Review Questions

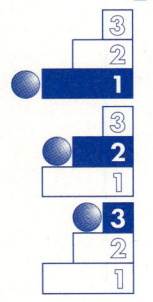

1. Do you need to `Load` a form into memory first before invoking the `.Show` method?

2. When a form is taken out of memory using the `Unload` statement, does it retain its place as part of the project?

3. Syntactically speaking, with regard to bringing forms into the workspace, why are `Load` and `Unload` *statements* and `.Show` and `.Hide` formal *methods* in object-oriented syntax?

21

The Window

In this chapter you see the properties that relate to the appearance of a window in the Visual Basic workspace. You also see examples of these properties—as you do for the other properties covered in Part V—being set with the Visual Basic design-time properties bar, as well as with source code.

What is This Thing Called, Love?

One of the primary intentions of the creators of windowed operating environments was for new users to be able to deduce the meaning and function of at least some of the on-screen controls without having to refer back to the instruction manual. Perhaps if the creators' intentions were fully realized, we in the instruction business would be out of a job. Nonetheless, there are those who have learned to operate the window "gadgets" and drop-down menus of Microsoft Windows without reading anything whatsoever beforehand. These people have become proficient Windows users, to some extent, without help. Yet many of these people aren't sure what the individual controls and gadgets are officially called.

Chapter 21 ◆ The Window

Some of these people—with good reason—might ask, "What does it matter what these things are called as long as we know how to use them properly?" If you went to a foreign country and didn't speak the language, you would still know how to use the telephone; likewise if your native environment is GEM, X/Window, or the Macintosh Finder and you're visiting the Windows environment, is it really necessary to know the name of the combo box, the control box, and the slider bar?

As a programmer in Visual Basic, you need to know what Microsoft calls the gadgets and controls of the individual windows because you will address them by name in source code. There is no universal convention for the names of visual controls in a windowed environment. For instance, what Microsoft calls a *scroll box*—the sliding grey square between the two arrows of a scroll bar—is what the Macintosh calls a *thumb*. (Microsoft isn't nearly as liberal with its choice of metaphors as is Apple. Perhaps this is for the best, because at least you won't have to set properties like *Thumb.Position*.)

Would Someone Open a Window?

Figure 21.1 points out the various elements of a window with which you're already familiar and shows Microsoft's names for those elements. At the upper-left corner is the window's *control box*, which when double-clicked closes the window. When clicked once, the control box offers the user options for manipulating and positioning the window, and generally offers the user access to the Windows Task Manager.

At the upper-right corner of this particular window, from left to right, are the *minimize* (down arrow) and *maximize* (up arrow) buttons for that window. Keep in mind that these two buttons, as well as these two terms, are not opposite to each other in this context. To minimize a window is to suspend the application for that window and to place its icon toward the lower-left corner of the Windows desktop. Execution of the application is resumed when this icon is double-clicked. By contrast, to maximize a window is to give that window full rein of the screen; this process does not change the execution state of the application. When the window is maximized, the maximize button is replaced with the *restore* button, which is marked with the up arrow on top of the down arrow.

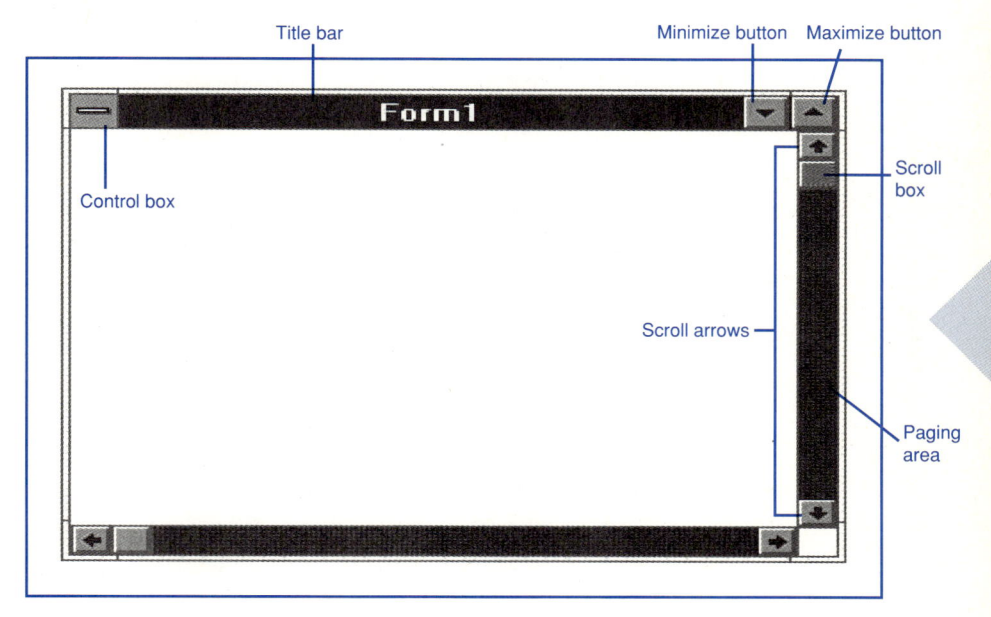

Figure 21.1. The parts of a Windows window.

You are already familiar with such commonly used graphic controls as the title bar—with which you can move the window as well as maximize and restore the window by double-clicking it. The sliding indicator between the two arrows on the scroll bar is the *scroll box*. The arrows are called *scroll arrows*. In many applications, clicking on the area between the scroll box and a scroll arrow scrolls the contents of the window in the direction of that arrow one *page*, or approximately one window-length of text or contents. Microsoft has not named the area between the scroll box and scroll arrow; so for the sake of my discussion, I call this area the *paging area*.

The parts listed here are the only parts of a window that are resources provided by Microsoft. *You* are supposed to conceive and design any other controls to operate the window in some fashion that you add to your Visual Basic form windows. In such cases, it is up to you to give your gadgets proper names.

The Fine Art of Property Setting

Throughout the rest of the book, but especially in Part V, I relate the various properties belonging to Visual Basic graphic objects, along with their possible settings. In many cases, properties for a graphic object are set *not* within the body of the source code, but by the programmer during programming, using the VB properties bar. This particular process is called *setting properties at design time*, meaning the application is not running, and perhaps source code is not yet entered into the application. Certain instructions can be used to set or change the properties of a graphic object while the application is running—while instructions are being executed. This process is called *setting properties at run time*.

When introducing each property term, I show you how the instruction that sets this property is phrased. I also show you the possible settings or range of settings for that term. Not all properties of a Visual Basic graphic object can necessarily be set at design time, nor can all properties of that object necessarily be set at run time. Therefore, example instructions are provided only where instructions for that property are supported. Nonetheless, because property terms are identified by their preceding period even if those properties are not supported in the source code, the period remains before each property when it is presented in general discussion.

With that in mind, here is the first of the properties that deal with window appearance and contents.

Form.ControlBox Property

The .ControlBox property is set to a true or false value, reflecting whether the window's control box will appear in the form for this window. By default, *form*.ControlBox is set to true (–1). The following VB instruction resets this property:

```
Form1.ControlBox = 0
```

where Form1 can be replaced by the name of the form being referred to. This property can also be reset or set at design time, although this setting takes effect only when the application is run.

The properties for showing the maximize and minimize buttons are set in a similar manner.

Form.MaxButton **Property**

The .MaxButton property is set to a true or false value, reflecting whether the window's maximize button will appear in the form for this window. By default, *form*.MaxButton is set to true (–1).

Form.MinButton **Property**

The .MinButton property is set to a true or false value, reflecting whether the window's minimize button will appear in the form for this window. By default, *form*.MinButton is set to true (–1).

The following two VB instructions will reset the preceding properties:

```
Form1.MaxButton = 0
Form1.MinButton = 0
```

where Form1 can be replaced by the name of the form being referred to. These properties can be set or reset at design time, although these settings take effect only when the application is run.

The reason you might not want a form to have a control box or minimize and maximize buttons is that some forms in a Visual Basic application serve the purpose of dialog boxes or file selectors. When you use a regular Windows application and select **O**pen... from the **F**ile menu on its menu bar, you most likely see some kind of file selector box. Such boxes generally do not have control boxes, and never have maximize and minimize buttons, because their functions are relevant only with respect to an application's main display window. *Boxes* such as dialog boxes and file selectors are considered to be agents of, and therefore are subservient to, the main application window. To minimize a window generally is a directive to minimize the *application* and proceed with operating some other application active within the Windows environment. Furthermore, because a file selector box is not officially a *task,* one usually doesn't need a control box to bring up the Task Manager using that box. Yet

273

Chapter 21 ◆ The Window

you may prefer to use a control box as an alternate `Cancel` button for a file selector. If you set the `.ControlBox` property for a file selector box to –1 (true), most users of your application probably know the purpose you intended for that control box.

Figure 21.2 depicts examples of the four window types supported by Visual Basic.

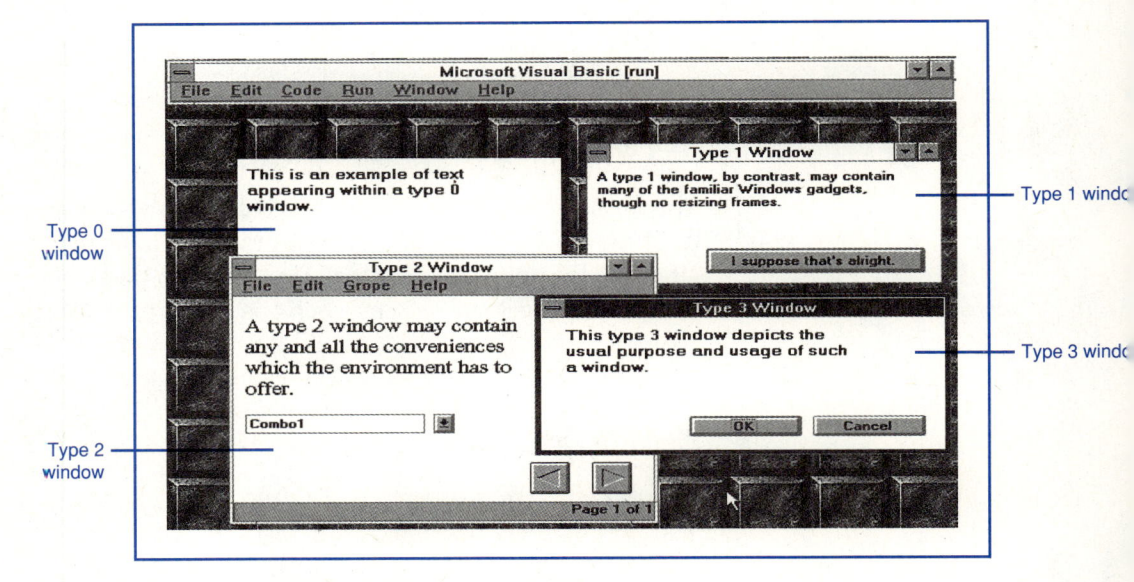

Figure 21.2. The four types of windows.

The *type 0* window is simply an unadorned box. It can contain controls, but such a window is generally not recognized by the user as a window. You can use type 0 for temporary messages, or "blurbs," which pop up on the screen for a moment and then disappear.

Window *type 1* may contain all the gadgets I've listed thus far, but does not have the surrounding window frame with which the user can resize the window. Type 1 may be necessary to display graphs on a fixed-coordinate system in which rescaling the image, or changing the proportion of x- to y-axis on that image, would render it meaningless or in some way reduce its information content. Type 1 is generally necessary when the window's size is critical to its operation. For instance, if the application was a calculator, you might not want the calculator panel to be resizable.

Window *type 2* in Figure 21.2 is the default window type for all forms created in the Visual Basic design area. Type 2 includes window frames with which the user can resize the form at any side or corner. *Type 3* windows are used by dialog boxes put forth by the Microsoft Windows environment. The size of a type 3 window is fixed. For that reason it contains no window frames or maximize and minimize buttons. It can, however, contain a control box that can operate as an optional `Cancel` button.

These four types should be distinguished from each other so the Visual Basic interpreter can have a better internal understanding of which *box* window belongs to which application. A dialog box is not generally considered a window by the user of the application; this is probably how it should be. The Microsoft Windows environment, however, as well as Visual Basic, sees every output region as a window. Therefore, it is helpful that windows intended to be *boxes* from the user's point of view be classified as such, so that the Windows environment can present such boxes to the screen in a more expedient fashion—in other words, so that each new dialog box is not interpreted by Windows as a newborn application.

The following is the property used to make distinctions between window types in Visual Basic.

Control.`BorderStyle` or *Form.*`BorderStyle` Property

The `.BorderStyle` property represents the internal classification of a form or control maintained by Visual Basic. As long as the name of the graphic object that is the antecedent of the property has been assigned as a form name (`.FormName`) or control name (`.ControlName`), the VB interpreter knows which set of categories—the form set or the control set—to apply to the graphic object.

The manipulability of a window or form on the Windows screen is indicated by its border style. Setting the style of a form's border with this property, therefore, simultaneously defines the operability—and thus, to some extent, the purpose—of that border.

Chapter 21 ◆ The Window

The purpose and function of graphic controls are already predefined, and are thus not affected through the setting of the `.BorderStyle` property.

The border styles recognized for controls and forms are defined in Table 21.1.

Table 21.1. Border styles for controls and forms.

Style	Definition
Control border styles	
0	No border
1	Fixed single (solid line)
Form border styles	
0	No border (totally confined to its present position)
1	Fixed single border (manipulable through use of window gadgets, although not resizable at run time)
2	Framed (resizable at run time)
3	Fixed double border (not resizable, although movable and closable using the control box)

Example

Here is a common use for a type 3 window. Suppose that on your main application form you have a button marked and called `Help`. You might need a dialog box to inquire about what the user needs help with. At design time, you've created an all-purpose dialog box having contents and purpose that can be defined at the time the user clicks a button in the main form. You have already given the dialog box the `.FormName` of `Dialog` and set its `.BorderStyle` to type 3, because you may not set this property at run time. Here is how the code for the `Help` button might look:

```
Sub Help_Click ()
Load Dialog
Dialog.HelpLine.Caption = "Enter a Help Subject:"
Dialog.Command1.Caption = "Index"
Dialog.Command2.Caption = "Find"
Dialog.Command3.Caption = "Close"
Dialog.Show
End Sub
```

The event this procedure is answering is a single click on the button called `Help`. The dialog is designed to be blank so the program can feed text into it for whatever purpose necessary and thus have a reusable dialog box. Notice that the text property-setting instructions fall between the instructions `Load Dialog` and `Dialog.Show`. When `Dialog` is loaded into memory (or whatever passes for memory at the time—see Chapter 20, "The Form"), the properties for all the controls are addressable by the program, although the form is not yet visible. When the textual properties are set, the dialog box can then be shown, and it will appear to have a specific purpose rather than a general one.

Notice also how `Dialog` is referred to by its `.FormName`, because this procedure belongs to a form outside of this one. In such cases where you refer to a graphic element of another form from within a form, each object is addressed by its "full name," using the syntax *Form.Object.Property*. This syntax is also used whenever a procedure within a general module addresses a graphic object within a form.

Now suppose you have another button on your main form which starts a process that searches for a certain instance of text in a document. Here's how the code for that button might appear:

```
Sub Search_Click ()
Load Dialog
Dialog.HelpLine.Caption = "Search for what text?"
Dialog.Command1.Caption = "Index"
Dialog.Command2.Caption = "Search"
Dialog.Command3.Caption = "Cancel"
Dialog.Show
End Sub
```

Chapter 21 ◆ The Window

This demonstrates another advantage to using generic forms and dialogs: the availability of transportable code. The preceding procedure is not that much different from the one before. For the most part, you needed to program the mechanics of the box display procedure only once. You could then use **C**opy and **P**aste from the **E**dit menu to move the content of procedure `Sub Help_Click ()` inside `Sub Search_Click ()`. Then you could edit the text and captions accordingly.

> **CAUTION:** Before these procedures can be executed again, the `Dialog` form must first be unloaded using `Unload Dialog`. The most convenient place for such an instruction to appear would be during an event such as `Cancel_Click ()`, which would be executed when the user exits the help or text search procedures with a button click. This way, when the instruction `Load Dialog` is executed again, a conflict does not occur.

Example

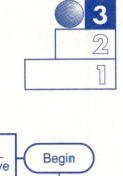

Here's an unusual type of control: Suppose in one corner of a form there is a clock or watch icon such as the WATCH02.ICO icon provided with Visual Basic. We want a procedure that displays the current time whenever the mouse pointer passes over this icon; the user doesn't necessarily have to click it, just make a sweeping maneuver over the icon. When the mouse pointer is over this area, the current time will "float" just next to it. Here's a procedure for such an odd but interesting control:

```
Sub Form_MouseMove (Button As Integer, Shift As Integer,
    x As Single, y As Single)
If x < 1035 And y < 1215 Then
    Clock.Top = MainForm.Top + x
    Clock.Left = MainForm.Left + y
    Clock.TimeNow.Caption = Time$
    Clock.Show
Else
    Clock.Hide
End If
End Sub
```

278

Visual Basic *By*
EXAMPLE

Here is the preceding procedure written in pseudocode:

Procedure awaiting a movement of the mouse pointer:
If the coordinates of the mouse pointer are within a given region, then
  The clock form's physical top coordinate is set to the mainform top coordinate plus the mouse pointer x coordinate.
  The clock form's physical left coordinate is set to the mainform left coordinate plus the mouse pointer y coordinate.
  The text of the clock form should be the current time.
  Now show the clock form.
Otherwise,
  Keep the clock form hidden.
End of condition.
End of procedure.

Figure 21.3 shows this procedure in action.

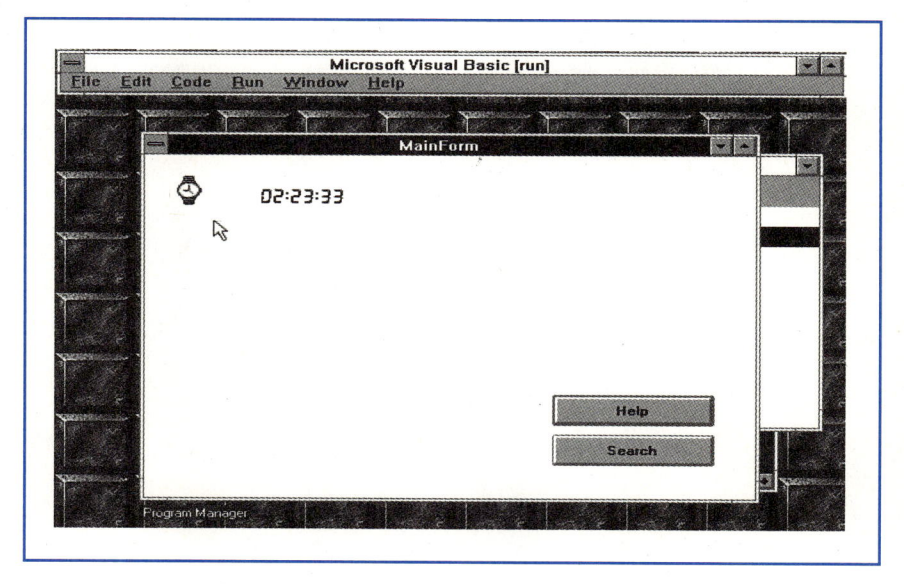

Figure 21.3. The automatic clock procedure.

279

In this procedure, `Clock.` is the name of a form with its `.BorderStyle` set to type 0 at design time. `Clock.` is just tall and wide enough to fit on one line, which is the one showing the current time. The watch icon appears at the upper-left corner of the main form. When the main form was invoked, its `Form_Load ()` procedure was executed; and somewhere within it is the instruction `Load Clock`, which brings the clock form into memory but does not display it on the screen.

The event that triggers execution here is `_MouseMove`; its procedure executes literally whenever the pointer is moved and the form containing the procedure is the active form. The event procedure, by nature, takes four parameters. The latter two of these parameters are the most important, because they return the mouse pointer position relative to the origin point of the *form* (not the whole screen) as integer variables `x` and `y`. When the position of the type 0 `Clock.` form is set, its coordinates will be relative to the *screen*, not to `MainForm.`, so the origin coordinates `.Top` and `.Left` of `MainForm` (1035, 1215) are added to the `x` and `y` values returned by the mouse pointer to obtain the physical screen coordinates where it will plot `Clock`.

This procedure loads the `Clock.` form but does not display it on-screen, yet its contents may still be set with the current time. `Clock.Show`, once it executes, instantly brings those contents to the screen. If the mouse pointer is not within the stated region, the `Else` portion of the clause is executed, and `Clock.Hide` will hide the form.

State Determination

In Chapter 20, "The Form," I discussed the many states a form or control might have with regard to memory. When in memory, a form might be maximized (given full rein of the screen), framed as a window among other windows, or minimized to an icon along the lower portion of the screen. Naturally, you might not want your application to plot anything urgent to a form that is currently minimized; so to determine what state the form's window is in at the moment, Visual Basic offers the following property:

Visual Basic *By*

EXAMPLE

Form.`WindowState` **Property**

The current setting of the `.WindowState` property is an integer that represents the operating state of the antecedent form as one of the following conditions:

- 0   Framed or bordered
- 1   Minimized; reduced to a representative icon
- 2   Maximized; unbordered, and given rein over the entire screen

Example

The `.WindowState` property can be used to manually set the operating state of a window from within a form or general module. Rarely would it be necessary to use this property to obtain information about the current form (the form in which this procedure resides). Because a form cannot await user events when it is in a minimized state, it is unnecessary for an event procedure to determine for itself whether its form is unminimized. However, suppose a routine, such as the one that plotted the type 0 clock form for the preceding procedure, appears within a general module. The context of a general module is such that it cannot automatically know the current operating state of any form in the procedure. As a result, if the routine appeared in a general module, it would need to be amended as follows:

```
If MainForm.WindowState <> 1 Then
    If x < 1035 And y < 1215 Then
        Clock.Top = MainForm.Top + x
        Clock.Left = MainForm.Left + y
        Clock.TimeNow.Caption = Time$
        Clock.Show
    Else
        Clock.Hide
    End If
End If
```

This way, if `MainForm.` is iconized, this routine will not execute.

281

Chapter 21 ◆ The Window

Summary

During the creation of a Visual Basic application, many of the properties of a form and its constituent controls are set at design time. If the value or content of these property settings is altered by the program, it is said that these properties are set at run time. Certain properties belonging to a form represent whether its window contains minimizing (reduction to an icon) and maximizing (expansion to full screen) buttons, as well as whether the form contains a control box in its upper-left corner. Whether these property settings are available for a particular form depends on the window type designated for that form.

A window's type is discernible by its border style. Window type 2, because it can have a `.WindowState` of both framed and maximized, is discernible by the resizing frames along its border. Type 2 is the default type in Visual Basic, and is generally used as an application's main window. A type 1 window is not resizable, and therefore has no resizing frames along its border; however, it contains all the other features of a type 2 window. A type 1 window is generally used for accessory or subsidiary programs such as calculators or control panels.

Window type 3 has a heavy border and provisions for a control box, although it has no minimize or maximize buttons. Its size is therefore fixed; as a result, type 3 windows are used most often for dialog boxes. Window type 0 has no window gadgets, provisions, or borders; as a result, this type is used for occasional or temporary text display. A window's type is represented within its `.BorderStyle` property, because the border of a window generally is representative of its purpose within the application.

The operating state of a window is represented by the `.WindowState` property. This property can be used to set the operating state of a form manually, although its usefulness in determining the current state through inference is generally restricted to procedures outside the context of a form.

Review Questions

State what would be the most convenient window type numbers to use as forms for the following purposes:

1. A variable-size graph-plotting area
2. A form made to resemble the control panel of a VCR or cassette tape player
3. A box that displays the definition of a word when that word is clicked
4. A window that warns the user that if he continues, vital data may be lost, and asks the user permission to proceed

22

Managing List Boxes

As I introduce you to the controls that comprise the standard repertoire of Visual Basic, I start by discussing the properties, methods, and events that are specific to list boxes. You see how items are added to a list box and how the operation of a list box differs from that of a combo box. Next, you examine Visual Basic's special provisions for directory-oriented list boxes.

Gaining Control

A *control* is a graphic object used for data acquisition and display.

Almost every Windows application uses the same standard set of visual controls. The fact that applications are by nature different from each other, and that the choices one makes when using such applications are therefore differentiated, should not mean that the act of making choices or selections is different from application to application. A *control* is a graphic object placed on a form specifically for the acquisition and display of data in a manner with which the user may easily become familiar.

A list should be identifiable as a list; similarly, states or conditions should be easily set with buttons. One objective of programming should be determining how many nonstandard selections or

285

choices can be represented in the program through familiar, standardized controls, and to what extent operations should be graphically represented in unique, nonfamiliar ways if such ways are more efficient.

Visual Basic gives programmers easy access to the most standard controls found within, and shared between, Windows applications. Through extensions to Visual Basic, it is possible to increase the amount and type of controls supported within a VB application; however, this chapter concentrates on the controls that are supported by the standard Visual Basic package.

List Boxes and Combo Boxes

What distinguishes the use of a drop-down list box from that of a drop-down menu is that the menu is generally used to present *command* selections, whereas the list box is used to present choices of items, settings, or conditions. The chosen item within a list is displayed within the single uppermost text line of the list box that is permanently visible. A *combo box* is a version of the text box control that includes some extra device for displaying or making choices that may allow the user to type his choice within the text line, especially in cases where the choice is not available in the list.

When a standard list box is placed onto a form at design time, by default the VB interpreter gives it the name `List`*n*, where *n* is the accession number of the list box; similarly, the default name given a combo box is `Combo`*n*. There is only one item in the VB toolbox for drawing both list boxes and combo boxes; the two items are actually distinguished with a property setting.

Combo`.Style` Property

The .Style property is set to an integer which denotes the appearance of a list on the form. Its possible settings are as follows:

0   A drop-down combo box with a down arrow button, having a list that is displayed only when that button is clicked. Its choice field is editable with the cursor.

Visual Basic *By*
EXAMPLE

1. A standard combo box without a down arrow button, having a list that is always displayed. Its choice field can be edited with the cursor.

2. A drop-down list box with a down arrow button, having a choice field that cannot be edited.

A list box begins its life on the form with no items in it. It is up to the source code to feed items into the list one by one.

.AddItem   Method

Syntax:

listname.AddItem *text$* [, *index%*]

.RemoveItem   Method

Syntax:

listname.RemoveItem *index%*

The .AddItem method places the textual contents of *text$* into the list or combo box that has the control name *listname*. By default, the text is placed at the end of the list. Optionally, the place of the new item in the list can be specified by number within *index%*. Items in a list are counted or indexed starting with 0; the value of *index%* must be no greater than the number of items in the list minus 1. You cannot add a string of items to a list from a text file.

The .RemoveItem method eliminates the item addressed by *index%* from the specified list or combo box.

Chapter 22 ◆ Managing List Boxes

Example

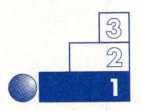

Assume that as a test you've placed a standard list box on a form. Have one button add an item to this list and another remove that item from it. Here is the code for both button-click procedures:

```
Sub Command1_Click ()
List1.AddItem "Test", 0
End Sub

Sub Command2_Click ()
List1.RemoveItem 0
End Sub
```

> **NOTE:** If your program has a cluster of .AddItem instructions in a sequence, and none of them specify a list index, the VB interpreter knows by default to add one item to the list after the other starting with item 0. If, however, you choose to specify index numbers directly with the .AddItem method, be sure you don't make any holes in the list, as you would if you attempt to add item 4 to the end of a two-item list. An error is generated upon such attempts.

When there are not more items assigned to a standard list box than can be displayed, the list box appears as a rectangle. At the moment the list box overflows, the VB interpreter adds a scroll bar to the right of the box automatically. A combo box at rest on the form appears as a single line of text with a down arrow button beside it. The list that drops below this line follows the same rules of display as the standard list box.

Example

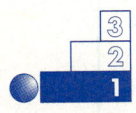

In the Expressor program I've used periodically throughout this book as an example application, a combo box appears with which the user selects a formula to be solved. Here is how the formula names are added to this list:

288

Visual Basic By EXAMPLE

```
Sub Form_Load ()
CalcList.AddItem "Surface Area of RC Cylinder"
CalcList.AddItem "Volume of RC Cylinder"
CalcList.AddItem "Zone Area of Sphere"
CalcList.AddItem "Force of Earth/Body Attraction"
CalcList.AddItem "Doppler Shift Transmitted Freq."
    .
    .
    .
End Sub
```

You will most likely want to place `.AddItem` instructions in the `Form_Load ()` procedure, because *seeding* the list is considered stage-setting for the form, and `Form_Load ()` is the stage-setting procedure that is automatically executed when the form is entered into memory.

Example

Thus far in the Expressor, I've developed five formulas for this application. If you had 105 instead, the repetitive invocations of `CalcList.AddItem` might become tiresome. Conceivably in the future, you could place the text descriptions for each formula within a string array and add each string to the list in sequence, as follows:

```
Sub Form_Load ()
For place = 0 To frmulas - 1
    CalcList.AddItem frmula$(place)
Next place
    .
    .
    .
End Sub
```

Here the variables that refer to Expressor formulas do not contain the letter *o* so that their names will not be confused with the keyword `Formula`.

When an item is added to a list, it is considered a property of that list, and therefore its contents and their aspects are addressed with property terms.

289

Chapter 22 ◆ Managing List Boxes

Object.List **Property**

The .List property is accessed in the manner of a control array; the contents of a list item at a particular index are addressed as .List(*index*). The property can be treated in the same manner as an array variable. Thus if a place in the list has been apportioned using .AddItem, the text contents of the list at an index can be assigned to a string variable as follows:

string$ = [*object*.]List(*index*)

For example:

ret$ = CalcList.List(5)

Likewise, the text contents of a list at an index can be changed by reversing the order of the equation:

[*object*.]List(*index*) = *string*$

Object.ListCount **Property**

The .ListCount property is always set to the number of items currently inhabiting the antecedent list or combo box; thus a list box with five items has a .ListCount of 5. The value of .ListCount - 1 is therefore the index of the last item in the list. This property cannot be set by the programmer.

Object.ListIndex **Property**

The .ListIndex property contains the index of the previously chosen item in the list. A choice can also be forced using this property, by assigning an index value to it. If no item is chosen, .ListIndex is set to –1 (not to be confused with the Boolean value for True in this context).

Example

In the Expressor, I used the `.ListIndex` property to determine which formula was chosen:

```
Sub ApplyFormula_Click ()
For in = 0 To 4
p(in) = Val(param(in).text)
Next in
ndx = CalcList.ListIndex + 1
If ndx = -1 Then GoTo The_end
On ndx GoTo f1, f2, f3, f4, f5
.
.
.
End Sub
```

Here the value of `CalcList.ListIndex + 1` is assigned to variable `ndx`. I added 1 so that the first formula addressed would be item 1 rather than item 0.

Visual Basic allows for items in a list box or combo box to be automatically sorted in alphabetical order, with digits falling before letters.

List.Sorted or *Combo*.Sorted Property

The `.Sorted` property denotes whether automatic sorting for a list box or combo box is set to true (–1) or false (0). This property can be set only at design time. When the `.Sorted` property for a list is set to true, the sort takes place *before* the list box is shown; sorting does not continue throughout the duration of the program. Therefore, if an `.AddItem` method is invoked that includes a specific index number, the item will appear in the list at the designated place, although this may mean that the list becomes unsorted. The value of the `.Sorted` property, however, is not affected by any addition made to the list at any place, regardless of whether the list actually does become unsorted.

Chapter 22 ◆ Managing List Boxes

Example

Here's a sample application with the sole purpose of testing your ability to manage lists. In the following test application, your form is a drop-down, noneditable combo box having a .Sorted property that is preset to true at design time. Clicking on a button adds an item to the list for this combo box, but the item will be out of order. As stated previously, this does not change the .Sorted property for this box, so you need a routine to tell you whether the list is actually in order.

Figure 22.1 shows this test procedure in its running state.

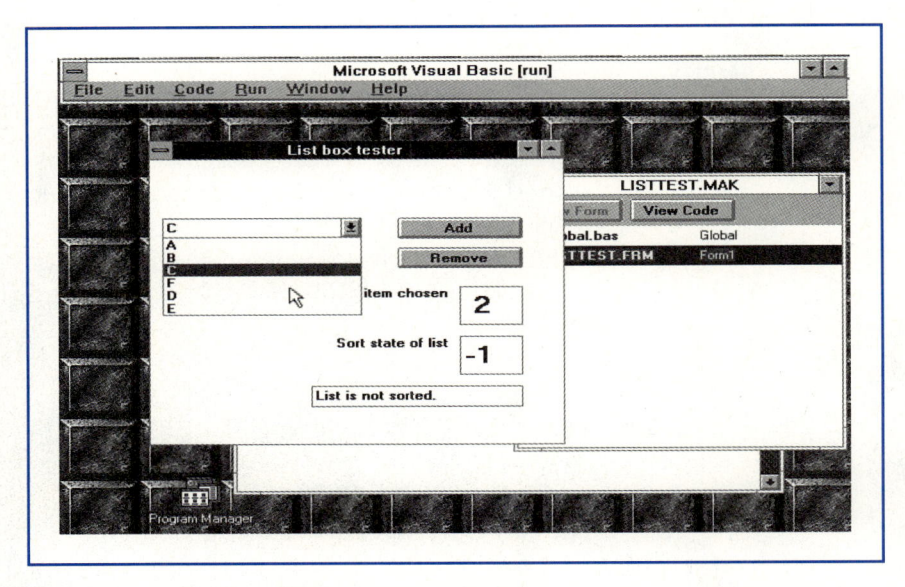

Figure 22.1. The combo box test procedure.

	PROJECT NAME	CONSTITUENT FILES
List Test Application	LISTTEST.MAK	LISTTEST.FRM

Object type	Property	Setting
Form	.Left	1050
	.Top	1200
	.Width	5130
	.Height	4725
	.Caption	List box tester
	.BorderStyle	1

292

Visual Basic By EXAMPLE

Object type	Property	Setting
Combo box	.Style .Sorted	2 True
Button	.Caption	Add
Button	.Caption	Remove
Text box	.CtlName .Text	Chosen (blank)
Text box	.CtlName .Text	SortState (blank)
Text box	.CtlName .Text	Message (blank)
Label	.Caption .Alignment	List item chosen 1 - Right Justify
Label	.Caption .Alignment	Sort state of list 1 - Right Justify

```
Sub Form_Load ()
Combo1.AddItem "E"
Combo1.AddItem "C"
Combo1.AddItem "A"
Combo1.AddItem "B"
Combo1.AddItem "D"
End Sub

Sub Command1_Click ()
Combo1.AddItem "F", 3
SortState.Text = Str$(Combo1.Sorted)
End Sub

Sub Command2_Click ()
Combo1.RemoveItem 3
SortState.Text = Str$(Combo1.Sorted)
End Sub

Sub Combo1_Click ()
```

293

```
Chosen.Text = Str$(Combo1.ListIndex)
SortState.Text = Str$(Combo1.Sorted)
End Sub

Sub Combo1_DropDown ()
For count = 1 To Combo1.ListCount - 1
    this_char$ = Left$(Combo1.List(count), 1)
    last_char$ = Left$(Combo1.List(count - 1), 1)
    If Asc(this_char$) < Asc(last_char$) Then
        Message.Text = "List is not sorted."
        Exit Sub
    End If
Next count
Message.Text = ""
End Sub
```

In the procedure `Form_Load ()`, five items are loaded into the list, obviously not in alphabetical order. When the procedure starts and `Form1` appears, clicking on the combo box's down arrow results in a display of a sorted list: A ¦ B ¦ C ¦ D ¦ E. The procedure `Command1_Click()` adds one item manually to this list, and certainly out of order, resulting in the following list: A ¦ B ¦ C ¦ F ¦ D ¦ E. `Command2_Click ()`, in turn, removes item number 3 (the fourth item) from the list. Both buttons place the textual form of the value of combo box property `.Sorted` in the text box `SortState`.

Procedure `Combo_Click ()` is executed whenever the user clicks on the area of the list. In other words, the event itself does not pay attention to the specific list item chosen, although that item may be determined through the procedure. In the case of this procedure, the `.ListIndex` of the chosen item is placed into the text box `Chosen`. and the value of Visual Basic's `.Sorted` property is placed within `SortState`. When F is added to the list out of order, the contents of `SortState` remain -1; the interpreter still thinks the list is sorted. You need to be able to tell when this list is in order and when it's not.

Here is procedure `Combo1_Click ()` written as pseudocode:

Visual Basic *By* EXAMPLE

> *Procedure for when the user clicks a list
>   item in the combo box:*
> *Place the alphanumeric form of the index of the
>   chosen item in the appropriate text box.*
> *Place the alphanumeric form of the state of the
>   .Sorted property in its appropriate text box.*
> *End of procedure.*

This is the purpose of procedure `Combo1_DropDown ()`. The event `_DropDown` occurs whenever the down arrow button of the combo box is clicked. This procedure is executed at that time, and renders a message to text box `Message`. if the contents of the list are not in order. The procedure starts a loop counting from index number 1 (the *second* item in the list) to the value of the `.ListCount` for this list—the number of items in it—minus 1, having a result that is the final index number for the list.

Pseudocode for the procedure `Combo1_DropDown ()` is as follows:

> *Procedure for when combo box 1 drops its list:*
> *Start counting from the index number of the second item
>   to that of the next-to-last item in the combo box.*
>   *Extract the first character of this list item.*
>   *Now extract the first character of the list item
>   just preceding it.*
>   *If this character falls beneath the order of the
>   last character in alphabetic sequence, then*
>   *Tell the user this list is not sorted.*
>   *Get out of this procedure.*
>   *End of condition.*
> *Count the next item.*
> *Clear the text box.*
> *End of procedure.*

Variable `count` is keeping count of the index number which the loop is currently processing. The first text character of this item is compared to the first character of the *previous* list item to determine whether it falls in sequence before the previous item, after that item, or is equivalent to that item. The function `Asc()` is used to derive the ASCII (actually the ANSI) code number for the extracted characters. The code numbers are then compared to each other. If the next

295

number in sequence is less than the previous one, the letter of the next item in sequence must fall before the previous one. The list must therefore be out of order. In such a case, a message to that effect is delivered to text box `Message.`, and the procedure is immediately exited because its purpose is served. If the loop completes itself totally, the list must therefore be in order. So the text contents of `Message.` are set to blank. The result of all this is that `Message.` blanks itself when the list is sorted.

The preceding procedure used a new event, which I introduce here.

*Combo*_DropDown **Property**

The `_DropDown` event is recognized whenever the user clicks the down arrow of the antecedent combo box. This event is reserved exclusively for such controls.

Taking on a Load

Three of the buttons found within the Visual Basic toolbox are dedicated to one relatively infrequent—although very important—programming purpose: the production of a file selector box. Such a window (most likely type 3) would be used to choose a file to load into memory, or to designate the directory location and file name of a file being saved to disk.

As you've seen already, three special list box graphic devices are available from the Visual Basic toolbar. The following properties pertain specifically to these devices:

Drive.Drive **Property**

The `Drive.Drive` property (this is not a typographical error) is set to the text of the selected item in the antecedent drive list box, the name of which need not necessarily be `Drive`. The format of this text is as follows:

```
drive:\ [volume_name]
```

The preceding is *not* the syntax of an instruction, but is instead the format of the textual setting of the .Drive property. The full volume name attributed to the drive device at the time it was formatted appears between square brackets following the device identifier.

Dir.Path **Property**

The .Path property is set to the text of the selected item in the antecedent directory list box. The format of this text is as follows:

`drive:\[subdirectory[\subdirectory. . . ]\]`

The text of the .Path property reflects the subdirectory path where a file resides, or where a search is being conducted for a file. The text does not contain the file name for a file.

File.FileName **Property**

The .FileName property is set to the text of the selected item in the antecedent file list box. The format of this text is as follows:

`filename.ext`

The text reflects only the name of the file itself with its three-letter extension, regardless of the location of that file.

File.Pattern **Property**

The .Pattern property is set to the search pattern, against which each file for the antecedent file list box is matched, to determine whether that file should appear in the list. Such a pattern can and usually does contain wildcard characters such as * and ? to stand for any number of characters or a single character, respectively.

Chapter 22 ◆ Managing List Boxes

Natural Selection

Our final example for this chapter uses all three categories of directory-oriented list boxes to construct a rudimentary yet all-purpose file selector box. It will be used as a form module that can be added to any VB project that requires a file selector. The reusable form we're aiming for appears as Figure 22.2.

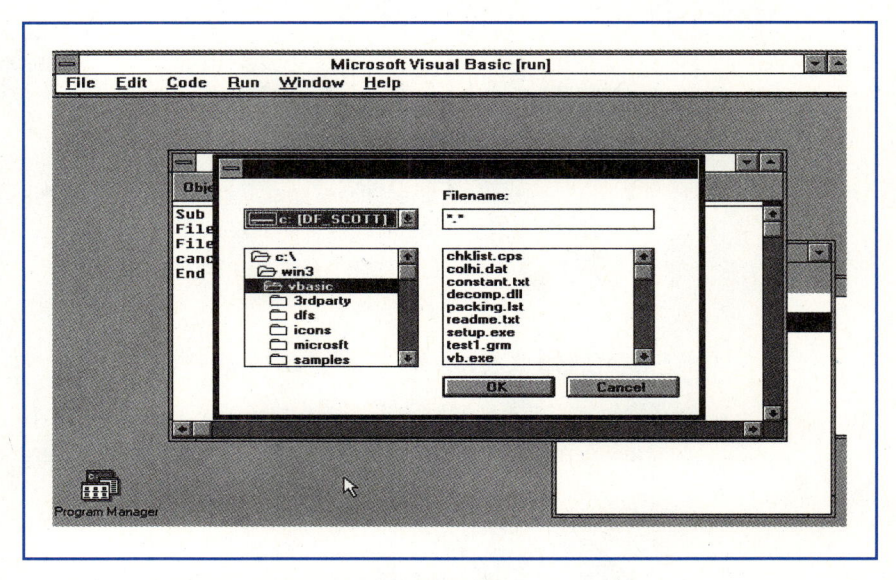

Figure 22.2. The sample file selector box.

Here is the listing for the generic file selector form:

	PROJECT NAME	*CONSTITUENT FILES*
File Selector Box	SELECTOR.MAK	SELECTOR.FRM

Object type	*Property*	*Setting*
Frame	.FormName	Selector
	.Caption	(blank)
	.BorderStyle	3

298

Object type	Property	Setting
Drive List Box	.Left	300
	.Top	450
	.Width	2115
	.Height	315
Path List Box	.Left	300
	.Top	1050
	.Width	2115
	.Height	1815
File List Box	.Left	2700
	.Top	1050
	.Width	2565
	.Height	1785
Text Box	.CtlName	Filename
	.Text	(blank)
Label	.Caption	Filename:
Button	.CtlName	OK
	.Caption	OK
Button	.CtlName	Cancel
	.Caption	Cancel

For the Selector to work cooperatively with other projects, you need to add the following line to the global module of the cooperating application:

```
Global TargetFile$, cancl As Integer
```

The remainder of the Selector's listing is as follows:

```
Sub Form_Load ()
File1.Pattern = "*.*"
Filename.Text = File1.Pattern
cancl = 0
End Sub
```

The initial search pattern is set to *.* (all file names), and the text box called `Filename.` reflects this patterning. Global variable `cancl` is a flag denoting whether the `Cancel` button is clicked, so the program that called the file selector will know if it is not supposed to look for a file name returned by the form. Because this is a global variable, it needs to be reset when the form starts.

```
Sub Drive1_Change ()
Dir1.path = Drive1.Drive
ChDrive Drive1.Drive
End Sub

Sub Dir1_Change ()
File1.path = Dir1.path
File1_Click
End Sub
```

The _Change event occurs in the preceding cases whenever the current contents of the choice lines in the drive and directory list boxes, respectively, are altered, whether by way of mouse or keyboard. Procedure `Drive1_Change ()` is invoked whenever the current choice in the drive list is changed; subsequently, it has the directory list alter itself to reflect the new drive being scanned, and tells DOS to change scanned drives as well.

```
Sub File1_Click ()
Filename.Text = File1.Filename
End Sub

Sub File1_DblClick ()
OK_Click
End Sub
```

When a file in the file list is clicked once, its name is entered into the `Filename.` text field. The user may then click OK to choose the file. If it is double-clicked, that means the file is chosen, and OK need not be clicked. We only want to write the choice procedure once, however, so we have procedure `File1_DblClick ()` branch to the following procedure:

Visual Basic By EXAMPLE

```
Sub OK_Click ()
pth$ = Dir1.Path
If Right$(pth$, 1) = "\" Then
    Filename.Text = pth$ + File1.Filename
Else
    Filename.Text = pth$ + "\" + File1.Filename
End If
TargetFile$ = Filename.Text
Unload Selector
End Sub
```

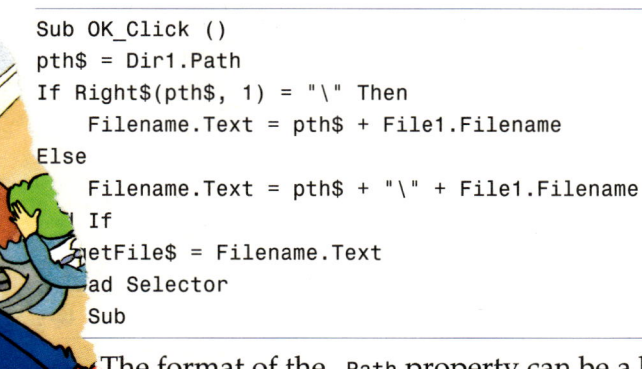

The format of the `.Path` property can be a bit confusing. If the current path being scanned is the root directory, the backslash appears at the end of the path, as in `C:\`. However, if the path is a subdirectory, the final backslash is omitted. Therefore, in order for the code to properly assess the location and file name returned by the Selector form, a backslash must be added to the path if the path doesn't have one yet. The file name is returned to the form that invoked Selector, within the global variable `TargetFile$`.

```
Sub Cancel_Click ()
TargetFile$ = ""
Unload Selector
End Sub
```

This procedure is executed in case the user clicks Cancel. The `cancl` procedure can't write out *cancel*, because that is a reserved word in Visual Basic. It is set to 1 and the file name return variable `TargetFile$` is set to a null string.

Here's how to operate this selector: The current list of accessible logical drives is made available from the drive combo box, which is operated like any drop-down combo box. To scan a different subdirectory, double-click the name of the directory in the directory list box. To close the subdirectory currently being scanned, click any other directory in the list. To choose a file, either click its name in the file list and click OK, or double-click its

301

It's Time for a Change

An extremely important event appears in a few of the preceding procedures: _Change.

*Object*_Change Event

The _Change event occurs whenever the contents of the antecedent graphic object are changed for any reason, whether by the program or by the user.

Some offshoots of the _Change event are reserved for directory list boxes and file list boxes. They are covered in the next few sections.

*Dir*_PathChange Event

The _PathChange event occurs whenever the path currently being scanned to obtain the contents of the antecedent directory list box is changed for any reason, whether by the program or by the user.

*File*_PatternChange Event

The _PatternChange event occurs whenever the pattern currently being applied against the current path to obtain matching files for the antecedent file list box is changed for any reason, whether by the program or by the user.

Summary

Visual Basic maintains provisions for list boxes as well as combo boxes, which are like list boxes except that they use extra graphic devices such as down-arrow buttons and often use editable text areas. The style of a combo box is set using the .Style property reserved for combo boxes.

Visual Basic *By* EXAMPLE

Items are added to and removed from a list or combo box using the `.AddItem` and `.RemoveItem` methods, respectively. When added to a list, the contents of a list item can be addressed using the property `.List`, generally in the manner of a control array. The property `.ListCount` registers the number of items currently inhabiting a list. The property `.ListIndex` returns the index or accession number of the previously chosen item from the list. Items in a list can be sorted in alphabetical and numerical order before they are displayed by presetting the `.Sorted` property for that list to –1 (true).

Visual Basic reserves three special types of list boxes for use in file selectors: drive or device lists, directory or path lists, and file lists. The VB interpreter fills these lists automatically with the current directory information gathered from DOS.

Review Questions

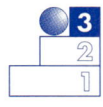

1. Assume it is 1959 and you have compiled a list of the United States within any kind of standard list box. You have 48 items in this list, and suddenly you receive word that two more items are to be added to the list. The `.Sorted` property for your list box is set to –1, and the list box is currently visible on screen. When you use `.AddItem` to add Alaska and Hawaii to your list box, *without* expressing any index number, what are the indices for your two new states?

2. Assume it is 1998 and you have compiled a list of the United States within any kind of standard list box. Columbia (formerly the District of Columbia) and Puerto Rico are comfortable in their new positions as states of the union, and the President has signed the executive order now officially making Guam a state as well. Sewing a 53-star flag with geometric symmetry is difficult enough; your job is to add Guam to your official list box of states. Assuming the `.Sorted` property for your list is set to –1 and the list box is not yet loaded into memory, what will the index be for the list entry for Guam?

303

Chapter 22 ◆ Managing List Boxes

Review Exercises

3 2 1 Borrowing some source code from the procedures used in this chapter, write a procedure that informs the user whether the list is sorted whenever a button is clicked.

23

Options and Scroll Bars

In this chapter I split the subjects down the middle. The first half of the chapter deals with the use of options and check boxes within a form, whereas the second half deals with the implementation of independent scroll bars. In the *Options* section, you learn more about control arrays and how a set of related controls can be directed using one source code procedure. In the *Scroll Bars* section, you see how scroll bars are best used to designate value shifts, ranges, and regions of an object being viewed.

Grouping Controls Within a Form

Setting an option dot beside a set of options in a form can be compared to choosing an item from a list. An options set generally offers the user a smaller degree of choice than a list box offers. Furthermore, the list of options in a set is always fixed.

What distinguishes a set of options from a set of check boxes is that multiple check boxes can be set or checked, whereas only one option dot in a set can be checked at a time.

> Multiple *check boxes* may be checked at one time.

305

Chapter 23 ◆ Options and Scroll Bars

Option buttons can only be set one at a time.

The Visual Basic interpreter considers all the option dots in a set to be related elements. If no subdivisions of the form exist, and if one option dot is set, another option dot elsewhere on the form is reset. Check boxes are not so interrelated, because several boxes in a form can be checked at one time regardless of subdivisions. A check box is generally used to set the binary state of some aspect or function of the program.

Figure 23.1 shows an accessory form for an application, with three option dots on the left and three check boxes on the right. Here you can see how their functions are distinguished; you can save a file in only one format, so only one option should be set for the `Save as:` group. Any or all of the boxes in the group on the right side can be set.

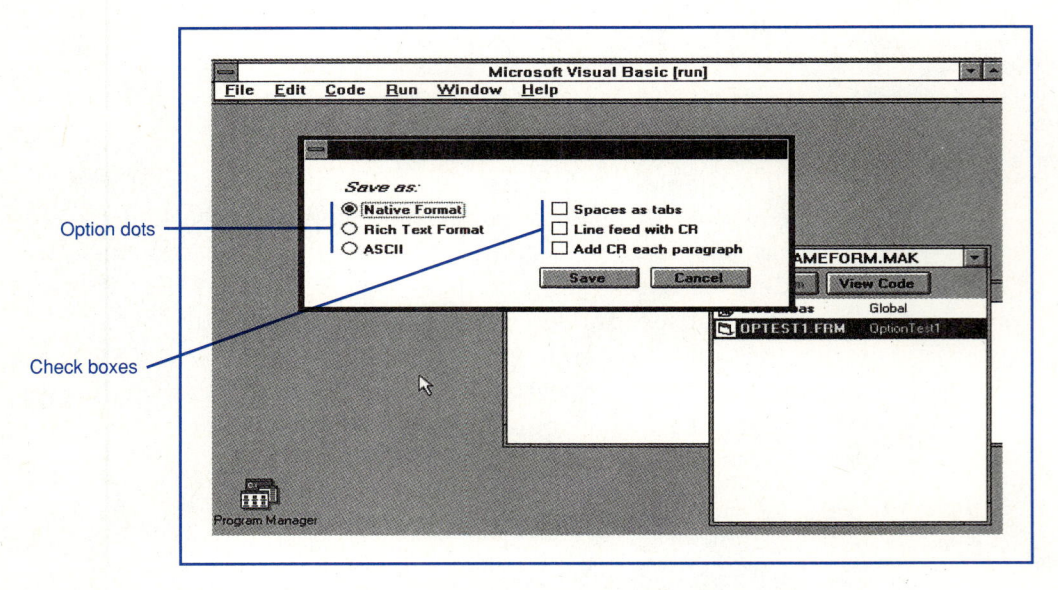

Figure 23.1. Option dots and check boxes compared.

A *frame* is used to separate groups of options from other parts of a form.

You can subdivide a form with a frame, wherein groups of options that are to be divided from other options in the form can be placed. A *frame* is a subdivision of a form which divides groupings of elements, such as options, from groups in other frames and groups elsewhere on the form.

306

Visual Basic *By* EXAMPLE

Adding a frame to a form is, in a sense, like putting a box within a box and having the "child" box be subordinate to the "parent" box. From the point of view of the programmers of Visual Basic, this isn't like placing a child within a parent; it *is* placing a child within a parent. For the controls placed within a frame to appear to belong together, they must fit entirely within that frame.

In order for a control to belong to a frame, or rather to be the "child" of that frame, it must be placed within that frame directly from the toolbox. A control cannot be drawn onto the main portion of a form, be dragged later into the area of a frame, and then *belong* to that frame. When a control belongs to a frame and the frame is moved, the control moves with it. When a control does not belong to a frame and the frame is moved, the control stays behind. Figure 23.2 shows the option dots from the preceding form recreated as part of a frame.

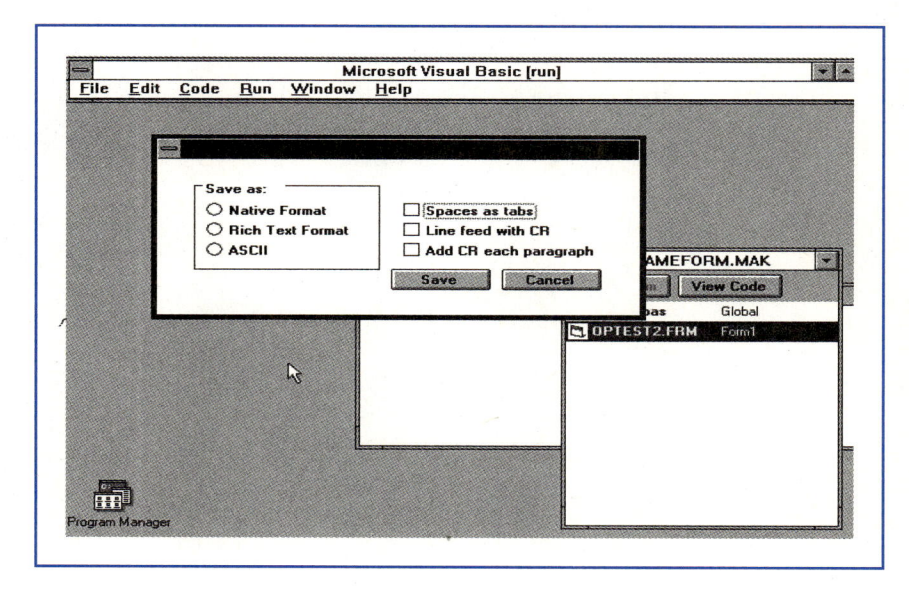

Figure 23.2. **To frame or not to frame.**

Now you can add another set of option dots to the form or another frame without those options being interrelated to those within this frame.

307

Chapter 23 ◆ Options and Scroll Bars

.Value is the property used to determine whether an option dot is set or a check box is checked.

Object.Value Property

The .Value property has different purposes with respect to the following types of antecedent objects: Check, Command, Option, and Scroll. In the case in which .Value refers to option dots, the setting of that property is true or false, reflecting whether the option is set or reset, respectively. In the case of check boxes, .Value is set to 0, 1, or 2—not true or false—reflecting whether the antecedent box is reset, set, or dimmed (made unavailable), respectively. In cases of buttons, .Value is set to true or false depending on whether the button is being pressed. In cases of scroll bars, .Value returns the relative position of the scroll box along the coordinate scale set for the antecedent scroll bar.

Keep in mind how the scroll bar uses .Value, because you test this property with scroll bars later in this chapter.

Example

Suppose you have a string variable in the preceding form which is set to a space when the check box marked Spaces as tabs is set. Here's a routine that assigns the proper value to the string variable:

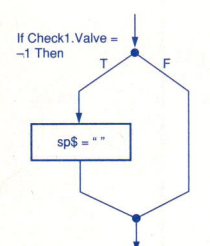

```
If Check1.Value = -1 Then
    sp$ = " "
End If
```

If the box is not checked, sp$ is left alone.

Example

Suppose the program determines which option dot from the preceding frame was set. Execution branches to any of three procedures as a result of setting the option dot and clicking the Save button. Here is a procedure that might determine how branching takes place:

308

Visual Basic By
EXAMPLE

```
Sub Save_Click ()
Select Case -1
    Case Option1.Value
        Standard_Save
    Case Option2.Value
        RTF_Save
    Case Option3.Value
        ASCII_Save
End Select
.
.
.
End Sub
```

Here's the above example written in pseudocode:

Procedure for clicking the Save option dot:
In case any of the following options are set:
  For the first option,
    Execute the procedure for standard saving.
  For the second option,
    Execute the procedure for RTF conversion.
  For the third option,
    Execute the procedure for ASCII conversion.
End of cases.
  .
  .
  .
End of procedure.

The `Select Case` clause compares all three `.Value` properties to logical truth (–1) for equality. Only one of these values is set to –1 because these are, after all, values for option dots. There can be, therefore, only one procedure branch.

309

Chapter 23 ◆ Options and Scroll Bars

Grouping Controls Within the Source Code

A *control array* is a set of similar, related controls that are referenced as a group.

At present, the VB interpreter sees each option dot and check box in the preceding form as a separate, individual control. Each dot and each box, therefore, has its own event procedure associated with it. In cases of options that are closely related to each other, it might be more convenient if the code for an options group could be reduced to one procedure. You can accomplish this by assigning each control in the options or check box set as part of a group that is addressable by one collective name, in the manner of an array variable. Such a group is called a *control array*. A control array is a set of similar, related controls in a form that are referenced together as a group, and that have an operation that is jointly defined by a single procedure in the source code.

In a control array, the graphic objects are grouped together and given a collective name, such as `Option1()`. The parentheses are included to distinguish that the control name refers to an array. A control array should consist of a group of graphic objects having nearly identical appearances and somewhat related purposes.

To design a control array:

1. Plot a control to the form that acts as a model for all the controls in the array. You can edit the textual contents of each control independently later.

2. Indicate the control and select **C**opy from the **E**dit menu.

3. To add the second control to the array, select **P**aste from the **E**dit menu. A dialog box appears.

4. This dialog box asks if you wish to create a control array (you'd think it would have guessed by now). Respond to the dialog box by clicking OK. The control array is now officially in existence.

5. The second element in the array appears in the upper-left corner of the form and is surrounded with indicator nodes. Drag this control to its proper position on the form. Its contents are identical to those of the copied control; at this time you may choose to edit the `.Text` or `.Caption` property for this control.

6. To add more elements to the array, select **Paste** from the **Edit** menu and repeat the preceding step.

7. To edit the `_Click` event procedure for this control array, double-click any control in the form.

Example

You can apply the control array procedure to the previous `Select Case` clause, so that the procedure branch can be made at the moment any of the option dots are set rather than waiting for the `Save` button to be pressed. Here's the revised procedure:

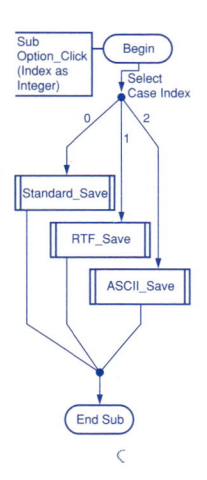

```
Sub Option_Click (Index as Integer)
Select Case Index
    Case 0
        Standard_Save
    Case 1
        RTF_Save
    Case 2
        ASCII_Save
End Select
End Sub
```

The event procedure is responded to as if all three controls in the array together constituted one big control called `Option`. When the Visual Basic interpreter creates a framework for the event procedure, it automatically places `Index as Integer` between the parentheses as both a declaration and a passed parameter. The index of the set option dot is returned within the variable `Index`. The `Select Case` clause now compares `Index` to the three possible values (0, 1, and 2) for equality. Because the option set has to be clicked for this procedure to execute, one of the branches must be made.

Scroll Bars

It's time to switch subjects and talk about scroll bars. In Visual Basic, the relative position of the scroll box between the two arrows is represented by a coordinate value stored within the property

`Scroll.Value`. Figure 23.3 depicts how the coordinate system of a horizontal scroll bar works.

Figure 23.3. The breakdown of a scroll bar.

The coordinate system of a scroll bar exists without regard to the scroll bar's current size. Consider each scroll bar as a number line extending from one integer (generally 0) to another. The minimum and maximum values along this line exist at the left and right, or top and bottom, points on this line. The number values at these points are assigned to properties `.Min` and `.Max`. There are therefore `Scroll.Max - Scroll.Min` coordinate points along this line. Again, the pixel length of a scroll bar has nothing to do with its coordinate system.

In the next few sections, I cover the property terms that can be attributed exclusively to a scroll bar.

Scroll`.Max` **and** *Scroll*`.Min` **Properties**

The `.Max` and `.Min` properties of a scroll bar are set to the maximum and minimum coordinate values of the scroll box along the bar. These properties can be set to any integer between –32,768 and 32,767, inclusive, as long as `.Max` remains greater than `.Min`. When set, the length of the scroll bar is divided into `.Max - .Min` intervals. Moving the scroll box along the bar thus sets `Scroll.Value` equal to the interval where the box currently rests.

Scroll`.SmallChange` **and** *Scroll*`.LargeChange` **Properties**

The value of `.SmallChange` represents the number of intervals the scroll box traverses along the bar when one of the arrow buttons is clicked on in the direction of that arrow. The value of `.LargeChange`, similarly, represents the number of intervals the scroll box traverses along the bar when the user clicks between the scroll box and one of the arrow buttons in the direction of that arrow. This zone of the scroll bar is often called the *paging area*.

Now that we know some things not only about arrays but how items within a range are represented on-screen, let's make some amendments to the NameForm application I introduced back in Chapter 8. The revised application can store lists of names within arrays, and uses a scroll bar as a device for selecting individual names from the array range. The revised NameForm form appears as shown in Figure 23.4.

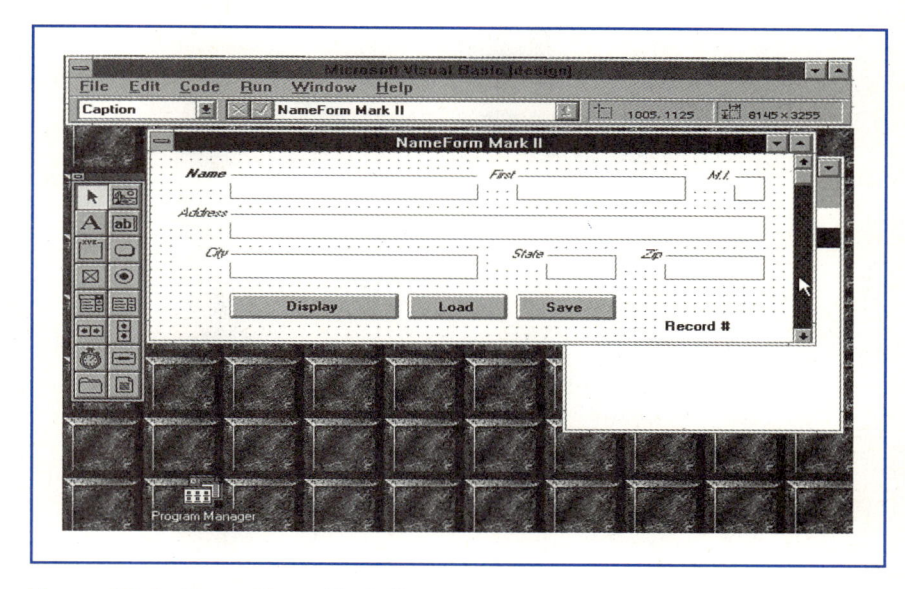

Figure 23.4. NameForm Mark II.

Here are the amended procedures for the revised application:

	PROJECT NAME	*CONSTITUENT FILES*
Name-only Record Entry System Mark II	NAMEFRM2.MAK	NAMEFRM2.FRM

General Module:

```
Option Base 1
Dim LstName$(1000), FrstName$(1000), MdInit$(1000), Adress$(1000),
    Cty$(1000), Stat$(1000), Zp$(1000)
Dim RecordNo As Integer
```

Chapter 23 ◆ Options and Scroll Bars

The first statement here, `Option Base 1`, resets the system for the sake of this program, so that the first address of an array is 1 and not 0. Notice the string array variable names chosen are each one letter removed from their text box equivalents on the form; this is because variable names and object names may not match. On the lowest line, `RecordNo` is dimensioned as a unit integer to be `Shared` throughout all procedures, not as an array variable. This is part of an alternate syntax which is new to Visual Basic.

```
Sub RecordShown_Change ()
RecordNo = RecordShown.Value
If RecordNo < 1 Then
    RecordNo = 1
End If
Reg$ = "Record #" + Str$(RecordNo)
Register.Caption = Reg$
LastName.Text = LstName$(RecordNo)
FirstName.Text = FrstName$(RecordNo)
MidInit.Text = MdInit$(RecordNo)
Address.Text = Adress$(RecordNo)
City.Text = Cty$(RecordNo)
State.Text = Stat$(RecordNo)
Zip.Text = Zp$(RecordNo)
End Sub
```

The key variable here is `RecordNo`; it ties all the elements of a record together. If you consider the data generated by this program to be a database, then `RecordNo` would be the sole relation in this base. The key instruction here is `RecordNo = RecordShown.Value`. This is where the sole index to all eight string array variables below this instruction is set to the interval value of the scroll box along the bar.

The event `_Change` signifies a movement of the scroll bar called `RecordShown` that was added to the form. This slider changes the visible record number, which is registered now as part of `Reg$` in a new label in the lower-right corner.

Here's the general concept of the preceding procedure, written as pseudocode:

Visual Basic *By*

EXAMPLE

Procedure for when the scroll bar value changes:
Change the current record number to reflect the scroll bar value.
If the registered scroll bar value is less than 1, then
   Make the record number 1.
End of condition.
For the register, place the record number beside the words "Record #."
Place this register in its proper position.
Change the textual contents of all the text boxes in the form to reflect the current values of each of their representative arrays for the current record number.
   .
   .
   .
End of procedure.

Here's the new `Form_Load ()` procedure for the application:

```
Sub Form_Load ()
RecordShown.Value = 1
RecordShown.SmallChange = 1
RecordShown.LargeChange = 10
RecordShown_Change
End Sub
```

You may remember, in every Visual Basic program, the procedure `Form_Load ()` executes automatically once the form is invoked. The control name for the scroll bar in this application is `RecordShown`. Its initial `.Value` is set to 1, because record number 1 (not number 0) is the first to be displayed. The `.SmallChange` property is set to 1 (the default anyway), which means the program proceeds to the next record in the list (`RecordNo + 1`) if you click the down arrow, or to the previous record (`RecordNo - 1`) if you click the up arrow. The `.LargeChange` property is set to 10, which makes 10 the value of *one page* of records. The records are now said to *page down* by 10.

```
Sub Address_Change ()
Adress$(RecordNo) = Address.Text
End Sub
```

Chapter 23 ◆ Options and Scroll Bars

```
Sub City_Change ()
Cty$(RecordNo) = City.Text
End Sub

Sub FirstName_Change ()
FrstName$(RecordNo) = FirstName.Text
End Sub

Sub LastName_Change ()
LstName$(RecordNo) = LastName.Text
End Sub

Sub MidInit_Change ()
MdInit$(RecordNo) = MidInit.Text
End Sub

Sub State_Change ()
Stat$(RecordNo) = State.Text
End Sub

Sub Zip_Change ()
Zp$(RecordNo) = Zip.Text
End Sub
```

With these brief procedures, whenever new text is typed into any of the text boxes on the form, the contents of the string array variable for the current record number changes automatically.

The way this program works now, you can set the scroll bar to any record number you choose and type a person's record for that number. You may then scroll to any other record number. When scrolling back to a filled record number, the record reappears.

Generally, a scroll bar is placed on the form as an independent control. Optionally, a scroll bar can be invoked as a part of a text box control, for cases in which the text within the box overflows the area of the box. The following invocation is made only at design time:

Text.ScrollBars **Property**

The .ScrollBars property is set to a two-bit binary value (not an editorial comment). Bit 0 on the right (the least significant bit) is set to 1 if the horizontal scroll bar for the antecedent text box is to be displayed. Likewise, bit 1 on the left (the most significant bit) is set to 1 if the vertical scroll bar for the text box is to be displayed. In decimal, the value of `.ScrollBars` can be set to any of the following:

- 0   No scroll bars (default)
- 1   Horizontal bar
- 2   Vertical bar
- 3   Both scroll bars

Summary

For each group of option dots that appears in a form, only one dot can be set at one time, thereby designating a single selection from a list. By contrast, many check boxes in a group can be set within a form at one time. Groups can be divided into subgroups by placing elements of those subgroups within a frame, which is a rectangular subdivision of a form. Each item in a list or group box has a `.Value` property attributed to it, which designates whether that control is currently set.

A control array is a formal grouping of controls addressed within the source code like an array variable, with a single name and a subscript index within parentheses. This is a different type of grouping from a graphic or frame grouping, in which related elements are drawn into a frame and are thus considered as resting on that frame.

A scroll bar is divided into equally spaced intervals numbered between its `.Min` and `.Max` property values. These intervals exist logically, regardless of the actual pixel length of the scroll bar in a form. Text boxes can have scroll bars apportioned to them using the `.ScrollBars` property, but these bars are not scroll bar controls by the formal definition.

Chapter 23 ◆ Options and Scroll Bars

Review Questions

1. Can a frame control be part of a control array?

2. If you drag a control into a frame, does it become part of a control array?

3. Can a control array exist partly within, and partly outside of, a frame?

4. Can you set the minimum value of a scroll bar belonging to a text box to another value?

Dialog Boxes

In this chapter you examine the creation and display of dialog boxes, which are brief windows the program uses to communicate with the user. Dialog box windows are not forms by the Visual Basic definition, so they are not designed beforehand. Instead, the contents of a dialog box are defined within the source code and are displayed using VB instructions.

Reaching into the Message Box

Dialog boxes are generally displayed for two purposes: to determine the user's response to a yes or no question, or to warn or notify the user of some occurrence within the program. The instruction used to display message boxes in Visual Basic is MsgBox.

MsgBox   Function or Statement

Function syntax:

response% = MsgBox (*message*$[, *code*%[, *title*$]])

Statement syntax:

MsgBox *message*$[, *code*%[, *title*$]]

The `MsgBox` instruction, however it is phrased, displays on-screen a dialog box containing the message that is presented as the argument `message$`. The value of the integer `code%` denotes specifically what contents besides the `message$` are to appear in the dialog box. The value of `code%` is evaluated binarily, with each bit in the binary value representing an element or style designation of the dialog box. This is a collective value, equal to the sum of any (or no) number from each of the following three sections.

Table 24.1. Message box contents codes.

Addend	Associated Feature
Button inclusion	
0	Display `OK` button.
1	Display `OK`, `Cancel` buttons.
2	Display `Abort`, `Retry`, and `Ignore` buttons.
3	Display `Yes`, `No`, and `Cancel` buttons.
4	Display `Yes`, `No` buttons.
5	Display `Retry`, `Cancel` buttons.
Icon inclusion	
16	Show red stop-sign (bad news) icon.
32	Show green question mark (query) icon.
48	Show yellow exclamation point (warning) icon.
64	Show blue *i* (information, please) icon.
Default button programming	
256	Make second button the default.
512	Make third button the default.

If *title$* is expressed, the contents of the title bar are set to *title$*; otherwise, the title is `Microsoft Visual Basic` by default.

If `MsgBox` is written as a function, the dialog box can return a value to the variable expressed as *response%*, designating which button the user pressed as a response to the dialog. This value can be any of the following:

Return value	Button pressed
1	OK
2	Cancel
3	Abort
4	Retry
5	Ignore
6	Yes
7	No

Example

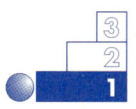

The following instruction displays a simple dialog box:

```
MsgBox "Project saved successfully."
```

The dialog box resulting from this statement appears in Figure 24.1.

Example

Here's a more complex dialog box, which elicits a response from the user:

```
message$ = "Proceeding will mean the contents of the
    current form will be cleared. Proceed anyway?"
response = MsgBox(message$, 324, "Visual Basic by Example")
```

321

Chapter 24 ◆ Dialog Boxes

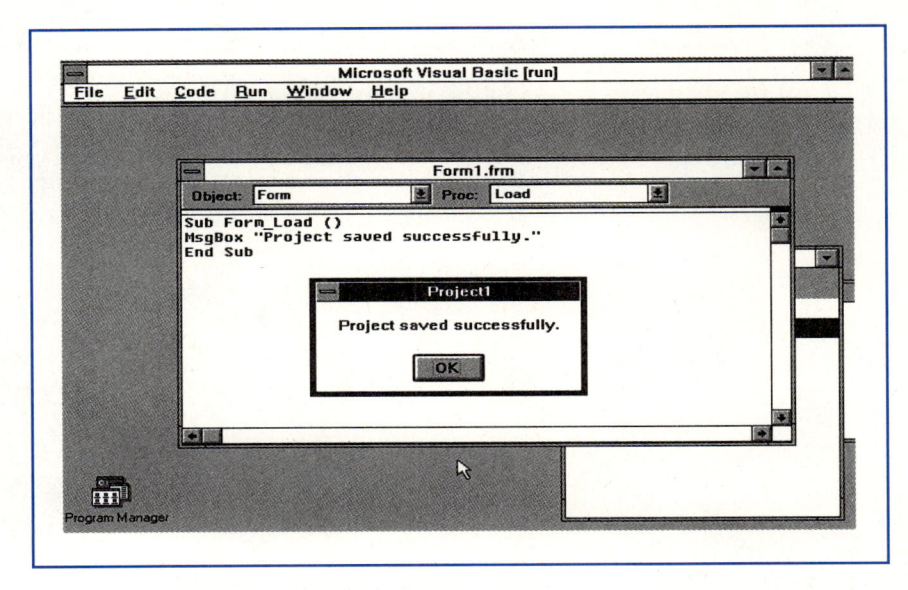

Figure 24.1. The simplest of dialog boxes.

In this instance, the message is long enough that, to keep the instructions shorter, it first is assigned to string variable `message$`. This is the first argument of the function (note the syntax). The value 324 is equal to 4 (display Yes, No buttons) plus 64 (show blue *i* icon) plus 256 (make second button the default). You could have expressed the second argument as 256 + 64 + 4 if you didn't want to strain your brain. The resulting dialog box appears as Figure 24.2.

Notice how the extra highlighting appears around the No button as a result of adding 256 to the second argument of the function. If the user clicks this button or presses Enter, the value 7 is returned to the variable `response`.

Dialog boxes in Visual Basic—just as they are in the rest of the Windows environment—suspend every other window on the screen until they have their response. Such a window is called *modal*.

By contrast, a *modeless* window allows other windows on the screen to be operated while it is active. These are two terms that don't seem to define themselves in the context of Windows, so try to memorize them.

> A *modal* window suspends the operability of every other window while it is operating and until it is exited.

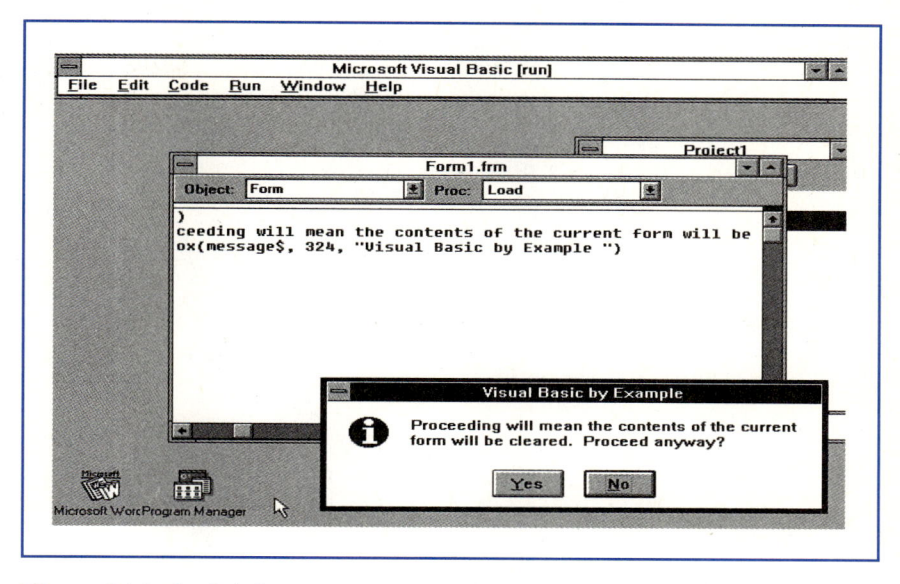

Figure 24.2. A slightly more complex dialog box.

The Input Box

One type of dialog box that receives *textual* input from the user is the *input box*, which is supported in Visual Basic with a function.

InputBox$()   **Function**

Syntax:

↳ *response*$ = InputBox$ (*message*$[, *title*$[, *default*$
   [, *xcoord*%, *ycoord*%]]])

The `InputBox$()` function uses the message within *message*$ as a prompt for a textual response, to be entered by the user on a text line appearing within the dialog box. The contents of this line are limited to a maximum of 31 characters, and may be seeded in advance by expressing *default*$. The title of the input box window can optionally be expressed as *title*$.

Normally, the input box appears in the center of the screen. To place it anywhere else on the screen, the origin point of the window can be expressed as coordinates *xcoord%*, *ycoord%*. An input box always contains two buttons: `OK` and `Cancel`. If the user clicks `Cancel`, the contents of *response$* will be a null string. If the user clicks `OK`, the contents of the text line are returned as *response$*.

Example

The following function places on the screen an input box that requests a password from the user:

```
message$ = "Enter a password:"
response$ = InputBox$(message$, "", "TRIPWIRE")
```

The second parameter in the function nullifies the title of the dialog box. The third parameter, `"TRIPWIRE"`, places a default password in the text line. The resulting input box appears as Figure 24.3.

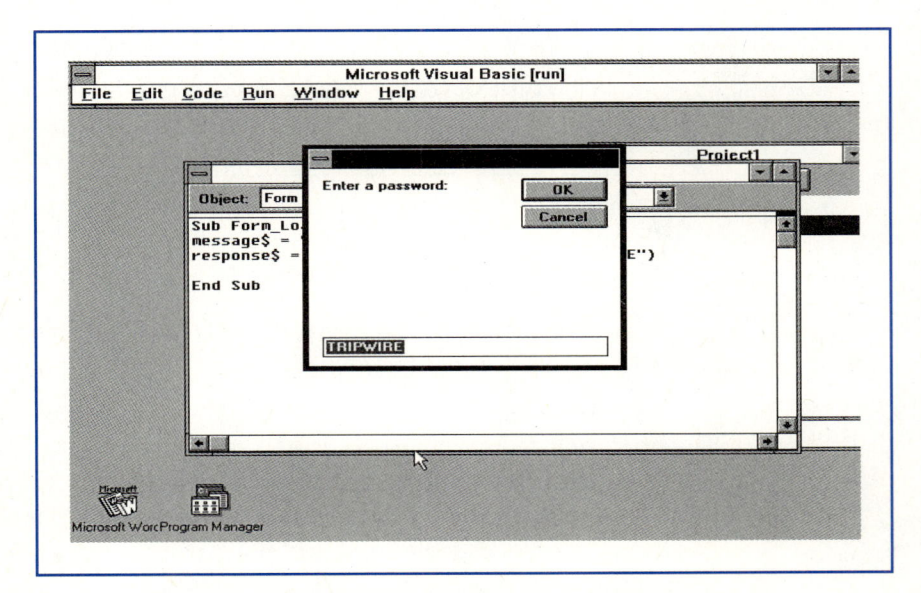

Figure 24.3. The password input box.

Notice that there is quite a bit of white space between the message text and the text line. The size of an input box is fixed, so this space is allotted for longer messages. Carriage return and line feed characters may be required within the message string for multiple lines.

Summary

A dialog box is not a form by the standard Visual Basic definition; instead, it is a temporary window provided as a resource of the Windows environment. The contents of this box are rendered to the `MsgBox` instruction, along with a sum value having binary or bitwise contents that reveal what buttons and icons inhabit the dialog box.

An input box is a type of dialog box that elicits a textual response from the user. Visual Basic's input boxes have a fixed size, and always have `OK` and `Cancel` buttons.

Review Questions

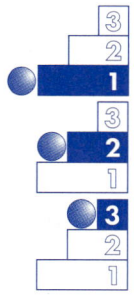

1. To elicit a textual response from the user, should you use a message box or an input box?

2. Using the `MsgBox` and `InputBox` terms, does the program display modal or modeless windows?

3. Why should a file selector box, such as `SELECTOR.FRM`, necessarily be a modal dialog box?

325

Control Manipulation and Organization

In this chapter you study the methods, events, and properties that relate to addressing, organizing, and manipulating graphic objects *in general*, in contrast to the control-exclusive instructions you've studied in the previous five chapters. Some of the instructions explained in this chapter have already been introduced to you through previous examples; this chapter formally establishes their purpose and function. You also see how to index, tag, and focus on controls in a form.

A Control by Any Other Name

As you've seen in several examples, a control on a form is addressed within the source code of a program by its control name. There are two other subsidiary properties Visual Basic provides for referring to a control, which are described in the following sections.

`Control`.`CtlName` Property

The `.CtlName` property for a control is set to an arbitrary name at design time. This property becomes the name that is stated to the left of the period when the graphic object is addressed within the source code of the program, using object-oriented syntax.

`Control`.`Index` Property

The `.Index` property is used to refer to elements of a control array, especially because all elements within an array share the same `.CtlName` property. The control is referred to by its designated array name. Following that, the index of a control within an array is stated as a subscript value within parentheses. Indices for controls within an array are designated in sequence at design time. Their sequence can also be reorganized at design time.

`Control`.`Tag` Property

The `.Tag` property for a control is set at design time to an arbitrary name other than its control name or index. By default, the `.Tag` for a control is a null string.

The `.Tag` property may not seem to be very useful in the context of Visual Basic. The control already has one name, and you may wonder why it needs a pseudonym. The reason for a second name is as follows: There will be times when you'd like to have a routine that *compares* one control to another, just as if that control were a variable of a specified data type. Visual Basic does recognize the data type `Control` for graphic objects inhabiting a form, so you can compare controls by using mathematical expressions. However, object-oriented syntax does not allow you to refer to objects *subjectively*. In other words, the control name of an object cannot be used as the subject of a comparison. To borrow a term from the NFL, this is what we would call *illegal procedure*.

The solution to this—albeit one that sounds more political than logical—is to create a second name for a control, when necessary, to act as its subjective name.

Visual Basic **By**

EXAMPLE

Looking at Things Subjectively

The purpose for the `.Tag` property is not at all self-explanatory, so I'll use a model. Assume the VB application you're writing is a children's game, where the child picks up "toy" symbols on the screen with the mouse and drops them into a box. These symbols are represented by VB icons. An event procedure is programmed to detect whenever a symbol is dropped into the box; but the way the interpreter works, the event is based around the box that the symbol is being dropped into, not the symbol that is being moved. With that in mind, your objective is to have our event procedure determine which toy entered the box. The box is the object of our event procedure; but the toy is the subject.

To ensure you're able to identify the subject, you need to assign `.Tag` property settings to each icon either at design time or within the `Sub Form_Load ()` or `Sub Main ()` procedure. With that out of the way, here's the event procedure:

```
Sub BigRedBox_DragDrop (Source As Control, x As Single,
    y As Single)
Select Case Source.Tag
    Case "Bear"
        Bear1.Picture = LoadPicture("C:\vbasic\icons\
            mine\hapybear.ico")
        Source.Parent.Message.Text = "Thank you."
    Case "Rocket"
        Rocket1.Picture = LoadPicture("C:\vbasic\
            icons\mine\blastoff.ico")
        Source.Parent.Message.Text = "We have liftoff."
    .
    .
    .
End Select
End Sub
```

The `_DragDrop` event occurs whenever a graphic object or control with drag capability is dragged and dropped on top of the antecedent object. The icons being dragged, from the interpreter's point of

329

Chapter 25 ◆ Control Manipulation and Organization

view, are picture boxes the contents of which may be established by means of the `LoadPicture()` function.

The key element of this procedure is on the very first line, at the declaration `Source As Control`. Up to now, you've declared variables `As Integer` or `As Double`, but in this instance `As Control` refers to a *structural* form of declaration, not to a numeric form. The toy being dragged into the box is a control; and here it may actually be declared as such using the term `As Control`. When this happens, all the property data associated with the control—size, position, and contents—are passed along with it.

With that in mind, here's the procedure as pseudocode:

Procedure awaiting a control to be dragged into the box:
Check to see what the tag of the source control is.
   In case its tag is "Bear"
     Load the happy bear picture into the control.
     Tell the parent form of the source control "Thank you."
   In case its tag is "Rocket"
     Load the blasting-off rocket into the control.
     Tell the parent form of the source control "We have liftoff."
.
.
.

End of cases.
End of procedure.

The choice of the term `Source` for the control data structure was arbitrary in this case, in the same way the choice of a variable name is arbitrary. In this procedure, all the properties that belong to the source control are copied and "absorbed," in a sense, by the term `Source`. Thus if `Object1.Tag = "Bear"` and the bear is the toy that was dragged, then once the drop occurs and this procedure executes, `Source1.Tag = "Bear"`.

The term `Parent.` in this procedure acts like a property for the sake of `Source.` but like an object from the point of view of `Message`, which is apparently a control that can have a `.Text` property of its own. Here is a closer look at this two-way term:

330

Visual Basic *By* EXAMPLE

> **Parent.**   **Object acting as Property**
>
> Syntax:
>
> *Source*.Parent
>
> The `Parent.` object is used to refer back to the parent form of a control whose constituent properties have already been passed to a procedure. This property passing takes place by way of declaring the data structure at the beginning of the procedure, in the form `Source As Control`. Once a control is passed to the procedure as if it were data, the control that was passed may be referred to by way of the indirect reference `Source.`, regardless of the type of control that was passed. `Source.` may then be used to refer to all the properties apportioned to the passed control. The properties of the form containing this control are therefore addressable from within the procedure as properties of `Parent`.

So in order to send a message back to the form to which the `Source.` control originally belonged, that form may be addressed within the procedure as `Parent.`, whatever the `.FormName` of the form may be. In this instance, `Message.` is an arbitrary name for a text box belonging to the parent form. You don't need to know the `.FormName` of the form, yet you do need to know the `.CtlName` of the object within that form in order to address it directly. Thus, the conglomerate reference `Source.Parent.Message.Text` refers to the text within a text box that is definitely called `Message`, residing in whatever the parent form is of whatever control was dragged into the box.

Pulling Tabs

One of the most difficult adjustments a long-time computer user has to make when migrating from DOS to the Microsoft Windows environment is remembering to press the Tab key when

331

entering text into a form with multiple fields. In most everyday DOS programs, the user can type text into a field, press Enter, and then enter text into the next field. In Windows, pressing Enter generally substitutes for clicking the default button, which in many forms is the OK button. If the Windows user presses Enter thinking the cursor will move to the next field, the Windows application might respond by assuming the entry of text for this form is complete. As a result, the form is stored as a formal record with a bunch of null fields.

In the first NameForm application listing, if you entered the text boxes into the form in the order they were presented, you should be able to enter text into one field at run time, press Tab, and proceed in sequence to the next logical field. In other words, you won't jump from the *last name* field to the *ZIP code* field. The Visual Basic interpreter maintains a *tab index* for each control, among other reasons, so that there is a logical sequence to the fields in a form.

Control.TabIndex Property

The .TabIndex property is set to the numerical place in the tabbing sequence of the antecedent control. By default, the tabbing sequence of controls in a form is established as their order of creation at design time; this sequence can be reorganized at design time or run time. Labels are assigned .TabIndex properties by default, although pressing Tab does not cause an indicator box to appear around the label as if it were an operable control. Labels and nonoperable controls are skipped in the tabbing sequence, regardless of their .TabIndex property settings.

Control.TabStop Property

The .TabStop property is a true or false flag designating whether the antecedent control can be indicated by pressing Tab during run time. By default, .TabStop is set to true (–1). A control can be a tab stop like a bench can be a bus stop. To designate that the tab route does not stop at the antecedent control—in a sense, to remove the bench from the bus stop, as it were—set its value to false (0).

Figure 25.1 shows the form for the NameForm application Mark II, along with the `.TabIndex` settings for each text field typed within their respective fields. All objects in Visual Basic have a `.TabIndex` property, even if it is not used, as in the case of labels and command buttons. The `.TabIndex` settings that are "missing" from Figure 25.1 are assigned to the other controls on the form.

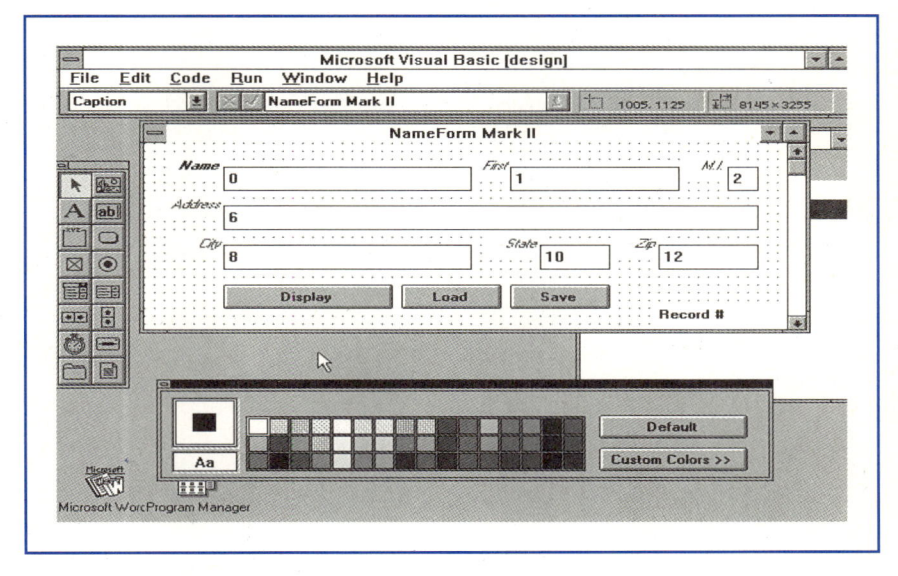

Figure 25.1. Your local tab stop route.

Suppose you want to add a field called `Company Name` between the middle initial field and the address field. You can easily make the form larger: Scoot the address, city, state, and ZIP code fields down and insert the company name field. The trouble is, the tab index for this new field will be 19, which falls above the tab index for the ZIP code field of 12. Having established the fact that the `.TabIndex` for the middle initial field is 2, you can logically reset the `.TabIndex` for the new company name field to 3. The indices for all successive controls are automatically scooted down one. The control that previously had the index of 3 is now bumped to 4. Figure 25.2 shows the amendments made to the form, along with their `.TabIndex` results.

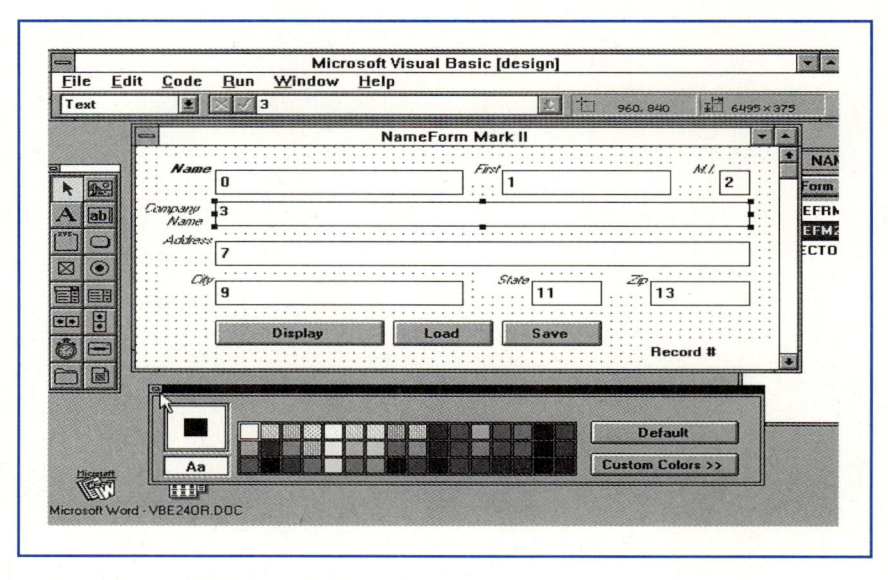

Chapter 25 ◆ Control Manipulation and Organization

Figure 25.2. A change in plan.

Monitoring Activity

A control *has the focus* when it is active and awaiting user input.

Arguably, few people choose to use the Microsoft Windows environment without a mouse. Microsoft did, however, at least program the Windows package so that a mouse was optional rather than required. In any window that has multiple fields and controls, Microsoft has the person who doesn't use a mouse press the Tab key repeatedly until the control the user wishes to operate is somehow indicated on the screen. If the control is a text box, the cursor appears within that box. If the control is a visual device, a *focus indicator* box appears around its caption. In Visual Basic, a control that *has the focus* is the control currently indicated by a hazy rectangle, designating that the control is active or awaiting input from the user. By default, the control within a form that has the focus first, is the first input-accepting control in the .TabStop sequence.

Acquiring the focus in VB is an event comparable to intercepting a football pass; event procedures may be executed for a control when it acquires the focus.

*Control*_GotFocus and *Control*_LostFocus Events

The _GotFocus event occurs whenever the antecedent control acquires the focus, as a result of the user indicating that control with the mouse or the Tab key, or by direct setting of the focus by the program. Acquiring the focus makes this particular control the active control for now. Consequently, the _LostFocus event occurs whenever the antecedent control loses the focus, assuming of course that it ever had the focus.

If necessary, the program can set the focus of a control manually, thus forcing on it the role of active control.

Control.SetFocus Method

Syntax:

Control.SetFocus

The .SetFocus method manually appoints the antecedent control to be the active control, thus giving it the focus.

Example

Suppose you add a Copy button to the NameForm application. Clicking it would copy the contents of the text field currently under the cursor—the control with the focus—to the system clipboard. The procedure needs to be able to determine what text box control contains the text to be copied. Here's how the procedure might appear:

```
Sub Copy_Click ()
copy$ = Screen.ActiveControl.Text
Clipboard.SetText copy$
End Sub
```

Here `ActiveControl.` refers reflexively back to whatever control currently has the cursor. For the sake of `.Text`, `ActiveControl.` is the object. To be a reflexive reference, however, `.ActiveControl` must be the *property* of something. Therefore, like `.Parent` in an earlier example, `.ActiveControl` is an object acting as a property. The VB interpreter has assigned it as the exclusive property of... well, everything in a sense. Everything in this sense is referred to by the object `Screen.`, which is the necessary object in order for `.ActiveControl` to fulfill its role as property. The reason for this is there can only be one active control on the Windows screen at any one time.

Here are the object terms used in the preceding example, along with any related terms:

ActiveControl. Object acting as Property

The `ActiveControl.` object, when used in conjunction with the universal reference `Screen.`, refers back to whatever control currently is active or has the focus, on any form.

ActiveForm. Object acting as Property

Likewise, the `ActiveForm.` object, when used in conjunction with `Screen.`, refers back to the currently active form. These terms are used as objects for the properties normally associated with the graphic objects they refer to and take the place of within instructions. From the point of view of `Screen.`, however, both `ActiveControl.` and `ActiveForm.` are treated as properties of the overall `Screen.` object.

Screen. Object

The `Screen.` object refers to the universal (screen-encompassing) coordinate system. It is used whenever a property of the whole screen, such as `.ActiveControl`, is invoked.

Clipboard. Object

The `Clipboard.` object acts as the antecedent object for all clipboard-specific methods within a procedure.

The preceding procedure was invoked with the occurrence of a type of event with which you are familiar. Here is a review:

*Object*_Click and *Object*_DblClick Events

The `_Click` event occurs when the user clicks the antecedent object, using the mouse. Likewise, the `_DblClick` event occurs when the user double-clicks the antecedent object.

Summary

A control appearing on a form can be assigned a `.Tag` property, which acts as its alias. Controls can be passed in the same manner as normal data (as parameters to procedures), as long as the control name is declared within the parentheses of the procedure's opening `Sub` statement as having data type `Control`. The form that contains the control passed as a parameter to the procedure can be addressed reflexively using the object/property hybrid term `Parent`.

All the controls on a form are given a `.TabIndex` property, which establishes the route the focus indicator bar takes when the user of the application repetitively presses the Tab key. The Tab key route

Chapter 25 ◆ Control Manipulation and Organization

follows the sequence established by the order of .TabIndex properties. This sequence is established by default at design time as the order of the controls' creation. When the user presses Enter while the focus indicator is over a control, he is operating that control as if he were using the mouse button. The control being operated on and being indicated is considered the active control, and therefore is said to *have the focus*. The form that contains the active control, likewise, is said to be the *active control*. A control can be rendered exempt from receiving the focus by setting the .TabStop property for that control to false (0).

The .ActiveControl and .ActiveForm can be addressed indirectly by using those terms. All properties and settings apply to these indirect references just as they would to their direct-reference antecedent objects. .ActiveControl and .ActiveForm relate back to the universal object Screen.

Review Questions

Using object-oriented syntax, write references for the following properties:

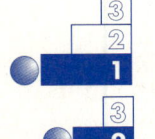

1. The contents of a text box called Surname

2. The tab index for an option dot called Group(1)

3. The alias for a picture called BobTheBear

4. A reflexive reference to the textual contents of the active control

5. A reflexive reference to a text box called Status passed as a parameter to a procedure

6. A reflexive reference to a text box called Status appearing within the active form

7. A reflexive reference to a text box called Status appearing in the same form as that which contains the control that was passed to the current procedure

Control Appearance

In this chapter you examine—or rather, in light of how far we've come, *review*—the properties and methods relating to the appearance, style, and positioning of graphic objects.

Front and Center

When I present a complete listing of a Visual Basic application, for each graphic object in the listing I always provide settings for the properties that describe where the object is and how big it is. Here are the definitions of those properties for your review:

`Form.Left` or `Control.Left` Property

The `.Left` property of a form is set to the distance in *twips* (1/1440 of a logical inch) between the origin point of the form and the leftmost edge of the screen. The origin point is the first user-addressable point in the upper-left corner of the form; if the form has borders, they appear around this point. The `.Left` property of a control is set to the distance in twips between the origin point of the control and the leftmost point on the form.

Form`.Top` or *Control*`.Top` Property

The `.Top` property of a form is set to the distance in twips between the origin point of the form and the uppermost edge of the screen. The `.Top` property of a control is set to the distance in twips between the origin point of the control and the uppermost point on the form.

Form`.Width` or *Control*`.Width` Property

The `.Width` property of a graphic object is set to the distance in twips between the two vertical sides of that object.

Form`.Height` or *Control*`.Height` Property

The `.Height` property of a graphic object is set to the distance in twips between the two horizontal sides of that object.

It is important to note that the length of a *logical inch* appears to change depending on the current screen resolution. The length of a logical inch appears to have been decided within a 640 x 480 coordinate system on, apparently, a 14-inch diagonal monitor; many SVGA, 8514a, and XGA graphics systems now are capable of resolutions of 800 x 600, 1024 x 768, and higher—which renders logical inches smaller and smaller as progress marches on.

When a control contains text, it's sometimes difficult for a new programmer to distinguish which controls have a `.Caption` property and which have a `.Text` property. A control can have only one or the other. Here are the distinguishing factors between the two properties:

Object.Caption **Property**

The .Caption property, with respect to a control, is set to the textual contents of the antecedent control having a type that is one of those listed previously. With respect to a form, the property refers to the textual contents of its title bar. This property can be set again at any time.

Forms, check boxes, command buttons, frames, labels, menus, and option buttons all have .Caption properties.

Object.Text **Property**

The .Text property is set to the textual contents of the antecedent control whose type is one of those listed immediately preceding this paragraph. With respect to list and combo boxes, the .Text property is set to the currently chosen item in the list. Combo, list, and text boxes all have .Text properties.

When a control is first created and placed on the form (how poetic), it starts its life as black on white. Described in greater detail, this is because the .ForeColor property of new controls is set by default to black and the .BackColor property is set by default to white.

Control.BackColor **and** *Control*.ForeColor **Properties**

The .BackColor property reflects the current background color of its antecedent object. The .ForeColor property represents the plotting color of text and graphical elements—such as borders—of its antecedent object. Both properties are expressed as six-digit hexadecimal values. These values digitally represent the color-mixing scheme currently in use. Because all graphics cards (and thus graphics card drivers) are not alike, the colors chosen for objects on the system on which the application is being programmed may not be identical (or even close) to the colors represented on some other system.

It's relatively difficult to express colors as six-digit hexadecimal (base 16) values—especially when you're not sure if those colors

Chapter 26 ◆ Control Appearance

will be the same when you move your VB application to a different system. Colors across systems and across graphics cards are generally similar. Keeping that in mind, here's how the `.ForeColor` and `.BackColor` properties of a graphic object can be set without having to resort to using the ABSCESSING application.

At the bottom of Figure 26.1 is a depiction of the Visual Basic color palette.

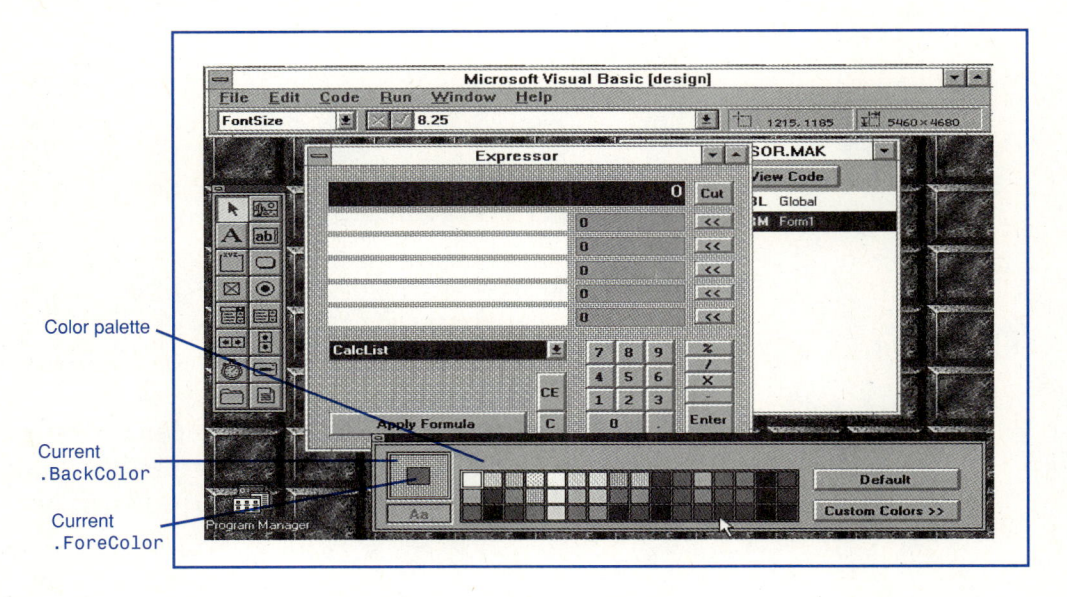

Figure 26.1. The VB color palette and color definition box.

At the upper-left corner of the color palette is a small box within a big box. The color of the small box represents the current color represented by `.ForeColor` for the graphic object currently indicated within the VB interpreter workspace. The color of the big box that contains the small box is the current color represented by `.BackColor` for the currently active object. Here is the graphical procedure for setting these properties.

To set color properties for an object at design time using the color palette:

342

- Indicate the graphic object to be recolored. If this object is a form, click any area within the form that is not inhabited by a control. If this object is a control, click that control so that it is surrounded by indicator nodes.

- To set the `.ForeColor` property for this object, click the smaller box inside the color palette once, then choose a color from the palette by clicking that color. The color change is immediately reflected in the VB workspace.

- To set the `.BackColor` property for this object, click the larger box inside the color palette containing the smaller box once, then choose a color from the palette by clicking that color. The color change is immediately reflected in the VB workspace.

Notice that in the color palette the sample text Aa appears below the two test boxes. This test is placed there to show how text set to the two chosen colors will appear within a form. In the Windows environment, regardless of how many colors are accessible from your current graphics card driver, Windows recognizes only as many as 32 actual colors for the immediate background behind text, and as many as 64 colors as mixtures for the remainder of the text area. Windows can then support as many as 256 colors for regions outside of those that are to contain text.

Summary

The `.Left` and `.Top` properties of a form denote the distance of that form's origin point from the leftmost and uppermost points, respectively, of the screen. The `.Left` and `.Top` properties of a control likewise denote the distance of that control's origin point from the leftmost and uppermost points, respectively, of the form in which the control resides.

When addressing text with a property, the term `.Text` is reserved for use in addressing the contents of text boxes, as well as list and combo boxes. The textual contents of all other types of controls, as well as the title bar of a form, are addressed by the term `.Caption`.

343

Chapter 26 ◆ Control Appearance

The .ForeColor of a graphic object is the foreground color used for its text as well as for most of its graphical content. The .BackColor of an object is the background color used for the area of that object not inhabited by text or graphics. Both properties are expressed as six-digit hexadecimal numbers; therefore, some programmers find it more convenient to set color properties at design time using the color palette.

Review Questions

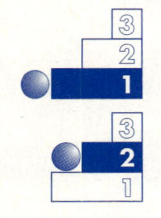

1. What is the foreground color of the default Windows text box?

2. In a picture box in which 50 white characters, representing stars, are placed geometrically on a blue field, what is the .BackColor setting for the picture box?

3. Editable text is addressed using what property term?

27

The Menu Bar

In this chapter you learn the procedure for adding a menu bar to a form, as well as how the menu hierarchy is maintained. You see individual menu items acting in place of graphic controls. Finally, you examine the properties that relate to menu items.

Le Menu

The menu bar is the one type of control that is not available through the Visual Basic toolbox. This is because the contents of a menu bar are not actually graphic objects. In fact, they are the only controls belonging to a form that are not graphic objects. They are addressable to some extent within the source code, however, using object-oriented syntax. On a Visual Basic menu bar, each menu selection is treated like a graphic control placed on the form. Selecting an item from a VB menu is treated the same way—in fact, with the same event name—as clicking a command button on a form.

Now, witness the creation of a menu bar for the application NameForm Mark III. In Chapter 25, "Control Manipulation," I added an extra line to this form; subsequently, I've had to change some of its procedures to read as follows:

Chapter 27 ◆ The Menu Bar

Declarations:

```
Option Base 1
Dim LstName$(1000), FrstName$(1000), MdInit$(1000),
   CompanyNam$(1000), Adress$(1000), Cty$(1000),
   Stat$(1000), Zp$(1000)
Dim RecordNo As Integer

Sub CompanyName_Change ()
CompanyNam$(RecordNo) = CompanyName.Text
End Sub
```

Now array variable `CompanyNam$()` is a regular part of the database table and receives its contents from the text box `CompanyName`.

```
Sub Display_Click ()
RecordNo = RecordShown.Value
FullName$ = FirstName.Text + " " + MidInit.Text + " "
   + LastName.Text
WorkPlace$ = CompanyName.Text
StreetAddress$ = Address.Text
Residence$ = City.Text + ", " + State.Text + "  " + Zip.Text
Next_Line$ = Chr$(13) + Chr$(10)
Envelope$ = FullName$ + Next_Line$ + WorkPlace$ +
   Next_Line$ + StreetAddress$ + Next_Line$ + Residence$
MsgBox Envelope$
End Sub
```

Here you see `CompanyName` also taking its rightful place in `Sub Display_Click ()`. Subsequently, I added one line to `Sub RecordShown_Change ()` to make `CompanyName` part of the formal record:

```
CompanyName.Text = CompanyNam$(RecordNo)
```

Menus are created through the use of a separate semimodal window called the *Menu Design window*. I say *semimodal* because no other Visual Basic feature is accessible while the Menu Design window is active, although features of the Windows environment outside of the design window are still usable. The Menu Design window is depicted in Figure 27.1.

Visual Basic *By*

EXAMPLE

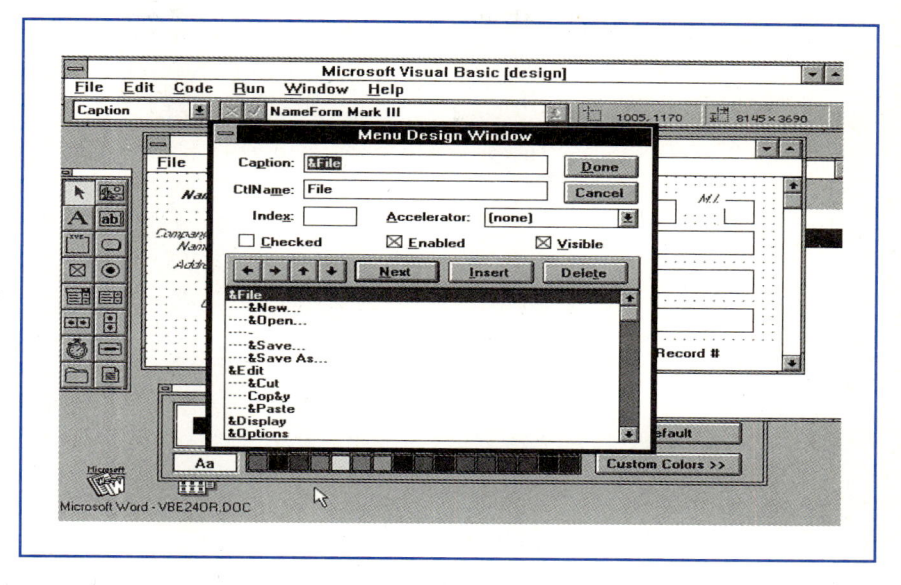

Figure 27.1. The Menu Design window at work.

Here is the procedure for using the Menu Design window. To create a menu bar for a form:

1. Indicate the form to receive the menu bar.

2. Select **M**enu Design Window from the **W**indow menu.

3. In this window is a large text box that acts as a type of outliner. The selections to appear within the menu at all levels appear here, displayed as a menu selection hierarchy as depicted in Figure 27.1. To add a menu category to this window, type the name of the category as it will appear on-screen into the text line marked `Caption:`. To assign a key to be paired with the Alt key as an alternate keystroke to this menu item, precede with an ampersand (&) the letter within the item caption that will act as the Alt pair key. For instance, the entry `&File` would assign Alt-F as the alternate keystroke to bring up the **F**ile menu.

4. Next, type the control name for this menu selection item in the line marked `CtlName:`. You have now set the two main properties of a menu selection item. A menu item has

347

.Caption and .CtlName properties just as a command button does. The .CtlName you just entered will act as the reference for this menu item within the source code.

5. To assign a Shift or Ctrl key combination as an alternate keystroke for this menu item, choose that keystroke from the combo box marked Accelerator:.

6. To set or reset any of the three true or false properties associated with this menu item, check or uncheck the box next to Checked, Enabled, or Visible.

7. To enter the menu item in the list, click the Next button.

8. To designate a menu item already on the list as subordinate to the category above it—as **O**pen is subordinate to **F**ile— click the right-arrow button in the window. This shifts the caption of this category four dots to the right, designating that item as belonging to a drop-down menu for the category above it. There can be up to five levels of submenus in a Visual Basic menu bar system.

9. To delete an item from the list, indicate that item and click the Delete button.

10. To add a space to the list for another item, indicate the item which currently occupies the space and click the Insert button.

11. To shuffle the order of a menu item in the list, first indicate that item. Next, click the up-arrow or down-arrow button to move that item up or down through the list.

12. To promote an item on the list to categorical rank, indicate the item to receive the promotion and click the left-arrow button.

13. To add a partition to a menu, create a menu item for the space where the partition is to appear. For the caption of that partition, type a hyphen (-). Unfortunately, you must also designate a control name for this hyphen, whether or not it's used as an actual control.

14. To abort menu bar creation, click the Cancel button.

15. When the menu bar is at an operable state and ready for testing, click Done.

Example

To experience the thrill of creating menu bars, go into the existing NameForm Mark II form and delete the buttons along the bottom. You may want to resize the form so that there's not so much blank space at the bottom. Next, using the procedure outlined previously, enter the following menu into the menu design window:

Captions	Control Names
&File	File
....&New...	FileNew
....&Open...	FileOpen
....-	hyphen1
....&Save...	FileSave
....&SaveAs...	FileSaveAs
&Edit	Edit
....&Cut	EditCut
....Cop&y	EditCopy
....&Paste	EditPaste
&Display	Display
&Options	Options
&GoTo	GetRecordNo

Previously, there was a button on this form which had a .Caption of *Display* and a .CtlName of *Display*. Now there is a menu item with the same name. Now that the button is gone, the procedure Sub Display_Click () originally attributed to that button automatically applies to the menu selection. Display is treated in this context as a graphic object, although it is not a graphic object. Figure 27.2 shows how NameForm looks with the addition of a menu.

Chapter 27 ◆ The Menu Bar

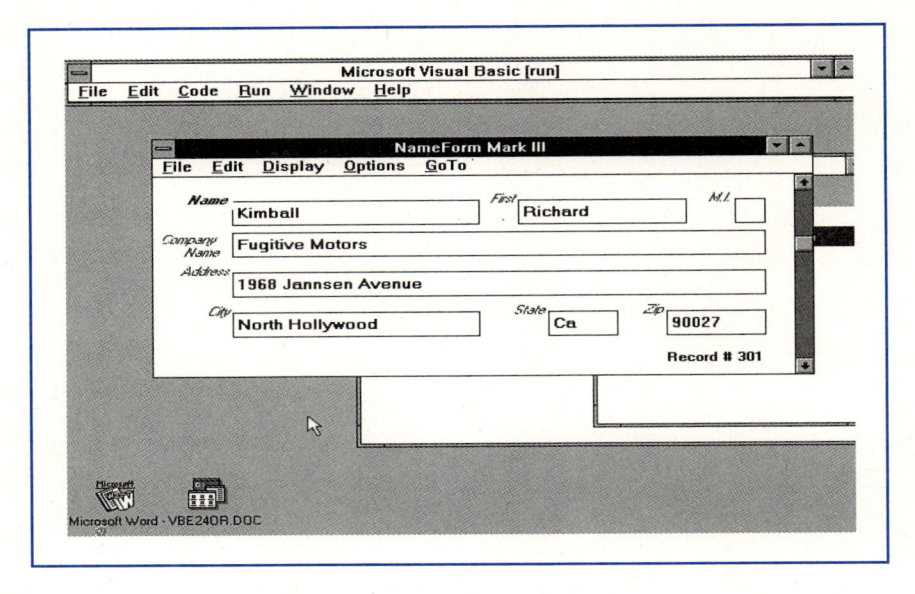

Figure 27.2. Would you like to see the menu?

The following are the three properties listed in the menu design window, designating the operative state of a control—and in this case, a menu selection is a control.

Control.Enabled Property

The .Enabled property is set to a true/false value designating whether the antecedent control is responsive to user events. By default, this property is set to true. To turn off a control but leave it within a form or greyed within a menu, you can set this property to false.

Control.Visible Property

The .Visible property is set to a true or false value that designates whether the antecedent control can be seen, in order to be responsive to user events. An invisible control is nonresponsive. By default, this property is set to true. To make this control disappear or to temporarily eliminate a selection from a menu, you can set this property to false.

Menu.Checked **Property**

This is the only property that is specific to menu items as controls. The .Checked property is set to a true or false value, designating whether a check mark appears beside the selection in a menu. This property does not change the effect of the menu or of any objects to which its event procedures may refer. It merely sets or resets a check mark beside the selection. Use this property to designate whether an option is set to *on* or *off*.

Summary

The menu bar is not a graphic object, nor are any of its constituent selections. Nonetheless, the menu bar is given object-oriented syntax within the source code of Visual Basic programs. Menus are created with the aid of the Visual Basic menu design window.

Review Questions

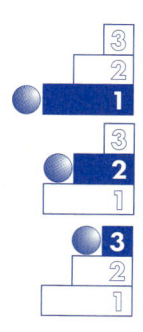

1. From a design point of view, why was a menu bar not included in the standard Visual Basic toolbox?

2. What does the ellipsis (...) in the .Caption of a menu command generally signify?

3. When an event procedure applies to a button and that button is removed from the form to be replaced with a menu command having the same .CtlName as the removed button, where did the event procedure "go" in the meantime while the replacement was taking place?

Dragging

In this chapter you learn how Visual Basic interprets and executes events that involve *dragging*. You may have used a computer with which you could delete files by dragging them to a "trash can" icon. This drag is accomplished by clicking the item to be deleted and holding down the index button of the mouse; dragging the pointer, keeping the index button held down, to the trash can; and releasing the button. The way Visual Basic interprets such events, certain controls on a form classified as *targets* act as the receivers of images of other controls. The receiving of these images is interpreted as a *drag* event. You learn how to program such events in this chapter.

Dragging Everything Out into the Open

When designing a form, the programmer moves a control on the form being designed by dragging the control to its new position. When the application containing that form is run later, it is said that the user can drag a control on top of another—like a file icon being dragged on top of a trash icon. Generally, such figures of speech require generations to develop. With respect to software, however, a generation is often scaled down to about a month.

Chapter 28 ◆ Dragging

A drag *operation copies an image from the control.*

When an application is running, *to drag a control* (in the way Microsoft uses the term) is to click and hold down the index button over a control, and then carry either a duplicate image of that control's border or a *drag icon* assigned to that control. A drag icon will follow the mouse pointer as it is dragged across the screen. The object on which the dragged image "lands" is considered the *target* object. The object where the image originated is considered the *source*.

Let's examine this act in more detail. Visual Basic controls in a form running in an application are, by nature, fixed in their place. The drag operation *does not move the control itself* from one place to another. Normally, if the user were to click and hold the mouse pointer over a control, nothing would happen. If the user were to release the button without moving the mouse, however, she could generate a `_Click` event. For the drag operation to be enabled for a control, its *drag mode* is set to 1. Now when the user clicks and holds the mouse pointer over the control, a hazy grey border appears around that control, which will follow the pointer as long as the index button is depressed (not to be taken psychologically).

As far as Visual Basic is concerned, all that has taken place thus far is just special effects without meaning. The drag event that actually initiates the execution of some code takes place at some point while the dragged image is over the target control; more to the point, the drag event takes place from the point of view of the target. If a control image is dragged on top of a control that isn't expecting this image to drop by, the entire operation is ignored. In other words, if dragging event procedures haven't been programmed for the target control, that control won't accept company.

The two drag events in the VB vocabulary are introduced here.

`Control_DragDrop` Event

The `_DragDrop` event for a control is recognized when the image from another control is dragged on top of it and the mouse button is released. The procedure for this event takes three parameters: the `Source` object where the dragged icon originated declared as having type `Control`, and the `X` and `Y` coordinates of the mouse pointer at the time of the drop.

Control_DragOver Event

The _DragOver event takes place for a control when the image from another control is dragged on top of it, regardless of whether the mouse button is released. The procedure for this event takes four parameters: the Source object where the dragging icon originated declared as having type Control, the X and Y coordinates of the mouse pointer at the time of the drop, and an integer that registers the state of progress of the drag operation. This integer is given any of the following values by the interpreter:

0   The pointer is entering the area of the target control.

1   The pointer is exiting the area of the target control.

2   The pointer is found to be within the area of the target control.

The dragging image for a control does not appear at run time by default; through a property, a control is informed of its drag capability.

Control.DragMode Property

The .DragMode property for a control is set to 1 to make that control automatically draggable at run time. By default, this property is set to 0, which means dragging can be enabled with source code, either one time only with the .Drag method, or through the remainder of the program with the instruction Control.DragMode = 1 until disabled with Control.DragMode = 0. Note that this property is a *flag* and not a Boolean true or false register, so .DragMode cannot be set to –1.

Example

You can put this process to the test with another practically useless application. I make a test form containing two pictures from the Visual Basic icon library: a file folder and a filing cabinet drawer. Because I intend for this application to be useless, this is all the form contains, as proven in Figure 28.1.

Chapter 28 ◆ Dragging

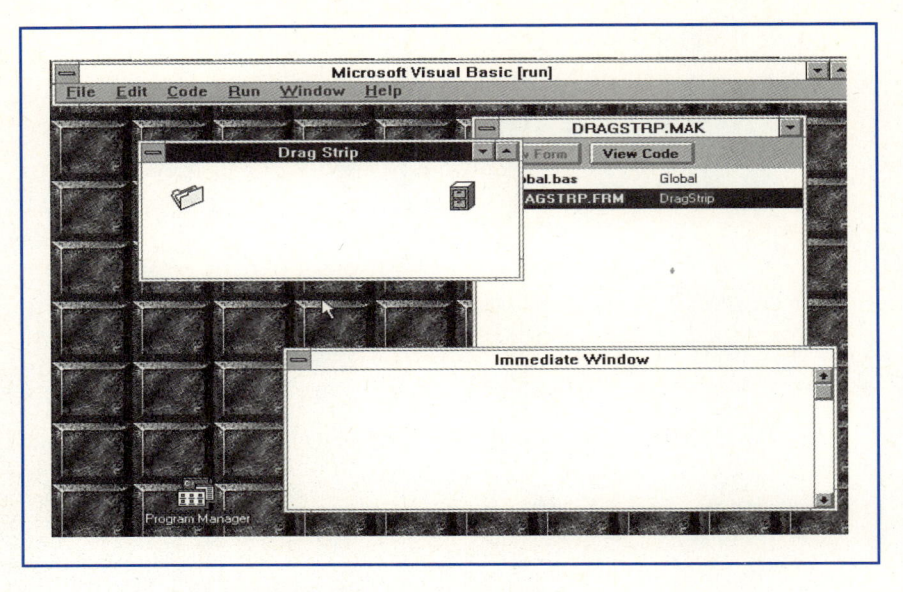

Figure 28.1. The Drag Strip test form in action.

The two controls depicted here are *picture boxes*, which can be of any size, but can be operated like buttons. At design time, picture boxes are created from the uppermost button to the right on the toolbox. The two icons shown here are \VBASIC\OFFICE \FOLDER02.ICO and \VBASIC\OFFICE\FILES03A.ICO, respectively. Although you call them *icons*, from the point of view of the Visual Basic interpreter, these are small picture boxes. If they each happened to be half the size of the screen, they would operate in the same manner.

To place a picture box on a form:

1. Click on the picture box button in the toolbox.

2. Move the pointer to the area of the form that will contain the picture box.

3. Click and hold the index button over one corner of the picture box area, drag the pointer to the opposite corner, and release the button. The picture box border appears on the form, surrounded by indicator nodes with which you can resize the box.

356

Visual Basic *By* EXAMPLE

4. To assign a picture or icon to this picture box, leaving the picture box indicated, choose the `Picture` property from the properties list in the VB main window. The settings list reads `(none)`.

5. At this point, what is normally the down-arrow button for the settings list now contains an ellipsis (...). To choose a picture to fit within the box, click the ellipsis button. A file selector box appears.

6. Visual Basic interprets PC Paintbrush (.PCX), Windows metafile (.WMF), and Windows icon (.ICO) formats for picture boxes. The file list in the selector box will show the files with these three extensions. Choose a picture file from this list. The picture will appear within the box flush-left against the top. You can crop it from the right and along the bottom.

Keeping that procedure in mind, here are the property settings for the test application.

"Drag Strip"
Drag Tester

PROJECT NAME *CONSTITUENT FILES*
DRAGSTRP.MAK   DRAGSTRP.FRM

Object Type	Property	Setting
Form	.Left	1035
	.Top	1200
	.Width	4650
	.Height	2175
	.FormName	DragStrip
	.Caption	Drag Strip
Picture box	.CtlName	Folder
	.Tag	Folder
	.Picture	FOLDER02.ICO
	.DragMode	1 - Automatic
	.BorderStyle	0 - None

357

Chapter 28 ◆ Dragging

Object Type	Property	Setting
Picture box	.CtlName	Cabinet
	.Tag	Cabinet
	.Picture	FILES03A.ICO
	.DragMode	1 - Automatic
	.BorderStyle	0 - None
Label	.Caption	(blank)
	.Alignment	1 - Right Justify

Note that setting the `.BorderStyle` property of a picture box does not have any bearing on its purpose or operation, as that property has with forms.

The challenge is to make it feasible for an image from the folder icon to be dragged over the cabinet icon and have the cabinet "know" it. Setting the properties as listed previously facilitates the dragging process for the folder icon automatically. What you need to do now is program the event procedure for the cabinet receiving the folder. Here is such a procedure:

```
Sub Cabinet_DragDrop (Source As Control, X As Single, Y As Single)
If Source.Tag = "Folder" Then
    Label1.Caption = "Folder received."
End If
End Sub
```

Here's pseudocode for the preceding procedure:

Procedure awaiting something to be dragged on top of the cabinet icon:
If the tag for that certain something is called "Folder," then
    Show on the form that the folder was received.
End of condition.
End of procedure.

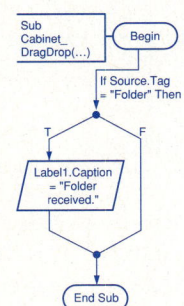

The three parameters passed here are automatically formed by the VB interpreter. `Source As Control` refers to all the properties of a control passed as data, and `X` and `Y` refer to the pointer location at the time of the drop. You don't use `X` or `Y` within this procedure; nonetheless, Visual Basic wants these parameters passed.

The procedure must determine what control was dragged on top of it, so it checks to see if the control's `.Tag` property is `Folder`. The `.CtlName` for this property is also `Folder`, but the VB interpreter doesn't allow you to refer to `Source.CtlName` in this context. The reason is that, because a control in one form can receive the image dragged from a control in another form within the same application, it is therefore possible for two controls in the application to have the same name. The two control names are distinguished by their root-form objects. That very distinguishing element is dropped, however, when the source is indirectly referred to using the `Source.` object. Therefore, to avoid the possibility of confusion, the `.Tag` property is used to refer to graphic objects by a name. For this reason, no two objects within an application can have the same tag.

> **NOTE:** Unlike the `.CtlName` property, the `.Tag` property is case-dependant, meaning that uppercase and lowercase letters are treated differently.

The way the procedure works currently, the image created while dragging the folder to the cabinet is a hazy grey border frame that follows the pointer. Microsoft was thoughtful enough to supply users with icons depicting everyday items in various states—for instance, open and closed folders, open and closed file drawers, and card files with cards being removed and cards being inserted. You can use one of these icons as a replacement for the generic-looking grey border.

Control.DragIcon **Property**

The .DragIcon property contains the file name of a picture or icon that Visual Basic will use as the dragging image for a control. When dragging is enabled for a control, and the user clicks and holds the pointer over the control having a .DragIcon property that has been set to an icon's file name, an image is shown. This is a black and white image derived from the icon clicked on, shown in place of the current pointer as long as the index button is depressed. This image can then follow the pointer to the target object of the drag.

For your purposes, the property Folder.DragIcon can be set to \VBASIC\OFFICE\FOLDER01.ICO, which depicts a closed folder as opposed to an open one. Now when the user clicks and holds over the open folder icon, the image of a closed folder follows the pointer.

Example

Similarly, you can use Microsoft's multiple-state icons to add a degree of animation to the form. Suppose that while the closed file folder is over the cabinet, one of its drawers opens. When the index button is released and the closed folder image disappears, the drawer closes. You can "open" the file drawer with the following procedure:

```
Sub Cabinet_DragOver (Source As Control, X As Single,
    Y As Single, State As Integer)
If Source.Tag = "Folder" Then
    Cabinet.Picture = LoadPicture
        ("c:\vbasic\icons\office\files03b.ico")
End If
End Sub
```

Instead of using the old-style conventional BASIC syntax that might look like LOADPIC "FILES03B.ICO", CABINET, LoadPicture() acts as a function rather than a command, returning a "value" in the form of a picture as a property setting for Cabinet.Picture.

Example

The current problem is that this animation is relatively untidy; I've left the file drawer open. You need to use the `LoadPicture()` function to close the drawer after the file is dropped onto it. You can amend the original Cabinet_DragDrop () procedure as follows:

```
Sub Cabinet_DragDrop (Source As Control, X As Single, Y As Single)
If Source.Tag = "Folder" Then
    Cabinet.Picture = LoadPicture
        ("c:\vbasic\icons\office\files03a.ico")
    Label1.Caption = "Folder received."
End If
End Sub
```

Here I've added a line that makes the file drawer revert to its closed state, by loading the original closed cabinet icon back into the picture box.

Example

One more untidy element remains: Suppose the closed folder icon passes over the file cabinet without being dropped into it. At the moment, the drawer would remain open. You can amend the _DragOver event routine so that it closes whenever you choose to ignore it:

```
Sub Cabinet_DragOver (Source As Control, X As Single,
    Y As Single, State As Integer)
If Source.Tag = "Folder" Then
    Cabinet.Picture = LoadPicture
        ("c:\vbasic\icons\office\files03b.ico")
End If
If State = 1 Then
    Cabinet.Picture = LoadPicture
        ("c:\vbasic\icons\office\files03a.ico")
End If
End Sub
```

361

Chapter 28 ◆ Dragging

Here is the pseudocode for the preceding code:

Procedure awaiting something to be dragged on top of the cabinet icon:
If the tag for that certain something is called "Folder," then
   Show on the form that the folder was received.
   Load the open cabinet icon as the cabinet image.
End of condition.
If the pointer has just left the cabinet area, then
   Reload the closed cabinet icon as this image.
End of condition.
End of procedure.

Here I've added a conditional clause that reloads the original closed cabinet icon whenever the pointer leaves the area of the picture box, regardless of what form the pointer has at the moment. Variable state here is supplied by the interpreter, and a value of 1 represents the state of having left the target object area.

Figures 28.2, 28.3, and 28.4 depict the animation sequence that takes place when the user clicks the folder icon, drags the folder image over the cabinet icon, and drops the folder into the cabinet.

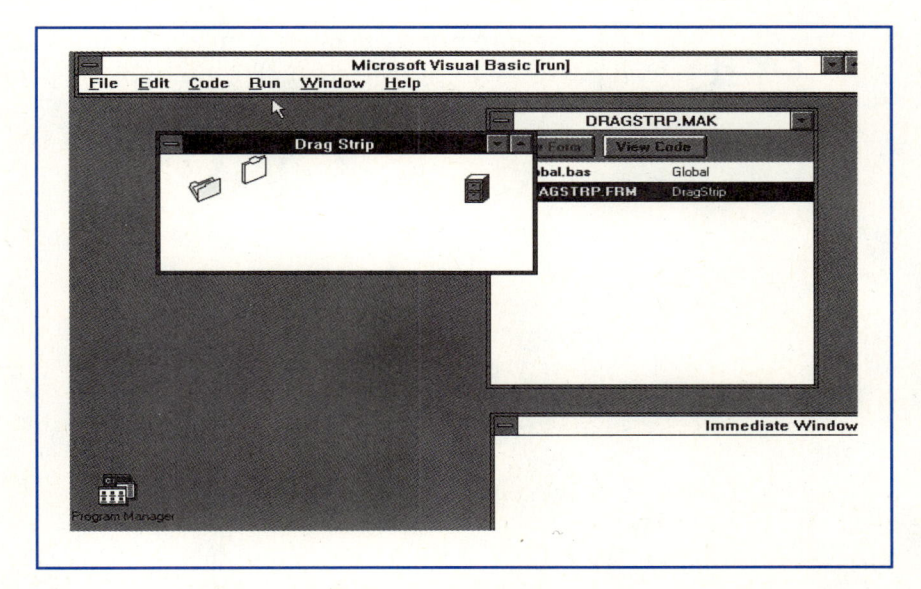

Figure 28.2. "Folder's" .DragIcon is engaged.

362

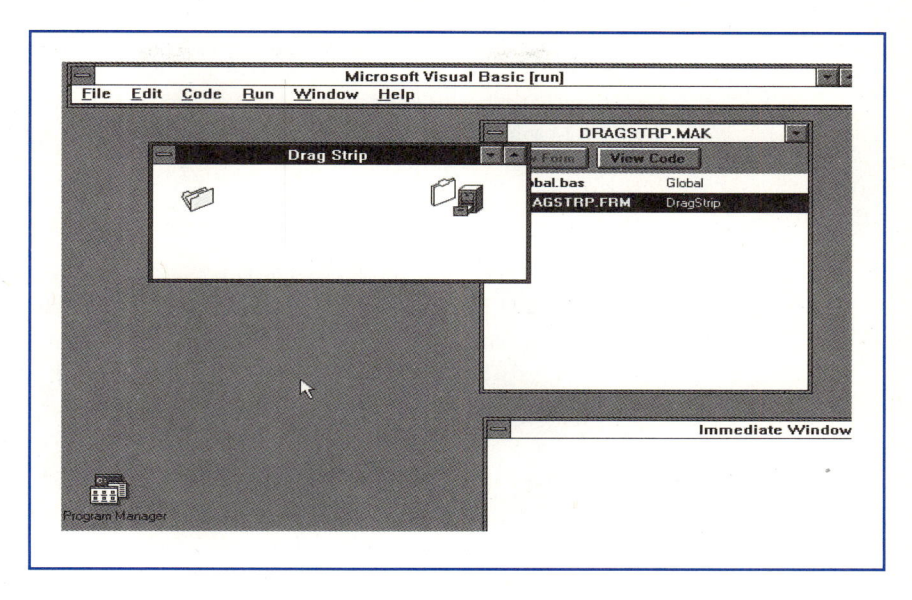

Figure 28.3. The `_DragOver` event makes the drawer open.

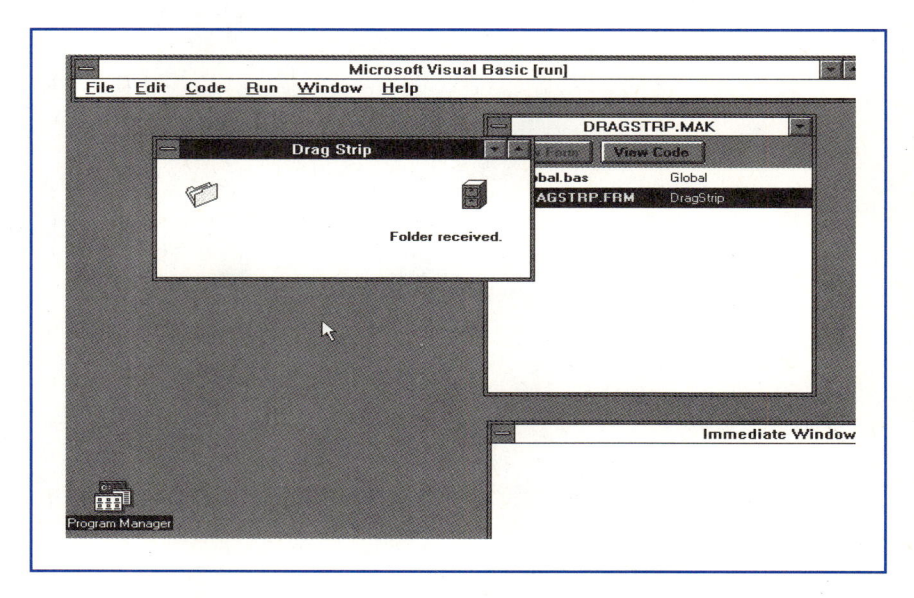

Figure 28.4. The `_DragDrop` event makes the drawer close.

Chapter 28 ◆ Dragging

An Idea for a Lock and Key

By skillfully using the Visual Basic picture box—which has, for the most part, the same events associated with it that a command button has—you may be able to invent your own type of control scheme that perhaps neither Visual Basic nor Windows itself has yet implemented. Here's an idea I've had in the back of my head for quite some time: Inventive programmers have, over the last decade of graphical programming, tried to concoct unique graphical mechanisms to better facilitate critical functions, such as file or record deletion, while keeping it not only foolproof but also practical. You can imagine what trouble could lay ahead for your user if you left a huge, unguarded `Erase` button in the middle of your form.

Generally, programmers invoke a dialog box that offers some last-second warning, such as, `Are you sure you want to delete this file? [Yes¦No]`. After seeing this dialog box a thousand times, I often begin to think it's purposefully trying to demean my (alleged) intelligence; after once hitting the big `Erase` button by accident, however, I'm glad that dialog box is there after all. Still, I envision a more graceful method to ensure against accidental deletion, or accidentally doing anything else, for that matter.

Figure 28.5 shows the Drag Strip test application modified for my purposes. The control on the right is a deletion icon that I created with the IconWorks application supplied with Visual Basic. Its `.CtlName` and `.Tag` are both `DeleteFile`. Its `.DragMode` has been set to 0, and its `.BorderStyle` is set to 1. The border style for this control implies its inaccessibility; you cannot use this control as long as there is a border around it. To take the border off, you must unlock it with the key. To unlock this control, you have to drag the key to the control.

The key, which is on the left, is Visual Basic icon SECUR06.ICO. Its `.DragIcon` is SECUR07.ICO, which floats above SECUR06.ICO. Its `.CtlName` and `.Tag` are both, understandably, `Key`. Its `.DragMode` remains set at 1.

364

Visual Basic *By*
EXAMPLE

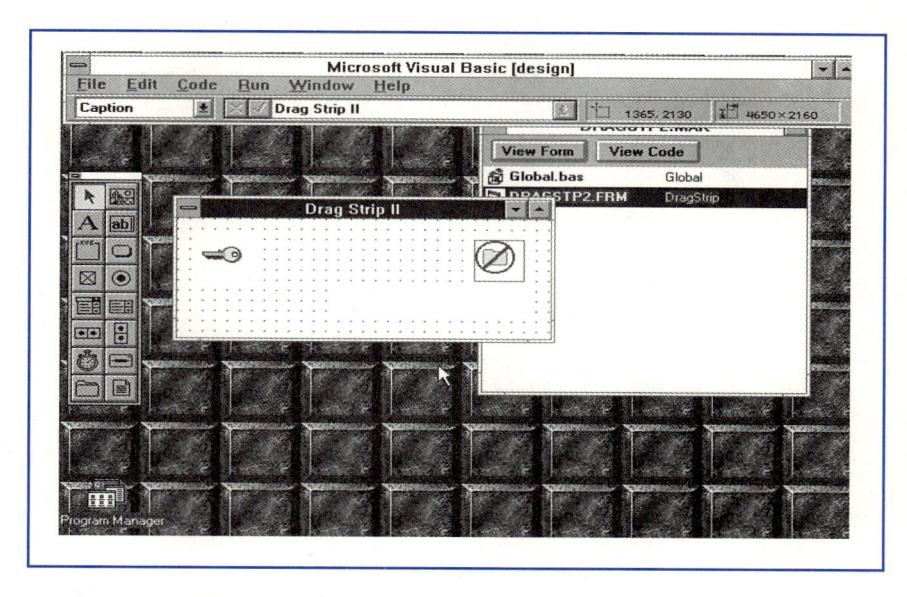

Figure 28.5. Keep this under lock and key for now.

Example

Here's how I rewrote the code of the original Drag Strip application to accommodate this new form of locked control. At the moment, the `DeleteFile` control needs no `_DragOver` event procedure. `DeleteFile` needs first to be able to detect whether the key was dragged on top of it.

```
Sub DeleteFile_DragDrop (Source As Control, X As Single,
    Y As Single)
If Source.Tag = "Key" Then
    DeleteFile.BorderStyle = 0
    Label1.Caption = "Clear to delete file."
End If
End Sub
```

365

Here is pseudocode for the preceding code:

Procedure awaiting something to be dragged on top of the lock icon:
If the tag of the received icon is "Key," then
  Take off the border from the lock.
  Tell the form the user can now delete the file.
End of condition.
End of procedure.

Notice that only the *clearance* to delete the file has been given, and the .BorderStyle for the DeleteFile control has been removed. Next I added the following event procedure:

```
Sub DeleteFile_DblClick ()
If DeleteFile.BorderStyle = 0 Then
    Label1.Caption = "File is deleted."
    DeleteFile.BorderStyle = 1
End If
End Sub
```

Here is pseudocode for the preceding code:

Procedure awaiting someone to double-click on this control.
If there is no border on this control, then
  Tell the form the file is deleted.
  Replace the border.
End of condition.
End of procedure.

Note that this procedure is only symbolic of a deletion; there are no erasure instructions here. The purpose of this application is merely to act as a model for a deletion control. Here you can assume that the deletion process takes place at roughly the area of the source code where the deletion notification takes place. The .BorderStyle is also reset, and the control is now locked. The deletion cannot take place unless the user double-clicks the DeleteFile control and the control has no border (.BorderStyle = 0).

Obviously, no one in his or her right mind would *accidentally* drag the key all the way to the deletion control and double-click it. Therefore, you don't really need any further safeguards on the back side of the activity, to paraphrase the Rev. Jesse Jackson, when you can concentrate on stating your objectives more clearly on the front side.

Example

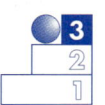

Here's another way to disable deletion for read-only files. Suppose the key's .DragMode is set back to automatic (1) as before, and has a .BorderStyle of 0—this way you don't have a situation in which the user locks the key. A check box is placed within the form, representing whether the file in question has a "read-only" status—if it does, the user is not allowed to delete it. Here's a procedure that bars the entire key-dragging procedure from being executed whenever the lock border is on and the read-only box is checked:

```
Sub DeleteFile_DragOver (Source As Control, X As Single,
    Y As Single, State As Integer)
If DeleteFile.BorderStyle = 1 And Check1.Value = 1 Then
    Source.Drag 0
End If
End Sub
```

This procedure introduces us to a new method:

.Drag Method

Syntax:

`Control.Drag integer%`

The `.Drag` method is used to manually start or stop the dragging process for a control, whether or not the `.DragMode` for that control is set. This is especially helpful if the control's `.DragMode` is set to 0 (manual) and by default cannot be dragged. The value of `integer%` can be any of the following:

0   Cancel dragging of the specified control.

1   Initiate dragging of the specified control, when the `.Drag` method appears within an event procedure for the antecedent control.

2   End dragging of the control and signal a `_DragDrop` event for that control.

367

Chapter 28 ◆ Dragging

Deletion at the OK Corral

A move operation relocates the control.

Finally, here is a wild twist to the prevalidation process: Suppose the form is to contain controls that are completely inoperable until they are moved to a marked region. Remember, to *drag* a control is not at all to *move* that control; VB shows an image being carried from the stationary control during the drag operation, while the control stays where it is.

The best way to have the source code move the control is to have a conventional drag-and-drop operation first, and then relocate the control to the position of the drop. Figure 28.6 shows a vastly modified Drag Strip application. Here the `DeleteFile` control takes the place of the key icon and will be the control that is moved. The place it will be moved to is a picture box containing no picture—only a pastel-shaded `.BackColor`. The `_DragDrop` event belongs to this shaded region. Since it is "OK" to activate controls as long as they can be found within this region, I call the region the *OK Corral*.

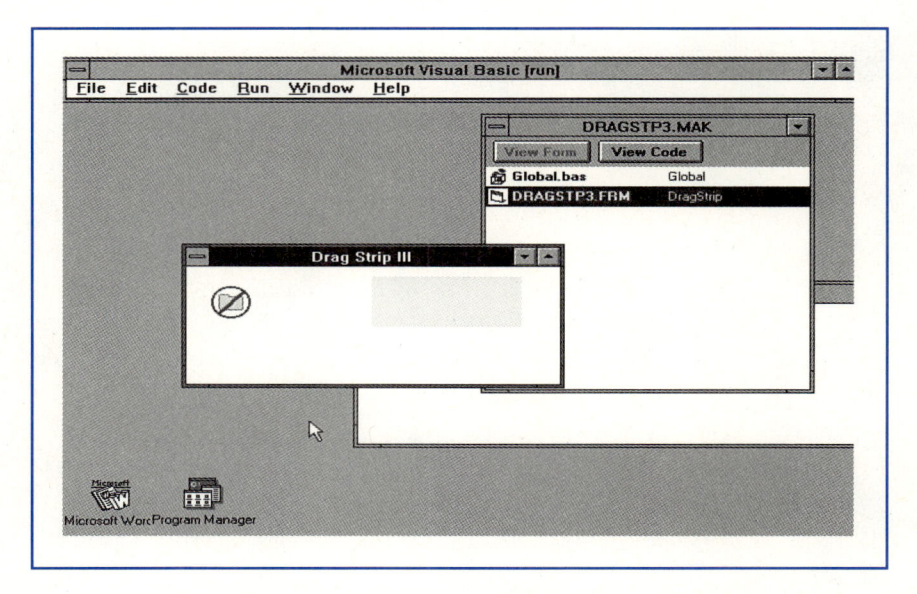

Figure 28.6. The OK Corral, as portrayed by the shaded region.

Visual Basic By EXAMPLE

The method that makes moving controls possible is explained by the following:

.Move   Method

Syntax:

Control.Move *left*[, *top*[, *width*[, *height*]]]

The .Move method moves the designated control on a form to the coordinate location on that form specified as the term's parameters. Only the *left* parameter needs to be specified, in order to move the control horizontally to the new twip position *left*. If *top* is specified, the control will be moved vertically as well. If *width* or *height* is specified, the control will be resized once it is moved.

For this procedure to work, you must declare certain information concerning the home position of the control and the deletion capability of the control at the form level. For this example, the statement Dim DelEnabled, stdx, stdy appears within the general procedures area of the form. These variables represent the deletion capability and the home coordinates of the DeleteFile icon, respectively. Within the form's Sub Form_Load () procedure, variables stdx and stdy are set to the .Left and .Top properties of the DeleteFile icon, respectively.

At design time, DeleteFile.DragMode is set to 1 (enabled), and OKCorral.DragMode is left at 0 (disabled). OKCorral is the picture box, and the crucial event procedures are attributed to that control. DeleteFile.DragIcon is set to the same image as DeleteFile.Picture. DeleteFile.Tag has been set to "DeleteFile" as well. These settings having been made, here's the new dropping procedure:

```
Sub OKCorral_DragDrop (Source As Control, X As Single, Y As
    Single)
If Source.Tag = "DeleteFile" Then
    Source.Move OKCorral.Left + X - 256, OKCorral.Top + Y - 256
    DelEnabled = 1
```

369

```
        Source.DragMode = 0
        Label1.Caption = "Clear to delete file."
    End If
End Sub
```

Here is the pseudocode for this procedure:

Procedure awaiting the receipt of a control:
*If the dragged control's tag is **DeleteFile**, then*
  Move the control to its new coordinates, accounting for the offset
    *making them relative to the location of **OKCorral**, plus the offset*
    for the distance between the corner and center of the moved control.
  Enable deletion.
  Turn off the draggability of this control.
  Tell the user he's clear to delete the file.
End of condition.
End of procedure.

The dropping coordinates x and y, automatically declared at the start of this procedure, are calculated by the interpreter relative to the object OKCorral, *not to the form*. The coordinates required for the .Move event are relative to the form; so to move the control to the coordinates passed to the procedure, you must first add the .Left and .Top coordinates of the OKCorral object itself to x and y.

Next, you need to make a correction to the way Visual Basic normally works. When an image is dragged into the OKCorral, it is dragged by the middle of the icon; so when the image follows the pointer, the middle of the image is at the pointer's hot spot. So when the pointer is within the area of OKCorral, the upper-left corner of the .DragIcon is above and to the left of the pointer position by about 256 twips. Yet, if you specify the current pointer position as the destination of the .Move event, the control will be replotted at the current pointer position starting at the control's *upper-left corner*, not the middle. To correct this problem for both x- and y-axes, 256 is subtracted from both coordinates so that the .Move event will move the *middle* of the control to the current pointer position, and not the corner.

The double-click procedure now belongs to OKCorral, as demonstrated by the following code:

Visual Basic *By* EXAMPLE

```
Sub OKCorral_DblClick ()
If DelEnabled = 1 Then
    Label1.Caption = "File is deleted."
    DeleteFile.Move stdx, stdy
    DeleteFile.DragMode = 1
    DelEnabled = 0
End If
End Sub
```

The `.Move` method is invoked here again, to return the control to its rightful place only if the form-level variable `DelEnabled` is set to 1. Figures 28.7, 28.8, and 28.9 depict this roundup at three stages of the sequence:

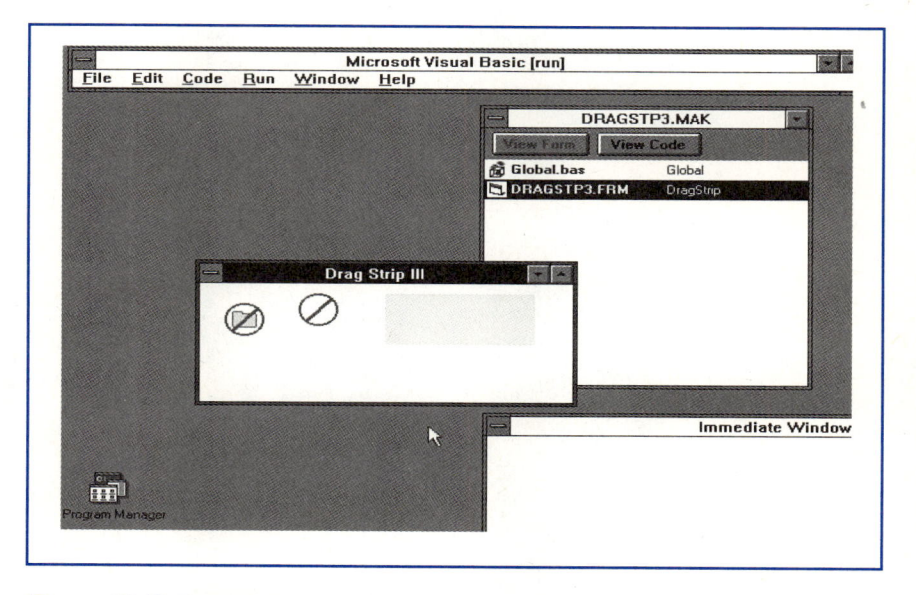

Figure 28.7. Dragging the `DeleteFile` icon into the `OKCorral`.

371

Chapter 28 ◆ Dragging

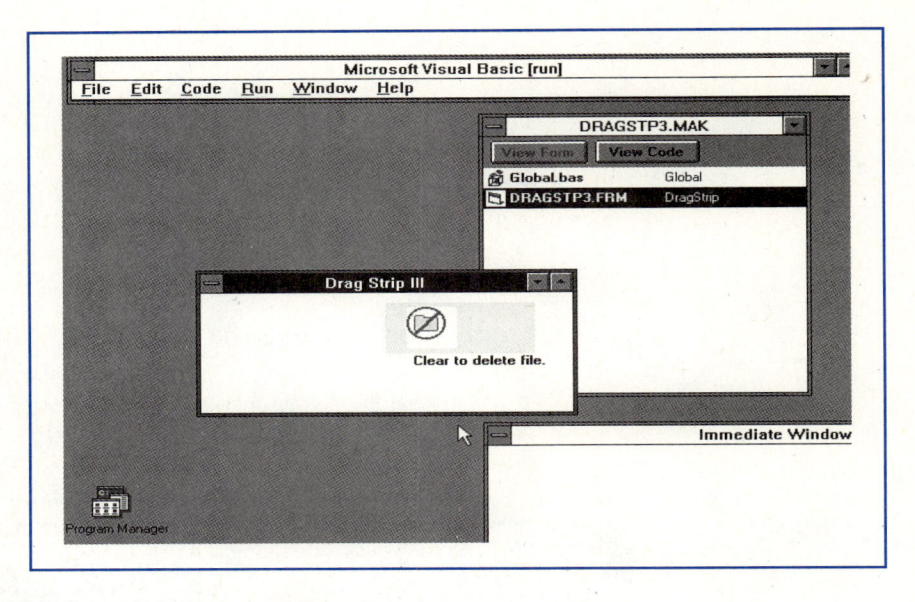

Figure 28.8. Having let go of `DeleteFile`.

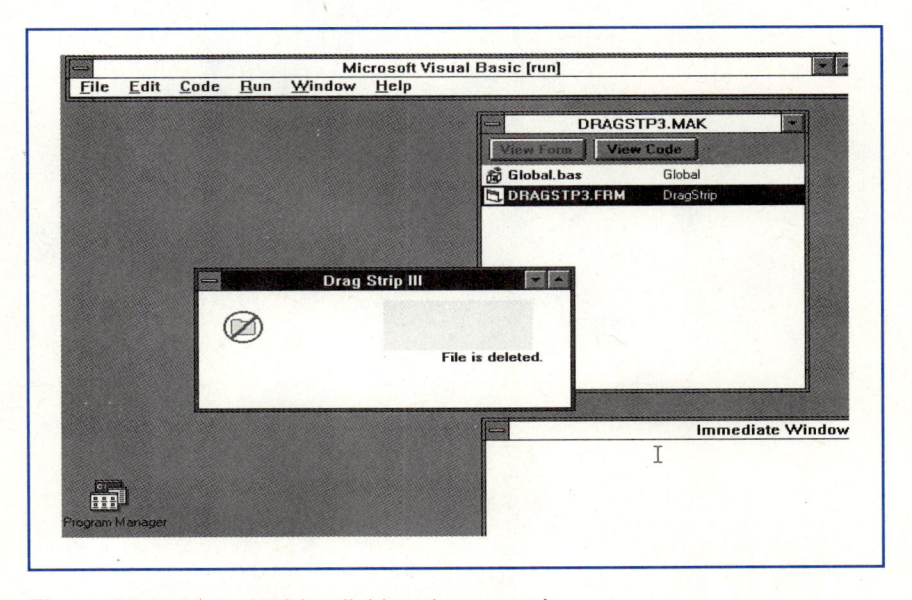

Figure 28.9. After double-clicking the control.

Summary

In graphical operations involving dragging, to drag a control is not the same operation as to move that control. During dragging, an image copied from the control follows the mouse pointer, although the control maintains its position. By contrast, moving a control relocates it to a new position. This image can be of either the border of the control being dragged or an icon referenced by the `.DragIcon` property. The control being dragged is considered the source; the destination object where the image is to land is considered the target.

Controls on a form may not be dragged by default; their `.DragMode` property can be set to 1 to initiate automatic dragging. Otherwise, any control can be made draggable within an event procedure for that control, using the `.Drag` method. While a control is draggable, events for clicking or double-clicking on that control are not recognized. Event procedures for dragging controls provide coordinate information that can be helpful in programming operations that actually move the control from one position on the form to another, using the `.Move` method.

Review Questions

1. What is the crucial difference between a *drag* operation and a *move* operation?

2. Is the event procedure awaiting the `_DragDrop` event always considered the target of the drop?

3. Are the coordinates stated within a `.Move` operation expressed relative to the screen, the current form, or the control to which the event procedure belongs?

Review Exercises

Using some of the preceding procedures as models, write procedures that use test controls that operate in the following manners:

Chapter 28 ◆ Dragging

1. An icon represents a file. Dragging its image inside a picture box places a border around that icon.

2. An icon represents a process to delete a file. Dragging a box around the icon enables deletion. Double-clicking the icon with the box around it initiates deletion.

The Timer

In this chapter you learn how the timer is used in Visual Basic as a control on a form to regulate *when* certain events can take place and *when* procedures can be executed. Normally, instructions in a procedure are executed once. By embedding instructions in a loop clause, or by expertly manipulating the various branches, instructions can be executed multiple times. There is a way within Visual Basic, however, to program instructions to be executed continually, periodically, or after a set interval. Unlike other languages, however, Visual Basic's continual execution mechanism is dependent on a specific graphic object: the timer object.

Where Did I Leave My Watch?

Just when you thought Visual Basic was esoteric enough, I have to introduce you to a graphic object that is not really an object. In the Microsoft Windows environment, each application running in the environment is given a brief slice of time in which to operate. Each application must then yield the balance of its time to the other application or to the environment itself, in much the same way congressmen are apportioned and exchange time on the floor of Congress. And while their Washington counterparts may debate,

Windows applications tend to argue with each other over how much time they are apportioned.

Partly because BASIC is such a popular language for programming or modeling time-intensive games, a mechanism must be maintained for keeping exact time. Yet with forms and modules in a Visual Basic application given indefinite time slices, depending on such incalculable factors as what computer the application is running on at the time, it would be rather difficult for the VB interpreter to keep perfect time for each running form. Therefore, Visual Basic maintains a laissez-faire attitude about timing, unless you as programmer specify otherwise. You can tell the VB interpreter directly to keep chronological (real-world) time for a particular form.

The way to do this is unusual, but effective. A *timer* is assigned to a form by clicking the timer button in the VB toolbox. The timer is then placed on the form to be timed as if that timer were a picture box. At design time, an image of a stopwatch appears where the timer is placed. At run time, however, this image will not be visible, so it really doesn't matter where the timer object is placed as long as it doesn't conflict with another graphic object. The user cannot operate the timer graphic object; it operates itself and generates an event by itself.

*Timer*_Timer **Event**

The _Timer event takes place for a form that contains a timer control, after each passing of a certain interval of time as specified within the *Timer*.Interval property.

> **CAUTION:** The Timer() function in Visual Basic refers to the time kept by the computer system clock, while the _Timer event refers to the time maintained by VB's simulated chronological timer. These are two different timing systems.

The .Interval property is the only property that is specific to a timer control.

Visual Basic *By* EXAMPLE

Timer.Interval **Property**

The .Interval property for a timer is the amount of time in milliseconds (thousandths of a second) the form's timer is to count before invoking a _Timer event. The property value ranges from 0 to 65,535 milliseconds, where 60,000 milliseconds equal one minute. The .Interval property is often set to 1000, so that events occur every second.

Example

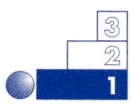

The most obvious use for the timer control is to have a form display the current real-world time. Assume a timer has been placed into a form. The .Interval property of this timer is set to 1000. Here is a procedure that displays the time as the caption of a label:

```
Sub Timer1_Timer ()
    TimeNow.Caption = Time$
End Sub
```

By itself or within another procedure, the line TimeNow.Caption = Time$ would be executed once, display the current time, and then become as useless as a stopped clock. With the preceding procedure, the _Timer event is generated regardless of what the user is doing at the time. The current time appears in the label TimeNow. once every second.

If you were more conservative with your time and wanted TimeNow to display the current time only every minute, you would reset the .Interval property to 60000, set the .Enabled property of the timer to true (–1) so that it might work, and rewrite the preceding procedure as follows:

```
Sub Timer1_Timer ()
    TimeNow.Caption = Right$(Time$, 5)
End Sub
```

Because the second hand is meaningless if the interval is set to minutes, you can use the Right$() function to extract the first five characters of Time$, leaving off the seconds digits.

Chapter 29 ◆ The Timer

Example

The `.Interval` property counts up to only one minute, five seconds, but that doesn't mean you can't keep certain elements of time independently. Suppose you have an application that maintains in memory a document that is being composed. You want this document to be backed up to disk every five minutes—regardless of what the user is doing at the moment—as a *background process*. Assuming the `.Interval` property is set to 60000 and the timer is `.Enabled`, here's how the branch to the back-up procedure might appear:

```
Sub Timer1_Timer ()
BranchClock = BranchClock + 1
If BranchClock = 5 Then
    BranchClock = 0
    Auto_Backup
End If
End Sub
```

Here's pseudocode for the above procedure:

Procedure awaiting a timer signal:
Add 1 to the number of minutes being kept.
If there are five minutes in the tally, then
   Reset the tally.
   Execute the backup procedure.
End of condition.
End of procedure.

With the `.Interval` set to minutes, the event procedure for `_Timer` is executed every minute. Each minute, a count of 1 is added to an accumulator variable `BranchClock`. When the minutes are five, the count is reset and the branch is made to the `Auto_Backup` procedure.

Summary

Normally, the Visual Basic interpreter doesn't time the execution of a form within a project in real-world time. To engage such timing for a form, a timer control is dragged into the form from the VB toolbox. This control is invisible at run time. When the timer is engaged by setting its `.Enabled` property to true (−1), the timer generates an event after each `.Interval` of milliseconds. An event procedure can be assigned to this event, called `Timer_Timer`.

Review Questions

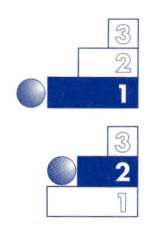

1. The maximum value of the `.Interval` property is roughly equivalent to how many minutes and seconds?

2. What terms, along with their delimiters (extra punctuation), are used to describe the following?

   A. The passing of the set Visual Basic interval

   B. The VB real-world chronometer

   C. The VB function that registers the passage of seconds since midnight

30

The Keyboard

In this chapter you learn how Visual Basic handles events related to the pressing and releasing of individual keys on the keyboard. To the left of your mouse (or to the right if you're left-handed) is a rather interesting device for processing user input that dates back to the 18th century. It's called a keyboard, and Visual Basic has not forgotten its existence. You see how the VB interpreter processes events related to the keyboard and individual key presses. You then examine ways keystrokes can be assigned as substitutes for graphic control inputs.

The Thing with All the Letter Buttons on It

Up to this point, you've used the keyboard to generate *text*, which is often composed of words typed into boxes. If you've ever played with Microsoft's Flight Simulator, you know that the keyboard can also be programmed as an elaborate control mechanism for simulations. If you're playing in Piper Cherokee mode and you throttle up, you hold down the plus key on your keyboard. Likewise, you use the minus key to throttle down. The longer the key is held down, the more the throttle is moved one way or the other.

Chapter 30 ◆ The Keyboard

Frankly, it historically has been difficult to program the keyboard for use as such a controller using standard BASIC. It wasn't so long ago that programmers such as I would use the PEEK command to look into a register of memory to see if a certain key was being held down; the *scan code* of the held down key often appeared in that memory address. This process is called *polling for keys* (generally, no cash prizes were awarded for guessing the right key). What this is, literally, is the search for the digital form of the electrical signal generated by a key touching a metal plate inside the keyboard unit.

The problem with polling in this way was that the execution of these polling routines was difficult to regulate. At first, before the advent of timers and statements such as ON TIMER GOSUB, the program had to branch to the key-polling subroutine whenever it could. There was no real way of regulating the specific time the polling took place. As a result, we had no intervals. Every once in a while, the program would branch, using GOSUB, to the key-polling subroutine. To make sure the keyboard was polled often, we included numerous GOSUB commands in the code. If we were programming a flight simulator (A flight simulator in BASIC? Are you kidding?) or something like it, when the user let go of whatever key acted as the throttle-up button, the program would not "know" the throttle-up was released until after the next GOSUB to the key-polling subroutine. By that time, the throttle may have increased by another 10 percent; and if you're leaking fuel, another routine might generate an explosion.

Later in BASIC's history, some manufacturers used the ON KEY GOSUB statement, which forced a branch to a subroutine whenever a key was pressed. Visual Basic's solution to the key-polling problem is to recognize key presses as events. The problem for the programmer is that VB events "belong" to controls. If the purpose for the keyboard is to operate controls on a form, it's no problem to assign a keypress event to a control. If the keypress is meant to affect some unseen value in memory, however, the objective for the programmer is to determine which control or which form module processes the event.

Here are the main events recognized for keypresses, in place of the old ON KEY command.

Control_KeyDown and Control_Keyup Events

The _KeyDown event for a form or control is recognized whenever that graphic object has the focus and a key is pressed on the keyboard. The _KeyDown event continues to be recognized for that control as long as that key remains depressed. Two parameters are passed to the procedure for this event: the scan code for the depressed key (not to be confused for the ASCII code value of the character the key generally represents) and an integer having a bitwise pattern that represents the depression state of the shifting key. This integer can take any of the following values:

    0   No shifting keys pressed

    1   Either Shift key pressed

    2   Either Ctrl key pressed

    3   Control + Shift pressed

    4   Alt key pressed

    5   Alt + Shift pressed

    6   Alt + Ctrl pressed

    7   Alt + Ctrl + Shift pressed

The _KeyUp event for a graphic object is recognized whenever that object has the focus and a key that had been depressed on the keyboard is released. Logically speaking, the event is recognized when the key scan code previously registered returns to 0. The procedure for the _KeyUp event is passed the same values by the VB interpreter as the _KeyDown event.

Example

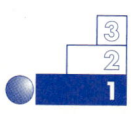

Suppose you need a quick procedure to register what the scan code is for a key, because the ASCII (ANSI) code for a character is not the same as the scan code for its corresponding key. All you need on the form is a simple text label and nothing else. Here's a procedure that returns the key scan code for any key pressed:

Chapter 30 ◆ The Keyboard

```
Sub Form_KeyDown (KeyCode As Integer, Shift As Integer)
Label1.Caption = Str$(KeyCode)
End Sub
```

Simply enough, the textual value of the key scan code is placed within `Label1`.

Suppose you want the contents of the label to clear itself when the depressed key is released. The following procedure might be added:

```
Sub Form_KeyUp (KeyCode As Integer, Shift As Integer)
Label1.Caption = ""
End Sub
```

Example

Earlier, I discussed a set of controls for "throttling" up and down using the keyboard. You can program such a control using the _KeyDown event and set up a scroll bar to represent the state of such a control in the form. Figure 30.1 depicts this form in action.

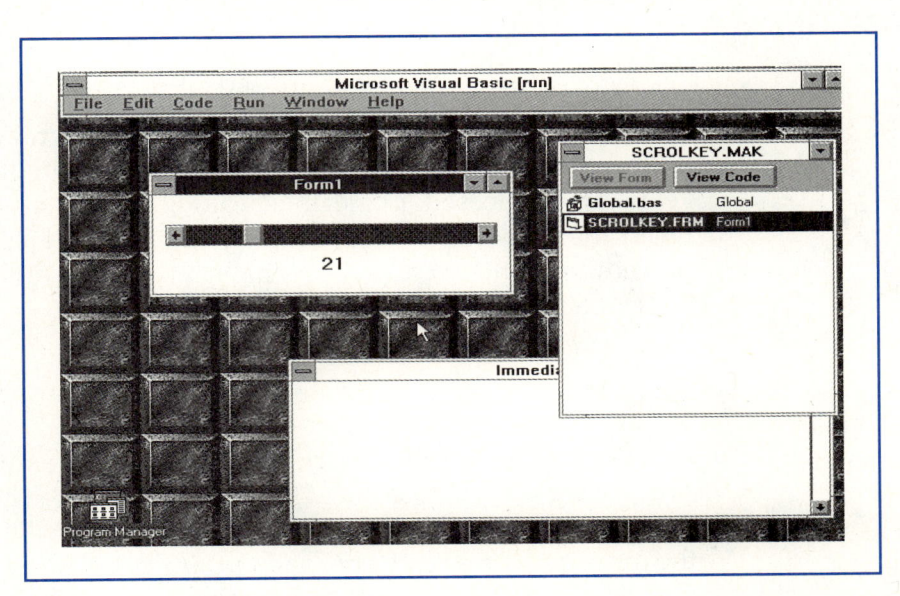

Figure 30.1. The scroll key form.

384

Visual Basic *By* EXAMPLE

"Scroll Key" Throttle Control Tester

PROJECT NAME
SCROLKEY.MAK

CONSTITUENT FILES
SCROLKEY.FRM

Object type	Property	Setting
Form	.Left	1095
	.Top	1545
	.Width	4485
	.Height	1905
Scroll bar	.Max	100
	.LargeChange	10
Label	.Alignment	2 - Center
	.FontSize	12

```
Sub HScroll1_KeyDown (KeyCode As Integer, Shift As Integer)
Sub HScroll1_KeyDown (KeyCode As Integer, Shift As Integer)
Select Case KeyCode
   Case 48
      If HScroll1.Min <= HScroll1.Value - HScroll1.LargeChange Then
         HScroll1.Value = HScroll1.Value - HScroll1.LargeChange
      End If
   Case 189
      If HScroll1.Min <= HScroll1.Value - HScroll1.SmallChange Then
         HScroll1.Value = HScroll1.Value - HScroll1.SmallChange
      End If
   Case 187
      If HScroll1.Max >= HScroll1.Value + HScroll1.SmallChange Then
         HScroll1.Value = HScroll1.Value + HScroll1.SmallChange
      End If
   Case 220
      If HScroll1.Max >= HScroll1.Value + HScroll1.LargeChange Then
         HScroll1.Value = HScroll1.Value + HScroll1.LargeChange
      End If
End Select
Label1.Caption = Str$(HScroll1.Value)
End Sub
```

The preceding procedure is a relatively more complex `Select Case` clause than you've utilized before. The clause compares the value of `KeyCode` to the key scan values of the 0, -, =, and \ keys, from top to bottom. The keys perform the following functions on the scroll box:

0	`.LargeChange` to the left
-	`.SmallChange` to the left
=	`.SmallChange` to the right
\	`.LargeChange` to the right

Each `Case` in the clause first checks to see if there is enough room to move the scroll box in the direction designated by the pressed key, using a subordinate conditional `If-Then` clause. If there is enough room, the scroll box is moved by adding the value of `HScroll1.SmallChange` or `.LargeChange` to `HScroll1.Value`, which represents the current scroll box position. When the `Select Case` clause is completed, that position is reflected in the label below the scroll bar.

You might find it easier to use ASCII code rather than key scan code to detect key presses. In such cases, Visual Basic supplies a key event that recognizes ASCII (ANSI) code.

*Control*_KeyPress Event

The _KeyPress event for a form or control is recognized whenever that graphic object has the focus and a key is pressed on the keyboard. The _KeyPress event does not continue to be recognized by default if the key is held down; however, if key repetition has been selected through the Windows Control Panel, continued depression of the key eventually causes Windows to repeat the key, thus making it appear to the VB interpreter that the _KeyPress event occurs repetitively. The ASCII code value of the character having its corresponding key pressed is the sole parameter passed to the procedure for this event.

Example

If it's easier for you to think in ASCII, the procedure introduced previously can be modified as follows:

```
Sub HScroll1_KeyPress (KeyAscii As Integer)
Select Case KeyAscii
   Case Asc("0")
      If HScroll1.Min <= HScroll1.Value - HScroll1.LargeChange Then
         HScroll1.Value = HScroll1.Value - HScroll1.LargeChange
      End If
   Case Asc("-")
      If HScroll1.Min <= HScroll1.Value - HScroll1.SmallChange Then
         HScroll1.Value = HScroll1.Value - HScroll1.SmallChange
      End If
   Case Asc("=")
      If HScroll1.Max >= HScroll1.Value + HScroll1.SmallChange Then
         HScroll1.Value = HScroll1.Value + HScroll1.SmallChange
      End If
   Case Asc("\")
      If HScroll1.Max >= HScroll1.Value + HScroll1.LargeChange Then
         HScroll1.Value = HScroll1.Value + HScroll1.LargeChange
      End If
End Select
Label1.Caption = Str$(HScroll1.Value)
End Sub
```

What immediately makes this procedure easier for programmers to implement is the fact that they can use the `Asc()` function to substitute for the ASCII value of the character in quotation marks, saving them from taking a trip to the ASCII table in Appendix A of this book. The cost of simplifying this procedure is the fact that it now runs a bit slower than its key scan code progenitor.

Chapter 30 ◆ The Keyboard

Substituting Buttons for Keys

Up to this point in the chapter, you've used keys from the keyboard to substitute for operating graphic controls. As you might expect, Visual Basic also gives you the option of using graphic controls as substitutes for keys. The way to do this is with a statement that *forces* keypresses to the system as if they came from the keyboard. This statement is then issued from an event procedure for the controls to substitute for the keys.

A program with redundant controls has many ways for the user to enter the same commands.

Why would you want something on the screen to substitute for something else that is right in front of you? Many modern applications utilize what are called *redundant controls,* or multiple ways to issue the same command to the program. In Visual Basic, as well as in any high-level language, you want to program an event procedure only once; but that procedure is dependent solely on a single event. If you want multiple events to execute the same procedure, you may want a way to easily tie a subsidiary event to the one that contains the main body of the code. If the keyboard is more important to the particular program and graphic controls are subsidiary, keystroke substitution may be a welcome tool. Here is the statement for forced keypresses:

SendKeys   Statement

Syntax:

SendKeys text$[, suspend%]

This statement sends the text contained in text$ to the system, one character after the other, as if each character in text$ were typed on the keyboard (but very fast). The control of the current form that has the focus will be the recipient of the text. If the cursor is within a text box, the text contained in text$ appears in that box as if the user typed that text manually. If the value –1 is specified for suspend%, execution of the Visual Basic application is suspended until Windows has processed all of the keys sent, and the keyboard buffer is empty.

Visual Basic *By* EXAMPLE

Example

To test this statement, I extended the Scroll Key application's form and added controls to it, as follows:

"Scroll Key" Throttle Control Tester

PROJECT NAME	CONSTITUENT FILES
SCROLKEY.MAK	SCROLKEY.FRM

Object Type	Property	Setting
Form	.Left	1095
	.Top	1530
	.Width	4485
	.Height	2505
Control Array Button	.CtlName	TapeControl
	.Caption	<<
	.Index	0
Button	.Caption	<
	.Index	1
Button	.Caption	>
	.Index	2
Button	.Caption	>>
	.Index	3

I then added the following procedure for the button control array:

```
    Case 1
        SendKeys "-"
    Case 2
        SendKeys "="
    Case 3
        SendKeys "\"
End Select
End Sub
```

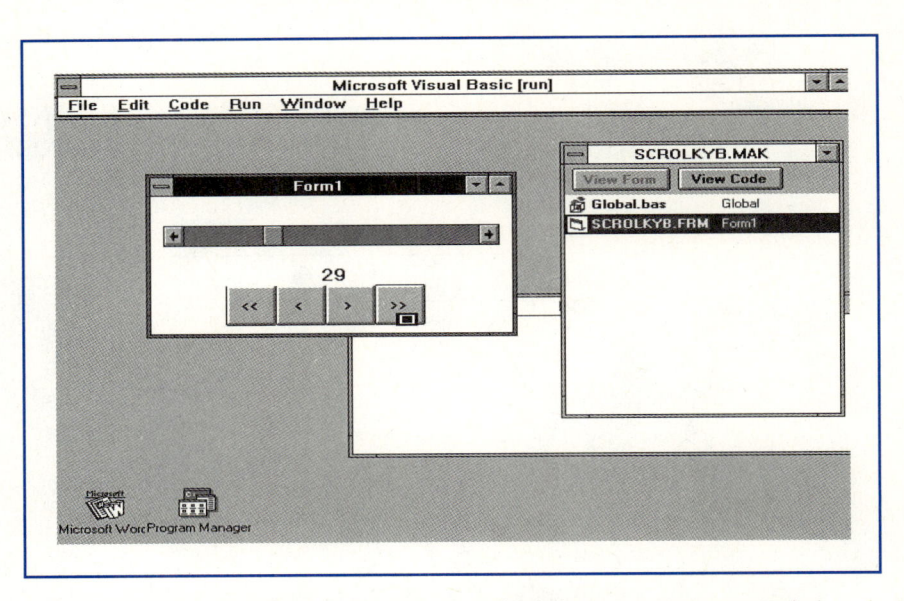

Figure 30.2 shows the cosmetic changes I made to the form.

Figure 30.2. Controls that act as keys, which in turn act as controls.

Pseudocode for the procedure is as follows:

Procedure awaiting a click on the **TapeControl** *button array:*
Set the focus to the horizontal scroll bar, taking it away from any of the buttons.
   In case the first button was pressed,
     Register a "0"
   In case the second button was pressed,
     Register a "–"
   In case the third button was pressed,
     Register a "="
   In case the fourth button was pressed,
     Register a "\"
End of cases.
End of procedure.

Here, the index of the button that was clicked passes to the event procedure for the control array. The `SelectCase` clause then sends the appropriate key for that index, using `SendKeys`. The procedure doesn't need to do anything more, because the event procedure that awaits keypresses will soon be executed, not knowing that the ASCII code is actually being sent by Visual Basic itself, disguised as the keyboard. As a result, you have efficient redundant controls. You can use both keyboard objects and graphic objects to perform the same events, without needing to use a branch statement or a remote procedure call from one event procedure to another.

Assigning Keystrokes to Buttons

When you operate a dialog box that contains the `OK` and `Cancel` buttons, pressing the Enter key generally substitutes for clicking `OK`, and pressing Esc substitutes for `Cancel`. Here, `Yes` and `No` buttons can be substituted for `OK` and `Cancel`; the two keys still perform much the same purpose. The VB interpreter cannot intuit which buttons in a form perform the yes/no functions, so it is informed which buttons can be assigned the Enter and Esc keystrokes with property settings.

Command.`Default` and *Command*.`Cancel` Properties

The `.Default` property for a button is set to true (−1) if the user can press Enter in place of clicking that button. Similarly, the `.Cancel` property of a button is set to true if the user can press Esc in place of clicking that button.

Example

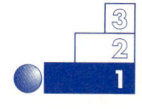

These properties generally do not require you to write any source code. Although they can be set at run time, computing etiquette generally dictates they be set at design time, so one default button is always the default button. In the `ScrollKey` application, for instance, if you wanted the > button (the *Play* button on a VCR or tape player) to be the default, you would set the property `TapeControl(3).Default = -1`.

Summary

Visual Basic recognizes events for keypresses that occur during the time a graphic object running in a VB application has the focus. While that object has the focus, the VB interpreter can await `_KeyDown`, `_KeyUp`, or `_KeyPress` events for that object. The latter event recognizes the ASCII (ANSI) code for the character corresponding to the key that was pressed, whereas the other two events recognize the key scan code for the particular key pressed, as returned to Windows by your computer's BIOS.

A `_KeyPress` event can be forced with the `SendKeys` statement, which makes it appear to Windows that a key on the keyboard was actually pressed. The default and cancelling keystrokes Enter and Esc, respectively, can be assigned to individual controls on a form with property assignments.

Review Questions

The procedure `Sub HScroll1_KeyDown` presented earlier in this chapter moved the scroll bar left or right based on the value of the key scan code passed to that event procedure by the VB interpreter itself. Knowing what you know about Visual Basic, Microsoft Windows, and key scan codes, speculate on the following: Suppose the user of this test program were to press at the same time two of the four keys being scanned for. What is most likely to happen?

1. Windows will add the bitwise values of the two scan codes, resulting in a sum that equals none of the four codes being searched for in the Select Case clause. None of the `Case`-dependent instructions will be executed.

2. The BIOS will scan for each key code in numerical order, so that one key is considered pressed before the other key is considered pressed, by virtue of that key's precedence in the code sequence.

3. The timing system of the computer will know one key was really pressed before the other one, rather than both being pressed at the same time. So, by virtue of the quickness of the computer's reflexes over the user's, one key will come out in front of the other.

4. The BIOS will apply priority to one key over the other, resulting in an implied hierarchy of key importance such that one key *blanks out* the other, making it more likely one key is considered "pressed" than another.

To find the answer to this question, I added a list box to the `ScrollKey` form called `KeyPresses`. At the end of procedure `Sub HScroll1_KeyDown`, I added this instruction:

```
KeyPresses.AddItem Str$(KeyCode)
```

Each time one of the scanned-for keys is pressed, its code is added to the list. By examining this list, you can determine the solution to the quandary I've presented to you.

31

The Mouse as Device

In this chapter you learn how Visual Basic processes events relating to the movement and position of the mouse pointer. You're used to processing a *click* as a quick press and release of the index button of the mouse. Visual Basic also recognizes a particular event for merely pressing and holding down a mouse button; likewise, it recognizes an event just for releasing the button. You study these events, and later you tinker with the coordinate system for the mouse pointer itself.

The Key to Your Mouse

In Chapter 30, "The Keyboard," I introduced you to the events the Visual Basic interpreter recognizes for the pressing of certain keys. VB also recognizes similar events for the pressing of the buttons on the mouse.

Chapter 31 ◆ The Mouse as Device

*Control*_MouseDown and *Control*_MouseUp Events

The _MouseDown event for a graphic object is recognized whenever that object has the focus and any mouse button is pressed. Four parameters are passed to the procedure for this event by the Visual Basic interpreter. The first is the state of the mouse buttons, assuming as many as three buttons for the mouse. This value can be set to any of the following:

1	Left button (default index button) pressed
2	Right button pressed
3	Left and right buttons pressed
4	Middle button pressed
5	Middle and left buttons pressed
6	Middle and right buttons pressed
7	Middle, left, and right buttons pressed

The second value passed to the _MouseDown event procedure reflects the current state of the shifting keys on the keyboard at the time the mouse button was registered as having been pressed. This value can be set to any of the following:

0	No Shift keys pressed
1	Either Shift key pressed
2	Either Ctrl key pressed
3	Shift and Ctrl pressed
4	Either Alt key pressed
5	Alt and Shift pressed
6	Alt and Ctrl pressed
7	Alt, Shift, and Ctrl pressed

The third and fourth values passed to the _MouseDown event procedure reflect the current mouse pointer coordinate location with respect to the graphic object to which this procedure is attributed.

The _MouseUp event for a graphic object is recognized whenever that object has the focus and the mouse button that was previously depressed is released. The _MouseUp event procedure is passed the same values by the VB interpreter as the _MouseDown procedure.

There is one more important event attributed to the mouse pointer: the event that occurs when the mouse pointer *moves* over a graphic object on the form.

> **CAUTION:** Some Windows mouse drivers do not recognize the middle button of a Logitech-brand or other three-button mouse, regardless of whether Visual Basic tries to recognize that button. As a result, a middle-button press might not be registered by the system, thus the VB interpreter would never see it.

Object_MouseMove Event

The _MouseMove event is recognized for a graphic object whenever that object currently has the focus and the mouse pointer is moved while it resides over the area of that object. The _MouseMove event can occur only on a file box, a label box, a list box, a picture box, or a form. The procedure for the _MouseMove event is passed four parameters, as described previously for the _MouseDown event.

Example

To see how these events work, here is an application that places a large arrow at a fixed position in the form. This arrow will point in the general direction that the mouse pointer is moving while the pointer is over the arrow. The objective of this application is to help facilitate a new type of control mechanism, whereby the direction the mouse is moved indicates a command to the program. Figure 31.1 depicts this application at run time.

Chapter 31 ◆ The Mouse as Device

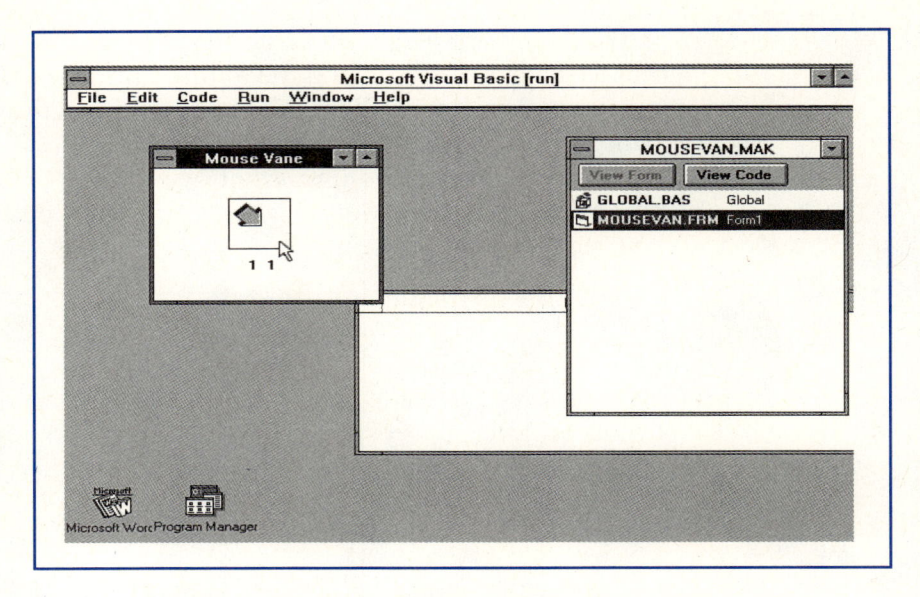

Figure 31.1. The mouse vane bloweth with the wind.

"Mouse Vane"
Mouse Direction
Tester

PROJECT NAME
MOUSEVAN.MAK

CONSTITUENT FILES
MOUSEVAN.FRM

Object type	Property	Setting
Form	.Left	1035
	.Top	1200
	.Width	2850
	.Height	2400
	.Caption	Mouse Vane
Picture Box	.CtlName	Vane
Label	.Alignment	2 - Center
	.Caption	(blank)

```
Sub Vane_MouseMove (Button As Integer, Shift As Integer,
    x As Single, y As Single)
Static lastx, lasty
If x > lastx Then xaxis = 1
If x < lastx Then xaxis = -1
If y > lasty Then yaxis = 1
If y < lasty Then yaxis = -1
Label1.Caption = Str$(xaxis) + " " + Str$(yaxis)
Select Case -1
    Case (xaxis = 1 And yaxis = 1)
        Vane.Picture = LoadPicture
            ("c:\win3\vbasic\icons\arrows\arw10se.ico")
    Case (xaxis = 1 And yaxis = -1)
        Vane.Picture = LoadPicture
            ("c:\win3\vbasic\icons\arrows\arw10ne.ico")
    Case (xaxis = -1 And yaxis = 1)
        Vane.Picture = LoadPicture
            ("c:\win3\vbasic\icons\arrows\arw10sw.ico")
    Case (xaxis = -1 And yaxis = -1)
        Vane.Picture = LoadPicture
            ("c:\win3\vbasic\icons\arrows\arw10nw.ico")
    Case (xaxis = 1 And yaxis = 0)
        Vane.Picture = LoadPicture
            ("c:\win3\vbasic\icons\arrows\arw07rt.ico")
    Case (xaxis = -1 And yaxis = 0)
        Vane.Picture = LoadPicture
            ("c:\win3\vbasic\icons\arrows\arw07lt.ico")
    Case (xaxis = 0 And yaxis = 1)
        Vane.Picture = LoadPicture
            ("c:\win3\vbasic\icons\arrows\arw07dn.ico")
    Case (xaxis = 0 And yaxis = -1)
        Vane.Picture = LoadPicture
            ("c:\win3\vbasic\icons\arrows\arw07up.ico")
End Select
lastx = x
lasty = y
End Sub
```

Chapter 31 ◆ The Mouse as Device

> **NOTE:** Depending on how you installed Visual Basic, the subdirectory locations of the supplied icons may be different than shown above.

Here's a sort of skeletal pseudocode for the preceding procedure:

Procedure awaiting the mouse pointer to move within the vane area:
Declare two variables to have their values maintained when this
  procedure is exited.
If the pointer's current x coordinate is greater than the previously
  registered x coordinate, then register a movement to the right.
If the pointer's current x coordinate is less than the previously
  registered x coordinate, then register a movement to the left.
If the pointer's current y coordinate is greater than the previously
  registered y coordinate, then register a downward movement.
If the pointer's current y coordinate is less than the previously
  registered y coordinate, then register an upward movement.
Display the registers for both directions.
Search for logical truth in the following cases:
   In the case of rightward and downward movement,
       Show a southeasterly pointing arrow.
   In the case of rightward and downward movement,
       Show a northeasterly pointing arrow.
       .
       .
       .

End of cases.
Register the current pointer coordinates as the old coordinates.
End of procedure.

400

In this application, the `MouseMove` event will not be recognized until the pointer enters the area of the picture box called `Vane`. At that point, the values `x` and `y` passed to the procedure by the VB interpreter are compared with two static variables `lastx` and `lasty` to see what the differences are. Variables `lastx` and `lasty` contain the previously recorded values of `x` and `y`, stored within those variables before the procedure was last exited. These variables were declared `Static` at the beginning of the procedure so that their values could be maintained upon its exit. If the current value of `x` is greater than that of `lastx`, the pointer must have moved to the right. Likewise, if the current value of `y` is less than that of `lasty`, the pointer must have moved upward.

The direction of the pointer's movement is stored in variables `xaxis` and `yaxis`. A negative value here refers to a lesser value on the coordinate scale of the axis; so an `xaxis` value of −1 refers to a leftward direction, and a `yaxis` value of −1 refers to an upward direction. Positive values refer to east and south movements, respectively. Zero values refer to no change in the axis. It would be relatively difficult for most people's hands to achieve a perfect zero-movement along either axis without making the arrow tip in some diagonal direction.

The `Select Case` clause loads an icon into picture box `Vane`, having a direction that corresponds with the direction of movement of the mouse. Here, logical expressions beside each `Case` are reduced, and their logically reduced values are compared with logical truth (−1) for equality. Finally, after `End Select`, the current states of the `xaxis` and `yaxis` values are shown in `Label1`.

Whither the Pointer?

The mouse pointer can be made to change appearance upon entry into the area of a graphic object. A special procedure or event is not necessary to accomplish this; it can be done through property settings.

Chapter 31 ◆ The Mouse as Device

Control.`MousePointer` **Property**

The `.MousePointer` property for a graphic object is set to an integer value that represents the default state of the mouse pointer whenever it enters the region of that object. On exiting the object region, the shape of the pointer either resumes its default state or the state designated by the `.MousePointer` property of its parent object. You generally set the `.MousePointer` property at design time. Its representative integer may be set to any of the following values:

- 0   Default state
- 1   Arrow: The standard Windows arrow
- 2   Cross: Thin cross hairs
- 3   I-Beam: The text locator pointer
- 4   Icon: (Not to be confused with an icon, despite its name) A square bullet
- 5   Size: A four-pointed arrow
- 6   Size NE SW: A two-pointed arrow directed northeast and southwest
- 7   Size NS: A two-pointed arrow directed north and south
- 8   Size NW SE: A two-pointed arrow directed north west and southeast
- 9   Size WE: A two-pointed arrow directed east and west
- 10 Up Arrow
- 11 Wait: The Windows hourglass symbol
- 12 No Drop: The circle-with-a-slash symbol indicating an object movement violation

Control.`Pointer` **Property**

The `.Pointer` property for a graphic object sets the shape of the mouse pointer to the state referred to by the representative integer, as defined above. This does not affect the `.MousePointer` property for that object; so the `.Pointer` property is useful for animation or temporary indication purposes. This property may only be set at run time.

Summary

Visual Basic maintains events that recognize when the mouse pointer is moved and when a mouse button is pressed. These events are each attributed to a graphic object, so such an event procedure can be executed only if its object currently has the focus. The shape and appearance of the mouse pointer on entering the area of a graphic object can be set at design time or during run time using property settings.

Review Questions

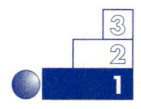

1. In the preceding `Sub Vane_MouseMove ()` event procedure, during run time, why is it so difficult to make the arrow within the picture box *not* point in a diagonal direction?

2. What is the *logical* difference between the `.MousePointer` property for an object and the `.Pointer` property for that object. In other words, how do the logical mechanisms for the two properties differ?

Part VI

Arithmetic Functions

Function Classification

Time now to turn your attention from the visually practical to the logically cerebral. In this chapter, you review what a Visual Basic function is and does. Before you start examining these functions in detail, you'll see how their return values can be classified as variable types.

The Function of the Matter

As you've learned thus far in this book, all a computer really does is perform logical operations. Literally, it compares two Boolean values and obtains the Boolean result. Because such operations mimic the appearance and behavior of mathematical operations at the base 2 level, logical comparisons and derivatives performed on one another repetitively and continually actually cause the computer to perform the same function as mathematics in the real world. Every mathematical function can somehow be described as a combination of logical comparisons, as discovered and proven by mathematicians such as George Boole and John von Neumann.

Chapter 32 ♦ Function Classification

A function is an arithmetic operation performed on a value, variable, or expression.

An expression is a mathematical comparison or combination of values.

When I say *function* in the context of the preceding paragraph, I refer to the role of mathematics in the modern world, and not the role of terms or instructions in Visual Basic. As defined in Chapter 3, a Visual Basic function is a more fundamental, less esoteric thing. A *function* is an arithmetic operation performed on a value, variable, or expression, having a result that is returned in a single variable.

An *expression* in this case is not a figure of speech. An expression is any of the following:

♦ An arithmetic comparison between two values, having a result that is expressed logically as a binary state

♦ One or more values or variables arithmetically joined by functions or functional operators

♦ An assignment of value to a variable through another value, variable, or another expression

An expression is a mathematical combination of values (or contents of strings, but not both) and functions. Fundamental mathematical functions are represented in Visual Basic by *operators* such as + and /. Functions such as the sine of an angle measurement or the ASCII code value of a character, however, are represented by abbreviated terms, each of which carries a set of parentheses. Within this set is the list of values or alphanumeric strings (or both) that the Visual Basic interpreter uses to derive a result.

A Visual Basic function is a term that is said to perform an operation on a set of values or textual contents. It is sometimes said to *yield* a result, which is stored within a variable that utilizes the function. In all Visual Basic instructions that include intrinsic functions, the function is stated within the right side of an equation. This equation acts as an *expression of assignment*, in that the solution of the equation is a result that is placed within a single variable. This variable is the only term on the left side of the equation. This expression takes on the following form:

```
variable=function()
```

Example

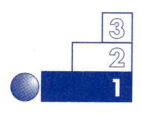

As an example, here's one of the simplest function assignments there is:

```
a# = sqr(2)
```

What you are doing is assigning the value of the square root of 2 to variable `a#`. Here, the intrinsic Visual Basic function is `sqr()`, which calculates the square root of whatever value or expression rests within its parentheses.

Some Visual Basic functions are not mathematical; in fact, a great many of them concern the manipulation of text. They operate in the same manner, because textual assignments can be formulated like equations. A text function can be distinguished easily from a value function, in that a text function always contains the `$` character before its parentheses. As an example:

```
c$ = chr$(65)
```

Here the character having ASCII code 65 is returned in the string variable `c$`. The character that `c$` now contains, by the way, is capital *A*.

Example

Often, a function contains more than one parameter, in which case these parameters are separated by commas as delimiters, as in the following example:

```
n$ = right$("D. F. Scott", 5)
```

Here, the `right$()` function extracts the rightmost five characters from my name and assigns them to variable `n$`. When strings are stated explicitly within a function as in `"D. F. Scott"`, you as programmer must resist the temptation to use correct English punctuation, which places the comma within the quotation marks. If the comma falls within the quotation marks, the VB interpreter assumes that comma to be the rightmost character in the string. When searching for a comma, the interpreter will not find one—it will instead find a 5 in the preceding example—and an error will be generated.

I Redeclare!

You now have been refamiliarized with all the fundamental terms necessary to discuss Visual Basic functions. Before going on with Part VI, Arithmetic Functions, I should introduce you to a series of statements that you may wish to use from time to time to make variable type distinction a little easier when you're creating your formulas:

DefCur, DefDbl, DefInt, DefLng, DefSng, DefStr   Statements

Syntax:

```
DefCur range[, range[, range. . . ]]
DefDbl range[, range[, range. . . ]]
DefInt range[, range[, range. . . ]]
DefLng range[, range[, range. . . ]]
DefSng range[, range[, range. . . ]]
DefStr range[, range[, range. . . ]]
```

These Deftype statements *do not* declare variables. Instead, they designate a range of the alphabet—as in A - Z—as reserved for a particular variable type, abbreviated by the letters following Def:

Cur	Currency
Dbl	Double-precision floating-point
Int	Standard integer
Lng	Long integer
Sng	Single-precision floating-point
Str	Alphanumeric string

Visual Basic *By* EXAMPLE

After you use a `Deftype` statement within a form's or module's declarations area, variables within that module declared informally or declared without establishing types, and having a first letter that falls within the range designated by the statement, will automatically be given the data type specified by the three-letter abbreviation *type*. Normally, informally declared variables are designated as single-precision floating-point variables. A `Deftype` statement can be used to override this distinction for variables that fall within certain ranges of the alphabet.

> **CAUTION:** Remember that unless declared otherwise (by formal statement or `Deftype` statement), a variable defaults to single-precision floating-point type.

Example

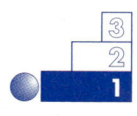

Many programmers, in the interest of memory conservation, override the single-precision default variable type with the following statement, placed within the declarations area of a Visual Basic application:

`DefInt a-z`

Now, every variable is given a default data type of `Integer`, as if it were declared `As Integer`. To give a variable a single-precision data type now, it can be declared `As Single` to override the integer distinction.

Some programmers like to reserve a letter or two for strings only, with such a statement as this:

`DefStr z`

From then on, the programmer could write equations of assignment like `z = "Argon gas"` and the interpreter would not generate an error. When a default data type is established for a range of variables using `Deftype`, the special character such as `#` or `$` is no longer necessary. This is acceptable for many programmers in the case of value variables; but because $ is often used as the sole distinction in text between a string and value variable, few programmers historically have used DefStr to avoid using the distinguishing character. History should not prevent you from taking your own course of action, however.

Summary

A function in Visual Basic is a mathematical operation performed on a set of values or alphanumeric strings, the result of which is returned within or assigned to a single variable. This variable is the sole element of the left side of the equation. The function exists somewhere within the right side of the equation, perhaps as part of a mathematical expression. A Visual Basic intrinsic function always has a set of parentheses for enclosing input parameters. The Deftype statement can be used to set the default data type for a variable before it is declared.

Review Questions

1. What is the conceptual difference between a function of arithmetic and a function of Visual Basic?

2. Would the instruction DefInt A-Z reserve single letters for use in integer variables?

3. Why are parentheses used in this book—even empty ones—to distinguish Visual Basic functions?

33

Conversion

In this chapter you are introduced to the intrinsic Visual Basic functions that take a single parameter of one type or form and convert it to a value or string of another type or form. These are generally the simplest of BASIC functions.

"Integize"

At times, you may need a value within a floating-point variable to be rounded to the nearest whole number, or perhaps you need to remove its fractional value altogether. Here are two functions for that purpose.

Int()   Function

Syntax:

`solution% = Int(expression)`

The `Int()` function rounds the logically simplified value of *expression* downward to the nearest integer or whole number. The result of this rounding is returned in the variable *solution%*.

Chapter 33 ◆ Conversion

Fix()   Function

Syntax:

solution% = Fix(*expression*)

The Fix() function removes any fractional value from the logically simplified value of *expression*, leaving an integer or whole number value. This value is returned in the variable *solution%*.

Example

Here is a "conversation" with the Visual Basic Immediate window (command-line interpreter), which should help to distinguish the difference (although there is little) between the Int() and Fix() functions:

```
a=4.9999
?int(a)
 4
?fix(a)
 4
a=-4.9999
    int(a)
-5
?fix(a)
-4
```

For a positive value of variable a, the Int() and Fix() functions return the same value. Yet for a negative value of a, the results of the two functions differ by 1. This is because Int() rounds the value downward to the nearest whole number (a downward direction increases a negative value). In contrast, Fix() simply removes the fractional value without performing any true arithmetic on the variable.

Example

A common use for the `Int()` function is to make values more manageable and tangible. Suppose, for instance, you have a loop clause that is executed as many times as there are miles between two points. The distance between those two points is found algebraically, and it is almost certain to contain a fractional value. A loop clause cannot be executed 8.26 times or a time and a half; there can be only a whole number of iterations. This whole number can be derived by rounding the distance using the `Int()` function, as follows:

```
distance# = Sqr(Abs((x2 - x1) ^ 2) + Abs((y2 - y1) ^ 2))
d% = Int(distance#)
For clomp = 1 to d%
    .
    .
    .
Next clomp
```

Here the loop clause is executed (`Int(distance#)`) times, without any fraction of a loop to worry about. Actually, Visual Basic loop clauses ignore fractional values if the `Step` value is assumed to be 1, anyway. This way, however, variable `d%` can be addressed within the clause.

String Conversions

Earlier in this book, you wrote an application that could, among other things, convert a base 10 value to base 16. Actually, there is a Visual Basic intrinsic function that can do that for you; but if I told you that in the beginning, you probably would not have learned as much about logic, would you? In any event, here are VB's base conversion string functions.

415

Chapter 33 ◆ Conversion

Hex$()   Function

Syntax:

*solution$* = Hex$(*num_expression*)

The `Hex$()` function solves for the value of *num_expression*, rounds that number down to the nearest integer, and finds the hexadecimal (base 16) value of the number. This number is returned as a string, especially because it may contain the digits *A* through *F* (10 through 15).

Oct$()   Function

Syntax:

*solution$* = Oct$(*num_expression*)

The `Oct$()` function works the same way as `Hex$()` does, but its solution is an octal (base 8) number. Although it contains only digits *0* through *7*, the solution is returned within a string variable *solution$*.

Example

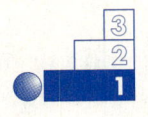

A conversation with the CLI shows the preceding functions in action:

```
num=1495
?Hex$(num)
5D7
?Oct$(num)
2727
```

As you discovered in an earlier chapter, Visual Basic (as well as Windows, DOS, and the BIOS itself) recognizes alphanumeric characters as numeric patterns. The patterns form a code that is called *ASCII* (pronounced *AS-key*) after the name of the standards document that defines it; however, Windows doesn't exactly adhere to this code 100 percent. Nonetheless, VB does maintain functions that convert a character to an ASCII (ANSI, really) value, and vice versa.

Asc ( ) — Function

Syntax:

`solution% = Asc("char$")`

where `char$` is a single character.

The `Asc()` function obtains the ASCII (actually the ANSI) code value for the character designated as `char$`. This value is returned within the variable `solution%`.

Chr$ ( ) — Function

Syntax:

`solution$ = Chr$(expression)`

where `expression` can be logically simplified to a legitimate ASCII code value.

The `Chr$()` function accepts the whole-number value of `expression` and looks up the ASCII (ANSI) code equivalent character for that value. This character is returned as the single-character contents of `solution$`.

Chapter 33 ◆ Conversion

Example

You may remember that I used the `Asc()` function back in Chapter 30, "The Keyboard," to determine which key was pressed and what instructions to execute as a response:

```
Sub HScroll1_KeyPress (KeyAscii As Integer)
Select Case KeyAscii
    Case Asc("0")
        If HScroll1.Min <= HScroll1.Value - HScroll1.LargeChange Then
            HScroll1.Value = HScroll1.Value - HScroll1.LargeChange
        End If
    Case Asc("-")
        If HScroll1.Min <= HScroll1.Value - HScroll1.SmallChange Then
            HScroll1.Value = HScroll1.Value - HScroll1.SmallChange
        End If
    Case Asc("=")
        If HScroll1.Max >= HScroll1.Value + HScroll1.SmallChange Then
            HScroll1.Value = HScroll1.Value + HScroll1.SmallChange
        End If
    Case Asc("\")
        If HScroll1.Max >= HScroll1.Value + HScroll1.LargeChange Then
            HScroll1.Value = HScroll1.Value + HScroll1.LargeChange
        End If
End Select
Label1.Caption = Str$(HScroll1.Value)
End Sub
```

Because I was lazy, I didn't bother to look up the ASCII values for the keys being polled. Instead, I invoked `Asc()` functions for the control keys.

Often, you need to convert a numeric value to string contents, and vice versa. Here are functions for those purposes:

Val()   Function

Syntax:

solution = Val(*string$*)

where string$ may be an expression that concatenates several strings. The first set of nonspace characters in the string, however, must be a set of digits, or any characters that the Visual Basic interpreter would normally use to distinguish fractional numbers. Decimal points are recognized as such characters.

The `Val()` function converts the first set of digits with number-delimiting characters in *string$* to a value that is placed within the variable *solution*. The first alphabetic character encountered within a string cancels the conversion process. A totally alphabetic character is therefore *converted* to 0. The contents of *string$* are unaffected by this conversion.

Str$() — Function

Syntax:

*solution$* = Str$(*value*)

The `Str$()` function converts the digits contained within *value* into an alphanumeric string, which is placed within the variable *solution$*. The value of the variable *value* is unaffected by this conversion.

Example

As you've learned, certain object properties are recognized as strings and others are recognized as values, without any distinguishing characters such as $ to help you out. With that in mind, a result value of an equation is often placed within a text box on a form. Text boxes can have only alphanumeric contents; they do not interpret values directly. The following conversion comes from the two-dimensional distance converter program from Chapter 6:

419

Chapter 33 ◆ Conversion

```
Sub Go_Click ()
x1 = Val(Box_x1.Text)
x2 = Val(Box_x2.Text)
y1 = Val(Box_y1.Text)
y2 = Val(Box_y2.Text)
d# = Sqr(Abs((x2 - x1) ^ 2) + Abs((y2 - y1) ^ 2))
Distance.Text = Str$(d#)
End Sub
```

Here, the derived distance value has to be converted into an alphanumeric string using `Str$()` before that solution can be displayed within the text box `Distance`.

Finally, here are five functions that convert values from one type to another:

CCur(), CDbl(), CInt(), CLng(), CSng() — Functions

Syntax:

solution = C*type*(*expression*)

where *type* is the abbreviation for the variable type being converted to, as introduced in Chapter 32.

The `Ctype()` functions solve for the logically reduced value of *expression* and then convert that expression to the specified variable type, even if that type requires more bytes than are necessary to represent the value. The result must be assigned to a variable having a type that is equivalent to the type being converted to.

Visual Basic By
EXAMPLE

Summary

Values can be rounded or truncated to whole-number values using the `Int()` and `Fix()` functions. Base 10 numbers can be converted to base 16 and base 8 using the functions `Hex$()` and `Oct$()`, respectively. The ASCII code value for a character can be obtained using `Asc()`; likewise, a character can be obtained from its ASCII code value using `Chr$()`. String contents are converted to a numeric value using `Val()`; likewise, a value is converted into a string using `Str$()`. Values can have their variable types converted and reassigned to a variable of a new type, using the `Ctype()` functions.

Review Questions

Using the functions introduced in this chapter, and without the aid of the computer, estimate the solutions to the following expressions:

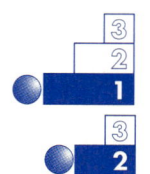

1. `Int(3.1415927)`
2. `Asc("A")`
3. `Chr$(Asc("z"))`
4. `Int(Asc("A"))`
5. `Val("1600 Pennsylvania Avenue")`

Practical Math

In this chapter you are introduced to the intrinsic Visual Basic functions that concern algebraic, trigonometric, and logarithmic calculations.

Algebraic Functions

Two functions that involve the sign of the numeric value (whether the value is positive or negative) are `Abs()` and `Sgn()`.

Abs() — Function

Syntax:

`solution = Abs(expression)`

The `Abs()` function returns the absolute value of the result of *expression*, within the variable *solution*. This is equivalent to the value of the original expression, unsigned.

Chapter 34 ◆ Practical Math

Sgn ( ) — Function

Syntax:

`solution% = Sgn(expression)`

The `Sgn()` function returns a value that represents the sign of the logically reduced value of *expression*, within the variable *solution%*. This representative value can be any of the following:

−1   if *expression* is negative

0   if *expression* = 0

1   if *expression* is positive

Example

By now, you're familiar with the two-dimensional distance-finding formula:

`d# = Sqr(Abs((x2 - x1) ^ 2) + Abs((y2 - y1) ^ 2))`

If you compare this distance formula with the one from algebra, you may wonder why I added the absolute value function to this formula in the first place. Assume x1 subtracted from x2 is a negative value; squaring that value should make it positive anyway. The absolute value of a negative number is a positive value. Yet it would appear that by squaring the two sets of subtracted values here, we would not need the `Abs()` function in the above example.

It appears that way, but such is not the case. For some reason, the VB interpreter can, and often does, maintain the negative sign if a negative value is squared. This may not be the case in your copy of Visual Basic (in other words, folks, we call this a *bug*) but during my testing, I removed erroneous results from formulas by using the `Abs()` function to remove the incorrect negative sign from squared negative values.

Also notable within this formula is the square root function.

424

Visual Basic *By*
EXAMPLE

Sqr()   Function

Syntax:

solution = Sqr(*expression*)

The Sqr() function returns the square root of the logically reduced value of *expression*, within the variable *solution*.

Visual Basic gives the user four functions that relate to trigonometry.

Sin(), Cos(), Tan(), Atn()   Functions

Syntax:

solution = Sin(*expression*)
solution = Cos(*expression*)
solution = Tan(*expression*)
solution = Atn(*expression*)

These four functions return the sine, cosine, tangent, and arctangent, respectively, of the logically reduced value of *expression*. This value is returned in the variable *solution* as a unit of *radians*, which are divisions of a circular arc.

Example

Because people have a tendency to think in terms of degrees, it will be necessary to convert degrees to radians—what Visual Basic uses to determine sines and cosines—before you can evaluate the trigonometric expression. A conversation with the Visual Basic CLI shows how you can do this:

Chapter 34 ◆ Practical Math

```
pi=3.1415927
deg = 90
?sin(deg*(pi/180))
 1
```

Finally, here are the two functions regarding logarithms:

Log(), Exp() — Functions

Syntax:

solution = Log(*expression*)
solution = Exp(*expression*)

The Log() function returns the natural logarithm of the logically reduced value of *expression*, within the variable *solution*. Likewise, the function Exp() returns the base of natural logarithm *e* raised to the power of the logically reduced value of *expression*, within the variable *solution*.

Summary

The absolute value of an expression is obtained with Abs(); likewise, the sign of that expression can be obtained with Sgn(). The square root of an expression is obtained with Sqr(). Visual Basic's trigonometric functions are Sin(), Cos(), Tan(), and Atn(). The natural logarithm of an expression is found with Log(). Likewise, the number to which natural logarithmic base *e* is raised to equal an expression's value is obtained with Exp().

Review Questions

If x = 6 and y = 9, solve for the following:

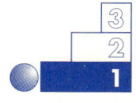

1. Abs(x - y)
2. Sgn(x - y)
3. Sgn(Abs(x - y))

35

String Functions

In this chapter you study how Visual Basic terms fashioned to resemble arithmetic functions actually operate on the contents of an alphanumeric string or string variable. For instance, you use VB string functions to alter or adjust the contents of strings so that they can be displayed better or stored within a record, or so that you can extract certain fragments of information from that record.

String of Pearls

When a function operates on a value stored within a variable, the contents of that variable are represented in a reserved region of the computer's memory. The location of this region may change from time to time, because it is the duty of Microsoft Windows to find the most convenient location for this region at any one time, with regard to such factors as how many other applications are inhabiting the environment and how much memory for data they require to operate.

When a function operates on the alphanumeric contents of a string variable, those contents are represented as a reserved region of the computer's memory. As you've seen in several previous chapters, each character of a string is represented as a pattern of bits. The code for this pattern is called ASCII (the American Standard

Code for Information Interchange, which is followed by much of the world outside of America). ASCII is a more logical pattern than, for instance, Morse Code. It is more *logical* because the equivalent code number for any given character can be easily determined arithmetically using binary logic rather than arbitrary guesswork.

Each character of an alphanumeric string is stored within one byte. Each byte of a string is generally stored in memory beside the other, in sequence. The region of memory containing the string has left and right "bounds," which are to some degree manipulable by the Visual Basic interpreter. You may remember from earlier study how variable values with different types (integer, double-precision, floating-point, and so on) are stored within regions of memory with differing bounds. In other words, a double-precision value can be stored within eight bytes, whereas an integer can be stored within two. To convert a double-precision value to an integer, from the point of view of the interpreter, is a process of moving the bounds and repositioning the value within those bounds, after shaving away the bytes containing the fractional portion of the value. Likewise, shaving away the trailing spaces from a string such as `"Sheffield[space][space][space][space][space]"` is accomplished by the interpreter's moving the bounds for the stored element of data. So the mechanisms for storing values and storing textual contents do not actually differ much from each other.

What is different in the way a string is contained from the way a value is contained is that the programmer has more control over the byte containment process with respect to strings. When you informally declare a variable as equalling a value, as in `pi = 3.1415927`, you've created a four-byte containment region. You can make it an eight-byte region by converting the value to double-precision using `Cdbl()`, but there would not be much point in doing so unless you were to add a more detailed fraction to the value. When you informally declare a string variable as containing specific contents, as in `ship$ = "Sheffield"`, you've created a nine-byte containment region. To make it into a 14-byte region, you can write an equation such as `ship$ = ship$ + "[space][space][space][space][space]"`. Likewise, you can change the upper bounds of the string by adding text to the beginning, as in `ship$ = "HMS[space]" + ship$`. (Note that the term `[space]` here substitutes for one character.)

Now you have an 18-byte region, although at first the trailing spaces may not appear to be of much use. However, suppose you're storing data to disk in the form of records containing vital information about, for instance, British Naval vessels of the Falklands War. A record in a random-access file is defined to be a precise number of characters long. Somewhere within each record is a specific 18-character region containing the name of a vessel. If the name of the vessel is less than the name of the region, the trailing spaces are necessary to separate the vessel's datum (item of data) from the next item in the record. This way, the name of the ship's captain doesn't bleed into the name of his vessel.

The type of control the programmer has over the string containment process can at first be likened to the type of control a person has over the contents of the IRS Form 1040 each April. When you as programmer realize there is logic behind the mechanism, however, you can more easily supply the logic for that mechanism. To explain: You've determined that the storage mechanism for string variables involves code. A coded value from 0 to 255 is stored within each byte of a string. Suppose you were to treat this value as a value by encoding vital information in sequence as characters and storing that data as a string rather than as an integer or, more wastefully yet, as a single-precision variable.

> **TIP:** To save memory, store some numbers as strings. If three low-value numbers are used to describe the state of some operation within the program, you can give the values for each state a character code. The characters can then be concatenated (joined together) and stored as a single string—as in `status$ = fuel$ + coolant$ + battery$`. What might have required six (or, informally declared, 12) bytes to represent now takes only three.

For the preceding tip, however, you would need to program the mechanism for storing the code as a procedure. If you use this mechanism for encoding an entire array of thousands of items, however, the memory you save may begin to be measured in kilobytes.

Perhaps the most important function relating to controlling a string variable in this manner is the Len() function.

Len() Function

Syntax:

`value% = Len(string_exp$)`

where `string_exp$` is any expression joining one or more strings of alphanumeric text.

The Len() function returns the number of characters currently being stored within the expressed string, in the numeric variable `value%`.

Example

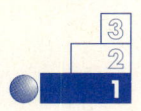

Here's the Len() function at work, as demonstrated through a conversation with the Visual Basic CLI:

```
ship$="Sheffield"
?len(ship$)
 9
```

The function simply counts the number of characters in the string.

Naturally, because Len() is a function like any other intrinsic Visual Basic function, its result can be assigned to a variable:

```
ship$="Sheffield"
ln=len(ship$)
?ln
 9
```

Example

> To *pad* a string is to fill it at the end with spaces or null characters to make it fit a given storage space.

Suppose a string array variable `nam$()` contains a list of surnames. The string space allocated for each datum in the array is only as long as the name contained within the string. For instance, the name *Enrik* is stored within a five-character string, whereas *Magnusson* is stored within a nine-character string. A record stored to disk contains a 25-character field for surnames called `n$()`, regardless of how long each surname is. When the length of each surname is less than 25, the right side of the string is to be *padded* with space characters. Here's a routine that supplies the padding:

```
For nam% = 1 to UBound(name$, 1)
    ln% = Len(nam$(nam%))
    pad% = 25 - ln%
    n$(nam%) = nam$(nam%) + Space$(pad%)
Next nam%
```

Here's the procedure translated into pseudocode:

Start counting from 1 to the number of names in the array.
  Assign the length of the name currently being counted to this variable.
  Subtract this length from 25.
  Place this many spaces at the end of the name before storing it.
Count the next name.

The loop clause uses the variable `nam%` to keep count as iterations proceed from 1 to the number of items in the array `nam$()`, as determined by the function `UBound()`. The length of each name in the array is found by the `Len()` function on the second line. This length is subtracted from 25—the length of each field to be stored to disk—to derive the number of spaces to be added to the end of the `nam$(nam%)` before it is added to `n$(nam%)`. The `Space$()` function adds a specific number of spaces to the end of `nam$(nam%)`.

433

Chapter 35 ◆ String Functions

Space$() — Function

Syntax:

`string$ = Space$(number%)`

The `Space$` function returns a series of *number%* space characters, within string variable *string$*.

The `Len()` function can be best put to use when invoked in a procedure that contains the other major string functions in the VB vocabulary.

Left$(), Right$() — Functions

Syntax:

`substring$ = Left$(string$, number%)`
`substring$ = Right$(string$, number%)`

The `Left$()` function extracts the first *number%* characters in sequence from the larger string *string$* and assigns those characters as contents of the smaller string variable *substring$*. Likewise, the `Right$()` function extracts the last *number%* characters of a string in sequence from the larger string *string$* and assigns those characters as contents of the smaller string variable *substring$*. In both functions, if *number%* is larger than the length of *string$*, the entirety of *string$* is returned in *substring$* without any characters added to either side of the string.

Example

Here you can see the `Right$()` function at work with the aid of the Visual Basic CLI:

Visual Basic By
EXAMPLE

```
ship$="Sheffield"
?right$(ship$,5)
field
```

Here the `Right$()` function counts the first five characters from the right of `ship$` toward the left and extracts those characters; however, the returned extracted characters are displayed from left to right and not backwards, as in *dleif*.

It's important to note that the `.Text` property of a text box and the `.Caption` property of a label or other graphic object that uses labels can be substituted for `string_exp$` in any of these functions. The VB interpreter treats the stated properties of graphic objects as if they were string variables, for the sake of these functions.

Example

The procedure I introduced previously did not take into account cases in which a person's surname is longer than 25 characters. Certainly the 25-character name is a rare case; but if the surname exceeds 25 characters, you really have no choice but to trim the longer name down to the first 25 characters. Here's how the trimming is determined and executed:

```
For nam% = 1 to UBound(nam$, 1)
    ln% = Len(nam$(nam%))
    If ln% <= 25 Then
        pad% = 25 - ln%
        n$(nam%) = nam$(nam%) + Space$(pad%)
    Else
        n$(nam%) = Left$(nam$(nam%), 25)
    End If
Next nam%
```

435

Chapter 35 ◆ String Functions

I've added an `If-Then-Else` clause that divides the naming operations into a true side and a false side. The true side will be executed when the length of nam$(nam%) is less than or equal to 25; the false side will be executed when the surname is too long to fit in the record. In such a case, the function `Left$()` is used to extract the leftmost 25 characters from nam$(nam%) and place them within n$(nam%). Note that I haven't been using the word *name* as a variable in these procedures; this is because `Name` is a reserved keyword in Visual Basic.

When people's names are stored to disk as a table using the preceding procedure, the padding of spaces attached to the names that are shorter than 25 letters allows each name to fit neatly into the slot or field created for each name. The procedure that retrieves these names knows where to look to retrieve a particular name in the sequence, because each stored field has a fixed beginning and ending byte location, regardless of the size of the data stored within the field. When the data is retrieved, however, you need to strip the trailing spaces from each name so that you won't have to mail envelopes with names that appear like these:

```
Lester              C.  Thurow
Robert              B.  Reich
Milton                  Friedman
```

Thankfully, Visual Basic gives you functions for automatically removing whatever spaces you may have padded each name with. They are `LTrim$()` and `RTrim$()`.

LTrim$(), RTrim$()   Functions

Syntax:

*string$* = LTrim$(*string_exp$*)
*string$* = RTrim$(*string_exp$*)

where *string_exp$* is any logical expression containing one or more concatenated strings or string variables.

Visual Basic *By* EXAMPLE

The `LTrim$()` function removes all spaces from the left side of the expressed string. Likewise, the `RTrim$()` function removes all spaces from the right side of the expressed string.

Example

After retrieving the padded names you stored to disk earlier, you can use `RTrim$()` to remove any trailing spaces from each name, as follows:

```
For nam% = 1 to UBound(n$, 1)
    nam$(nam%) = RTrim$(n$(nam%))
Next nam%
```

Notice that you don't have to use any arithmetic here to *remove* the spaces from the end of the name; the VB interpreter knows, when given the directive by `RTrim$()`, to search for any trailing spaces that may exist and purge them.

The `Lset` and `Rset` pair of statements is used to justify text within strings that contain spaces as padding, so that the padding can be bunched up on one side of the strings or the other.

Lset, Rset   Statements

Syntax:

```
LSet field$ = entry$
RSet field$ = entry$
```

The `LSet` and `RSet` statements assign the textual contents already assigned to *entry$* to a string full of spaces: *field$*. The length of *field$* is not changed; instead, spaces within *field$* are replaced by the contents of *entry$*. The `LSet` statement enters *entry$* within *field$* starting at the leftmost character of *field$*, thus creating a left-justified field. Likewise, the `RSet` statement enters *entry$* within

437

Chapter 35 ◆ String Functions

field$* starting at the rightmost character of *field$, creating a right-justified field. If there are more characters in *entry$* than there are in *field$*, only the leftmost characters of *entry$* appear in *field$* for both statements. The length of *field$* remains the same.

String of Strings

Earlier, I introduced the function String$() as a function for placing a certain number of spaces into a string variable, generally as *padding*. A related function, derived from earlier in BASIC's history, is String$().

String$() Function

Syntax 1:

*word$* = String$(*number%*, "*char$*")

Syntax 2:

*word$* = String$(*number%*, *ascii_char%*)

The String$() function issues a designated *number%* of repeated characters as the string variable *word$*. Under Syntax 1, the single character to be repeated is expressed as *char$*, between quotation marks. Under Syntax 2, the single character to be repeated is expressed as the ASCII code equivalent of the character that is expressed as *ascii_char%*.

Example

Assume you're designing a printout for a price sheet for your retail store. Your price sheet will show retail prices for items you sell, line by line. After the name of each item, you'd like a series of

438

asterisks linking the item to its price. You don't know in advance how long the item name will be, nor how many characters will constitute the price. Here's a procedure that determines how many asterisks you would need to use between the item name and its price, for a line that's 66 characters long:

```
For nam% = 1 To UBound(item$, 1)
    li% = Len(item$(nam%))
    prce$(nam%) = "$" + Str$(price(nam%))
    lp% = Len(prce$(nam%))
    numast = 66 - li% - lp%
    PriceList.Print item$(nam%); String$(numast, "*"); prce$(nam%)
Next nam%
```

Here's pseudocode for this procedure:

Count from the first to the last item in the array.
   Acquire the length of the current item in characters.
   Make the price string equal to "$" joined with the alphanumeric form of the price of the current item.
   Acquire the length of this new price string.
   The number of asterisks between these two strings will be 66 minus the length of both strings.
   Print to the price list the current item's name, the number of asterisks required, and the current price.
Count the next item.

The lengths of the item name string and price string are assigned to variables `li%` and `lp%`, respectively. Variable `prce$` is created here by concatenating a dollar sign with the string-converted form of the price value. Visual Basic requires the names of string variables to be different from the names of value variables, so the *i* was removed from *price* in `prce$`. Naturally, the string must be created before its length is obtained. I used variable `numast` to determine the number of asterisks necessary to fill the space between the item name and the price so that both appear flush left and right on the price list. The `.Print` method then prints three items in succession, the second being a string of asterisks formed by the function `String$(numast, "*")`.

Chapter 35 ◆ String Functions

String$() is one example of what in old BASIC was called a *command function*, which was the term for a function that performs the role of a command. The interpreter is told to produce a row of characters of a specified type. Two similar functions that qualify as command functions by the old definition are LCase$() and UCase$().

LCase$(), UCase$() — Functions

Syntax:

*string$* = LCase$(*string_exp$*)
*string$* = UCase$(*string_exp$*)

The LCase$() function converts all alphabetic characters appearing within the expressed string or string concatenation *string_exp$* to lowercase letters. Likewise, the UCase$() function converts all alphabetic characters appearing within the expressed string or string concatenation *string_exp$* to uppercase letters.

Example

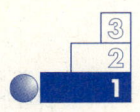

A conversation with the Visual Basic CLI demonstrates the use of both preceding case conversion functions:

```
ship$="Sheffield"
ship$=ucase$(ship$)
?ship$
SHEFFIELD
ship$=lcase$(ship$)
?ship$
sheffield
```

In the Midst of Strings

Up to now, we've been working with functions that concentrate on either the left or right side of the string, or the whole string.

Visual Basic *By*
EXAMPLE

There will most certainly be instances in your programming career when you'll need to know whether the user entered a particular string of characters someplace within the *middle* of a large text box. Here is a function that determines not only if that text was entered, but where it appears:

InStr() **Function**

Syntax:

position& = InStr([*first_char&*], *string_exp1$*, *string_exp2$*)

The InStr() function initiates a search for the string or string concatenation expressed by *string_exp2$*, within the larger *string_exp1$*. The length of *string_exp2$* must be less than 65,536 characters. If the search turns up a match, the number of the character in the larger string where the first character of the smaller string appears is returned as long integer variable *position&*. The first character of the larger string is considered character number 1. If the smaller string does not appear exactly within the larger string, or if *string_exp2$* is larger than *string_exp1$*, the function returns a null value (0). If the long integer *first_char&* is expressed, the search begins with that character position of the larger string. The value of *first_char&* may be no larger than 65,535.

> **NOTE:** Even though *first_char&* is a four-byte long integer, the Visual Basic interpreter can only search a string that is less than 65,536 characters long. It might seem that, because 65,536 requires only two bytes for representation, this wouldn't be the case; but VB interprets two-byte integer values using one extra sign bit for positive and negative values. Thus with two bytes, VB can only count from -32,768 to 32,767. To count any higher, VB requires the next class of variable, that being a four-byte integer.

Chapter 35 ◆ String Functions

Example

As an example of the `InStr()` function, assume you have an application called `App` with a search-and-replace text function. When you select that function from the menu, a dialog box form pops up requesting the text to look for in the body of a document called `Document`, and the text to replace it with. This dialog box has a `.FormName` of `Replacer`; its procedure, which starts the search-and-replace operation, is as follows:

```
Sub Start_Click ()
srch$ = SearchText.Text
rplc$ = ReplaceText.Text
If Len(srch$) = 0 Or Len(rplc$) = 0 Then
    Replacer.Hide
    Exit Sub
End If
trgt$ = App.Document.Text
pos = InStr(trgt$, srch$)
If pos = 0 Then
    MsgBox "Text not found.", 0, ""
    Exit Sub
End If
App.Document.SelStart = pos - 1
App.Document.SelLength = Len(srch$)
App.Document.SelText = rplc$
Replacer.Hide
End Sub
```

Here's pseudocode for this procedure:

Procedure awaiting a click on the Start button:
Acquire the text to search for from a text box.
Acquire the text it is to be replaced with, from the other text box.
If the length of either specimen of text is 0, then
   This must be a "pocket cancel," so take this dialog box off the screen and
   Exit this procedure.
End of condition.

Take the text from the document.
Find the place where the search text begins within the target text.
If the search text is not there, then
 Notify the user.
 Get out of this procedure.
End of condition.
Otherwise, start to indicate the beginning of the search text in the document.
Extend the selector for the length of the search text.
Replace the selected text with the replacement string.
Remove this dialog box from the screen.
End of procedure.

The first thing this procedure does is assign the text being searched for to the variable `srch$`. If the user did not type anything into this box (`If Len(srch$) = 0`), then there's no point in searching for nothing. The dialog box is hidden and the procedure is exited.

For the sake of this example, the entire document is assigned to variable `trgt$`. Now the crucial `Instr()` function is invoked, searching for the first instance of `srch$` within `trgt$`, starting with character number 1 and proceeding one character at a time. Variable `pos` should contain the location of the first character where `srch$` was located within `trgt$`; but if `pos = 0`, evidently the search string doesn't exist within the target, and a message box is displayed to that effect.

When the procedure finds a match for `srch$` within `trgt$`, the found text is automatically selected as a property `.SelText` of the text box and it is replaced by making that property equal to the replacement string `rplc$`. The text selection properties are covered in depth in a later chapter.

The preceding example demonstrates how search-and-replace functions work when you know precisely what text you're searching for. Assume you need a procedure that searches for an element of text based upon its *construction*, not its contents. Say, for instance, you're looking for a ZIP code—not a specific one, just any ZIP code. You know a ZIP code is at least five digits appearing next to one another. You can't use `Instr()` to search for unknown text, so you'll probably need to employ the help of the following function:

Chapter 35 ◆ String Functions

`Mid$()` ### Function

Syntax:

*substring$* = Mid$(*string$*, *start_pos&*, *number%*)

The `Mid$()` function extracts a *number%* of characters from a string in sequence from the larger string *string$*, starting at character position *start_pos&* counting from the left of *string$*. The extracted characters are then assigned to the smaller string variable *substring$*.

Example

Here's a procedure that looks for anything resembling a ZIP code:

```
Sub Zip_Click ()
total = Len(Document.Text)
trgt$ = Document.Text
For pos = 1 To total - 4
    If Mid$(trgt$, pos, 1) > Chr$(48) And Mid$(trgt$, pos, 1)
        < Chr$(57) Then
        zipfind = zipfind + 1
        If zipfind = 5 Then
            Document.SelStart = pos - 5
            Document.SelLength = 5
            zp$ = Document.SelText
            MsgBox "Possible ZIP code " + zp$ +
                " found at position " + Str$(pos - 5), 0, ""
        End If
    Else
        zipfind = 0
    End If
Next pos
End Sub
```

444

Pseudocode for this procedure is as follows:

Procedure awaiting a click on the Zip button:
Find the length of the entire document.
Call the text of this document the target string.
Count from the first to the fourth from the last character in the document.
  If the character at this position is a digit, then
    Add one to the potentiality that this is a ZIP code.
    If this potentiality equals 5 digits, then
      Indicate the text at this point.
      Indicate five characters from this point.
      Place the indicated text in a string variable.
      Tell the user this may be a ZIP code, and where it was found.
    End of condition.
  Otherwise,
    Strike any hope of this being a ZIP code.
  End of condition.
Count the next character.
End of procedure.

This procedure belongs to the main form, not to a dialog box. First, the length of the text typed into `Document` is obtained and assigned to variable `total`. The text itself is assigned to `trgt$`. The loop clause keeps a count of characters called `pos`, starting with the first character and ending with the fifth from the end—because ZIP codes are five characters long. Within the loop clause is a conditional clause using the `Mid$()` function, which tests to see if the specified single character `Mid$(trgt$, pos, 1)` has an ASCII value between 48 and 57—which would make that character a digit. If it is indeed a digit, one is added to an independent counter variable `zipfind`.

When `zipfind = 5`, the procedure has found five digits in a row. The digits then are extracted from behind the current count position `pos - 5` and are displayed in an appropriate message box. If the procedure did not find enough digits in sequence, `zipfind` is reset to 0.

In Visual Basic, the term `Mid$` can also be used as a statement, which in effect reverses the order of the transaction in the `Mid$()` function:

445

Chapter 35 ◆ String Functions

> **Mid$** **Statement**
>
> Syntax:
>
> Mid$(*string$*, *start_pos&*[, *number&*]) = *substring$*
>
> The Mid$ statement replaces the text currently assigned to *string$*, starting at cursor position *start_pos&* counting from the left, with the text contained within *substring$*. If *number&* is expressed, that number of characters are removed from *string$* and replaced with the first *number&* characters from the left of *substring$*.

Summary

A string variable is stored in memory with each byte representing a character of the string. Unlike the storage techniques given a numeral value, string contents in memory are given left and right bounds that can be manipulated by changing the contents of the string. The length of a string in memory is returned with the Len() function.

A sequence of spaces is created using the command function Space$(). Similarly, a sequence of any single character is created using String$(). Leading and trailing spaces can be trimmed from a string using the LTrim$() and RTrim$() functions, respectively. A smaller string can be entered into a larger string full of spaces. That larger string's contents can be justified using the LSet and RSet statements. Any string's alphabetic characters can be converted to upper- or lowercase using UCase$() and LCase$(), respectively.

The leftmost and rightmost portions of any string can be extracted and assigned to another string variable, using Left$() and Right$(), respectively. A number of characters from the middle of any string can be extracted and assigned to another string variable using the Mid$() function. A number of characters within the middle of any string can be replaced by a sequence of characters from another string using the Mid$ statement. The character position of the first instance of a smaller string within a larger string can be obtained by using the Instr() function.

Review Questions

Assume srch$ is assigned the following string contents:

`When in the course of human events`

Without using the computer as an aid, determine the result of the following functions:

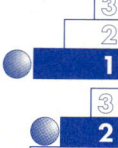

1. Left$(srch$, 4)
2. Right$(srch$, 7)
3. Mid$(srch$, 4, 1)
4. Mid$(srch$, 9, 4)

Suppose you invoke the following instruction:

`Mid$(srch$, 6) = "in, of, and around"`

5. What are the current contents of srch$?

Composite Variable Types

In this chapter you experiment with creating your own variable types and declaring variables using those types. You then use your personal types to pass composite variables to and from procedures.

The Composition of Variables

Microsoft uses the term *user-defined variables* to describe variable types that are defined by the programmer. This distinction does not initially make a great deal of sense, because I've already defined the *user* as the person who operates the programs that have variables that are defined, if not altogether created, by the *programmer*. I could use the term *programmer-defined variables*, but what I am really talking about are variables that *contain* other variables.

A *composite variable* in Visual Basic is a container for multiple numeral, string, or other composite variables, addressed together as one unit using a single arbitrarily-defined term and invoked within an instruction using object-oriented syntax.

In a composite photograph, multiple images of one object viewed from different angles appear on the same page. In a composite drawing sketched by a police artist, portions of generic faces are

> A *composite variable* is a programmer-defined combination of numerals and strings that is treated as a single variable.

combined to produce a likeness of a suspect. Similarly, a composite variable in Visual Basic is made up of other variables. In the same way a composite photo is really more than one photo, and a composite drawing is really comprised of pieces of more than one face, a composite variable is made up of more than one variable. More to the point, it is not really a variable; it is merely addressable as if it were a variable.

Earlier I introduced you to the variable type `Control`, which represents graphic objects that have properties that are indirectly passed to generic procedures. You may remember you used the variable `Source` as an example of passing the properties of a graphic object to a procedure by declaring within the `Sub` statement of that procedure `Source As Control`. From then on, you could refer to such properties as `Source.Text` and `Source.Top`, and be indirectly referring to a graphic object having a control name that is *not* `Source`. The properties belonging to the object are referred to using object-oriented syntax throughout the generic procedure, as if the control name of the object were `Source`.

The mechanism of a composite variable in Visual Basic is similar to the `Control` declaration mechanism. Suppose, for instance, that you use four variables throughout an application to refer to aspects of one real-world item, such as a transaction in your personal checkbook. Using Visual Basic's composite variable mechanism, you can declare these aspect variables to be *properties* of checkbook transactions. In doing so, you've rendered transactions to be, to some extent, virtual *objects* in the context of your application; thus it seems natural to use object-oriented syntax to refer to your checkbook properties, as in `Transaction.Number`, `Transaction.Recipient`, or `Transaction.Debit`.

Referring to properties in this manner does not, however, mean that `Transaction.` becomes an object by the formal definition of the term used in computing. If it did, you would be able to use the programming language to construct methods such as *Transaction.Record* or *Transaction.Cancel*, and call such methods as directives to your application as if they were keywords in the language vocabulary. Visual Basic does not contain facilities for programmer-defined methods; therefore, composite variables cannot be true objects—at least not in the current release.

The declarative statement used to create composite variables is the `Type-End Type` statement.

Type-End Type Statement

Syntax:

```
Type typename
    variable As existing_type
    [variable As existing_type]
        .
        .
        .
End Type
```

The `Type-End Type` clause is used within the global module of an application to declare programmer-defined composite variable types for that application. The *typename* for the composite variable is arbitrarily defined by the programmer, although it must not be a reserved keyword, a declared variable name, or a term used in the program for any other purpose.

Each variable that will comprise the composite variable is listed within the clause. Listings of variables here do not count as declaratives; these variables must be declared elsewhere in the program. The invocation of each variable here is only meant as a reservation for its place within the composite variable being declared. The type of variable being listed must be specified; this type can be any numeral value or string variable type, or any previously declared composite type, but not an array variable.

Chapter 36 ◆ Composite Variable Types

Example

One of the most common uses for composite variables is to describe shapes, especially rectangles. Suppose the following composite declaration appears in the global module of an application:

```
Type Rectangle
    origx As Integer
    origy As Integer
    deltax As Integer
    deltay As Integer
End Type
```

Evidently the purpose of `Type Rectangle` is to describe the upper-left corner of a rectangle and the rectangle's length and width. On purpose, I am not using the recognized property terms `.Left`, `.Top`, `.Width`, or `.Height` as variables belonging to the composite, to help prove the point that composite variable types are indeed defined by the programmer.

At the bottom of a test form module, a single button appears that has the caption and control name `Draw`. Within the general declarations area of this form module is the following line:

```
Dim the_box As Rectangle
```

This is the first example of actually dimensioning a variable as a composite type. Variable `the_box` can now be addressed within the source code using object-oriented syntax, as in using `the_box.origx` to refer to the origin point of the box along the x-axis.

Now suppose you have the following procedure for the sole button:

```
Sub Draw_Click ()
the_box.origx = 1000
the_box.origy = 1000
the_box.deltax = 1500
the_box.deltay = 1500
display the_box
End Sub
```

452

There will definitely be a fixed box within this form; the application does nothing else but plot this box. Now that the box's coordinates are set, the call is placed to a procedure called `display`. Notice that I've created four parameters, but the only parameter passed to procedure `display` is `the_box`.

Here is the listing for procedure `display`:

```
Sub display (object As Rectangle)
Line (object.origx, object.origy)-(object.deltax,
    object.deltay), , B
End Sub
```

Notice that all four parameter names—`origx`, `origy`, `deltax`, and `deltay`—appear within this procedure without having to appear within the parentheses of the `Sub` procedure declaration. The only parameter appearing there is `object`, which was declared to be of type `Rectangle`. Notice I did not call this "object" `the_box`. This is to demonstrate that `object.` now refers to `the_box` *indirectly*, in the same way that `Source.` in the previous examples referred to a graphic object indirectly. Another object with another name—perhaps `another_box`—could at some later time be passed to this procedure, and `object.` would refer to that object indirectly, as well. The result is that a box is plotted to the form.

Example

You can now modify the preceding application so that you can draw a shaded grey box on the form by dragging a solid black line around where you want the box to appear. Assume you have a blank form on the screen—no controls, no gadgetry, and no need for a specific form size. Here is the source code for the box-drawing program:

Chapter 36 ◆ Composite Variable Types

	PROJECT NAME	*CONSTITUENT FILES*
Box Test	BOXTEST.MAK	BOXTEST.GBL
	BOXTEST.FRM	BOXTEXT.GBL

```
Type Rectangle
    origx As Integer
    origy As Integer
    deltax As Integer
    deltay As Integer
End Type
```

General Declarations Area:

```
Dim downx As Integer, downy As Integer, oldx As Integer,
    oldy As Integer
Dim the_box As Rectangle
```

Here I've added four new array variables for keeping track of where the user first pressed the mouse index button and the last known position of the mouse pointer.

```
Sub Form_MouseDown (button As Integer, Shift As Integer,
    X As Single, Y As Single)
downx = X
downy = Y
Line (downx, downy)-(X, Y), RGB(0, 0, 0), B
oldx = X
oldy = Y
End Sub
```

This procedure is executed the moment the user presses the index button. A solid black, unfilled rectangle is plotted to the form, albeit a small one.

```
Sub Form_MouseMove (button As Integer, Shift As Integer,
    X As Single, Y As Single)
If button = 1 Then
    Line (downx, downy)-(oldx, oldy), RGB(255, 255, 255), B
    Line (downx, downy)-(X, Y), RGB(0, 0, 0), B
    oldx = X
    oldy = Y
End If
End Sub
```

When the mouse pointer moves, you want the solid black rectangle to move with it, keeping its origin rooted at the point where the user first pressed down the index button. A white rectangle is plotted over the old black one, and a new black one is plotted in its place.

```
Sub Form_MouseUp (button As Integer, Shift As Integer,
    X As Single, Y As Single)
the_box.origx = downx
the_box.origy = downy
the_box.deltax = X
the_box.deltay = Y
display the_box
End Sub
```

When the index button is released, the `downx` and `downy` variables declared at the form level are assigned as properties of the composite variable `the_box`. The call is made to `display the_box`, and only one parameter is passed.

General Procedures Area:

```
Sub display (object As Rectangle)
Line (object.origx, object.origy)-(object.deltax, object.deltay),
    RGB(128, 128, 128), BF
End Sub
```

I modified the `Line` method slightly so that it would display a grey filled rectangle (display mode BF, with all due respect to B. F. Skinner). At this point the rectangle is displayed and the program goes back to its state of waiting for another rectangle to be drawn.

While experimenting with this test program, you'll note that some of the white replotting lines cut into the existing grey shaded boxes. In later chapters, I show you how to overcome such graphic anomalies.

Chapter 36 ◆ Composite Variable Types

Summary

A composite variable is a container for several other non-array variables. The term for this variable is established by the programmer, as long as it does not conflict with a reserved Visual Basic keyword or another variable, graphic object, or line-labeling term currently in use within the source code. When a composite variable type is declared within the global module, component variables can be addressed as properties of the composite variable, as if the composite were an object.

The `Type-End Type` clause is used to declare composite variables; it can appear only within the global module of a VB application. The variables listed within the clause are not declared by the clause; they are declared elsewhere.

Review Questions

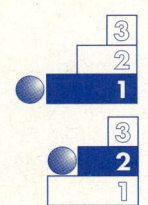

1. Can a composite variable include both string and value variables?

2. Composite variables use object-oriented syntax for addressing individual elements. If at one point the value of one element of a composite variable is set to the value of a regular variable, and the value of that regular variable changes later in the program, does the value within the composite variable change as well?

3. Because a composite variable is not a variable, why is it called a *composite variable*?

The Random-Number Generator

In this chapter you experiment with one of the more intriguing features of this or any other high-level programming language, the part that appears to act for the most part on its own: the interpreter's generator for "random" numbers. As a Visual Basic programmer, you use randomization to set up conditions for experiments, as well as create the random element for tests, simulations, and games.

Whether 'tis by Chance or by Circumstance...

Having thoroughly expounded on the logical processes of computing thus far in this book, it would seem there could be no process within a computer that could possibly take the random element into account. It would seem so because it *is* so; in fact, there is no true random-number generator within any computer, or any interpreter or compiler. Rather than skip to the next chapter, however, you should note that there is a logical function within Visual Basic that *appears* to generate random numbers with no specific inputs or parameters passed to it. The Rnd() function is one of the

Chapter 37 ◆ The Random-Number Generator

oldest functions in the BASIC language, and it seems to have been unscathed by the more purposeful path of progress:

Rnd ( ) — Function

Syntax:

`number# = Rnd[(process#)]`

where *process#* is any double-precision floating-point number, the sign of which, when *process#* is expressed, is crucial to the generation process.

The `Rnd()` function returns what appears to be, for all intents and purposes, a random double-precision floating-point number between 0 and 1. The value of *process#* affects the random number generation process. A particular "random" number is generated for each *process#* value passed to the function, if *process#* < 0. A particular sequence of random numbers may exist within an application for each number generation, in which case the same sequence is generated each time the application is executed. The next number in this sequence can be generated if *process#* > 0, or if *process#* is omitted altogether. The previous random number is regenerated if *process#* = 0.

The random number generation process in Visual Basic is actually dependent on the current value yielded by the `Timer` function. The result is a sequence of numbers that appears to be random when pulled out of the proverbial hat. After running applications that use random numbers again and again, however, you might notice that the same sequence of randomization appears each time. This would get a little frustrating for the programmer trying to maintain a constant level of difficulty for a blackjack game.

This repeated-sequence problem is easily solved through the invocation of the `Randomize` statement.

Randomize Statement

Syntax:

`Randomize[(seed%)]`

The `Randomize` statement *reseeds* the random-number generator for an application. In other words, it changes some of the constants in the random generation algorithm so that a different sequence of random numbers can be generated, thus eliminating the possibility of number prediction. If `seed%` is expressed, a particular sequence of random numbers referred to by `seed%` is initiated. If `seed%` is omitted, a "random" seed is initiated, the choice of which seed value is based on the current state of the random-number generator itself.

Example

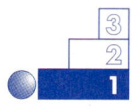

You can see that the generator really does appear to pick numbers out of a hat, as demonstrated by this conversation with the CLI appearing in the Visual Basic Immediate window:

```
?rnd(1)
 .7055475
?rnd(1)
 .533424
?rnd(1)
 .5795186
?rnd(1)
 .2895625
?rnd(1)
 .301948
```

Each time the same function is invoked, and each time a different response is generated. It is possible, however, that a program that invoked the random-number generator five times would, throughout several executions, generate the same *sequence* of "random" numbers each time, unless the `Randomize` statement appears somewhere toward the beginning of the program, perhaps in `Sub Form_Load ()` or `Sub Main ()`.

Chapter 37 ◆ The Random-Number Generator

The following function returns a random integer value between 0 and 15:

```
rnum = Int(Rnd * 15)
```

The value returned by `Rnd()` (or `Rnd` without parentheses, if you prefer) will always be between 0 and 1. Thus, if you multiply the value by 15, the result will always be between 0 and 15. Making this result into an integer allows the interpreter to pick a number between 0 and 15.

A similar function can be used to pick a capital letter between *A* and *Z*:

```
letr = Int(Rnd * 26) + 65
letr$ = Chr$(letr)
```

The ASCII code value for character *A* is 65. The 26 uppercase letters in the alphabet fall in the ASCII code from 65 to 90, in sequence. After picking a number from 0 to 25, the result is added to 65 to obtain an uppercase letter from the ASCII code, which is assigned to string variable `letr$`.

Example

It's inevitable that, at some time in the career of the game programmer, she will use the random-number generator to shuffle cards. If you assume the standard deck contains 52 cards (54 if you count jokers), it would be easy to pick a single card out of the deck with the function `Int(Rnd * 52) + 1` (not counting card number 0). The shuffling process, however, from the point of view of the computer, picks 52 random cards from this deck successively. We can't say `For card = 1 to 52` and have the randomizing process merely repeat itself, because it's possible that the interpreter could pick the same card more than once. The shuffled deck can have only one instance of each card; each time that card is picked for the new deck, some indicator must remain to prevent the card from being picked again.

```
Randomize
For plac = 1 To 52
choose:
    extract = Int(Rnd(1) * 52) + 1
    If slot(extract) = 1 Then GoTo choose
    card(plac) = extract
    slot(extract) = 1
Next plac
```

Here is the procedure translated into pseudocode:

Reseed the random-number generator.
Start counting card places from 1 to 52.
   Pick a card between 1 and 52.
   If this number has been chosen before then go back
   and pick another card.
   Otherwise, assign this card number to the deck.
   Record this card as having been chosen once.
Count the next card.

Here you assume that each card number is representative of a particular card; for instance, card number 1 could be the ace of spades.

Summary

Random number generation is accomplished in Visual Basic through the use of the `Rnd()` function. A set sequence of random numbers exists virtually for each application, although that sequence can be replaced with another sequence using the `Randomize` statement. Each random number generated by the VB interpreter has a value between 0 and 1; this value can be multiplied and made into an integer, resulting in the appearance of the computer picking a whole number from a specified range.

Chapter 37 ◆ The Random-Number Generator

Review Questions

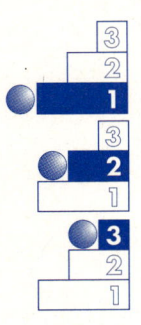

1. In the expression `Rnd(1) * 72`, the function randomizes a number between 0 and what?

2. Why are the parentheses in the `Rnd()` function optional?

3. Can the `Randomize` seed for the random number generator be a random number?

Part VII

Text

38

Conventional Output

In this chapter you are introduced—and in many cases, reintroduced—to the statements, functions, and properties of Visual Basic that concern text production. In Visual Basic, the most well-known of BASIC instructions—PRINT—makes its appearance as the `.Print` method. Microsoft uses a character descriptor code among nearly all of its Windows applications that describes for the application or interpreter the output format for an alphanumeric string. You study this code in this chapter, and some examples are presented here utilizing the code in `.Print` methods with the `Format$()` function.

In Search of Finer `.Print`

Observing the BASIC programming language from the point of view of a computing historian is in many ways like a designer or engineer observing the history of a model of car having a shape and function that have changed over the decades—for instance, the Ford Thunderbird or the Pontiac LeMans. When a model of car is drastically altered from a two-seater sports coupe (the '57

Chapter 38 ◆ Conventional Output

Thunderbird) to a long, six-passenger, four-door sedan (the '63 Thunderbird), the people behind the reengineering of the product say such changes are necessary to suit people's needs in a progressing society. The same is said when a model of car is drastically altered from a long, six-passenger, four-door sedan (the '79 LeMans) to a two-seater sports coupe (the '89 LeMans).

We who have witnessed the redesign of literally everything merchandisable know the need for change is most prevalent in the minds of engineers. The '57 Thunderbird was a perfectly good car. The time came, however, to design another car, or else lay off a perfectly good team of engineers. In computing, the need for change is far more frequent than in the automotive industry, perhaps because the rapid growth of computing as an industry fostered within its participants a more advanced level of impatience. A central processing unit can be blazingly fast until the advances in technology make it look chillingly slow by comparison. Still, some degree of permanence—call it heritage—remains in the design and engineering of a computing device, even when its performance is raised by another exponential factor in its redesign. The Intel 386 CPU utilizes much of the same logic in its design as its distant ancestral progenitor, the Intel 4004—which was used in the mid-'70s to control traffic lights.

I drive a 1983 Datsun 280ZX. In and of itself, that has little to do with Visual Basic, except for the following: In tracing the design history of the Z, I find the '83 model a comfortable blend of the newer engineering prevalent in the late '80s models and the heritage of the "Ladybird" Z in the early '70s models. I like taking notice of what design elements remain intact over the years, and what elements are replaced in the interest of progress or better architecture. BASIC has been my programming language like the Z has been my car. In Visual Basic, there are hardly any remnants of the old BASIC language that haven't been shrouded within the new and brighter latticework of logical design progress; but from the depths, an element or two does peer out into the modern world, a remnant covered in layer upon layer of reengineering and revision. One such remnant is the `.Print` method.

.Print   Method

Syntax:

```
[Object.]Print [expression1{;¦,} expression2{;¦,}
    . . . expression[{;¦,}]
```

where each *expression* consists of any valid, logically interpretable mathematical or string expression. A mathematical expression, in this case, is comprised of one or more values or variables combined arithmetically using operator symbols such as + or function terms such as Int(). A string expression is comprised of one or more elements of text, whether they be alphanumeric phrases, string variables, or string functions such as Right$(). Multiple-element string expressions can be concatenated using the + operator. Text that is to be printed literally must appear within double quotation marks, as in "Hello". Double quotation marks themselves can be printed using the function Chr$(34), the function itself appearing *outside* of any quotation marks. Likewise, you can express other special characters not appearing on the keyboard by using the Chr$() function.

The .Print method displays the logically reduced form of each expression in its expression list. If *Object.* is specified, the recipient of the printed text is either the stated graphic object, such as Form1, or an output device, such as Printer. If *Object.* is allowed by the interpreter to be omitted, printing is directed to the form window to which the procedure containing the .Print method belongs. The recipient *Object.* cannot be omitted from the instruction if the .Print method appears within the context of a general module. If the recipient *Object.* belongs to a form other than the one containing the .Print method, the form name is specified before the object name, with both names separated from each other by a period.

The semicolon and comma as delimiters have specific uses with respect to the .Print method. Each expression in the list is separated from the others by one of these delimiters. If two expressions are separated from each other by a semicolon, the text of both expressions will be printed next to each other (side by side). If two expressions are separated from each other by a comma, the interpreter will insert a tabulation character at the end

Chapter 38 ◆ Conventional Output

of the first expression before printing the start of the second. A tabulation is equivalent to 14 *columns* or, to borrow a term from typography, 14 *ens,* where an *en* is the average width of a letter in the currently chosen font.

The Visual Basic interpreter recognizes a virtual cursor for the graphic objects that receive text using the .Print method. This cursor's coordinate position is registered within properties of the graphic object, called .CurrentX and .CurrentY. Whenever a .Print method has completed execution, it by default leaves the virtual cursor at the beginning (by default, the left side) of the line immediately following the one just printed. If the .Print method is closed with a semicolon, the cursor position is set at the immediate end of the text just printed, without the interpreter executing a *carriage return* to the next line. If the .Print method is closed with a comma, the cursor is tabulated to the next 14-column stop and will remain there without the interpreter executing a *line feed* to the next line.

If the .Print method appears on a line by itself, a carriage return with a line feed is generated. In other words, the "print head" is set to the far left by the carriage return, and one line down by the line feed—like what happens when you press the Return key on an electric typewriter. The virtual cursor's position is set at the beginning of the next line below the previously printed one.

Print seems like a simple enough instruction until you try to explain it to somebody. Part of the reason the instruction is so complex today is because functionality has been added to it over time since 1964. Remember, when BASIC was first compiled on a college mainframe, the PRINT command was the language's only instruction for direct visual output. In other words, PRINT did all the display work for BASIC, back before the advent of point-addressable graphics. On many systems, the only display device for the computer was the printer.

Imagine an old Digital Equipment DECwriter. This was, for the most part, an oversized typewriter on stilts; it did include a full typewriter keyboard. For many terminal systems, the DECwriter was the input/output device. For this reason, the PRINT command in BASIC and the WRITE command in FORTRAN developed a typewriter-like mode of operation, keeping track of such things as carriage position, tab stops, and line feeds. A carriage return was—and still is—a character in the ASCII code.

Visual Basic maintains three categories of objects, which are distinguished from each other by their capability to receive text. The first category is a graphic object to be used specifically as a control. Text is assigned to such control devices by setting their `.Caption` properties as equivalent to that text, as in the following instruction:

> Graphic objects used as *controls* have text set with their `.Caption` property.

```
Command1.Caption = "Cancel"
```

The user cannot edit on-screen the text that is assigned as a `.Caption`. The second category of object is the text box, which is generally used as an explicitly marked area or field for the entry or display of text. Text is assigned to this category by setting its `.Text` property equivalent to that text; conversely, text can be acquired from a text box by assigning its `.Text` property to a string variable, as in the following instruction:

> Text boxes have their text set with the `.Text` property.

```
name$ = Surname.Text
```

So, the primary difference between the operation of a text box and a captioned control is that the text box is a *receptacle* for user-entered text, thus making text exchange within the source code a two-way process. Text is *acquired* from a text box as easily as it can be assigned to it, by merely reversing the order of items in the equation.

The type of object that can take advantage of the `.Print` method can best be thought of as a *terminal*, like the old DECwriter. In essence, each time you create a new form or picture box, you're creating for all intents and purposes a new terminal. This is how Microsoft Windows thinks of such objects as well; in fact, making the single terminal that is your computer's BIOS into multiple virtual terminals is the primary purpose of Microsoft Windows. The textual rules of each terminal you create within the Windows environment are still based in large part on the way old terminals like the DECwriter used to work.

In the Visual Basic scheme of things, the Immediate window— the object name of which is, rather unaffectionately, `Debug.`—is the last remnant of the old terminal communication device for conversing with the BASIC command-line interpreter. The Debug. device can be used as an output device when all else fails. The following example shows a statement that could be used in the event of a benchmark program "erroring out:"

```
Debug.Print "Error after";iter;"iterations",stag;"stage."
```

The semicolons here have the interpreter print the value of the stated variables beside the text. Since these are values, the interpreter knows to add spaces between the text and values, so it isn't necessary here to include an extra space within the quotation marks. The comma after each literal expression (text appearing within quotation marks) has the interpreter "press Tab"—in other words, tabulate to the next tab stop on the line.

Another way to space elements of text from each other is through the use of functions. One of the oldest BASIC functions for such purposes is Tab().

Tab() Function

Syntax:

Tab(*column%*)

The Tab() function is used to move the text cursor to the specified *column%*. A column at any one time is equivalent to roughly the average width of every character in the type style and size currently being used, which is often the width of the lowercase *n*.

A related function is Spc().

Spc() Function

Syntax:

Spc(*spaces%*)

Visual Basic *By*
EXAMPLE

The `Spc()` function is used to move the text cursor a specified number of *spaces%* to the right. A space at any one time is the width of the space character for the type style and size currently being used.

Example

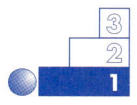

The difference between the `Tab()` function and the `Spc()` function becomes evident when you print using proportionally spaced fonts. Here are two instructions containing text to be printed within the same text box, using a proportionally spaced *Helvetica* font. Figure 38.1 shows the results of the following instructions:

```
Picture1.Print "Schorr"; tab(45); "Daniel"
Picture1.Print "Schorr"; spc(45); "Daniel"
```

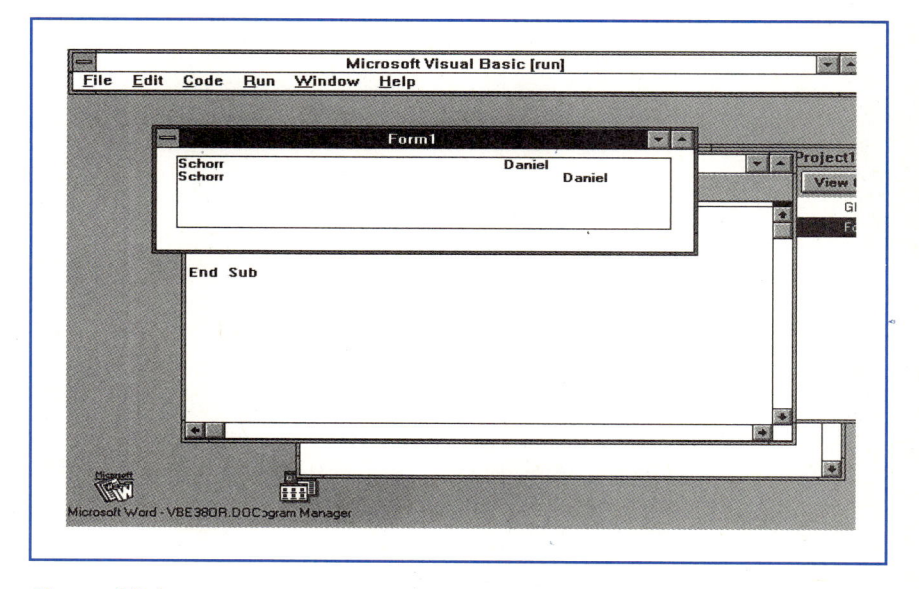

Figure 38.1. Daniel Schorr. You've seen him tabulated. Now see him spaced out.

471

Chapter 38 ◆ Conventional Output

One more terminal-control command from the old days making its appearance as a Visual Basic method is .Cls.

.Cls   Method

Syntax:

[*Object*.]Cls

The .Cls method clears the specified graphic object of any printed or plotted contents, textual or graphic. If *Object*. is not specified, the form within which the .Cls procedure appears is cleared.

Example

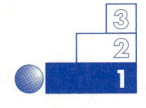

Nothing can be simpler than clearing the contents of a picture box:

Picture1.Cls

Gobbledygook Made Logical

As mentioned earlier in this chapter, Microsoft has developed a text descriptor language for describing the appearance, display, or printing format of an element of text. Microsoft uses this language or some derivative of it in most of its Windows applications, including Visual Basic. This format descriptor code used to be prevalent in the old PRINT USING statement, which assigned an appearance format to the text of a value or numeric variable that followed the word USING. This term doesn't appear in Visual Basic; in its place is a separate function—not a statement—that states the appearance format for a specified value.

Visual Basic *By*

EXAMPLE

Format$()   Function

Syntax:

*string$* = Format$(*value*[, *descriptor$*])

The Format$() function converts a numeric *value* to an alphanumeric string, in the same manner as the Str$() function. If *descriptor$* is not specified, the Format$() function stops here; otherwise, it applies an appearance format, described using Microsoft's number format descriptor code, as the format for this value. If *descriptor$* is to be written out, it must appear within quotation marks; otherwise, the descriptor can be assigned to a string variable in advance, using an equation.

Examples

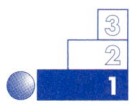

Several characters act as number formatters in Microsoft's code. Instead of listing them all like some programmer's manual-rewriting service, I show you examples of some of these format descriptors in action, using the Visual Basic CLI as a guide.

```
number=12.95
text$=format$(number, "0000.00")
print text$
0012.95
```

Each zero within the descriptor saves an absolute place in the text string for a digit, whether or not a value exists for the place of that digit. The preceding descriptor will definitely display a four-digit whole-number, two-digit fractional-number value. The period in the descriptor reserves the place for the decimal point.

```
text$=format$(number, "####.##")
print text$
12.95
```

473

The use of the pound sign (#) within a descriptor holds a place for a digit in the converted text, unless no value exists for that digit.

```
text$=format$(number, "$####.##")
print text$
$12.95
```

A dollar sign within the descriptor places a dollar sign within the text at that place.

```
text$=format$(number, "$#000.00")
print text$
$012.95
```

Zero placeholders and pound sign placeholders can be mixed within a descriptor, although the results may be confusing.

```
text$=format$(number, "*******$#######.##")
print text$
*******$12.95
```

Asterisks and other symbolic characters can be used as leading or trailing characters within a descriptor.

```
text$=format$(number, "###%")
print text$
1295%
text$=format$(number,"###.##%")
print text$
1295.%
```

The percentage sign used in a descriptor places a percentage sign within the converted text; however, the value before the percentage sign is then multiplied by 100.

```
number=1563534
text$=format$(number, "###,###,###,###")
?text$
1,563,534
```

Commas can be used as delimiters for every thousandth place in a base 10 value.

Visual Basic *By* EXAMPLE

You may remember from Chapter 10, "Time and Date," how the internal variable Now maintains the current system time and date in a single-precision floating-point number.

```
?now
 33539.1968634259
?format$(now,"mm/dd/yy")
10/28/91
```

The current month, day, and date can be extracted from this internal variable using combinations of ms, ds, and ys. Two of each appearing together return digital displays.

```
?format$(now,"dd mmmm yyyy")
28 October 1991
```

Four ms together spell out the month, and four ys together display the entire year.

```
?format$(now,"dd/mm/yy")
28/10/91
```

For the benefit of Europeans, the day and month can be formatted in reverse order.

```
?format$(now,"dd mmm yy")
28 Oct 91
?format$(now,"mmm dd yyyy")
Oct 28 1991
```

There are countless other ways to format dates.

```
?format$(now,"hh:mm:ss")
04:47:20
```

Combinations of hs, ms, and ss can be used for expressing time. The Visual Basic interpreter somehow knows to distinguish the mm of time from the mm of date.

```
?format$(now,"h:m:s")
4:47:36
```

Chapter 38 ◆ Conventional Output

Single characters here display the time with leading zeros removed.

```
?format$(now,"h:mm:ss AM/PM")
4:48:42 AM
?format$(now,"hh:mm:ss a/p")
04:49:05 a
```

These are two examples of expressing a.m. and p.m.:

```
?format$(now,"dd mm yy hh:mm:ss A/P")
28 10 91 04:49:34 A
```

The underscore character is used here as a lead-in character. Dates and times can be combined on the same line.

Example

```
number=-15.5
?format$(number, "##.##;(##.##)")
(15.5)
```

The semicolon is used here to separate the format for negative values from the format for positive values. Here you're telling the interpreter to display negative values within parentheses.

Example

```
fmt$="##.##;(##.##);"+chr$(34)+"Zero"+chr$(34)
?fmt$
##.##;(##.##);"Zero"
number=0
?format$(number,fmt$)
Zero
```

This final example is perhaps a bit confusing. The format descriptor language conceived by Microsoft allows the programmer to display any textual string within the descriptor, as long as that text is enclosed in quotation marks. However, quotation marks cannot be assigned as part of a string using the normal equation, because in Visual Basic an equation used to assign text requires that text to be placed in quotation marks. Therefore, you can only use the function `Chr$(34)` to assign a quotation mark as part of a string. In the preceding example, the concatenation was assigned to `fmt$`.

The second semicolon in the descriptor is used for specifying the appearance format for a zero value. In this case, the descriptor string `fmt$` contains the text string `"Zero"`. Now the `Format$()` function will spell out *Zero* whenever the value is zero; otherwise, the value appears in accountants' format.

Summary

`.Print` manifests itself in Visual Basic as a method, which dispatches text to a specific graphic object or output device. The `.Print` method can print multiple items in sequence, separated by delimiters having functions that were derived from the earliest use of the `PRINT` command in old BASIC for TTY terminals.

Visual Basic maintains three categories of text-receiving graphic objects. The first is the command control object, which receives its text by assignment to the property `.Caption`. The second is the interactive text box, which receives its text by assignment to the property `.Text`. The third is the virtual terminal, which is the conventional primary output area for textual processes and interaction. This area receives its text from the `.Print` method. Virtual terminal display areas are handled as if they were display typewriter pages with carriage returns and tab stops.

Microsoft uses a format descriptor code for describing the textual appearance of numbers and values. A measure of this code is supported by Visual Basic, through the `Format$()` function.

Chapter 38 ◆ Conventional Output

Review Questions

What `Format$()` descriptor could be used to display the following text, given the values listed:

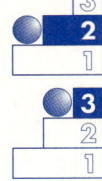

1. `value = .15, text$ = "15%"`

2. `value = 365.5, text$ = "****365.50"`

3. `value = Now, text$ = "5 PM"`

4. `value = 0, text$ = "Unchanged"`

5. `value = Now, text$ = "by 8:00 PM tonight at the earliest."`

39

Textual Properties

In this chapter you briefly examine the properties of text that belongs to graphic objects. You then further investigate the notion of the *virtual cursor* that accompanies all objects that the Visual Basic interpreter sees as *virtual terminals*. Finally, you experiment with two methods for judging how much space text to be printed will consume within a graphic object.

Font Characteristics

The Visual Basic program uses the screen font and printer font generation system supplied to it as a resource by Microsoft Windows. Some Windows users prefer to use third-party print manager programs such as Adobe Type Manager, in which case their screen and printer fonts should appear significantly clearer and should have more detailed characteristics such as true italicization. In any event, only the most general characteristics of a font or type style as supported by the standard font generation system of Windows are supported by Visual Basic.

Object.FontName or *Printer*.Fontname Property

The .FontName property is set to the precise text of a name from the list of fonts currently maintained by Microsoft Windows. When this property is set, the font used for printing or assigning text to a form, graphic object, or the printer is referred to by this name.

Object.FontSize or *Printer*.FontSize Property

The .FontSize property is set to the approximate point size available for a font that has its current .FontName supported by Windows and that is currently the chosen .FontName for printing or assigning text.

Label.Alignment Property

When a font is chosen for a textual label to appear in a form, its alignment can be set by a property called the .Alignment property.

The .Alignment property for a label is set to an integer that describes how the text within that label is aligned. The property can be set to any of the following values:

- 0   Left justification (default)
- 1   Right justification
- 2   Centered

True-False Font Properties

After a font name is chosen for an *Object* or *Printer*, five true-false properties describing the appearance of that font can be addressed: .FontBold, .FontItalic, .FontStrikethru, .FontTransparent, and .FontUnderline.

These five properties are set to Boolean values of –1 (true) or 0 (false) depending on their state. For command and interactive controls, setting these properties at run time immediately changes the on-screen appearance of the fonts within those controls. For virtual terminals (form, printer, and picturebox), setting these properties at run time changes the way text *to be printed* will appear, although the appearance of text already printed will remain as it is.

By setting the .FontTransparent property to false, each character to be displayed or printed will carry with it a surrounding block background of an assigned .BackColor. By setting the .FontStrikethru property to true, each character to be displayed or printed will have a slash mark or other mark through it, although only if this characteristic is available for the chosen font. By default, the .FontBold and .FontTransparent properties for a new graphic object are set to true; the .FontItalic, .FontStrikethru, and .FontUnderline properties are set to false.

The Curse of the Missing Cursor

In programming the Test Text search-and-replace form in Chapter 35, "String Functions," you may remember I included a few instructions in one of the procedures for extracting the text being searched for from the paragraph after it was located:

```
Sub Start_Click ()
srch$ = SearchText.Text
If Len(srch$) = 0 Then
    Searcher.Hide
    Exit Sub
End If
trgt$ = App.Document.Text
pos = InStr(trgt$, srch$)
If pos = 0 Then
    MsgBox "Text not found.", 0, ""
    Exit Sub
```

Chapter 39 ◆ Textual Properties

```
End If
App.Document.SelStart = pos - 1
App.Document.SelLength = Len(srch$)
found$ = App.Document.SelText
Searcher.Hide
MsgBox "Search string '" + found$ + "' found at position"
    + Str$(pos) + "."
End Sub
```

The VB interpreter maintains an internal location of a cursor for a text box object at all times. In the preceding example, the location of this cursor can be addressed with respect to the index of the specific character that currently resides to its right. You can set the cursor's location by assigning an index to it, and then use it to *select* and extract a region of text with property settings.

Combo.SelStart or *Text*.SelStart Property

The .SelStart property is set to a value that designates where the cursor will appear within the text in a text box. This is where extraction from this body of text begins. Each character of text within the box has its own index number, starting with character 1 at the beginning of the text. Setting the value of .SelStart places the cursor to the right of the indexed character; setting it to 0 places it at the beginning of the text. The cursor position is also referred to as the *insertion point*.

Combo.SelLength or *Text*.SelLength Property

The .SelLength property is set to the number of characters being extracted to the right of the cursor position .SelStart. This text "selection" is normally invisible to the user at run time.

Object.SelText or *Text*.SelText Property

The .SelText property is set to the contents of the text being extracted from the text box. This text does not appear indicated on the screen as if the user marked this text with the mouse; the extraction process is invisible to the user. Setting the .SelStart and .SelLength properties of a text box automatically sets the .SelText property to the characters starting at position .SelStart and extending for .SelLength characters.

Making It All Fit

Suppose you want an element of text, which you plan to print to a picture box, to take up all the space it can within that box. Visual Basic provides you with two methods for discerning the width and height of text for the given .FontName and .FontSize for a picture box or form, *before* it is printed there.

Object.TextHeight and *Object*.TextWidth Methods

Syntax:

value% = [*Object*.]TextHeight(*string$*)
value% = [*Object*.]TextWidth(*string$*)

The .TextHeight and .TextWidth methods are invoked to some extent like functions, although they are expressed using object-oriented syntax. These methods return the predicted height and width, respectively, of the text expressed in *string$* as it might appear within the specified *Object* when it is printed there using the .Print method. These values are returned within the integer *value%* as if the methods were functions. These methods work only with virtual terminal objects such as a picture box or form, or the printer device. If *Object* is not specified, the form containing the currently executing procedure is assumed.

In much the same way the interpreter maintains a `.SelStart` property containing the cursor position for a text box, two properties are maintained for a form or picture box containing the current cursor coordinates: `.CurrentX` and `.CurrentY`.

Object.CurrentX or *Printer*.CurrentX and *Object*.CurrentY or *Printer*.CurrentY Properties

The `.CurrentX` and `.CurrentY` properties for a virtual terminal graphic object are set by the current coordinates of the cursor for that object. By default, these coordinates are expressed graphically as twips, unless the `.ScaleMode` property for the object is set otherwise. The settings for these properties are relative to the current coordinate scale for the graphic object or device.

Each time a `.Print` method is invoked, the `.CurrentX` property for the object receiving the text is increased by a certain number of twips (or whatever units are in use at the time). At the end of the `.Print` method instruction, assuming no trailing delimiters appear at the end, the cursor moves to the next line, in so doing increasing the `.CurrentY` property of the object. By default, the `.CurrentX` property is then reset to 0.

Summary

The Visual Basic interpreter borrows its resources for font and type style control from Microsoft Windows. The settings for the `.FontName` and `.FontSize` properties are supplied to the interpreter by Windows as resources. The bold, italic, strikethrough, transparency, and underline styles for any Windows font, if they are available, can be set using VB properties that have settings that are Boolean values.

The position of the cursor among text appearing within a text box can be set using the `.SelStart` property. If text is to be extracted from this cursor position forward, the number of characters to be extracted can be expressed as the `.SelLength` property. The extracted text thus becomes the `.SelText` property.

The predicted width and height of text to be printed within a form or picture box can be obtained using the `.TextWidth` and `.TextHeight` methods, respectively. These methods are expressed within an equation almost in the manner of functions, although with object-oriented syntax. The current cursor coordinates within a virtual terminal object are accessible through the `.CurrentX` and `.CurrentY` properties.

Review Questions

1. Why are there no `.CurrentX` or `.CurrentY` properties for a standard text box?

2. Suppose you set the `.SelStart` property to any positive number, and then set the `.SelLength` property to any positive number, what would describe the current contents of the `.SelText` property?

40

The Printer

In this chapter you begin to direct Visual Basic output to the `Printer.` device. This device has a few properties and methods that are specific to the printer.

Hard Copy

Like a form or a picture box, Visual Basic considers the printer to be a *virtual terminal* that receives text using the `.Print` method in the manner of an old TTY or DECwriter terminal printer. To print to the printer from any procedure appearing within any module, address the printer as demonstrated in the following line:

```
Printer.Print "This is an example line of text."
```

Printer.Page Property

The printer as device has a few extra characteristics attributed to it by the VB interpreter. Each application is distributed its own printing process, beginning at page one. The current page number is stored within a property specific to the printer.

Chapter 40 ◆ The Printer

The `Printer.Page` property is set to the current page number maintained by the VB interpreter for an application. Each time an application starts running, the `.Page` property is set to 1. The interpreter assumes a single document is being created for this application at any one time. Each time a page is finished printing, the `.Page` property is incremented.

Printer.NewPage — Method

Syntax:

`Printer.NewPage`

The `.NewPage` method is invoked to eject the page currently being printed. This ejection signal is held within the Windows Print Manager until it dispatches that signal to the printer at an appropriate time. The `.Page` property for the application's internal document is automatically incremented.

To state that the end of a document has been reached, the `.EndDoc` method is invoked.

Printer.EndDoc — Method

Syntax:

`Printer.EndDoc`

The `.EndDoc` method is invoked to signal the completion of the application's internal document and to send the ejection signal for the last page to the Windows Print Manager. The `.Page` property for the application's internal document is automatically reset to 1.

While printing to the printer takes place, the VB interpreter maintains `.CurrentX` and `.CurrentY` properties for the printer's internal "cursor." These cursor coordinates are not expressed in rows and columns, but in graphic coordinates according to the coordinate scale currently set for the printer.

Example

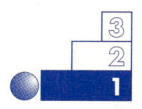

Here's a routine that prints the printer's current coordinate scale to the printer:

```
Printer.Print "Current .ScaleLeft ="; Printer.ScaleLeft
Printer.Print "Current .ScaleTop ="; Printer.ScaleTop
Printer.Print "Current .ScaleWidth ="; Printer.ScaleWidth
Printer.Print "Current .ScaleHeight ="; Printer.ScaleHeight
Printer.EndDoc
```

A twip, when printed on most printers, consumes about 1/72 of a square inch.

For a laser printer that emulates a Hewlett-Packard LaserJet II+, the default `.ScaleWidth` property setting is 11520 and the default `.ScaleHeight` is 15120. Divided by 80 columns per page, you find that `Printer.CurrentX` is increased by 144 *printer twips* for each character printed. Likewise, divided by 60 lines per page, you find that `Printer.CurrentY` is increased by 252 printer twips each time a carriage return or line feed is generated. The printer's internal scale can be manually reset by altering the `.ScaleWidth` and `.ScaleHeight` properties for the `Printer`.

Font Selection

A font installed in Microsoft Windows is intended to have the same general style and appearance on-screen as it does on the printer. Nonetheless, Visual Basic maintains two separate lists of fonts, one for the screen and one for the printer. Both lists have two properties associated with them.

[Screen].Fonts or [Printer].Fonts Property

The `.Fonts()` property behaves as an array that contains the name of each installed font in Microsoft Windows, in whatever order the current Windows font maintenance system has set for that list. This property array is likely to be different for each computer system.

Chapter 40 ◆ The Printer

[*Screen*].FontCount or
[*Printer*].FontCount **Property**

The .FontCount property contains the current number of fonts installed in Microsoft Windows. This property also is likely to be different for each computer system.

Example

Here's a test routine that sets the current printer font to the last font installed in Windows:

```
lastfont = Printer.FontCount
Printer.FontName = Printer.Fonts(lastfont)
```

The number of fonts installed is returned in the variable lastfont, which is used as an array pointer to the last font in the list, .Fonts(lastfont).

Sound

If the standard AT computer bus was a more sonically versatile system, I would be more than pleased to devote an entire section of this book to the topic of sound. Unfortunately, the only sound device that comes standard on all AT-bus computers is the little beeper device. Windows makes use of this device only infrequently, when it forces the beeper to make a noise called a *beep*, which in Version 3.0 actually sounds like a Dutch wooden shoe clomping against concrete. (The improvement made to Version 3.1 is that it now sounds like a plastic whistle blown from a bathtub.) Here is the entire Visual Basic vocabulary for activating this powerful clomping device:

Beep Statement

Syntax:

`Beep`

The `Beep` statement forces a *beep* noise from the computer system. This statement takes no parameters, because in Windows there is only one beep.

The Windows Applications Program Interface is capable of being programmed for beeps of different frequencies and intervals, although the API vocabulary is not a regular part of the VB vocabulary.

Summary

The Visual Basic interpreter maintains an internal printed document for each application. It therefore maintains a page count for that document as the property `Printer.Page`, which is incremented each time the page is ejected using the `Printer.NewPage` method, and is reset to 1 each time the document is closed using the `Printer.EndDoc` method.

The "cursor" position for the printer is maintained within the `Printer.CurrentX` and `Printer.CurrentY` properties. The settings for these properties are expressed in *printer twips,* which correlate to the current scale set for the printer. This scale can be altered using the `Printer.ScaleHeight` and `Printer.ScaleWidth` properties.

Microsoft Windows maintains two font lists for both the `Screen.` and `Printer.` devices. The lists are both addressable as property arrays, using the `.Fonts()` property. The number of fonts currently installed in the particular Windows environment where the interpreter is running is returned using the `.FontCount` property.

`Beep` makes the computer beep.

Chapter 40 ◆ The Printer

Review Questions

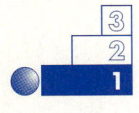

1. After printing the famous line from Paddy Cheyevsky's play *Network*, "I'm mad as hell and I'm not going to take it anymore!" what is the value of `Printer.CurrentX`?

2. Suppose we placed a semicolon to the right of the quotation mark closing the line. What would the value of `Printer.CurrentX` be then?

3. If Microsoft Windows is supposed to facilitate a what-you-see-is-what-you-get text composition environment—where what you see on-screen corresponds to a high degree to what's going to be printed—then how come Visual Basic maintains two different lists of names for fonts belonging to the screen and the printer?

Review Exercise

Write a routine that makes the properties `Printer.CurrentX` and `Printer.CurrentY` addressable as if they were column and row values, respectively.

Part VIII

Bitmapped Graphics

Picture Boxes

In this chapter you study the operation of picture boxes when they are utilized to display graphic images rather than just text. You see what properties are used to point the graphic contents of a picture box to a stored image file.

Picture.*Picture* Revisited

When a picture box is used to display graphics from an image file, that image is considered to be the background for that object. Any text to be printed to that object using the `.Print` method appears on top of the image. Placing an image within a picture box does not affect the values of `.CurrentX` and `.CurrentY` for that box.

The property that lists the file name for a background image—with all due respect to Mr. Rogers — is the `Picture.Picture` property.

Picture.*Picture* Property

The `.Picture` property is set to the file name of the image that appears as the background for the antecedent picture box object. This file name may have a .BMP (Windows Bitmap), .ICO (standard icon), or .WMF (Windows Metafile) extension. The picture is aligned with the upper-left corner of the picture box. If the image is wider or taller than the picture box, the image is said to *hang* beyond the right and bottom edges of the box, respectively.

To set the background image of a picture box at design time:

1. On the form, indicate the picture box to receive the image.

2. Choose the `Picture` property from the properties list of the Visual Basic main window. The property settings bar reads `(picture)`, and the drop-down arrow button beside the settings bar becomes an ellipsis (...) button.

3. To choose a file name for this picture, click the ellipsis button. A file selector box appears.

4. Choose a file name from the list presented and click OK. The image file chosen is loaded immediately into the picture box, and will be displayed on the form as design continues.

To load an image file into the picture box at run time, a *command function* is used.

`LoadPicture()` — Function

Syntax:

`[Form.]Picture = LoadPicture("filename$")`

where `filename$` refers to a file having extension .BMP (Windows bitmap), .ICO (standard icon), or .WMF (Windows metafile).

The `LoadPicture()` function loads the specified image file into the picture box designated on the left side of the equation.

After the image within the picture box has been altered, it can be resaved to disk using the complementary `SavePicture` statement.

496

SavePicture Statement

Syntax:

SavePicture [*object.*]*property*, *filename$*

where *filename$* refers to a file having extension .BMP (Windows bitmap), .ICO (standard icon), or .WMF (Windows metafile); and *property* refers either to the .Image or .Picture property of the specified object, or the object to which the procedure containing the statement currently belongs.

The SavePicture statement saves to disk either the .Picture or .Image currently residing in the designated picture box *object.*, using the *filename$* given. If the .Image property is specified, then regardless of the filename or extension expressed, the image will be saved as a Windows bitmap file, which is more commonly given a .BMP extension. If the .Picture property is specified, the picture will be saved in its current format within the picture box, which may be a Windows bitmap, a standard icon, or a metafile.

Example

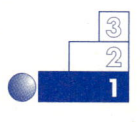

In the first Drag Strip test application in Chapter 28, I had the image of a folder be dragged by the mouse into the area of a picture box, which had the image of a file cabinet loaded into it. As the folder image crossed the boundaries of the picture box, another image was loaded into the box, making the file cabinet appear to open:

```
Sub Cabinet_DragOver (Source As Control, X As Single,
    Y As Single, State As Integer)
If Source.Tag = "Folder" Then
    Cabinet.Picture = LoadPicture
        ("c:\win3\vbasic\icons\office\files03b.ico")
End If
If State = 1 Then
    Cabinet.Picture = LoadPicture
        ("c:\win3\vbasic\icons\office\files03a.ico")
End If
End Sub
```

Chapter 41 ◆ Picture Boxes

When the pointer crossed over the image back into the regular form area, the original file cabinet image was reloaded into the picture box.

Example

You may also remember that I used the `LoadPicture()` function liberally in the Mouse Vane test application in Chapter 31. There, a small picture contained the image of an arrow pointing in the direction that the mouse pointer was moving at any one time. This arrow picture was loaded from the library supplied by Microsoft with the Visual Basic package:

```
Sub Vane_MouseMove (Button As Integer, Shift As Integer,
    x As Single, y As Single)
Static lastx, lasty
If x > lastx Then xaxis = 1
If x < lastx Then xaxis = -1
If y > lasty Then yaxis = 1
If y < lasty Then yaxis = -1
Select Case -1
    Case (xaxis = 1 And yaxis = 1)
        Vane.Picture = LoadPicture
            ("c:\win3\vbasic\icons\arrows\arw10se.ico")
    Case (xaxis = 1 And yaxis = -1)
        Vane.Picture = LoadPicture
            ("c:\win3\vbasic\icons\arrows\arw10ne.ico")
    Case (xaxis = -1 And yaxis = 1)
        Vane.Picture = LoadPicture
            ("c:\win3\vbasic\icons\arrows\arw10sw.ico")
    Case (xaxis = -1 And yaxis = -1)
        Vane.Picture = LoadPicture
            ("c:\win3\vbasic\icons\arrows\arw10nw.ico")
    Case (xaxis = 1 And yaxis = 0)
        Vane.Picture = LoadPicture
            ("c:\win3\vbasic\icons\arrows\arw07rt.ico")
    Case (xaxis = -1 And yaxis = 0)
        Vane.Picture = LoadPicture
            ("c:\win3\vbasic\icons\arrows\arw07lt.ico")
    Case (xaxis = 0 And yaxis = 1)
```

```
        Vane.Picture = LoadPicture
↳           ("c:\win3\vbasic\icons\arrows\arw07dn.ico")
    Case (xaxis = 0 And yaxis = -1)
        Vane.Picture = LoadPicture
↳           ("c:\win3\vbasic\icons\arrows\arw07up.ico")
End Select
lastx = x
lasty = y
End Sub
```

As made obvious by this example, the `LoadPicture()` function can be invoked any number of times during an application's run time for a single picture box.

Summary

The background image currently loaded into a picture box object is registered by its file name, appearing as the `.Picture` property for that object. An image can be loaded into a picture box at design time by setting this `.Picture` property. An image can be loaded into a picture box at run time using the `LoadPicture()` function; likewise, an altered image can be saved from a picture box to disk using the `SavePicture` statement.

Review Questions

1. What is the difference, in Visual Basic terms, between an *image* and a *picture*?

2. Speculate why `LoadPicture()` is a function and `SavePicture` is a statement.

Plotting

In this chapter you learn how to draw images directly into forms and picture boxes using the Visual Basic plotting mechanism. For every form and picture box within a VB application, the interpreter maintains a *virtual pen*, which makes certain elements of the drawing process simulate using a plotter device, giving the appearance of drawing with ink on paper. The VB interpreter knows how to move this pen from place to place, change pen colors, and draw a few rudimentary shapes. First, however, you look at the origins of the Visual Basic coordinate system.

You Have to Draw the Line Someplace

Microcomputers of the late 1970s and early 1980s used their own fixed-screen coordinate systems so programmers would know, in a sense, where to draw the line. The coordinate systems of the first microcomputer BASIC implementations used parameter pairs to address individual pixels or pixel blocks on the screen. The block at the upper-left corner of the screen was generally addressed as (0, 0). Because people dealt with relatively low-resolution television sets for output back then, the lower-right block was generally some

Chapter 42 ◆ Plotting

value like (128, 64). Line-plotting statements such as the ones pioneered by AppleSoft BASIC utilized two pairs of these x- and y-axis coordinates as beginning and end points. More advanced BASICs utilized circle-plotting statements that used perhaps two pairs of coordinates representing the "corners" of the circle-plotting area, or one pair representing the center and a third value for the radius of the circle. BASIC interpreters were considered advanced if they could draw circles like this.

Actually, the concept of addressing points on the screen or cursor locations with parameter pairs really was quite advanced for the mid-1970s, because minicomputer and mainframe computer programmers generally weren't afforded such tools on their own systems. Arguably, the major advances in programming languages premiered on home computers like the Apple II, the TRS-80, and the Atari 400/800 long before the big computer companies of today considered such innovations to have any purpose beyond the recreational.

One major reason parameter pairs were so innovative is as follows: At times, programmers wanted to plot data to just one rectangular region of the screen. On character-based minicomputers, plotting to the screen always began in the upper-left corner. The screen-plotting mechanism was as graphically complex as typing a picture of something on your portable typewriter; text and graphic blocks were "typed" to the screen. To get something to appear in the middle of the screen, like typing something in the middle of a piece of paper, the programmer had to carriage return down several lines and then tab to the right several spaces. These lines and spaces could be programmed in advance as y- and x-axis offset coordinates, respectively. The PRINT command could return the carriage the number of lines in the offset variable OY, and the TAB() function could space the cursor to the right for the number of spaces in the offset variable OX.

With home microcomputers, variables OX and OY (or variables with other names but the same purpose) could be addressed within parameter pairs as *geometric* offsets. While the environment of character-based minicomputers existed within a virtual IBM Selectric II typewriter, the environment of such pioneering graphic computers as Apple's and Atari's was Cartesian geometric space, which gave not only programmers but also mathematicians a great deal more freedom of expression. The technique they utilized was to have OX and OY serve as offset intervals from the *origin* point (0, 0). These offsets allowed for the creation of a *virtual origin* of a semi-independent plotting region of the screen. By plotting to a point such as (75 + OX, 25 + OY) in effect, a point (75, 25) virtually exists in the programmer's mind relative to this semi-independent region. The programmer could then comfortably ignore OX and OY for now, concentrating on the region as if it was a screen unto itself.

Perhaps you've guessed what I'm leading up to. Later interpreters, using BASIC as well as other languages, allowed for the declaration of these independent regions without the use of offset variables within the plotting statement. No one is sure who gets the credit for first naming these declarable regions *windows*.

So it was, arguably, that windows were created as programmer conveniences, and not as the ease-of-use devices that certain marketing divisions might have us believe. Let's face it, computers are really no easier to use today than they ever were. They are, in fact, far more complex devices than they were five years ago, although their complexity has merely become more understood by the public at large. Windows themselves have made computers more complex by introducing a new order of multiplicity to the computing environment. By having more than one of something within a computer in the first place, the computing environment is established.

Windows Within Windows

Visual Basic maintains a coordinate system for the Screen. object at large, although this system is not intended for direct plotting. In other words, you can't draw a line from the absolute upper-left corner of the screen to the lower-right corner unless you find a way to expand the drawing area of a form so that it consumes the entire screen, and then plot to that form as if it were the screen. Screen coordinates in Visual Basic are reserved for the positioning of forms. Each form then has its own coordinate system. As you've seen, graphic objects are positioned relative to the coordinates of the form rather than those of the screen. Picture boxes, as you learned in the previous chapter, have their own coordinate systems, which are separate and independent from the form.

Chapter 42 ♦ Plotting

> A *twip* is a plotting point that is considered independently of pixels.

The coordinate system used by Visual Basic is extraordinarily versatile. The "blocks" it uses, by default, are actually smaller in geometric configuration space than pixels themselves. The screen coordinate system is thus independent of the screen itself. Each point along this system is considered a *twip*. A twip is a plotting point as interpreted in memory by Microsoft Windows, within a relative coordinate system that exists independently from the physical pixel-based coordinate system of the screen.

Microsoft boldly postulates that there are 1440 twips to the inch. Exactly what size screen Microsoft used to obtain this measurement has not been discerned, although you might assume they used a 15-inch diagonal color VGA monitor because there are more of these in production than any other type. Still, some VGA cards produce images to the same monitor that have different sizes than others. Also, varying screen resolutions often change the dimensions of the on-screen image. You may be lucky enough to have a beautiful 20-inch display; if you do, however, the twips themselves won't know it. So let's say there are roughly 1440 twips to the inch, give or take several hundred.

In all graphical computers, each unit in the coordinate system is represented in memory by a certain number of bits. Usually, the combination of bits for a pixel represents, using binary coding, the color of the pixel at that point. This is true for most VGA graphic systems. Memory within these systems is specially apportioned for the VGA card itself so that the motherboard's main memory can be used for other purposes. Here in the main memory, Windows maintains a representation of the screen that has a greater resolution than the actual screen. Visual Basic is capable of allocating segments of main memory for itself to maintain images that have a greater resolution than the screen. This way, if the graphics hardware of the computer changes and the screen drivers are advanced to go with it, the screen representation can be rescaled to fit the new screen without drastically altering the VB program.

The Color Scheme

In Visual Basic, as with every graphical computer devised to date, when you plot a point of a particular color to a specified location, you change the bitwise pattern of the portion of memory that corresponds to that point. The new pattern then represents the new color of that point. Visual Basic maintains a variety of methods for determining which color is to be plotted. As you might have guessed, the system Visual Basic uses is far more complex than choosing a color for a box on your Apple II.

Utilizing the same philosophy that says the programmer should have more points available for plotting than there are pixels, Visual Basic makes it possible for the programmer to have more color *values* available than there may be colors. Generally, Windows screen drivers mix existing colors to form patterns that represent in-between colors. These patterns are formed with multiple pixels in the hope that your eye will perform the role of color blender. As a result, you cannot possibly plot a point to the screen using any one of 16,777,216 colors, although the RGB() function acts as if you can.

RGB( ) Function

Syntax:

`color& = RGB(red%, green%, blue%)`

where `red%`, `green%`, and `blue%` are integers with the range 0 to 255, representing the intensity of each primary color in the mixture.

The RGB() function returns a single long integer value that is a mathematical combination of the three input parameters and represents for the Visual Basic interpreter a specific color-mixture value. Each parameter represents the amount of its optical primary color used in the mixture. The greater the parameter value, the brighter the primary color for the mixture.

Using optical mixing, yellow is comprised of a full blend of red and green.

Because it's doubtful you'd want to look up a particular color from a table of 16,777,216 choices, this function comes in handy. When blending colors optically, using light rather than pigment, the three primary colors are red, blue, and *green.* For some people, mixing colors in this manner may be a bit foreign at first. Optically, a full blend of red and green forms *yellow.* Using the RGB() function, the brightest yellow obtainable would be represented as RGB(255, 255, 0), where the 0 stands for no blue. White in this case would be represented as RGB(255, 255, 255), and a middle, cold grey would be RGB(128, 128, 128).

It might appear at first that such color blendings make available to the programmer every color imaginable, but this is in fact not true. No optical cathode ray tube yet has been able to generate a true emerald green or leaf green, a warm grey, or a cobalt blue. Conceivably, you do have every color in the rainbow available to you, but keep in mind that browns are not in the rainbow. You could use pattern blending to try to simulate brown; however, what you really get is a warm but dark form of red, formed by patterning red pixels against black ones—using, for instance, RGB(45, 10, 0). The green here can be used to dull down the brightness of the red somewhat. Too much green, however, generates yellow specks in the mixture. If you try (as I have) to simulate burnt sienna or raw umber, you will most likely fail (as I have).

If you're familiar with programming using the BASIC interpreter that came with your version of DOS, or if you've used Microsoft QuickBASIC, you've probably become accustomed to the CGA color registers for plotting to the fixed coordinate system of DOS' character-based screen. Visual Basic provides a function that simulates these registers for those who have them already engrained in their brains. It is the QBColor() function.

QBColor()   **Function**

Syntax:

color& = QBColor(*register%*)

The QBColor() function returns a long integer value representing for the Visual Basic interpreter a color mixture roughly equivalent to the value of the color *register%* used in Microsoft QuickBASIC for plotting to the CGA screen. The parameter *register%* can take any of the values in Table 42.1. In this table, the values are shown next to their RGB() functional equivalents.

Visual Basic *By* EXAMPLE

Table 42.1. QuickBASIC and RGB color conversion chart.

QB Color Value	QB Color	RGB Color
0	Black	RGB(0, 0, 0)
1	Blue	RGB(0, 0, 191)
2	Green	RGB(0, 191, 0)
3	Dark Cyan	RGB(0, 191, 191)
4	Red	RGB(191, 0, 0)
5	Magenta	RGB(191, 0, 191)
6	Dark Yellow	RGB(191, 191, 0)
7	Page White	RGB(191, 191, 191)
8	Grey	RGB(64, 64, 64)
9	Bright Blue	RGB(0, 0, 255)
10	Bright Green	RGB(0, 255, 0)
11	Bright Cyan	RGB(0, 255, 255)
12	Bright Red	RGB(255, 0, 0)
13	Bright Magenta	RGB(255, 0, 255)
14	Bright Yellow	RGB(255, 255, 0)
15	Bright White	RGB(255, 255, 255)

In most computer systems, plotting to or *setting* a point to a certain color changes the bitwise value of the location in memory that corresponds directly to the specified point. This setting in memory is what changes the color of the pixel on screen. In Visual Basic, the coordinate systems are entirely relative. Setting a specified twip changes the bitwise value of the location in memory that corresponds to the twip. The point on the screen that corresponds to the twip coordinates, however, is determined relatively, not directly, with internal offsets as well as a variable coordinate scale.

The method used to set a twip to a certain color is the *Object*.PSet method.

Object.PSet   Method

Syntax:

[*Object*.]PSet [Step](*twipx!*, *twipy!*)[, *color&*]

    The .PSet method sets the color value of a coordinate point represented by the coordinates (*twipx!*, *twipy!*). If the point currently is visible on-screen, the pixel relative to that point along the current twip coordinate system will have its color value set. If the point is not visible on the screen, the point in memory will be set anyway, and the change (if any) will be reflected on-screen when that point is made visible.

    If *Object*. is specified, the method sets the point value relative to the coordinates of the specified object. Otherwise, the coordinate system of the form containing the method is assumed. If *color&* is specified, the .PSet method sets the color value of the point to any long integer value in the range 0 to 16,777,215, representing a color or color pattern recognized by Microsoft Windows. The value of *color&* can be represented by the function RGB() or QBColor(). To *reset* a point—to give it the background color value—the property term .BackColor can be used as *color&*. If *color&* is not specified, the .PSet method will set the point's color value to the value of the .ForeColor property of the specified object.

    If Step is included in the method, the coordinate system expressed in (*twipx!*, *twipy!*) is considered by the VB interpreter to be relative to the last point plotted, or to (0, 0) if no point has been plotted. The last point plotted within a graphic object can be obtained through the .CurrentX and .CurrentY properties for that object.

    The width and height of the point plotted with .PSet can be set in advance with the .DrawWidth property of the object receiving the point. The point can be plotted as an invisible point—existent although unseen—by setting the .DrawStyle of the object to 5.

    The following may be a bit confusing, so read carefully: The coordinate system used in Visual Basic graphics methods is the twip coordinate system, which is manually scalable by the programmer. If you can imagine the screen as a grid full of pixels, overlay in your mind a finer, more detailed grid representing twips. A pixel is a filled rectangular area on the pixel system. A twip, by contrast, is an intersection point between two logically interpreted axis lines. Figure 42.1 shows the conceptual difference between the pixel system and the twip system.

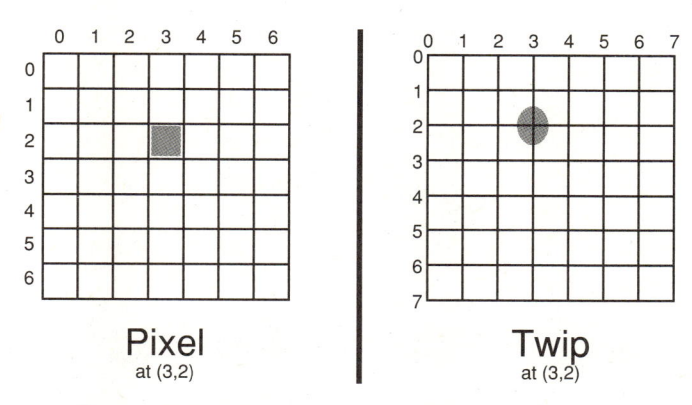

Pixel at (3,2)

Twip at (3,2)

Figure 42.1. The two coordinate systems of Visual Basic.

> A *twip* is plotted along an intersection point in memory, whereas a *pixel* is plotted within a fixed space.

If you play board games, perhaps you'll better understand the pixels versus twips dilemma through the aid of the following analogy: Imagine that each point plotted by a Visual Basic graphics method is a chess piece. The pixel coordinate system would be like chess, where the piece would occupy the center of a space or square. The twip coordinate system, by contrast, is like Chinese checkers, where each piece sits on the intersection between lines along the board. Instead of occupying a space, the Chinese checkers piece occupies a point.

What's important about this analogy is this: An intersection point *does not constitute a measurable area.* There is therefore no unit of spatial measurement called a twip, whereas a pixel consumes space and therefore can be used as an area measurement. When a method such as .PSet is used to set the color value of a twip coordinate, the pixel—or even *pixels*—nearest that twip coordinate are set to the new color. If the .DrawWidth of each point or line within a picture box or form is set to greater than 1, then as Figure 42.2 shows, a block of pixels having an approximate center that is at or near the twip coordinates is set to the new color.

509

Chapter 42 ◆ Plotting

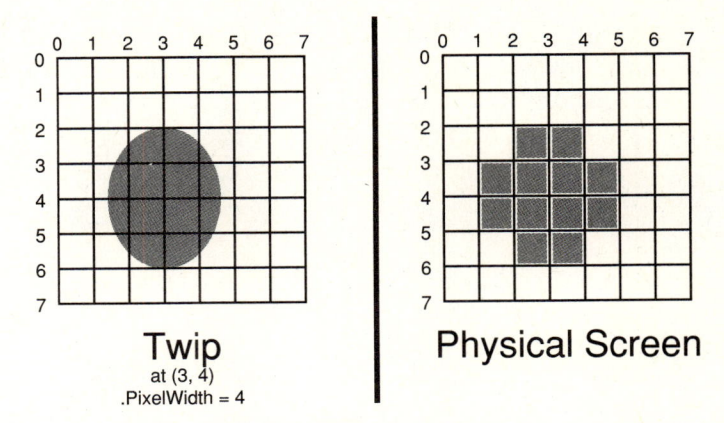

Figure 42.2. Plotting a block of pixels along a twip.

Perhaps Lewis Carroll would appreciate the inherent beauty of plotting blocks of pixels along a twip having its point marked with .PSet. To quote his equally gibberish-like *Jabberwocky*, "All mimsy were the borogoves, and the mome raths outgrabe."

The Plot So Far

Here's a routine that plots a dotted diagonal line to the object Picture1.:

```
For plt = 0 To 50 Step 5
    Picture1.PSet (plt, plt)
Next plt
```

There are 11 dots in this line because the interpreter counts from 0 to 50 by fives, starting with 0. Here the value of variable plt represents both the x- and y-axis values for the .PSet method. So, for each iteration of the loop clause, the plot point is spaced as many twips down as to the right. Twips are considered by Visual Basic to be relatively square. Depending on the screen driver and graphics hardware you're currently using, pixels on the screen should be square as well—in other words, a block of pixels plt wide and plt high should appear geometrically equilateral.

Example

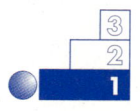

Suppose the diagonal dotted line is to extend from some unknown point where plotting has taken place previously. You could use the Step extension to have the virtual pen jump to a location relative to the previous plot coordinates, as follows:

```
For dot = 1 to 11
    Picture1.PSet Step (5, 5)
Next dot
```

This routine produces a dotted line identical in form to the one generated by the routine above it, although its plot position starts at the point returnable as (Picture1.CurrentX, Picture1.CurrentY). In other words, it starts at the last point that received a plot, or at (0, 0) if no plotting has taken place. With each iteration, the .PSet method steps the pen five spaces to the right and five spaces down. You can express 5 both times as a constant, because each Step takes place relative to the point precedingly plotted. The method uses .CurrentX and .CurrentY (although not explicitly) as offsets for the relative coordinate system—modern equivalents of the OX and OY variables from the historical example earlier in this chapter.

There is, thankfully, a more direct method for drawing a line, using the *Object*.Line method.

Object.Line   Method

Syntax:

[*Object*.]Line [[Step](*twipx1!*, *twipy1!*)]
-[Step](*twipx2!*, *twipy2!*)[, *color&*][, B][F]

The .Line method sets the color value of a linear series of all addressable twips represented in memory extending from the coordinates (*twipx1!*, *twipy1!*) to (*twipx2!*, *twipy2!*). The two coordinate pairs are always separated by a hyphen. The color value for each twip in the series will be set regardless of whether it is visible at present. If any or all of the specified twips are invisible or obstructed by some other graphic object, their color values will be set anyway, and the change (if any) will be reflected on-screen when those twips are made visible.

Chapter 42 ◆ Plotting

If `Object.` is specified, the method sets the twip values relative to the coordinates of the specified object. Otherwise, the coordinate system of the form containing the method is assumed. The form the line takes is returnable through the properties `.DrawStyle` and `.DrawWidth`, where `.DrawStyle` represents the type of hatching used in the line (if any) and `.DrawWidth` represents the relative width of the line drawn.

If the first coordinate pair is omitted, the interpreter assumes the line to extend from the last plotted point to the coordinates specified by the second pair, which cannot be omitted. The hyphen remains in the method instruction, nonetheless. The last point plotted within a graphic object can be obtained through the `.CurrentX` and `.CurrentY` properties for that object. If no points have been plotted for that object, initial coordinates of (0, 0) are assumed.

If `Step` is included before the first pair of coordinates, those coordinates are assumed to be relative to the last point plotted before the instruction was executed, as represented within `.CurrentX` and `.CurrentY`. If `Step` is included before the second pair of coordinates, those coordinates are assumed to be relative to the first pair of coordinates.

If `color&` is specified, the `.Line` method sets the color values of the twips in the series to any long integer value in the range 0 to 16,777,215, representing a color or color pattern recognized by Microsoft Windows. The value of `color&` can be represented by the function `RGB()` or `QBColor()`. To *reset* the points in a linear series—to give them the background color value—the property term `.BackColor` can be used as `color&`. If `color&` is not specified, the `.Line` method sets the series' color value to the value of the `.ForeColor` property of the specified object.

If `B` is included toward the end of the `.Line` method, the instruction will not draw just a line, but it will draw a *box* with opposite corners that are expressed as the two pairs of coordinates. In other words, the box will extend from point (`twipx1!`, `twipy1!`) to (`twipx2!`, `twipy1!`), to (`twipx2!`, `twipy2!`), to (`twipx1!`, `twipy2!`), and back to (`twipx1!`, `twipy1!`). Only coordinate sets 1 and 2 need to be specified. If `F` is included beside `B`, the box will be filled with the color used to plot the box itself. If `F` is *not* included beside `B`, the box will be filled with the color and pattern obtainable through the `.FillColor` and `.FillStyle` properties, which may be different from the color used to plot the box. By default, the filling color and pattern are transparent. If B or BF is included and *color&* is omitted, the comma used as a delimiter for *color&* remains, as in , ,BF.

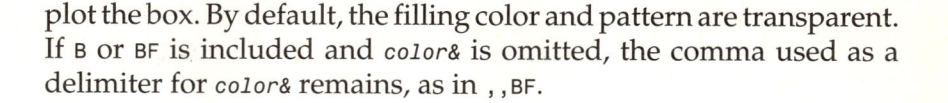

The last few sentences may have been confusing, so here is an explanation: If you specify a B *alone* within the .Line method, you have transformed the method into a box-drawing method. The graphic object receiving the box has a .FillColor and .FillStyle, which are currently set to the independent color and style reserved for closed shapes produced by graphics methods. If you specify BF within the .Line method—the F standing for *filled*—you are telling the interpreter to *ignore* the current .FillColor and .FillStyle for the object receiving the box and to fill the box *solidly* with whatever color was used to draw the box, whether it was taken from the .ForeColor property or stated as the optional *color&* parameter.

The Plot Thickens

The preceding discussion mentioned four properties, each of which may affect the outcome of the .Line method: the .DrawStyle property, the .DrawWidth property, the .FillColor property, and the .FillStyle property.

Form.DrawStyle, *Picture*.DrawStyle, or *Printer*.DrawStyle Property

The .DrawStyle property is set to a value that represents the style of line to be produced by the next method, which draws a series of points to an object. This property can take any of the following values:

0 ─────── (Solid)

1 ─ ─ ─

2 ----

3   — - — -

4   — - - —

5   (Invisible)

6   ———— (Solid, although entirely inside the area of a box)

Form.DrawWidth, *Picture*.DrawWidth, or *Printer*.DrawWidth **Property**

The .DrawWidth property is set to the width in pixels of any lines or points to be plotted to the antecedent object using graphics methods.

Form.FillColor, *Picture*.FillColor, or *Printer*.FillColor **Property**

The .FillColor property is set to the RGB color to be reserved for all closed shapes to be produced with graphics methods. The default value for .FillColor is 0 (black).

Form.FillStyle, *Picture*.FillStyle, or *Printer*.FillStyle **Property**

The .FillStyle property is set to the fill pattern to be reserved for all closed shapes to be produced with graphics methods. The value of .FillStyle can take any of the values depicted in Figure 42.3. The default setting for .FillStyle is 1, for transparency.

Visual Basic *By* EXAMPLE

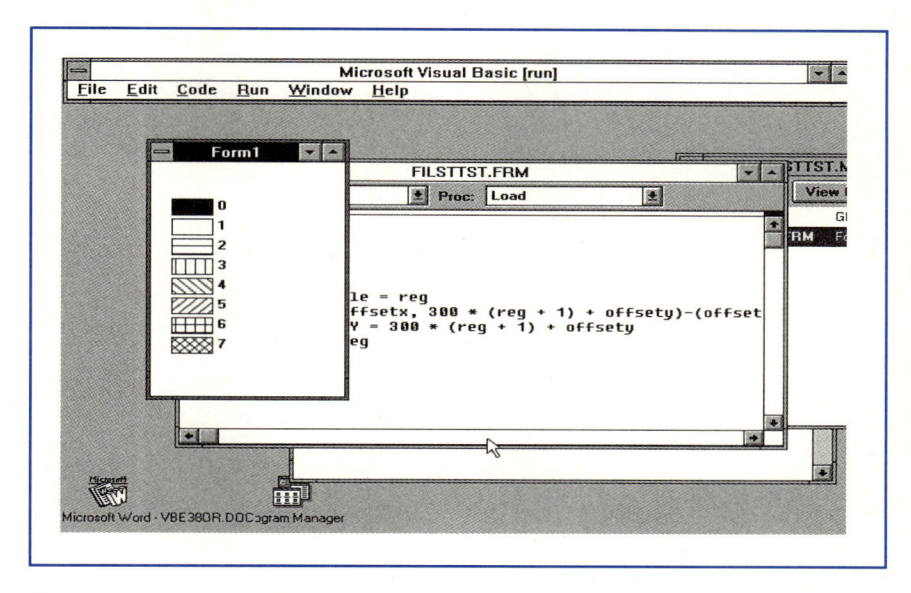

Figure 42.3. The settings for .FillStyle.

Example

Here is the listing of the routine used to generate the form in Figure 42.3:

```
Sub Form_Load ()
Form1.Show
offsetx = 250
offsety = 250
For reg = 0 To 7
    Form1.FillStyle = reg
    Form1.Line (offsetx, 300 * (reg + 1) + offsety)
      - (offsetx + 500, 300 * (reg + 1) + offsety + 250), , B
    Form1.CurrentY = 300 * (reg + 1) + offsety
    Form1.Print reg
Next reg
End Sub
```

515

Here is the procedure translated into pseudocode:

*Show **Form1**, although it's empty at the moment.*
Set two offset variables for the x- and y-axes to 250, so that you can have left and top margins.
Start counting from 0 to 7.
  *Set the .**FillStyle** to the current count value.*
  *Draw a box spaced out **offsetx** twips from the left, 500 twips long and 250 twips high, starting at (300 times the number of boxes drawn) twips down from the top margin **offsety**, leaving a space of 50 twips between boxes.*
  Set the y-axis value of the virtual pen so that it's aligned with the top of the box just plotted.
  Print the current count value.
Count the next value.
End of procedure.

The preceding procedure can be modified to show all the available color registers obtainable using the function `QBColor()`:

```
Sub Form_Load ()
Form1.Show
offsetx = 250
offsety = 250
For reg = 0 To 15
    Form1.Line (offsetx, 300 * (reg + 1) + offsety)
        - (offsetx + 500, 300 * (reg + 1) + offsety + 250),
        QBColor(reg), BF
    Form1.CurrentY = 300 * (reg + 1) + offsety
    clr& = Form1.Point(offsetx, 300 * (reg + 1) + offsety)
    Form1.Print clr&, Hex$(clr&)
Next reg
End Sub
```

In this procedure, the vacancy between the two adjacent commas in the `.Line` method of the previous procedure is filled with `QBColor(reg)`. By specifying this color directly, you're telling the interpreter to overlook the `.ForeColor` it would normally use for drawing this object; however, `.ForeColor` is not changed. By including the F after the B, you're telling the interpreter to overlook also the `.FillColor` and `.FillStyle` normally reserved for closed shapes, and to instead use the specified color to fill the object solidly.

So that you can see what the RGB color registers look like as decimal and hexadecimal numbers, I had these numbers printed next to their respective boxes using the `Form1.Print` method. The RGB color was obtained from within the box area through the use of the `Object.Point` method, which detects the color of any designated point.

Object.Point — Method

Syntax:

`color& = [Object.]Point(twipx!, twipy!)`

The `.Point` method acts like a function in that it returns the RGB color value of a pixel nearest the specified twip coordinates, within the long integer `color&`. The method is specified, however, using object-oriented syntax. If `Object.` is included in the instruction, the coordinate system of the specified object is used. Otherwise, the system of the form currently containing the instruction is assumed.

The `.Line` method is used whenever you want to draw a box; in other words, there is no *.Box* method in Visual Basic, although there are BOX statements in other versions of BASIC. In a similarly odd fashion, to draw an arc or a curved line, you invoke the `.Circle` method.

Object.Circle — Method

Syntax:

`[Object.]Circle [Step](twipx!, twipy!), radius![, color&]`
↳ `[, ang_start!, ang_end!][, aspect!]`

The `.Circle` method plots a series of points in a curve, all of which geometrically converge around a center point specified as `(twipx!, twipy!)`. By default, these points take the form of a circle; however, by specifying the latter three optional parameters, you can plot an arc or ellipse instead.

517

Unless *aspect!* is specified, each point in the series is plotted at a distance of *radius!* twips from the center coordinates. If `color&` is specified, the series is plotted in the specified color. The `RGB()` and `QBColor()` functions can be used to determine the value of `color&`. If `color&` is omitted, the series is plotted using the color set as the `.ForeColor` property setting of the object receiving the plot.

If *ang_start!* and *ang_end!* are specified, plotting of the circle begins at a point that forms an angle *ang_start!* radians relative to the center point and extends to a point that forms an angle *ang_end* radians relative to the center point. The radian range specifiable for these parameters is (−2 * Pi) − (2 * Pi). If neither parameter is specified, the curve is plotted as a closed shape, as either a circle or an ellipse. As such, the shape is filled with a pattern and color specified as the current values of the `.FillStyle` and `.FillColor` properties. By default, the fill style for an object is transparent (1) and the fill color is black (0).

The value of *aspect!*, when specified, represents the ratio of height to width for the series, for use in plotting noncircular arcs or ellipses. A 4:1 ratio of height to width is represented as an *aspect!* of 4, which forms a tall ellipse. Conversely, a 1:4 ratio is represented as an *aspect!* of .25, which forms a squat ellipse. In cases where *aspect!* is specified, the value of *radius!* becomes, geometrically speaking, half the length of the *major axis* of the ellipse—being the widest obtainable diameter of the ellipse.

If `Step` is included with the `.Circle` method, the coordinate pair following `Step` is interpreted as being relative to the last point plotted, or to `(0, 0)` if no point has previously been plotted. The last point plotted within a graphic object is returnable within the properties `.CurrentX` and `.CurrentY`.

Example

The `QBColor()` function test procedure can be converted to plot ellipses rather than boxes, as follows:

```
Sub Form_Load ()
Form1.Show
Form1.FillStyle = 0
offsetx = 250
offsety = 250
For reg = 0 To 15
    Form1.FillColor = QBColor(reg)
    Form1.Circle (offsetx + 250, 300 * (reg + 1) + offsety
      + 125), 250, QBColor(reg), , , .5
    Form1.CurrentY = 300 * (reg + 1) + offsety
    Form1.CurrentX = Form1.CurrentX + 300
    clr& = Form1.Point(offsetx + 250, 300 * (reg + 1)
      + offsety + 125)
    Form1.Print clr&, Hex$(clr&)
Next reg
End Sub
```

Here, the coordinate pair from the old `.Line` method was modified so that plotting takes place around the center. No angles were specified within the `.Circle` instruction, so the shape is closed and is thus filled solid because I set `Form1.FillStyle` to 0 (solid). The aspect ratio is .5, so the ellipse is half as high as it is wide.

Because plotting ends at the bottom of the ellipse, I had to space `.CurrentX` out a little to make room for the text. The `.Point` method now obtains the color value from the center of the ellipse rather than from the upper-right corner of the box. Figure 42.4 is an example of what you should see.

Chapter 42 ◆ Plotting

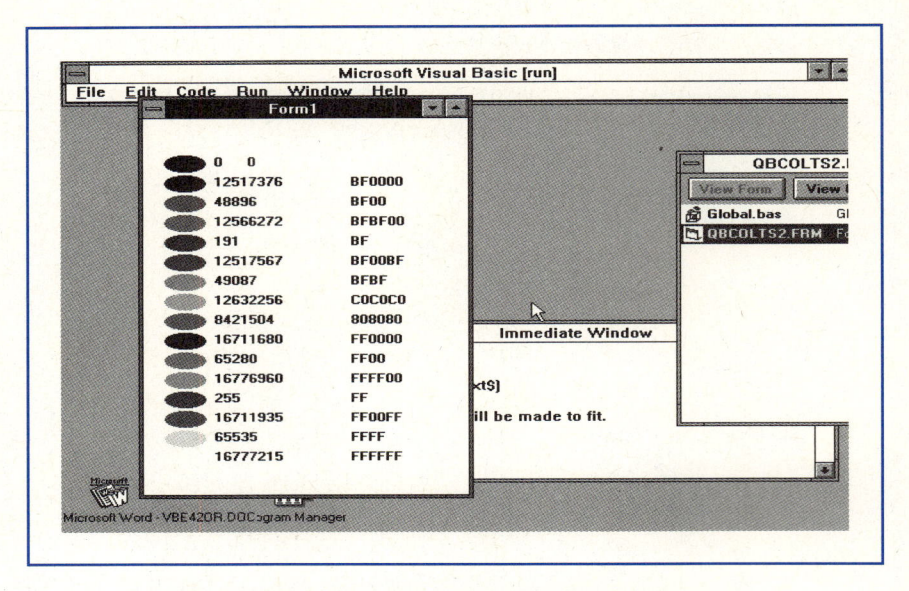

Figure 42.4. The QuickBASIC-style watercolor paintbox.

Summary

The Visual Basic coordinate system is based on a grid of twips. A twip point is really an intersection point on the coordinate grid, so the system uses true Cartesian geometric coordinates. The twip coordinate system is separate from the pixel coordinate system. The pixel or pixels set with a bitmapped graphics method are set nearest the twips addressed by the statement.

Visual Basic supports all of Windows' 16,777,216 logical colors, although graphics hardware has yet to support that many colors. Instead of specifying a color register from the more than 16 million available, VB offers the RGB() and QBColor() functions as substitutes for color numbers, providing access to VGA color mixtures and CGA color register numbers, respectively.

The .PSet method is used to plot a point to a form, a picture box, or the printer. The .Line method is used to plot a line or series of points; however, it can also be used to plot filled and unfilled boxes. Unless otherwise specified within the instruction itself, the .Line method relies on the .DrawStyle, .DrawWidth, .FillColor, and .FillStyle properties for the graphic object receiving the plot to determine the appearance of the plotted line or shape.

The color of the pixel nearest any specified twip location can be obtained using the .Point method. A circle, ellipse, or unclosed arc can be drawn using the .Circle method. If starting and ending angles are specified using this method, an arc is plotted; otherwise, a shape is plotted having a .FillStyle and .FillColor that both rely on the property settings for the object receiving the shape.

Review Questions

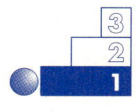

1. Does the .PSet method affect the values of properties .CurrentX and .CurrentY?

2. Does the .Point method affect the values of properties .CurrentX and .CurrentY?

3. Assume you've plotted a line to a picture box using the .Line method, which uses the twip coordinate system. As a result, the image within the picture box contains a line between two points. If you use the .Move method to magnify that image, making the line *bigger*, does the line therein become also *thicker* or merely *broader*?

Review Exercises

1. Write a procedure that draws a circle gradually, as if it is being drawn with a compass and pen. Use the .Circle method and specify the start and end angles of the arc being drawn. **Hint:** Use a loop clause that counts the current value of the end angle.

2. Write a procedure that continually resets the .FillColor property for a picture box so that it fades from white to black gradually.

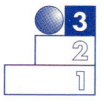

3. Write a project that lets the user draw a circle to a form by clicking and holding down the index button over the center of the circle, extending the pointer as far as the radius of the circle, and then releasing the pointer. Use the box-drawing method from Chapter 31, "The Mouse as Device," as a model.

521

Part IX

Error Trapping and Debugging

Image Scaling and Integrity

In this chapter you study the properties that direct the Visual Basic interpreter to maintain the image integrity of a form or picture box. You also experience the thrill of resizing a picture box while it is running, and having its coordinate system rescale itself to meet the current box size. You do all of this, mind you, at warp speed.

Integrity Properties

Two properties maintained within the Visual Basic vocabulary tell the interpreter what course of action to take if certain adjustments are made to the image or control: .AutoSize and .AutoRedraw.

Label.AutoSize or *Picture*.AutoSize Property

The .AutoSize property for a label or picture box is set to a value of true (−1) or false (0), indicating whether the VB interpreter is to resize that control if its contents become larger than the control's designated space allows. If the property is set to true, the interpreter automatically resizes the image or label to fit the contents as snugly as possible.

Form.AutoRedraw or *Picture*.AutoRedraw **Property**

The .AutoRedraw property for a form or picture box is set to a value of true (−1) or false (0), indicating whether the interpreter is to maintain a persistent bitmap of the specified image in memory. If the property is set to true, whenever another object is moved by process or user-directed motion to an area that partially or totally overlaps the antecedent object of the property, the graphic portion of that object will be retained in memory. When the portion is no longer obstructed, the interpreter replots the graphic contents to the object automatically. If the .AutoRedraw property is set to false, whenever another object is moved to an area that obstructs the antecedent object, the obstructed portion is in effect erased from the object. In such a case, however, when the object is no longer obstructed, the _Paint event will be generated, and a _Paint event procedure may be invoked to refresh or repair the contents of the obstructed object.

Here is the event currently being discussed:

*Form*_Paint or *Picture*_Paint **Event**

The _Paint event for a form or picture box is recognized when the .AutoRedraw property for that object is set to false (0), and the once partially or totally obstructed antecedent object is partly or totally freed from obstruction. This allows the program to redraw the object manually, thus conserving memory for other purposes.

Rescaling

As discussed earlier, the twip coordinate system is at the same time precise and somewhat confusing. Other optional coordinate systems are available for any graphic object, which you can select with a property setting:

[*Object*].ScaleMode or [*Printer*].ScaleMode Property

The `.ScaleMode` property for a *virtual terminal* graphic object is set to one of eight integer values, representing the type of coordinate system being used for the antecedent object. This value can be one of the following:

- 0   User-defined. This setting takes place automatically when the programmer sets the scale for the antecedent object to a variable value.
- 1   Twip coordinate system (default).
- 2   Points. There are approximately 72 points per inch on a 15-inch-diagonal monitor.
- 3   Pixel coordinate system, determined using the current screen resolution of Microsoft Windows.
- 4   Twelve-pitch character-based system, representing 12 characters to the inch horizontally and six lines to the inch, when printed to a standard printer device.
- 5   Inches, again assuming a 15-inch-diagonal monitor.
- 6   Millimeters.
- 7   Centimeters.

Mode 2 is especially helpful when you are creating a page layout application. Mode 3 is provided for those who are more comfortable with pixel-to-pixel plotting. Mode 4 works best with picture boxes that will contain text only, and for the `Printer.` object. Modes 5 through 7 are helpful when you plot images to the screen that will be represented on paper using more definite units of measurement.

Four properties are available to the programmer for defining a particular coordinate scale for an object:

Chapter 43 ◆ Image Scaling and Integrity

.ScaleLeft, .ScaleTop, .ScaleWidth, and .ScaleHeight Properties

The .ScaleLeft and .ScaleTop properties are set to the coordinate pair representing the point at the upper-left corner of the antecedent *Object* or *Printer*. The .ScaleWidth property represents the number of x-axis divisions in the coordinate scale of the antecedent object. Likewise, the .ScaleHeight property represents the number of y-axis divisions in the coordinate scale of the antecedent object.

These properties can alternately be set with a method:

[*Object*.]Scale — Method

Syntax:

[*Object*.]Scale [(*origx*, *origy*)-(*extx*, *exty*)]

The .Scale method sets the coordinate pair for the upper-left corner of the antecedent object to (*origx*, *origy*) and the coordinate pair for the lower-right corner of the object to (*extx*, *exty*). If both pairs of coordinates are omitted, the scale for the object is reset to the default twip coordinate scale.

Example

To demonstrate rescaling at work, I've created an application that generates a moving star pattern, like those you'd see in science fiction movies (only slower). The form itself can be set to any size, although it is vital that a timer control be placed within the form someplace, in order to give the user time to resize the form while it's running. After each resizing, the star pattern will stretch or be squashed to fit the new form size, by setting the scale properties for the form.

Visual Basic *By*
EXAMPLE

	PROJECT NAME	CONSTITUENT FILES
"Stars" Resizable Starfield Generator	STARS.MAK	STARS.FRM

General declarations area:

```
Dim Xoom(15), Yoom(15), Rangle(15), Zang(15), Lax(15),
   Lay(15), Voom(15), Hypo(15), Lum(15), Brite(15)
Dim rbrite As Integer, gbrite As Integer

Sub Form_Load ()
Timer1.Interval = 500
ViewScreen.ScaleMode = 3
ViewScreen.Scale (0, 0)-(320, 200)
ViewScreen.Show
starbloom
End Sub
```

Here the `.FormName` is `ViewScreen`. The interval for the timer control is set to 500 milliseconds (half a second). The screen will be replotted now every half-second. The scale is set to `pixelline`, using virtual 320 x 200 coordinates.

```
Sub starbloom ()
For bloom = 0 To 15
  Rangle(bloom) = Int(Rnd(1) * 359)
  Zang(bloom) = Int(Rnd(1) * 10)
  Lum(bloom) = Int(Rnd(1) * 255) + 1
  Brite(bloom) = Lum(bloom)
  Voom(bloom) = Zang(bloom) / Lum(bloom)
  Hypo(Bang) = Int(Rnd(1) * 5)
Next bloom
End Sub
```

529

Chapter 43 ◆ Image Scaling and Integrity

The procedure `starbloom()` is invoked to generate the parameters for the first 15 stars. The stars all start out in the center of the form and zoom out toward you. The angle of their trajectory is described by `Rangle(bloom)`. The amount of stable visible speed for each star is described by `Zang(bloom)`, whereas the amount of visible speed increase as the star comes "closer" to you is described by `Voom(bloom)`. `Lum(bloom)` is the stable color of each star, whereas `Brite(bloom)` is the visible color of the star as it comes closer to you. `Hypo(bloom)` is an extra speed multiplication factor that can give the star an extra shove toward you, for the illusion of perspective.

```
Sub Timer1_Timer ()
For Bang = 0 To 15
  If Lax(Bang) > 0 Then
    ViewScreen.PSet (Lax(Bang), Lay(Bang)), RGB(0, 0, 0)
  End If
  Xoom(Bang) = 160 - Sin(Rangle(Bang)) * (Hypo(Bang)
      * (Zang(Bang) * Voom(Bang)))
  Yoom(Bang) = 100 - Cos(Rangle(Bang)) * (Hypo(Bang)
      * (Zang(Bang) * Voom(Bang)))
  ViewScreen.PSet (Xoom(Bang), Yoom(Bang)), RGB(Brite(Bang),
      Brite(Bang), Brite(Bang))
  Lax(Bang) = Xoom(Bang)
  Lay(Bang) = Yoom(Bang)
  Zang(Bang) = Zang(Bang) + .3
  Hypo(Bang) = Hypo(Bang) + 1
  Brite(Bang) = Brite(Bang) + 1
  If Brite(Bang) > 255 Then Brite(Bang) = 255
  If Xoom(Bang) < 0 Or Yoom(Bang) < 0 Then
    Revive
  End If
  If Xoom(Bang) > 319 Or Yoom(Bang) > 199 Then
    Revive
  End If
Next Bang
End Sub
```

By now, you may have become accustomed to trigonometrically extracting (x, y) coordinates from angle and radius values. The coordinate pair in this case is (`Xoom(Bang)`, `Yoom(Bang)`). Notice that this is the first Visual Basic application in this book with its own sound effects—this should make up for the lackluster `Beep` statement. The "old" plot values are stored in (`Lax(Bang)`,`Lay(Bang)`), and the zooming factors are increased to make the next plot for each star appear closer to you. `Brite(Bang)` is also augmented to make the star brighter with each plot.

```
Sub Revive ()
  Rangle(Bang) = Int(Rnd(1) * 359)
  Zang(Bang) = Int(Rnd(1) * 10)
  Lum(Bang) = Int(Rnd(1) * 255) + 1
  Brite(Bang) = Lum(Bang)
  Voom(Bang) = Zang(Bang) / Lum(Bang)
  Hypo(Bang) = Int(Rnd(1) * 5)
End Sub
```

This procedure is used to create a new star each time one wanders off the edge of the form.

```
Sub Form_Resize ()
ViewScreen.Cls
ViewScreen.ScaleHeight = 200
ViewScreen.ScaleWidth = 320
End Sub
```

Here is the crucial rescaling procedure in its entirety. Each time the `_Resize` event is allowed to occur, the screen is cleared and the scale of the image is reset to 320 units across and 200 units down.

Summary

You can tell the Visual Basic interpreter whether to resize a picture box or label to fit oversized contents, by means of the `.AutoSize` property. You can also tell the interpreter whether to automatically replot the contents of a bitmapped object after it is cleared from obstruction, by means of the `.AutoRedraw` property. If this property is set to false, the contents of the cleared object can still be redrawn manually through the `_Paint` event procedure for that object.

You can select a special coordinate scale for a *virtual terminal* graphic object by setting the `.ScaleMode` property for that object.

Chapter 43 ◆ Image Scaling and Integrity

When an object is rescalable, its upper-left corner coordinates can be described as (`Picture1.ScaleLeft, Picture1.ScaleTop`). The number of x-axis divisions for an object can be set using `.ScaleWidth`. Likewise, the number of y-axis divisions for an object may be set using `.ScaleHeight`. All four of the scale properties can be set simultaneously with the `.Scale` method.

Review Questions

1. What is the functional difference between making a picture box's contents larger with the `.Move` method and making the contents larger with the `.Scale` method?

2. What output device would benefit most from setting the `.ScaleMode` property to 4?

3. In Cartesian coordinate geometry, a line on a graph having a y-axis value that increases is a line pointing *upward* from your point of view—assuming the graph is turned "right-side up." In all of Visual Basic coordinate systems for the screen, a line having a y-axis value that increases is a line pointing *downward*. The most likely reason for this is one of engineering; speculate on what that reason might be.

44

Registering Errors

In this chapter you are introduced to the error-trapping mechanism of Visual Basic. Normally, when an error occurs during the processing of a program, the interpreter alerts the user to this fact with an alert box, and the process may shut down. However, the programmer may wish to include methods for taking corrective steps to solve manageable problems before the process shuts down. In such cases, Visual Basic offers the programmer error traps, which send execution of the program to a specific routine. You will learn how to invoke these routines in this chapter. Later, you'll examine conditions in which even the most advanced error traps may not be of much help.

To Err Is Not Only Human

A *computing error* is the result of any process that fails to perform in the manner in which it was intended or designed.

One of the common definitions that most requires altering when translated into the realm of computing is that of the word *error*. An error in computing is not necessarily an error in one's judgment or a syntax error. An error in computing is the result of any process that failed to perform in the manner in which it was intended or designed, and which by its nature or in the interest of preventing disaster prevents logical program execution from continuing.

Chapter 44 ◆ Registering Errors

The graphical control system of Windows is designed to be almost foolproof; there are few ways a user can crash a program using the conventional Windows controls. Graphical processes may cause errors to occur. For instance, in the STARS.MAK application I programmed for Chapter 43, I spent about an hour tracking down the source of an error that was generated when, for some reason, the coordinates for a star jumped from the maximum x-value of 320 to 1900. I'm not even sure I found the source of the error, but my patchwork apparently fixed the problem.

Errors are a natural part of programming; in fact, they're necessary. Without errors, it's nearly impossible for the programmer to know what course of action to take when developing a program. A flurry of errors might help the programmer know when a particular course of action is unworkable. If I program an application from an idea in my head and the program compiles right the first time without generating any errors...folks, something is wrong. I hate to sound paranoid (especially with the number of people who will be after me if I admit that I am), but when I see errors being generated by my programs right at first, I know the process of programming is actually coming along rather smoothly.

In earlier editions of BASIC, programmers generally had to program error-trapping routines that waited for the user to make an error, such as responding to the numeric INPUT command WHAT IS YOUR CURRENT AGE IN YEARS? with the alphanumeric phrase NONE OF YOUR BUSINESS. The Microsoft Windows system of user input is such that user-generated errors are minimized; the function Val(Text1.Text) that extracts a numeral value from a text box, for instance, can ignore alphanumeric characters and search only for numbers. In a way, this is a major advance for computing. Yet on the other hand, it now takes a deliberate process on the part of the programmer to determine whether letters really were entered into a numeric field by accident.

Still, errors are generated for the most part by faults in the source code. A programmer should let these faults occur. Covering them with an error trap that ignores the fault could lead to a processing catastrophe later in the program. Perhaps it is best for the programmer to add error-trapping routines to the code of the program last, after it appears that the application's source code is foolproof.

Visual Basic *By*
EXAMPLE

Baiting the Trap

Here's how an error-trapping routine works: A statement is placed within a procedure, setting branching to a particularly labeled line whenever an interpreter-recognized error occurs. When that happens now, processing is not stopped in the normal manner, but instead execution branches immediately to the statement following the error label in the procedure, regardless of what instruction caused the error. Here is the statement that baits the proverbial trap:

On Error [GoTo ¦ Resume] Statement

Syntax:

`On [Local ]Error {GoTo label¦Resume Next¦GoTo 0}`

The `On Error` branching statement sets an error trap that, when invoked for the first time within an application, forces execution of the current procedure to jump to a specified line label, whenever any error occurs that would normally suspend or interrupt the normal process of execution. As long as the procedure continues to execute without trouble, branching to the label immediately takes place on the occurrence of an error.

The phrase `On Error GoTo 0` is used to terminate an error trap and allow the Visual Basic interpreter to again suspend execution in the case of a serious error. The phrase `On Error Resume Next` is included as a way of allowing the programmer to tell the interpreter to ignore any errors that may come along, and to resume execution with the next instruction following the one that caused the error.

The keyword `Local` is provided as an option for users of other Microsoft BASIC compilers. Its invocation within a Visual Basic error trap has no effect, however, because all Visual Basic error traps exist on the local level, anyway.

535

Chapter 44 ◆ Registering Errors

The instruction that takes the program out of the error trap routine and back into the main body of the program is the `Resume` statement.

Resume   Statement

Syntax:

`Resume {[0] ¦ Next ¦ label}`

The `Resume` statement is reserved for the end of error trap routines within a procedure. Invoked on a line by itself or accompanied by a 0, the statement sends execution back to the statement that caused the error that sprung the trap. The formerly erroneous statement is then reexecuted to see if it generates the same error a second time.

The phrase `Resume Next` sends execution back to the statement immediately following the one that caused the error. The phrase `Resume label` sends execution back to the statement immediately following the specified `label`.

Example

Because the controls and instructions of Visual Basic are far more versatile than they once were, it is less necessary to program error-trapping routines now than at any time in the past. Besides, branching can take place only to labels within the same procedure that contained the error. Still, an error trap may be necessary for such potential errors as trying to find a specific file name on disk and not finding it, as modeled by the following procedure fragment:

```
Sub FileFind (filepath$)
    On Error GoTo NoFile
    Selector.Show 1
    Open targetfile$ For Input As #1
        .
        .
        .
```

```
NoFile:
    If Err <> 53 Then
        msg$ = Error$(Err)
        MsgBox (msg$, 16)
        Stop
    Else
        msg$ = "File " + targetfile$ + " not found."
        MsgBox (msg$, 16)
        Resume Next
    End If
    .
    .
    .
Exit Sub
```

Here is pseudocode for the error trap routine, starting at the line marked by the label `NoFile`:

If the error is not a file-not-found error, then
   Tell the user what the error actually is.
   Place this error message in a message box.
   Stop the program.
Otherwise,
   Tell the user what file wasn't found.
   Tell the user this in a message box.
   Resume the program where it left off.
End of condition.

Suppose it is possible for the file selector box invoked by the instruction `Selector.Show 1` to return a nonexistent file name to the routine that invoked it. If such a travesty occurs, instead of stopping execution altogether, a branch is made to the line `NoFile`. At this time, the internal variable `Err` is polled to see if the error number generated was error 53 (file not found). If the error was any number other than 53, an error message is generated to that effect, and execution is manually forced to `Stop`. If `Err` is 53, the name of the file that wasn't found is added to the message box before it is displayed. The `Resume Next` reverse branch statement enables execution to continue, however, with the line following the one that caused the error.

537

Chapter 44 ◆ Registering Errors

> **NOTE:** Using the SELECTOR.FRM we created in Chapter 22, it is impossible for the selector to generate a nonexistent file name unless the user typed it specifically. If the file name is selected from a directory list, that file must exist because its name appeared in the directory. Conceivably, however, the file may be corrupt, resulting in one of many possible error values.

The preceding fragment introduced us to a number of error-related instructions.

Err — Internal Variable

The internal variable Err is set by the interpreter to the value of the last error that occurred during processing of the program. If no error has occurred, Err = 0. This variable can be set to any value by the programmer for use in simulating error conditions when testing the applicability of error-trapping routines. Setting the value of Err manually, however, does not result in the automatic generation of an error.

Error$() — Function

Syntax:

*string$* = Error$(*ercode%*)

where *ercode%* is an integer value corresponding to a valid error code. Internal variable Err can be used as *ercode%*.

The Error$() function returns a text string describing the error code that is passed to the function, within the string variable *string$*.

Two more instructions round out Visual Basic's error-related vocabulary: The Error statement and the Erl internal variable.

Error — Statement

Syntax:

`Error ercode%`

where `ercode%` is an integer value corresponding to a valid error code. Internal variable `Err` can be used as `ercode%`.

The `Error` statement forces the VB interpreter into believing that the error specified by `ercode%` has occurred. This statement is particularly useful when you test the applicability of error-trapping routines.

Erl — Internal Variable

The internal variable `Erl` is set by the system to the number of the line that last generated the error, assuming the programmer uses the old BASIC method of numbering lines—which is supported by Visual Basic as an option. If an application doesn't have line numbers, this variable is useless.

> **TIP:** You can choose to program one large error-handling procedure for your entire application. Each of the other procedures may have a different `On Error` branch statement that leads to a routine within the error-handling procedure. You could then have each routine consist of two statements: a call to the global error handler and a `Resume` statement designating where execution is to proceed.

Chapter 44 ◆ Registering Errors

"We Sing the Song of the Sewer..."

If you're an Art Carney fan, you're probably singing the preceding song now; however, this song is also the official anthem of professional debuggers. Errors are relatively nice because you can trap them, tame them, and release them using error-trapping routines. Bugs are not so nice. Generally, bugs cause things to go wrong with the program, although from the interpreter's point of view, everything is proceeding fine. Sometimes a mess is in the eye of the beholder, and a computer doesn't have eyes.

> A *bug* is an error that cannot be detected by the interpreter.

A program bug, technically speaking, is not an error. A bug could lead to the generation of errors, but there's really no way the interpreter can track the presence of a bug. A *bug* in computing is the result of any process that failed to perform in the manner for which it was intended or designed, which cannot be detected automatically by the interpreter or compiler, and thus by its nature allows logical program execution to continue along a potentially disastrous course.

While I was testing Visual Basic for this book, I programmed an application wherein I would plot a point to the screen using a mouse pointer I programmed manually, and a device I called the compass would echo the direction in which I was moving the pointer. While I was developing this project, my program contained a few bugs that were difficult to find. For days, whenever I plotted a point, my compass control would register that point as being located 180 degrees in the other direction from where it actually was. From the computer's point of view, nothing was going wrong. Let's face it, it was doing exactly what it was told to do. Bugs are not necessarily examples of instructions being misexecuted. Often they happen because the interpreter followed instructions to the letter.

I discovered the source of the bug by using my favorite Visual Basic tool: The Immediate window. As I've described it before, this window is in fact a command line interpreter, the primary purpose of which is perhaps best summarized by its object name, `Debug`. Using the CLI, I can break an operation in progress and quiz the interpreter regarding the status of the program and its individual variables. Figure 44.1 shows a typical CLI operation in progress, working to debug a problem that came up in the execution of one of the procedures.

Visual Basic *By*
EXAMPLE

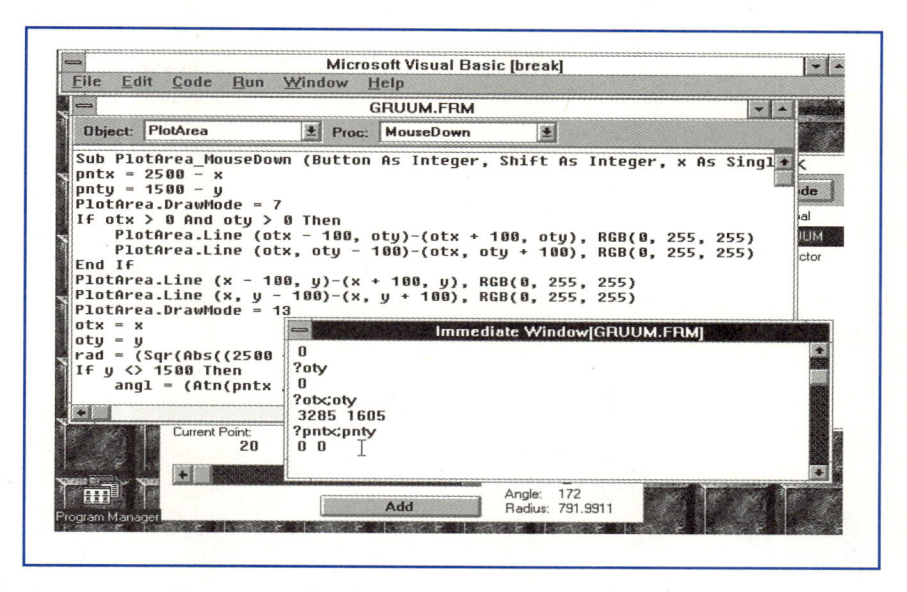

Figure 44.1. My test application on the operating table.

In Figure 44.1, notice the instruction line in the procedure window that has the hazy grey box around it. This is the line that was being executed when the program was suspended, either by selecting **B**reak from the **R**un menu or by pressing Ctrl-Break on the keyboard. On my keyboard, the Break key doubles as the Pause key (although I've never seen it pause anything).

After suspending execution with Ctrl-Break, I set the *breakpoint* for this routine by indicating the instruction line to receive the breakpoint and pressing the F9 key. A breakpoint is an instruction line that temporarily forces execution of the program to be suspended immediately following execution of that line.

Figure 44.2 shows an example of a proper breakpoint for the preceding routine.

> A *breakpoint* immediately suspends the program after it is executed.

541

Chapter 44 ♦ Registering Errors

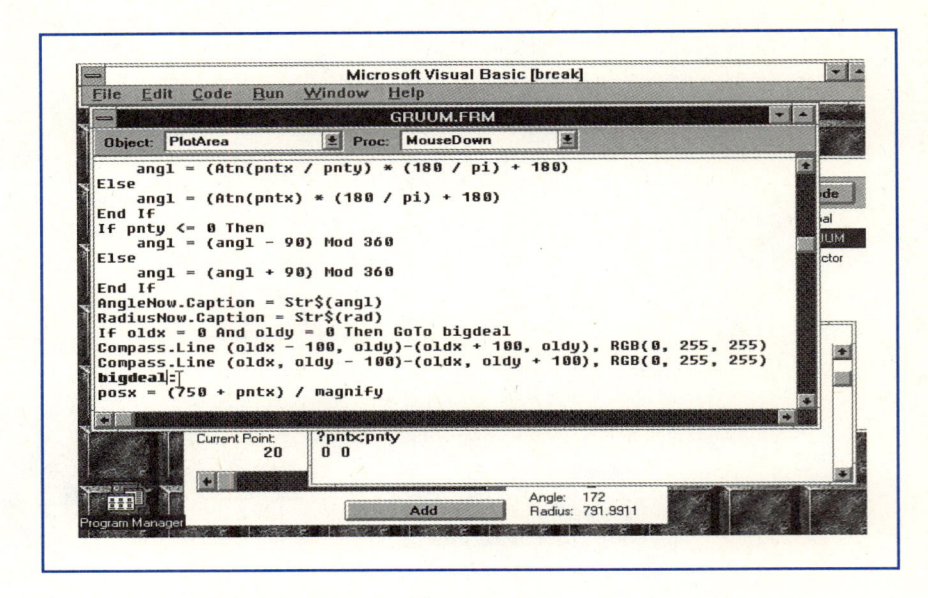

Figure 44.2. No big deal from my vantage point.

To set the breakpoint for an instruction line:

1. While the program is in suspension, indicate the instruction line to receive the breakpoint by placing the cursor within that line and pressing the F9 key.

2. When you run the program, execution stops after the breakpoint line as if there were a Stop statement following the line.

With the breakpoint having suspended the program, you can now use the Immediate window to quiz the current state of the program. This isn't a well-known fact, but the Immediate window can be used to execute small programs. As in the old BASIC interpreters, you can use colons to separate instructions typed to a single line within the CLI. The programmer can then enter a small loop clause to a line, like the one I used to determine what was wrong with the point values of the stars in my STARS.MAK project in Chapter 43:

```
for b=1 to 15:?xoom(b),yoom(b):next b
```

Here I can use abbreviated syntax and lowercase letters, and the ? stands in place of the `Print` command.

You can use the Immediate window also to resume execution at any procedure heading by typing that heading as an instruction line, as if it were a procedure call in the program. Using the CLI, I was able to suspend execution of my point-plotting application, set a breakpoint, add an offset to the current angle value, and re-execute the program to see what the problems were. I determined that I could re-edit the second and third lines of the procedure so that the offsets were subtracted *from* x and y, and not the other way around. What was wrong, you see, was that I had used a - mathematical operator where I should've used a +.

No debugging system is automatic, in the same way no spelling checker for your word processor can spot every possible error. For a spelling checker to be able to correct all errors, it would have to know the context in which the word you intended to spell should appear. One of the most commonly misspelled words I've found in editing other people's copy, for instance, is *you're*. It seems correct from *your* vantage point, but in the sentence "*Your* going too far," or "Why, *your* much thinner than you were," you can plainly see there are two misspelled words. A spelling checker cannot know that, since the misspelled words are words nonetheless.

Similarly, for Visual Basic to spot my mathematical operator bug, it would have to estimate what geometry I had intended for my program. From my point of view, I made an error; from the interpreter's, everything is proceeding smoothly. This is what differentiates a bug from an error in computing; if things did not proceed smoothly, then a formal error would be generated, and could possibly be trapped.

> Bugs are non-trappable, because the interpreter cannot recognize them.

Summary

An error is a fault in the processing of a program that suspends or terminates execution. Despite the negative connotation of the term, errors help the programmer determine whether the logical structure of a procedure being developed is workable. Suspension or termination of a program's execution can be intercepted with a procedural error trap. The error trap branch is baited using the

Chapter 44 ◆ Registering Errors

phrase `On Error GoTo`. Within this error trap routine, the internal variable `Err` can be used to determine what error occurred, and `Error$(Err)` can be used to generate a system-defined error message. The `Resume` statement terminates an error-trapping routine. A bug is a failure on the part of the program to operate in the manner in which it was intended, though it may be operating in the manner in which it was designed.

Review Questions

1. Would the instruction `Form1.Line xbeg, ybeg, xend, yend` generate a bug or an error?
2. Would the instruction `circ = 2 * pi / r` for calculating the circumference of a circle generate a bug or an error?

Review Exercises

Program a routine or procedure for the file selector box SELECTOR.FRM that determines whether a file name exists before it sends the value of `targetfile$` to the application that invoked it. Use an error trap and the internal error variable `Err`.

Part X

Physical Data

Sequential Access

In this chapter you examine the mechanism used by the BASIC programming language for storing user-created data to disk as files. This mechanism has changed little since the early 1970s, even with its inclusion in Visual Basic. You see how DOS file names are assigned to Visual Basic as ordinal numbers, which serve to represent data *channels*. These channels are opened and closed like the locks on a dam. When opened, data flows through the *stream*. In this chapter, you learn how to "turn the locks" and manage the stream.

The Hydrodynamics of Data Files

Most applications you will ever use create stored files for one purpose or another. BASIC programs themselves are files; a Visual Basic program can be comprised of several files. Yet up to this point, I haven't discussed how the Visual Basic application produces files *outside* of itself, in the manner and format specified within the program. It may seem unusual at first, but originally BASIC could not be programmed to produce files for the user other than its own source code file. The reason was not lack of foresight on the part of its designers, but the fact that operating systems used by relatively

Chapter 45 ◆ Sequential Access

inexpensive computers of the mid-1960s stored memory on rotating drums, so that the single program running at the time was *the* file. It was only in the 1970s when BASIC started to be used on computers that had memory that was more *solid-state*—reliant more on electrical currents than on centrifugal force—that a BASIC program was capable of being instructed to produce files.

> A *database* is data stored structurally as records of related entries.

All applications that produce and utilize their own data files—regardless of the language they're programmed in—are said to have their own *database*. A well-structured database includes a small portion of data that describes how the rest of the data relates to each other. The mechanics of BASIC data files were invented, for the most part, in 1970, at about the same time E. F. Codd was developing the concepts of modern databases for IBM. Because BASIC couldn't wait for Dr. Codd, the data file storage mechanism chosen for the language was somewhat blind to the structure and relationships between the elements of data being stored.

> A *channel* is a logical device that maintains the flow of data between the interpreter and an output device.

In a sense, the data storage and retrieval mechanism for BASIC-produced files is little more than a verbally commanded tape recorder. For a sequential-access file (the subject of this chapter) each element of data is stored to disk in a stream, one datum after the other. This stream is referred to as a *channel*, which is a throwback term to the first file-maintaining small systems of the 1970s. A channel is a logically interpreted device (in other words, not a tangible, physical entity) for maintaining the flow of data between the interpreter and an output device or storage unit.

The sequential-access mechanism works like this: A channel is opened with the `Open` statement, and this channel is rendered an ordinal number—for instance, `#1`. Each element of data is "printed" to this channel, one datum after the other, using the statement `Print #1`. No data concerning the physical makeup or construction of the file is included with this data. There's simply a bunch of raw numbers printed to magnetic media with the same technical consideration given to them that a typewriter gives the individual letters it types on a page.

A sequential-access data file is always read in the same way it was written—beginning-to-end, one datum after the other. When the file is created, the first 1000 elements may be names of people, the second 1000 may be their addresses, the third may be their cities of origin, and so on. These elements can be stored in this order using the `Print #` statement. So that the recalled data elements retain the same meaning and purpose in the program after they are loaded back into memory from disk, each element must be reloaded in exactly the order in which it was saved. So in this instance, the 1000 names would be reloaded first, followed by the 1000 addresses and the 1000 cities. A program could not open the file and have it immediately pick out just the addresses. In fact, if you wanted just the addresses, after you opened the file using the `Open` statement, you'd need to read the 1000 names anyway to get to the 1000 addresses.

This may seem like an archaic manner in which to store data... and for many of us, well, it is. However, assume you're writing a program that maintains several array variables to describe the main portion of data in memory—for instance, a vector-plotted drawing like you'd find in a CAD program. In such cases, the data is pertinent only in its entirety; half the number of vector plots in a drawing would result, no doubt, in a senseless drawing. In such cases in which it is more convenient to dump the entire image of data from memory to disk in one lump, sequential-access techniques prove to be convenient. In cases in which an individual item of data is important itself—for instance, somebody's address in a list—sequential access is rather cumbersome. *Random-access* data storage is less cumbersome, although it is far more complex. I reserve discussion of that technique for Chapter 46, "Random Access."

Example

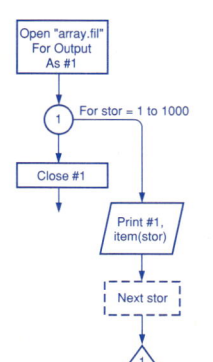

For now, here's how an array of 1000 items is stored to disk using sequential access:

```
Open "array.fil" For Output As #1
For stor = 1 To 1000
    Print #1, item(stor)
Next stor
Close #1
```

Chapter 45 ◆ Sequential Access

Here's pseudocode for this procedure:

Open a storage file for the arrays generated thus far, make this an output file for sequential access, and give this file channel 1.
Count from 1 to 1000, the maximum number of units in the array.
  Store the array value for this count to disk, using channel 1.
Count the next item.
Close the channel.

Here you see the modern incarnation of the old BASIC ordinal file system. A channel is opened and given ordinal number 1. The `Open` statement links #1 with the file name `array.fil`. As a result, anything that is sent through the channel using `Print #1` is written to that file. When the array is depleted, the channel is closed.

The `Open` statement is the primary statement behind all data file access operations.

Open   Statement

Syntax:

```
Open filename$ [For mode] [Access restriction] [locktype]
   As [#]channel% [Len = bytelength%]
```

The `Open` statement initiates a channel for the transfer of data between the Visual Basic interpreter and a physically stored file. The DOS file name of this file is specified as *filename$* and may contain the complete file storage path. The channel number associated with this file is expressed as *channel%* and can be any integer between 1 and 255. The choice of numbers here is completely arbitrary; a lower-numbered channel need not be opened previously before a higher number is chosen. After the `Open` statement is used to assign a channel number to a file name, any data transfer instruction that refers to this number affects the file attributed to the number by the `Open` statement. A pound sign before the channel number is optional to maintain syntax compatibility with earlier versions of BASIC.

The term represented by *mode* specifies the type of data transfer being established. This term can be stated as any of the following:

550

Sequential access:

    Output   Opens a channel for sequential data output to the specified file, starting at the beginning of the file. If the file does not currently exist at the time of the `Open` statement's execution, the file is created; otherwise, it is overwritten.

    Append   Opens a channel for sequential data output to the specified file, beginning at the point just following the last datum entered into the existing file. If the file does not currently exist at the time of the `Open` statement's execution, the file is created; however, with `Append`, an existing file is never overwritten.

    Input   Opens a channel for sequential data input to the specified file, in the order the data was output, starting with the beginning of the file.

Random access:

    Random   Opens a channel for data exchange using random-access mode. In this mode, data can be written to or read from a file at any specifiable point at any time. This is the default mode for channel initiation, and is assumed if *mode* is omitted from the `Open` statement.

Binary access:

    Binary   Opens a channel for data exchange using binary file mode. In this mode, individual bytes of data—for instance, pixels in an image or characters in a document—can be written to or read from a file at any specifiable point at any time.

The optional parameter *restriction* following `Access` may include either or both of the terms `Read` and `Write`, specifying any extra restrictions to be placed on file access, especially with regard to running the VB application over a network. The optional term *locktype* that follows is used to specify any access restrictions for

Chapter 45 ◆ Sequential Access

clients attempting to open the same data file already opened by another client in the network. The term `locktype` can be stated as `Shared` to allow any other client access to the open data file, `Lock Read` to prevent every other client from reading the data file while it's open, or `Lock Write` to prevent every other client from writing to the data file while it's open. These two terms are especially—and in many ways exclusively—helpful in networking environments, for use in "steering" a data file so that all clients in the network can obtain access to the most current version of the file, and no single client can override the changes made to that file by another client.

The term `Len = bytelength%` is used in random access mode to establish the fixed character length, in bytes, of each element of data being exchanged between the interpreter and the data file. Random access uses fixed field lengths to establish the beginning and end of a data item within a file; by default, this length is set to 128 bytes. Sequential access, by contrast, relies on the program to know the sequence in which each item was stored to the file, and to know in turn the field length of each item in the sequence. The methodology is that if the program knows in advance the precise contents of a file being recalled from disk—as it must with sequential access—it must know, as a result, the byte length of each item in that file. The term `Len = bytelength%` is used optionally in sequential-access mode to establish the length of the internal memory buffer being used to house characters being exchanged between the interpreter and data file. By default, this length is set to 512 bytes.

Obviously, this is an extremely complex statement, and it will probably require all of this and the following two chapters to explore every permutation of `Open`. By stark contrast, the statement's counterpart on the reverse side of the channel control operation is extremely simple.

Close Statement

Syntax:

`Close [#]channel1%[, channel2%, . . . channeln%]`

The `Close` statement terminates access to the data files that have names that were attributed by the `Open` statement to the `channel%` numbers listed. Any read or write instructions following `Close` pertaining to the channel numbers stated just previously within `Close` will generate errors. Access to files using those numbers can only be reinstated using an `Open` instruction. `Close` cancels any association between the stated numbers and the file names attributed to them by the `Open` instruction, so the numbers can be used again for any other file names. Pound signs are optional before each channel number. Should no channel numbers be specified, all open channels are closed.

In Windows, data that is stored to a file may not actually make it to disk, but instead may go to an in-between region—a sort of astral plane of the computing psyche. This *buffer zone,* as it is actually called, is retained in memory until it is full. At this time only the buffer is stored in one lump to disk, unless the `Close` statement is executed. At `Close`, the entire buffer is stored to disk whether or not it is full.

Example

Suppose you have data in memory that contains the names of the 50 United States, along with each state's governor's name, total population, total measurement of land mass, and official state bird. Here's one way you could save all that data to disk using a sequential-access technique:

Chapter 45 ◆ Sequential Access

```
Open "50states.dta" For Output As #2
For state = 1 To 50
    Print #2, name$(state)
Next state
For state = 1 To 50
    Print #2, pop(state)
Next state
For state = 1 To 50
    Print #2, mass(state)
Next state
For state = 1 To 50
    Print #2, bird$(state)
Next state
Close #2
```

At some later date, when you've just started running the program and memory is clear, you would load all that data back into memory using the following routine:

```
Open "50states.dta" For Input As #3
For state = 1 To 50
    Input #3, name$(state)
Next state
For state = 1 To 50
    Input #3, pop(state)
Next state
For state = 1 To 50
    Input #3, mass(state)
Next state
For state = 1 To 50
    Input #3, bird$(state)
Next state
Close #3
```

Your choice of numbers for both Open statements is not extremely important, as long as that choice remains constant throughout the data exchange process and doesn't conflict with any other existing open channel number. What must remain identical in both instances is the order data is stored and retrieved from the file. Visual Basic does not include a database management system (although third-party manufacturers do produce DBMS facilities for VB). Neither the programmer nor the user, therefore, can access a data file like you can with, for instance, Structured Query Language—SELECT * POPULATION FROM 50STATES.... In other words, you can't contact a portion of data by the category it falls under; Visual Basic has no provisions for categorization of data. It cannot know *what* data is being stored and retrieved; it can only keep track of *where* that data is. Using sequential access, you narrow the definition of *where* to *wherever the next datum resides.*

The preceding two routines were written more for ease of reading by human beings than for ease of interpretation by Visual Basic. The Output routine stores each list of 50 in sequence in its entirety before storing the next list. One good reason, perhaps, for dividing this sequence into individual loops is so that functions specific to the variables being stored can be easily placed and isolated. For instance, there are two numeric array variables in the preceding routines. If these variables are being retrieved from text box fields in a form, however, the text from those boxes will need to be converted into numeric variables before it can be stored as values. The routines would be converted as follows:

```
Open "50states.dta" For Output As #2
For state = 1 To 50
    Print #2, name$(state)
Next state
For state = 1 To 50
    pop = Val(pop$(state))
    Print #2, pop
Next state
For state = 1 To 50
    mass = Val(mass$(state))
    Print #2, mass
Next state
For state = 1 To 50
    Print #2, bird$(state)
Next state
Close #2
Open "50states.dta" For Input As #3
For state = 1 To 50
    Input #3, name$(state)
Next state
For state = 1 To 50
    Input #3, pop
```

```
        pop$(state) = Str$(pop)
Next state
For state = 1 To 50
    Input #3, mass
    mass$(state) = Str$(mass)
Next state
For state = 1 To 50
    Input #3, bird$(state)
Next state
Close #3
```

Notice how in both of the preceding routines, when writing the numeric values to disk and reading them from the disk, you did not need to specify the variable as an array. The values in the `Input` routine were restored first to simple numeric variables and then assigned to string arrays. Visual Basic does not keep track of the variable name associated with the data stored to disk, only the variable type. You could use a variable with a different name to restore data that was stored to disk. It is essential, however, that the variable you use is declared, either explicitly or informally, to be the same type as the one you used to store the data to disk.

The reason for this necessity is as follows: Each variable type has a different amount of bytes reserved for storage in memory. When you use the `Print #` statement (to be explained in detail momentarily), the contents of the data are printed digit-by-digit to a *text file*, in the same manner used by the .`Print` method for a *virtual terminal* graphic object. So, instead of saving an image of data to disk as it appears in memory, `Print #` saves the textual equivalent of that data. You can go into that file with a text editor such as Notepad, and the file appears with precisely the same contents it would have if the data were printed to a graphic object.

When reading this file back into memory, the VB interpreter has no idea what it sees at the moment. The only clue it has about what each character represents is the variable type of the `Input #` statement for the variable that is supposed to hold the converted value in memory. The interpreter determines the beginning and end of each printed element in the file by looking for its surrounding space characters. In the midst of an opening and closing space is an alphanumeric string that is extracted into memory. The interpreter then performs its own covert form of the `Val()` function to convert this string back to a value, if the variable type expressed in `Input #` is numeric. The results of this translation will not correspond with the data as it was printed to the file if the variable type expressed in `Input #` is not the same as it was in `Print #`. The interpreter will use the wrong number of bytes to store the value conversion.

Here are the two data storage and retrieval instructions I've been discussing:

Print # Statement

Syntax:

```
Print #channel%, expression1[{;¦,} expression2]
    [. . . {;¦,} expressionn]
```

where each *expression* can either be logically reduced to a numeric value or expressed as an alphanumeric concatenation of one or more elements of text.

The `Print #` statement prints the text of the values or contents of each expression in the list to a text file that acts as the data file attributed to the integer *channel%*. This channel number must have been opened previously with the `Open` statement for `Output` or `Append` and attributed to a specific file name found within the `Open` statement. `Print #` will print text to a file with this file name. The form of this text will be exactly as it would appear if it was printed to a graphic object or to the printer, using the `.Print` method.

> **CAUTION:** A pound sign *must* precede the *channel%* number so that the interpreter can better distinguish this statement from the `.Print` method.

If a semicolon appears before an expression, printing of the expression to the file takes place immediately at the present character pointer position—thus canceling any carriage return or line feed before printing begins. If a comma appears before an expression, printing of the expression to the file is to take place at the beginning of the next print zone. Because no text font is assumed for printing

Chapter 45 ◆ Sequential Access

to a disk file—because you're not dealing with images or appearance specifically—a print zone begins every 14 characters.

The current character position within the file is maintained by the interpreter for each open channel until the Close statement is executed for that channel, thus closing the file. Multiple Print # statements executed in sequence for the same channel number will have their results appear within the file associated with that channel, in the same sequence.

Input # Statement

Syntax:

`Input #channel%, variable1[, variable2, . . . variablen]`

The `Input #` statement reads data from a textual data file whose `channel%` number was previously opened for `Input` by the `Open` statement, and whose file name was previously specified within the `Open` statement. The pound sign is required to distinguish the `Input #` statement from the old BASIC `Input` statement, although that particular statement is no longer supported by Visual Basic. Each textual element from the file is assigned to the variables in the `Input #` instruction's list, in sequence. If the variable being assigned a datum from the file is a numeric variable, the interpreter will automatically attempt to convert the text string associated with that variable to a numeric value before assigning a value to the variable.

Example

Now that you know more about the nature of printing to a sequential-access file, you can modify the two `Print #` and `Input #` routines for greater efficiency, as follows:

Visual Basic *By* EXAMPLE

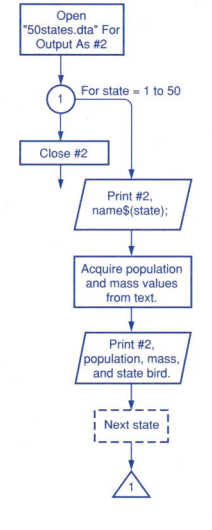

```
Open "50states.dta" For Output As #2
For state = 1 To 50
    Print #2, name$(state);
    pop = Val(pop$(state))
    mass = Val(mass$(state))
    Print #2, pop, mass,
    Print #2, bird$(state)
Next state
Close #2
```

```
Open "50states.dta" For Input As #3
For state = 1 To 50
    Input #3, name$(state); pop, mass, bird$(state)
    pop$(state) = Str$(pop)
    mass$(state) = Str$(mass)
Next state
Close #3
```

A *record* is a logical grouping of related elements of data within a data file or database.

In both cases, you're using single loops to govern both the storage mechanism and the retrieval mechanism. In so doing, each item of information is interleaved into the others, so that the data entries for each state appear on the same "line" within the text file. You can officially consider this grouping of related elements to be a *record*.

Example

The previous examples assume the program knows in advance how many records of related data will be entered into application memory. Suppose you were to extend the program, however, such that the application would store information about the individual counties or boroughs in each state. You really don't want to have to create 50 different array variables for the states. Instead, it would be more convenient for you to create two-dimensional array variables, of which the first dimension represents a state and the second dimension represents a county. You then let the data file decide for you, after the data is loaded into memory, how many counties each state has. Here are the storage and retrieval routines you might write for storing each county or borough's name, land area, and county seat:

559

Chapter 45 ◆ Sequential Access

```
Open "counties.dta" For Output As #4
For state = 1 To 50
    Print #4, counties(state)
    For lc = 1 To counties(state)
        Print #4, cname$(state, lc), mass(state, lc),
            cseat$(state, lc)
    Next lc
Next state

Open "counties.dta" For Input As #5
For state = 1 To 50
    Input #5, counties(state)
    For lc = 1 To counties(state)
        Input #5, cname$(state, lc), mass(state, lc),
            cseat$(state, lc)
    Next lc
Next state
```

In the preceding pair of routines, each state has a variable apportioned to it called `counties()` that keeps count of the number of counties or boroughs in the state. By looking at the `Print #4` routine, you can see that the number of counties per state is stored to disk *first.* Following that is a list of as many names, land masses, and bastions of power as there are counties in the state currently being counted. Because the `lc` loop counts only to the number of counties registered to be in the current state and then stops, you can be certain that in the "semi-cloned" `Input #5` routine, the loading loop will "know" in advance how many counties to load in memory before it initiates the loop. This number is always the first number in a county *cluster.* After the cluster is loaded, the file pointer points to the next number of counties automatically. You can also guarantee from the identical way you've structured the saving and loading routines that `Input #5, counties(state)` always picks up the number of counties for the current state, and not a county name by mistake.

One of the dangers in using this method of storage is that, when reading character files into memory, the sequential-access loader treats commas and semicolons as delimiters. You can easily store the sequence of characters *Washington, D.C.* to disk using `Print #`, but the comma after the *n* will cause the interpreter to think *Washington* is the entire data field. What's worse, *D.C.* is likely to become the start of the next data field, and chances are that the District of Columbia itself will show up as a ZIP code, and all the fields to follow will be one datum off.

In a strange way, the cause of this problem is also the solution to it, as I explain with `Write #`.

Write # Statement

Syntax:

`Write #channel%, expression1[, expression2 . . , expressionn]`

where each *expression* can either be logically reduced to a numeric value or expressed as an alphanumeric concatenation of one or more elements of text.

The `Write #` statement prints the text of the values or contents of each expression in the list to a text file that acts as the data file attributed to the integer `channel%`. This channel number must have been opened previously with the `Open` statement for `Output` or `Append` and attributed to a specific file name found within the `Open` statement. `Write #` will print text to a file with this file name. This text will be in the form of an *ASCII-delimited* data file as used by the *mail merge* feature of many word processors. All elements will be separated from each other by commas, and all alphanumeric strings will be enclosed within quotation marks. Commas and any punctuation other than quotation marks themselves that are intended to appear within a string will be enclosed within the quotation marks.

> **CAUTION:** A pound sign *must* precede the `channel%` number in the `Write #` statement. Commas are used within the `Write #` statement only to separate data items; they do not affect the "printing" position of that data in the text file generated by the interpreter. You *cannot* use semicolons as delimiters within `Write #`.

Chapter 45 ◆ Sequential Access

Sequential Data as Pages

When outputting character-based data to the printer, you can set the coordinate system for the `Printer.` object for characters rather than graphic points (`Printer.Scalemode = 4`). You then have a general understanding of the `.Height` and `.Width` of the printed page, with regard to character spacing. A stored sequential access file is, in essence, a printed page, although Visual Basic maintains no height property for that page. Visual Basic does, however, maintain an optional column width, which is resettable by means of a statement, but not a property.

Width #   Statement

Syntax:

`Width #channel%, columns%`

The `Width #` statement sets the "printing" width of a sequential access file whose `channel%` is currently open by means of the `Open` statement. The setting is made to a specified number of `columns%` from 0 to 255. Once the interpreter has stored `columns%` number of characters to an open file, it automatically generates a carriage return and line feed character. "Printing"—or storage of entries to the file—then begins on the following line. If `columns%` is zero, no lines are assumed, and text is presumed to wrap around without carriage returns until its termination.

Assuming `Width #` is set to a reasonable amount, we then have access to the `Line Input #` statement:

Line Input #   Statement

Syntax:

`Line Input #channel%, string$`

The `Line Input #` statement reads a line of text from a sequential access file, and stores it in memory within the variable *string$*. A line of text in this instance is defined as a continuous stream of characters that end with a carriage return. This character is assumed to be the end-of-line character. If no such break occurs in the file, or if `Width #` was not used to specify the line width of the sequential data file, then `Line Input #` could be used to assign the entire textual contents of the data file to string variable *string$*.

Summary

All applications that use data in one form or another operate a database. A database management system maintains the categorical and relational information about elements of data. Visual Basic has no such system. It can only open channels for data and maintain their throughput and positioning in a file.

The appearance of a Visual Basic stored data file is a page, although one that seems to be "printed" to disk. In fact, the statement `Print #` is the primary statement for printing a sequential-access record to disk. A channel is opened with the `Open` statement. If the access mode is specified as `Output`, using sequential access, data can be "printed" to this file or "written" to this file with more descriptive delimiters using `Write #`.

Review Questions

1. What is the operational difference between the `Print #` statement and the `Write #` statement?

2. What is the operational difference between the `Input #` statement and the `Line Input #` statement?

3. Why is printing to the screen or printer accomplished with the `.Print` method, and printing to a file accomplished with the `Print #` statement?

Chapter 45 ◆ Sequential Access

Review Exercises

1. Suppose you're writing an astronomy program in which the user catalogs the celestial objects she happens to view with her telescope. Write a routine that stores to disk all the objects the user has cataloged thus far, along with their celestial catalog names and observed magnitudes and brightnesses.

2. Suppose the astronomer sees planets, stars, galaxies, or other celestial phenomena. Given the fact that the description criteria for each category is different, but you don't have it all on-hand at the moment, write a routine that saves a sequential-access file for all objects observed in the skies thus far. Have the saving and loading routines differentiate between the celestial objects, so that each time a new type of object is sighted, the individual content and structure of the object is chosen and utilized by the program.

46

Random Access

In this chapter you witness the other primary method of storing and retrieving data as files in Visual Basic—the random-access method. This involves the storage of related data elements as records and the retrieval of each record by number, although not necessarily in sequence. One record can be pulled out of a file at random, which is where the access method gets its name. You also see the binary-access method in action, in which data are stored and retrieved byte-by-byte into memory rather than datum-by-datum.

Yippie I/O

In the real world of file storage, people do not open up a cabinet and read word-for-word the contents of every file that falls before the one their looking for. If that were so, people with last names beginning with Z would probably be the last to receive their tax refunds. Random-access file storage should perhaps be called *rational access,* because each element of data has its own recognized place or location within the file, and the element can be called at any time by specifying that location.

We actually use the term *random access* often in our lives, especially with regard to memory—as in RAM. In random-access memory, you can address, acquire, and store a byte of data by

Chapter 46 ◆ Random Access

referring to its location—or in terms of memory, its address. When programming in assembly language, data are addressed by their byte location, and often for arithmetic operations certain elements of data are copied into *registers,* which on paper appear to be variables.

Normally in BASIC, a variable refers to a location in memory where the data reside or, in the case of an alphanumeric string, begin to reside. Many versions of BASIC allow you to address this memory location directly with the VARPTR statement; but Visual Basic does not and cannot support this statement, because Microsoft Windows frequently shifts the location of the data frames for an application in memory without notifying any of those applications. Microsoft employs what can best be called a "Data Relocation Program" for segments of data in which the data have grown too large for the segment.

The invocation of a Visual Basic variable is an example of random access, technically speaking. Such an invocation is merely an indirect way of referring to an element of memory by its address—except for the fact that in Windows, that address keeps changing. Notice that in the sequential data access technique, you actually employ random access anyway. You use sequential access to place all the data that had been stored on disk into *memory*, and from there you can access any element of it randomly. The subscript of the array into which you loaded the data serves as the address of that element—so you have random access whether you want it or not.

In the random-access data storage and retrieval technique, you're merely being more up-front about what technique you use to address data. The access takes place from the disk or stored file rather than from memory; you use the Put # and Get # statements rather than Print # and Input # to retrieve and store, respectively, an element of data by its address. You therefore directly address the disk rather than the memory, and save the VB application a bit of work.

Here is the statement used to write data to a random-access file, described in detail:

Put # Statement

Syntax:

`Put #channel%, [location&], variable`

The `Put #` statement writes the contents of the specified *variable* to a random-access data file, previously opened with the statement `Open...As Random` or `Open...As Binary`, and whose *channel%* number is designated by that `Open` statement. The term *variable* cannot be replaced with an expression or a value. In the instance of the `Put #` statement, only a variable may be explicitly stated. Only one variable can be included; the VB interpreter does not recognize lists of variables for this statement.

When using the random-access technique, if *location&* is stated, the *variable* contents are assumed to be written to the element position in the list numbered *location&* from the beginning of the file. If an element already exists at that position, it is replaced for the contents of *variable*. If *location&* is not stated, the comma that holds the place where *location&* would have been stated must remain to distinguish its purpose in this statement from that of *variable*.

The Visual Basic interpreter maintains a file pointer for each data file opened with the `Open` statement. This pointer registers the location where the next data element will be written. In random access, if *location&* is omitted, writing takes place to the location currently being pointed to by the file pointer. After writing to a random- or binary-access file takes place, the file pointer registers the location just following the preceding write. Therefore, if a `Put #` statement writes to some *location&* in the middle of an existing file, after the write the file pointer will increment itself to the next location in the middle of that file. In other words, the default location of the file pointer when *location&* is not specified is *not* at the end of a random-access file in Visual Basic.

If the value of *location&* is beyond the value where any data has been written to the file, the contents of the data at locations previous to *location&* may be erroneous. It is legal, however, to specify a storage *location&* that is far greater than the number of elements in the file.

Chapter 46 ◆ Random Access

The length in stored bytes of each element is, by default, 128 bytes. You can respecify this length with the Len = *length%* portion of the Open statement for that file. This is considered the field length of each element in the file. Each field can be from 1 to 32,767 bytes in length, and all fields within a random-access file have identical lengths. This many bytes are written to the file each time Put # is executed, regardless of the byte length of the specified *variable*. An alphanumeric string cannot be longer than the number of bytes in the field length minus two, to account for a string descriptor value. Each time Put # is executed, the number of bytes in the field length is added to that pointer to maintain that pointer's current absolute location.

When using the binary-access technique—when the data file was opened using Open...As Binary—the value of *location&*, when specified, represents the absolute byte number within the open file. This byte number acts as an absolute address. Elements of a binary-access file do not have identical lengths; so the Put # statement writes exactly as many bytes to the binary-access file as are used to store the specified *variable* in memory. If *location&* is not specified, writing takes place at the next byte address in the sequence.

> **CAUTION:** The binary-access method does not write descriptors to a file specifying the beginning and end of a variable's contents or value. It is therefore possible to accidentally (or purposefully) write bytes as data *in the midst of* a previously stored element, thus invalidating that element. Binary access should therefore be used only for nonrecord data, such as long textual documents and bitmapped images.

Figure 46.1 depicts the differences between random- and binary-access storage. In the upper panel, a random-access file has been opened with a field length of 16, specified within the Open statement using Len = 16 at the end. Two variables are stored to this file using Put #. The first is a double-precision floating-point variable consuming eight bytes of memory, and the second is the string form of the file name *CUOMO1.DTA*, which is 10 characters long. With the random-access file, the eight-byte value is stored within a 16-

byte field, leaving an excess of eight bytes. The 10-character string is then stored within another 16-byte field, with two characters included as a string descriptor, leaving an excess of four bytes.

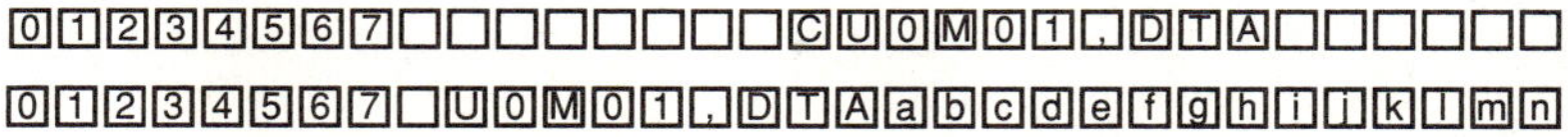

```
0 1 2 3 4 5 6 7 □ □ □ □ □ □ □ □ C U O M O 1 . D T A □ □ □ □ □
0 1 2 3 4 5 6 7 □ U O M O 1 . D T A a b c d e f g h i j k l m n
```

Figure 46.1. The two addressable data storage schemes.

In the lower panel of Figure 46.1, a binary-access file has been opened, and such files have no fixed field lengths. Here, the same two variables are being stored to the file using the same `Put #` statement. The eight-byte value is stored to eight bytes of the file, leaving the file pointer at the next byte. The ASCII value of the 10 characters in *CUOMO1.DTA* are stored immediately following the eight-byte value. The file pointer then rests at the byte just following the *A*.

Keep these two panels in mind as I introduce the statement that reloads variables from a data file into memory.

Get # Statement

Syntax:

```
Get #channel%, [location&], variable
```

The `Get #` statement reads the contents of the specified *variable* from a random-access data file, previously opened with the statement `Open...As Random` or `Open...As Binary`, and whose *channel%* number was designated by that `Open` statement. The term *variable* cannot be replaced with an expression or a value. In the instance of the `Get #` statement, only a single variable can be explicitly stated by itself, not a list of variables.

When using the random-access technique, if *location&* is stated, the *variable* contents are assumed to be read from the element position in the list numbered *location&* from the beginning of the file. If *location&* is omitted and a comma holds the empty space where *location&* would have appeared, reading takes place at the location currently being pointed to by the file pointer. After reading from a random- or binary-access file, the file pointer registers the location just following the preceding read. Therefore, if a `Get #` statement reads from some `location&` in the middle of an existing file, after the read the file pointer will increment itself to the next location in the middle of that file.

If the value of `location&` is beyond the location where any data have been written to the file, any value read from that nonexistent position will be zero, and any string read from that position will be null. It is legal, however, to specify a storage `location&` that is far greater than the number of elements in the file.

When using the binary-access technique to load a value into memory, the `Get #` statement reads exactly as many bytes to the binary-access file as are used to represent the specified value `variable` when it is loaded into memory. When loading an alphanumeric string and assigning its contents to a string variable in memory using binary access, the number of characters loaded into memory is exactly the number of characters currently belonging to that string variable. In other words, if contents have yet to be assigned to a string variable and its official contents are null (`string$ = ""`), a `Get #` statement will not load any characters into the specified string variable.

If `location&` is not specified, reading takes place at the next byte address in the sequence.

> **CAUTION:** If the variable type stated within `Get #` is different from the type used when storing that variable to the binary-access file using `Put #` earlier, the value or contents of the `Get #` variable will be erroneous. It is therefore important that the instruction pattern of the binary-access loading routine be somewhat similar to that of the binary storage routine.

Visual Basic By EXAMPLE

> A *field* is any container for an element or item of data.

In some of the preceding descriptions, I've introduced the concept of *fields,* or regions of data. A field is any container for an element or item of data, whether it be any of the following three things:

A graphic object for the display of that datum

A region of memory reserved for that datum

A region of a file reserved for that datum

> A *table* is a combination of data and data structures, such as field names and relations.

In true database management, a category of data—such as *last name* or *amount owed*—is addressed by its field name. Visual Basic has no native database manager, although the random-access data files it creates have field lengths that are fixed by the `Open` statement. These field lengths are not stored along with the data, however, but are determined within the source code. Because these field lengths are a necessary component for the structure of a formal database *table,* Visual Basic is said not to manage a *formal* database. A table is a stored database component consisting of data, along with the structure of that data, such as field names and relations.

One of the primary differences between the sequential- and random-access techniques is that random access is *bidirectional*—you can read to and write from the same channel. With sequential access, the mode `Output` or `Input` is specified first, setting the direction of the data stream in advance. With random access, there is no data stream; the file pointer is positioned wherever you want, and data is either sent to or acquired from that position. The file pointer then scoots over one element, so it knows that a sequence exists. In random access, however, the sequence of data elements in a file does not govern how that data is accessed.

For instance, suppose the application has a form on the screen that contains fields for data about one of the 50 states. To acquire this data, the user types the two-letter postal abbreviation for a state into a field marked `Postal Abbr.`, which is a text box. The user then clicks a button marked `Reference`, and the application is then directed to acquire the rest of the data for that state from the file. In memory is a string array variable that acts as a sort of directory; within each element of the array is a postal abbreviation. If the abbreviation typed matches an abbreviation in the array, the array subscript

Chapter 46 ◆ Random Access

value for that abbreviation will be used to acquire the record of that state from a file.

Example

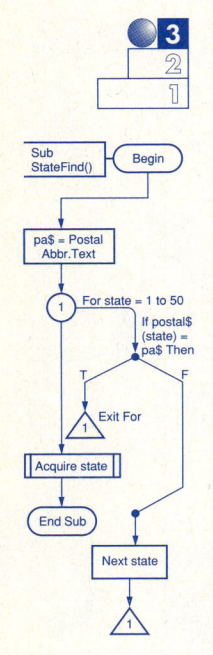

Here's how the procedure for determining which record is loaded might appear:

```
Sub StateFind ()
pa$ = PostalAbbr.Text
For state = 1 to 50
    If postal$(state) = pa$ Then Exit For
Next state
Acquire state
Exit Sub
```

First, the contents of the postal abbreviation field are copied to string variable `pa$`. The loop clause then compares these contents to those within the array `postal$(state)` and continues to execute this comparison as long as the contents are *not* equivalent to each other. When they become equivalent, the loop is exited and control is passed to `Sub Acquire ()`, a procedure that loads data about the state into memory. Assume that earlier in the program the following instruction was executed:

```
Open "50STATES.DTA" For Random As #1 Len = 48
```

As you move from procedure to procedure, channel #1 is still open. You can address the file for channel #1 using `Sub Acquire ()` as follows:

```
Sub Acquire (state As Integer)
locat = (state - 1) * 4
Get #1, locat, name$(state)
StateName.Text = name$(state)
Get #1, , pop
pop$(state) = Str$(pop)
Population.Text = pop$(state)
Get #1, , mass
mass$(state) = Str$(mass)
LandMass.Text = mass$(state)
```

```
Get #1, , bird$(state)
Bird.Text = bird$(state)
End Sub
```

The first order of business is to determine where the record for this state starts. The way the example works thus far, there are four fields per record. When the first state's record (Alabama's, if you're proceeding alphabetically) was saved to the file 50STATES.DTA, the file pointer started at location 0. After all four elements of that record were saved, the pointer was at location 4 waiting for the next record to be saved. The pointer position is therefore at a location four times the value of the state being saved minus 1. The formula `locat = (state - 1) * 4` thus returns the proper file pointer location for the state being loaded into memory.

The first element of the record is loaded into the string array variable `name$()` using `Get #` and specifying the starting file pointer location `locat` directly. From then on, each time an element is loaded, the pointer location is automatically incremented, so you don't need to specify a pointer location variable again for the rest of the loading procedure. In the preceding procedure, after each element is loaded into its appropriate string array variable, the text of that element is also displayed within the form on the screen.

Is This On the Record?

If you're comparing the choice of terms this book uses to discuss random access with the choice of terms in the manuals that were supplied with your copy of Visual Basic, you may be confused at the moment, and with good reason. To dispel the confusion, here's an explanation: The term *record* is used universally to describe a grouping of related elements of data. This is the technical definition of *record* subscribed to worldwide, especially by programmers of database management systems. Microsoft uses the term *record* only with respect to Visual Basic to describe an element of data being written to or read from a file—or what is still sometimes called a *datum*. This choice was probably made because the term *record* has been used historically—however incorrectly—by the originators of BASIC to describe a datum stored to a random-access file.

Because authors and publishers have a duty to describe the operations of more applications and interpreters than just Visual Basic, we chose to adhere to the universal definition of *record* rather than the specific definition. This way, each time you jump from one application's "world" to the next application's "world," you don't find yourself rewriting the dictionary.

Another reason we adhere to the universal definition of *record* is because Visual Basic has provisions for the creation of formal records for use in random-access files. This is done by invoking a `Type` clause within the VB application's global module. This clause contains the structure of a formal record—the grouping of related elements of data. We can then use `Put #` to write a record of several elements of data to a disk file using just one variable.

Example

Here's how a `Type` clause might appear within the global module of our 50 States program:

```
Type StateData
    name As String * 24
    pop As Long
    mass As Long
    bird As String * 16
End Type
Global StateRecord as StateData
```

When declaring a string as in `String * 24`, you set the length of the declared string. Formal data records using "user-defined" composite variable types may not include strings of variable length, because a formal random-access record must have a fixed length for it to be recogized as a record. Array variables may not be invoked within a `Type` clause; but in the case of the revised 50 States program, you no longer need array variables because the record arrays are kept on disk now rather than in memory. The active record number is still kept in variable `state`; however, the value of `state` is now also the value of the current file pointer location, assuming record number 0 is a null record.

Assume now that, someplace in the application, you invoke the following instructions:

```
RecLength = Len(StateData)
Open "50STATES.DTA" For Random As #1 Len = RecLength
```

Normally, the `Len()` function is used to return the length of a string variable; but in this instance, it may also be used to return the byte length of a composite variable. In this case, `RecLength` is now 48, and that value is now assigned as the length of the formal records accessed through channel #1. Our storage routine for a state's data may now appear as follows:

```
StateRecord.name = StateName.Text
StateRecord.pop = Val(Population.Text)
StateRecord.mass = Val(LandMass.Text)
StateRecord.bird = Bird.Text
Put #1, state, StateRecord
```

This is the entire storage routine. The contents of the currently displayed form are transferred to constituent variables invoked as properties of an object `StateRecord`. You can use object-oriented syntax to address these variables because they were previously included within a `Type` clause that attributed them to `StateRecord` as if that were an object. The values and contents of these variables having been set, `StateRecord` now contains a complete record for the state. It is stored to disk at location number `state`; translation from state number to location number does not need to take place.

You can now modify `Sub Acquire ()` to work in the reverse:

```
Sub Acquire (state As Integer)
Get #1, state, StateRecord
StateName.Text = name
Population.Text = Str$(pop)
LandMass.Text = Str$(mass)
Bird.Text = bird
End Sub
```

Once `StateRecord` is loaded into memory, the contents and values of its four constituent variables follow.

575

Chapter 46 ◆ Random Access

Summary

After opening a file in Random access mode using the Open statement, data elements can be stored to and retrieved from a designated file at random from any location within the boundaries of the file, and at any time. Random access is bidirectional, whereas sequential access is unidirectional—either Input or Output/Append. Opening a file in Binary access mode allows for the storage and retrieval of individual bytes from a file, rather than elements of data in the form of variables.

The Put # statement is used to write the value or contents of a single variable to a random-access file, either at a specified location within the file or at the point just following the last recorded writing to that file. The Get # statement is used to retrieve data from a random-access file, from a specified location or just after the last location read from or written to.

A data element within a random-access file has a fixed field length, specified within the Open...As Random statement using the optional Len term. If Len is not included in the Open statement, the field length is set to 128 bytes. A record is a collection of related data elements. An entire record can be stored within this single field, as long as the constituent variables within that record have fixed field lengths themselves. The constituent variables of a record can be specified within a Type clause in the global module of a Visual Basic application.

Review Questions

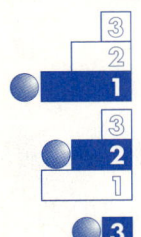

1. What is the maximum length of an alphanumeric string within a random-access data element?

2. Using the formal database model, if a set of records defined by a Type clause can be considered a table, a variable within the clause may be considered what?

3. What is the value returned by Len(Precinct) if the Type clause is expressed as follows:

```
Type Precinct
    name As String * 36
    seat As String * 25
    latitude As Single
    longitude As Single
    PopRegistered As Long
End Type
```

Data File Attributes

In this chapter I introduce you to the functions that you can use to retrieve data *about* a data file, or, in other words, functions that return the attributes of that file. Later, you learn an alternate method for retrieving individual bytes from a stored data file in either sequential- or binary-access mode.

Now Then, Let's See... Where Exactly Are We?

As you've seen thoroughly demonstrated in the previous two chapters, the Visual Basic interpreter maintains a file pointer for each open data channel. This pointer is a value in memory—not a variable—which registers the current location where an element of data would be read from a file or would be stored to a file. Because Visual Basic does not see stored data files as formal structures with stored field lengths, attributes, and relations, practically the only control the programmer has over the data-transfer process is through this file pointer.

Chapter 47 ◆ Data File Attributes

Perhaps the simplest file pointer control function to comprehend is the one that tells you whether you've reached the end of the proverbial rope.

EOF ( ) Function

Syntax:

`variable% = EOF(channel%)`

The `EOF()` function returns whether the file pointer for a specified `channel%` is currently within its boundaries. If the file pointer has reached the *End Of the File*, `EOF()` returns a Boolean value of true (−1). If there are still more data elements or bytes to be read within an open data file, `EOF()` returns false (0). The function works only on files which have a `channel%` opened previously with the `Open` statement, and are currently considered open by the interpreter. The pound sign before `channel%` is *omitted* for this function.

Example

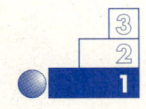

One common use of the `EOF()` function is in loading the contents of a sequential-access file into array variables in memory when the number of data elements within the file has not been determined. Here is an example routine that loads the contents of a sequential-access file of any length into an array variable, assuming that variable has been dimensioned for a high enough value:

```
Open "test.fil" For Input As #1
While EOF(1) = -1
    Input #1, item(test)
    test = test + 1
Wend
```

You could have used a `For-Next` loop within the preceding routine, but only if you knew ahead of time or could specify indirectly within a variable the number of elements within the data file—because you'd have to count from 1 to *something%*. Here variable test is incremented manually, and the While-Wend loop executes until the end-of-file register is set to true.

The Visual Basic interpreter maintains values for the last location written to or read from a data file, as well as the *next* location. These are not to be confused with each other.

Loc ( ) Function

Syntax:

location& = Loc(*channel%*)

The Loc() function returns the location of the previous storage to or retrieval from an open data file, the *channel%* number of which is specified between the parentheses. For random-access files, the Loc() function returns the number of the previous data element or record, where 1 is the number of the first element in the file. For sequential-access files, Loc() returns a rounded value equivalent to the current byte location of the data pointer—not the element or record location—divided by 128. For binary-access files, Loc() returns the location of the byte previously written to or read from the data file. The pound sign before *channel%* is omitted for this function.

Seek ( ) Function

Syntax:

location& = Seek(*channel%*)

The Seek() function returns the location of the file pointer within an open data file, the *channel%* number of which is specified between the parentheses. This pointer location is where the next read or write operation will take place. For random-access files, Seek() returns the number to be given the next data element written to or read from the data file. For sequential- and binary-access files, Seek() returns the byte location where the next character of data will be written to or read from the data file. The pound sign before `channel%` is omitted for this function.

Example

Suppose your application maintains a random-access data file. A record of related data elements within this file is grouped informally—in other words, without the aid of the `Type` clause. A cluster of individual elements, each with a small, fixed data length, comprise a record. You may have a procedure that, at some time, needs to know whether the current file pointer is in the midst of a record or at the beginning of one. You can use the following routine fragment to determine this state:

```
lc = Seek(1)
If lc / reclength = Int(lc / reclength) Then
    Rem Beginning of Record
    .
    .
    .
Else
    Rem Midst of Record
    .
    .
    .
End If
```

The total number of data elements within a complete random-access data file *must* be a multiple of the number of data elements in a complete record in that file. It therefore follows that if the record length does not evenly divide into the element location of the file pointer, the pointer must not be at the beginning of a new record.

You can use the `Seek #` statement, which is related to the `Seek()` function, to set the current location of the file pointer manually.

Seek # Statement

Syntax:

`Seek [#]channel%, location&`

The `Seek #` statement sets the location of the pointer for a data file, where the next read or write operation will take place, to a specified `location&`. The data file is specified by its designated `channel%`, which was given to that file when it was opened using the `Open` statement. The value of `location&` may be specified as greater than the actual current length of the file. In such cases, the interpreter will generate null values for all locations between the final location and the stated `location&`.

For random-access files, the value of `location&` is set to the data element number where a variable is to be written when `Put #` is invoked next, or to the data element number where it is to be read when `Get #` is invoked next. For sequential- and binary-access files, the value of `location&` is set to the byte address of the next character to be written to or read from the data file. The pound sign before the `channel%` number is optional.

Example

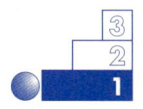

Perhaps the most common use for the `Seek #` statement is to set the current file pointer to element #1 of a file, as with the following instruction:

`Seek #1, 1`

Data Process Control

A *buffer* is an area of memory where data are temporarily stored.

When storing information to a data file, the data usually wait within a data *buffer* before they actually are sent to disk. A buffer is a holding area in memory consisting of a fixed number of bytes, reserved for data that are to be sent to some device—often a disk file—at some later time, generally when the buffer is full.

583

Chapter 47 ◆ Data File Attributes

The purpose of a buffer in this case is to speed writing operations to a file, because writing to an address in memory is much faster than writing to a single location on a disk, and writing several data elements to a single location on a disk *once* is much faster than writing several data elements to *several* locations on that disk at different times. In sequential access, specifying the `Len =` option in the `Open` statement sets the size of this buffer in memory; by default, it is set to 512 bytes, or half of a kilobyte..

Each open channel has its own memory buffer apportioned to it. Part of what the `Close` instruction does is flush the memory buffer apportioned for the stated channel number. Until the `Close` instruction is executed, the image of the data file that the VB interpreter sees may not be equivalent to the image of the data file on the disk itself. Updates of the physical file on disk take place only when the buffer is full; after each update, the buffer is emptied. *Caching* in microcomputer hardware is similar to buffering in software, in that hard-coded registers are reserved for holding data that are to be transferred to another device. Because transferring data all at once is always faster than transferring one unit at a time, processing is noticeably expedited..

The only danger in batch-storing is that, in the event of a fatal error or a system crash, the logical image of the data in memory is lost and the non-updated physical image of the data remains. You can use the `Reset` statement at the end of a program, during an error-trapping routine, or before loading a new document file into memory to shut down data transfer officially and to make the physical data image equivalent to the logical image.

Reset   Statement

Syntax:

`Reset`

The `Reset` statement shuts down all data-transfer processes by flushing the contents of all open data buffers to their apportioned `Open` files and closing all open channels without having to invoke `Close` statements for those channels.

Here are the rest of Visual Basic's general file maintenance functions:

LOF() — Function

Syntax:

`length% = LOF(channel%)`

The `LOF()` function returns the length in bytes of the open file whose `channel%` appears between the parentheses. The pound sign before `channel%` is omitted for this function.

FreeFile — Function

Syntax:

`channel% = FreeFile`

The `FreeFile` function returns the lowest-valued available unopened channel number, within the variable `channel%`. You can then use this variable within an `Open` statement that may follow. The `FreeFile` function requires no parentheses.

FileAttr() — Function

Syntax:

`setting% = FileAttr(channel%, attribute%)`

When `attribute%` is stated as 1, the `FileAttr()` function returns a value that describes the data file access mode assigned to the specified data channel. This value can be any of the following:

585

Chapter 47 ◆ Data File Attributes

1	Sequential `Input`
2	Sequential `Output`
4	`Random`
8	Sequential `Append`
32	`Binary`

When `attribute%` is stated as 2, the `FileAttr()` function returns a value representing the file's handle or access number attributed to it by the Microsoft Windows environment. You can use this handle in conjunction with instructions to the Windows Application Program Interface.

Unformatted Data Input

Visual Basic maintains one function (not a statement, mind you) for the acquisition of data from a file—any file—that may not necessarily be a file in one of the three regular VB formats. This statement can be used to acquire characters from a regular text file and convert those characters into usable data later.

`Input$()` Function

Syntax:

*string$* = Input$(*numchars%*, [#]*channel%*)

The `Input$()` function is used to acquire raw data from a file, the data elements of which, if indeed there are any, are not distinguished from each other in any way that is immediately recognizable by the Visual Basic interpreter. After the data are acquired, it is up to the VB application to interpret the data and find a purpose for them.

The function retrieves *numchars%* number of alphanumeric characters from a data file which has a *channel%* number apportioned to it by the `Open` statement for sequential `Input` or `Binary` access. The

Visual Basic *By* EXAMPLE

current file pointer is moved to the byte following the last one read by `Input$()`. The string is retrieved and assigned to the string variable *string$*. Each byte in the retrieved string is treated as an alphanumeric character that can be converted to a value between 0 and 255 with the `Asc()` function. This function is not available for files opened for `Random` access. The pound sign before *channel%* is optional for this function.

Example

Suppose you have a file selector box that contains a preview line, which shows the first 85 characters of a text file currently being highlighted within the file directory box. Here is a routine that would display the first line:

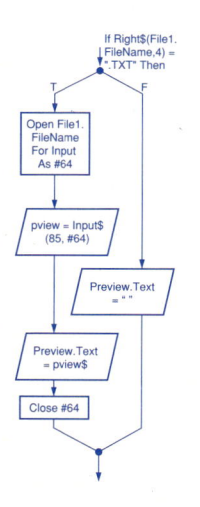

```
If Right$(File1.FileName, 4) = ".TXT" Then
    Open File1.Filename For Input As #64
    pview$ = Input$(85, #64)
    Preview.Text = pview$
    Close #64
Else
    Preview.Text = ""
End If
```

Here is the preceding routine written as pseudocode:

If the file currently being highlighted is a text file, then
    Open that file as a data file, give it channel number 64, and pretend it is a sequential-access input file.
    Retrieve the first 85 characters from channel #64.
    Place those characters within the preview text box.
    Close the channel, because you need no more characters.
Otherwise,
    Clear the preview text box, because you're not reading a conventional text file.
End of condition.

587

Chapter 47 ◆ Data File Attributes

Summary

The `EOF()` function is used as a flag to determine whether the final element of a data file has been read. The `Loc()` function is used to return the file pointer location of the element that has just been read, whereas the `Seek()` function is used to return the file pointer location of the element that is about to be read. The `Seek #` statement is used to position that pointer to a specific location. The file pointer location for a sequential- or binary-access file is a byte address within the data file, whereas the location for a random-access file is a data element number, regardless of the length of that element.

The `LOF()` function is used to return the length in bytes of an open file. The `FreeFile` function is used to return the first available unopened file channel. The `FileAttr()` function is used, for the most part, to determine the file-access mode attributed to an open channel.

The `Input$()` function is used for files that appear to be opened for sequential or binary access, for acquiring a specified number of characters from any file, whether or not it is a formal Visual Basic data file. This function bypasses the standard access techniques for sequential and binary access.

Review Questions

Assume a text file is comprised in its entirety of the following:

```
We hold these truths to be self-evident: that all men
are created equal...
```

Only one space follows the colon, by the way. This file has been opened and given a channel number with the following instruction:

```
Open "CONSTITU.DTA" For Input As #5 Len = 512
```

1. What is the current value returned by `LOF(5)`?

2. What are the contents of `c$` after invoking the instruction `c$ = Input$(7, #5)`?

3. After invoking the preceding instruction, what is the value returned by `Loc(5)`?

4. What is the current value returned by `Seek(5)`?

5. Suppose the instruction `Seek #5, 32` is executed. What are the contents of `c$` now?

6. What are the contents of `c$` after executing the instruction `c$ = Input$(7, #1)`?

48

Formal Records

In this chapter you witness the latest update of the NameForm application that you have continually amended throughout the book to make the application serve its promised purpose. You use random-access techniques to make the application store its data not to arrays in memory as it has been doing, but to a physical data file on disk.

Making NameForm Work

I've added some essential features to NAMEFRM4.FRM, as you can see in Figure 48.1.

Because the form itself has changed so drastically, this chapter contains a listing of the procedures of the application that were changed or added to produce NameForm Mark IV.

591

Chapter 48 ◆ Formal Records

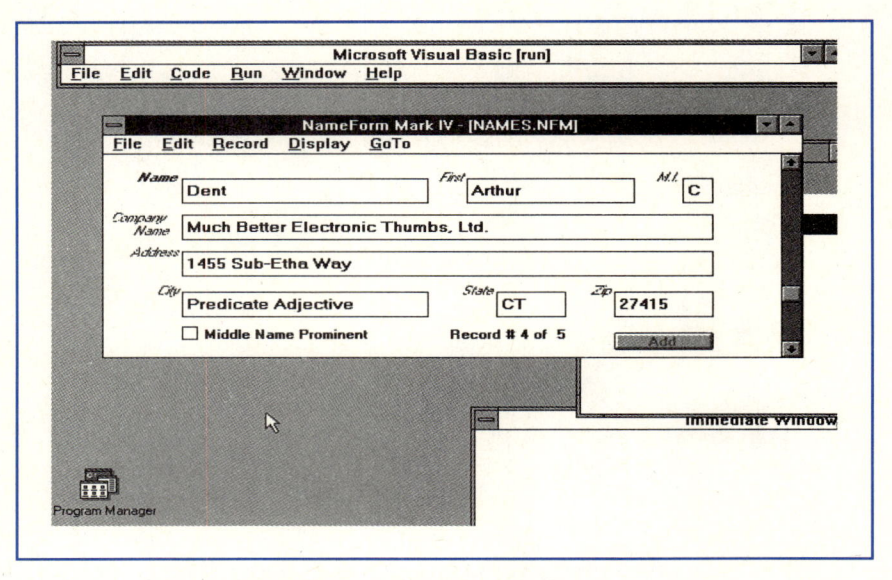

Figure 48.1. NameForm Mark IV, in all its glory.

	PROJECT NAME	CONSTITUENT FILES
NameForm Mark IV Mailing List Manager	NAMEFRM4.MAK	NAMEFRM4.GBL NAMEFRM4.FRM SELECTOR.FRM

NAMEFRM4.GBL Global Module:

```
Option Base 1
Global TargetFile$, cancl As Integer, prmpt$, filename$, pattern$
Type NameRecord
    LastName As String * 30
    FirstName As String * 20
    MidInit As String * 3
    CompanyName As String * 50
    Address As String * 50
    City As String * 20
    State As String * 5
```

```
       Zip As String * 10
       MidProm As Integer
End Type
Global CurRecord As NameRecord
```

    The first `Global` statement here contains variables that you will use for SELECTOR.FRM, the file selector box you created in Chapter 22. Within the type clause is the new record format for each name to be stored in the random-access file. `NameRecord` acts as the formal record type, whereas `CurRecord` acts as the "object" for all the attributes listed within the type clause. Notice the fixed length of all variables declared as type `String` within the `Type` clause.

NAMEFRM4.FRM:

Object type	*Property*	*Setting*
Form	.Left	930
	.Top	1110
	.Width	8655
	.Height	3750
	.FormName	NameForm
	.Caption	NameForm Mark IV
Menu	*Control Name*	*Caption*
	File	&File
	FileOpen	----&Open
	FileSort	----&Sort
	hyphen1	----
	FileSaveMerge	----Save as &Mail Merge
	FileTrim	----&Trim
	Edit	&Edit
	EditCopy	----Cop&y
	EditClear	----Clea&r
	Record	&Record
	RecordInsert	----&Insert
	RecordDelete	----&Delete
	Display	&Display
	DisplayFirst	----&First NameFirst
	DisplayLast	----&Last Name First¦
	GoToRecord	&GoTo

Chapter 48 ◆ Formal Records

Object type	Property	Setting
Text box	.CtlName .Caption	LastName (blank)
Text box	.CtlName .Caption	FirstName (blank)
Text box	.CtlName .Caption	MidInit (blank)
Text box	.CtlName .Caption	CompanyName (blank)
Text box	.CtlName .Caption	Address (blank)
Text box	.CtlName .Caption	City (blank)
Text box	.CtlName .Caption	State (blank)
Text box	.CtlName .Caption	Zip (blank)
Label	.Caption .FontItalic .Alignment	Name True 1 - Right Justify
Label	.Caption .FontBold .FontItalic .Alignment	First False True 1 - Right Justify
Label	.Caption .FontBold .FontItalic .Alignment	M.I. False True 1 - Right Justify
Label	.Caption .FontBold .FontItalic .Alignment	Company Name False True 1 - Right Justify

Object type	Property	Setting
Label	.FontBold	False
	.FontItalic	True
	.Alignment	1 - Right Justify
Label	.Caption	City
	.FontBold	False
	.FontItalic	True
	.Alignment	1 - Right Justify
Label	.Caption	State
	.FontBold	False
	.FontItalic	True
	.Alignment	1 - Right Justify
Label	.Caption	Zip
	.FontBold	False
	.FontItalic	True
	.Alignment	1 - Right Justify
Label	.CtlName	Register
	.Caption	(blank)
	.Alignment	1 - Right Justify
Scroll bar	.CtlName	RecordShown
	.Min	1
	.Max	1
	.LargeChange	10
	.Value	1
Check box	.CtlName	MidName
	.Caption	Middle Name Prominent
	.Value	0
Button	.CtlName	Add
	.Caption	Add
	.Enabled	False

595

Chapter 48 ◆ Formal Records

Declarations Section:

```
Dim RecordNo As Integer, MaxRecord As Integer
Dim sortarray() As Integer
```

Variable `RecordNo` holds the current record number in the sequence stored to disk. `MaxRecord` contains the highest record number in the file. Previously, you dimensioned array variables for 1000 units each; by keeping all the records within a random-access file, you relieve memory of its duty to maintain the record image. Array `sortarray()` keeps the image of the data table in memory, so it can be sorted alphabetically later. I cover that topic in Chapter 49, "Sorting."

```
Sub Form_Load ()
filename$ = "NAMES.NFM"
LoadFile
End Sub
```

The default file to be scanned from disk is called NAMES.NFM. Mind you, you're not loading this file into memory; you're simply loading individual records into the form, one at a time. You use the .NFM extension for NameForm files. This file will be *opened* but not *loaded*. Note the distinction.

```
Sub LoadFile ()
Open filename$ For Random As #1 Len = 190
If LOF(1) > 190 Then
    Do
        Get #1, MaxRecord + 1, CurRecord
        MaxRecord = MaxRecord + 1
    Loop Until CurRecord.FirstName = "~*End" Or MaxRecord >
        LOF(1) / 190
Else
    CurRecord.FirstName = "~*End"
    Put #1, 2, CurRecord
    CurRecord.MidProm = 0
```

```
        CurRecord.FirstName = ""
        Put #1, 1, CurRecord
        MaxRecord = 1
End If
titl$ = "NameForm Mark IV - [" + UCase$(filename$) + "]"
NameForm.Caption = titl$
RecordNo = 1
RecordShown.Max = MaxRecord
RecordShown.Value = 1
If RecordNo < MaxRecord Then
        Add.Enabled = 0
Else
        Add.Enabled = -1
End If
ShowRecord
End Sub
```

You're in the general procedures area now. This is a crucial procedure, so take a look at it in pseudocode:

Start of the **LoadFile** procedure:
Open a file having the name that the user selected from SELECTOR.FRM a moment ago, or whatever some other procedure is passing as a default name. You'll call this a random-access file having a length of 190 bytes per record. If the file doesn't exist yet, create it.
If there appears to be more than one record in this file, then
   Repeat the following until told to stop:
      See if you can grab the record that resides at a location one higher than the one you know so far to be the highest location.
      Add 1 to that highest location tally.
   Repeat the preceding instructions until you reach a dummy record marked ~*End or until the maximum record tally appears to be beyond that which is logically feasible for this record, given its limited length.
Otherwise, because this is obviously a new file,
   Create a dummy first name ~*End.

Save this dummy first name to the physical end of the file, which is record #2.
Clear the middle-name-prominence register.
Clear the dummy first name field.
Save this clean-slate record as the first record of this new file.
Set the logical maximum record number in memory to 1.
End of condition.
Create a new title for this form, containing the current file name of the open file.
Assign this title to the title bar of the form.
Call this the first record number in the file.
Set the scroll bar so that its maximum registerable value is exactly that kept by the logical maximum record tally.
Set the scroll bar slider value to 1.
If the current record number is less than the maximum number, then
    *Disable the **Add** button.*
Otherwise,
    *Enable the **Add** button.*
End of condition.
Branch to the procedure that shows the current record.
End of procedure.

The `Open` statement is found as the first instruction of `SubLoadFile ()`. I placed the instruction here rather than in `Form_Load` because there may be more than one occasion during the run time of the program when a data file will be opened. It is best to make your code reusable whenever possible—such is the purpose of modularization in the first place.

To be honest, this procedure used to be part of `Sub Form_Load ()` until, on second thought, I cut it and pasted it here. Much of programming is accomplished after second thought on the part of the programmer. Of course, after that comes third thought.

One such third thought was the `Add` button, which you didn't see in the earlier chapters. The original incarnation of NameForm had 1000 blank records stored in memory. You could add a record at any location at any time. With Mark IV, I had `MaxRecord` store only the number of records that had been entered into the file, taking into account that the last record in the file would always be a blank record; after filling it in, the next record could be created and made blank. It then occurred to me that there is no way the application can know for sure whether a record is "filled in" completely unless the record is *told*. Thus, I decided to incarnate the `Add` button.

The initial presence of the `Add` button in the form created a problem: Just what does *Add* mean? You already have a menu selection for inserting a record in the midst of a file and scooting the other records one position to the right. To add is therefore not to insert. *Add* can therefore only mean that the currently displayed record must be added to the end of the file. If the scroll bar doesn't show that the file pointer is at the end of the file, however, what purpose does the button serve? It occurred to me then that the `Add` button should be disabled if you're not looking at the final record in the file, thus the presence in `Sub LoadFile ()` of the conditional clause `If RecordNo < MaxRecord Then`....

Now when `Sub LoadFile ()` is first called by `Sub Form_Load ()`, for the first time in the program's history, the file pointer will most certainly be at the end of the file NAMES.NFM, because the only record officially in the file is blank. The `Add` button is therefore enabled. However, `Sub LoadFile ()` will be called throughout the execution of the application, in which case there may be occasions where the button should be disabled by setting its `.Enabled` property to 0.

Placing the End in the Middle

When you save a Visual Basic record to a disk-based data file, you can imagine the process being similar to carving that record in a marble wall. To delete the record carved on the face of the wall, you could deface the record by carving the entire marble face down until all that's left is a blank record. The face on which the record is carved, however, does not go away. You cannot delete a random-access data record and its field in Visual Basic.

Chapter 48 ◆ Formal Records

When the user of the NameForm application deletes a record by selecting **D**elete from the **R**ecord drop-down menu (the procedure for that selection follows later), the contents of all the records following the deleted one are extracted using `Get #1` and rewritten at a location one below the previous location. The record that previously existed one ahead of the deleted record now inhabits the deleted record's space. Variable `MaxRecord` is decremented by one, so for the moment it would appear there is one less record in the table. Suppose, however, that the user were at some later time to reload the data table. The table would appear to contain just as many records as it did before the deletion. This is because the record at the end of the file—the one that should have been axed because its contents moved one location down in sequence—never really goes away. There is no instruction to delete this record. To tell you the truth, there never has been one in standard versions of BASIC. The language has never been considered a database manager.

Now, the way many formal database tables are structured once they are stored to disk, there are often several bytes of structural information at the very beginning regarding the lengths of each record and the mathematical relations between them. I didn't place any structural information about the data at the beginning of the NameForm data file, because this information would constitute a record itself. This record would rest at position 1, which would make the first real record rest at position 2. Explaining to the interpreter that the first record is number 2 in a series takes a modicum of arithmetic; and the more unnecessary compensative arithmetic you can avoid, the better.

Physical records are stored to disk; *logical* records are manipulated in memory.

Instead I had the application write a false record—one whose `.FirstName` is `~*End` and which contains nothing else—at a record location just one past the value of `MaxRecord`. When assessing the length of a data table, you could invoke a formula that takes the number of bytes in the record—`LOF(1)`—and divides that figure by the length of each record—`190`. In fact, I did invoke this formula as a precautionary measure within the `Do-Loop` clause in `Sub LoadFile ()` a while back. The result of this formula is the number of *physical* records within the file. This takes into account, however, all the defaced or deleted records hanging at the end of the file that you don't want any more. By having a dummy ~*End record just after the last *logical* record in the file (and who has a first name like ~*End, anyway?), any process, such as sorting, which assesses the number of records within the open file will know to not look at or beyond the record marked with ~*End. No defaced record will therefore ever be accidentally loaded into the NameForm form.

Variable RecordNo will be used as a pointer to the current record number, or the number of the record that should be displayed. The way you'll use RecordNo in the future, the variable will be set to the record number to be displayed first. Immediately that record will be loaded into the record variable CurRecord. For now, RecordNo should point to record number 1, the first in the sequence. The .Max property of the scroll bar is set so that it cannot scroll past the maximum record number MaxRecord; subsequently, the .Value of the scroll bar is set to 1, again representing the first record. The Add button conditional clause then appears here, enabling the button if the currently shown record is the last in the sequence. The current record can be the first *and* the last, of course, if there's only one record in the file.

From here, control is passed to a procedure ShowRecord:

```
Sub ShowRecord ()
Get #1, RecordNo, CurRecord
Reg$ = "Record #" + Str$(RecordNo) + " of " + Str$(MaxRecord)
Register.Caption = Reg$
LastName.Text = RTrim$(CurRecord.LastName)
FirstName.Text = RTrim$(CurRecord.FirstName)
MidInit.Text = RTrim$(CurRecord.MidInit)
CompanyName.Text = RTrim$(CurRecord.CompanyName)
Address.Text = RTrim$(CurRecord.Address)
City.Text = RTrim$(CurRecord.City)
State.Text = RTrim$(CurRecord.State)
Zip.Text = RTrim$(CurRecord.Zip)
MidName.Value = CurRecord.MidProm
End Sub
```

The first instruction in this sequence is the crucial `Get #1` statement, which retrieves the record numbered `RecordNo` in the sequence to the record variable `CurRecord`. At the bottom of the form is a label called `Register` that now shows not only the current record number, but also the total number of records in the file. The nine elements of the record variable `CurRecord` are each assigned to text box and check box objects within the form. Notice here how record components and graphic objects can share the same name.

Notice for each alphanumeric component of `CurRecord` assigned to a `.Text` box, you used the function `RTrim$()`. Remember in the `Type` clause how you declared certain component variables `As String` with asterisks denoting the fixed length of each string. When a string of characters shorter than this fixed length is assigned to one of these variables, the interpreter fills the rest of the space with space characters. These characters become part of the record. So when that record is redisplayed, those space characters become part of the display. This isn't noticeable at first until you try to edit the name and find that the cursor can be positioned far beyond the end of each element that is redisplayed. This really becomes visible when you select **D**isplay and the envelope form of the current record has lots of extra space in it. I therefore used `RTrim$()` to trim the rightmost spaces from each textual element being placed in a text box—which is the primary purpose of the `RTrim$()` function.

The one check box I've added to the main form, marked `Middle Name Prominent`, is reserved especially for people like F. Lee Bailey, C. Everett Koop, and J. Fred Muggs (arguably a nonperson) who prefer to spell out their middle names and abbreviate their first names. In such instances, you can swap the first and middle names, as in *Lee F. Bailey*, and set the check box. When copying the name and vital information to `Envelope$`, the program will then know to swap the first and middle names.

```
Sub Address_Change ()
CurRecord.Address = Address.Text
End Sub
```

```
Sub City_Change ()
CurRecord.City = City.Text
End Sub

Sub CompanyName_Change ()
CurRecord.CompanyName = CompanyName.Text
End Sub

Sub LastName_Change ()
CurRecord.LastName = LastName.Text
End Sub

Sub MidInit_Change ()
CurRecord.MidInit = MidInit.Text
End Sub

Sub State_Change ()
CurRecord.State = State.Text
End Sub

Sub Zip_Change ()
CurRecord.Zip = Zip.Text
End Sub
```

Each of these procedures is executed after the text box values within the form change. This can happen when a character is typed within the box; so if you're entering a seven-letter surname within graphic object `LastName`, the value of component variable `CurRecord.LastName` would change seven times. There's also this new procedure to consider:

```
Sub MidName_Click ()
CurRecord.MidProm = MidName.Value
End Sub
```

This changes the only value variable within the record variable `CurRecord`.

Chapter 48 ◆ Formal Records

```
Sub Add_Click ()
Put #1, RecordNo, CurRecord
RecordNo = RecordNo + 1
MaxRecord = MaxRecord + 1
ClearForm
CurRecord.FirstName = "~*End"
Put #1, MaxRecord + 1, CurRecord
RecordShown.Max = RecordShown.Max + 1
RecordShown.Value = RecordNo
If RecordNo = MaxRecord Then
    CurRecord.FirstName = ""
    Put #1, RecordNo, CurRecord
End If
ShowRecord
End Sub
```

If the Add button is enabled, you must be entering the last record in the sequence. After clicking this button, the first Put # statement places the record CurRecord at the current RecordNo location. Because this is at the end of the file (otherwise you wouldn't have clicked this button), RecordNo, MaxRecord, and RecordShown.Max (the maximum scroll value) are each incremented. The record just added replaces—or more descriptively, *overwrites*—the dummy ~*End record. The next order of business is to add a new dummy record to the location just following the logical end of the file. The scroll bar is then manually moved to the end of the file at RecordNo, which was just incremented.

Toward the end, Sub Add_Click () places a call to Sub ClearForm():

```
Sub ClearForm ()
FirstName.Text = ""
LastName.Text = ""
MidInit.Text = ""
CompanyName.Text = ""
Address.Text = ""
City.Text = ""
State.Text = ""
Zip.Text = ""
MidName.Value = 0
End Sub
```

The operation of this procedure is nearly as self-evident as its purpose. All the text boxes are set to null values and the check box is unchecked.

```
Sub RecordShown_Change ()
Put #1, RecordNo, CurRecord
RecordNo = RecordShown.Value
If RecordNo < MaxRecord Then
    Add.Enabled = 0
Else
    Add.Enabled = -1
End If
ShowRecord
End Sub
```

The other way a record is officially stored to a file is by changing the value of the scroll box. Remember that the data file now acts in place of memory, so if you cleared the form or replaced its contents before you stored the current contents to disk, the record just typed would be lost. For that matter, no records with nonblank contents would even exist for the data file, because every time the scroll bar was moved, the record's contents would be overwritten before the record could be saved. The displayed record could only be overwritten by an existing one, which must be blank anyway because a nonblank record could not be saved. I could go on with this forever, but it would only fill our hearts with despair and pessimism. The solution to the problem is to save the record to disk each time a scroll bar change is registered, before the current record numbers are updated.

After the `Put #1` statement is executed, the new record number is obtained from the current value of the scroll bar. Again, the `.Enabled` property of the `Add` button is determined by whether the last record in the sequence is chosen.

In keeping with a new tradition started by Microsoft, I've given menu selections names that are concatenations of the menu category and command—for instance, `FileOpen`. There are a few exceptions here, such as when a control name would be too long or would be the same as a Visual Basic reserved word. Here are some of the menu procedures for NameForm Mark IV:

```
Sub FileOpen_Click ()
prmpt$ = "Choose a file to open:"
pattern$ = "*.nfm"
Selector.Show 1
filename$ = targetfile$
If cancl = 1 Then Exit Sub
cancl = 0
Close #1
LoadFile
End Sub
```

This procedure executes if the user selects **O**pen from the **F**ile menu. The way this particular program works, a file is *opened* but it is not *saved,* the reason being that records are saved to an open file along the way. To create a new file, you *open* that file as if it already existed. Thus, you don't need a New... selection within the NameForm Mark IV menu.

This procedure basically operates the file selector box. The way SELECTOR.FRM works now, you can pass a special prompt to it through the global variable `prmpt$`, and you can pass the default file extension for your files—in this case, *.NFM—to the selector through the global variable `pattern$`. After the Selector's modal dialog completes execution, it returns two global variables—`targetfile$` (the name of the chosen file) and `cancl`—to the main form. If the value of `cancl` is 1 then evidently the user clicked the Selector's Cancel button, so the file-opening operation aborts. If the user clicked OK, the existing random-access file closes and the call is made to procedure `Sub LoadFile ()`, which I listed earlier.

```
Sub FileSaveMerge_Click ()
prmpt$ = "Name of mail merge file:"
pattern$ = "*.mrg"
Selector.Show 1
If cancl = 1 Then Exit Sub
filename$ = targetfile$
Open filename$ For Output As #2
```

```
For ConvRec = 1 To MaxRecord
    Get #1, ConvRec, CurRecord
    Write #2, RTrim$(CurRecord.LastName),
        RTrim$(CurRecord.FirstName), RTrim$(CurRecord.MidInit),
        RTrim$(CurRecord.CompanyName), RTrim$(CurRecord.Address),
        RTrim$(CurRecord.City), RTrim$(CurRecord.State),
        RTrim$(CurRecord.Zip), CurRecord.MidProm
Next ConvRec
Close #2
ShowRecord
End Sub
```

As discussed in Chapter 45, "Sequential Access," Visual Basic maintains an alternate command for saving sequential-access data elements to a file that can be interpretable by word processors with mail merge features. Selecting Save from the File menu as Mail Merge allows the user to create a second file that mirrors the current one, although its format is a sequential mail merge file rather than a VB random-access file.

The Selector is used again to obtain the file name, and this time the user is still allowed to enter into the `Filename:` box a name that does not yet exist in the directory. If the chosen file does exist, in this case invoking `Open #2...As Output` overrides its existing contents entirely. Both channels #1 and #2 are now open simultaneously, so you can `Get` data from one file and `Write` it to the other. The immediate problem with this is that record variables declared with a `Type` clause may not be addressed within sequential-access statements. It therefore follows that every component variable to `CurRecord` must be written to the sequential file individually, although they can be expressed within a list, unlike with the `Put #` statement.

In `FileSaveMerge_Click ()`, a loop clause is initiated from the beginning to the last record in a random-access file. Within the loop, a record is obtained, and its constituent variables are trimmed of their trailing spaces and then written to channel #2 using `Write #`. Notice I didn't affect the value of `RecordNo`, so after the translation operation is complete, the current record is again displayed (if for some reason it ever left), and I've returned to business as usual.

Chapter 48 ◆ Formal Records

```
Sub GoToRecord_Click ()
recno$ = InputBox$("Go to which record number?", "Go To. . .")
RecordNo = Val(recno$)
RecordShown.Value = RecordNo
ShowRecord
End Sub
```

Selecting the `GoTo` category is an alternate method for changing the currently displayed record number. Using this procedure, you can easily type the new number into an input box. This value is then assigned to `RecordNo`, the program manually updates the scroll bar, and calls `ShowRecord`, which brings this new record to the screen.

```
Sub EditCopy_Click ()
c$ = Envelope$(RecordNo, 1)
Clipboard.SetText c$
End Sub
```

One other useful purpose for this program is for copying a single name to the clipboard so that you can paste it to another application—for instance, a word processor, perhaps for the top of business correspondence. Selecting **Copy** from the **Edit** menu places the text of the current record within the clipboard, first by placing a call to the new `Function` procedure:

```
Function Envelope$ (rec As Integer, order As Integer)
Get #1, rec, CurRecord
If Asc(Left$(CurRecord.MidInit, 1)) <> 0 Then
    Separator$ = " " + RTrim$(CurRecord.MidInit) + " "
Else
    Separator$ = " "
End If
If order = 1 Then
    If MidName.Value = 0 Then
        FullName$ = RTrim$(CurRecord.FirstName) +
          Separator$ + RTrim$(CurRecord.LastName)
```

```
        Else
            FullName$ = RTrim$(CurRecord.MidInit) + " " +
                RTrim$(CurRecord.FirstName) + " " +
                RTrim$(CurRecord.LastName)
        End If
    Else
        If MidName.Value = 0 Then
            FullName$ = RTrim$(CurRecord.LastName) +
                ", " + RTrim$(CurRecord.FirstName) + Separator$
        Else
            FullName$ = RTrim$(CurRecord.LastName) +
                ", " + Separator$ + RTrim$(CurRecord.FirstName)
        End If
    End If
    WorkPlace$ = RTrim$(CurRecord.CompanyName)
    StreetAddress$ = RTrim$(CurRecord.Address)
    Residence$ = RTrim$(CurRecord.City) + ", " +
      RTrim$(CurRecord.State) + " " + RTrim$(CurRecord.Zip)
    Next_Line$ = Chr$(13) + Chr$(10)
    Envelope$ = FullName$ + Next_Line$ + WorkPlace$ +
      Next_Line$ + StreetAddress$ + Next_Line$ + Residence$
End Function
```

Here's the preceding procedure in pseudocode:

Function for generating a name for the envelope:
Get from channel 1 the specified record number, and call that the current record.
If the middle initial field has a real character in it, then
　Make the separator string that middle initial sandwiched between two spaces.
Otherwise,
　Make the separator string just a space.
End of condition.
If the last name order is to fall last, then
　If the middle name prominence check box is not checked, then
　　The full name is a concatenation of the first name, the separator, and the last name in that order.

Chapter 48 ◆ Formal Records

> Otherwise,
> > The full name is concatenation of the middle initial, a space, the first name, another space, and the last name in that order.
> End of this condition.
> However, if the last name comes first,
> > If the middle name prominence check box is not checked, then
> > > The full name is a concatenation of the last name, a comma and space, the first name, and the separator in that order.
> > Otherwise,
> > > The full name is a concatenation of the last name, a comma and space, the separator, and the first name in that order.
> > End of this condition.
> End of the major condition.
> Acquire the workplace from the appropriate field.
> Acquire the address from the appropriate field.
> The residence is a concatenation of the city, a comma and space, the state, two spaces, and the ZIP code.
> The "next line" string is a carriage return and line feed joined together.
> The full envelope string is a concatenation of the full name, "next line," the workplace, "next line," the street address, "next line," and the residence.
> End of function.

The `Envelope$()` function creates a long, concatenated string comprised of the contents of all the fields of a designated record `rec`, combined as they might appear typed on an envelope. This record `rec` may be the current record or one not currently shown. You may remember the general structure of this function from seeing its forebear `Sub ShowEnvelope ()` in NameForm Mark I.

The first conditional clause checks to see what are the contents of the `Middle Name` field. In many cases, this field will be left blank. If it is blank, its numeric value will be considered to be 0. Zero just happens to be the terminating character for alphanumeric strings for some Windows and Visual Basic functions; thus if you added a 0 to the middle of the long, concatenated string, Windows might mistake that string as ending in the middle. Thus I created a string `Separator$`, which will have meaningful, nonzero contents even if the middle name field is left blank.

One of the parameters this function takes is `order`, which determines whether the last name is to come first (0) with a comma separating it and the first name, or whether the last name is to fall last (1). Another conditional clause has been added so that F. Lee Bailey's feelings won't be hurt by receiving mail addressed to Lee F. Bailey. If `MidProm.Value` is set to 1 in the form (if it's checked), the clause puts `Separator$` in the middle of the name; otherwise, it puts `Separator$` at the beginning of the name. The conditional clause surrounding that one places the last name last or first, depending on the value of `order`.

The carriage-return (`Chr$(13)`) and line-feed (`Chr$(10)`) characters are used here so that the person's name and address don't appear all on one line when pasted to the other application. After you tack the rest of the fields onto the end, the result is `Envelope$`, which is passed back to the calling body of the application.

```
Sub DisplayFirst_Click ()
c$ = Envelope$(RecordNo, 1)
MsgBox c$, 0, "Preview"
End Sub

Sub DisplayLast_Click ()
c$ = Envelope$(RecordNo, 0)
MsgBox c$, 0, "Preview"
End Sub
```

There are now two different **D**isplay preview selections, depending on whether you want to see the first or last name first. Selecting the **D**isplay category allows the user to preview the currently displayed record pointed to by `RecordNo` as it would appear typed on an envelope, before it's copied to the clipboard. The 0 in the `MsgBox` instruction means you need nothing else within the message box but an OK button.

```
Sub EditClear_Click ()
ClearForm
End Sub
```

You can manually call the procedure for clearing the current form by selecting Clear from the Edit menu. Remember that the event procedures for each text box, such as `Sub Address_Change ()`, execute whenever the contents of the form change as a result of any action, even if that action is made by the program and not the user. Therefore, clearing the form causes all the `_Change` event procedures to execute in turn. So by clearing the screen, you clear the current record.

```
Sub RecordDelete_Click ()
If RecordNo < MaxRecord Then
    For mve = RecordNo To MaxRecord
        Get #1, mve + 1, CurRecord
        Put #1, mve, CurRecord
    Next mve
End If
ClearForm
If RecordNo = MaxRecord Then
    RecordNo = RecordNo - 1
End If
If MaxRecord > 1 Then
    MaxRecord = MaxRecord - 1
    RecordShown.Max = RecordShown.Max - 1
Else
    Put #1, 1, CurRecord
End If
ShowRecord
End Sub
```

Finally, there are the relatively ingenious procedures for deleting a record from a data file and inserting a record into the middle of it. In random access, you can `Get #` and `Put #` records using the same open channel. With sequential access, by contrast, an accessed file is locked into either being read or written to. The `For-Next` loop clause counts every record numbered between the current `RecordNo` and the last logical `MaxRecord` and keeps that count within variable `mve`. The loop then takes the record just ahead of the counter location using `Get #1` and uses it to overwrite the record at the current location using `Put #1`. Remember, this includes the dummy `~*End` record. At the first iteration of this loop, the current record saved to disk is overwritten by the record that follows it in the sequence. Temporarily, there are two copies of the same record next to each other, until the next iteration of the loop, when the record that follows overrides the older copy.

At the last iteration of the loop, there are temporarily two copies of the final physical record. Because this is the dummy ~*End record, there's no problem. The final conditional clause makes the current record blank only if there's only one record in the file anyway, and that's the one that was deleted. Otherwise, the maximum logical record tally and current record number are both decremented.

```
Sub RecordInsert_Click ()
For mve = MaxRecord + 1 To RecordNo Step -1
    Get #1, mve, CurRecord
    Put #1, mve + 1, CurRecord
Next mve
ClearForm
Put #1, RecordNo, CurRecord
MaxRecord = MaxRecord + 1
RecordShown.Max = RecordShown.Max + 1
End Sub
```

Select Insert from the Record menu when you want to place a new record—at the moment, one that hasn't been typed in—at the location currently registered by the scroll bar. Remember, when the user types data, it's automatically considered to be part of the current record, and not some future record. If you programmed an insertion routine to add a record having contents that appeared within the form, at the point currently indicated by the scroll bar you would have two copies of the same record. You see, when the current record is moved to make way for the new one, the current form contents represent the record that was moved. If you have the current form contents also represent the record that is being inserted, you have two copies of the same record.

For this procedure, you have a loop clause that is to some extent the reverse of the one you programmed for the Delete routine. Here variable mve counts backward from the absolute last record in the file (including the dummy record) to the current record number. The record pointed to by mve is then acquired from the file using Get #1, and then is copied to the location just following the current location using Put #1. On the first iteration of this loop, one record is added to the end of the file: a copy of the final record. After the loop clause is completed, the form is cleared and stored as the current record. You have therefore made space, literally, for a new record.

```
Sub FileTrim_Click    ()
Open "~temp.fil" For Random As #2 Len = 190
plc = 1
tmp = RecordNo
Do
    Get #1, plc, CurRecord
    Put #2, plc, CurRecord
Loop Until CurRecord.FirstName = "~*End"
Close #2, #1
Kill filename$
Name "~temp.fil" As filename$
Open filename$ For Random As #1 Len = 190
RecordNo = tmp
ShowRecord
End Sub
```

Finally, this procedure was added as the only way to get rid of the trailing blank or dummy records from a data file containing numerous deletions. A second shadow file is opened called *~temp.fil* and is given channel #2. Each record from #1 is copied to #2 in exactly the same location, until the dummy ~*End is reached and the Do-Loop clause ceases. At that time, both channels #2 and #1 are closed; the file once belonging to #2 now has exactly as many records as it should, without any blank trailing records.

Next, the old #1 data file is deleted from the disk using the Kill instruction. The Name instruction then renames *~temp.fil* to whatever file name was being used previously, and then that file name is reopened as #1. Channel #1 now points to a new file; after this procedure is exited, however, the rest of the application never knows the difference.

Summary

This is the second time in this book that you've seen the NameForm application listed; this time, you've seen a more mature form of the program. It is one thing to program a working Visual Basic application, but the point at which the programmer decides the job of programming an application is complete may be purely arbitrary. There are always more and more new ideas that can be implemented in code. Perhaps this is why in the realm of commercial software there are so many packaged applications with skyrocketing version numbers.

Review Questions

1. When a record is "erased" from a random-access data file, how many fewer records are there now than there were before?

2. Why is it inconvenient to place a data file descriptor at the beginning of a random-access data file, even though such construction makes sense for a normal database?

3. Why is there no Save button or menu selection in the NameForm application?

49

Sorting

In this chapter you take an excursion into one of the more fun aspects of computing, if you share my enthusiasm about procedural logic. Career programmers appreciate the beauty of *sorting algorithms,* or mathematical procedures with which you can sort an array of unsorted contents. Yet when these algorithms are put on paper, with all their numbers, letters, and arrows, attempting to grasp the concepts that govern all this symbolism generally makes the newcomer feel like he's jumped aboard a train moving at full speed. This feeling is, in fact, close to reality, in that to understand procedural algebra, you have to learn to be fast.

In this chapter, you see a Visual Basic application that uses three sorting algorithms and demonstrates how the sorting process takes place. Unfortunately, this book can show you only still images, so there is a measure of comprehension that cannot be imparted here by reading alone. However, the application presented herein, after you type it and run it from the interpreter, gives you *moving patterns* depicting the sorting process at work. Such pictures are worth about three or four chapters full of words, because you can see the gears and wheels of the algorithmic mechanism at work.

Chapter 49 ◆ Sorting

Programming as Locomotion

Figure 49.1 depicts The Sort Contest, in which three sorting algorithms are pitted against each other in a time trial. The program creates three arrays of 100 elements, each of which contains a random integer value between 1 and 100. Each element is unique, so for this particular program, no two array elements have the same value.

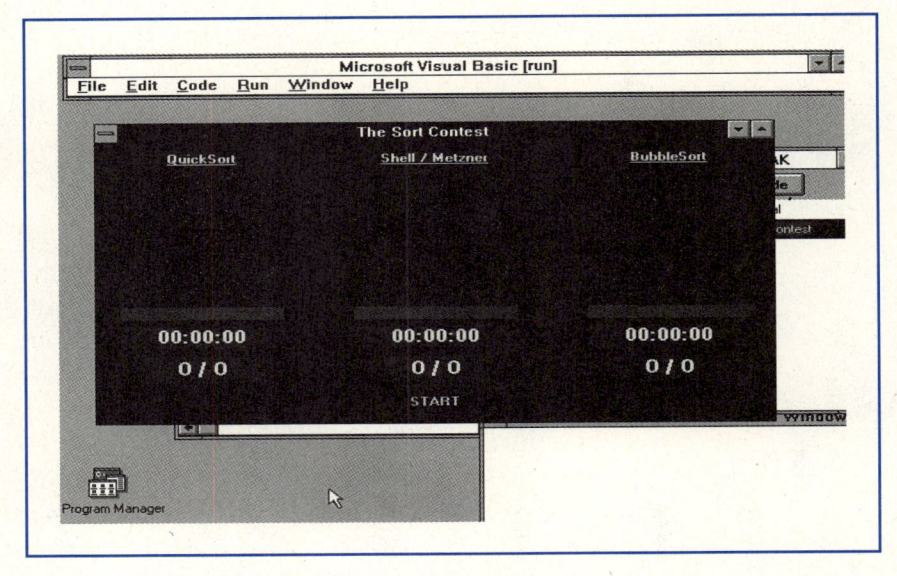

Figure 49.1. The Sort Contest playing field.

An *algorithm* is a real-world process that can be simulated using procedural algebra.

The three black blocks within the form are graphs of the array's contents. The y-axis represents the array elements, whereas the x-axis represents the value stored within each element—from left to right, from 1 to 100. After these three arrays are sorted, their values equal 1, 2, 3, and so on. But perhaps more importantly, the array points plotted as scattered dots within these blocks will gradually come together to form a straight diagonal line from the upper-left corner to the lower-right corner, like grains of sand falling into the folds of an origami sculpture. How the "grains" form this single-file line tells the story of each sorting algorithm. An *algorithm* is any real-world process having inherent operators that can be encoded as numbers and processes that can be simulated using procedural algebra.

The three algorithms in the contest are QuickSort, Shell/Metzner, and BubbleSort. QuickSort is so named for its (alleged) speed. As you'll see, the name should perhaps be reconsidered, although the algorithm has unchallenged efficiency. The Shell/Metzner sort was named for its two originators, and not for the "shell game" passing sequence. BubbleSort is named for the pattern it forms, "bubbling" high-valued elements toward the bottom of the array. You will see how the algorithm earned its name.

The idea for this chapter came from two articles from two old (*very* old in this business) back issues of *Creative Computing* magazine. I give credit to Howard Kaplon's May 1983 article, "A Comparison of Sorts, Revisited," and David G. Schwaegler's July 1983 article, "Low-Res Sort Display." In those days, *low-res* referred to the lowest graphic resolution of the Apple II—which was literally 40 x 40 pixels. Ponder working in that resolution for a moment, especially as you examine the following multitude of numbers:

The Sort Contest

PROJECT NAME: SORTCONT.MAK

CONSTITUENT FILES: SORTCONT.FRM

Object type	Property	Setting
Form	.Left	390
	.Top	1005
	.Width	8400
	.Height	4740
	.FormName	SortContest
	.Caption	The Sort Contest
	.BorderStyle	1 - Fixed Single
	.BackColor	&H00400000&

Control array	Property	Setting
Picture boxes	.CtlName	SortPlot
	.BackColor	&H00000000&
	.AutoRedraw	False
	.Index	0

Chapter 49 ◆ Sorting

Control array	Property	Setting
	.CtlName	SortPlot
	.Index	1
	.CtlName	SortPlot
	.Index	2
Labels	.CtlName	Sorted
	.Caption	SORTED
	.Alignment	2 - Centered
	.BackColor	&00000080&
	.ForeColor	&000000FF&
	.Index	0
	.CtlName	Sorted
	.Caption	SORTED
	.Index	1
	.CtlName	Sorted
	.Caption	SORTED
	.Index	2
Labels	.CtlName	Clock
	.Caption	00:00:00
	.Alignment	2 - Centered
	.BackColor	&H00C00000&
	.ForeColor	&H0000FFFF&
	.FontName	Tms Rmn
	.FontSize	13.5
	.Index	0
	.Index	1
	.Index	2

620

Visual Basic *By* EXAMPLE

Control array	Property	Setting
Labels	.CtlName	Iterations
	.Caption	0 / 0
	.Alignment	2 - Centered
	.BackColor	&H00FF0000&
	.ForeColor	&H0000FFFF&
	.FontSize	13.5
	.Index	0
	.Index	1
	.Index	2
Label	.Caption	QuickSort
	.FontUnderline	True
	.Alignment	2 - Centered
	.BackColor	&H00800000&
	.ForeColor	&H0000FFFF&
Label	.Caption	Shell / Metzner
	.FontUnderline	True
	.Alignment	2 - Centered
	.BackColor	&H00800000&
	.ForeColor	&H0000FFFF&
Label	.Caption	BubbleSort
	.FontUnderline	True
	.Alignment	2 - Centered
	.BackColor	&H00800000&
	.ForeColor	&H0000FFFF&
Label	.CtlName	Start
	.Caption	START
	.Alignment	2 - Centered
	.BackColor	&H00000000&
	.ForeColor	&H0080FFFF&

General Declarations Area:

```
Dim unit(100, 2) As Integer
Dim StartTime As Double
Dim oldx1 As Integer, oldy1 As Integer, oldx2 As Integer,
    oldy2 As Integer
Dim newx1 As Integer, newy1 As Integer, newx2 As Integer,
    newy2 As Integer
Dim done As Integer
Dim comp(2), swic(2)
Dim p(100) As Integer, w(100) As Integer
```

The set of three arrays is called `unit()`. The second dimension of the array refers to the three panels, which are themselves indexed from 0 to 2. `StartTime` will be a double-precision value used in keeping the elapsed time of each sort. The two sets of integer variables `old`n and `new`n are used in plotting over the old element points in each graph and plotting new element points. The `old` series will remove the points that have been moved or swapped by the algorithm, whereas the `new` series will be used in plotting their new positions after the positions of two points in the array have been exchanged.

Array variables `comp()` and `swic()` keep track of how many comparisons and how many element-pair swaps or switches have been made for each algorithm, again numbered 0 to 2. Array variables `p()` and `w()` are reserved especially for the QuickSort algorithm, which uses them to develop subarrays. QuickSort sorts small portions of the large array first. To develop those small portions, it needs something to hold the smaller arrays.

```
Sub Form_Load ()
SortContest.Show
Randomize
For panel = 0 To 2
    SortPlot(panel).Scale (1, 1)-(100, 100)
Next panel
SortContest.Refresh
RackEmUp
ShowPlots
End Sub
```

When the main form is loaded into the workspace, it is immediately displayed. Otherwise, the user would wonder why nothing seemed to happen for a minute or so. It takes a little while for the program to seed each array, and the VB interpreter tends to treat its graphical duties as less important than its mathematical ones. Thus, the seeding of the arrays actually prevents the form from being shown for a little while, unless you invoke the instruction `SortContest.Show`. The instruction `SortContest.Refresh` enables you to display the other graphical elements in the form, before the interpreter goes about its business of seeding the arrays.

The plotting scale for each panel is set by the `.Scale` method within the loop clause. Procedure `Sub RackEmUp ()` is the procedure that seeds the three arrays; `Sub ShowPlots ()` displays the initial patterns for these arrays within the three blocks.

```
Sub RackEmUp ()
For cell = 1 To 100
MakeCell:
    vl = Int(Rnd(1) * 100) + 1
    For chk = 1 To cell - 1
        If vl = unit(chk, 1) Then GoTo MakeCell
    Next chk
    For rack = 0 To 2
        unit(cell, rack) = vl
    Next rack
Next cell
End Sub
```

I intend to make each element within each array unique, so that no two values match, and so that the final diagonal line will be perfectly straight and not flawed. This way, you won't miss out on the full experience. Each of the three cells is seeded with the same set of values, in the interest of fairness. Variable `vl` draws a random number between 1 and 100. This number is then checked against those previously allocated within one of the arrays (they're all identical, remember) to see if there's a matching pair. If there is, the procedure jumps back to the instruction following the label `MakeCell:` and draws another number. This flip-flop process continues until an original number finally is drawn. When that happens, all three of the arrays are seeded with that value. This process is iterated 100 times until the arrays are full.

Chapter 49 ◆ Sorting

```
Sub ShowPlots ()
For lin = 1 To 100
    For panel = 0 To 2
        SortPlot(panel).PSet (unit(lin, panel), lin),
            QBColor(11)
    Next panel
Next lin
End Sub
```

This procedure plots all the points within the three blocks. Notice that `SortPlot` is a control array of picture boxes, so it bears a subscript on its back, in the form of `(panel)`. The two loops count for the y-axes of each chart first—from 1 to 100—and for each of the three panels second-indexed from 0 to 2. Each point is plotted using the `.PSet` method. Within the parentheses, the `unit()` value acts as the x-axis parameter, whereas the line count variable `lin` acts as the y-axis parameter.

```
Sub Start_Click ()
If done = 1 Then
    ResetPlot
End If
qsort
ssort
bsort
done = 1
End Sub
```

There's only one event procedure for this application, concerning whether the user clicks the `Start` label. Labels in Visual Basic have all the necessary properties of buttons; they just don't have the beveling and animation that Windows gives buttons. In certain cases where, for instance, grey might clash with the interior design of the rest of your form, you might prefer to use a label rather than a formal button for use as a control.

```
Sub ResetPlot ()
For panel = 0 To 2
    SortPlot(panel).Line (1, 1)-(100, 100), QBColor(0), BF
    SortPlot(panel).Refresh
```

```
    comp(panel) = 0
    swic(panel) = 0
Next panel
RackEmUp
ShowPlots
End Sub
```

I added this procedure as one of those "on third thought" additions to the program. What it does is clear and reset the panels, so the sort procedures can be run a second or third time after the first set of iterations is completed.

Dive! Dive! Dive!

You now enter the heart of the program: the sort algorithms themselves. The QuickSort algorithm is executed first in the application, but because it is the most difficult to explain—and by far the longest—I save it until last.

The BubbleSort Algorithm

I start with the easiest algorithm to explain: BubbleSort.

```
Sub bsort ()
StartTime = Now
Dim j As Integer, k As Integer, l As Integer, t As Integer
For l = 1 to 100
    j = l
    For k = j + 1 To 100
        comp(2) = comp(2) + 1
        If unit(k, 2) <= unit(j, 2) Then
            j = k
        End If
    Next k
    If l <> j Then
        swic(2) = swic(2) + 1
        t = unit(j, 2)
        oldx1 = unit(j, 2)
        oldy1 = j
```

```
                unit(j, 2) = unit(l, 2)
                oldx2 = unit(l, 2)
                oldy2 = l
                newx1 = unit(j, 2)
                newy1 = j
                unit(l, 2) = t
                newx2 = unit(l, 2)
                newy2 = l
                ShowTime 2
                ShowIter 2
                OverPlot 2
                NewPlot 2
            End If
        Next l
        ShowTime 2
        ShowIter 2
        Light 2
    End Sub
```

The BubbleSort algorithm is deceptively simple. I know it doesn't look that way now, but give me a few paragraphs and it will. BubbleSort starts with the first element in the array. It considers this—represented by variable l—the element to currently sort. The only real job BubbleSort has is to find the lowest-valued element from the remainder of the array. So a comparison location variable j is created, and its initial value is set to precisely that of l. Variable k is used in a loop clause that counts from the element of the array just following j to the last element: 100. The comp(2) instruction is like a referee for the sake of the contest; you'll see such comp instructions taking note of when a comparison operation is made.

The loop clause counts to see if there's any value lower than that currently held within the unit() array at position j. If there is, j is set to the location of that lowest value; however, the loop isn't exited yet. Instead, it continues to the end to see if there's an even lower value. The result of this loop is that j contains the address of the lowest value in the remainder of the array. Note how the mechanism works here: Before the For-Next begins, the value of j is set to the value of l. Within the loop, if the conditional clause finds there's a lower value in the kth unit than there is in the jth unit, j is made equal to k. After the loop clause, j is tested to see if it still equals k—in other words, to see if the conditional clause was activated. If the two values are no longer equivalent, the conditional clause must have found a lower value, now pointed to by j. This value is swapped with the one to which 1 currently points; so the lowest possible comparison address contains the lowest possible value. Variable 1 is then incremented, and all the elements behind 1 are considered *sorted*. The comparison process then continues with the new element pointed to by 1. You can say 1 acts as a sort of zipper—which leads one to wonder why this wasn't named *ZipperSort*.

The result of the swap between the array elements at locations 1 and j is that element j must now contain a higher value than it did. As the sorting process continues, the values that 1 has not touched toward the end of the array tend to grow higher in value. The higher values are said to *bubble* toward the high end, which is how this sort algorithm gets its name.

Figure 49.2 is a comic strip version of BubbleSort as a series of descriptive panels. Here we have an array of 10 elements rather than 100 elements.

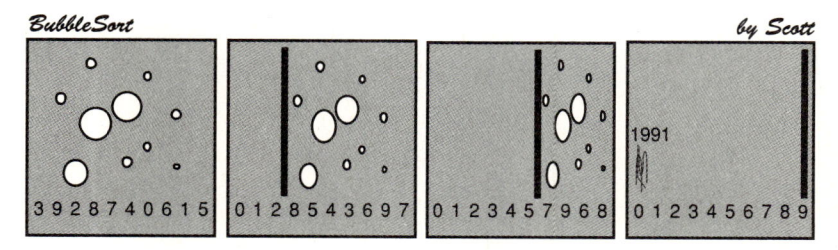

Figure 49.2. BubbleSort's debut comic strip, issue #1: Sure to be a collector's item.

The Shell/Metzner Sort Algorithm

The next algorithm on the discussion list is Shell/Metzner. It is not the fastest, nor is it the least complex, although it certainly may be the most elegant:

Chapter 49 ◆ Sorting

```
Sub ssort ()
Dim m As Integer, j As Integer, i As Integer, t As Integer
StartTime = Now
m = 100
While m > 0
    m = m \ 2
    For i = m To 99
        For j = (i - m + 1) To 1 Step -m
            comp(1) = comp(1) + 1
            If unit(j, 1) <= unit(j + m, 1) Then Exit For
            swic(1) = swic(1) + 1
            t = unit(j, 1)
            oldx1 = unit(j, 1)
            oldy1 = j
            unit(j, 1) = unit(j + m, 1)
            newx1 = unit(j, 1)
            newy1 = j
            oldx2 = unit(j + m, 1)
            oldy2 = j + m
            unit(j + m, 1) = t
            newx2 = unit(j + m, 1)
            newy2 = j + m
            ShowTime 1
            ShowIter 1
            OverPlot 1
            NewPlot 1
        Next j
    Next i
Wend
ShowTime 1
ShowIter 1
Light 1
End Sub
```

Here, variable `j` is again a pointer to the value in this array that is being tested, whereas `i` is a pointer to the value to which the `j`th array value is being compared. Variable `m` acts as a sort of *spanner*, which is used to continually divide the array in half, forming smaller and smaller segments. The Shell/Metzner algorithm swaps values between these segments, so that the lower-ordered segments contain the lower values. As `m` is continually divided by 2 and the segment size is halved, the values in each segment are compared to those in all the segments before it. If a lower-ordered segment contains a higher value than that in the higher-ordered segment, the two values are swapped. The new positions for those values may not be their final resting places when the array is entirely sorted, but the point is that *they're closer than they were before.* With the segment size becoming continually smaller and the distance between swapped elements becoming narrower, each element will continue to be nudged closer and closer to where it eventually belongs. When m cannot be halved any more, the array must be sorted.

Figure 49.3 shows the Shell/Metzner process at work on a 10-value array. In Panel A, the array is divided into two five-unit segments, and the values in the latter segment are compared to those in the former. Variable m contains the segment size, which is currently 5. Variable i will count all the elements from the beginning of the second segment to the end of the array; this is the key variable of the primary For-Next loop in the preceding procedure. Variable j acts as a pointer to all elements within the array that are *n* segment-sizes (multiples of m) behind the element to which i points. If the former segment element i points to is higher in value than the latter segment element j points to—regardless of what those values actually are—the two values are swapped.

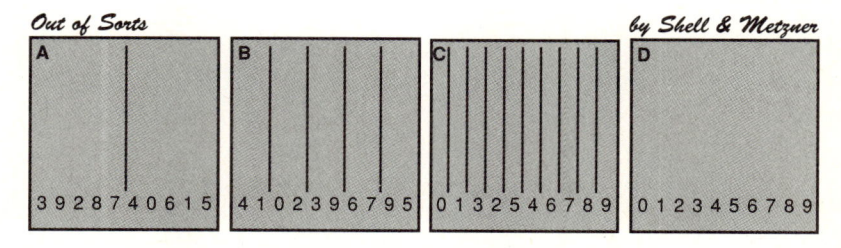

Out of Sorts *by Shell & Metzner*

A	B	C	D
3 9 2 8 7 4 0 6 1 5	4 1 0 2 3 9 6 7 9 5	0 1 3 2 5 4 6 7 8 9	0 1 2 3 4 5 6 7 8 9

Figure 49.3. A sorting algorithm that relies solely on hindsight.

In Panel B, the array is divided into four two-unit segments. The swapping process continues as the distance between swaps becomes continually narrower. In Panel C, there are 10 single-unit segments. By this time, there are generally few swaps necessary. By Panel D, the array is sorted.

Chapter 49 ◆ Sorting

The QuickSort Algorithm

The QuickSort algorithm is by no means quick to explain. It consists of a complex series of several procedures that repeat less often, rather than a simpler series of fewer procedures that repeat more often. This is a relatively difficult concept to grasp; in fact, perhaps our art department might supply us with an "expanding brain" icon to use in such instances as this. Because the algorithm's incarnation in Visual Basic is so large, I'll take the listing of Sub qsort () in small segments:
Part 1:

```
Sub qsort ()
Dim i As Integer, j As Integer, b As Integer, l As Integer,
    t As Integer, r As Integer, d As Integer
StartTime = Now
k = 1
p(k) = 1
w(k) = 100
l = 1
d = 1
r = 100
```

A *stack* is a list of data elements stored from the bottom up and read from the top down.

The array being sorted by the QuickSort algorithm is continually broken into subarrays—which are like the segments in the Shell/Metzner algorithm, except that these subarrays are sorted independently from the rest of the array. The upper and lower bounds of each subarray are maintained within array variables p() and w(), respectively. These array variables don't contain the subarrays themselves, merely their starting and ending locations with respect to the main array. Borrowing a term from assembly language, we say that these two array variables define the *stack*, or the ongoing list of smaller arrays to be independently bubble-sorted. The bubble sort takes place only when the subarray has been divided and subdivided until it is conveniently small.

Figure 49.4 depicts the QuickSort technique with a 25-element array. Panel A of the figure shows the algorithm starting with element 1, which for now is the leftmost element in the array. Variables l and r are placemarkers, with r currently pointing to the rightmost element of the array. These two placemarkers are scooted toward the middle of the array as the algorithm progresses, like the plates of a trash compactor drawing closed. Variable d is a register depicting whether the direction of the comparison (the definition of which I provide momentarily) is to the left (–1) or the right (1).

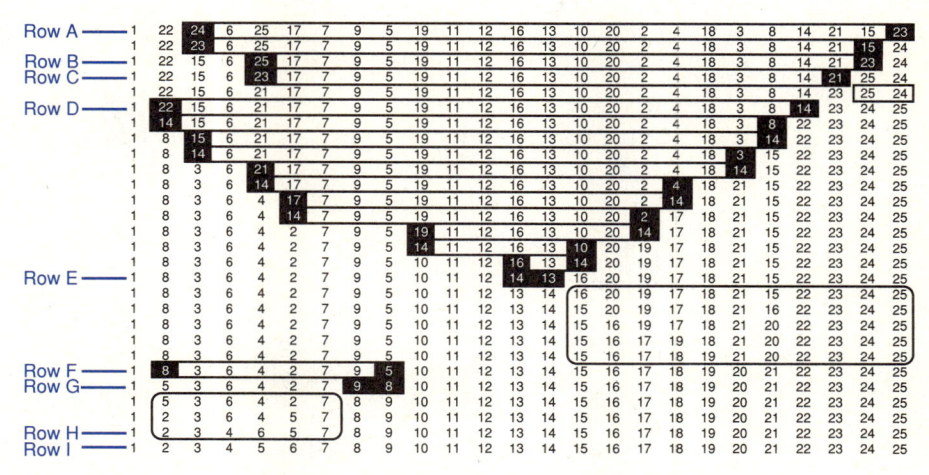

Figure 49.4. The long, drawn-out story of QuickSort.

QuickSort looks first to the right of element 1 to see if there's any value lower than that of 1. The element being compared to 1 is j. Row B shows QuickSort counting backwards by one from the rightmost element r until it finds a lower value than 1. When it finds that value, QuickSort swaps the values of element 1 and element j, and then makes variable r point to where the element that was 1 now resides. The rightmost "compactor" has been moved toward the center. You also know for a fact that every element to the right of r is greater in value than r, so you've already made significant progress.

Row C shows QuickSort now looking to the left of element r to see if there's a value higher than that of r. The element being compared to r is i. In Row C, you can see QuickSort is counting forward now by one from element 1, which is for the moment the leftmost element in the array. When that higher value is found, QuickSort swaps that value with that of r, and then makes variable 1 point to the element that was r. The leftmost compactor is now actively moving toward the center, and every element that falls before element 1 is now lower in value than 1.

At Row D, QuickSort looks to the right of element l again, counting backward by one from where it last left element r until it finds a value that is lower than l. This value is then swapped with l, and r is set to point to the element that was l. This flip-flop continues until the point when compactors collide. This happens at Row E. When r and l are next to each other, every element behind l is lower in value than that of l, and every element ahead of r is higher in value than that of r. Mind you, the array isn't sorted yet, but it's certainly far closer to being sorted with only a few swaps having taken place.

Variables l and r now divide the array into two segments. You can cast the left segment aside for the moment and concentrate on the right one. Variables l and r now divide the array into two segments. You can cast the left segment aside for the moment and concentrate on the right one. The segment to the right of the collision point undergoes a BubbleSort. Once that is done, at Row F, l and r are set to the left and right locations of the unsorted part of the leftmost segment, and the back-and-forth swapping process starts all over again. At Row G, l and r have collided again, dividing this subarray into two smaller segments. The segment to the right is already sorted, so the BubbleSort process works on the small segment to the left. By Row I, the entire 25-element array is sorted.

Here's how I implemented this concept in Visual Basic:
Part 2:

```
Do
toploop:
    If r - l < 9 Then GoTo bubsort
    i = l
    j = r
    While j > i
        comp(0) = comp(0) + 1
        If unit(i, 0) > unit(j, 0) Then
            swic(0) = swic(0) + 1
            t = unit(j, 0)
            oldx1 = unit(j, 0)
            oldy1 = j
            unit(j, 0) = unit(i, 0)
            oldx2 = unit(i, 0)
```

```
            oldy2 = i
            newx1 = unit(j, 0)
            newy1 = j
            unit(i, 0) = t
            newx2 = unit(i, 0)
            newy2 = i
            OverPlot 0
            NewPlot 0
            ShowTime 0
            ShowIter 0
            d = -d
        End If
        If d = -1 Then
            j = j - 1
        Else
            i = i + 1
        End If
    Wend
```

The main part of the procedure is implemented in the form of a `Do-Loop` clause, which is exited when no more subarrays are left to be sorted. The algorithm keeps a running tally `k` of how many array portions have yet to be sorted. When the value of `k` reaches 0, the loop is exited.

The first `If-Then` conditional statement checks to see if the distance between the right and left boundaries `r` and `l` is less than 9. If it is, execution branches to the bubble sort routine. Assuming you haven't branched, comparison element pointers `i` and `j` are set to the left and right boundary pointer values for the time being.

Within the `Do-Loop` clause is a subordinate `While-Wend` loop that will execute only as long as the right element `i` is to the right (naturally) of the left element `j`. The preceding comparison clause tests to see if the value of the left element, held within `unit(i, 0)`, is greater than the value of the right element within `unit(j, 0)`. If it is, a swap is made using `t` as a temporary variable, as you've seen in the two earlier algorithms.

> **NOTE:** BASIC aficionados: There is no SWAP instruction in Visual Basic.

After the swap is made, four calls are placed to routines that update the display. Following those calls, the direction register d is negated with the instruction d = -d. This is because after the swap is completed, QuickSort looks the other direction, behind the swap, as explained earlier. If d = -1 (left), then after the instruction, d = 1 (right). Following the end of the conditional clause, this directional variable d determines whether the right variable j is decremented or the left variable i is incremented. The same unit(i, 0) > unit(j, 0) comparison can be made repetitively within the While-Wend loop. The only mechanical difference concerns the direction of the comparison, and that difference is handled by being able to negate variable d.

Part 3:

```
j = j + 1
k = k + 1
If i - 1 < r - j Then
    p(k) = j
    w(k) = r
    r = i
Else
    p(k) = l
    w(k) = i
    l = j
End If
d = -d
GoTo toploop
```

After the loop clause is completed, the "compactor doors" will have collided. The job of QuickSort now is to divide the main array into a subarray, starting the process again with new left and right boundaries. Variable j is incremented so that you don't have a situation in which the same comparison is performed twice. One is added to the tally variable k, meaning you have one more subarray to evaluate. The comparison expression

```
i - 1 < r - j
```

determines whether you should now look left (true) or right (false). The true side of the clause sets up the boundaries for right-side evaluation, whereas the false side sets up the boundaries for left-side evaluation. The directional register d is negated yet again, and a direct branch is made to the label `toploop` where the `While-Wend` loop begins again.

Part 4:

```
bubsort:
    If r - l > 0 Then
        For i = l To r
            b = i
            For j = b + 1 To r
                comp(0) = comp(0) + 1
                If unit(j, 0) <= unit(b, 0) Then b = j
            Next j
            If i <> b Then
                swic(0) = swic(0) + 1
                t = unit(b, 0)
                oldx1 = unit(b, 0)
                oldy1 = b
                unit(b, 0) = unit(i, 0)
                oldx2 = unit(i, 0)
                oldy2 = i
                newx1 = unit(b, 0)
                newy1 = b
                unit(i, 0) = t
                newx2 = unit(i, 0)
                newy2 = i
                OverPlot 0
                NewPlot 0
                ShowTime 0
                ShowIter 0
            End If
        Next i
    End If
    l = p(k)
    r = w(k)
    k = k - 1
Loop Until k = 0
ShowTime 0
ShowIter 0
Light 0
End Sub
```

You may recognize the BubbleSort procedure by now. For safety's sake, the procedure executes only if the distance between

635

Chapter 49 ◆ Sorting

boundaries r and l is greater than 0. Each BubbleSort array for this particular incarnation of the QuickSort algorithm can be as many as eight elements wide, so there's really not much for this segment of the program to do. Toward the end of the BubbleSort section, the left and right boundaries for the next sort section are reset to the next values from the stack arrays p() and w(), and one is subtracted from the tally of subarrays to be sorted, which is variable k.

The Do-Loop clause exits when this tally k equals 0—in other words, when there are no more subarrays to sort. The display is updated one last time, and the procedure ends.

Finally, there are a few "housekeeping" procedures to be considered, reference to which was made in each of the three sort algorithm procedures:

```
Sub ShowTime (panel As Integer)
elapsed# = Now - StartTime
tim$ = Format$(elapsed#, "hh:mm:ss")
Clock(panel).Caption = tim$
Clock(panel).Refresh
End Sub

Sub ShowIter (panel As Integer)
disp$ = LTrim$(Str$(comp(panel))) + " / " +
   LTrim$(Str$(swic(panel)))
Iterations(panel).Caption = disp$
Iterations(panel).Refresh
End Sub

Sub OverPlot (panel As Integer)
SortPlot(panel).PSet (oldx1, oldy1), QBColor(0)
SortPlot(panel).PSet (oldx2, oldy2), QBColor(0)
End Sub

Sub NewPlot (panel As Integer)
SortPlot(panel).PSet (newx1, newy1), QBColor(15)
SortPlot(panel).PSet (newx2, newy2), QBColor(15)
SortPlot(panel).PSet (newx1, newy1), QBColor(11)
SortPlot(panel).PSet (newx2, newy2), QBColor(11)
End Sub

Sub Light (panel As Integer)
Sorted(panel).ForeColor = QBColor(14)
```

```
Sorted(panel).BackColor = QBColor(12)
Sorted(panel).Refresh
End Sub
```

Sub `ShowTime ()` interrupts the sort procedure every so often to show the user the elapsed time; similarly, Sub `ShowIter ()` shows the user the number of iterations executed thus far. In order for a point within one of the panels to move from place to place, Sub `OverPlot ()` erases the old point (plots a black dot over it), and Sub `NewPlot ()` places it in its new position on the panel. Sub `Light ()` (pardon the physics pun) is executed at the end of the sort, to show that the sort is in fact complete.

Allow me a measure of poetic license to give you a preview of what you'll see when you run this application. After you click the long, black START button (actually a textual label working in place of a button), the QuickSort panel will start first. If you've ever cooked homemade rock candy, you're familiar with taking a pan of boiling sugar-water, hanging a string down into the pan, and setting it off the fire. As the water cools, the sugar forms hard crystals onto the string, which are about finger-size by the next morning, when the mixture has entirely cooled.

In your mind, scatter several grains of sugar within a black, square pan, and say that by clicking START you've set the pan off the fire, letting the mixture cool. As you watch, groups of sugar crystals will collect themselves in square-shaped regions. Like the way ice crystals form over a cold pond, you'll notice one large square region dividing itself slowly into two smaller square regions side-by-side, like diamonds pulling themselves apart from each other. When a region has become too small to bisect itself, it zips itself closed into a tight line. Remember, the perfectly tight diagonal line is an indicator that the array is completely sorted—the first pixel is at the first position, the second pixel just below it is at the second position, the third is at the third, and so on. So perhaps QuickSort's is the panel that most closely resembles a biochemical process.

The Shell/Metzner sort panel is next. For the most part, it looks like a baker folding bread dough into a roll, layer by layer. Remember that Shell/Metzner maintains a spanning variable m that helps determine the distance between each swap and is halved with each reexecution of the loop. You'll actually see m narrowed as the clump of sugar grains becomes tighter and tighter. At the last, from top to bottom this collected bunch of grains—almost in a straight line now—is pinched together cluster by cluster, as if by a finger and a thumb.

Finally, there's the large-scale form of the BubbleSort, the no-holds-barred, down-and-dirty, let's-get-this-puppy-sorted algorithm. As stated earlier, I think you could rename this procedure *ZipperSort* because the algorithm, in one step, zips this diagonal line closed from top to bottom.

On the display beneath each panel is a series of numbers, one of which obviously is the time it took your computer to perform this sort routine. Keep in mind that your computer's application wasn't sorting this array every moment while the program was running. It was also keeping track of the operating system, monitoring all the input devices to see if you're trying to tell the computer something, and first and foremost, updating the display as well as this clock.

Two numbers appear below the clock, separated by a slash mark. The number on the left shows the total amount of comparisons performed so far during the algorithm's run, whereas the number on the right shows the number of comparisons resulting in swaps. These are the values that the referee variables `comp()` and `swic()` tallied, respectively. Having the algorithm keep track of these things naturally increases the time it takes to perform the sort. A lot of factors in this contest slow down the sorts themselves. What is important here is the proportion between the final times, so that you can judge the relative speed of one algorithm against the others.

Algorithmic Logic Versus Archie Bunker

In this chapter, I've been discussing the simulation of real-world processes, which is, after all, the purpose of algorithms. It may not seem that the procedures demonstrated here are performed in the real world in precisely the same manner. You may not employ a spanning variable, for instance, when sorting the various books on your bookshelf. Yet for any process that you perform regularly and repetitively that you think you can do in your sleep, your mind has probably worked out a standard operating procedure that makes the process simple enough that you don't have to think much about it. This may be a matter more for psychologists than programmers, but it is likely that if you were to write this process, it would be mathematical to some degree.

When a repetitive real-world process becomes so mathematical as to be logically encodable, then what code is necessarily the *right* code? In pondering this question, I'm reminded—would you believe it?—of a sketch from the American situation comedy *All in the Family,* in which Archie Bunker attempts to explain to his son-in-law Michael how "real" people don their shoes and socks. The argument begins when Michael puts a sock and a shoe on one foot, then a sock and a shoe on the other. Archie insists this is to a great degree un-American, and that the proper procedure is to put on both socks first. Michael argues that it doesn't matter what process you choose as long as you get yourself dressed. Archie responds that it matters because one way is *right* and the other isn't.

You can laugh at this because in the back of your mind, you probably can substitute Archie and his shoe closet for someone within your own work environment who makes similar arguments on behalf of more complex, but just as easily encodable, procedures. Perhaps you've proposed similar arguments yourself. My first job was in a public library sorting books most of the day, which perhaps is why I can relate so well to sorting algorithms. In hindsight, I realize that after a few years of sorting books without concentrating solely on the fine art of sorting books, one procedure I had adopted was like the QuickSort algorithm. If the books were already laid out on a table or set on a shelf, I would start at the left side, take one book that was out of alphabetical order, place it in relative order someplace to the right, then take a book in the immediate vicinity of the one I just placed and move it someplace to the left. I found this swapping procedure enjoyable, and I probably realized at some time during my tenure that this procedure could be explained logically as a program. When a new library aide was being trained, I would try to give her all the sorting techniques I had worked out. On a few occasions I would hear in response, "What does it matter *how* you do something, as long as the job is done well in the end?"

The original intent of the *Creative Computing* articles I mentioned earlier was to determine what constituted efficiency in sorting: simplicity or complexity. At the time (1983), the experts seemed to conclude that complexity led to efficiency, as demonstrated by sort times that showed the QuickSort algorithm as being far faster

Chapter 49 ◆ Sorting

than the BubbleSort, a much simpler technique. The reason cited for this was that the BubbleSort performed far more comparisons than did the QuickSort, and thus took much more time. Yet as the contest application provided here will attest, the BubbleSort algorithm now seems to be much faster than the QuickSort.

The reason for this, I originally concluded, was that the BubbleSort algorithm performed far more comparisons, was more repetitive, and therefore took more time. To my surprise, however, I was wrong; the real reason was something of an illusion created by the staging of the contest itself. Calls to the Windows screen input/output functions consume time; the QuickSort procedure, by virtue of its construction, places more I/O calls than does the BubbleSort procedure. Once you've become thoroughly enamored with the graphical part of this procedure, try this simple test: From each of the three sort procedures, remove the following cluster of four lines:

```
ShowTime 2
ShowIter 2
OverPlot 2
NewPlot 2
```

Note that this cluster appears in the QuickSort procedure twice. What happens as a result is that the sort procedures still work, although you only see the timed results without actually witnessing the arrays being sorted. You learn then that the QuickSort procedure actually does live up to its name.

What this little revelation taught me was that efficiency in computing really depends upon the coordination of those elements we choose to call efficient. Raw ingenuity has proved here that the most efficient way of working can easily become the *least* efficient if another process, with which it works in conjunction, slows it down. Suppose these sort elements represented records in a random-access data file, and instead of I/O calls to the screen I was placing calls to that file. The QuickSort algorithm—arguably the most efficient of the three—may have been the slowest for my particular application, depending on how I implemented it. In other words, a sock and a shoe and a sock and a shoe may not be the most efficient method after all *if* we're trying to coordinate that method with, say, eating breakfast or shaving. The interrelationship of efficient processes does not necessarily result in an efficient process.

BubbleSorting and the Real World

One legitimate purpose for the BubbleSort algorithm can be found by rewriting it for the NameForm application and having it sort the names in the data file by last name first, first name second, and so on. Here's how it looks:

```
Sub FileSort_Click ()
Dim j As Integer, k As Integer, l As Integer, t As Integer,
    seed As Integer
ReDim sortarray(MaxRecord)
tmp = RecordNo
RecordNo = MaxRecord
If Asc(Left$(LastName.Text, 1)) > 0 Then
    Put #1, RecordNo, CurRecord
End If
For seed = 1 To MaxRecord
    sortarray(seed) = seed
Next seed
Do
    l = l + 1
    If l = MaxRecord Then Exit Do
    j = l
    For k = j + 1 To MaxRecord - 1
        If Envelope$(k, 0) <= Envelope$(j, 0) Then
            j = k
        End If
    Next k
    If l <> j Then
        t = sortarray(j)
        sortarray(j) = sortarray(l)
        sortarray(l) = t
    End If
Loop
Open "~temp.fil" For Random As #2 Len = 190
For replac = 1 To MaxRecord - 1
    Get #1, sortarray(replac), CurRecord
    Put #2, replac, CurRecord
```

```
Next replac
Close #2, #1
Kill filename$
Name "~temp.fil" As filename$
Open filename$ For Random As #1 Len = 190
RecordNo = sortarray(tmp)
ShowRecord
End Sub
```

Visual Basic is quite kind in the way it allows you to evaluate the "value" of such things as words and even sentences. The "value" of such alphanumeric strings, in this case, is the relative position of each string in the alphabet. This value isn't really representable numerically, but if a$ = "Aaron" and b$ = "Zenith", the expression a$ < b$ would evaluate logically to be true (–1), because *Aaron* falls below *Zenith* alphabetically.

The result of this form of alphabetic expression is that you can add the BubbleSort routine to the NameForm application without a great deal of reorganization. I have created an array variable sortarray() that contains the number of each record in the current data file, listed in the order in which each record will appear in the sorted data file. At the beginning of the procedure, sortarray() is seeded with an integer value equal to its own subscript; thus sortarray(1) = 1, sortarray(2) = 2, and so on. You never load every data record from the file into memory all at once. Instead you invoke the comparison

```
If Envelope$(k, 0) <= Envelope$(j, 0)
```

which places two calls to the procedure Function Envelope$(). This way, only two records need to be loaded into memory at any one time.

The mechanism of the sort proceeds as if it were sorting numbers, although the comparison is made between the contents of the two Envelope$ strings. The 0 parameter here causes Function Envelope$() to return a concatenation of all the elements of the form, with the last name of the person placed first, followed by the first name and middle initial (or middle initial and first name if the box is so checked). The swap is performed not between the names, but between the numbers that represent them within sortarray(). After the `Do-Loop` clause is completed, `sortarray()` acts as a list of all the name swaps that will take place now within the physical data file.

You may remember from the procedure `Sub FileTrim ()` in Chapter 48 how a second data file was created using the `Open` statement, and only the meaningful records were copied into that file. Both files were then closed. Then the original file was deleted, the newly created file was given the file name of the old file, and the new file was reopened. After the procedure was exited, the rest of the application would never know a switch had taken place. A similar process is found at the end of `Sub FileSort_Click ()`. This time, the file *~temp.fil* is created and given channel #2. The loop being counted by variable `replac` goes through the `sortarray()` list and retrieves from the existing record the data file found at the current place within the array list. So, if `sortarray(1) = 23`, the first record retrieved will be the 23rd. Each record is then written to the second data file in sequence, with the end result being that the second file is a sorted form of the first one. Both files are then closed with the `Close` statement, and the first file is deleted. The second file is then given the name of the first one. The file that was being viewed at the time `Sub FileSort_Click ()` was called is retrieved from its new position in the `sortarray()` and is given to procedure `Sub ShowRecord ()` for redisplay.

Summary

To best understand the mechanics of an algorithm, you should consider how your own mind naturally *simplifies*—not complicates—the real-world process that the algorithm is designed to simulate. A repetitive task that you perform in your everyday life is something that you may even say you don't think about while you're doing it. Yet what may actually be happening is that your brain is conjuring the most logical way for you to perform this task with relatively little attention being paid to it by you.

Mathematics is a creation of human beings, not an element found in nature. Yet when human processes are simplified so that they can be explained or encoded, the method behind those processes becomes mathematical in nature. It therefore follows that the more mathematical a process is, the simpler it is. To give the more logical portion of your everyday work task to the computer to perform and to have the computer expedite your work in turn is how you *automate* that task. It should be your objective as a programmer to automate existing tasks, not to create new ones unless those new processes give the user more insight into the nature of his work, or can be used as recreation.

Review Questions

1. The Shell/Metzner sort algorithm assumes that when its "viewing window" variable m can no longer be divided evenly in half, the array must be sorted. How can the algorithm be so sure?

2. Why is the BubbleSort algorithm so crucial to the success of the QuickSort algorithm, within which it plays a role?

Part XI

The Operating System

Devices and Directories

In this chapter you learn about the instructions of the Visual Basic vocabulary that parallel to some extent many of the instructions used in MS-DOS. You also study some of the formal properties that Visual Basic attributes to file names and directories, using information supplied to VB by DOS through Windows.

Dust off Your Hard-Sector Disk Drives

The first brand of mass-market microcomputers to support an optional floppy drive was the Apple II; Stephen Wozniak was codesigner of the first "Disk II" drives. The second such brand was the TRS-80 Model I Level II—assuming the owner of that computer was rich enough to afford at least 16K of RAM and an adaptor called the Expansion Interface. Floppy disk drives in the year 1979, you see, were considered *expansions*. Microsoft wrote the first BASIC interpreters for the Apple II. The company also codeveloped both Disk Basic and the TRSDOS operating system with Tandy.

Chapter 50 ◆ Devices and Directories

Microsoft borrowed from BASIC inventors Kemeny and Kurtz the idea of having the command line of the computer act as both BASIC interpreter and operating system command line. Back in 1979, Microsoft developed a list of terms for TRSDOS called the *system command library.* Many of these terms survive today as part of MS-DOS; others that did not survive have managed to hold on to life, would you believe, as part of Visual Basic.

Three disk directory-related VB instructions with direct parallels in MS-DOS are ChDir, MkDir, and RmDir.

ChDir   Statement

Syntax:

ChDir *directory$*

The ChDir statement changes the currently active DOS directory path to *directory$*, provided that the string is a validly interpretable MS-DOS device directory no longer than 128 characters.

MkDir   Statement

Syntax:

MkDir *directory$*

The MkDir statement creates an MS-DOS directory or subdirectory and renders its name as *directory$*. Should *directory$* not contain a device identifier, then the device to contain the directory is assumed to be the currently active storage device. If *directory$* has multiple tiers, all subdirectories, with the exception of the final one in the list, are presumed to already exist. MkDir can be used only to add one new directory tier on top of the existing one.

Visual Basic *By*
EXAMPLE

RmDir   Statement

Syntax:

RmDir *directory$*

The RmDir statement removes an MS-DOS directory or subdirectory from the device that is either stated or implied within *directory$*. RmDir can be used only to remove a subdirectory one tier above that of the currently active MS-DOS directory path. The directory is assumed to be empty; if it isn't, it cannot be deleted.

In MS-DOS, to change devices from one identifier to another, you type the identifier letter followed by a colon. In Visual Basic, the lack of a keyword would violate the command structure, so Microsoft has added the ChDrive statement.

ChDrive   Statement

Syntax:

ChDrive *device$*

The ChDrive statement changes the currently active MS-DOS storage device to the one referred to in *device$*. This string must be exactly two characters long and must contain the device identifier letter followed by a colon.

To determine what the active MS-DOS subdirectory is—because Visual Basic does not have a command prompt per se—you are provided with a function.

649

Chapter 50 ◆ Devices and Directories

CurDir$() Function

Syntax:

*directory$* = CurDir$[(*device$*)]

The CurDir$ returns a currently active MS-DOS directory path, as *directory$*. If *device$* is specified, the function will return the last-used directory path for the specified device, whether or not the device is recognized by MS-DOS as the current drive. If *device$* is omitted, the function will return the current directory for the current drive or device.

In Chapter 22, I introduced the SELECTOR.FRM file selector, which contained Visual Basic's special provisions for a device, path, and file directory. I've used this form in a few applications since then. Within it is a file list box called File1, which shows just the file names and extensions of all the current files for the specified directory, indicated to the immediate left of the file box within a directory path list box called Dir1.

MS-DOS maintains four *attributes* for each file in its system, which describe four aspects of that file as well as DOS can for 20th century technology. These very aspects can be applied by Visual Basic as properties of the file list box, so that the box can have the capability of showing otherwise invisible files or files with particular qualities assigned to them by DOS. You can address them from the DOS command line by using the ATTRIB command. I discuss the supported properties in the following paragraphs.

File.Normal Property

The .Normal property for a file list box is set to true (−1) by default, enabling the list to display the files that do not have special MS-DOS attributes. When this property is set to false (0), only those files that have at least one of the four special properties attributed to them by DOS will be displayed within the file list box.

File.Hidden **Property**

When set to true (−1), the .Hidden property of a list box enables it to display files that were manually attributed as hidden using the MS-DOS ATTRIB command, and that would not otherwise be displayed in a normal directory listing.

File.ReadOnly **Property**

When set to true (−1), the .ReadOnly property of a list box enables it to display files that are designated within MS-DOS as unchangeable or undeletable.

File.System **Property**

When set to true (−1), the .System property of a list box enables it to display any files within a root directory list belonging to the operating system. For most recent editions of Microsoft MS-DOS, IO.SYS and MSDOS.SYS qualify as system files. These files are written to a disk when it is formatted using the FORMAT command with the /S option.

File.Archive **Property**

When set to true (−1), the .Archive property of a list box enables it to display any files with archive bits recognized by MS-DOS as set. The archive bit is generally reserved for use by the BACKUP and RESTORE utilities of MS-DOS, for them to determine which files previously have been backed up.

As a frequent DOS user, you probably already understand the general principles governing these instructions. Rather than concentrate on the construction of DOS, I spend the next few pages reconstructing the SELECTOR.FRM reusable file selector form, using the keywords described previously. The Selector, as you know, behaves as a sort of dialog box; but as an added enhancement to this form, I demonstrate how to give this dialog box its own subordinate dialog box. Figure 50.1 shows the revised Selector in its

Chapter 50 ◆ Devices and Directories

design state. Note how a message appears to be obstructed by the path and file list boxes. This is part of the secret of manual dialog box creation.

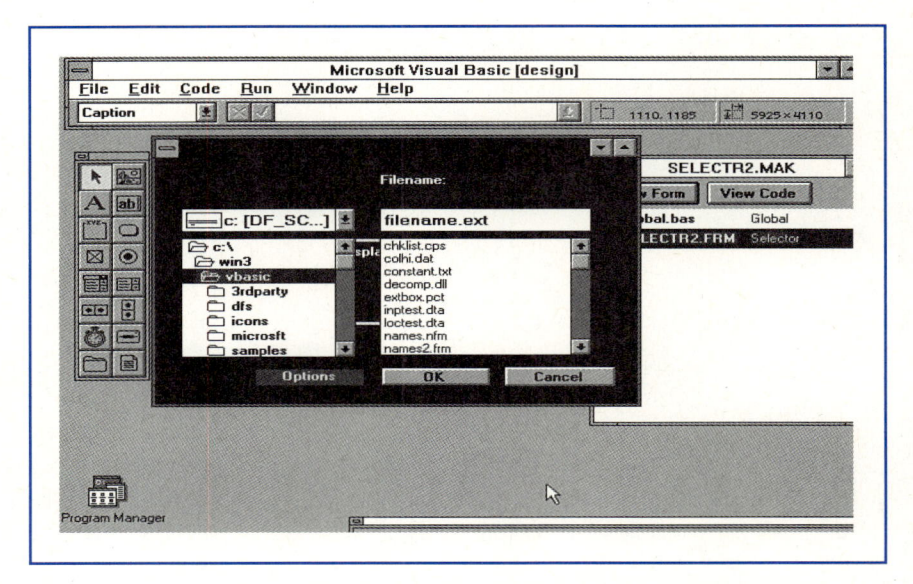

Figure 50.1. The Selector Mark II, conspiring to cover evidence.

	PROJECT NAME	CONSTITUENT FILES
The Selector, Mark II	SELECTR2.MAK	SELECTR2.FRM

Object type	Property	Setting
Form	.Left	1110
	.Top	1170
	.Width	5925
	.Height	4125
	.FormName	Selector
	.Caption	(blank)
	.BorderStyle'	3 - Fixed Double
	.BackColor	&H00400000&

Visual Basic *By* EXAMPLE

Object type	Property	Setting
Drive list box	.CtlName	Drive1
	.FontSize	9.75
Path list box	.CtlName	Dir1
File list box	.CtlName	File1
	.FontBold	False
Text box	.CtlName	Filename
	.FontSize	9.75
	.ForeColor	&H00800000&
	.BorderStyle	1 - Fixed Single
Text box	.CtlName	Prompt
	.BackColor	&H00C00000&
	.ForeColor	&H00FFFFFF&
Picture box	.CtlName	OptPanel
	.BackColor	&H0000FFFF&
	.Enabled	False
	.Visible	False
Frame	.CtlName	OptFrame
	.Caption	File Display Options
	.BackColor	&H00800000&
	.ForeColor	&H00FFFFFF&
Label	.CtlName	Archive
	.Caption	Archive
	.FontBold	False
	.BackColor	&H00800000&
	.ForeColor	&H00FFFF80&
Label	.CtlName	Hidden
	.Caption	Hidden
	.FontBold	False
	.BackColor	&H00800000&
	.ForeColor	&H00FFFF80&

Chapter 50 ◆ Devices and Directories

Object type	Property	Setting
Label	.CtlName	Normal
	.Caption	Normal
	.FontBold	False
	.BackColor	&H00800000&
	.ForeColor	&H00FFFF80&
Label	.CtlName	ReadOnly
	.Caption	Read Only
	.FontBold	False
	.BackColor	&H00800000&
	.ForeColor	&H00FFFF80&
Label	.CtlName	Systm
	.Caption	System
	.FontBold	False
	.BackColor	&H00800000&
	.ForeColor	&H00FFFF80&
Button	.CtlName	OKOpt
	.Caption	OK
	.FontBold	False
	.BackColor	&H00800000&
Button	.CtlName	OK
	.Caption	OK
	.Default	True
	.BackColor	&H00800000&
Button	.CtlName	Cancel
	.Caption	Cancel
	.Cancel	True
	.BackColor	&H00800000&
Label	.CtlName	Options
	.Caption	Options
	.BackColor	&H000000FF&
	.ForeColor	&H0000FFFF&
	.Alignment	2 - Centered

General Declarations Area:

```
Dim arc As Integer, hid As Integer, nor As Integer,
    rdo As Integer, sys As Integer
```

These form-level variables will contain the settings for the five DOS file attributes, generally set by means of the DOS ATTRIB command.

```
Sub Form_Load ()
File1.pattern = pattern$
Filename.Text = File1.pattern
Dir1.Path = CurDir$
cancl = 0
If prmpt$ = "" Then
    Prompt.Caption = "Filename:"
Else
    Prompt.Caption = prmpt$
End If
If optout = 1 Then
    Options.Enabled = 0
    Options.Visible = 0
End If
nor = -1
arc = (extras And 1) > 0
hid = (extras And 2) > 0
rdo = (extras And 4) > 0
sys = (extras And 8) > 0
Normal.FontBold = nor
Normal.ForeColor = QBColor(15)
If arc Then
    Archive.FontBold = arc
    Archive.ForeColor = QBColor(15)
End If
If hid Then
    Hidden.FontBold = hid
    Hidden.ForeColor = QBColor(15)
End If
If rdo Then
    ReadOnly.FontBold = rdo
    ReadOnly.ForeColor = QBColor(15)
End If
```

Chapter 50 ◆ Devices and Directories

```
If sys Then
    Systm.FontBold = sys
    Systm.ForeColor = QBColor(15)
End If
End Sub
```

Here's skeletal pseudocode for this procedure:

Procedure awaiting the form to be loaded:
Assign the global file pattern as the pattern for this selector.
Assign this pattern temporarily as the selected filename.
Set the search path to the current DOS subdirectory.
Reset the cancel flag.
If no prompt has been given the selector, then
  Make the prompt "Filename:"
Otherwise,
  Make the prompt the contents of the global prompt string.
End of condition.
If the options are not to be seen now, then
  Disable the options subwindow controls.
  Make this subwindow invisible.
End of condition.
Set the normal flag to true.
Set the next four attributes relative to whether the extras value, paired logically with the bitwise place assigned each attribute, is greater than 0.
Set the "Normal" font to bold if nor is –1.
Make the "Normal" font brighter.
As for all the other attributes, if they are shown to exist, then
  Set the font where they are listed to bold.
  Make their font color brighter white.
End of conditions.
End of procedure.

The new version of the Selector receives its input from four global variables as well as the `CurDir$` function, written here without parentheses in order to obtain the currently active DOS directory. The global variables are supplied to SELECTR2.FRM by the larger application that includes it in its .MAK project file. Variable `pattern$`

contains the search pattern for each file name in the list, which can include wild-card characters such as `*` and `?`. An instructional message is sent to the Selector as `prmpt$`. That message is displayed in the label area that currently reads `Filename:`. If `prmpt$` has not been set in advance, this is what the label will continue to read. Variable `optout` is a flag that tells the Selector whether to display a special red button marked `Options`, which is displayed by default.

> The term *bitwise* refers to any method of interpreting numbers or values using the binary system.

Variable `extras` is the first one you've created that operates in a *bitwise* fashion. This variable contains four pieces of true or false information, as its lowermost or *least significant* four bits. Each bit has a binary place value equivalent to 2 raised to the power of the number of the place counting from the right, starting at 0. Thus, the 0th bit at the far right symbolizes the 2^0 place, or 1. Next to it is the 2^1 place, or 2.

Selector II maintains five variables that describe the current state of the five properties of the file list box, as explained earlier. Variable `nor` represents the `.Normal` property; the Selector assumes that to be true (-1) by default. The initial states requested for the other four properties are passed bitwise in `extras`. Because the variable actually contains four symbolic values for one numeric value, to extract one symbolic value from the lot, the others are masked out by comparing the bit within `extras` you're interested in, with the binary place for that bit.

The result of the Boolean `And` comparison is a single symbolic value; the other three bits will be 0. If the `extras` bit and the comparison bit are set (1), the resulting bit will be set (1) as well. In all other cases, the bit will be reset (0). In the meantime, the result can contain only as many as one bit set out of four, so numerologically speaking, the result is still some power of 2. You may have that one bit you want; the trouble is, it's not at any place where you know you can get your hands on it. To make this into a real Visual Basic true/false value, with a -1 you can sink your Booleans into, the `And` comparison is placed within parentheses so that it solves first, and the result of that comparison is then itself compared to see if it is greater than 0. If it is, the result is Boolean true (-1). You can now use this result to set the aspects and properties of variables and graphic objects related to this variable that require Boolean true/false values—for instance, `Archive.FontBold = arc`.

The condition `If arc Then` evaluates true if `arc` contains a non-zero value—in other words, if it *exists*. Selector II returns two global variables to the calling body of the application: the file or path that the user selected `targetfile$`, and a true/false value `cancl` that registers whether the user clicked the `Cancel` button rather than the `OK` button. All five global variables must be declared within the global module of the application that contains SELECTR2.FRM; preferably, `extras` and `cancl` should be declared `As Integer`. These variables should not be declared within the Selector form itself, because if they were, they would be treated as form-level variables, and variables of the same name used by other procedures could not be used to pass data to the Selector form.

Data is passed between the Selector and the rest of the application with global variables rather than by parameter passing, because of the peculiar passing pattern perpetrated by Visual Basic. A procedure attributed to a form can pass parameters to another procedure within that form or to a procedure in a general module, but not to a procedure attributed to another form within the same application. In other words, a branch can make a direct connection to the trunk, but not to another branch. Conceivably, a procedure could be adapted within a general module acting solely as a *relay*, receiving the parameters from one form procedure and passing them to the Selector form procedure.

For a form procedure to invoke the Selector form, you have the four global variables seeded and ready. As a result of the user selecting **Load** from the **File** menu, or some other similar directive, the instruction `Selector.Show 1` is placed within the form's event procedure. The Selector is a part of the current project file, although until necessary it is considered unloaded. Once brought on-screen using the `.Show` method, it is considered loaded, and for that reason the Selector's `Sub Form_Load ()` procedure is executed. The `1` as a method for the `.Show` method tells Visual Basic to suspend all other inputs related to its own application, until the shown form is unloaded again. So the visible behavior of the application is no different than if it were possible to pass parameters between form modules.

Here are the event procedures for making selections from the Selector's three list boxes:

```
Sub Drive1_Change ()
Dir1.Path = Drive1.Drive
ChDrive Drive1.Drive
End Sub

Sub Dir1_Change ()
File1.Path = Dir1.Path
File1_Click
End Sub

Sub File1_Click ()
Filename.Text = File1.Filename
End Sub

Sub File1_DblClick ()
OK_Click
End Sub
```

Notice in `Sub Drive1_Change ()` that the `ChDrive` instruction was necessary to tell DOS that you are examining a different device now, whereas in `Sub Dir1_Change ()` a `ChDir` command was not necessary. You can keep any path for the current device that does not have to correspond with the current DOS directory path. This path may not be applicable, however, if the device being searched is not the same as the device DOS currently considers active.

```
Sub OK_Click ()
topofproc:
pth$ = Dir1.Path
If File1.Filename = "" Then
    fil$ = Filename.Text
Else
    fil$ = File1.Filename
End If
If Right$(pth$, 1) = "\" Then
    Filename.Text = pth$ + fil$
Else
    Filename.Text = pth$ + "\" + fil$
End If
TargetFile$ = Filename.Text
On Error GoTo Oops
```

Chapter 50 ◆ Devices and Directories

```
Open TargetFile$ For Binary As #1
Close #1
ChDir Dir1.Path
Unload Selector
Exit Sub
Oops:
If Err = 53 Then
    MsgBox "File cannot be found", 32
Else
    MsgBox "ERROR:  " + Error$(Err)
End If
On Error GoTo 0
Resume Outahere
Outahere:
End Sub
```

You may remember you needed the second conditional clause to correct what appeared to be a problem with how Visual Basic records the current path as its own properties. Toward the end of the procedure, note that I've added the ChDir instruction, for the sake of the calling application that now can use Dir1.Dir as its default directory. You've probably noticed that in many Windows applications the file name of a document being edited appears in the title bar of its window, along with the path where that document's file resides (if that path is different from the currently active DOS path). Loading a document into memory will change the DOS path to the one that contains the document file being loaded; ChDir performs that directory change on behalf of the application.

I've added an error trap to this procedure, based in large part upon the "file not found" trap example presented in Chapter 44. In this instance, the procedure actually tries to open the TargetFile$ as a binary data file through channel #1. It really doesn't intend to retrieve any binary data from this file at all; the whole point of attempting to open the file is to determine whether it actually exists. If it does, then the error trap is avoided, and the channel is immediately closed. If the file does not exist, the trap is sprung, and execution resumes at the start of the trap routine, marked Oops. The nature of the error is reported to the user, the trap is reset, and the procedure is exited.

```
Sub Cancel_Click ()
cancl = 1
TargetFile$ = ""
Unload Selector
End Sub
```

The other option, of course, is for the user to click `Cancel`; if the user does so, the `cancl` variable is set to 1 for the sake of the application that will be checking it. I left out the *e* on purpose because *Cancel* is a reserved word in Visual Basic.

As promised, here is how you can program a manual dialog box for use inside what is, for most intents and purposes, a dialog box. In Selector II, I've added a "red button" marked `Options`; this is in fact not a formal command button, but a text label painted red that happens to have the `_Click` event associated with it. Here's the procedure for that event:

```
Sub Options_Click ()
Dir1.Enabled = 0
File1.Enabled = 0
OptPanel.Visible = -1
OptPanel.Enabled = -1
End Sub
```

> **TIP:** As a matter of convenience, many people insert `Const` declarations into the Global module for recurring values such as –1 for TRUE and 0 for FALSE. For example, you could add `Global Const FALSE=0` and also `Global Const TRUE=-1` to the Global module for this application and then make the appropriate changes.

The directory and file list boxes are turned off for now, but they are not taken off the screen. For a moment they'll be overwritten; Windows makes the choices in the file list box grey until the box is reenabled. Back in Figure 50.1, you may remember a partly obstructed message hiding behind these two list boxes. This obstructed object is a picture box object called `OptPanel`. As the preceding listing

Chapter 50 ◆ Devices and Directories

shows, it contains a frame object, within which are five text labels and a button. Together, these smaller objects comprise what appears to be another dialog box, as depicted in Figure 50.2.

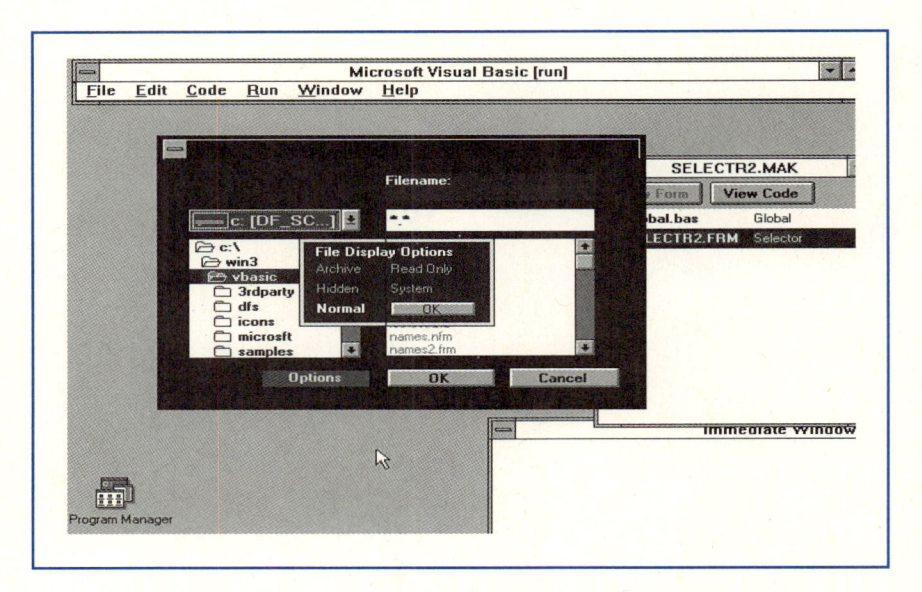

Figure 50.2. A miniature, really small, "fun size" dialog.

Because you had a minimum of space to work with, you needed a way to symbolize the true/false setting for five properties in a minimum of space. To place five check boxes in this mini-dialog box would make it unnecessarily large. The method for symbolism I chose instead was to have each reset (0) property be displayed in nonbold, pastel blue text, and each set (–1) property in a bold white text. Clicking the text itself toggles its state, as well as the property for that state. The OK button is more self-explanatory; after users experiment with this type of manual control, however, they'll probably experience what programmers call the *oh-now-I-get-it* phenomenon, which generally carries with it a measure of self-satisfaction from figuring out something neat.

Here are the event procedures for clicking the individual items of text:

```
Sub Archive_Click ()
If arc = 0 Then
    arc = -1
    Archive.ForeColor = QBColor(15)
Else
    arc = 0
    Archive.ForeColor = &HFFFF80
End If
Archive.FontBold = arc
End Sub

Sub Hidden_Click ()
If hid = 0 Then
    hid = -1
    Hidden.ForeColor = QBColor(15)
Else
    hid = 0
    Hidden.ForeColor = &HFFFF80
End If
Hidden.FontBold = hid
End Sub

Sub Normal_Click ()
If nor = 0 Then
    nor = -1
    Normal.ForeColor = QBColor(15)
Else
    nor = 0
    Normal.ForeColor = &HFFFF80
End If
Normal.FontBold = nor
End Sub

Sub ReadOnly_Click ()
If rdo = 0 Then
    rdo = -1
    ReadOnly.ForeColor = QBColor(15)
Else
    rdo = 0
    ReadOnly.ForeColor = &HFFFF80
End If
```

Chapter 50 ◆ Devices and Directories

```
ReadOnly.FontBold = rdo
End Sub

Sub Systm_Click ()
If sys = 0 Then
    sys = -1
    Systm.ForeColor = QBColor(15)
Else
    sys = 0
    Systm.ForeColor = &HFFFF80
End If
Systm.FontBold = sys
End Sub
```

All five procedures work the same way, as demonstrated by the following pseudocode:

Start of procedure:
If the setting is false, then
    Make the setting true.
    Turn the text white.
Otherwise,
    Make the setting false.
    Turn the text pastel blue.
End of condition.
Make the boldness of the text whatever the setting is now.
End of procedure.

All that's left is to have the miniature OK button deliver these property settings to their respective list boxes:

```
Sub OKOpt_Click ()
OptPanel.Visible = 0
OptPanel.Enabled = 0
Dir1.Enabled = -1
File1.Enabled = -1
File1.Archive = arc
File1.Hidden = hid
File1.Normal = nor
File1.ReadOnly = rdo
File1.System = sys
End Sub
```

Visual Basic *By* EXAMPLE

The panel is made invisible and disabled again, meaning that the user won't accidentally click some invisible element of the panel and have it be mysteriously indicated. The directory path and file list boxes are reenabled, and their properties are set in accordance with the variables with which the mini-dialog box was working.

Notice that this mini-dialog box was not a form itself, but an integral part of the Selector form. In fact, Visual Basic considers this box to be "smack dab" in the middle of the form at all times, though invisible and disabled most of the time. When designing this dialog box, however, make sure the frame is drawn within the area of the picture box and not elsewhere on the form, and that the labels and button are drawn within the area of the frame and not elsewhere. This way the interpreter will attribute all these subordinate *child* objects as belonging to the *parent* object, so when the parent is disabled, so are its children. Also, you won't have a bunch of floating, disabled text in the middle of your form.

Murder or Mere Deletion? You Decide!

Finally, let me briefly touch on the matter of *killing* files. Had MS-DOS retained the vocabulary of its forebears, it is possible we would be much more brutal computer users than we are today. Visual Basic maintains the old BASIC command line interpreter instruction for the deletion of files.

`Kill` Statement

Syntax:

`Kill pattern$`

The `Kill` statement deletes the files within the currently active MS-DOS directory path that have file name patterns that match the one specified as *pattern$*. The pattern can contain wild-card characters `*` and `?`. This statement takes effect immediately, without any confirmation.

665

Chapter 50 ◆ Devices and Directories

On a far more sane note, the old form of the MS-DOS RENAME command is also supported by VB.

Name Statement

Syntax:

Name *oldfilename$* As *newfilename$*

The Name statement renames a file within the currently active MS-DOS directory from *oldfilename$* to a new name *newfilename$*. Neither file name can be specified as patterns, so wild-card characters are not allowed. If a file with the name *oldfilename$* does not exist within the current directory, an error is generated.

Example

You may remember from the NameForm IV application that after I had created a perfectly sorted data file, I shamelessly killed the old one and gave the new file the name of the old one:

```
    .
    .
    .
Open "~temp.fil" For Random As #2 Len = 190
For replac = 1 To MaxRecord - 1
    Get #1, sortarray(replac), CurRecord
    Put #2, replac, CurRecord
Next replac
Close #2, #1
Kill filename$
Name "~temp.fil" As filename$
Open filename$ For Random As #1 Len = 190
RecordNo = sortarray(tmp)
ShowRecord
End Sub
```

Variable `filename$`, if you remember, was a form-level variable containing the name of the file currently being edited. The `Name` statement, immediately following the `Kill` statement, assigns this new file name to the existing *~temp.fil*.

Finally, there is the matter of a function that makes the attempt to extract a concrete file name with just a pattern to go on.

Dir$()   **Function**

Syntax:

*filename$* = Dir$(*pattern$*)

The `Dir$()` function returns the first available file name within a directory having a file name pattern that matches the one specified as *pattern$*. This string can contain device identifiers, subdirectories, and wild-card characters. If a device and path are specified, the function returns the first available file name for that path; otherwise, it returns the first available file name within the currently active MS-DOS directory. In this case, the first available file name is the first name on the DOS list; however, that list may be sorted. DOS generally sorts file names within a directory in the order in which those names were inserted into that directory, with the most recent files last. Your particular computer system, however, may behave differently.

Example

With the abundance of utility programs such as directory sorters and disk optimizers, which arrange DOS directories as they themselves so choose, it is impossible to actually simulate this function for the sake of this book and tell you what the results will be. However, I can suggest that `Dir$()` be used to supply file names to an application where only a pattern was provided. You could modify one of the procedures in SELECTR2.FRM, for instance, to look up the first file matching the current pattern if the user did not choose a specific file name:

Chapter 50 ◆ Devices and Directories

```
Sub OK_Click ()
pth$ = Dir1.Path
If File1.Filename = "" Then
    If Filename.Text = "" Then
        fil$ = Dir$(Dir1.Path)
    Else
        fil$ = Filename.Text
    Endif
Else
    fil$ = File1.Filename
End If
.
.
.
End Sub
```

Here the procedure returns at least a valid file name for the current path if no specific file name was chosen, using `Dir$()` within an embedded conditional clause.

Summary

Visual Basic recognizes the currently active MS-DOS subdirectory, which would display within a prompt if Windows had such a prompt. In any event, the `ChDir`, `MkDir`, and `RmDir` statements are supported, and they operate in the same manner as their DOS function counterparts. In addition, the `ChDrive` instruction was added for changing the currently active DOS storage device identifier. In lieu of the DOS command prompt, the `CurDir$()` function returns the full form of the currently active DOS directory path.

A file list box has five properties that designate which files with special DOS attributes may be visible within this box. These attributes are directly accessible using the DOS `ATTRIB` command. The `.Normal` property for a file list box allows that box to display the files with no special attributes. The `.Hidden`, `.ReadOnly`, `.System`, and `.Archive` properties for a file list box allow it to display files that have, for one reason or another, those particular attributes set.

A file can be deleted from a DOS directory using the `Kill` statement and renamed using the `Name` statement. The `Dir$()`

function (not to be confused with CurDir$()) returns the first file name in a DOS directory list that matches the specified pattern.

Review Questions

1. In the following example from Sub Form_Load (), why are the values being used in the Boolean comparisons all powers of 2?

    ```
    arc = (extras And 1) > 0
    hid = (extras And 2) > 0
    rdo = (extras And 4) > 0
    sys = (extras And 8) > 0
    ```

2. Why did the error trap at the end of Sub OK_Click () end in the following manner?

    ```
    On Error GoTo 0
    Resume Outahere
    Outahere:
    End Sub
    ```

Windows Instructions

In this chapter you study the instructions that are designed to perform the housekeeping roles for the Microsoft Windows environment before you proceed to the final and more esoteric topics of this book. You look first at the instructions that control and monitor the current operative state of Windows and Windows applications. You proceed to the instructions that override Visual Basic's tendency to place priority on mathematical operations rather than graphical operations. I close with a look at the system clipboard and the methods that send data to and retrieve data from this logical device.

Environmental Control

As Microsoft's Programmers Guide to Visual Basic demonstrates, a completed VB application can be *compiled* to an .EXE file that can be run from a command line, or from Program Manager or File Manager. This .EXE file is not an executable file, mind you, because it does not contain executable code by the standard definition. Instead, the VB interpreter produces *intermediate p-code*

Chapter 51 ◆ Windows Instructions

(processor code) that's interpreted at run time through the use of an accessory program that is automatically called by the Visual Basic compiled .EXE file, currently called VBRUN100.DLL. A Windows .DLL file is a *dynamic link library*.

The Windows Program Manager—as well as PM substitutes—contains an optional command line that can be invoked by selecting **R**un from the **F**ile menu from the PM main window. To run a Visual Basic compiled .EXE file, you can type its path and file name at this command line. So, like a DOS application, Microsoft has allowed Visual Basic applications to be endowed with command options, in the form of switches or parameters. These options are typed beside the file name of the VB compiled application to be run, separated from that file name by a lone space. This string of options can be acquired by using the Command$ function.

Command$ — Function

Syntax:

`string$ = Command$`

The Command$ function returns the alphanumeric string of characters typed by the user at the time the Visual Basic application was invoked, containing any commands or switches to be parsed (that is, isolated and interpreted) by the application. This string is entered by selecting **R**un from the **F**ile menu from Program Manager or File Manager (or many of their substitutes) and typing this string beside the name of the application in the command line.

If the application is still in its interpretive stage, Visual Basic can be launched, an application can be loaded and run automatically, and the Command$ can be entered by typing

`[device:][\path\]vb /run filename$ /cmd com$`

at the command line, where `com$` is the string that will be accepted by the VB interpreter as Command$. If the application is in its compiled state (.EXE), it can be invoked by typing

`[device:][\path\]filename$ com$`

at the command line. In either case, com$ is returned by the Command$ function. If no command options are typed, or if the application or the VB interpreter was invoked by double-clicking an icon, Command$ will be a null string. The Command$ function takes no parentheses.

Example

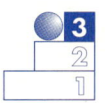

You could retrofit the Sort Contest application so that a command line option could let the user designate how many units will appear in each array, rather than the default 100. One of the procedures you would have to rewrite appears as follows:

```
Sub RackEmUp ()
If Command$ = "" Then
    units = 100
Else
    units = Val(Command$)
End If
For cell = 1 To units
MakeCell:
    vl = Int(Rnd(1) * units) + 1
    For chk = 1 To cell - 1
        If vl = unit(chk, 1) Then GoTo MakeCell
    Next chk
    For rack = 0 To 2
        unit(cell, rack) = vl
    Next rack
Next cell
End Sub
```

Mind you, you would then have to change the part of the application that scales the plotting panels and redimensions the temporary sort array. Such repetitive replacement of a constant for a variable is rather academic for now, and perhaps too redundant to be covered here in detail.

On the reverse side of the equation, Visual Basic is capable of sending a command line to DOS itself for the launching of an application.

Chapter 51 ◆ Windows Instructions

Shell()   Function

Syntax:

`taskid% = Shell(filename$[, window%])`

The `Shell()` function executes a program that has its name specified as `filename$`. If this string contains no device data or path data, the file is assumed to exist within the current DOS directory. The file name must have an extension of .BAT, .COM, .EXE, or .PIF; otherwise, an error will be generated. If `filename$` is to be stated outright rather than represented by a string variable, its text must be enclosed within quotation marks.

The value of `window%`, when specified, represents the operative state of the application's main window, assuming the application is a Windows application. If the program referred to by `filename$` is a DOS application, the settings for `window%` that would place the application in an independent window will be ignored, and the DOS application will have full rein over the screen. The value of `window%` can be set to any of the following:

1   Independent window given the focus

2   Minimized icon given the focus

3   Maximized window given the focus (a maximized window must have the focus by default)

4   Independent window without the focus

7   Minimized icon without the focus

None of these states is considered the default state, because the state of some Windows applications at startup is dependent on the state designated for their main windows by their own .INI files.

The function returns an integer value `taskid%` that is a serial number of sorts that identifies the application for the sake of the Windows environment, as well as all other applications that seek to "get in contact" with this application through the Windows Applications Program Interface.

This isn't an entirely perfect function, especially in situations where a DOS program you've used this statement to call has an environment of its own. When the DOS application is supposed to look to subsidiary files for information concerning how it is supposed to operate, DOS may look instead to the directory last accessed by Windows, rather than the directory belonging to the DOS application. On not seeing the subsidiary files, the DOS application assumes those files don't exist, and it may either run "blank" or not run at all. Before using `Shell()` you can, for safety's sake, invoke the `ChDir` statement to change the active directory to the one that contains the DOS application to be launched.

If a Windows application other than the VB application has been loaded into the workspace, the `AppActivate` statement can pass the focus to it.

AppActivate   Statement

Syntax:

AppActivate *titlebar$*

The `AppActivate` statement passes the focus within the Windows environment to the window or icon whose title matches *titlebar$* character-for-character, although uppercase letters can be substituted for lowercase letters and vice versa. This window may belong to the Visual Basic application, to the VB interpreter, or to some other Windows application. Such cross-application window activation may be necessary for the VB application to direct the other application to perform a directive with a Dynamic Link Library. If *titlebar$* is to be stated outright rather than represented by a variable, it must be enclosed within quotation marks.

When your computer system is booted and DOS is loaded into memory, within the CONFIG.SYS file is generally a series of *environmental variables* that describe some aspect of DOS's operation within this specific computer. Environmental variables are set using

Chapter 51 ◆ Windows Instructions

MS-DOS's SET `var = command`. You're probably familiar with the PATH setting for granting certain DOS subdirectories access to DOS files, or with the TEMP variable, which tells programs such as Windows where to store temporary files. The settings for such environmental variables, if any, can be retrieved by Visual Basic using the following function:

Environ$() Function

Syntax 1:

`string$ = Environ$(envterm$)`

Syntax 2:

`string$ = Environ$(place%)`

The `Environ$()` function is used to return the environmental variable settings currently employed by MS-DOS within its specific computer. If Syntax 2 is employed, `place%` refers to an ordinal position within a list maintained by MS-DOS for environmental variables. The contents of `string$` will be set to the name of the variable, followed by an equal sign, then the alphanumeric setting for that variable. The result is a line that appears much as it would following the SET command of the computer's AUTOEXEC.BAT file. If no variable exists for the specified `place%`, `string$` is set to a null string. If Syntax 1 is employed, `envterm$` refers to a specific environmental variable to be found in the MS-DOS list. The contents of `string$` will be set to the alphanumeric setting for the specified variable. If no setting exists for the specified variable, the contents of `string$` will be set to a null string.

`Environ$()` can be especially useful in determining the current settings for PATH. If the compiled VB application places some calls to DOS itself, it may need the PATH environmental variable to point to its own location on the current disk, so that it can access DOS.

Which Events Take Precedence?

When I programmed the Sort Contest application, as you may have noticed, I included the .Refresh method at opportune places. This is because the Windows environment gives mathematical operations a higher priority than graphical operations, in an attempt to support real-time operations in which math cannot wait for the screen to update itself. When the Sort Contest is active, you'll notice that even keyboard input is put on hold momentarily, with the exception of pressing Ctrl-Break to stop the program. You can manually override this priority momentarily, and have the form or constituent object update itself using the .Refresh method.

Object.Refresh — Method

Syntax:

[*Object*.]Refresh

Invoking the .Refresh method for a graphic object suspends mathematical operations in progress momentarily and allows Windows to perform any appearance-changing operations on the stated *Object*. This object may not be the Screen. universal object, because that is handled independently by Windows.

Example

Here's one instance in which I used .Refresh to have the Sort Contest stop sorting for a moment, just long enough for it to tell the user how it's doing:

```
Sub ShowIter (panel As Integer)
  disp$ = LTrim$(Str$(comp(panel))) + " / " +
    LTrim$(Str$(swic(panel)))
  Iterations(panel).Caption = disp$
  Iterations(panel).Refresh
End Sub
```

This is the part of the application that showed how many actual comparisons and swaps were made. This information could be sent to the label area by setting the `.Caption` property. As far as Visual Basic was concerned, that property was set and updated. Trouble is, it is now the job of Windows to update this object, and it won't get the call to do so while the VB interpreter is busy sorting. This is why I added the `.Refresh` method following the setting of the `.Caption` property.

One other function, `DoEvents()`, is available so that all pending events—especially user input—can be processed before mathematical operations are to continue.

DoEvents()   Function

Syntax:

forms% = DoEvents()

The `DoEvents()` function suspends all pending operations within the running VB application, allowing Windows to update all graphic objects, read all holding user inputs, and then pass control for a few moments to the other applications in the Windows workspace for whatever business they are waiting to perform in the background. In effect, this directs the currently running VB application to yield the floor to all other background processes until they have signaled their completion.

On an almost unrelated note, `DoEvents()` returns the integer value *forms%* that is equivalent to the number of forms currently loaded within the workspace of the Visual Basic application.

System Clipboard Management

I've already used the methods for facilitating cut-and-paste operations several times throughout this book. From the point of view of management of the system clipboard, this process might best be called "set-and-get" rather than "cut-and-paste." It has been several months since writers in the computing business have taken time to appreciate the power of the system clipboard in computing and how it seems to be able to handle data in differing formats—raw text, rich text, object graphics, bitmaps—without users having to set these formats themselves.

You'll probably appreciate this even more now as a programmer, especially because it is your job to maintain the format of the data going into and out of the system clipboard. Microsoft Windows recognizes certain integer values as representative of clipboard data formats; these values are in turn recognized by Visual Basic. They are listed in Table 51.1.

Table 51.1. Windows' clipboard data formats.

Data type	Const name	Value
Text	CF_TEXT	1
Standard bitmap	CF_BITMAP	2
Windows metafile	CF_METAFILE	3
Device-independent bitmap	CF_DIB	8
Dynamic link	CF_LINK	48,896 (&HBF00)

The *device-independent bitmap* format uses scalable bitmaps, with more color capacity than most video drivers are capable of handling.

A *standard bitmap* is an image represented photographically, in which pixels are represented binarily as on/off states. The original Windows icons for versions 1 and 2 used the default black-and-white format for the standard bitmap, which is now called the *device-dependent bitmap* in retrospect. With Windows 3 came the *device-independent bitmap* format, which was first of all easily scalable for many different output devices, and furthermore used an RGB lookup table to produce colors.

Chapter 51 ◆ Windows Instructions

A DIB bitmap can have more colors than you do—the format is ready for some of the new 32,000-color Windows video drivers being produced as we go to press.

A Windows metafile is a combined element of object-oriented graphics, produced by lines proceeding in specifiable vectors, along with filled shapes and colored areas. The new edition of Microsoft Draw being shipped with some Windows applications enables the user to produce metafile images for importing into the main application. Metafiles are described logically by instruction rather than by numeric representation. In other words, the metafile tells Windows how to draw the image rather than what to draw.

The dynamic link format is reserved for pasting data to an application, although a link is still retained to the application that created the cut data in the first place. There are six methods reserved by Visual Basic for controlling the contents of the system clipboard.

Clipboard.SetText   Method

Syntax:

`Clipboard.SetText string$[, format%]`

The `.SetText` method places the text currently referred to as *string$* on the system clipboard. By default, this text is assumed to be of data format 1 unless specified as &HBF00, in which case the text is assumed to be part of a dynamic link operation.

Clipboard.SetData   Method

Syntax:

`Clipboard.SetData Object.{Image | Picture}[, format%]`

The `.SetData` method assigns to the system clipboard the `.Picture` (bitmap on the form) or `.Image` (bitmap in memory) referred to using object-oriented syntax. By default, the image is assumed to be a standard bitmap of data format 2; however, formats 3 and 8 are also supported.

Clipboard.GetText() — Method

Syntax:

`string$ = Clipboard.GetText (format%)`

The `.GetText` method acts in the manner of a function, in that it returns the current textual contents of the system clipboard within `string$`. If `format%` is specified as either type 1 or &HBF00 (dynamic link), the contents of the clipboard are returned to `string$` whether or not that format was intended for those contents.

Clipboard.GetData() — Method

Syntax:

`Object.Picture = Clipboard.GetData (format%)`

The `.GetData` method acts in the manner of a function in that it returns the `.Image` or `.Picture` contents of the system clipboard and assigns those contents as the `.Picture` property of the specified `Object`. If `format%` is stated as data format 2, 3, or 8, the contents of the clipboard will be assigned to the `.Picture` property regardless of whether that data was designed to be image data.

Chapter 51 ◆ Windows Instructions

`Clipboard.GetFormat()` — Method

Syntax:

`Boolean% = Clipboard.GetFormat (format%)`

The `.GetFormat` method acts in the manner of a function in that it returns within the integer variable `Boolean%` a true/false value indicating whether the data currently residing on the system clipboard is of the specified `format%`.

`Clipboard.Clear` — Method

Syntax:

`Clipboard.Clear`

The `.Clear` method clears the current contents of the system clipboard.

Example

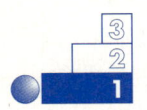

In the Expressor application, I used a clipboard method to place on the clipboard the number currently in the readout:

```
Sub EditCut_Click ()
Clipboard.SetText readout.Caption
End Sub
```

Example

At any time, an instruction can be invoked that takes the text currently indicated by the user within a large text box and copies it to the system clipboard:

682

```
Clipboard.SetText Text1.SelText
```

Now, if you want to make this operation an Edit-and-Cut operation rather than an Edit-and-Copy operation, you might want to add the following instruction:

```
Text1.SelText = ""
```

At some later point, should you want this clipped text inserted at the current cursor location, you can invoke the following:

```
Text1.SelText = Clipboard.GetText()
```

Notice that the parentheses are left within the `Get` operations but omitted within the `Set` operations.

Summary

A Visual Basic application can take command-line arguments just like a DOS application. If it does accept such arguments, they can be retrieved into a variable using the `Command$` function. Another DOS or Windows application can be launched from a Visual Basic application using the `Shell()` function. Focus can be passed to another form or to another application's window or icon using the `AppActivate` statement. The current state of your computer's AUTOEXEC.BAT environmental variables can be obtained using the `Environ$()` function.

Microsoft Windows, by nature, schedules mathematical operations above user input and graphical events. To have Visual Basic mathematical operations pause momentarily to update the appearance of a graphic object, use the `.Refresh` method for that object. To refresh everything in sight, as well as to let background operations and applications have a moment to work, use the `DoEvents()` function.

The Microsoft Windows system clipboard maintains one text format, three image formats, and a special format reserved for dynamic linking. The `.SetText` and `.SetData` methods for the `Clipboard.` object are used to acquire data from an object and place it on the system clipboard. Likewise, the `.GetText` and `.GetData` methods are used to place data from the clipboard on a qualifying object. The `.GetFormat` method is used to acquire the format number of the data currently maintained by the system clipboard. The `.Clear` method is reserved

Chapter 51 ◆ Windows Instructions

specifically for use with the `Clipboard.` object; it is used, naturally, to clear the clipboard of its contents.

Review Questions

1. *Parsing* describes what type of process?

2. The `.Refresh` method is used to have the Visual Basic interpreter suspend its mathematical processes until it fully updates the antecedent graphic object. Instructions to graphically alter this object generally will have been processed, though not yet executed. Why doesn't it seem VB processes all instructions in the sequence in which they were written?

In Closing

With these paragraphs, you come to the end of a very long intellectual journey. When Will Durant used to close one of his volumes of *The Story of Civilization*, he thanked his reader for being so patient, for having the courage to plod through the dull points in history, and in essence to say that it was worth the Dark Ages to reach the Renaissance. He would also tell his reader that he had not yet reached the end, that there were further volumes to follow.

That to some extent is the case with "The Story of Computing," because in this business we must make the attempt to produce a new volume virtually tomorrow. We hope that this particular volume has been an awakening of sorts, a stirring within you of the need to make art out of something as uninterpretably simple and as potentially trivial as logic. I hope that you can make some use of these tools so that we may provide a measure of artistry in a realm of existence that can certainly make use of it. Feel free to use, modify, and distribute the routines, programs, and applications presented in this book however you wish. I appreciate your curiosity, your patience, and your time. Until the next volume, I wish you the best of luck and bid you all the energy and time you need to take your everyday business and, with the aid of this marvelous machine, make sense of it all.

ASCII/ANSI Code Chart

The following table lists the values that represent alphanumeric characters for the Visual Basic interpreter. The table shows the basis of the character code of the American National Standards Institute (ANSI). This code has been adapted by Microsoft for use with Microsoft Windows, so it contains some elements of the all-encompassing ANSI code as well as some elements of ASCII (American Standard Code for Information Interchange) on which the ANSI code is partly based. This table assumes you have installed the English code table for your copy of MS-DOS.

Character	*Hex code*	*ANSI code*
Backspace	&H08	8
Tab	&H09	9
Line feed	&H0A	10
Carriage return	&H0D	13
Space	&H20	32
!	&H21	33
"	&H22	34

Appendix A ◆ ASCII/ANSI Code Chart

Character	Hex code	ANSI code
#	&H23	35
$	&H24	36
%	&H25	37
&	&H26	38
'	&H27	39
(	&H28	40
)	&H29	41
*	&H2A	42
+	&H2B	43
,	&H2C	44
-	&H2D	45
.	&H2E	46
/	&H2F	47
0	&H30	48
1	&H31	49
2	&H32	50
3	&H33	51
4	&H34	52
5	&H35	53
6	&H36	54
7	&H37	55
8	&H38	56
9	&H39	57
:	&H3A	58
;	&H3B	59
<	&H3C	60
=	&H3D	61
>	&H3E	62
?	&H3F	63
@	&H40	64
A	&H41	65
B	&H42	66
C	&H43	67
D	&H44	68
E	&H45	69
F	&H46	70
G	&H47	71

Character	Hex code	ANSI code
H	&H48	72
I	&H49	73
J	&H4A	74
K	&H4B	75
L	&H4C	76
M	&H4D	77
N	&H4E	78
O	&H4F	79
P	&H50	80
Q	&H51	81
R	&H52	82
S	&H53	83
T	&H54	84
U	&H55	85
V	&H56	86
W	&H57	87
X	&H58	88
Y	&H59	89
Z	&H5A	90
[	&H5B	91
\	&H5C	92
]	&H5D	93
^	&H5E	94
_	&H5F	95
`	&H60	96
a	&H61	97
b	&H62	98
c	&H63	99
d	&H64	100
e	&H65	101
f	&H66	102
g	&H67	103
h	&H68	104
i	&H69	105
j	&H6A	106
k	&H6B	107
l	&H6C	108

Appendix A ◆ ASCII/ANSI Code Chart

Character	Hex code	ANSI code
m	&H6D	109
n	&H6E	110
o	&H6F	111
p	&H70	112
q	&H71	113
r	&H72	114
s	&H73	115
t	&H74	116
u	&H75	117
v	&H76	118
w	&H77	119
x	&H78	120
y	&H79	121
z	&H7A	122
{	&H7B	123
|	&H7C	124
}	&H7D	125
~	&H7E	126
'	&H91	145
'	&H92	146
"	&H93	147
"	&H94	148
°	&H95	149
–	&H96	150
—	&H97	151
Space	&HA0	160
¡	&HA1	161
¢	&HA2	162
£	&HA3	163
⊗	&HA4	164
¥	&HA5	165
¦	&HA6	166
§	&HA7	167
¨	&HA8	168
©	&HA9	169
ª	&HAA	170
«	&HAB	171

Character	Hex code	ANSI code
¬	&HAC	172
-	&HAD	173
®	&HAE	174
¯	&HAF	175
°	&HB0	176
±	&HB1	177
²	&HB2	178
³	&HB3	179
´	&HB4	180
µ	&HB5	181
¶	&HB6	182
•	&HB7	183
¸	&HB8	184
	&HB9	185
º	&HBA	186
»	&HBB	187
¼	&HBC	188
½	&HBD	189
¾	&HBE	190
¿	&HBF	191
À	&HC0	192
Á	&HC1	193
Â	&HC2	194
Ã	&HC3	195
Ä	&HC4	196
Å	&HC5	197
Æ	&HC6	198
Ç	&HC7	199
È	&HC8	200
É	&HC9	201
Ê	&HCA	202
Ë	&HCB	203
Ì	&HCC	204
Í	&HCD	205
Î	&HCE	206
Ï	&HCF	207

Appendix A ◆ ASCII/ANSI Code Chart

Character	Hex code	ANSI code
Ð	&HD0	208
Ñ	&HD1	209
Ò	&HD2	210
Ó	&HD3	211
Ô	&HD4	212
Õ	&HD5	213
Ö	&HD6	214
×	&HD7	215
Ø	&HD8	216
Ù	&HD9	217
Ú	&HDA	218
Û	&HDB	219
Ü	&HDC	220
Ý	&HDD	221
Þ	&HDE	222
ß	&HDF	223
à	&HE0	224
á	&HE1	225
â	&HE2	226
ã	&HE3	227
ä	&HE4	228
å	&HE5	229
æ	&HE6	230
ç	&HE7	231
è	&HE8	232
é	&HE9	233
ê	&HEA	234
ë	&HEB	235
ì	&HEC	236
í	&HED	237
î	&HEE	238
ï	&HEF	239
ð	&HF0	240
ñ	&HF1	241
ò	&HF2	242
ó	&HF3	243

Character	Hex code	ANSI code
ô	&HF4	244
õ	&HF5	245
ö	&HF6	246
÷	&HF7	247
ø	&HF8	248
ù	&HF9	249
ú	&HFA	250
û	&HFB	251
ü	&HFC	252
ý	&HFD	253
þ	&HFE	254
ÿ	&HFF	255

The _KeyPress event is recognized whenever a standard ANSI character—not including function keys or control keys—is pressed once on the keyboard. The returned value will be one of those listed in the preceding table. By contrast, a key code is recognized continually by the _KeyUp and _KeyDown events *while* a key on your keyboard is being pressed. This key may be one of those in the preceding ANSI table, although it may also be a key that is not represented by the ANSI code, such as the Ctrl key or Print Screen. These other keys are listed within the CONSTANT.TXT file supplied with your copy of Visual Basic, as declarations of constants that can be attached to the global module of your VB application.

B

Answers to Review Questions

The following is a listing of answers to the Review Questions at the end of each chapter. You can obtain answers to Review Exercises through the disk offer. See the disk offer page at the back of this book for more information.

Chapter 1 Answers

1. Because BASIC is designed to more closely approximate the language used by people, whereas a low-level language is designed to more closely approximate the logic of the computer.

2. An instruction.

3. Machine language.

4. MS-DOS, or whatever acts as your computer's operating system.

5. Realistically speaking, a computer does not receive information; it can't be informed of anything because information implies the presence of a reasoning capability that the

computer does not have. The instruction does, however, inform the human reader that a symbolic reference or variable called a will be used to represent the numeral value 6, and it tells the person to think of a as being equal to 6—to replace a for 6 in his mind. The BASIC language thus performs a dual purpose: It informs the human reader while it instructs the computer. This is another reason why we consider BASIC a high-level language.

Chapter 2 Answers

1. A project.
2. Buttons.
3. An underscore character (_).
4. `_Click`; in other words, the term following the underscore character.
5. The title bar, where you'll find the term [design] if the application is being constructed or written, [run] if it's currently running, or [break] if the program is currently in suspension.
6. Design mode.
7. .FRM, the extension given form modules.

Chapter 3 Answers

1. `f = 6`
2. `Int(a + b + c)`
3. `good = 1`
4. 3.
5. A subroutine.

Chapter 4 Answers

1. Whenever you press a calculator key from 1 through 9, that digit appears in the display, moving any other digits before it to the left. The 0 key works in a similar manner, except that if the display already reads 0, no digits are added. Because there was an exception, the 0 key was excluded from the control array. It could have been included, although you would need to add a special conditional statement to the procedure, such as `Select Case 0`, that would determine whether the key pressed was in fact the 0 key. The period or point key is not handled at all like a digit, so it should remain outside the control array.

2. In standard calculator notation, or *algebraic notation*, the user enters the mathematical function *before* entering the value to which that function pertains. As a result, when entering the expression *5 + 8 – 6*, the addition of *8* to *5* takes place when the user presses the *minus* key just before pressing *6*. This makes algebraic notation a confusing procedure to implement. In Reverse Polish notation, the preceding expression would be entered as *5 Enter 8 Enter 6 – .* The function takes place at the time the user presses the function key. This makes it possible in Visual Basic for a procedure to be executed on pressing a command button that acts as the function key.

Chapter 5 Answers

1. A value.

2. A statement.

3. A statement or expression of assignment.

4. 32.

5. The sign of a value in memory consumes one bit, thus reducing its maximum absolute numeric value by a power of two. If one bit isn't being used to store the sign of the value,

it can be used to store a digit, thus increasing the capacity of that value by a power of two. Furthermore, you can imagine dividing the number of representable values in half, resulting in the negative side and the positive side; but you would be forgetting zero, which is a value that is neither negative or positive. The number of representable values in a byte is always an even number, but 0 is one value and 1 is an odd number. It must, therefore, take space from one side or the other, negative or positive; computer designers chose the positive side. This is why a byte can represent –256 but not +256.

Chapter 6 Answers

1. A. x = 47.2
   B. x = 3.333333
   C. x = 48

2. A. v = (3.1415927 / 3) * r ^ 2 * h
   B. P = F / (1 + i) ^ n

Chapter 7 Answers

1. –1
2. –1
3. 0
4. –1
5. –1
6. 0
7. 0

Chapter 8 Answers

1. `Ardwight`
2. `94201`
3. `WallaceArdwight` (Notice that no space separates the two.)
4. `5151 Back o' the Bay Way`
5. `Oakland, CA  94201`
6. `Wallace T. Ardwight`
   `5151 Back o' the Bay Way`
   `Oakland, CA  94201`
7. `Wallace T. Ardwight`
   `Oakland, CA  94201`
8. `Mr. or Ms. Wallace T. Ardwight`

Chapter 9 Answers

1. Nebraska.
2. A bishop.
3. 400.
4. `Dim Aspen() As Double`

Chapter 10 Answers

1. `DateSerial()`
2. `TimeSerial()`
3. `TimeValue()`
4. `TimeValue()`

Appendix B ◆ Answers to Review Questions

Chapter 11 Answers

1. The sixth power.
2. Zero.
3. No, because any number to the zeroth power is 1, and 1 divides into every integral (whole) number evenly.

Chapter 13 Answers

1. The `End Sub` statement closes a procedure, whereas the `Exit Sub` statement forces an exit from that procedure before its `End Sub` statement is executed.
2. `End` by itself ends the entire program; no other statement does that.

Chapter 15 Answers

1. 15
2. 3
3. `"Go"`
4. 0
5. `" "`

Chapter 16 Answers

1. `For-Next`
2. `Do-Loop Until`
3. `Do While-Loop`

Chapter 17 Answers

1. The interpreter "errors out;" naturally, it generates a `Return without GoSub` error.

2. Any form of `Do-Loop` constructs using `While c < 4` as a qualifier, or a `While c < 4. . . Wend` loop.

3. Any form of `Do-Loop` constructs using `Until c = 4` as a qualifier.

Chapter 18 Answers

1. The global module.

2. `Sub Form_Load ()`.

3. Either `Form2.Show` or `Load Form2`.

4. After the interpreter clears and resets the workspace, absolutely nothing. No instructions are executed whatsoever. The project rests in limbo.

Chapter 19 Answers

1. A function in computing combines arithmetic functions to derive a single result value, whereas a statement merely changes the operative state of the program without returning a value. Because all instructions in Visual Basic are arithmetic operations in one form or another, the instruction that calls the `Function` routine must be mathematical in nature as well. Because this instruction is stated in the form of an equation, and the equation contains an obvious result value location, the instruction fulfills all the requirements of a function in computing. Thus a call to a procedure that returns a value is a function. For that matter, all function procedures in computing—whether they are written in Visual Basic or assembly language—must be called by some body of the source code, so all functions are in turn *function calls.*

Appendix B ◆ Answers to Review Questions

2. The `Call` statement places a call to a procedure that is not considered a function, because no value is returned. Values are passed to this `Sub` procedure, however, and those values are declared at the beginning of the `Sub` procedure within parentheses. During this book, I've specified functions and function calls with parentheses, as in `Len()`, even when I don't state any parameters. Programmers do this to distinguish the role of the instruction as a function or function call. If you left parentheses around the `Sub` (non-function) procedure call, you would be violating the syntax of functions. By *including* parentheses in the `Call` syntax, you are specifying parameters using standard syntax not for the name of the `Sub` procedure, but for the word `Call` itself.

Chapter 20 Answers

1. No. If the form has not been loaded yet using the `Load` statement, the `.Show` method performs that duty on behalf of `Load`.

2. Yes. `Unload` only takes the form out of the workspace and out of memory.

3. In the object-oriented methodology, an object can be referred to as such only if it has the memory constructs associated with it that make the item `object`-ive. Those constructs do not exist when the object is not in memory. Object-oriented syntax thus cannot be used to refer to a nonexistent object. `Load` and `Unload` are both non-object-oriented because the forms and graphic elements to which they refer do not exist in memory yet, and thus do not have objective constructs associated with them.

Chapter 21 Answers

1. 2
2. 1

3. 0

4. 3

Chapter 22 Answers

1. Alaska would be state #49, and Hawaii would be state #50, regardless of the .Sorted state of the list.

2. Guam will be the 11th item in the list, because it has yet to be loaded into memory, and you're accounting for the State of Columbia.

Chapter 23 Answers

1. Yes. They will still be considered independent objects, although they will be referenced using the same procedure.

2. No. A control is made part of a frame by creating it within the frame area. If it was created outside the frame, then the VB interpreter always considers it to be outside the frame.

3. Visually it can, but logically a control cannot "half-belong" to a frame.

4. A scroll bar created as a result of setting the .ScrollBars property of a text box cannot be set to a minimum or maximum value.

Chapter 24 Answers

1. An input box.

2. Modal.

3. Because the program, by displaying a file selector box, evidently needs a file name in order for its process to continue, it is generally safer to suspend any other inputs to the program until such a file name is delivered.

Appendix B ♦ Answers to Review Questions

Chapter 25 Answers

1. `Surname.Text`
2. `Group(1).TabIndex`
3. `BobTheBear.Tag`
4. `Screen.ActiveControl.Text`
5. `Source.Status.Text`
6. `Screen.ActiveForm.Status.Text`
7. `Source.Parent.Status.Text`

Chapter 26 Answers

1. Black.
2. Blue.
3. .Text.

Chapter 27 Answers

1. A menu bar is not a positionable object one can place on a form using a pointer, thus you should not use a pointer graphically to invoke a menu bar within a form.
2. A dialog box follows the selection of this menu command.
3. The general procedures area of the form that contained the removed button, and now contains the menu command.

Chapter 28 Answers

1. A drag operation leaves the dragged control where it is and carries a *copy* of the control. A move operation actually relocates the control to a new location.

2. Yes. The procedure responds only to drops into the region it inhabits, thus making it the target.

3. Coordinates are relative to the control, and must be offset by means of additive arithmetic if they are to be made relative to the form or the screen.

Chapter 29 Answers

1. About 1:05.536.

2. A. `_Timer`
   B. `Timer`
   C. `Timer()`.

Chapter 30 Answers

1. The scan code values are not functionally additive. The BIOS doesn't think in decimal numbers anyway, so if there was any summing of the two, the result would be Boolean rather than decimal.

2. Most likely the first key pressed out of a sequence, no matter how closely together the sequence was pressed, will be the first key scanned; however, the lower BIOS values do take precedence.

3. You have to read this question carefully to be able to answer it logically. If you understand the problem logically, you understand something about the art and theory of programming. Mechanically speaking, one key takes precedence over the other. The faster the computer is at scanning, the more adept it is at determining which key came first...or shall I say, *appearing* to determine which key came first. The BIOS code at its lowest level scans for only one key at a time. At no time does it consider which came first, because it never deals with two values at the lowest level. Thus the computer's quick reflexes have nothing to do with which key will take precedence over the other.

4. By virtue of the scanning sequence, yes, one key higher up in the sequence will have "authority" over another. This is not a hierarchy by virtue of one key's assumed importance over another, however, just its sequence.

Chapter 31 Answers

1. The way this particular procedure is written, the only way a nondiagonal arrow could appear is if the movement of the mouse along either axis is absolute zero. In other words, you'd have to move the mouse perfectly straight to get the arrow to point in a nondiagonal direction.

2. The .MousePointer property, set at design time, represents a default state; whereas the .Pointer property, set at run time, represents a temporary state.

Chapter 32 Answers

1. A function of arithmetic is any operation that can be expressed symbolically and that changes the state or value of something. In trigonometry, for instance, a "true" function is any operation that can be solved logically as a single value for any one unit of time. A graph of such a function, therefore, may only show one point plotted for any vertical line along the graph. A Visual Basic function is representative of a low-level process within the interpreter. It represents an arithmetic function, and logically "returns" an explicit value. It thus *simulates* an arithmetic function, although it may not actually be calculating that function specifically.

2. Not in Visual Basic, as this instruction might in some other dialects of BASIC. In Visual Basic, the instruction reserves all variables of single or multiple letters beginning with the letters *A* through *Z* as being integer variables by default, unless stated otherwise.

3. Because the Timer control, the _Timer event, and the `Timer()` function, for instance, can be confused with each other if not for the extra punctuation provided in this book.

Chapter 33 Answers

1. 3
2. 65
3. `"z"`
4. 65
5. 1600

Chapter 34 Answers

1. 3
2. –1
3. 1

Chapter 35 Answers

1. `"When"`
2. `" events"`
3. `"n"`
4. `"the "`
5. `"When in, of, and around the course of human events"`

Chapter 36 Answers

1. Yes, both types can be included within a `Type-End Type` clause.

Appendix B ◆ Answers to Review Questions

2. No. Although Visual Basic uses object-oriented syntax here, it does not use object-oriented *structure* in its composite variables.

3. Because when an element of a composite variable is referenced, that reference takes the same place in an equation that a conventional variable normally takes.

Chapter 37 Answers

1. Between 0 and 1. Read the question carefully. The multiplication by 72 takes place after the randomization rather than during the randomization.

2. Most of the time, you will be using the function as if it were written Rnd(0). Omitting the parentheses along with the "dummy parameter" makes using this function a bit easier.

3. Yes, as long as that number is rounded to a short (two-byte) integer expression.

Chapter 38 Answers

1. "##%"

2. "****000.00"

3. "h AM/PM"

4. "##.##;(##.##);Unchanged"

5. Chr$(34) + "by " + Chr$(34) + "h:mm AM/PM" + Chr$(34) + " tonight at the earliest." + Chr$(34)

Chapter 39 Answers

1. Regardless of how many lines of text you may see in a text box, the VB interpreter considers the contents of all text boxes as if they were written out in one long, straight line.

2. At this point, the .SelText property would automatically be set to the contents of the selected characters in the text box. No equation is necessary.

Chapter 40 Answers

1. Zero. After printing the line, the interpreter executes a carriage return with line feed, resetting the .CurrentX value to 0.

2. 53. The semicolon stops the interpreter from resetting .CurrentX. If you were to print anything else using the .Print method, it would appear just to the right of the exclamation point.

3. Many laser printers have internal fonts and font cartridges that have no corresponding fonts in Windows. Some Windows laser printer drivers therefore use "best-guess estimate" fonts to represent those in the printer; however, those estimate fonts have different names and metrics than the real printer fonts. You must therefore keep the lists separate.

Chapter 41 Answers

1. A Visual Basic image is the bitmap in memory that represents, point by point, what you see on the screen. A VB picture, by comparison, is a more abstract concept, which describes not only what you see, but also the file format in which it is presented.

2. When a picture or image is loaded into an object, the graphic object is the recipient. Its content property is set to the contents of the image; so those contents are most easily represented almost as they were a value, or as a *function* that appears to substitute for a value. When a picture or image is saved to disk, by contrast, the file is the recipient. A file is not an object, so object-oriented syntax does not apply. You have to rely therefore on the older style of BASIC syntax. In other words, you must phrase the instruction as a "command." The statement form is therefore used here.

Appendix B ◆ Answers to Review Questions

Chapter 42 Answers

1. Yes, because the .PSet method makes a direct plot to the object.

2. No, because the .Point method does not plot to the object, but simply makes a request of that object.

3. Yes, the line does become thicker. Geometrically speaking, because the .Line method plots between two intersection points, it might seem that stretching those points has nothing to do with the thickness of the line between them. Yet once the point is plotted, the *image* of the picture box is set as a bitmap; and the .Move method magnifies that bitmap, not its underlying coordinate system.

Chapter 43 Answers

1. Does not affect the internal coordinate system for that image; .Scale does affect that system.

2. The printer, because a .ScaleMode of four selects elite pitch type, or 12 characters to the inch. Because an inch on your screen cannot be reasonably estimated by your program, although an inch on your printer *can* be estimated, the printer benefits most by this .ScaleMode setting.

3. All cathode ray tube scanning systems in the world start at the upper-left corner of the screen, scan a line toward the right, and then skip to the line below starting at the left side—the way you're reading the lines in this book now. From an engineering standpoint, to place the origin point at the bottom and proceed upward would be backward.

Chapter 44 Answers

1. An error, because this is not the proper syntax for the .Line method. Two sets of parentheses are missing.

2. A bug, because the division operator in the instruction should be a multiplication operator, but the interpreter has no way of knowing the programmer's original intentions.

Chapter 45 Answers

1. The `Print #` statement creates text on disk that has the same format as if the same text were printed to the screen or printer using the `.Print` method. The `Write #` statement, by contrast, places all data entries within quotation marks and separates each entry with a comma, in order for applications with "mail-merge" features to be able to import this data.

2. The `Input #` statement retrieves data entries from disk that have been saved using the `Print #` statement. These entries have the same length after the `Input #` is executed as they had after the `Print #` was executed. The `Line Input #` statement inputs a string of characters—rather than an explicit entry—that is terminated by a carriage return.

3. The screen, its constituent graphic objects, and the printer all have properties and therefore can be expressed using object-oriented syntax. Printing thus becomes a method with respect to them. A data file is governed not by Windows but by DOS, and has no properties. Thus, you must express instructions regarding files using the older style of BASIC syntax.

Chapter 46 Answers

1. 32,765 bytes, which is the maximum length of the actual element minus two for the descriptor.

2. A field.

3. 73 bytes.

Appendix B ◆ Answers to Review Questions

Chapter 47 Answers

1. 74

2. `"We hold"`

3. 7

4. 8

5. `"We hold"`. The `Seek` statement does not affect the contents of a string variable.

6. `" these "` with spaces around the word. The `Input$` function starts inputting characters beginning at the current `Seek()` position.

Chapter 48 Answers

1. None. There is merely a blank record in place of the erased one. NameForm Mark IV has a procedure for covering blank records with the contents of the record immediately following it.

2. The interpreter would consider the header as a formal record, making the first real record #2 in the count rather than #1.

3. Each record is considered saved once the user enters it or corrects it. The random-access data file is modified periodically by the program.

Chapter 49 Answers

1. The final integer that `m` can possibly be made equal to is 2. When `m = 2` in this procedure, the algorithm is sorting only two elements of the array at any one time. By this time, the value `i` immediately following the sort value `j` in the list can

be either 1 less than or 1 greater than the sort value. If `i` is 1 less than `j`, the two values are swapped. At this iteration, the array can be sorted no further.

2. All the QuickSort portion of the algorithm does is group numbers together that have values that are very close to one another. The BubbleSort algorithm is required to sort those small groups, or subarrays.

Chapter 50 Answers

1. The variable `extras` simultaneously represents four true/false states, by virtue of an arbitrarily-selected bitwise place in the base 2 form of the value for each state. The powers of 2 represent the value of 2 raised to each state's place.

2. The error trap mechanism is disengaged with `On Error GoTo 0`. Still, the trap routine has to end, and it may only do so by executing a `Resume` statement, which is a branch. The statement must appear, even though the point being branched to immediately follows the branch.

Chapter 51 Answers

1. When a command line or an instruction is *parsed*, its more important terms are isolated by the interpreter from its less important or unrecognized terms. Then the interpreter can determine how the syntax of the instruction forms a statement or command.

2. The Visual Basic interpreter processes all instructions in the order in which they were written. In processing, however, some of the job of updating the graphic environment is passed on to Windows, which may choose to stand by until VB's mathematical operations—which Windows considers more important—are completed first.

713

Complete Source Code Listings of Major Applications

In this appendix, you will find the complete listings for the major applications covered in this book. If you would like to save some time by not typing the examples, you can order a disk that includes all the code listings in this book, along with some additional programs. See the disk offer page located at the back of this book for more details.

The Expressor—Custom Calculator

The following files make up the EXPRESOR.MAK project:

EXPRESOR.GBL—Global Module

```
Global readout_value As Double, combine_value As Double
Global ready As Integer
```

Appendix C ◆ Complete Source Code Listings of Major Applications

EXPRESOR.FRM—Main Form

Object type	Property	Setting
Form	.Left	1128
	.Top	204
	.Width	5436
	.Height	4692
	.Caption	Expressor
	.BorderStyle	1 - Fixed Single
	.BackColor	&H00FF8080&
Label	.CtlName	Readout
	.Caption	0
	.BackColor	&H00FF0000&
	.FontName	Courier
	.FontSize	15
	.ForeColor	&H00FFFFFF&
Button	.CtlName	EditCut
	.Caption	Cut

Control array	Property	Setting
Label	.CtlName	ParamText
	.Caption	(blank)
	.Index	0
	.BackColor	&H00FFFFFF&
	.ForeColor	&H00FF0000&
	.FontBold	False
	.FontSize	8
	.BorderStyle	0 - None
	.Index	1
	.Index	2
	.Index	3
	.Index	4

Visual Basic *By* EXAMPLE

Control array	Property	Setting
Text box	.CtlName	Param
	.Caption	0
	.BackColor	&H00FFFF00&
	.ForeColor	&H00000000
	.Index	0
	.Index	1
	.Index	2
	.Index	3
	.Index	4

Control array	Property	Setting
Button	.CtlName	StoreBank
	.Index	0
	.Index	1
	.Index	2
	.Index	3
	.Index	4
List box	.CtlName	CalcList
	.BackColor	&H00C00000&
	.ForeColor	&H00FFFFFF&
	.Sorted	False
Button	.CtlName	ApplyFormula
	.Caption	Display
Button	.CtlName	ClearEntry
	.Caption	CE
Button	.CtlName	ClearAll
	.Caption	C

717

Appendix C ♦ Complete Source Code Listings of Major Applications

	Control array	Property	Setting
	Button	.CtlName	ButtonPos
		.Caption	1
		.FontName	Courier
		.Index	1
		.Caption	2
		.Index	2
		.Caption	3
		.Index	3
		.Caption	4
		.Index	4
		.Caption	5
		.Index	5
		.Caption	6
		.Index	6
		.Caption	7
		.Index	7
		.Caption	8
		.Index	8
		.Caption	9
		.Index	9
	Button	.CtlName	Button0
		.Caption	0
		.FontName	Courier
	Button	.CtlName	ButtonPoint
		.Caption	.
		.FontName	Courier
	Button	.CtlName	Percent
		.Caption	%
	Button	.CtlName	DividedBy
		.Caption	/
	Button	.CtlName	Times
		.Caption	X

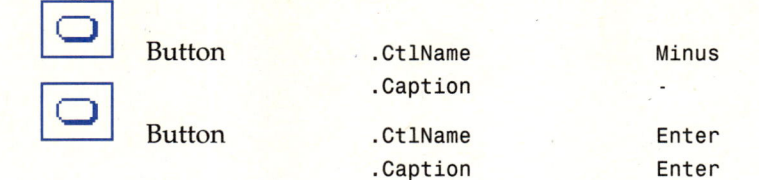

Visual Basic By EXAMPLE

	Button	.CtlName	Minus
		.Caption	-
	Button	.CtlName	Enter
		.Caption	Enter

General Declarations— The Expressor

```
Dim label$(15, 4), p(4)
Dim readout_value As Single, solution As Single
Const PI = 3.1415927
Const GRAV = 6.6732E-11
```

Event Procedures—The Expressor

```
Sub Form_Load ()
CalcList.AddItem "Surface Area of RC Cylinder"
CalcList.AddItem "Volume of RC Cylinder"
CalcList.AddItem "Zone Area of Sphere"
CalcList.AddItem "Force of Earth/Body Attraction"
CalcList.AddItem "Doppler Shift Transmitted Freq."
label$(0, 0) = "Radius of right circular cylinder"
label$(0, 1) = "Height of cylinder"
label$(1, 0) = "Radius of right circular cylinder"
label$(1, 1) = "Height of cylinder"
label$(2, 0) = "Radius of sphere"
label$(2, 1) = "Height of zone"
label$(3, 0) = "Mass of Earth"
label$(3, 1) = "Mass of body in Earth's grav. field"
label$(3, 2) = "Radius of Earth"
label$(3, 3) = "Distance of body above Earth's surface"
label$(4, 0) = "Observer velocity"
label$(4, 1) = "Source velocity"
label$(4, 2) = "Observed frequency"
label$(4, 3) = "Velocity of wave"
End Sub
```

Appendix C ♦ Complete Source Code Listings of Major Applications

```
Sub ApplyFormula_Click ()
For in = 0 To 4
p(in) = Val(param(in).text)
Next in
ndx = CalcList.ListIndex + 1
If ndx = -1 Then GoTo The_end
On ndx GoTo f1, f2, f3, f4, f5
GoTo display_result
f1:
solution = surf_area_rccyl(p(0), p(1))
GoTo display_result
f2:
solution = volume_rccyl(p(0), p(1))
GoTo display_result
f3:
solution = zone_sphere(p(0), p(1))
GoTo display_result
f4:
solution = force_att(p(0), p(1), p(2), p(3))
GoTo display_result
f5:
solution = dopp_shift(p(0), p(1), p(2), p(3))
display_result:
readout.caption = Str$(solution)
The_end:
End Sub
```

```
Sub ButtonPos_Click (Index As Integer)
If ready > 0 Then
    If ready < 20 Then
        readout.caption = readout.caption + Right$(Str$(Index), 1)
        ready = ready + 1
    End If
Else
    readout.caption = Right$(Str$(Index), 1)
    ready = 1
End If
assess_readout
End Sub
```

```
Sub Button0_Click (Index As Integer)
If ready > 0 Then
    If ready < 20 Then
        readout.caption = readout.caption + "0"
        ready = ready + 1
    End If
End If
assess_readout
End Sub
```

```
Sub Button_Point_Click (Index As Integer)
Static point_lock As Integer
If point_lock = 0 And ready < 20 Then
    readout.caption = readout.caption + "."
    point_lock = 1
    ready = ready + 1
End If
assess_readout
End Sub
```

```
Sub CalcList_Click ()
For n = 0 To 4
    ParamText(n).caption = label$(CalcList.ListIndex, n)
Next n
Clear_Params
End Sub
```

```
Sub ClearAll_Click ()
readout.caption = "0"
readout_value = 0
combine_value = 0
ready = 0
End Sub
```

```
Sub ClearEntry_Click ()
readout.caption = "0"
readout_value = 0
ready = 0
End Sub
```

Appendix C ◆ Complete Source Code Listings of Major Applications

```
Sub EditCut_Click ()
Clipboard.SetText readout.caption
End Sub

Sub Enter_Click ()
assess_readout
readout_value = readout_value + combine_value
combine_value = readout_value
readout.caption = Str$(readout_value)
ready = 0
End Sub

Sub Minus_Click ()
assess_readout
readout_value = readout_value - combine_value
combine_value = readout_value
readout.caption = Str$(readout_value)
ready = 0
End Sub

Sub Times_Click ()
assess_readout
readout_value = readout_value * combine_value
combine_value = readout_value
readout.caption = Str$(readout_value)
ready = 0
End Sub

Sub DividedBy_Click ()
assess_readout
If readout_value <> 0 And combine_value <> 0 Then
    readout_value = readout_value / combine_value
End If
combine_value = readout_value
readout.caption = Str$(readout_value)
ready = 0
End Sub

Sub Percent_Click ()
readout_value = readout_value / 100
readout.caption = Str$(readout_value)
ready = 0
End Sub
```

Visual Basic By EXAMPLE

```
Sub StoreBank_Click (Index As Integer)
param(Index).text = readout.caption
ready = 0
End Sub
```

General Procedures— The Expressor

```
Sub assess_readout ()
readout_value = Val(readout.caption)
End Sub

Sub Clear_Params ()
For pl = 0 To 4
param(pl).text = ""
Next pl
ClearAll_Click
End Sub

Function dopp_shift (vo, vs, fo, c)
dopp_shift = ((c + vo) / (c - vs)) * fo
End Function

Function force_att (me, mb, r, y)
force_att = -GRAV * ((me * mb) / ((r + y) ^ 2))
End Function

Function surf_area_rccyl (r, h)
surf_area_rccyl = (2 * PI) * r * h
End Function

Function volume_rccyl (r, h)
volume_rccyl = PI * (r ^ 2) * h
End Function

Function zone_sphere (r, h)
zone_sphere = 2 * PI * r * h
End Function
```

Appendix C ◆ Complete Source Code Listings of Major Applications

NameForm Mark IV—Mailing List Manager

The following files make up the NameForm Mark IV program:

NAMEFRM4.GBL—Global Module

```
Option Base 1
Global TargetFile$, cancl As Integer, prmpt$, filename$,
    pattern$
Type NameRecord
    LastName As String * 30
    FirstName As String * 20
    MidInit As String * 3
    CompanyName As String * 50
    Address As String * 50
    City As String * 20
    State As String * 5
    Zip As String * 10
    MidProm As Integer
End Type
Global CurRecord As NameRecord
```

NAMEFRM4.FRM—Main Form

Object type	Property	Setting
Form	.Left	930
	.Top	1110
	.Width	8655
	.Height	3750
	.FormName	NameForm
	.Caption	NameForm Mark IV

Visual Basic *By* EXAMPLE

Menu	Control Name	Caption
	File	&File
	FileOpen	----&Open
	FileSort	----&Sort
	hyphen1	-----
	FileSaveMerge	----Save as &Mail Merge
	FileTrim	----&Trim
	Edit	&Edit
	EditCopy	----Cop&y
	EditClear	----Clea&r
	Record	&Record
	RecordInsert	----&Insert
	RecordDelete	----&Delete
	Display	&Display
	DisplayFirst	----&First Name First
	DisplayLast	----&Last Name First
	GoToRecord	&GoTo

Object type	Property	Setting
Text box	.CtlName	LastName
	.Caption	(blank)
Text box	.CtlName	FirstName
	.Caption	(blank)
Text box	.CtlName	MidInit
	.Caption	(blank)
Text box	.CtlName	CompanyName
	.Caption	(blank)
Text box	.CtlName	Address
	.Caption	(blank)
Text box	.CtlName	City
	.Caption	(blank)
Text box	.CtlName	State
	.Caption	(blank)
Text box	.CtlName	Zip
	.Caption	(blank)

Appendix C ◆ Complete Source Code Listings of Major Applications

Object type	Property	Setting
Label	.Ca/ption	Name
	.FontItalic	True
	.Alignment	1 - Right Justify
Label	.Caption	First
	.FontBold	False
	.FontItalic	True
	.Alignment	1 - Right Justify
Label	.Caption	M.I.
	.FontBold	False
	.FontItalic	True
	.Alignment	1 - Right Justify
Label	.Caption	Company Name
	.FontBold	False
	.FontItalic	True
	.Alignment	1 - Right Justify
Label	.Caption	Address
	.FontBold	False
	.FontItalic	True
	.Alignment	1 - Right Justify
Label	.Caption	City
	.FontBold	False
	.FontItalic	True
	.Alignment	1 - Right Justify
Label	.Caption	State
	.FontBold	False
	.FontItalic	True
	.Alignment	1 - Right Justify
Label	.Caption	Zip
	.FontBold	False
	.FontItalic	True
	.Alignment	1 - Right Justify
Label	.CtlName	Register
	.Caption	(blank)
	.Alignment	1 - Right Justify

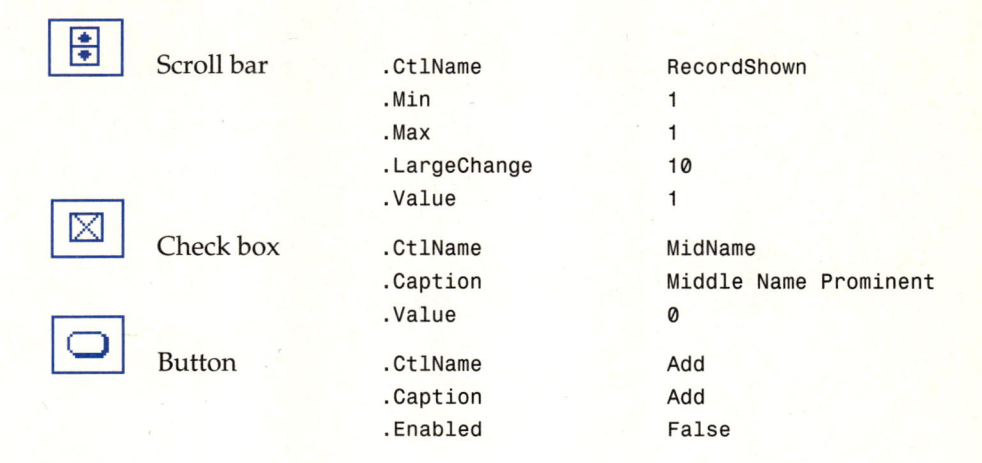

Scroll bar		.CtlName	RecordShown
		.Min	1
		.Max	1
		.LargeChange	10
		.Value	1
Check box		.CtlName	MidName
		.Caption	Middle Name Prominent
		.Value	0
Button		.CtlName	Add
		.Caption	Add
		.Enabled	False

General Declarations—NameForm Mark IV

```
Dim lastline As Integer, lhght As Integer, llft As Integer,
    lastmark As Integer
Dim RecordNo As Integer, MaxRecord As Integer
Dim sortarray() As Integer
```

Event Procedures—NameForm Mark IV

```
Sub Form_Load ()
filename$ = "NAMES.NFM"
LoadFile
End Sub

Sub Address_Change ()
CurRecord.Address = Address.Text
End Sub

Sub City_Change ()
CurRecord.City = City.Text
End Sub
```

Appendix C ◆ Complete Source Code Listings of Major Applications

```
Sub CompanyName_Change ()
CurRecord.CompanyName = CompanyName.Text
End Sub

Sub LastName_Change ()
CurRecord.LastName = LastName.Text
End Sub

Sub MidInit_Change ()
CurRecord.MidInit = MidInit.Text
End Sub

Sub State_Change ()
CurRecord.State = State.Text
End Sub

Sub Zip_Change ()
CurRecord.Zip = Zip.Text
End Sub

Sub MidName_Click ()
CurRecord.MidProm = MidName.Value
End Sub

Sub Add_Click ()
Put #1, RecordNo, CurRecord
RecordNo = RecordNo + 1
MaxRecord = MaxRecord + 1
ClearForm
CurRecord.FirstName = "~*End"
Put #1, MaxRecord + 1, CurRecord
RecordShown.Max = RecordShown.Max + 1
RecordShown.Value = RecordNo
If RecordNo = MaxRecord Then
    CurRecord.FirstName = ""
    Put #1, RecordNo, CurRecord
End If
ShowRecord
End Sub

Sub DisplayFirst_Click ()
c$ = Envelope$(RecordNo, 1)
```

```
MsgBox c$, 0, "Preview"
End Sub

Sub DisplayLast_Click ()
c$ = Envelope$(RecordNo, 0)
MsgBox c$, 0, "Preview"
End Sub

Sub EditClear_Click ()
ClearForm
End Sub

Sub RecordDelete_Click ()
If RecordNo < MaxRecord Then
    For mve = RecordNo To MaxRecord
        Get #1, mve + 1, CurRecord
        Put #1, mve, CurRecord
    Next mve
End If
ClearForm
If RecordNo = MaxRecord Then
    RecordNo = RecordNo - 1
End If
If MaxRecord > 1 Then
    MaxRecord = MaxRecord - 1
    RecordShown.Max = RecordShown.Max - 1
Else
    Put #1, 1, CurRecord
End If
ShowRecord
End Sub

Sub RecordInsert_Click ()
For mve = MaxRecord + 1 To RecordNo Step -1
    Get #1, mve, CurRecord
    Put #1, mve + 1, CurRecord
Next mve
ClearForm
Put #1, RecordNo, CurRecord
MaxRecord = MaxRecord + 1
RecordShown.Max = RecordShown.Max + 1
End Sub
```

729

Appendix C ◆ Complete Source Code Listings of Major Applications

```
Sub FileTrim_Click ()
Open "~temp.fil" For Random As #2 Len = 190
plc = 1
tmp = RecordNo
Do
    Get #1, plc, CurRecord
    Put #2, plc, CurRecord
Loop Until CurRecord.FirstName = "~*End"
Close #2, #1
Kill filename$
Name "~temp.fil" As filename$
Open filename$ For Random As #1 Len = 190
RecordNo = tmp
ShowRecord
End Sub

Sub RecordShown_Change ()
Put #1, RecordNo, CurRecord
RecordNo = RecordShown.Value
If RecordNo < MaxRecord Then
    Add.Enabled = 0
Else
    Add.Enabled = -1
End If
ShowRecord
End Sub

Sub FileOpen_Click ()
prmpt$ = "Choose a file to open:"
pattern$ = "*.nfm"
Selector.Show 1
filename$ = targetfile$
If cancl = 1 Then Exit Sub
cancl = 0
Close #1
LoadFile
End Sub

Sub FileSaveMerge_Click ()
prmpt$ = "Name of mail merge file:"
pattern$ = "*.mrg"
Selector.Show 1
```

730

```
        If cancl = 1 Then Exit Sub
        filename$ = targetfile$
        Open filename$ For Output As #2
        For ConvRec = 1 To MaxRecord
            Get #1, ConvRec, CurRecord
            Write #2, RTrim$(CurRecord.LastName),
                RTrim$(CurRecord.FirstName), RTrim$(CurRecord.MidInit),
                RTrim$(CurRecord.CompanyName), RTrim$(CurRecord.Address),
                RTrim$(CurRecord.City), RTrim$(CurRecord.State),
                RTrim$(CurRecord.Zip), CurRecord.MidProm
        Next ConvRec
        Close #2
        ShowRecord
        End Sub

        Sub GoToRecord_Click ()
        recno$ = InputBox$("Go to which record number?", "Go To. . .")
        RecordNo = Val(recno$)
        RecordShown.Value = RecordNo
        ShowRecord
        End Sub

        Sub EditCopy_Click ()
        c$ = Envelope$(RecordNo, 1)
        Clipboard.SetText c$
        End Sub

        Sub FileSort_Click ()
        Dim j As Integer, k As Integer, l As Integer, t As Integer,
            seed As Integer
        ReDim sortarray(MaxRecord)
        tmp = RecordNo
        RecordNo = MaxRecord
        If Asc(Left$(LastName.Text, 1)) > 0 Then
            Put #1, RecordNo, CurRecord
        End If
        For seed = 1 To MaxRecord
            sortarray(seed) = seed
        Next seed
        Do
            l = l + 1
            If l = MaxRecord Then Exit Do
            j = l
```

Appendix C ◆ Complete Source Code Listings of Major Applications

```
        For k = j + 1 To MaxRecord - 1
            If Envelope$(k, 0) <= Envelope$(j, 0) Then
                j = k
            End If
        Next k
        If l <> j Then
            t = sortarray(j)
            sortarray(j) = sortarray(l)
            sortarray(l) = t
        End If
Loop
Open "~temp.fil" For Random As #2 Len = 190
For replac = 1 To MaxRecord - 1
    Get #1, sortarray(replac), CurRecord
    Put #2, replac, CurRecord
Next replac
Close #2, #1
Kill filename$
Name "~temp.fil" As filename$
Open filename$ For Random As #1 Len = 190
RecordNo = sortarray(tmp)
ShowRecord
End Sub
```

General Procedures— NameForm Mark IV

```
Sub LoadFile ()
Open filename$ For Random As #1 Len = 190
If LOF(1) > 190 Then
    Do
        Get #1, MaxRecord + 1, CurRecord
        MaxRecord = MaxRecord + 1
    Loop Until CurRecord.FirstName = "~*End" Or MaxRecord >
      LOF(1) / 190
Else
    CurRecord.FirstName = "~*End"
    Put #1, 2, CurRecord
    CurRecord.MidProm = 0
    CurRecord.FirstName = ""
```

```
        Put #1, 1, CurRecord
        MaxRecord = 1
End If
titl$ = "NameForm Mark IV - [" + UCase$(filename$) + "]"
NameForm.Caption = titl$
RecordNo = 1
RecordShown.Max = MaxRecord
RecordShown.Value = 1
If RecordNo < MaxRecord Then
    Add.Enabled = 0
Else
    Add.Enabled = -1
End If
ShowRecord
End Sub

Sub ShowRecord ()
Get #1, RecordNo, CurRecord
Reg$ = "Record #" + Str$(RecordNo) + " of " + Str$(MaxRecord)
Register.Caption = Reg$
LastName.Text = RTrim$(CurRecord.LastName)
FirstName.Text = RTrim$(CurRecord.FirstName)
MidInit.Text = RTrim$(CurRecord.MidInit)
CompanyName.Text = RTrim$(CurRecord.CompanyName)
Address.Text = RTrim$(CurRecord.Address)
City.Text = RTrim$(CurRecord.City)
State.Text = RTrim$(CurRecord.State)
Zip.Text = RTrim$(CurRecord.Zip)
MidName.Value = CurRecord.MidProm
End Sub

Sub ClearForm ()
FirstName.Text = ""
LastName.Text = ""
MidInit.Text = ""
CompanyName.Text = ""
Address.Text = ""
City.Text = ""
State.Text = ""
Zip.Text = ""
MidName.Value = 0
End Sub
```

Appendix C ◆ Complete Source Code Listings of Major Applications

```
Function Envelope$ (rec As Integer, order As Integer)
Get #1, rec, CurRecord
If Asc(Left$(CurRecord.MidInit, 1)) <> 0 Then
    Separator$ = " " + RTrim$(CurRecord.MidInit) + " "
Else
    Separator$ = " "
End If
If order = 1 Then
    If MidName.Value = 0 Then
        FullName$ = RTrim$(CurRecord.FirstName) +
            Separator$ + RTrim$(CurRecord.LastName)
    Else
        FullName$ = RTrim$(CurRecord.MidInit) + " " +
            RTrim$(CurRecord.FirstName) + " " +
            RTrim$(CurRecord.LastName)
    End If
Else
    If MidName.Value = 0 Then
        FullName$ = RTrim$(CurRecord.LastName) +
            ", " + RTrim$(CurRecord.FirstName) +
            Separator$
    Else
        FullName$ = RTrim$(CurRecord.LastName) +
            ", " + Separator$ +
            RTrim$(CurRecord.FirstName)
    End If
End If
WorkPlace$ = RTrim$(CurRecord.CompanyName)
StreetAddress$ = RTrim$(CurRecord.Address)
Residence$ = RTrim$(CurRecord.City) + ", " +
   RTrim$(CurRecord.State) + " " + RTrim$(CurRecord.Zip)
Next_Line$ = Chr$(13) + Chr$(10)
Envelope$ = FullName$ + Next_Line$ + WorkPlace$ +
   Next_Line$ + StreetAddress$ + Next_Line$ + Residence$
End Function
```

The Selector Mark II—File Selector Form

The following files make up the Selector Mark II file selection form:

SELECTR2.FRM—Main Form

Object type	Property	Setting
Form	.Left	1110
	.Top	1170
	.Width	5925
	.Height	4125
	.FormName	Selector
	.Caption	(blank)
	.BorderStyle	3 - Fixed Double
	.BackColor	&H00400000&
Drive list box	.CtlName	Drive1
	.FontSize	9.75
Path list box	.CtlName	Dir1
File list box	.CtlName	File1
	.FontBold	False
Text box	.CtlName	Filename
	.FontSize	9.75
	.ForeColor	&H00800000&
	.BorderStyle	1 - Fixed Single
Text box	.CtlName	Prompt
	.BackColor	&H00C00000&
	.ForeColor	&H00FFFFFF&
Picture box	.CtlName	OptPanel
	.BackColor	&H0000FFFF&
	.Enabled	False
	.Visible	False

Appendix C ◆ Complete Source Code Listings of Major Applications

	Frame	.CtlName	OptFrame
		.Caption	File Display Options
		.BackColor	&00800000&
		.ForeColor	&H00FFFFF&
	Label	.CtlName	Archive
		.Caption	Archive
		.FontBold	False
		.BackColor	&H00800000&
		.ForeColor	&H00FFFF80&
	Label	.CtlName	Hidden
		.Caption	Hidden
		.FontBold	False
		.BackColor	&H00800000&
		.ForeColor	&H00FFFF80&
	Label	.CtlName	Hidden
		.Caption	Hidden
		.FontBold	False
		.BackColor	&H00800000&
		.ForeColor	&H00FFFF80&
	Label	.CtlName	ReadOnly
		.Caption	Read Only
		.FontBold	False
		.BackColor	&H00800000&
		.ForeColor	&H00FFFF80&
	Label	.CtlName	Systm
		.Caption	System
		.FontBold	False
		.BackColor	&H00800000&
		.ForeColor	&H00FFFF80&
	Button	.CtlName	OKOpt
		.Caption	OK
		.FontBold	False
		.BackColor	&H00800000&
	Button	.CtlName	OK
		.Caption	OK
		.Default	True
		.BackColor	&H00800000&

Visual Basic *By*
EXAMPLE

Button	.CtlName	Cancel
	.Caption	Cancel
	.Cancel	True
	.BackColor	&H00800000&
Label	.CtlName	Options
	.Caption	Options
	.BackColor	&H000000FF&
	.ForeColor	&H0000FFFF&
	.Alignment	2 - Centered

General Declarations— The Selector Mark II

```
Dim arc As Integer, hid As Integer, nor As Integer, rdo
    As Integer, sys As Integer
```

Event Procedures— The Selector Mark II

```
Sub Form_Load ()
File1.pattern = pattern$
Filename.Text = File1.pattern
Dir1.Path = CurDir$
cancl = 0
If prmpt$ = "" Then
    Prompt.Caption = "Filename:"
Else
    Prompt.Caption = prmpt$
End If
If optout = 1 Then
    Options.Enabled = 0
    Options.Visible = 0
End If
nor = -1
arc = (extras And 1) > 0
hid = (extras And 2) > 0
rdo = (extras And 4) > 0
```

737

Appendix C ◆ Complete Source Code Listings of Major Applications

```
    sys = (extras And 8) > 0
    Normal.FontBold = nor
    Normal.ForeColor = QBColor(15)
    If arc Then
        Archive.FontBold = arc
        Archive.ForeColor = QBColor(15)
    End If
    If hid Then
        Hidden.FontBold = hid
        Hidden.ForeColor = QBColor(15)
    End If
    If rdo Then
        ReadOnly.FontBold = rdo
        ReadOnly.ForeColor = QBColor(15)
    End If
    If sys Then
        Systm.FontBold = sys
        Systm.ForeColor = QBColor(15)
    End If
    End Sub

    Sub Drive1_Change ()
    Dir1.Path = Drive1.Drive
    ChDrive Drive1.Drive
    End Sub

    Sub Dir1_Change ()
    File1.Path = Dir1.Path
    File1_Click
    End Sub

    Sub File1_Click ()
    Filename.Text = File1.Filename
    End Sub

    Sub File1_DblClick ()
    OK_Click
    End Sub

    Sub OK_Click ()
    topofproc:
    pth$ = Dir1.Path
```

```vb
        If File1.Filename = "" Then
            fil$ = Filename.Text
        Else
            fil$ = File1.Filename
        End If
        If Right$(pth$, 1) = "\" Then
            Filename.Text = pth$ + fil$
        Else
            Filename.Text = pth$ + "\" + fil$
        End If
        TargetFile$ = Filename.Text
        On Error GoTo Oops
        Open TargetFile$ For Binary As #1
        Close #1
        ChDir Dir1.Path
        Unload Selector
        Exit Sub
        Oops:
        If Err = 53 Then
            MsgBox "File cannot be found", 32
        Else
            MsgBox "ERROR:   " + Error$(Err)
        End If
        On Error GoTo 0
        Resume Outahere
        Outahere:
        End Sub

        Sub Cancel_Click ()
        cancl = 1
        TargetFile$ = ""
        Unload Selector
        End Sub

        Sub Options_Click ()
        Dir1.Enabled = 0
        File1.Enabled = 0
        OptPanel.Visible = -1
        OptPanel.Enabled = -1
        End Sub
```

Appendix C ◆ Complete Source Code Listings of Major Applications

```
Sub Archive_Click ()
If arc = 0 Then
    arc = -1
    Archive.ForeColor = QBColor(15)
Else
    arc = 0
    Archive.ForeColor = &HFFFF80
End If
Archive.FontBold = arc
End Sub

Sub Hidden_Click ()
If hid = 0 Then
    hid = -1
    Hidden.ForeColor = QBColor(15)
Else
    hid = 0
    Hidden.ForeColor = &HFFFF80
End If
Hidden.FontBold = hid
End Sub

Sub Normal_Click ()
If nor = 0 Then
    nor = -1
    Normal.ForeColor = QBColor(15)
Else
    nor = 0
    Normal.ForeColor = &HFFFF80
End If
Normal.FontBold = nor
End Sub

Sub ReadOnly_Click ()
If rdo = 0 Then
    rdo = -1
    ReadOnly.ForeColor = QBColor(15)
Else
    rdo = 0
    ReadOnly.ForeColor = &HFFFF80
End If
ReadOnly.FontBold = rdo
End Sub
```

```
Sub Systm_Click ()
If sys = 0 Then
    sys = -1
    Systm.ForeColor = QBColor(15)
Else
    sys = 0
    Systm.ForeColor = &HFFFF80
End If
Systm.FontBold = sys
End Sub
```

```
Sub OKOpt_Click ()
OptPanel.Visible = 0
OptPanel.Enabled = 0
Dir1.Enabled = -1
File1.Enabled = -1
File1.Archive = arc
File1.Hidden = hid
File1.Normal = nor
File1.ReadOnly = rdo
File1.System = sys
End Sub
```

Glossary

algorithm Any real-world process having inherent objects and elements, however tangible, that can be represented by linguistic or numeric code, and having procedures that can be simulated using terms acquainted with logic.

alphanumeric Having the quality of containing either letters or digits, or both.

antecedent The graphic object referred to by a property or method, generally written following the period that separates it from the graphic object with which it is associated.

application An operational program or set of cooperative programs within the computer environment having a work product that is a specific document or set of documents.

argument A value or variable used within a function or formula. This term is often synonymous with *parameter*.

array A list or set of related values or alphanumeric contents, collectively referred to by a common term.

ASCII The American Standard Code for Information Interchange. This is the most widely used code for transmission and storage of alphanumeric data in a bitwise form within or between computers.

binary   Representable using as many as two digits. This term also refers to the base 2 numeral system.

binary access   A method of storing data to and retrieving it from a device, whereby the structure of the data is not a factor, and data is interpreted only as single bits, bytes, or characters.

binary state   The minimum unit of value in a computer, which can be described as either true (−1 or 1, depending on the interpreter) or false (0).

bit   Short for *binary digit*, which is the elementary unit of value within a computer, representing a logical state of true (1 or ON) or false (0 or OFF). Mechanically, it represents the presence of electrical current.

bitmap   A group of related values which, when represented on the screen as pixels rather than characters, forms an image.

blit   Short for *block transfer*, it is an instantaneous relocation of a grouping of memory contents from one region to another.

Boolean operator   A term used to represent the comparison of one binary value to another, the intent being to derive a single binary value as a result.

branching   To direct the interpreter to suspend execution of the normal sequence of instructions and resume the sequence at some other specified point in the program.

break   A suspension of the operating state of the program.

breakpoint   An instruction line temporarily scheduled to force execution of the program to be suspended immediately following the execution of that line.

buffer   A holding area in memory consisting of a fixed number of bytes, reserved for data that is to be sent to some device—often a disk file—at some later time, generally when the buffer is full.

bug   The result of any process that failed to perform in the manner for which it was intended or designed, although it cannot be detected automatically by the interpreter or compiler. Thus by its nature, a bug allows logical program execution to continue along a potentially disastrous course.

button   A control or graphic object used for passing directives or commands to the program.

byte   The primary memory storage unit for all forms of data in a computer system, comprised of eight binary digits (bits).

caption   A non-editable element of text appearing within a form or graphic object.

channel   A logically interpreted device (in other words, not a tangible, physical entity) for maintaining the flow of data between the interpreter and an output device or storage unit.

check box   A graphic control used to represent an on/off or true/false state, the setting of which is chosen by the user.

child   An object or element belonging to, or residing within, a greater *parent* element.

clause   1. A compound instruction that contains one or more subordinate instructions and is distributed in a single group over more than one line.   2. Any set of instructions, the execution of which is dependent on the value of a variable in a mathematical expression.

client   The receiver or requester of the primary block of data in a communications link.

clipboard   The logical device maintained by Microsoft Windows, which retains an element of data being transferred between locations.

combo box   A control that enables a user to choose an item from a list or type a choice that may not appear on that list.

composite variable   A container for multiple numeral, string, or other composite variables, addressed together as one unit using a single, arbitrarily defined term and invoked within an instruction using object-oriented syntax.

condition   A mathematical test, stated in the form of an expression, used to determine the order of execution of the program.

constant   A term that stands in place of a value in an expression, having its value set once and only once.

Glossary ◆ Visual Basic

context The "understanding" the interpreter has of which variables and functions of a procedure pertain only to that procedure, which values and variables are exchanged between this procedure and the one that called it, and which variables and functions pertain to the program as a whole. In other words, the relative degree to which one component of a program pertains to the rest of that program.

control A graphic object placed on a form specifically for purposes of data acquisition and display, in a manner that easily can be made familiar to the user.

control array A set of similar, related controls in a form that are referenced together as a group, and the operation of which is jointly defined by a single procedure in the source code.

conversation The term for a Dynamic Data Exchange communication between two applications currently running within the Windows environment.

cursor A marker indicating the point within a document or textually oriented control where new characters will appear after they are typed; also called the *caret*.

database Any stored group of data elements containing the structure by which those elements are related to each other.

decimal A number that can be represented using as many as 10 digits. The term also refers to the base 10 numeral system.

declaration **1.** The first statement in a program to assign a legitimate value to a variable. **2.** An instruction that introduces a procedure or process and defines the context of that process.

default The state of an object, device, or memory construct that is presumed beforehand if no instructions to alter that state have been processed.

delimiter A character of punctuation used to distinguish elements of an expression from each other, or to separate them from each other.

design time The period of the Visual Basic interpreter's execution during which the programmer composes the application.

dialog box   A window having the purpose of obtaining at least one element of user input. It is often abbreviated as *dialog*.

document   The primary data product of an application as it is represented in memory.

Dynamic Data Exchange   Microsoft's term for interapplication communication within the Windows environment.

dynamic link   An established channel of communication between two or more Windows applications, whereupon all applications joined by the link recognize the same element of data, and any change to that data made by one application is recognized immediately by all other applications sharing the link.

Dynamic Link Library   A file containing programs that can be accessed by any participating Windows applications using standardized functional terms, by means of a dynamic link.

environment   The logical and often graphical facilities one program provides another for easier, more efficient operation.

equation   A statement of equality that assigns a value—whether it is a numeral or an arithmetically derived value—to a variable.

error   The result of any process that fails to perform in the manner it is intended or designed, and which by its nature or in the interest of preventing disaster prevents logical program execution from continuing.

event   A unit of user input, utilizing any of the available devices attached to the computer system, which triggers the execution of a procedure in response.

expression   **1.** An arithmetic comparison between two values, the result of which is expressed logically as a binary state.   **2.** One or more values or variables arithmetically joined by functions or functional operators.   **3.** An assignment of value to a variable with another value, variable, or another expression.

field   Any container for an element or item of data, whether it be a graphic object for the display of that datum, a region of memory reserved for that datum, or a region of a file reserved for that datum.

Glossary ◆ Visual Basic

floating-point   The storage format for a possibly fractional value, having its decimal point position stored in memory as a separate value.

focus   The state of a graphic object indicated on-screen by a hazy rectangle, which designates that the control is active or awaiting input from the user.

form   The input/output window for Visual Basic applications, and the container for graphic objects that act as controls.

formula   An algebraic expression of equality that states the relationships between qualities, quantities, or other such values, whether they are known or unknown.

frame   A subdivision of a form that divides groupings of elements, such as options, from groups in other frames and elsewhere on the form.

function   An arithmetic operation performed on a value, variable, or expression, the result of which is returned in a single variable.

global module   The primary module for variable and structural declarations in a Visual Basic project, recognized by all other modules within the application.

graphic device   Any mechanical or logical unit having the purpose of displaying data as both characters and images.

graphic object   A data structure that can be represented visually and behaves to some degree as a device that receives user input and displays result data.

handle   The accession number given a logical device by the operating system or environment, used to identify that device within the program.

hexadecimal   A number that can be represented using as many as 16 digits. This term also refers to the base 16 numeral system.

icon   A functionally symbolic representation of a form, window, device, or application.

image   The visual interpretation of a segment of values in memory.

index   The value represented by a subscript of an array.

instruction   Any complete directive made within a program, comprised of a keyword and any parameters, terms, or delimiters associated with that directive.

integer   Any whole number that has no fractional value.

integrity   The measure of the logical correspondence between data and the information it is intended to represent.

interpreter   Any program that receives a set of compound, high-level instructions from the programmer and instantly translates them into more rudimentary instructions that are easier for the computer to understand and execute.

iteration   One repeated cycle of execution of the instructions in a loop clause, or any repetitious body of instructions.

keyword   A term having its use reserved for instructions. It cannot be used for variables or labels.

label   A non-instruction written on a line by itself and succeeded by a colon, designating a branching point.

library   A set of process names that are treated as procedure names by Visual Basic, but which are actually calls to processes within a Dynamic Link Library outside of Visual Basic.

list box   A control that allows one or more items to be chosen from a list, often a scrollable list.

local   The minimum scope of a variable or composite structure, which limits its references to the confines of a single procedure.

logical context   A program structure that simulates an electronic device for the sake of any routine that directs data to it for output.

logical reduction   The act of obtaining the solution value to an expression by reducing the elements of that expression through arithmetic combination.

loop   A sequence of instructions that are executed repetitively either for a specified count or until a condition is evaluated true.

maximize To bring a reduced icon back into the workspace, as the form or window associated with that icon.

menu bar The area of a form or window below the title bar where categorical command or directive choices are listed.

meta-application A single task formed by the cooperation of several application components working in conjunction within the same environment.

metafile A method of representing vectored, object-oriented graphics within the Windows environment.

method An instruction that directs the interpreter to perform a programmed action on a graphic object.

minimize To reduce a form or window to its associated icon temporarily, thus suspending its primary execution.

modal An attribute of a window which suspends the operability of every other window until it is exited.

module A complete set of procedures along with form contents and properties, stored within a single file.

multitasking The planned or scheduled cooperation of multiple programs within a single computer system, with the capability for single elements of data to be recognized by those multiple programs during the same session.

nest The special indentation of typesetting optionally given to a set of dependent instructions within a clause.

object In object-oriented syntax, a data structure that combines the contents and attributes of the data, along with the encoded form of its function.

octal Numbers that can be represented using as many as eight digits. This term also refers to the base 8 numeral system.

operator A symbol that represents a mathematical function combining, comparing, or equating two values.

option dot A control, generally one of a set of such controls, used to represent the user's single choice of all the elements within a collected set.

parameter   A value or variable passed to a procedure from outside that procedure.

parent   The greater object or element with which another object or element is associated.

phrase   Any functional combination of terms within an instruction or routine.

pixel   The minimum unit of measurement or plotting in the physical screen coordinate system.

pointer[1]   The logical device operated by the mouse, used for indicating elements on the screen.

pointer[2]   **1.** A value that represents the location in memory where a value or contents of a variable are stored.   **2.** Any logical value that represents the location or position where another value can be obtained.

precision   Refers to the number of bytes used to represent a variable's value.

procedure   The core component of a Visual Basic application, the purpose of which is to logically describe or model at least one task or mathematical function, passing its results to some other component.

program   The symbolic form of a task, or any computing process that is described logically in a uniformly interpretable code.

project   All the files that collectively comprise a Visual Basic application.

property   An attribute of a graphic object that is addressable by name using object-oriented syntax, and can be described by a value or term.

random access   A mode for storing data to and retrieving it from a device, either physical or logical, whereby data can be written to or read from a region or file at any specifiable point, at any time.

record   A logical grouping of related elements of data within a data file or database.

Glossary ◆ Visual Basic

relation The mathematics that symbolically join two or more elements or fields of a database.

RGB Refers to a method of mixing red, green, and blue colors optically.

routine Any arbitrarily bounded sequence of instructions within a body of source code.

run time The period in which instructions within the source code of the program are executing.

scope The extent to which the reference of a variable is applied across the various divisions of the source code of a program.

scroll bar A sliding graphic device having the purpose of representing a value within a minimum and maximum range.

sequential access A mode for storing data to and retrieving data from a physical device in an absolute, specifiable sequence.

server The sender of the primary block of data in a communications link.

setting A term that represents the state, appearance, or some aspect of a graphic object.

source code The written text of a program in its native language.

statement An instruction that specifies a change or deviation in the operating status of the program.

static Used to describe a variable or structure local to a procedure, having its value or contents maintained by the interpreter on exiting that procedure, for use when the procedure is entered again.

string A sequence of any number of bytes that are interpreted jointly as text or alphanumeric characters.

subroutine A set of instructions within a procedure that can be executed repetitively, can be called by name, and when ended can force a branch back to the instruction just past the one that called it.

subscript An integral value or variable within an array variable that represents the place or position of a value in the array's list or table.

syntax   The arrangement of terms within an instruction or clause.

tab sequence   The arbitrarily designated order of graphic objects within a form, representing the sequence in which the focus passes through those objects during run time, when the user presses the Tab key.

table   A stored database component consisting of data, along with the structure of that data, such as field names and relations.

tag   Refers to the alias name arbitrarily given to a graphic object.

title bar   The uppermost bar of a form or window, which generally contains the title of that window.

twip   A plotting point as interpreted in memory by Microsoft Windows, within a relative coordinate system that exists independently from the physical pixel-based coordinate system of the screen.

variable   An arbitrarily named term that represents a unit of data in memory that can be altered by the program.

virtual terminal   Any graphic object capable of receiving input and output in the manner of a standard computer terminal.

workspace   The area of the screen where forms and Visual Basic tools reside—but may not necessarily appear—during an application's run time.

Index

Symbols

\# (pound sign), 474, 550, 557, 561
$ (dollar sign), 120, 474
% (percentage sign), 474
   integer symbol, 92
& long integer symbol, 92
&H symbol, 158
– operator
   subtraction, 97
   unary, 49
' (apostrophe), 186
, (comma), 467, 474, 557, 561
" " (double quotation marks), 467
   null string symbol, 213
( ) parentheses, 98-104, 241
   with Boolean operators,
      116-117
* (multiplication) operator, 97
+ operator
   addition, 97
   concatenation, 123

. (period), 473
... (ellipsis), 65
/ operator
   division, 97
   slash, 49
: (colon), 55, 222
; (semicolon), 467, 557, 561
< (less than) operator, 111
<= (less than or equal to)
     operator, 111
= operator
   assignment, 49
   comparison, 49
   equal to, 111
> (greater than) operator, 111
>= (greater than or equal to)
     operator, 111
? (Print statement) shortcut, 100
[] (brackets), 65
^ (exponentiation) operator, 97
_ underscore character, 36
{} (braces), 65

Index

A

`Abs()` function, 423-424
`Acquire ()` procedure, 572-575
active state, 265
`ActiveControl.` object as property, 336
`ActiveForm.` object as property, 336
`.AddItem` method, 287-289
addition (+) operator, 97
address numbers, changing default lower bounds, 170
`Address_Change ()` procedure, 315, 602
algebra, procedural, 60
algorithms, 618
    BubbleSort, 625-627, 640-643
    QuickSort, 630-640
    Shell/Metzner, 627-629
    sorting, 618, 625
`.Alignment` property, 480
allocating array variables dynamically, 138-139
alphanumeric strings, 429-431
    assigning to string variables, 570
    comparing to values, 119-120
    converting numeric values, 76, 472-477
AND Boolean operator, 113-117
annuities, future values, 54-55
ANSI (American National Standards Institute) codes, 121, 687-693
antecedents, 266
apostrophe ('), 186
`AppActivate` statement, 675
applications, 15
    hierarchy of divisions, 50-52
    launching applications from within, 673-675
    NameForm, 591-614
    passing focus to other applications, 675
`ApplyFormula_Click ()` procedure, 291
`.Archive` property, 651
`Archive_Click ()` procedure, 663
arcs, drawing, 517-519
arctangent, 425
arguments, 241
arithmetic
    modulo, 158
    operators, 96-97
array elements, 618
array variables, 133-134, 574
    allocating units equal to number of records, 139-140
    changing default lower bounds address numbers, 170
    changing sizes, 138-139
    declaring, 134-138
    sequential-access file, loading, 580
arrays
    allocating same lengths as files, 139-140, 144
    control, 74-75, 212-213, 310-311
    dividing, 634
    erasing contents, 138
    establishing bounds, 140-141
    one-dimensional (lists), 135
    redimensioning, 138-139
    seeding, 623
    sequential-access, saving, 549-550
    sorting, 627-638
    swapping, 629
    three-dimensional (three-axis tables), 136
    two-dimensional (tables), 136

As `Control` expression, 330
As `Integer` expression, 137-138
As *type* expression, 241
`Asc()` function, 417-418, 587
ASCII (American Standard Code for Information Interchange) code, 121-122, 687-693
   converting values with characters, 416-418
   detecting key presses with, 386-387
ASCII-delimited data files, 561
assignment
   (=) operator, 49
   expressions, 48-49, 122, 408-410
   statements, 92-93
`Atn()` function, 425
ATTRIB command, 650
attributes
   files, 650
   identifying in names, 40
automation, 15
`.AutoRedraw` property, 526
`.AutoSize` property, 525-526
axes, 136
   setting divisions, 527-528

B

Babbage, Charles, 154
`.BackColor` property, 341-343
background
   backing up disks in, 378
   images in picture boxes, 495-499
   operations, suspending current applications for, 678
backing up disks, 378
bar charts, creating, 211
.BAS file extension, 245
base conversion string functions, 415-416

BASIC
   commands, *see* commands
   history of, 465-466
   programming, comparing to Visual Basic, 57-61
batch-storing, 584
`Beep` statement, 490-491
`BigRedBox_DragDrop ()` procedure, 329-330
binary
   number system, 109
   operators, 96
   states, 47-48, 107-110
   system, 155
   values, comparing, 113-117
Binary value, 585
binary-access
   files, 568
      returning byte location, 581
   storage, 569-570
bitmaps, 679-680
bits (binary digits), 107, 155
bitwise, 657
.BMP (Windows Bitmap) file extension, 495-497
Boole, George, 154
Boolean operators, 113-117
border styles, 276
`.BorderStyle` property, 275-276
bounds, establishing for arrays, 140-141
boxes, drawing, 512-513
braces ({}), 65
brackets ([]), 65
branching, 221-223
   arguments for local jumping, 228-229
   comparing `Sub` and `Function` procedures, 253-256
   conditional, 196-197
   `GoSub`, 229-232

757

Index

`GoTo`, 223-228
  sequential, 232-233
breakpoints, 541-542
BubbleSort algorithm, 619, 625-627, 640-643
buffer zone, 553
bugs, 540-543
buttons
  adding to forms, 35-38
  animated effects, 33
  captions, 39-41
  checking status of, 308-309
bytes, 90, 109
  returning locations, binary-access files, 581
`ByVal` expression, 241, 259

C

`Cabinet_DragDrop ()` procedure, 358-361
`Cabinet_DragOver ()` procedure, 360-362, 497-498
caching, 584
calculating
  depreciation, 99-100
  future values of annuities, 54-55
  zones of spheres, 57-61
calculators, Cartesian, 100-104
`Call` statement, 253-255
`.Cancel` property, 391-392
`Cancel_Click ()` procedure, 301, 661
`.Caption` property, 39-41, 341, 435
captions in graphic objects, 340-341
carriage returns, 127-128, 468
Cartesian calculators, 100-104
catabolizing code, 17
central processing units (CPUs), 24

CGA color registers, 506-507
`_Change` event, 302
channels, 548
  buffers, 584
  closing, 552-557, 584
  opening, 550-557
  reading to, 571
  returning numbers, 585
  writing from, 571
character representation, 121
characters
  ASCII code, 121-122
  control, 127
  converting with ASCII values, 416-418
  finding number stored in strings, 432
  padding strings with repeat, 438-440
charts, bar, 211
`ChDir` function, 660
`ChDir` statement, 648
`ChDrive` statement, 649
Check box tool, 35
check boxes
  checking status of, 308-309
  comparing to option dots, 305-306
  grouping within source code, 310-311
`.Checked` property, 351
chess, game of, 214
`Chr$()` function, 127, 417
chronological timers, 375-378
`.Circle` method, 517-518
`City_Change ()` procedure, 316, 603
clauses, 56, 189-194
  closing, 175
  conditional, 56, 190
  loop, 56-57

multiple-evaluative, 197-203
Select Case, 64
Type, 574
.Clear method, 682
ClearForm () procedure, 604
CLI, *see* Immediate window
_Click event, 337
clipboard
    controlling contents, 679-683
    data formats, 679-680
Clipboard. object, 337
Clipboard.Clear method, 682
Clipboard.GetData ()
    method, 681
Clipboard.GetFormat ()
    method, 682
Clipboard.GetText () method, 681-683
Clipboard.SetData method, 680-681
Clipboard.SetText method, 680-683
clock icon, 278-280
Close statement, 552-553
closing
    channels, 552-557, 584
    programs, clauses, or procedures, 175
.Cls method, 472
codes
    ANSI, 687-693
    ASCII, 121-122, 687-693
    catabolizing, 17
    intermediate p-code, 18, 673
    object, 18
    writing efficient, 74-76
colon (:), 55, 222
colors
    filling
        boxes, 512-513
        shapes, 514-515

in graphic objects, 341-343
lines, 512
mixing values, 504-510
obtaining for specified points, 517
columns, setting widths, 562
combination, expressions of, 48-49
Combo box tool, 35
combo boxes, 286-296
Combo.SelLength property, 482
Combo.SelStart property, 482
Combo.SelText property, 483
Combo.Sorted property, 291-296
Combo.Style property, 286-289
Combo_DropDown property, 296
Combo1_Click () procedure, 294-295
Combo1_DropDown () procedure, 295
comma (,), 467, 474, 557, 561
Command button tool, 35
Command$ function, 672-673
command-line
    arguments
        retrieving, 672-673
        sending to DOS, 673-675
    interpreter (CLI), *see* Immediate window
Command.Cancel property, 391-392
Command.Default property, 391-392
Command1_Click () procedure, 288
Command2_Click () procedure, 288
commands
    BASIC
        DEF FN, 242
        GOSUB, 382

759

Index

ON KEY, 382
PEEK, 382
PRINT, 465, 468-469
PRINT USING, 472
RUN, 31
DOS
ATTRIB, 650
SET, 676
File Add Module, 245
File Make EXE File..., 42
File New Module..., 245
File New Project..., 86
File Save As, 245
File Save Project As..., 41
File Save Project..., 41
parsing, 672
Run Break, 86
Run End, 32
Run Start, 31, 86
comments, 186-187
`CompanyName_Change ()` procedure, 346, 603
comparison
(=) operator, 49
expressions, 48, 113
for equality, 197-200
compilers, 19
composite variables, 449-455
compound instructions, 46
computers, 16-17
environment, 23-25
interacting with users, 20-22
concatenation (+) operator, 123
conditional
branches, 196-197
clauses, 56, 190
conditions, 189
`Const` statement, 168
constants, 84, 168-169
context
of code, 164
procedures, 52

control
arrays, 74-75, 212-213, 310-311
box, 270
characters, 127
programs, 23
`Control.BackColor` property, 341-343
`Control.BorderStyle` property, 275-276
`Control.CtlName` property, 328
`Control.DragIcon` property, 360
`Control.Enabled` property, 350
`Control.ForeColor` property, 341-343
`Control.Height` property, 340
`Control.Index` property, 328
`Control.Left` property, 339
`Control.MousePointer` property, 402
`Control.Pointer` property, 402-403
`Control.SetFocus` method, 335
`Control.TabIndex` property, 332-333
`Control.Tag` property, 328-330
`Control.Top` property, 340
`Control.Visible` property, 350
`Control.Width` property, 340
`Control_DragDrop` event, 354
`Control_DragMode` property, 355
`Control_DragOver` event, 355
`Control_GotFocus` event, 335
`Control_KeyDown` event, 383
`Control_KeyPress` event, 386
`Control_KeyUp` event, 383
`Control_LostFocus` event, 335
`Control_MouseDown` event, 396-397
`Control_MouseMove` event, 397
`Control_MouseUp` event, 396-397
`.ControlBox` property, 272
`.ControlName` property, 248

controls, 285-286
  border styles, 276
  captions versus text, 340-341
  colors, 341-343
  combo boxes, 286-296
  comparing to other controls, 328-331
  control names, 328
  dragging, 353-367
  grouping
    within forms, 305-309
    within source code, 310-311
  indexing, 328
  list boxes, 286-296
  locking, 364-372
  menu bars, 345-351
  moving, 368-372
    focus between, 334-337
  redundant, 388
  tagging with subjective names, 328-330
  text-receiving capabilities, 469
  timers, 375-378
coordinate geometry, 100-104
coordinates, 501-504
`Cos()` function, 425
cosine, 425
CPUs (central processing units), 24
`.CtlName` property, 328
`Ctype()` functions, 420
`CurDir$()` function, 650
currency conversion factor, 200
`.CurrentX` property, 484
`.CurrentY` property, 484
cursors
  determining positions
    in picture boxes and forms, 484
    in printers, 488-489
    in text boxes, 482
  programming to extract text, 481-483
  tabbing, 470-471
  virtual, 468
cylinders, area of, 256-257

D

data, 20
  buffers, 583-584
  fields, 571
  files
    ASCII-delimited, 561
    locking, 551-552
    storing, 583-584
  objects, *see* graphic objects
  passing, 658
  raw, acquiring, 586
  storing, 566
  transfer types, 550-551
  types, setting defaults for variables, 410-412
  writing to random-access file, 567-569
data file access mode, describing, 585
databases, 548
  managers, 14
`Date$` internal variable, 149-150
dates
  as text, 149-150
  converting strings to signature value formats, 150-151
  extracting from signatures, 144-145
  formatting, 475-476
  reconstructing signatures from, 147-148
`DateSerial()` functions, 147-148
`DateValue()` function, 150-151
datum, 573
`Day()` function, 144-145

Index

`_DblClick` event, 337
debugging, 540-543
decimal system, 153-158
declaring
  procedures, 52, 241-244
  variables, 85
    array, 134-138
    formally, 161-163
    global, 658
DEF FN command, 242
`.Default` property, 391-392
`Def`*type* statements, 410-412
`DeleteFile_DblClick ()`
  procedure, 366
`DeleteFile_DragDrop ()`
  procedure, 365-366
`DeleteFile_DragOver ()`
  procedure, 367
deleting
  directories, 649
  files, 665
  items from combo or list boxes, 287-289
  padded spaces from strings, 436-437
  records, 600-601, 612
delimiters, 98-104
depreciation, 99-100
descriptor code, format, 472-477
design state, 264
  setting properties, 272
device-dependent bitmaps, 679
device-independent bitmaps, 679
diagonal lines, plotting, 510-511
dialog boxes
  Help, creating, 276-277
  input boxes, 323-325
  manual, programming, 661-664
  message boxes, 319-322
`Dim` statement, 134-140, 164-165

`Dim variable()` statement, 138-139
dimensioning variables, 134-138
`Dir$()` function, 667-668
`Dir.Path` property, 297
`Dir_PathChange` event, 302
`Dir1_Change ()` procedure, 300, 659
directories
  changing, 660
    DOS, 648
    paths, 650
  creating DOS, 648
  removing, 649
Directory list box tool, 35
directory list boxes, 297-301
`Display_Click ()`
  procedure, 346
`DisplayFirst_Click ()`
  procedure, 610
`DisplayLast_Click ()`
  procedure, 610
dividing arrays, 634
division (/) operator, 97
.DLLs (dynamic link libraries), 672
`Do-Loop` loop clause, 217-219
documents, counting pages when printing, 487-488
`DoEvents()` function, 678
dollar sign ($), 120, 474
Doppler shift formula, 257-258
DOS (disk operating system), 24
  commands, *see* commands
  directories, 648
double quotation marks (" "), 467
drag icons, 354
`.Drag` method, 367
drag mode, 354
`_DragDrop` event, 354
dragging controls, 353-367
`.DragIcon` property, 360

_DragMode property, 355
_DragOver event, 355
Draw_Click () procedure, 452
drawing
   arcs, 517-519
   boxes, 512-513
   ellipses, 517-519
   lines, 511-512
      curved, 517-519
   rectangles, 52-54
.DrawStyle property, 513-514
.DrawWidth property, 514
Drive list box tool, 35
drive list boxes, 296-301
Drive.Drive property, 296-297
Drive1_Change () procedure, 300, 659
drives, floppy, 647
_DropDown event, 296
dynamic link
   format, 680
   libraries (.DLLs), 672
dynamically allocating, 138-139

E

EditClear_Click () procedure, 611
EditCopy_Click () procedure, 608
EditCut_Click () procedure, 682
eject codes, sending to printers, 230-231
ellipses
   drawing, 517-519
   vertical, 64
ellipsis (...), 65
Else expression, 192-197
ElseIf expression, 192
embedded loop clauses, 214
.Enabled property, 350

End statement, 175-178
.EndDoc method, 488
ending project execution, 32
Envelope$ () procedure, 608-610
Envelope$() function, 610
Environ$() function, 676
environment, graphical, 24
environmental variables, retrieving settings, 675-676
EOF() function, 580
equal (=)
   assignment operator, 49
   comparison operator, 49
equal to (=) operator, 111
equality comparisons, 197-200
equations, 49, 87, 95-96
   passing parameters between, 258-259
   string variables in, 122-129
Erase statement, 138
Erl internal variable, 539
Err internal variable, 538
Error statement, 539
Error$() function, 538
errors, 533-534
   comparing to bugs, 543
   trapping, 535-539
event-driven languages, 36-37
events, 30, 37, 185-186
   _Change, 302
   _Click, 337
   _DblClick, 337
   _DragDrop, 354
   _DragOver, 355
   _DropDown, 296
   _GotFocus, 335
   _KeyDown, 383
   _KeyPress, 386
   _KeyUp, 383
   _LostFocus, 335
   _MouseDown, 396-397

Index ◆

    `_MouseMove`, 397
    `_MouseUp`, 396-397
    naming convention, 40
    `_Paint`, 526
    `_PathChange`, 302
    `_PatternChange`, 302
    `_Timer`, 376
.EXE files, 19, 42
    running, 672
`Exit Do` statement, 217
`Exit` statement, 176-178
`Exp()` function, 426
exponentiation (^) operator, 97
exponents, creating series, 56-57
expressions, 48-49, 85
    `As Control`, 330
    `As Integer`, 137-138
    `As` *type*, 241
    `ByVal`, 241, 259
    comparison, 48, 113
    `Else`, 192-197
    `ElseIf`, 192
    `Lock Read`, 552
    logically reducing, 198-199
    mathematical, 408
    of assignment, 48-49, 408-410
        and string variables, 122
    of combination, 48-49
    `On`, 232-233
    `Shared`, 165, 552
    `Static`, 242
    `To`, 136
    `Until`, 218-219
    `While`, 217-219
Expressor, 68-70

F

fields, 571
    lengths, 571
        random-access files, 568
    moving between, 331-333
File Add Module command, 245
file list boxes, 297-301, 657
File Make EXE File...
    command, 42
File New Module...
    command, 245
File New Project... command, 86
file pointers, 573, 580
    locating, 582
    locations
        returning, 581
        setting, 583
    writing to, random-access
        files, 567
File Save As command, 245
File Save Project As...
    command, 41
File Save Project... command, 41
file selector boxes, 296-301, 606
`File.Archive` property, 651
`File.FileName` property, 297
`File.Hidden` property, 651
`File.Normal` property, 650
`File.Pattern` property, 297
`File.ReadOnly` property, 651
`File.System` property, 651
`File_PatternChange` event, 302
`File1_Click ()` procedure,
    300, 659
`File1_DblClick ()` procedure,
    300, 659
`FileAttr()` function, 585-586
filed state, 264
`FileFind ()` procedure, 536-538
`.FileName` property, 297
`FileOpen_Click ()`
    procedure, 606
files
    attributes, 650
    binary-access, 568
    data
        acquiring, 586
        ASCII-delimited, 561

deleting, 665
displaying, 651
erasing, 138
.EXE, 19, 42
   running, 672
extensions
   .BAS, 245
   .BMP (Windows Bitmap), 495-497
   .FRM, 41
   .ICO (standard icon), 495-497
   .MAK, 41
   .WMF (Windows Metafile), 495-497
image, 495-499
loading default, 596
names, 666-667
   error trap for not finding, 536-538
   locating, 667
opening, 596, 606
random-access
   length, 568
   writing, 567-569
reading, 580
returning length, 585
sequential access, printing to, 557-561
sorting, 214-216
storing, 565-575
   records, 605
unchangeable, 651
undeletable, 651
Files list box tool, 35
FileSaveMerge_Click () procedure, 606-607
FileSort_Click () procedure, 641-642
FileTrim_Click () procedure, 614
.FillColor property, 514
.FillStyle property, 514-515
FirstName_Change () procedure, 316
Fix() function, 414
floating-point numbers, 90
floppy drives, 647
focus
   indicator boxes, 334
   moving between controls, 334-337
   passing to Windows applications, 675
.Font property, 124
.FontBold property, 480-481
.FontCount property, 490
.FontItalic property, 480-481
.FontName property, 480
fonts
   screen and printer, 489-490
   setting properties, 479-481
.Fonts property, 489-490
.FontSize property, 480
.FontStrikethru property, 480-481
.FontTransparent property, 480-481
.FontUnderline property, 480-481
footers, sending to printers, 230-231
For-Next loop clause, 208-216
For-Next loops, 612
For-Next statement, 208-209
.ForeColor property, 341-343
form modules, 28, 51, 247-249
Form.AutoRedraw property, 526
Form.BorderStyle property, 275-276
Form.ControlBox property, 272
Form.DrawStyle property, 513-514
Form.DrawWidth property, 514

Index

Form.FillColor property, 514
Form.FillStyle property, 514-515
Form.FormName property, 265-266
Form.Height property, 340
Form.Left property, 339
Form.MaxButton property, 273
Form.MinButton property, 273
Form.Top property, 340
Form.Width property, 340
Form.WindowState property, 281
Form_KeyDown () procedure, 384
Form_KeyUp () procedure, 384
Form_Load () procedure, 247-248, 289, 299, 515-516, 519, 596, 622-623, 655-656
Form_MouseDown () procedure, 454
Form_MouseMove () procedure, 278-279, 454-455
Form_MouseUp () procedure, 455
Form_Paint event, 526
Form_Resize () procedure, 531
format descriptor code, 472-477
Format$() function, 473-477
formats
    clipboard data, 679-680
    dates and times, 475-476
    signature value, converting date and time strings to, 150-151
.FormName property, 248, 265-266
forms
    adding buttons to, 35-38
    border styles, 276
    determining cursor positions, 484
    displaying, 266-267
    hiding, 267
    image integrity, 525-526
    loading, 266
        into workspace, 247-248
    moving between fields, 331-333
    NameForm, 123-129
    naming, 265-266
    rescaling, 528-531
    states of existence when loading into workspace, 263-265
    subdividing with frames, 306-307
    unloading, 267-268
formulas, 85
Frame tool, 34
frames, 29-30, 306-307
FreeFile function, 585
.FRM file extension, 41
Function procedure, 54-55, 156-157
    calling, 254-258
Function statement, 242-244
functions, 49-50, 183, 407-410
    Abs(), 423-424
    Asc(), 417-418, 587
    Atn(), 425
    ChDir, 660
    Chr$(), 127, 417
    Command$, 672-673
    Cos(), 425
    Ctype(), 420
    CurDir$(), 650
    DateSerial(), 147-148
    DateValue(), 150-151
    Day(), 144-145
    Dir$(), 667-668
    DoEvents(), 678
    Envelope$(), 610

Environ$(), 676
EOF(), 580
Error$(), 538
Exp(), 426
FileAttr(), 585-586
Fix(), 414
Format$(), 473-477
FreeFile, 585
Hex$(), 416
Hour(), 145-146
Input$(), 586-587
InputBox$(), 323-324
InStr(), 441-443
Int(), 413-415
intrinsic, 50
LBound(), 140-141
LCase$(), 440
Left$(), 434-435
Len(), 432-434, 575
LoadPicture(), 496-499
Loc(), 581
LOF(), 585
Log(), 426
LTrim$(), 436-437
Mid$(), 443-445
Minute(), 146
Month(), 145
MsgBox, 319-321
Oct$(), 416
QBColor(), 506-507
RGB(), 505-507
Right$(), 76, 409-410, 434-435
Rnd(), 457-460
RTrim$(), 436-437, 602
Second(), 146
Seek(), 581-582
Sgn(), 424
Shell(), 673-675
Sin(), 425-426
Space$(), 433-434
Spc(), 471

Sqr(), 409, 425
Str$(), 76, 419-420
String$(), 438-440
SubLoadFile (), 598-599
Tab(), 470-471
Tan(), 425
Timer(), 376
TimeSerial(), 147-148
TimeValue(), 151
UBound(), 140-141
UCase$(), 440
user-defined, 242-243
Val(), 418-419
Weekday(), 144-145
Year(), 145
future values of annuities, 54-55
Future_Click procedure, 54-55

G

general modules, 28, 52, 245-247
geometric offsets, 502
geometry, coordinate, 100-104
Get# statement, 569-573
.GetData () method, 681
.GetFormat () method, 682
.GetText () method, 681-683
global
   modules, 28, 51
      order of execution, 245
   scope, 166-168, 256
   variables, 658
      declaring, 658
      determining local versus,
         71-73
Global statement, 167-168
Go_Click () procedure, 420
GOSUB command, 382
GoSub statement, 229-232
_GotFocus event, 335
GoTo keyword, 46
GoTo statement, 46-47, 223-228

Index

`GoToRecord_Click ()`
    procedure, 608
graphic objects, 32-35, 184-186
    assigning keystrokes to
        buttons, 391-392
    captions versus text, 340-341
    clearing contents, 472
    colors, 341-343
        and patterns, 514-515
    displaying forms, 266-267
    hiding forms, 267
    identifying attributes in
        names, 40
    in control arrays, 212-213
    keys for operating, 383-387
    loading forms, 266
    naming forms, 265-266
    pausing mathematical operations to update screen
        appearance, 677-678
    positioning and appearance
        on-screen, 339-340
    states of existence, 264-265
    substituting buttons for keys,
        388-391
    unloading forms, 267-268
graphical environment, 24
graphics, coordinate system for,
    210-211
greater than (>) operator, 111
greater than or equal to (>=)
    operator, 111

H

H.P. (Hewlett Packard) notation,
    76-77
`.Height` property, 340
Help dialog box, creating,
    276-277
`Help_Click ()` procedure, 277

`Hex$()` function, 416
hexadecimal system, 155-156
`.Hidden` property, 651
hidden state, 265
`Hidden_Click ()`
    procedure, 663
`.Hide` method, 267
high-level languages, 16
Horizontal scroll bar tool, 35
`Hour()` function, 145-146
`HScroll1_KeyDown ()`
    procedure, 385-386
`HScroll1_KeyPress ()`
    procedure, 418

I-J

.ICO (standard icon) file
    extension, 495-497
icons
    drag, 354
    folder and cabinet, 360-363
    lock and key, 364-367
`If` keyword, 46
`If-Then` statement, 46-47, 113,
    191-197
    comparing to Select Case
        statement, 201
image
    files, displaying graphics from,
        495-499
    integrity, 525-526
Immediate window, 86-87, 100,
    469-470
    debugging with, 540-543
implied loops, 157
incremented variables, 208
`.Index` property, 74-75, 328
Indy race car simulator, 224-226,
    231-232
information, 20

Input # statement, 558-561
input boxes, 323-325
Input$() function, 586-587
InputBox$() function, 323-324
InStr() function, 441-443
instructions
   clauses, 56
   compound, 46
   nested, 56
   phrases, 46
   syntax, 63-65
Int() function, 413-415
integers, 135
   (%) symbol, 92
integrity, image, 525-526
intermediate p-code, 18, 671
interpreters, 17-19
   listing current projects, 65-66
   VBRUN100.DLL, 19
   Visual Basic, 567, 581
.Interval property, 376-377
intrinsic functions, 50
iterations, 208

K

keyboard
   assigning keystrokes to
      buttons, 391-392
   history, 381-382
   keys for operating graphic
      objects, 383-387
   substituting buttons for keys,
      388-391
_KeyDown event, 383
_KeyPress event, 386
keys
   detecting presses with
      ASCII code, 386-387
      scan codes, 383-384
   polling for, 382
   Tab, 331-333

_KeyUp event, 383
keywords
   GoTo, 46
   If, 46
   Let, 92-93
   Local, 535
   Name, 436
   Then, 46
Kill statement, 665
kilobytes (K), 91

L

Label tool, 34
Label.Alignment property, 480
Label.AutoSize property,
   525-526
labels, 55, 222-223, 624
   resizing, 525-526
languages, 16
   catabolizing code, 17
   event-driven, 36-37
   high-level, 16
   low-level, 16
LastName_Change () procedure,
   316, 603
LBound() function, 140-141
LCase$() function, 440
.Left property, 339
Left$() function, 434-435
Len() function, 432-434, 575
less than (<) operator, 111
less than or equal to (<=)
   operator, 111
Let keyword, 92-93
libraries, 245
Light () procedure, 636
line feeds, 127-128, 468
Line Input # statement,
   562-563
.Line method, 511-513

lines
  curved, 517-519
  diagonal, 510-511
  drawing, 511-512
  setting style and width, 513-514
List box tool, 35
list boxes, 286-301
`.List` property, 290
`List.Sorted` property, 291-296
`.ListCount` property, 290
`.ListIndex` property, 290-291
lists, 135
`Load` statement, 266
`LoadFile()` procedure, 596-598
loading
  array variables
    sequential-access file, 580
  default files, 596
  forms, 266
    into workspace, 263-265
  records, 596
`LoadPicture()` function, 496-499
`Loc()` function, 581
local
  context, 52
  scope, 54, 163-166, 255
  variables, determining global versus, 71-73
`Local` keyword, 535
location& values, 583
`Lock Read` expression, 552
locking
  controls, 364-372
  data files, 551-552
`LOF()` function, 585
`Log()` function, 426
logarithms, 426
logical
  inches, 340
  operators, 110-112

logically reducing expressions, 198-199
long integer (&) symbol, 92
loop clauses, 207-208
  `Do-Loop`, 217-219
  embedded within loops, 214
  `For-Next`, 208-216
  terminating execution, 176
loops, 56-57
  `For-Next`, 612
  implied, 157
  `While-Wend`, 581
`_LostFocus` event, 335
low-level languages, 16
`LSet` statement, 437-438
`LTrim$()` function, 436-437

M

machines, 16
mail merge, 561
`Main ()` procedure, 246-249
.MAK file extension, 41
markup ratios, 88-90
mathematical
  expressions, 408
  operations, pausing to update screen appearance, 677-678
`.Max` property, 312
`.MaxButton` property, 273
maximize button, 270
megabytes (M), 91
memory
  buffer zone, 553
  solid-state, 548
  states of existence, graphic objects, 264-265
menu
  bars, 345-351
  design windows, 346-349
`Menu.Checked` property, 351
message boxes, 127-128, 319-322

metafile images, 680
methods, 184
    `.AddItem`, 287-289
    `.Circle`, 517-518
    `.Clear`, 682
    `.Cls`, 472
    `.Drag`, 367
    `.EndDoc`, 488
    `.GetData ()`, 681
    `.GetFormat ()`, 682
    `.GetText ()`, 681-683
    `.Hide`, 267
    `.Line`, 511-513
    `.Move`, 369
    `.NewPage`, 488
    `.Point`, 517
    `.Print`, 466-470
    `.PSet`, 507-508
    `.Refresh`, 677-678
    `.RemoveItem`, 287-289
    `.Scale`, 528
    `.SetData`, 680-681
    `.SetFocus`, 335
    `.SetText`, 680-683
    `.Show`, 266-267
    `.TextHeight`, 483
    `.TextWidth`, 483
microcomputers, coordinate systems, 501-503
Microsoft Windows 3.0, *see* Windows
`Mid$` statement, 445-446
`Mid$()` function, 443-444
`MidInit_Change ()` procedure, 316, 603
`MidName_Click ()` procedure, 603
`.Min` property, 312
`.MinButton` property, 273
minimize button, 270
`Minute()` function, 146

`MkDir` statement, 648
modal windows, 322
modeless windows, 322
modes
    data file access, 585
    drag, 354
modular scope, 164-166, 256
modularization, 598
modules, 50
    form, 28, 51, 247-249
    general, 28, 52
    global, 28, 51
    order of execution, 244-247
    origins, 239-241
modulo arithmetic, 158
`Month()` function, 145
mouse pointer
    changing appearance, 401-403
    moving, 397-401
    pressing mouse buttons, 395-397
`_MouseDown` event, 396-397
`_MouseMove` event, 397
`.MousePointer` property, 402
`_MouseUp` event, 396-397
`.Move` method, 369
moving
    controls, 368-372
    mouse pointer, 397-401
MS-DOS, *see* DOS
`MsgBox` function or statement, 319-321
`.MultiLine` property, 128
multiple-evaluative clause, 197-203
multiplication (*) operator, 97

N

`Name` keyword, 436
`Name` statement, 666-667

Index

NameForm
  application, 591-614
  form, 123-129
  Mark IV, 592-598
    menu procedures, 605-606
naming files, 666-667
nested instructions, 56, 190
networks, locking data files, 551-552
`.NewPage` method, 488
`NewPlot ()` procedure, 636
non-array variables, 164
`.Normal` property, 650
`Normal_Click ()` procedure, 663
notation
  H.P. (Hewlett Packard), 76-77
  Reverse Polish, 76-77
  T.I. (Texas Instruments), 76-77
Now internal variable, 143
null string (" ") symbol, 213
numbers
  base 10, converting to other bases, 156-158
  binary system, 109
  floating-point, 90
  random, 457-461
  rounding or removing fractions, 413-415
  square root, 424-425
numeric values
  converting with strings, 418-420
    alphanumeric, 472-477
  signs, 423-424

O

object code, 18
Object Management Group, 184
object-oriented syntax, 183-184
`Object.Caption` property, 341
`Object.Circle` method, 517-518
`Object.CurrentX` property, 484
`Object.CurrentY` property, 484
`Object.FontBold` property, 480-481
`Object.FontItalic` property, 480-481
`Object.FontName` property, 480
`Object.FontSize` property, 480
`Object.FontStrikethru` property, 480-481
`Object.FontTransparent` property, 480-481
`Object.FontUnderline` property, 480-481
`Object.Line` method, 511-513
`Object.List` property, 290
`Object.ListCount` property, 290
`Object.ListIndex` property, 290-291
`Object.Point` method, 517
`Object.PSet` method, 507-508
`Object.Refresh` method, 677-678
`[Object].Scale` method, 528
`[Object].ScaleHeight` property, 527-528
`[Object].ScaleLeft` property, 527-528
`[Object].ScaleMode` property, 527
`[Object].ScaleTop` property, 527-528
`[Object].ScaleWidth` property, 527-528
`Object.Text` property, 341
`Object.TextHeight` method, 483
`Object.TextWidth` method, 483
`Object.Value` property, 308-309
`Object_Change` event, 302

Object_Click event, 337
Object_DblClick event, 337
objects
  as property
    ActiveControl., 336
    ActiveForm., 336
    Parent., 330-331
  categories of, 469-470
  Clipboard., 337
  Screen., 337
  target, 354
Oct$() function, 416
octal system, 156
OK_Click () procedure, 301, 659-660, 668
OKCorral_DblClick () procedure, 371
OKCorral_DragDrop () procedure, 369-370
On Error [GoTo | Resume] statement, 535
On expression, 232-233
ON KEY command, 382
one-dimensional arrays, 135
Open statement, 550-552
opening
  channels, 550-557
  files, 596, 606
operators
  − unary, 49
  + (concatenation), 123
  / (slash), 49
  = (equal)
    assignment, 49
    comparison, 49
  arithmetic, 96-97
  binary, 96
  Boolean, 113-117
  delimiters, 98-104
  logical, 110-112
  order of precedence, 97-98

Option Base statement, 170
Option button tool, 35
option dots
  checking status of, 308-309
  comparing to check boxes, 305-306
  grouping within source code, 310-311
Option_Click () procedure, 311
Options_Click () procedure, 661
OR Boolean operator, 115-117
origin point, 503
output devices, sending text to, 469-470
OverPlot () procedure, 636

P

p-code, 18, 671
  files, compiling projects into, 42
.Page property, 487-488
pages
  counting when printing, 487-488
  footers and eject codes, sending to printers, 230-231
  windows, 271
paging area, 313
_Paint event, 526
parameters, 52, 241
  command-line, retrieving, 672-673
  parsing, 672
  passing, 658
  order, 256-259
Parent. object, 330-331
parentheses (), 98-104, 241
  with Boolean operators, 116-117

Index

PATH environmental
 variable, 676
.Path property, 297, 301
_PathChange event, 302
paths, directories, 650
.Pattern property, 297
_PatternChange event, 302
patterns, filling shapes with,
 514-515
PC DOS, *see* DOS
PEEK command, 382
pens, virtual, 501
percentage sign (%), 474
period (.), 473
phrases, 46
Picture box tool, 34
picture boxes, 356-358
 background images, 495-499
 determining
  cursor positions, 484
  width and height of text, 483
 image integrity, 525-526
Picture.AutoRedraw
 property, 526
Picture.AutoSize property,
 525-526
Picture.DrawStyle property,
 513-514
Picture.DrawWidth
 property, 514
Picture.FillColor
 property, 514
Picture.FillStyle property,
 514-515
Picture.Picture property,
 495-496
Picture_Paint event, 526
pixels
 comparing to twips, 510
 obtaining colors for specified
  points, 517

pneuma, 200
.Point method, 517
.Pointer property, 402-403
polling for keys, 382
pound sign (#), 474, 550, 557, 561
precedence, order of for
 operators, 97-98
precision, variable, 90-92
Print # statement, 558-561
PRINT command, 465-469
.Print method, 466-470
Print statement, 100
PRINT USING command, 472
Print# statement, 557
printer twips, 489
Printer.CurrentX property, 484
Printer.CurrentY property, 484
Printer.DrawStyle property,
 513-514
Printer.DrawWidth
 property, 514
Printer.EndDoc method, 488
Printer.FillColor
 property, 514
Printer.FillStyle property,
 514-515
Printer.FontBold property,
 480-481
[Printer].FontCount
 property, 490
Printer.FontItalic property,
 480-481
Printer.FontName property, 480
[Printer].Fonts property,
 489-490
Printer.FontSize property, 480
Printer.FontStrikethru
 property, 480-481
Printer.FontTransparent
 property, 480-481
Printer.FontUnderline
 property, 480-481

Printer.NewPage method, 488
Printer.Page property, 487-488
[Printer].ScaleHeight
    property, 527-528
[Printer].ScaleLeft property,
    527-528
[Printer].ScaleMode
    property, 527
[Printer].ScaleTop property,
    527-528
[Printer].ScaleWidth
    property, 527-528
printers
    fonts, 479-481, 489-490
    receiving text, 487-489
    sending page footers and eject
        codes, 230-231
printing, 466-468
    text, 561
    to sequential-access files,
        557-561
procedural algebra, 60
procedures, 52-54
    Acquire (), 572-575
    Address_Change (), 315, 602
    ApplyFormula_Click (), 291
    Archive_Click (), 663
    BigRedBox_DragDrop (),
        329-330
    Cabinet_DragDrop (),
        358-361
    Cabinet_DragOver (),
        360-362, 497-498
    Cancel_Click (), 301, 661
    City_Change (), 316, 603s
    ClearForm (), 604
    closing, 175
    Combo1_Click (), 294-295
    Combo1_DropDown (), 295
    Command1_Click (), 288
    Command2_Click (), 288

CompanyName_Change (),
    346, 603
declaring, 52, 241-244
DeleteFile_DblClick (),
    366
DeleteFile_DragDrop (),
    365-366
DeleteFile_DragOver (),
    367
Dir1_Change (), 300, 659
Display_Click (), 346
DisplayFirst_Click (), 610
DisplayLast_Click (), 611
Draw_Click (), 452
Drive1_Change (), 300, 659
EditClear_Click (), 611
EditCopy_Click (), 608
EditCut_Click (), 682
Envelope$ (), 608-610
executing, 248-249
File1_Click (), 300, 659
File1_DblClick (), 300, 659
FileFind (), 536-538
FileOpen_Click (), 606
FileSaveMerge_Click (),
    606-607
FileSort_Click (), 641-642
FileTrim_Click (), 614
FirstName_Change (), 316
Form_KeyDown (), 384
Form_KeyUp (), 384
Form_Load (), 247-248,
    289-299, 515-519, 596,
    622-623, 655-656
Form_MouseDown (), 454
Form_MouseMove (), 278-279,
    454-455
Form_MouseUp (), 455
Form_Resize (), 531
Function, 54-55, 156-157
Future_Click, 54-55

775

Index

Go_Click (), 420
GoToRecord_Click (), 608
Help_Click (), 277
Hidden_Click (), 663
HScroll1_KeyDown (), 385-386
HScroll1_KeyPress (), 418
LastName_Change (), 316, 603
Light (), 636
LoadFile(), 596-598
Main (), 246-249
MidInit_Change (), 316, 603
MidName_Click (), 603
NewPlot (), 636
Normal_Click (), 663
OK_Click (), 301, 659-660, 668
OKCorral_DblClick (), 371
OKCorral_DragDrop (), 369-370
Option_Click (), 311
Options_Click (), 661
order of execution, 244-247
OverPlot (), 636
parameter passing order, 256-259
RackEmUp (), 623, 673
ReadOnly_Click (), 663
RecordDelete_Click (), 612
RecordInsert_Click (), 613
RecordShown_Change (), 314-315, 605
Rect_Draw, 52-53
ResetPlot (), 624
Revive (), 531
rewriting, 75-78
Save_Click (), 309
Search_Click (), 277
ShowIter (), 636
ShowPlots (), 624
ShowRecord (), 601
ShowTime (), 636
starbloom (), 529-530
Start_Click (), 442-443, 481-482, 624
State_Change (), 316, 603
StateFind (), 572
Sub, 52-53
   calling explicitly, 253-256
Systm_Click (), 664
terminating execution, 176
Timer1_Timer (), 377-378, 530-531
Vane_MouseMove (), 399-401, 498-499
windows, 29
writing first, 73-74
Zip_Change (), 316, 603
Zip_Click (), 444-445
programmers interacting with computers, 20-22
programming, 16-17
   catabolizing code, 17
   comparing BASIC to Visual Basic, 57-61
   determining global versus local variables, 71-73
   elements representing numerically as values, 70-71
   end to beginning, 70
   in Reverse Polish Notation, 76-77
   instructions versus real-world instructions, 181-182
   manual dialog boxes, 661-664
   objective, 13-15
   rewriting procedures, 75-78
   writing
      efficient code, 74-76
      first procedure, 73-74
programs, 15-16, 50
   closing, 175
   control, 23
   generating, 17-18
   graphical environment, 24

moving star pattern, 528-531
purposeful versus operational elements, 73
structure, 23-25
suspending execution, 176
user, 23
see also applications
projects
  elements, 27-30
  ending execution, 32
  listing current, 65-68
  running, 31-32
  saving, 41-42
properties, 184-185
  `ActiveControl.` object as, 336
  `ActiveForm.` object as, 336
  `.Alignment`, 480
  `.Archive`, 651
  `.AutoRedraw`, 526
  `.AutoSize`, 525-526
  `.BackColor`, 341-343
  `.BorderStyle`, 275-276
  `.Cancel`, 391-392
  `.Caption`, 39-41, 341, 435
  `.Checked`, 351
  `.ControlBox`, 272
  `.ControlName`, 248
  `.CtlName`, 328
  `.CurrentX`, 484
  `.CurrentY`, 484
  `.Default`, 391-392
  `.DragIcon`, 360
  `_DragMode`, 355
  `.DrawStyle`, 513-514
  `.DrawWidth`, 514
  `.Drive`, 296-297
  `_DropDown`, 296
  `.Enabled`, 350
  entering settings from project listings, 66-67
  `.FileName`, 297
  `.FillColor`, 514
  `.FillStyle`, 514-515
  `.Font`, 124
  `.FontBold`, 480-481
  `.FontCount`, 490
  `.FontItalic`, 480-481
  `.FontName`, 480
  `.Fonts`, 489-490
  `.FontSize`, 480
  `.FontStrikethru`, 480-481
  `.FontTransparent`, 480-481
  `.FontUnderline`, 480-481
  `.ForeColor`, 341-343
  `.FormName`, 248, 265-266
  `.Height`, 340
  `.Hidden`, 651
  `.Index`, 74-75, 328
  `.Interval`, 376-377
  `.LargeChange`, 312-313
  `.Left`, 339
  `.List`, 290
  `.ListCount`, 290
  `.ListIndex`, 290-291
  `.Max`, 312
  `.MaxButton`, 273
  `.Min`, 312
  `.MinButton`, 273
  `.MousePointer`, 402
  `.MultiLine`, 128
  naming convention, 40
  `.Normal`, 650
  `.Page`, 487-488
  `Parent.` object as, 330-331
  `.Path`, 297, 301
  `.Pattern`, 297
  `.Picture`, 495-496
  `.Pointer`, 402-403
  `.ReadOnly`, 651
  `.ScaleHeight`, 527-528
  `.ScaleLeft`, 527-528
  `.ScaleMode`, 527
  `.ScaleTop`, 527-528
  `.ScaleWidth`, 527-528

Index

.ScrollBars, 316-317
.SelLength, 482
.SelStart, 482
.SelText, 483
setting, 38-39, 272
.SmallChange, 312-313
.Sorted, 291-296
.Style, 286-289
.System, 651
.TabIndex, 332-333
.TabStop, 332
.Tag, 328-330, 359
.Text, 341, 435
.Top, 340
.Value, 308-309
.Visible, 350
.Width, 340
.WindowState, 281
.PSet method, 507-508
Put# statement, 567-569

Q

QBColor() function, 506-507
QuickSort algorithm, 619, 630-640
   developing subarrays, 622

R

race car simulator, 224-226, 231-232
RackEmUp () procedure, 623, 673
radians, 425-426
random numbers, 457-461
Random value, 586
random-access
   data storage, 566-569
   files
      field length, 568
      returning previous data elements, 581
      technique, bidirectional, 571

Randomize statement, 458-461
ratios, markup, 88-90
reading
   files, 580
   variable contents, 569-570
.ReadOnly property, 651
ReadOnly_Click ()
     procedure, 663
real-world time, 377
record-entry system, 123-129
RecordDelete_Click ()
     procedure, 612
RecordInsert_Click ()
     procedure, 613
records, 559, 573
   adding, 599, 604-605
   allocating array variable units, 139-140
   clearing current, 611
   components, 602
   deleting, 600-601, 612
   displaying, 602
   inserting, 599, 612-613
   loading, 596
   locating, 573
   numbers
      changing, 608-610
      current, 596
   retrieving, 602
   saving, 605
   trimming, 602
RecordShown_Change ()
     procedure, 314-315, 605
Rect_Draw procedure, 52-53
rectangles, drawing, 52-54
ReDim statement, 138-140
redundant controls, 388
reflexive references, 336
.Refresh method, 677-678
registers, 566
relays, 658
Rem statement, 186-187

.RemoveItem method, 287-289
Reset statement, 584
ResetPlot () procedure, 624
restore button, 271
Resume statement, 536
Return statement, 231-232
Reverse Polish Notation, 76-77
Revive () procedure, 531
RGB() function, 505-507
right triangles, area of, 254-255
Right$() function, 76, 409-410, 434-435
right-circular cylinders, area of, 256-257
RmDir statement, 649
Rnd() function, 457-460
rounded value equivalents, sequential-access files, 581
routines, 55, 227
   timing executions, 148-149
RSet statement, 437-438
RTrim$() function, 436-437, 602
Run Break command, 86
RUN command, 31
Run End command, 32
Run Start command, 31, 86
running state, 31-32, 265
   setting properties, 272

S

Save_Click () procedure, 309
SavePicture statement, 496-497
saving
   picture box images, 496-497
   projects, 41-42
   sequential-access
      arrays, 549-550
      data elements, 607
scale divisions, setting, 527-528
.Scale method, 528
.ScaleHeight property, 527-528
.ScaleLeft property, 527-528
.ScaleMode property, 527
.ScaleTop property, 527-528
.ScaleWidth property, 527-528
scan codes, detecting key presses, 383-384
scope, 163, 255-256
   global, 166-168
   local, 54, 163-166
   modular, 164-166
   static, 166-167
Screen. object, 337
[Screen].FontCount property, 490
[Screen].Fonts property, 489-490
screens
   coordinates, 503-504
   fonts, 489-490
scroll
   arrows, 271
   bars
      checking status of, 308-309
      coordinate systems, 311-312
      in text boxes, 316-317
      paging area intervals, 312-313
      setting coordinate values, 312
      using, 313-316
   boxes, 270-271
      changing values, 604
Scroll.LargeChange property, 312-313
Scroll.Max property, 312
Scroll.Min property, 312
Scroll.SmallChange property, 312-313
.ScrollBars property, 316-317
Search_Click () procedure, 277

Index

searching for
  and replacing text, 481-483
  file names, 669
  records, 573
  strings within strings, 440-443
  text, 277
  unknown text in strings, 443-446
`Second()` function, 146
seconds elapsed since midnight, 148-149
seeding arrays, 623
`Seek#` statement, 582-583
`Seek()` function, 581-582
`Select Case` clause, 64
`Select Case` statement, 197-203
Selector II, 657-659
Selector Mark II, 652-656
`.SelLength` property, 482
`.SelStart` property, 482
`.SelText` property, 483
semicolon (;), 467, 557, 561
`SendKeys` statement, 388
Sequential Append value, 586
sequential branching, 232-233
Sequential Input value, 586
Sequential Output value, 586
sequential-access, 548-549
  closing channels, 552-557
  files
    loading into array variables, 580
    returning rounded value equivalents, 581
  opening channels, 550-557
  saving data, 606
  setting column widths, 562
  storing
    arrays to disk, 549-550
    lines of text in memory, 562-563

SET command, 676
`.SetData` method, 680-681
`.SetFocus` method, 335
`.SetText` method, 680-683
settings, 185
`Sgn()` function, 424
Shared expression, 165, 552
shell, 70
`Shell()` function, 673-675
Shell/Metzner sort algorithm, 619, 627-629
`.Show` method, 266-267
`ShowIter ()` procedure, 636
`ShowPlots ()` procedure, 624
`ShowRecord ()` procedure, 601
`ShowTime ()` procedure, 636
signatures, 144
  extracting date and time information, 144-147
  reconstructing from date and time information, 147-148
`Sin()` function, 425-426
sine, 425
slash (/) operator, 49
`.SmallChange` property, 312-313
solid-state memory, 548
sort algorithms, 625
`.Sorted` property, 291-296
sorting, 617-643
  algorithms, 618
  arrays, 627-638
  files, 214-216
  list or combo box items, 291-296
  names, 641-642
sound, 490
source code, 16
`Space$()` function, 433-434
spaces
  inserting in concatenated strings, 127

780

padded, 433-434
    justifying text within strings, 437-438
    removing from strings, 436-437
spanners, 628
`Spc()` function, 471
spheres, calculating zones, 57-61
`Sqr()` function, 409, 425
square root, 424-425
standard bitmaps, 679
star pattern program, 528-531
Star Trek, 137-138
`starbloom ()` procedure, 529-530
`Start_Click ()` procedure, 442-443, 481-482, 624
startup procedures, 246-247
`State_Change ()` procedure, 316, 603
`StateFind ()` procedure, 572
statements, 46-47, 183
  `AppActivate`, 675
  `Beep`, 490-491
  `Call`, 253-255
  `ChDir`, 648
  `ChDrive`, 649
  `Close`, 552-553
  `Const`, 168
  `Deftype`, 410-412
  `Dim`, 134-140, 164-165
  `Dim variable()`, 138-139
  `Do-Loop`, 217-218
  `End`, 175-178
  `Erase`, 138
  `Error`, 539
  `Exit`, 176-178
  `Exit Do`, 217
  `For-Next`, 208-209
  `Function`, 242-244
  `Get#`, 569-573
  `Global`, 167-168
  `GoSub`, 229-232
  `GoTo`, 46-47, 223-228
  `If-Then`, 46-47, 113, 191-197, 201
  `Input #`, 558, 559, 560-561
  `Kill`, 665
  `Line Input #`, 562-563
  `Load`, 266
  `LSet`, 437-438
  `Mid$`, 445-446
  `MkDir`, 648
  `MsgBox`, 319-321
  `Name`, 666-667
  of assignment, revising as formal, 92-93
  `On Error [GoTo | Resume]`, 535
  `Open`, 550-552
  `Option Base`, 170
  `Print`, 100
  `Print#`, 557-561
  `Put#`, 567-569
  `Randomize`, 458-461
  `ReDim`, 138-140
  `Rem`, 186-187
  `Reset`, 584
  `Resume`, 536
  `Return`, 231-232
  `RmDir`, 649
  `RSet`, 437-438
  `SavePicture`, 496-497
  `Seek#`, 582-583
  `Select Case`, 197-203
  `SendKeys`, 388
  `Static`, 166-167
  `Stop`, 83, 176-178
  `Sub`, 241-242
  `Type-End Type`, 451-452
  `Unload`, 267-268
  `Width #`, 562
  `Write #`, 561

states
- active, 265
- binary, 47-48, 107-110
- design, 264
- filed, 264
- hidden, 265
- running, 265
- unloaded, 264-265
- virtual, 265

`Static` expression, 242
static scope, 166-167, 256
`Static` statement, 166-167
`Stop` statement, 83, 176-178
storage
- binary-access, 569-570
- random-access, 569

storing
- files, 565-575
- to data files, 583-584

`Str$()` function, 76, 419-420
string variables, 119-122
- in equations, 122-129
- length, 575

`String$()` function, 438-440
strings, 429-431
- base conversion, 415-416
- concatenated, 610
- converting
  - numeric values with alphanumeric, 472-477
  - with numeric values, 418-420
- extracting partial strings from, 434-435
- length, 574
- null (" ") symbol, 213
- padded
  - justifying text within, 437-438
  - removing spaces, 436-437
  - with repeat characters, 438-440
  - with spaces, 433-434
- searching for
  - number of characters stored, 432
  - strings, 440-443
  - unknown text, 443-446
- values, 642

`.Style` property, 286-289
`Sub` procedure, 52-53
- calling explicitly, 253-256

`Sub` statement, 241-242
`SubLoadFile()` function, 598-599
subprograms, 240-241
subroutines, 55, 229-232
subscripts, 134
subtraction (–) operator, 97
swapping arrays, 629
`.System` property, 651
system
- command library, 648
- date and time, 149-150

`Systm_Click()` procedure, 664

T

T.I. (Texas Instruments) notation, 76-77
Tab key, 331-333
`Tab()` function, 470-471
`.TabIndex` property, 332-333
tables, 136
- dimensioning, 136
- three-axis, 136

`.TabStop` property, 332
`.Tag` property, 328-330, 359
`Tan()` function, 425
tangent, 425
target objects, 354

text
  alphanumeric
    comparing to values, 119-120
    converting to numeric values, 76
  boxes
    determining cursor positions, 482
    scroll bars, 316-317
    text-receiving capabilities, 469
  dates and times as, 149-151
  determining width and height, 483
  fonts, 479-481
  in graphic objects, 340-341
  justifying within padded strings, 437-438
  lines of, storing in memory, 562-563
  printing, 561
    to sequential-access files, 557-561
  programming cursor to extract, 481-483
  searching for, 277
    unknown, 443-446
  sending to
    output devices, 469-470
    printers, 487-489
  tabbing, 470-471
Text box tool, 34
.Text property, 341, 435
Text.ScrollBars property, 316-317
Text.SelLength property, 482
Text.SelStart property, 482
Text.SelText property, 483
.TextHeight method, 483
.TextWidth method, 483

Then keyword, 46
three-axis tables, 136
three-dimensional arrays, 136
thumb, 270
time signature, 144
Time$ internal variable, 150
Timer internal variable, 148-149
Timer tool, 35
Timer() function, 376
Timer.Interval property, 376-377
Timer_Timer event, 376
Timer1_Timer () procedure, 377-378, 530-531
timers, 375-378
times
  as text, 149-150
  converting strings to signature value formats, 150-151
  displaying, 278-280
  extracting from signatures, 145-147
  formatting, 475-476
  reconstructing signatures from, 147-148
TimeSerial() functions, 147-148
TimeValue() function, 151
timing routine executions, 148-149
To expression, 136
toolbox, 33-35
.Top property, 340
trailing zeros, 91
trapping errors, 535-539
triangles, right, 254-255
trigonometric functions, 425-426
trimming records, 602
twips, 210-211, 504
  comparing to pixels, 510
  obtaining colors for specified points, 517

783

Index

printer, 489
setting to colors, 507-508
two-dimensional arrays, 136
`Type` clause, 574
`Type-End Type` statement, 451-452

U

`UBound()` function, 140-141
`UCase$()` function, 440
unary (–) operator, 49
underscore (_) character, 36
`Unload` statement, 267-268
unloaded state, 264-265
Until expression, 218-219
user programs, 23
user-defined
   functions, 242-243
   variables, 449
users interacting with computers, 20-22

V

`Val()` function, 418-419
`.Value` property, 308-309
values
   array elements, 618
   assigning to variables, 87-90
   Binary, 585
   comparing
      binary, 113-117
      to alphanumeric text, 119-120
   converting
      alphanumeric text to, 76
      between types, 420
   passing back to programs, 242-244
   Random, 585
   representing program elements numerically as, 70-71
   rounding or removing fractions, 413-415
   scroll boxes, changing, 605
   Sequential Append, 585
   Sequential Input, 585
   Sequential Output, 585
   strings, 642
`Vane_MouseMove ()` procedure, 399-401, 498-499
variables, 21, 46, 60, 84, 657
   array, 133-134
   assigning values to, 87-90
   composite, 449-455
   data, storing, 566
   declaring, 85
      formally, 161-163
   determining global versus local, 71-73
   dimensioning, 134-138
   environmental, retrieving settings, 675-676
   global, 658
   incremented, 208
   internal
      `Date$`, 149-150
      `Erl`, 539
      `Err`, 538
      `Now`, 143
      `Time$`, 150
      `Timer`, 148-149
   naming, 213
   non-array, 164
   parameter passing order, 256-259
   precision types, 90-92
   reading contents, 569-570
   scope, 163-168, 255-256

setting default data types, 410-412
string, 119-129
length, 575
user-defined, 449
value of undeclared, 87
writing to random-access data files, 567
VBRUN100.DLL interpreter, 19
vertical ellipses, 64
Vertical scroll bar tool, 35
virtual
cursors, 468
determining positions in text boxes, 482
programming to extract text, 481-483
origins, 503
pens, 501
state, 265
terminals, 469
coordinate system types, 527
.Visible property, 350
Visual Basic
interpreters, 17-19, 567, 581
programming, comparing BASIC to, 57-61
with Windows, 24-25
vital information, 123-129
von Neumann, John, 154-155
von Neumann machines, 154

W

Weekday() function, 144-145
While expression, 217-219
While-Wend loop, 581
Width # statement, 562
.Width property, 340

Windows, 24-25
applications, passing focus to, 675
Version 3.0, 24-25
windows
determining operating state, 281
elements, 270-271
history, 502-503
Immediate, 86-87, 469-470
menu design, 346-349
modal, 322
modeless, 322
procedure, 29
setting appearance and contents properties, 272-274
types, 274-280
.WindowState property, 281
.WMF (Windows Metafile) file extension, 495-497
workspace, loading forms into, 263-265
Write # statement, 561

X-Z

x-axis divisions, setting, 527-528
XOR Boolean operator, 115

y-axis, 618
setting divisions, 527-528
Year() function, 145

zeros, trailing, 91
ZIP codes, searching for, 444-445
Zip_Change () procedure, 316, 603
Zip_Click () procedure, 444-445
zones of spheres, calculating, 57-61

785

Computer Books from Que Mean PC Performance!

Spreadsheets

1-2-3 Beyond the Basics	$24.95
1-2-3 for DOS Release 2.3 Quick Reference	$ 9.95
1-2-3 for DOS Release 2.3 QuickStart	$19.95
1-2-3 for DOS Release 3.1+ Quick Reference	$ 9.95
1-2-3 for DOS Release 3.1+ QuickStart	$19.95
1-2-3 for Windows Quick Reference	$ 9.95
1-2-3 for Windows QuickStart	$19.95
1-2-3 Personal Money Manager	$29.95
1-2-3 Power Pack	$39.95
1-2-3 Release 2.2 QueCards	$19.95
Easy 1-2-3	$19.95
Easy Excel	$19.95
Easy Quattro Pro	$19.95
Excel 3 for Windows QuickStart	$19.95
Excel for Windows Quick Reference	$ 9.95
Look Your Best with 1-2-3	$24.95
Quattro Pro 3 QuickStart	$19.95
Quattro Pro Quick Reference	$ 9.95
Using 1-2-3 for DOS Release 2.3, Special Edition	$29.95
Using 1-2-3 for Windows	$29.95
Using 1-2-3 for DOS Release 3.1+, Special Edition	$29.95
Using Excel 4 for Windows, Special Edition	$29.95
Using Quattro Pro 4, Special Edition	$27.95
Using Quattro Pro for Windows	$24.95
Using SuperCalc5, 2nd Edition	$29.95

Databases

dBASE III Plus Handbook, 2nd Edition	$24.95
dBASE IV 1.1 Qiuck Reference	$ 9.95
dBASE IV 1.1 QuickStart	$19.95
Introduction to Databases	$19.95
Paradox 3.5 Quick Reference	$ 9.95
Paradox Quick Reference, 2nd Edition	$ 9.95
Using AlphaFOUR	$24.95
Using Clipper, 3rd Edition	$29.95
Using DataEase	$24.95
Using dBASE IV	$29.95
Using FoxPro 2	$29.95
Using ORACLE	$29.95
Using Paradox 3.5, Special Edition	$29.95
Using Paradox for Windows	$26.95
Using Paradox, Special Edition	$29.95
Using PC-File	$24.95
Using R:BASE	$29.95

Business Applications

CheckFree Quick Reference	$ 9.95
Easy Quicken	$19.95
Microsoft Works Quick Reference	$ 9.95
Norton Utilities 6 Quick Reference	$ 9.95
PC Tools 7 Quick Reference	$ 9.95
Q&A 4 Database Techniques	$29.95
Q&A 4 Quick Reference	$ 9.95
Q&A 4 QuickStart	$19.95
Q&A 4 Que Cards	$19.95
Que's Computer User's Dictionary, 2nd Edition	$10.95
Que's Using Enable	$29.95
Quicken 5 Quick Reference	$ 9.95
SmartWare Tips, Tricks, and Traps, 2nd Edition	$26.95
Using DacEasy, 2nd Edition	$24.95
Using Microsoft Money	$19.95
Using Microsoft Works: IBM Version	$22.95
Using Microsoft Works for Windows, Special Edition	$24.95
Using MoneyCounts	$19.95
Using Pacioli 2000	$19.95
Using Norton Utilities 6	$24.95
Using PC Tools Deluxe 7	$24.95
Using PFS: First Choice	$22.95
Using PFS: WindowWorks	$24.95
Using Q&A 4	$27.95
Using Quicken 5	$19.95
Using Quicken for Windows	$19.95
Using Smart	$29.95
Using TimeLine	$24.95
Using TurboTax: 1992 Edition	$19.95

CAD

AutoCAD Quick Reference, 2nd Edition	$ 8.95
Using AutoCAD, 3rd Edition	$29.95

Word Processing

Easy WordPerfect	$19.95
Easy WordPerfect for Windows	$19.95
Look Your Best with WordPerfect 5.1	$24.95
Look Your Best with WordPerfect forWindows	$24.95
Microsoft Word Quick Reference	$ 9.95
Using Ami Pro	$24.95
Using LetterPerfect	$22.95
Using Microsoft Word 5.5: IBM Version, 2nd Edition	$24.95
Using MultiMate	$24.95
Using PC-Write	$22.95
Using Professional Write	$22.95
Using Professional Write Plus for Windows	$24.95
Using Word for Windows 2, Special Edition	$27.95
Using WordPerfect 5	$27.95
Using WordPerfect 5.1, Special Edition	$27.95
Using WordPerfect for Windows, Special Edition	$29.95
Using WordStar 7	$19.95
Using WordStar, 3rd Edition	$27.95
WordPerfect 5.1 Power Macros	$39.95
WordPerfect 5.1 QueCards	$19.95
WordPerfect 5.1 Quick Reference	$ 9.95
WordPerfect 5.1 QuickStart	$19.95
WordPerfect 5.1 Tips, Tricks, and Traps	$24.95
WordPerfect for Windows Power Pack	$39.95
WordPerfect for Windows Quick Reference	$ 9.95
WordPerfect for Windows Quick Start	$19.95
WordPerfect Power Pack	$39.95
WordPerfect Quick Reference	$ 9.95

Hardware/Systems

Batch File and Macros Quick Reference	$ 9.95
Computerizing Your Small Business	$19.95
DR DOS 6 Quick Reference	$ 9.95
Easy DOS	$19.95
Easy Windows	$19.95
Fastback Quick Reference	$ 8.95
Hard Disk Quick Reference	$ 8.95
Hard Disk Quick Reference, 1992 Edition	$ 9.95
Introduction to Hard Disk Management	$24.95
Introduction to Networking	$24.95
Introduction to PC Communications	$24.95
Introduction to Personal Computers, 2nd Edition	$19.95
Introduction to UNIX	$24.95
Laplink Quick Reference	$ 9.95
MS-DOS 5 Que Cards	$19.95
MS-DOS 5 Quick Reference	$ 9.95
MS-DOS 5 QuickStart	$19.95
MS-DOS Quick Reference	$ 8.95
MS-DOS QuickStart, 2nd Edition	$19.95
Networking Personal Computers, 3rd Edition	$24.95
Que's Computer Buyer's Guide, 1992 Edition	$14.95
Que's Guide to CompuServe	$12.95
Que's Guide to DataRecovery	$29.95
Que's Guide to XTree	$12.95
Que's MS-DOS User's Guide, Special Edition	$29.95
Que's PS/1 Book	$22.95
TurboCharging MS-DOS	$24.95
Upgrading and Repairing PCs	$29.95
Upgrading and Repairing PCs, 2nd Edition	$29.95
Upgrading to MS-DOS 5	$14.95
Using GeoWorks Pro	$24.95
Using Microsoft Windows 3, 2nd Edition	$24.95
Using MS-DOS 5	$24.95
Using Novell NetWare, 2nd Edition	$29.95
Using OS/2 2.0	$24.95
Using PC DOS, 3rd Edition	$27.95
Using Prodigy	$19.95
Using UNIX	$29.95
Using Windows 3.1	$26.95
Using Your Hard Disk	$29.95
Windows 3 Quick Reference	$ 8.95
Windows 3 QuickStart	$19.95
Windows 3.1 Quick Reference	$ 9.95
Windows 3.1 QuickStart	$19.95

Desktop Publishing/Graphics

CorelDRAW! Quick Reference	$ 8.95
Harvard Graphics 3 Quick Reference	$ 9.95
Harvard Graphics Quick Reference	$ 9.95
Que's Using Ventura Publisher	$29.95
Using DrawPerfect	$24.95
Using Freelance Plus	$24.95
Using Harvard Graphics 3	$29.95
Using Harvard Graphics for Windows	$24.95
Using Harvard Graphics, 2nd Edition	$24.95
Using Microsoft Publisher	$22.95
Using PageMaker 4 for Windows	$29.95
Using PFS: First Publisher, 2nd Edition	$24.95
Using PowerPoint	$24.95
Using Publish It!	$24.95

Macintosh/Apple II

Easy Macintosh	$19.95
HyperCard 2 QuickStart	$19.95
PageMaker 4 for the Mac Quick Reference	$ 9.95
The Big Mac Book, 2nd Edition	$29.95
The Little Mac Book	$12.95
QuarkXPress 3.1 Quick Reference	$ 9.95
Que's Big Mac Book, 3rd Edition	$29.95
Que's Little Mac Book, 2nd Edition	$12.95
Que's Mac Classic Book	$24.95
Que's Macintosh Multimedia Handbook	$24.95
System 7 Quick Reference	$ 9.95
Using 1-2-3 for the Mac	$24.95
Using AppleWorks, 3rd Edition	$24.95
Using Excel 3 for the Macintosh	$24.95
Using FileMaker Pro	$24.95
Using MacDraw Pro	$24.95
Using MacroMind Director	$29.95
Using MacWrite Pro	$24.95
Using Microsoft Word 5 for the Mac	$27.95
Using Microsoft Works: Macintosh Version, 2nd Edition	$24.95
Using Microsoft Works for the Mac	$24.95
Using PageMaker 4 for the Macintosh	$24.95
Using Quicken 3 for the Mac	$19.95
Using the Macintosh with System 7	$24.95
Using Word for the Mac, Special Edition	$24.95
Using WordPerfect 2 for the Mac	$24.95
Word for the Mac Quick Reference	$ 9.95

Programming/Technical

Borland C++ 3 By Example	$21.95
Borland C++ Programmer's Reference	$29.95
C By Example	$21.95
C Programmer's Toolkit, 2nd Edition	$39.95
Clipper Programmer's Reference	$29.95
DOS Programmer's Reference, 3rd Edition	$29.95
FoxPro Programmer's Reference	$29.95
Network Programming in C	$49.95
Paradox Programmer's Reference	$29.95
Programming in Windows 3.1	$39.95
QBasic By Example	$21.95
Turbo Pascal 6 By Example	$21.95
Turbo Pascal 6 Programmer's Reference	$29.95
UNIX Programmer's Reference	$29.95
UNIX Shell Commands Quick Reference	$ 8.95
Using Assembly Language, 2nd Edition	$29.95
Using Assembly Language, 3rd Edition	$29.95
Using BASIC	$24.95
Using Borland C++	$29.95
Using Borland C++ 3, 2nd Edition	$29.95
Using C	$29.95
Using Microsoft C	$29.95
Using QBasic	$24.95
Using QuickBASIC 4	$24.95
Using QuickC for Windows	$29.95
Using Turbo Pascal 6, 2nd Edition	$29.95
Using Turbo Pascal for Windows	$29.95
Using Visual Basic	$29.95
Visual Basic by Example	$21.95
Visual Basic Programmer's Reference	$29.95
Windows 3.1 Programmer's Reference	$39.95

For More Information,
Call Toll Free!
1-800-428-5331

*All prices and titles subject to change without notice.
Non-U.S. prices may be higher. Printed in the U.S.A.*

que

Learn programming
By Example with Que!

C By Example
Jack Purdum

This is the best way to learn C outside the classroom! Short chapters help beginners learn the language one small step at a time.

Version 1.0

$21.95 USA
0-88022-813-X, 650 pp., $7^{3}/_{8}$ $9^{1}/_{4}$

More *By Example* Books From Que

QBasic By Example
Version 1.0
$21.95 USA
0-88022-811-3, 650 pp., $7^{3}/_{8}$ x $9^{1}/_{4}$

Turbo C++ 3 By Example
Version 3
$21.95 USA
0-88022-812-1, 650 pp., $7^{3}/_{8}$ x $9^{1}/_{4}$

Turbo Pascal 6 by Example
Version 6
$21.95 USA
0-88022-908-X, 650 pp., $7^{3}/_{8}$ x $9^{1}/_{4}$

Visual Basic By Example
Version 1
$21.95 USA
0-88022-904-7, 650 pp., $7^{3}/_{8}$ x $9^{1}/_{4}$

que

To Order, Call: (800) 428-5331
OR (317) 573-2500

Only Que gives you the most comprehensive programming guides!

**DOS Programmer's Reference,
3rd Edition**
Through DOS 5.0
$29.95 USA
0-88022-790-7, 1,000 pp., 7³/₈ x 9¹/₄

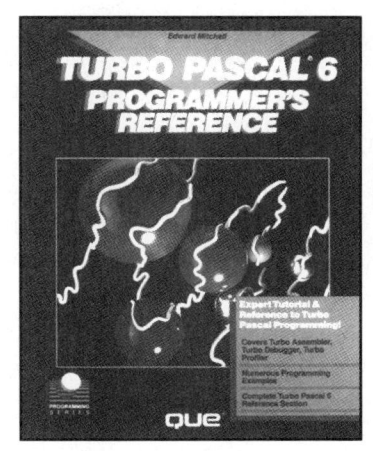

**Turbo Pascal 6
Programmer's Reference**
Version 6
$29.95 USA
0-88022-862-8, 1,000 pp., 7³/₈ x 9¹/₄

**Borland C++
Programmer's Reference**
*Latest Versions of Borland C++
and Turbo C++*
$29.95 USA
0-88022-714-1, 900 pp., 7³/₈ x 9¹/₄

Clipper Programmer's Reference
Clipper 5.01
$29.95 USA
0-88022-677-3, 800 pp., 7³/₈ x 9¹/₄

FoxPro Programmer's Reference
Version 2.0
$29.95 USA
0-88022-676-5, 1800 pp., 7³/₈ x 9¹/₄

Paradox Programmer's Reference
Latest Version
$29.95 USA
0-88022-705-2, 800 pp., 7³/₈ x 9¹/₄

UNIX Programmer's Reference
AT&T UNIX System V
$29.95 USA
0-88022-536-X, 750 pp., 7³/₈ x 9¹/₄

**Visual Basic
Programmer's Reference**
Version 1
$29.95 USA
0-88022-859-8, 800 pp., 7³/₈ x 9¹/₄

**Windows 3.1
Programmer's Reference**
Version 3.1
$29.95 USA
0-88022-787-7, 1,400 pp., 7³/₈ x 9¹/₄

To Order, Call: (800) 428-5331
OR (317) 573-2500

Complete Computer Coverage from A to Z!

The Ultimate Glossary of Computer Terms—Over 200,000 in Print!

Que's Computer User's Dictionary, 2nd Edition

Que Development Group

This compact, practical reference contains hundreds of definitions, explanations, examples, and illustrations on topics from programming to desktop publishing. You can master the "language" of computers and learn how to make your personal computers more efficient and more powerful. Filled with tips and cautions, *Que's Computer User's Dictionary* is the perfect resource for anyone who uses a computer.

IBM, Macintosh, Apple, & Programming

$10.95 USA

0-88022-697-8, 550 pp., $4^{3}/_{4}$ x 8

"Dictionary indeed. This whammer is a mini-encyclopedia...an absolute joy to use...a must for your computer library..."
Southwest Computer & Business Equipment Review

que

To Order, Call: (800) 428-5331 OR (317) 573-2500

D. F. Scott's
VISUAL BASIC SOURCEDISK

Source Code Disk Offer!

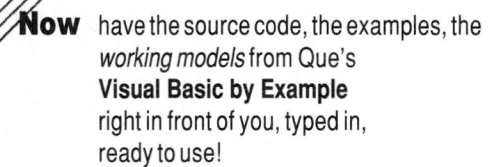

Now have the source code, the examples, the *working models* from Que's **Visual Basic by Example** right in front of you, typed in, ready to use!

Plus **Expressor II** — a scientific formula calculator with an x/y chart generator that exchanges charts using the Windows Clipboard

Plus Explore the realm of artificial intelligence with **Visual Reversi** — actually watch the game think!

Plus A rotational clip art generator for use with your CAD applications

Plus **Ultimate Trek** — a space strategy game in real time with both friends and foes who fight using true AI algorithms and physical principles!

Offer by The D. F. Scott Company

Disk: **$19.95**

High-density
☐ 5 1/4"
☐ 3 1/2"
Check one.

Oklahoma residents add **6%** sales tax

Shipping and handling charges:

$5.00 US and Canada
US$10.00 International orders

All shipping via Federal Express

Send a photocopy of this page along with your payment in US dollars by ☐ Check   ☐ Money order

made payable to:

**The D. F. Scott Company
PO Box 57377
Oklahoma City, OK 73157 USA**

Please allow two weeks for delivery.

Please print your delivery address below:

Name

Company

Address

City   **State/Province**   **Zip/Postal**

Free Catalog!

Mail us this registration form today, and we'll send you a free catalog featuring Que's complete line of best-selling books.

Name of Book _____

Name _____

Title _____

Phone ( ) _____

Company _____

Address _____

City _____

State _____ ZIP _____

Please check the appropriate answers:

1. Where did you buy your Que book?
   - ☐ Bookstore (name: _____)
   - ☐ Computer store (name: _____)
   - ☐ Catalog (name: _____)
   - ☐ Direct from Que
   - ☐ Other: _____

2. How many computer books do you buy a year?
   - ☐ 1 or less
   - ☐ 2-5
   - ☐ 6-10
   - ☐ More than 10

3. How many Que books do you own?
   - ☐ 1
   - ☐ 2-5
   - ☐ 6-10
   - ☐ More than 10

4. How long have you been using this software?
   - ☐ Less than 6 months
   - ☐ 6 months to 1 year
   - ☐ 1-3 years
   - ☐ More than 3 years

5. What influenced your purchase of this Que book?
   - ☐ Personal recommendation
   - ☐ Advertisement
   - ☐ In-store display
   - ☐ Price
   - ☐ Que catalog
   - ☐ Que mailing
   - ☐ Que's reputation
   - ☐ Other: _____

6. How would you rate the overall content of the book?
   - ☐ Very good
   - ☐ Good
   - ☐ Satisfactory
   - ☐ Poor

7. What do you like *best* about this Que book?
   _____
   _____

8. What do you like *least* about this Que book?
   _____
   _____

9. Did you buy this book with your personal funds?
   - ☐ Yes   ☐ No

10. Please feel free to list any other comments you may have about this Que book.
    _____
    _____
    _____

─────── que ───────

Order Your Que Books Today!

Name _____

Title _____

Company _____

City _____

State _____ ZIP _____

Phone No. ( ) _____

Method of Payment:

Check ☐   (Please enclose in envelope.)

Charge My: VISA ☐   MasterCard ☐   American Express ☐

Charge # _____

Expiration Date _____

Order No.	Title	Qty.	Price	Total

You can **FAX** your order to **1-317-573-2583**. Or call **1-800-428-5331, ext. ORDR** to order direct.
Please add $2.50 per title for shipping and handling.

Subtotal _____

Shipping & Handling _____

Total _____

─────── que ───────

NO POSTAGE
NECESSARY
IF MAILED
IN THE
UNITED STATES

BUSINESS REPLY MAIL
First Class Permit No. 9918   Indianapolis, IN

Postage will be paid by addressee

que®

11711 N. College
Carmel, IN 46032

NO POSTAGE
NECESSARY
IF MAILED
IN THE
UNITED STATES

BUSINESS REPLY MAIL
First Class Permit No. 9918   Indianapolis, IN

Postage will be paid by addressee

que®

11711 N. College
Carmel, IN 46032